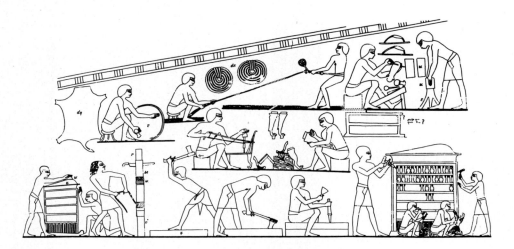

ABOVE: Line drawing from a painted scene in the tomb of the Vizier
Rekhmirē, Thebes, showing carpenters at work.

BELOW: Stacking chairs by Arne Jacobsen, for Fritz Hansens Eft.,
Copenhagen.

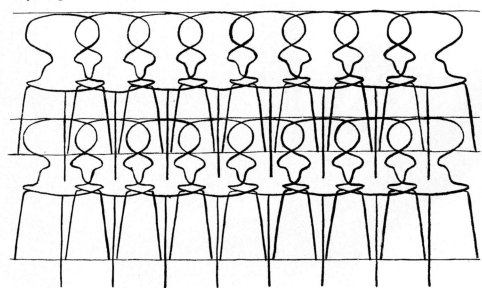

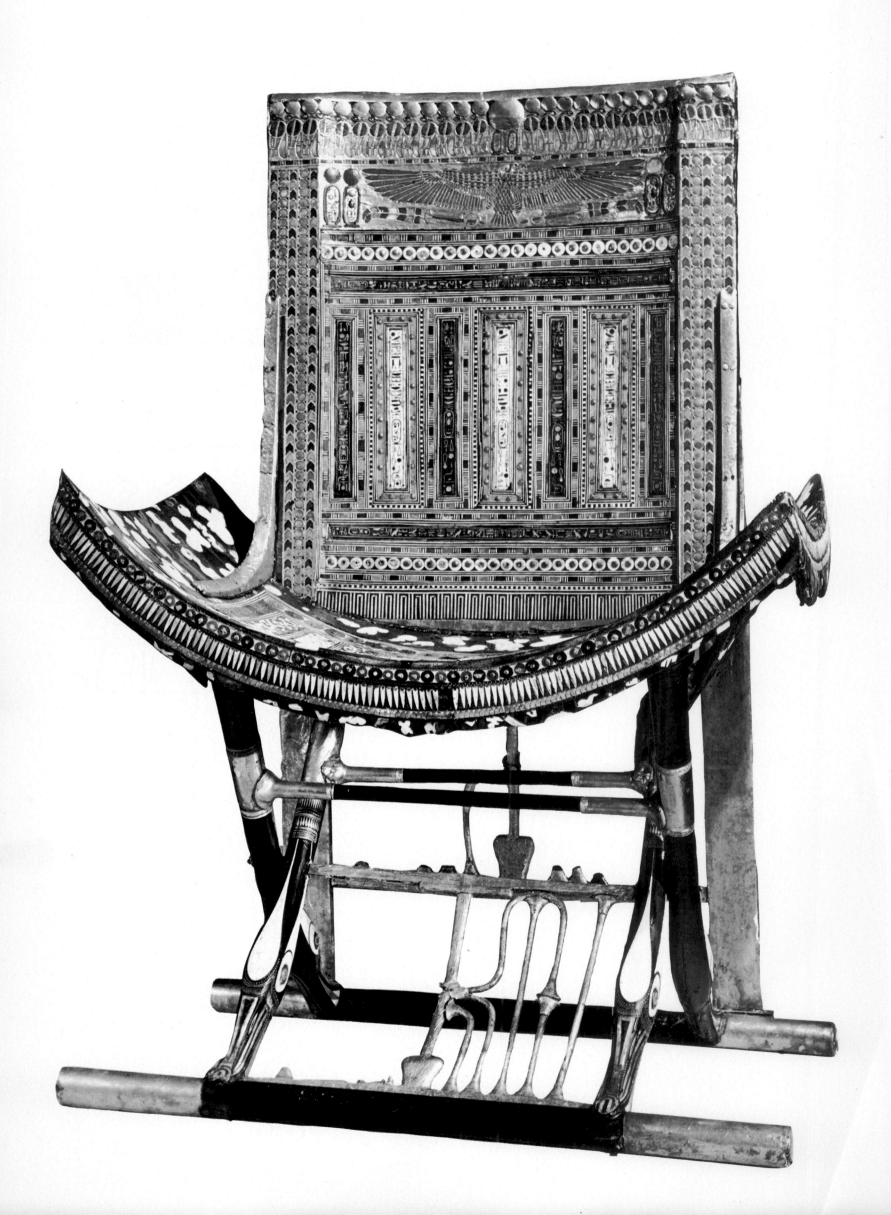

WORLD FURNITURE

An illustrated history from earliest times
edited by Helena Hayward

Douglas Ash

Yvonne Brunhammer

Laurence Buffet-Challié

Joseph T. Butler

Andrew Ciechanowiecki

Anthony Coleridge

Serge Grandjean

Charles Handley-Read

John R. Harris

Helena Hayward

J. Hillier

Hugh Honour

John Hunt

Hans Huth

E. T. Joy

Joan Liversidge

Bozenna Maszkowska

Margaret Medley

P. W. Meister

Clifford Musgrave

Th. H. Lunsingh Scheurleer

Herwin Schaefer

Robert C. Smith

Peter Thornton

Hamlyn
London · New York · Sydney · Toronto

Frontispiece:

The Ecclesiastical Throne from the tomb of
Tutankhamūn, now in the Cairo Museum,
(New Kingdom, 18th dynasty). The throne
is in the form of a folding stool with rounded
sloping back. The legs are of ebony inlaid
with ivory and ornamented with gold
mounts, the front members terminating in
ducks' heads. The seat is also of ebony inlaid
with ivory coloured in imitation of animal
skins. The back is partially overlaid with gold
foil inlaid with faience, glass, semi-precious
stones and panels of ebony and ivory.

Photograph by F. L. Kenett © George Rainbird Ltd.

Published by
The Hamlyn Publishing Group Limited
Astronaut House, Feltham, Middlesex, England

© Copyright The Hamlyn Publishing Group Limited 1965.

First softback edition 1981
ISBN 0 600 34262 X

Printed and bound in Spain
by Graficromo, S. A. - Córdoba

Contents

COLOUR PLATES

INTRODUCTION

Furniture is not only useful, and much of it essential to civilised living, but often it is also a form of art. Modern designers have to come to terms with the first of these aspects much more realistically than has been necessary in the past. Today a well-designed interior must be practical and exclude the superfluous. Limited space must be used ingeniously and a sense of clarity is needed as a setting for efficient living. Furniture must fulfil a specific purpose and need little care or attention. At the same time, costs must be kept down, for in the modern world there are many luxuries competing for favour. Inevitably, function and economy are of the first importance.

In the past, designers of furniture, serving the needs of royalty, nobility, landowners or rich merchants, were not inhibited by such conditions. From the Renaissance until the early 19th century, the art of the cabinet-maker was highly valued. Function was not the first consideration and interiors did not always have to be practical. They expressed in various ways the particular needs of society and a survey of WORLD FURNITURE reveals some wholly different and, to modern eyes, astonishing roles which furniture has been called upon to play.

In the Renaissance, fine furniture and interiors were designed to emphasise not only the riches, but also the learning and wisdom of their owners. Artists in every field exploited rare materials and used exacting techniques. Frederick, Duke of Urbino, was one of the most learned patrons of the arts of the late 15th century, and the little *studio* in his palace reflected his intellectual distinction. Decorated with inlaid panels in variously coloured woods, its *trompe l'oeil* designs suggested *objets d'art*, musical instruments or pieces of armour, the subtle deception arousing wonder and admiration. As connoisseurs in an expanding world, Renaissance princes and merchants collected, with equal enthusiasm, books, curiosities, pictures, furniture and scientific instruments. These treasures were displayed in rooms which were, in themselves, expressions of learning and skill. Curios were also housed in the splendid cabinets-on-stands of the 16th and early 17th centuries made in Italy, South Germany, the Netherlands, France and Spain. Miniature palaces of this kind were fitted with rows of little drawers, which, in turn, were mounted with semi-precious stones, inlaid panels or carved plaques of ivory, ebony or boxwood. They were virtually works of art, rather than practical cupboards, and their purpose was not to furnish a room in any utilitarian sense, but to exhibit learning and taste. No modern designer would countenance such displays of virtuosity. Yet so highly prized were these pieces that a superb cabinet, made at Augsburg, set with brilliantly contrived inlaid panels, was proudly brought home as war booty by the Commander of the Swedish troops in the Thirty Years' War. Included in his loot was also a chair of chiselled steel, once a worthy gift to the Emperor Rudolf II. It was ornamented with sculptured scenes depicting the four great monarchies of the world, as a compliment to the Emperor. Such scholarly attention to detail and wealth of allusion delighted Renaissance Europe.

The increasing affluence of the late 17th and 18th centuries encouraged a rather different attitude towards the role that furniture could play. The architect now took charge in matters of interior decoration and his task was to provide a balanced and sumptuous setting to enhance royal splendour and personal grandeur. Furniture became a vital decorative feature and was deployed, almost in a military sense, in a carefully planned architectural scheme. Generous scale and expensive materials were essential. Louis XIV himself spent vast sums on furniture of silver. Gifts of silver furniture were grandiose, but not unusual gestures, and in England, Charles II commissioned for Nell Gwynn a splendid silver bed, of which the silver weighed more than 3,000 ounces and was valued at the time at over £1,000. The king had earlier been presented by the City of London with a side table, a mirror and a pair of candlestands of embossed silver. Such suites were architectural features and were intended to form an integral part of the interior decoration. They were not to be casually moved from the position allotted to them and they were certainly not for use.

As decorative features, furniture also assumed the roles of sculpture and painting. Side tables, console tables or candlestands were supported on carved figures or leafy scrolls. Even chairs, set in stiff array round the walls of state apartments, borrowed the attributes of sculpture. Those of the Venetian carver, Antonio Corradini, were virtually composed of carved nymphs, and reject any practical role. In a similar way, the late 17th-century brilliantly coloured marquetry cabinets of the Low Countries and France, depicting great vases of flowers, birds and butterflies, fulfilled the function of paintings or tapestries.

As the 18th century advanced, furniture became increasingly important as a form of artistic expression in both sculptural and pictorial terms. Indeed, in Paris, cabinet-makers were among the most highly paid artists of the day. In the 1760s, for example, few paintings were commissioned for a price as high as £1,000. Roentgen, on the other hand, received £3,200 for the famous bureau ordered by Louis XVI in 1779 and, a few years later, Madame du Barry purchased a commode, mounted with Sèvres porcelain plaques, for the same figure—each the equivalent today of approximately £38,000. These were the standards of the fashionable world—a world which accepted furniture as a form of art and deemed it vital to the maintenance of social prestige.

The purpose of this book is to illustrate the history of furniture as an art in relation to its background, and to trace the various styles in which it developed. As in the parallel arts of architecture, sculpture and painting, furniture styles have followed international movements over the course of time. For this reason, the book is arranged according to periods. The first chapters, covering the Classical, Early Medieval and Gothic worlds, contain material which is vital to the understanding of later developments and form a basis upon which much of the book depends. Europe and America have constantly looked back to Antiquity. Classical features such as columns, capitals, acanthus leaves or lion masks have been re-introduced, on various terms, in later ages. Occasionally, in the course of history, fashionable taste has sought to revive the forms or the spirit of Gothic furniture, and familiar Gothic characteristics,

such as tracery or crockets, have been re-interpreted. Although furniture designers have thus sought inspiration basically from Ancient and, more rarely, from Medieval sources, the main stream of development has also, at times, been freshened by impulses from the Arab world and from the Far East. Not, however, until the late 19th and early 20th centuries did the first furniture designers of the modern movement break with these traditions to find new and original idioms.

It is within the framework of broad stylistic changes through the centuries that national cultures must be considered. Ideas have constantly flowed from country to country and from East to West. Fashions have spread in a number of ways: as a sequel to military conquest, in the movement of craftsmen from one land to another, in the general use of engraved designs, and by the traffic in furniture itself as part of international trade. Yet, despite these links, most pieces of furniture disclose a national identity. To define these national characteristics, the chapters of this book are divided, where possible, into sections, each devoted to a particular country, whose achievements in furniture design have contributed to the general development. Too little furniture survives to make a sub-division into countries practicable in the Middle Ages. But from the Renaissance to the 19th century, country sections are included in each chapter in order of relevance in the chain of stylistic development. For example, Italy appears first in the Renaissance chapter, followed by France, while France leads the way in the 18th and Britain in the 19th century. A separate chapter has been devoted to the Far and Middle East, for though the arts of China and Japan have frequently aroused intense interest and have inspired imitators in Europe, the true virtues of Oriental furniture have often eluded Western understanding and Eastern cultures have tended to remain curiously isolated and remote. A general chapter on modern furniture, on an international basis, followed by a short appendix on primitive furniture, concludes the book. Only in a survey of this breadth can the pattern of constantly interweaving influences be revealed and the wide range of the art of the furniture-maker be truly appreciated.

For valuable help in obtaining material for illustrations, grateful acknowledgements are due to Norman Adams, Ltd., H. Blairman & Sons, Ltd., Christie, Manson and Woods, Ltd., *The Connoisseur*, Hotspur, Ltd., Jas. A. Lewis & Son, Mallett & Son (Antiques) Ltd., Mayorcas Ltd., Sotheby & Co., Temple Williams, Ltd., Wolsey (Antiques) Ltd., and particularly to Knoll Associates Inc., New York. I must also express my deep indebtedness to Miss Elizabeth Aslin of the Victoria and Albert Museum, London, Dr Tove Clemmensen of the National Museum, Copenhagen, Mr J. F. Hayward of the Victoria and Albert Museum, London, Mr Niels Lassen of the Royal Danish Embassy, London, Mr John Crowther of the Council of Industrial Design, London, Mr David Stockwell of Wilmington, Delaware, Professor Ole Wanscher of the Royal Academy of Fine Arts, Copenhagen, for constructive advice in the preparation of this book. To Miss Ann Hill, who has assisted me so ably and with tireless energy, I owe a special debt of thanks.

HELENA HAYWARD

Apulian volute *krater* by the 'Darius painter'. 4th century B.C. Museo Nazionale, Naples

I EGYPT, GREECE, ROME

EGYPT

John R. Harris

Approximate dates B.C.: beginning of 1st dynasty c. 3000;
Old Kingdom c. 2700–2200 (4th dynasty c. 2610–2500);
Middle Kingdom c. 2050–1785 (12th dynasty c. 1990–1785);
New Kingdom c. 1575–1075 (18th dynasty c. 1575–1310).

The furniture of Pharaonic Egypt, which at its best attained a degree of sophistication unparalleled in the ancient world until the heyday of Imperial Rome, is well known both from actual examples and from innumerable representations. Not only have many pieces been preserved almost intact in the dry climate of the Nile Valley, but tomb reliefs and paintings, statues and funerary models provide important evidence of much which has not survived, particularly from earlier times. Depiction of furniture as such is indeed unusual, but individual items are often shown among offerings and mortuary equipment, in carpenters' workshops, and most frequently in use, as for example in banqueting scenes. In nearly every case, however, such representations reflect the living conditions of the upper classes, and most extant pieces are likewise from the tombs of the comparatively rich, for as late as the New Kingdom, at the height of Egypt's prosperity, possession of any but the humblest furniture was something of a status symbol.

The Egyptians were used to sitting and sleeping on the ground or on mats of reed, rush, papyrus, halfa grass and palm fibre, and even in the 18th dynasty guests at a feast would often squat upon such mats. Mud brick divans too served as both seat and bed, and in earlier periods many quite prosperous individuals slept on no more than a simple roll of linen. Thus, although beds and other fragments have in fact survived from the 1st dynasty, furniture is altogether rare in tombs of the Old and Middle Kingdoms, the only significant finds being the funerary equipment of Hetepheres, of the 4th dynasty, and some ornate toilet boxes of the 12th. From the New Kingdom, on the other hand, more has been preserved, and not only in tombs, although the most impressive collections do come from three burials of the 18th dynasty —those of the overseer of works Kha and his wife Meryet, of Yuya and Tuyu the grandparents of Akhenaten, and of Tutankhamūn. Of these the furniture from the intact tomb of Kha and Meryet is of particular interest, providing a clear picture of how the home of a well-to-do official of the New Kingdom might be equipped. The principal items were two beds with their head-

rests and bedding, a single chair, a collection of stools of varying design—about a dozen in all, two or three small tables and a few stands, and numerous boxes and baskets. The larger boxes, several of which were elaborately painted, contained quantities of linen, a tall chest accommodated Meryet's wig, and smaller caskets held phials of eye-paint and other toilet requisites. There were also cosmetic preparations in vases and jars, and a small 'work-basket' with some personal trinkets, though most of the baskets were packed with food, which was also stored in pottery vessels. A group of metal utensils included pitchers, a jug and basin, and one or two ring stands, and there was also a large lamp with a separate pedestal.

The earliest Egyptian beds were probably crude timber affairs corded with grass or fibre, but by the 1st dynasty they were already more refined, with rectangular frames and short legs simply shaped or in the form of bull's feet, of which fine ivory examples survive. Beds of this type, the ends of the longer timbers often carved in the form of papyrus culms, were also typical of the Old Kingdom, though the bull's hooves gradually gave way to lion's paws and there were other, more practical, modifications. The frame, frequently spanned with a hide or skin, was as a rule raised rather higher, sometimes with longer legs at the head so that it sloped down to the foot, which might be fitted with a board. The footboard was not essential however, being absent, for example, on beds with lion masks at the head, a form known also from the Middle Kingdom, as well as on a rather unusual type of couch which was without legs at the foot and sloped quite sharply. New Kingdom beds had no appreciable slope, but the frame, spanned with woven cord, was often gently concave, and sometimes of such a height that a mounting block was necessary. Ordinary beds might have simple legs, but animal legs, usually those of a lion, were the rule for beds of quality, even the folding 'camp' bed in Tutankhamūn's tomb having feet of this design. Footboards were often richly decorated with carved openwork figures, inlay and gilding, but the head was generally unadorned, and there was never a headboard. Bedding consisted

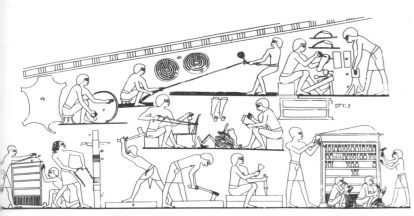

1 *Above*: Portion of a painted scene depicting craftsmen at work. Below, carpenters are engaged on a chair and two shrines, while above are leather workers, two of them seated upon three-legged stools. The tools used by the carpenters include adzes, axes, a bow drill, two kinds of chisel, mallets, sandstone rubbers and a saw. New Kingdom (18th dynasty). Tomb of the vizier Rekhmirē, Thebes

2 *Right*: Detail of a funerary procession, with servants bearing furniture. The items include (from right to left): strutted stands supporting small shrines and cosmetic vessels; a chair, painted black with yellow bracket and red cushion; four boxes, with black framework, white lining and red panels (see illustration 15); a bed, black with yellow bracket, on which are a mattress or roll of bedding and a headrest; a strutted stool (see illustration 9). New Kingdom (18th dynasty). Tomb of the vizier Ramose, Thebes

3 Furniture piled in the antechamber of the tomb of Tutankhamūn. On the further funerary couch is a large box with barrel-shaped lid, and beneath it are the king's throne and footstool (see illustration 5) and a small shrine. On the nearer couch are a white painted wooden bed and a chair of wood and papyrus, with another chair beneath. In front are two stools (see illustrations 9, 11) a white painted box, a footstool and a stool of wood and papyrus. New Kingdom (18th dynasty). Tomb of Tutankhamūn, Thebes (the objects now in the Cairo Museum)

4 Part of a banquet scene, the ladies, below, seated upon cushioned chairs, one with the legs painted blue (see illustration 13), the men, above, upon strutted stools (see illustration 9) and a folding stool (see illustration 11). The floor is covered with mats. Three of the ladies rest their feet upon a footstool, and beneath the seats are bowls supported upon low pottery stands. New Kingdom (18th dynasty). Tomb of two sculptors, Nebamūn and Ipuky, Thebes

5 Scene on the back of the throne of Tutankhamūn, the wood overlaid with gold foil and decorated with silver, faience (glazed quartz frit), glass and semi-precious stones. The king is seated upon a chair of normal height padded with a cushion or roll of linen, his feet resting upon a footstool; on the right is a stand supporting a tray. New Kingdom (18th Dynasty). Cairo Museum (tomb of Tutankhamūn)

chiefly of linen, which could be folded to form a mattress, though padded mattresses may also have been known. Pillows, however, were not used as such, the head being supported on a crescent-shaped headrest, sometimes inscribed with the owner's name, with possibly a linen pad for greater comfort.

At what date seats, as distinct from primitive thrones, were first evolved is uncertain, but light stools of papyrus and bent wood were probably known before the 1st dynasty, and fragments from several royal tombs of this period are evidence of more developed wooden stools and chairs. By the beginning of the Old Kingdom two principal classes of seat may be distinguished, one evidently based on wicker construction, the other closely related to the early dynastic beds, and possibly derived from them. The first type, with square legs and arched bent wood braces, was usually backless (i.e. a stool), though variants with a very low back or batten and with a higher back were also known, the latter a definite chair. The second type, consisting of a frame, decorated with papyrus culm terminals behind, and legs, shaped like those of a bull (or later a lion), was also backless at first, but from the 4th dynasty had more often a low back, the high-backed form remaining somewhat unusual. Armchairs, which seem to have been exceptional before the 4th dynasty, were also of the animal leg type, and were somewhat awkwardly styled, with high straight backs and arms up to the armpits. From some of the individual stools and chairs were developed double benches on which man and wife are shown seated, those represented in tomb reliefs being mostly doublets of the low-backed 'semi-chair' with animal legs.

Although the simpler type of stool and its derivatives became obsolete, several Old Kingdom forms were preserved into the Middle Kingdom and others, such as the folding stool, were introduced. The high-backed chair was no longer so rare, and the back was sometimes sloped for greater comfort, the design of armchairs being similarly improved, with better proportioning of the back and arms.

A certain variation in the height of both stools and chairs is noticeable in all periods, but particularly in the New Kingdom, when low seats raised only some nine inches from the ground were apparently no less popular than those of more normal height. Of the various types of seat in use at this period perhaps the most characteristic was a light stool with four slender legs braced by rails and struts. Such stools were generally of papyrus or thin wooden laths and often painted white, though some more ornate examples were of costly woods left plain or inlaid, and might have thicker, carved legs and decorative bracing. Also quite common was the folding stool, the crossed legs of which usually terminated in duck's heads or, less frequently, lion's claws. The seat was probably of skin or leather stretched over curved battens, though this was sometimes imitated in solid wood. The type of three-legged stool used by workmen was found in the home as well, and rough stools formed simply of four legs joined by rails, around which the seat was corded, were usual in less wealthy households. Some ordinary chairs too were of rough leg and rail construction, with slatted backs, but those of better quality were differently designed, the basis being a seat or frame spanned with cord or thongs, to which the legs and back, made separately, were attached. As a rule the legs were shaped like a lion's, and the back was either flat and straight or, more often, rounded and slightly sloping, with vertical supports behind. Armchairs were of similar basic design, with arms generally of elbow height and somewhat concave in profile, though chairs without arms seem always to have been preferred. While usually flat, the seats of some chairs and stools, notably those spanned with solid wood, were shaped in an easy curve, and pads of linen or cushions of linen or leather stuffed with feathers might be added for greater comfort. Cushions served also as footstools, though these were often of wood or papyrus, and something like an ottoman with cushioned top is known from representations. Of several fine chairs that have survived none is more elegant than that in the Louvre, which might almost have served as a model for the *Directoire* style of the late 18th century.

Tables were invariably small, mere stands to raise things from the ground, and larger tables to seat several were quite unknown. In early times food was served on circular stone platters with a small support or foot, from which developed the 'offering-table' with taller pedestal shown in funerary reliefs and later copied in

wood and metal. Baskets, trays and bowls were also supported
on ring stands of pottery or papyrus, and, from the Old Kingdom, vessels and the like were placed upon four-legged stands
and racks of papyrus, wood and even metal. During the New
Kingdom, stands of this type were common, their form being not
unlike that of the strutted stool, though often with much longer
legs. Other forms of small table, including some with three legs,
were also known, and gaming boards might be equipped with
special table-like stands or be independent units with legs
attached—the oldest games tables.

Although drawers were incorporated in gaming boards and
toilet boxes, and shrines such as held divine figures were basically
cupboards, neither chests-of-drawers nor cupboards were developed for domestic use, perhaps because the possibilities of
shelving were not appreciated. The earliest surviving cabinet
with doors is of late date and may not necessarily be a piece of
household furniture. In the absence of anything more advanced,
possessions were kept in boxes and baskets, the commonest items
in house or tomb, the former being used chiefly for linen, clothing and personal effects, while the latter could contain almost
anything, but especially food. Baskets were of palm fibre, halfa
grass, rush and similar materials, coiled spirally and bound by a
sewing strip (not woven on a stake-frame as in Europe), and
were generally round or oval with domed lids, varying in size
according to purpose. Most boxes and chests, whether of wood,
papyrus or reed, were rectangular, with short feet, though a few
had longer legs and some small caskets were elaborately shaped.
Boxes with internal divisions and fittings were made to hold
jewellery, wigs and toilet requisites. Lids were usually flat, gabled,
barrel-shaped or sloped to a slight arch in front, and were often
detachable, accommodated, if at all, by means of battens, flanges,
grooves and other simple devices. Lids pivoting sideways on a
single peg were not, however, uncommon on small boxes, and
larger lids might open upwards on pivots engaging in the sides of
the box, the use of metal hinges dating from the 18th dynasty.

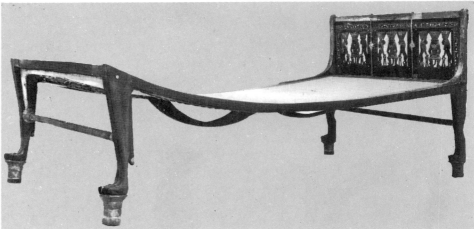

6 *Top right*: Furniture (restored) from the funerary equipment of Queen
Hetepheres, mother of Khufu. A bed with detachable inlaid footboard and
silvered headrest, and a low armchair with straight back and high arms
stand beneath a canopy designed to take hangings. The framework of bed,
chair and canopy is overlaid with gold foil, which alone survived, the
original wood having perished. The find also included a carrying chair, a
second, inlaid, armchair, a curtain box, an inlaid chest and a gilded jewel
box. Old Kingdom (4th dynasty). Cairo Museum

7 *Above right*: Ebony bed spanned with woven cord painted white, the
footboard framing openwork figures and bearing an inscription inlaid with
ivory. Parts of the footboard and its decoration are gilded, as are the bases
of the legs and the bracket strengthening the union of legs and frame. New
Kingdom (18th dynasty). Cairo Museum (tomb of Yuya and Tuyu)

8 *Right*: Folding bed of light wood spanned with woven cord and painted
white, the three sections joined by heavy bronze hinges. New Kingdom
(18th dynasty). Cairo Museum (tomb of Tutankhamūn)

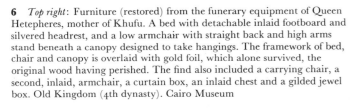

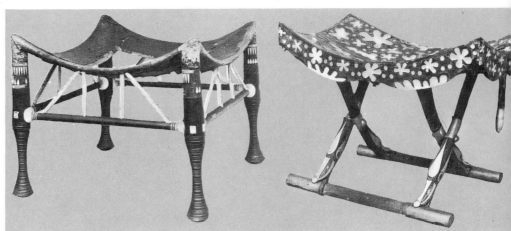

9 *Left*: White painted wooden stool with
strutted framework, one of the commonest forms
during the New Kingdom (see illustration 4)
New Kingdom, (18th dynasty). Cairo Museum
(tomb of Tutankhamūn)

10 *Above*: Ebony stool with ivory struts and
inlaid ornament. The plaques masking the
mortices for the rails are coloured red, and the
seat was originally of red leather. New Kingdom.
British Museum, London

11 Folding stool of ebony inlaid with ivory and
ornamented with gold mountings, the legs
terminating in duck's heads and the seat
patterned in imitation of an animal's skin. The
seat being solid, the stool does not fold as it would
if spanned with real skin or leather. New
Kingdom (18th dynasty). Cairo Museum
(tomb of Tutankhamūn)

12 *Left*: Low wooden chair with seat of woven cord and flat, straight back panelled and decorated with strips of ebony and ivory inlay. New Kingdom. British Museum, London. 13 *Centre*: Wooden chair of normal height with seat of interlaced hide strips and rounded, sloping back panelled and decorated with strips of ebony and ivory inlay. The legs are painted blue (see illustration 4). New Kingdom. Louvre, Paris.

14 *Above* Armchair of normal height, of a red wood, with seat of woven cord and rounded, sloping back veneered and decorated with gold leaf on gesso. The decoration on the arms, and the two heads are also gilded, but the bases of the legs, the bracket strengthening the union of legs and seat and four panels on the reverse of the back are silvered. New Kingdom (18th dynasty). Cairo Museum (tomb of Yuya and Tuyu)

Flat lids and the lids of gabled boxes were sometimes divided, with the leaves hinged independently and opening from the centre. Although lids might be fastened by rotating snecks or bolts running in staples, boxes could not be 'locked' except by lashing cord around projecting knobs and sealing the binding with clay.

Other articles of furniture were few, but every household had its pots and pans. These were mostly of coarse pottery, but in the richer homes might be of stone, chiefly alabaster, or metal—including perhaps one or two purely decorative pieces. In most houses too there will have been a basin and ewer of water for washing the hands and to cool the heat of the day, a brazier to warm the chill night, and lamps to light it. The floors of rooms were generally covered with mats, and the walls sometimes decorated with patterned hangings which could also be used as screens. But in all, the furnishing of even the most prosperous homes, though colourful, was sparse, as indeed is usual in hot climates, and any Egyptian room would have seemed bare to modern eyes.

A Note on Materials and Techniques

Apart from papyrus and other fibres, whose use antedated carpentry and continued throughout dynastic times, the principal materials for furniture were native timbers, acacia, sycamore-fig, tamarisk and sidder, though woods such as cedar, cypress and juniper were imported from Syria, and ebony (*Dalbergia melanoxylon*, not true ebony) from countries to the south. Since native woods could not provide sizeable plants or panels, a 'patchwork' technique was evolved, small irregular pieces being united by flat tongues or dowels, cramps and pegs, lacing, and occasionally by tongue and groove, used also for panelling. Mortice and tenon joints and dovetailing were common, and corners were formed by several types of mitre, pegged or lashed, like butt joints, with cord or thongs. Metal pins and nails, though earlier used to fasten metal to a wooden core, were not employed in carpentry until the 18th dynasty. Flaws were plugged and patched, and poor wood was often surfaced with gesso and painted, sometimes to imitate more valuable materials. Veneer and inlay too might mask inferior timber, the elements generally of ebony and ivory, thin slips of which were also used for marquetry. Decoration of sheet gold, foil and leaf, the last on gesso, was not uncommon on luxury furniture, and silver was similarly applied, though rarely before the New Kingdom. Thin inlay, marquetry and metal foil were glued in place, sheet metal was rivetted, and thicker inlay pegged, exposed pegs and rivets being sometimes adapted as ornament. The carpenter's tools were simple, namely adzes, axes, the bow-drill, two kinds of chisel, mallets, sandstone rubbers and pull-saws, the blades of copper and later bronze and the handles of wood. The plane was unknown, smoothing being done with adzes and rubbers, and the lathe was not introduced until a later date.

15

16

5, 6, 7, 14

6, 7, 12, 13, 14

1

15 Boxes of a common wood coated with gesso and painted in imitation of more valuable materials, the black framework representing ebony, the white lines ivory inlay, the red panels framed by the lines probably cedar, and some yellow details gilding (see illustration 2). The smaller chequered panels on the right hand box imitate marquetry of ivory and ebony with some blue (for faience or glass) in the border. New Kingdom (18th dynasty). Cairo Museum (tomb of Yuya and Tuyu)

16 Box of common wood veneered with ivory and ebony and decorated with panels of marquetry composed of thin slips of the same materials. When found, the box contained miscellaneous items of jewellery. New Kingdom (18th dynasty). Cairo Museum (tomb of Yuya and Tuyu)

GREECE, ROME

Joan Liversidge

The palatial interiors and fine furnishings of the ancient Greek world have long vanished. But Homer's *Odyssey* can still evoke the splendours of the early palaces and suggest an ideal vision of formal grandeur. Such descriptions, however, give no detailed picture of the furniture itself, while virtually no moveable pieces from pre-Hellenic Greece survive to help us. Fortunately both sculptured reliefs and painted vases show scenes from mythology and contemporary events. By exploiting all such interesting and attractive sources of information, we can build up some knowledge of domestic furniture and changing taste.

Many of the forms in use in Egypt and the Near East were adopted in Greece but it is clear that certain new features developed. The bed, for example, completely abandoned the vertical footboard and small separate headrest which had been usual in Egypt. It now served not only for sleep at night but also for reclining on at mealtimes. It thus became a very important piece of furniture.

Adequate supplies of timber existed and these couches were decorated with inlays of fine woods, gems and precious metals while the feet were of silver or ivory. The frames were simply strung with cords or leather thongs. But the wool or linen mattress and pillow covers, sometimes perfumed and woven in multicoloured designs, lent an air of glamour. Sometimes the supports were in the form of animal legs. Much more common from the 8th century B.C. onwards were couches with rectangular legs. The earliest examples are shown on the Geometric Dipylon vases. Here the rectangular posts flare outwards at the top. As time advanced the legs at the head sometimes had a decorative finial which would help to prop up the pillows. From the early 6th century B.C. more substantial supports were decorated with painted or inlaid palmettes. These seem to have been a Greek innovation. Frequently the space between the palmettes became a narrow neck, weakening the legs structurally but relieving their rather heavy appearance. The couch legs projected above the level of the seat, the pair at the head end often being higher than those at the foot and crowned with volutes. The mattress was spread over this raised end, helping to keep the pillows in position and so acting as the earliest form of couch rest.

Although less popular, couches with turned legs continued a tradition already known in Egypt. They are also shown on 8th-century Geometric vases and they continued in fashion well into the Roman period. How these Egyptian and early Greek legs were turned is uncertain but the lathe is known to have been adopted in Greece sometime after the 7th century B.C., probably from the Middle East, and the turned leg in consequence became more and more elaborate. At first the legs were thick near the top, narrowing to a flaring foot with moulded rings at intervals, until the lower parts, if the artists depicted them accurately, became dangerously thin. At the head the legs rose above the frame to support a headrest. Later, turned legs grew more elegant. The well-proportioned upper and lower halves were gently curved and connected by a simple boss, or the rounded top of the leg was joined to a tall foot.

In Greece, individual seats ranged from the throne to the

17 *Above*: Detail of a Greek black-figured *hydria* showing Heracles feasting after overcoming the Nemean lion. He is reclining on a couch which has rectangular legs carved at the base in such a way that only a narrow section links the legs with the feet, while the mattress and pillows are covered with striped material. In front of the couch is a rectangular table. The hero's sword hangs on the wall, his club is against the couch leg and his quiver of arrows leans against the table. From Vulci, *c.* 520–510 B.C. British Museum, London

18 *Below*: Detail of a Greek red-figured *kylix*, painted with a scene showing three men drinking together and signed by the painter Douris. The guests are reclining on couches and are being served by two slaves. The couches have turned legs and low headrests, and beside each is a table with two legs at one end and one at the other on which food and wine could be placed. From Vulci, *c.* 500–470 B.C. British Museum, London

19 Detail of a Greek black-figured *kylix* showing Zeus. The throne upon which he is seated has a serpent-head back, and armrests terminating in large lotus buds, while the supports are in the form of animal legs. The elaborate hangings and the footstool in front lend pomp to the scene. 6th century B.C. British Museum, London

20 Detail from an Apulian volute *krater* by the 'Darius painter'. The Emperor Darius is seated on a splendidly decorated throne, the rectangular panel at the back surmounted by two winged figures of Victory. The throne has low armrests and is supported on rectangular legs. 4th century B.C. Museo Nazionale, Naples

21 *Above*: Attic marble relief on the base of a statue, showing a cat and dog fight. The man on the right is seated on a folding stool, the supports in the form of animal legs. *c.* 510–500 B.C. National Museum, Athens

22 *Right*: Marble gravestone of Hegeso showing an elegant *klismos* and small footstool. Greek, 2nd half 5th century B.C. National Museum, Athens

folding stool. Thrones, as in Egypt, were reserved for deities or people of importance. But early Greek examples, often ornamented with rosettes, volutes or palmettes, betray a more adventurous sense of form. Some were backless but others had

19 high backs, occasionally with lotus bud or palmette finials. These appear on a series of 'Hero Reliefs' from Sparta. There were also thrones with low backs, sometimes in the shape of the fore part of a horse or a lion's head, or terminating in volutes, or the heads of swans or serpents. These startlingly varied sculptural forms which gave the carver a superb opportunity, were repeated on the supports of the armrests and on the stretchers, which were gradually coming into use. These were sometimes in the form of triton's or ram's heads. Throne legs, too, could be in the form of animal legs, while others were simply turned. But by the 5th century B.C. the rectangular leg seems to have been the more popular. As time advanced a taste for ornamentation developed. Fourth-century thrones, like couches, were more

20 richly adorned, and that of the Emperor Darius, depicted on an Apulian *krater* of the period, is elaborately decorated.

22 In the home the favourite type of chair was the *klismos*. Homer tells us that it was used by goddesses but numerous vase paintings show it predominant in scenes of daily life. It is considered to be a Greek invention, possibly a development of the Egyptian chairs or Greek thrones with animal legs. It consists of a plaited seat standing on curved legs, with a back composed of three uprights fitted into a curved board at shoulder level. Light and comfortable, it was easily carried about, and by the 5th century when its curves achieve ideal proportions, it has become a most graceful and delightful piece of furniture. Unhappily later *klismoi* develop much deeper backboards which cause them to appear clumsy. This tendency can be seen in the

23 chairs of the two councillors who sit behind King Darius on the Naples *krater*.

21 The *diphros* was another seat of Egyptian origin used by both gods and mortals. It consists of a stool without a back standing on four turned legs, sometimes strengthened with stretchers. As is the case with thrones and couches, the legs increase in elaboration as time goes on. The simpler, earlier forms appear on the Parthenon frieze. A lower stool, often with undecorated legs, was also used by workmen or servants. Another low seat seems to have consisted of a rectangular box, the sides painted in several colours with geometric designs or occasional figures.

21 The folding stool, (*diphros okladias*) increased in popularity and Athenaeus tells us how slaves followed their masters about, carrying them. The birds' head decoration and the stretchers joining the feet, which are common features of Egyptian stools, disappear and are replaced by animal legs, often very bandy, ending either in lion paws turning inwards or hooves turning outwards. Some cross-legged stools, such as the one occupied by

23 Detail from an Apulian volute *krater* by the 'Darius painter', showing two councillors seated on *klismoi*. The legs show a marked flare and the backboards are much deeper than in the previous example. The animal skin covering the seat of the chair on the left is clearly visible. 4th century B.C. Museo Nazionale, Naples

24 *Below*: Detail from an Apulian volute *krater* by the 'Darius painter' showing a stool with crossed legs, a modification of the folding stool, the supports united by a boss in the form of a mask. Museo Nazionale, Naples

25 *Right*: Etruscan bronze candelabrum from which lamps could be hung on chains. This piece, with its winged Cupid supporting the shaft and imaginative use of animals and birds, offered the sculptor an opportunity for inventive display. 3rd century B.C. Museo Etrusco Gregoriano, Vatican

26 Bronze *fulcrum* (headrest) encrusted and inlaid with silver. From a Roman couch, 1st century A.D. The mule's head has a silver collar and the winged maenad wears a silver wreath and panther skin. The panel between is ornamented with silver inlay depicting a Dionysiac scene. Tomb of Amiterno, Museo dei Conservatori, Rome

27 The barrel-shaped chair was developed in Etruscan times, the back curving round to form arms. This terracotta model shows how such chairs would have been carried out in bronze. Staatliche Museen, Berlin

28 Monument surmounting the funerary urn of the Etruscan, Arnth Velimnes Aulis, showing a couch with rests in the form of swan heads and necks and beside it a long, low footstool supported by lions. An air of luxury is sustained by the generous grandeur of the textile coverings. 2nd century B.C. Tomb of the Volumnii, Perugia

29 Roman sarcophagus showing a mourning scene for a young girl. She lies on a couch with a high back and sides supported on turned legs. A low footstool is beside her and one mourner is seated on a folding stool while another occupies a high-backed chair. 2nd century A.D. British Museum, London

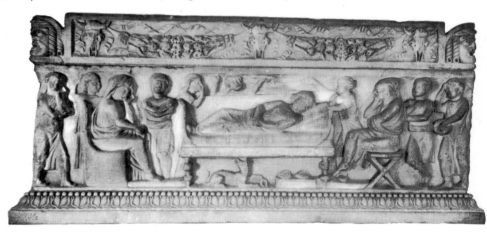

24 a Persian treasurer receiving tribute in the bottom row on the Naples *krater*, have such marked curves and substantial seats that they may not have folded at all, or the usual leather seat may have been replaced by one which lifted off and was carried separately.

20, 23, 24 The Darius *krater* also shows a number of footstools accompanying the various types of seats. These gave the sitter both comfort and dignity. They also provided a convenient and elegant means of mounting a couch. Some were merely pieces of wood resting on plain rectangular feet but they soon developed bow legs with lion-paw feet, sometimes with decorative motifs added on the narrow sides between the paws. Other footstools resemble a shallow upturned box with sides ornamented in various ways.

Tables were used rather more by the Greeks than by the Egyptians. They were small and light and used chiefly at meal-17, 18 times, being pushed under the couch when not in use. Vase paintings show that the Greeks used to hang their possessions on the walls, so cupboards and sideboards were not needed. Bronze and marble table legs have survived but wood must have been the usual material. The Greeks seem to have developed an attractive little round table found from the 4th century B.C. This was a type, much admired in Neo-Classical Europe so many centuries later, supported on three deer legs terminating in hooves.

Chests continued to be used for holding clothing, household equipment and valuables. They varied in size and closely re-

sembled Egyptian prototypes. A fine series of Greek chests used as coffins have been found in Egypt and the Crimea. Small model chests of terracotta or bronze are also occasionally found. From about the end of the 5th century B.C. the Etruscans developed a circular casket or coffer (*cista*) of wood or bronze which is frequently found in graves. The bronze examples are beautifully engraved with lively scenes and they stand on low feet, often of the lion-paw type.

The *cista* may have been of Italic origin, but on the whole Etruscan household furnishing was much the same as Greek. Tomb paintings and objects found in graves suggest an atmosphere of luxury. The Etruscans made an increased use of bronze and numerous bronze tripods and tall candelabra for lamps or candles preserved in Italy start a sequence which lasts from the 7th century B.C. to the 4th century A.D. The candelabra stood on three short, often bandy legs with claw feet, sometimes ornamented with leaves. The shafts, supported on sculptured figures, were decorated in various ways, sometimes with animals 25 climbing up them.

The larger pieces of furniture included a new and more comfortable type of chair on a barrel-shaped base with a back 27 curving round to form arms. A mood of greater splendour is evoked by the 2nd-century B.C. bed of the Etruscan Arnth Velimnes Aulis. The head- and footrests are decorated with 28 swans, and the turned legs appear to have bronze mounts. The couches of Hellenistic and Roman date also have turned legs of wood or bronze and examples survive from Rome, Hercu- 26

Small box on tall legs, from the tomb of Tutanhkamūn, now in the Cairo Museum, (New Kingdom, 18th dynasty). The framework, inlaid with bands of inscription, is of ebony with fitted panels of a red wood, probably cedar, the openwork hieroglyphs below being of ebony and gilt wood. The lid opens on bronze hinges, and the two knobs, positioned for tying and sealing, are also gilt. The box which was evidently intended to hold articles of fine linen, was one of a pair.

Ebony gaming board and stand, from the tomb of Tutankhamūn, now in the Cairo Museum. The stand is in the form of a small couch with lion-paw feet mounted upon a sledge. The pedestals beneath the feet and the brackets bracing the legs and frame are gilt. The games board is reversible, faced with ivory on both playing surfaces, but differently divided, into thirty squares and twenty respectively. Within the board was a drawer, now lost, which held the ten playing pieces (five a side), and the knuckle bones or gaming rods with which the moves were thrown. These too are missing, the pieces shown here belonging in fact to another set.

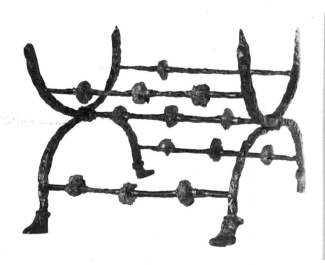

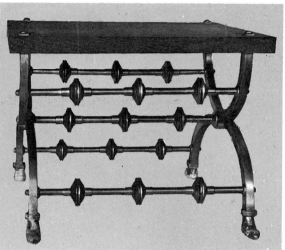

30, 31 Roman cross-legged stool of iron joined by five stretchers ornamented with brass bosses and with bronze sandalled human feet. Excavated at Nijmegen, Holland. On the right, a modern reconstruction. Rijksmuseum Kam, Nijmegen

laneum and Pompeii. By the end of the 1st century A.D. these couches ceased to have such elaborate headrests. Instead, the characteristic Roman couch with high back and sides makes its appearance. Legs were of varying height, still turned and sometimes standing on bases, and mattresses became increasingly thicker. These couches appear in funeral scenes on tombstones and sarcophagi, not only in Italy but all over the Roman Empire, a notable series being found in the Rhineland. Some have decorated couch rails and fine striped mattress covers. Low footstools were used both with these couches and with chairs and folding stools.

The spread of Roman civilisation round the Mediterranean and across Europe, ensured the adoption of Roman forms of furniture far beyond the frontiers of Italy. Actual examples of Roman straight-legged folding stools of iron and bronze have been recovered from graves in Belgium and England. One found in Italy at Ostia is silver plated. A heavier form of cross-legged stool of iron with bronze sandalled feet was discovered at Nijmegen, Holland. Tripods, consisting of three or four legs connected by crossbars which moved up and down on slides and supported either a tray or a bowl, were favourite items of Roman bronze furniture, developed from the earlier Greek models. A silver tripod from the treasure found at Hildesheim, Germany, stands on three pairs of sandalled feet, the bearded heads at the top of the legs supporting a circular tray. Other tripods did not fold, and several very luxurious bronze examples of this type survive from Pompeii.

Other Roman seats for individuals were based upon Greek prototypes. There is the *diphros* with turned legs, and a heavier version of the Greek *klismos*. Chairs deriving perhaps from Etruscan examples with rounded backs and rounded or rectangular bases, were also popular. One from Trier provides evidence that they were also made of wicker work. Women were particularly fond of them when nursing infants or at their toilet. Business men sometimes preferred more upright chairs with panelled sides. A straight-backed bench with panelled seat frequently appears where groups of mother goddesses are represented.

32 *Above*: Roman folding tripod of silver, from the Hildesheim Treasure. It is interesting to recall that the decorative feature of the pairs of human feet upon which the tripod is supported was revived, with other Classical motifs, in the early 19th century. Early 1st century A.D. Staatliche Museen, Berlin

33 *Below*: Stone relief showing a woman at her toilet. She is seated on a chair with a high rounded back which was clearly made of wicker work. It was a favourite chair in the later Roman period. Early 3rd century A.D. Trier Museum

Wall painting from the house of Marcus Lucretius Fronto at Pompeii, c. A.D. 30, illustrating the courtship of Venus and Mars. In the background the high couch has a mattress and pillow with striped covers and a scrolled headpiece supports the pillow. Venus sits on a *klismos*, the sabre legs of which are visible, and her feet rest on a low footstool. The chair also has elaborate draperies and gold tassels.

Wall painting in the house of the Vettii at Pompeii, dating from the 3rd quarter of the 1st century A.D. The walls are decorated in the so-called 'Fourth Style' of Pompeii, in which the architectural vistas are divided into two stages. At ground level the painting imitates a frieze of brightly coloured marble slabs, against which couches would have been set. Perspectives of distant architecture flank the big square paintings which illustrate mythological scenes. Here the sculptor Daedalus is shown bringing his wooden cow to Pasiphaë. Pasiphaë is seated on a throne, and in the foreground a carpenter is working at his bench.

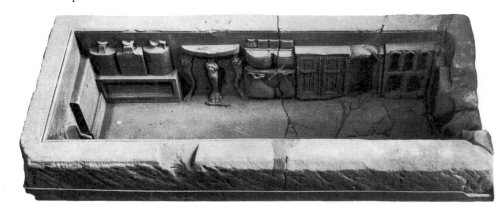

35 *Below*: Interior of a stone sarcophagus showing furniture belonging to the dead person and including a table or bench, console table supported on three legs with lion-paw feet surmounted by lion masks, cupboards with panelled doors and shelves. Provincial Roman, early 3rd century A.D. From

34 *Above*: Bronze tripod with claw feet, the circular top supported on winged sphinxes. From the Temple of Isis at Pompeii. This exceptionally fine piece is an example of the Roman taste for elaborate decoration. Museo Nazionale, Naples

36 Stucco ceiling from the Tomb of the Valerii, late 2nd century A.D. The scenes in the roundels, reflecting doctrines of immortality, represent the soul being carried to the Island of the Fortunate. This type of graceful, low relief in stucco inspired late 18th-century architects and recalls the work of Robert Adam.

The small round tables with animal legs developed by the Greeks became increasingly popular. Of bronze, marble, silver or rare imported woods, especially citrus, the curved legs were now much decorated. An example of probable Hellenistic date, now in Brussels, is supported by legs surmounted by swans rising out of acanthus foliage. Lion or panther heads and claw feet enliven a whole series of Roman tables found in Italy and in the provinces, while in England, fragments occur decorated with griffin heads, with dogs or hares sometimes climbing up the legs to meet them. These are made of Kimmeridge shale, a Dorset slate, and they show how widespread Mediterranean fashions in furniture had now become.

Rectangular four-legged tables continued in use, the legs joined by stretchers. They were convenient as stands or low seats, and plainer types were employed in kitchens or workshops. In Italy a new fashion resulted in the appearance of large tables with rectangular tops of wood or marble placed on uprights consisting of marble slabs, elaborately carved with fabulous beasts such as winged griffins, flowers and leaves. They were, perhaps, the sideboards which we know from literary sources and which were introduced into Roman households, probably from the East. They were not used as dining tables, and the small round tables continued in use in the dining room. Late in the Roman period the larger table of sigmoid shape (*mensa lunata*) was also a piece of dining room furniture. Other articles of Roman furniture included bronze or silver candelabra, substantial chests set on low feet and embellished with bronze mounts, and the newly-invented cupboards with shelves.

A selection of the household equipment of an early 3rd-century Roman provincial villa is clearly depicted on the interior of the sarcophagus found at Simpelveld. In the provinces extravagant articles of furniture may have been lacking, but painted walls and mosaics existed and the surviving reliefs and occasional fragments of furniture show that a good standard of solid comfort had been attained. In Italy itself this furniture was made of the most luxurious materials possible. Combined with multicoloured curtains, cushions and bedcovers, animated wall paintings and brilliant mosaics, the rooms presented a gorgeous spectacle. Indeed, such was the feeling of the ancient world for style and sophistication that it has never ceased to present a mysterious attraction to Western civilisation.

37 *Below*: Magnificent marble table support carved to represent winged lions with rams' horns. 1st century A.D. This type of table support was imitated in Italy in the Renaissance and also inspired many northern Baroque examples. Surviving Roman marble and stone tables were studied with academic fervour by architects in the early 19th century. House of Cornelius Rufus, Pompeii

Eleventh-century Byzantine ivory showing Christ enthroned. He is seated in a chair of framed squared timbers with a rounded back carved with a rope moulding. The uprights are enriched with jewels and the finials elaborately carved. The footstool has a carved and moulded frieze supported on acanthus foliage. The seat is supplied with a large, bolster-like pillow. Museo Civico, Bologna

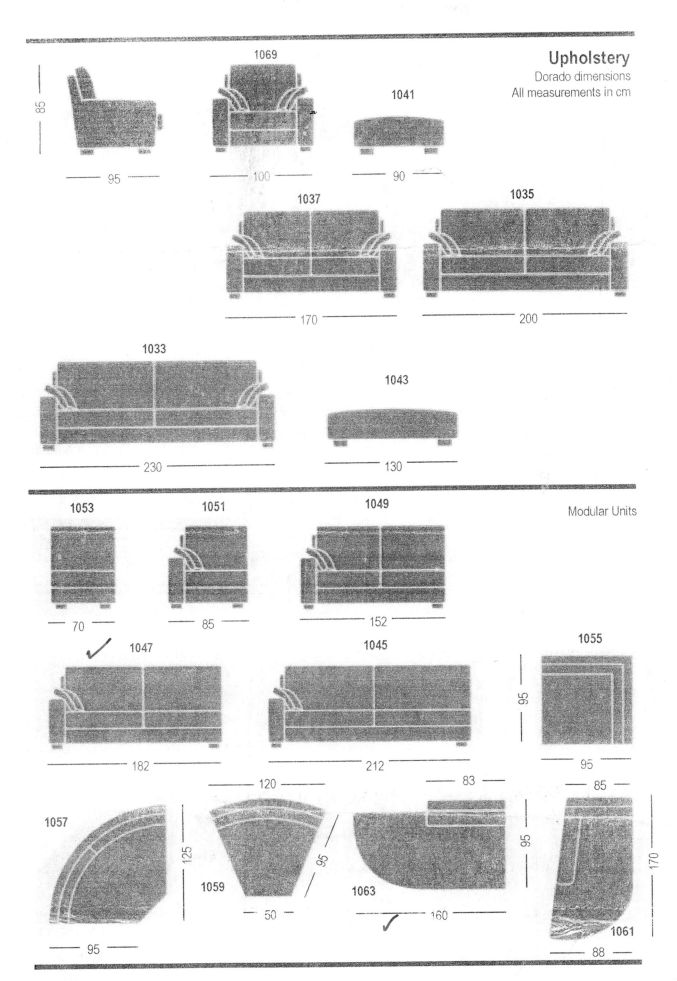

Upholstery
Dorado dimensions
All measurements in cm

85

95

1069

100

1041

90

1037

170

1035

200

1033

230

1043

130

Modular Units

1053

70

1051

85

1049

152

1047

182

1045

212

1055

95

95

85

1057

95

120

1059

50

125

95

1063

160

83

95

170

1061

88

£2800

The **Furniture** Union
Bankside Lofts 65 Hopton Street London SE1 9LR Tel 020 7928 5155 Fax 020 7928 5253

Upholstery
Dorado range

Sofas available are sizes 170, 200, 230 cm in length.

The Dorado is a solid wood structure with stress resistant polyurethane foam and heat bonded polyurethane fibre faced with adhesive velveteen. Springing by means of reinforced elastic straps. Seat and back cushions in stress resistant polyurethane foam, covered in 100% hollow soft polyester fibre.
Solid wood feet walnut or cherry stained. Fully removable covers, except the leather option.
Various sizes available as well as a modular option. Armchair also available in this range.

Dorado Range
Modular Units

The **Furniture** Union
Bankside Lofts 65 Hopton Street London SE1 9LR Tel 020 7928 5155 Fax 020 7928 5253

II BYZANTINE
AND EARLY MEDIEVAL

BYZANTINE AND EARLY MEDIEVAL

John Hunt

38 6th-century Byzantine mosaic lunette illustrating episodes from the life of Abraham. In the centre he offers a meal to the angels who came to announce the birth of his son. The angels are seated at a table with three loaves of bread before them. The table is simply constructed of squared timbers with two sets of rails. The angels rest their feet upon the lower rails. Presbytery of San Vitale, Ravenna

The barbaric invasions of the 5th century brought final collapse to the Roman Empire in the West. But the traditions of Classical art were not to be entirely overwhelmed and two factors helped to maintain them: the rise of Christianity and the founding of Byzantium. The gradual ascendancy of Christian civilisation in the Mediterranean had meant that already in the 3rd and 4th centuries Christians had begun to adapt and make use of Classical art. In the large towns of the Greco-Roman world painters and sculptors worked both for a pagan and an increasingly large Christian clientele. Christian artists took over Classical figure subjects and *putti*; tritons and nereids decorated Christian sarcophagi.

It was on a basis of Christian belief that Constantinople was founded early in the 4th century and the Imperial residence transferred to the new Eastern capital. Here, on the shores of Asia Minor, Greek culture had remained dominant and the workshops of the Imperial Court were now to provide for the needs of a Christian society still imbued with the most refined Hellenistic taste amidst the ruins of the Classical world. But the new Empire borrowed from the East such Oriental features as rigid, hieratic figures and luxurious but formal, abstract ornamentation.

These two traditions, the solemn hieratic approach of the East and the grace and refinement of Hellenism, formed the basis of Byzantine art. Slowly, a wholly un-Classical delight in colourful surface ornamentation as against Classical naturalistic forms was to transform the style into the art of the Middle Ages.

Evidence of the furniture in use derives almost exclusively from manuscript illustrations, ivories and mosaics. From these we can see that certain types of furniture, chairs and tables for example, continued to be made in the fashion developed through centuries of Classical art. But much of the legacy of antiquity was abandoned. All those lovely subtle curving shapes seen in Greek and late Roman furniture, the rounded backs and the sweeping sabre legs have vanished, only to be artificially resuscitated in the late 18th and 19th centuries. Instead, manuscripts and mosaics show interior scenes in either churches or palaces, which are rigidly formalised. The atmosphere of regal splendour suited the Byzantine vision of Christ and the Apostles as imperial and princely beings and was reflected in the fashions of the Court. The monasteries, too, were furnished with splendour and comfort, if one can judge by the lavish use of textile hangings.

Furniture may be divided into two main types—that produced by a joiner, and the more accomplished productions of the cabinet-maker. Functional furniture of joined wood must have existed in the houses of farmers and peasants but all evidence of this has vanished although some furniture shown in illustrations seems to be a throw-back to primitive forms. But one precious legacy of the lost Classical world inherited by the Byzantine Empire was the skilled craft of the cabinet-maker; both manuscripts and mosaics provide vivid evidence of this.

The furnishings most constantly depicted are chairs and thrones. The latter are usually architectural in form and suggest massive constructions of heavy timber, covered with ornamental paintings and with cushioned seats. Others are more simple, the legs, back and seat rails evidently housed together with mortice and tenon joints.

Desks in the form of a table on turned feet, with a flat top for writing instruments and an upper lectern for scrolls or book were sometimes decorated with crocketing and the doors of the

39 *Above*: Byzantine ivory figure of the Virgin enthroned, 10th–11th century. Her chair has a curious lobed back of oriental flavour, ornamented with an engraved design of large flowers which are repeated upon the ends of the bolster behind her back. Formerly in the Stroganoff Collection, Milan

40 *Above right*: Page from a Byzantine Gospel Book, late 12th century. The Evangelist is seated on an X folding chair of which one member on each side is prolonged upwards to form a back. The footstool has an arcaded base and the circular writing table of cupboard-like form has arched and panelled doors within which are writing instruments. From the top of the table a hinged and movable upright supports the decorated and painted book rest. Apostles MS 531, Walters Art Gallery, Baltimore

41 *Above*: 6th-century Byzantine ivory throne, known as the 'Throne of Maximian', a splendid example of the use of ivory in furniture. The precious material has been used in the place of wood, and the main members are carved with running designs of animals and birds amid fruit and foliage scrolls. The art of the carver is revealed in the framed and mitred panels, boldly worked in high relief with the figures of St John the Baptist and Apostles, and scenes from the life of Christ. Museo Archivescovile, Ravenna

42 *Left*: *The Last Supper*, an illustration from the 6th–7th century Codex Purpureus. Christ and the Apostles lie upon couches which surround a semi-circular table. They recline in the Classical manner on one elbow, the other hand being used to take the food. The edge of the table is provided with a long bolster or cushion to support the arms, and the hangings on the table and couches are painted with birds. Rossano Cathedral, Italy

chest-like lower part were often panelled and painted. This combination of desk and lectern in one unit was apparently a favourite Byzantine fashion. Such lecterns vary in form and suggest that there was no lack of small convenient pieces to supply the needs of leisure or study. They seem usually to have been of wood, elaborately painted with geometrical devices. Some had a single hinged stem, allowing a variety of positions for the book rest. The table beneath was sometimes round, perhaps with a cupboard in it, standing upon three feet.

Some chairs and stools were of X-form, with a slung leather seat between the supports. This type of seat has a long Classical history. The upper terminals of the X-supports were often elaborately ornamented and turned, or were formed as beasts' heads, perhaps lions, while the lower ends became claw feet or paws. These X-chairs were generally of metal but illustrations also show heavier wooden examples, elaborately painted. Simple frame stools and painted benches were common, constructed of four uprights, decorated with knobs and turned feet with connecting seat and foot rails. Sometimes the top oversails, converting the stool into a small table and the legs are evidently morticed into the under part. Turned legs are also found, either plainly cylindrical or elaborately moulded. Footstools were a natural accompaniment to seats and all shapes and sizes were used, some of wood, some of metal, the top occasionally enriched with cushions.

Tables followed Classical models and were of stone or metal. Examples with four slender legs joined by X-shaped stretchers, are constantly shown placed beside seated figures of evangelists in manuscript illustrations. Wooden tables were round, square or rectangular, some of them elaborate examples of cabinet-
making, with framed and panelled cupboards beneath. Small

tables, too, with a drawer in the frieze and stretchers on three sides are to be seen in manuscripts, the front stretcher being absent to accommodate the feet of the writer. Dining tables were occasionally large and circular or semi-circular, the guests reclining around it on couches in the Classical manner.

Chests and boxes abounded, from the small trinket box to the large oblong coffer which might also serve as a bench or bed. Besides the primitive slab-sided box, framed and panelled examples were in use, often decorated with painting, or with elaborate intarsia of various woods or even plated with ivory. Gold and silver inlay, perhaps combined with ivory, was employed for the smaller and more precious containers.

Simple beds and couches continued the Classical tradition, but the metal forms with graceful curved headpieces seem to have been abandoned. The mosaics of St Mark's, Venice, show magnificent structures, the bed surmounted by a canopy supported by columns and enclosed within curtains.

Cupboards have an ancient lineage from antiquity, and the Byzantine world was rich in all forms of press and cupboard, from simple wall shelving to elaborate examples of the cabinet-
maker's craft. Some were of architectural form with pilasters and pediments, or enriched with paintings and colour. Book-
cases with open shelves and cupboards below were also made.

In contrast with the Eastern Empire, where Classical traditions mingled with the Orient, Western Europe, slowly recover-
ing from the chaos of the great invasions, sheltered only in royal Courts and favoured monasteries any remnant of the traditions of Classical luxury and comfort. The old skills had been almost entirely swept away. The structure of daily life had to be built anew and the household arts slowly to develop out of the old primitive forms and shapes.

40

50

*Plate facing
page 32*

42

*Plate facing
page 32*

*Plate facing
page 32*

Although the furnishings found in the ship burials of Oseberg and Gogstad in Scandinavia, had a certain magnificence, they provide evidence of the clean sweep which the migrations had made of Classical tradition. The ships themselves are magnificent specimens of the carpenter's skill developed over many generations but the furnishings are primitive joiner's work. Starting from a fresh beginning, therefore, the forms of Western furniture were simple. Primitive chairs were made of short logs or branches, the end sharpened and fixed into holes in the adjoining members. Nowhere was there any hint of cabinet-making or panelled framework. Instead, ideas, forms and construction were borrowed directly from the craft of the stone-mason. One of the favourite combinations was that of turned members, made to simulate stone columns, with semi-circular arches, to form arcaded sides and back to ceremonial chairs. All these were further enriched with the universally popular painted decoration of brilliant colours and gilding on a gold or coloured ground. These chairs were a prerogative of great princes and nobles and indicated their ruling position. They were not even to be used by women or guests. The countrymen and peasants still sat on the primitive three-legged stool or box.

The cataclysmic change in the economy of Western Europe which followed the passing of Roman rule radically changed the way of life of even the very rich. The shortage of coinage and the change in the distribution of peoples in the early Middle Ages, left huge areas unpopulated. Spain and Portugal were a no man's land; Germany had but few centres of population. Large parts of France were almost uninhabited. Even the largest towns had only a few thousand inhabitants. These conditions forced the big landowner, who alone with great prelates and a few merchants were sufficiently cultured to demand and own furniture, to range incessantly through the land. Chairs, tables and beds had to be made so that they could be taken apart and easily packed and transported. Much of the furnishings of fine castles took the form of hangings and curtains and tapestries, with a wealth of cushions to soften the hardness of chest or stone window-seat. The great standing cupboard, or the high table, might not accompany the lord on his journeys but the walls of his castle would certainly be left cold and bare, the windows without glass, barred only by shutters, until the family returned from their ceaseless round of visits.

Chests and boxes of all sizes were the commonest articles of furniture. The most primitive form was simply composed of four vertical boards with a base, and a lid. It served as a receptacle, a stool, a chair, a work table and so on; the construction being modified by the addition of side uprights into which the front and back boards were housed, thereby raising the bottom from the floor. Designs in chip carving were popular in the Romanesque period, but the finest and most effective decoration was the use of architectural motifs, columns and arcading. These were heightened with colour.

Chairs occupied a peculiarly ceremonial position, both in secular and lay use. Elaborate throne chairs of stone and bronze are architectural constructions rather than furniture, but thrones of wood were common. Chairs were often composed of turned

43 Scandinavian chair, bench and desk of remembered Romanesque form, *c.* 1200. The construction is of turned uprights into which the stiles and rails are housed by means of mortice and tenon joints. The decoration consists of designs of simply turned wooden billets and primitive arcading, the flat surfaces being further decorated with incised lines and hatching, forming arcading and lozenges. Vallstena Church, Gotland, Sweden

44 Page from a Carolingian Gospel Book, *c.* 870, showing Charles the Bald enthroned. The Emperor's throne is constructed of squared timbers with rounded finials to the front and back supports. The back is in several registers, and the front appears to be pierced with keyhole arcading. All the stiles and rails of the throne are brilliantly painted with simulated jewelling. Codex Aureus, folio 5v, from the Convent of St Emmerau, now in the State Library, Munich

45 The Evangelist St Mark. St Mark's throne is a bench of rectangular form, the thickened top and footrest painted with a scroll design and the front with jewelled panels and lobate panels at the ends. The high back is humped like a camel with two heads, and covered with a voluminous hanging. His writing desk, with its table top carrying an inkwell, is of turned reel-and-bead design, with a foliate foot and capital. Painted columns with bell bases support the canopy above the throne. Codex Aureus, folio 59r, State Library, Trier

46 Mid-13th-century walnut chest of primitive plank construction, the single unit of the front disguised with two rows of arcading in chip carved technique, the supports decorated with roundels above carved Romanesque arches of several orders, forming the legs. This chest or hutch would originally have been enriched with colour. Between the two rows of arcading are engraved the words: *Ave Maria Gracia Plena.* Musée de Valère, Sion, Switzerland

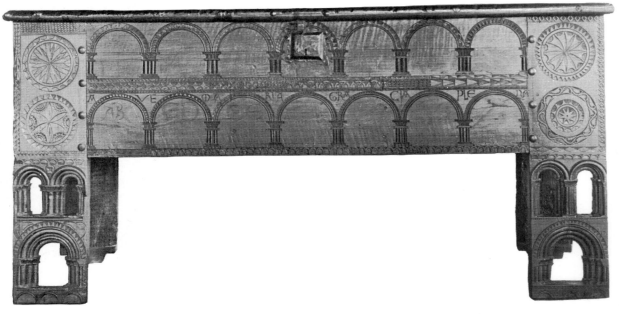

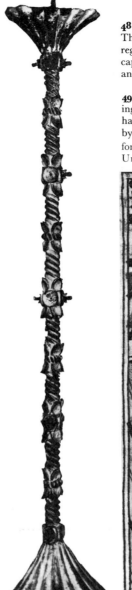

48 *Left*: One of a pair of 12th-century painted wooden altar candlesticks. The fluted circular bases support roped columns with carved knops at regular intervals. The knops are alternately of leaf and flower form and the capitals are fluted like the bases. Burrell Collection, Glasgow Art Gallery and Museum

49 *Below*: Laurence of Durham, from a mid-12th-century manuscript. His ingenious chair and writing desk combined is made of squared timbers and has a high back and arcaded decoration to the sides. The desk is supported by two uprights which are hinged to the back members of the seat, and fall forward into slots at the top of the front legs of the chair. Cossin V.III.L, University Library, Durham

47 Seated Virgin from a 12th-century Adoration scene. The Virgin's chair has high turned legs and a low curved back, the sides being filled with panels pierced with plate tracery of alternating circles and diamonds. Her simple footstool has pierced arcaded sides and a cushioned top. La Charité-sur-Loire, Nièvre, France

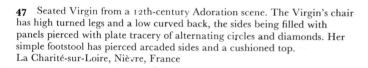

50 *Left*: 12th-century boxwood folding stool, the so-called Stool of S. Ramon. The sides and rails of the double X-form are brilliantly and crisply carved with interlaced foliage. The upper terminals have stylised lion heads with animals and plants in their mouths and the lower ends have paw feet. The simple form is overlaid with trailing plant stems and is curiously reminiscent of Scandinavian style. Cathedral of Roda de Isabeña, Huesca, Spain

51 *Right*: 12th-century French manuscript illustration of the *Marriage at Cana*. The wedding guests are seated at a long table. As was the custom, the supports are completely concealed by the elaborately draped table cloth. In the lower register the servants draw water from a well, and climb a ladder to the feast above with the filled water pots on their shoulders. A cupboard containing more pots stands on the left. The doors are of solid plank construction with elaborate iron hinges, while the top of the cupboard is decorated with a painted band beneath a pediment with three pierced lancets. Cotton MS, Nero C.IV Psalter folio 17r, British Museum, London

52 *Above*: 12th-century stone sculpture showing a Nativity scene. The Virgin lies in a bed, the squared uprights with ball finials carrying rails forming a frame for the arcaded back and front, within which the mattress lies. There is a gap in front to enable the occupant to get out of bed more easily. Tympanum of the West Portal, Chartres Cathedral

54 Painted sacristy cupboard, *c.* 1200. The cupboard is simple joiner's work of massive timbers with single plank sides and plank doors. The primitive form is completely overlaid with an elaborate and brilliantly painted composition in colour upon a gesso ground. The painting, which decorates the cupboard both inside and out, consists of the figures of saints upon the sides and doors, while the lower supports and bottom frieze are treated with a Romanesque design of foliage showing much oriental influence. Cathedral Museum, Halberstadt

members and were elaborately painted. They sometimes had high backs, the uprights decorated with finials, and armrests. Footstools of simple form accompanied them. Other necessary articles were writing desks and lecterns and standing candle-sticks.   49, 53, 48

Folding stools of X-form were still endowed with the official   50 dignity of their Classical prototypes and were used as seats of estate and circumstance for secular and lay ceremonial use. Four-legged stools with turned or rectangular members were brilliantly painted, while benches of the same form and construction were also found in the castles of the rich and houses of the well-to-do merchants. Benches were not always used solely as seats. Gregory of Tours records that King Chilperic when seated with Bishop Bertrand, had before him a bench upon which were bread and other food.

The tables in use in Romanesque times were of various shapes. The greater number appear to have been movable and supported upon trestles. Some had semi-circular tops and during meals were covered with cloths and hangings.

Cupboards and presses, apart from plain wall shelving were   51 made in the simplest fashion of planks without framework or panel construction. Here again, brilliant polychrome decoration concealed the crude carpentry.   54

After chairs, beds were the most elaborately made and decorated articles of furniture. Also composed of turned members, elaborately framed together they were masterpieces of turnery. Another form was based upon chest construction, with square   52 supports at the head and foot and board-like sides. Both had curtains and hangings suspended from rods or from a framework around the bed. These standing beds, denuded of their hangings, were probably left in the empty castle during the lord's frequent absences. Contemporary documents constantly refer to 'trussing' beds or camp beds, which could be folded and transported with ease, and which were evidently very popular even with the nobility. Couches and day beds, and beds upon wheels were other variants, and mention of a couch with cords, presumably to support the mattress, occurs in a contemporary life of St Thomas of Canterbury.

Romanesque furniture, with its carved architectural decoration and vivid colouring was formal and splendid. It was only slowly to give way in the 13th century to the new soaring elegance of the Gothic style.

In medieval times, cloisters and passage ways in religious houses were also used for work and study. One side would be divided up with wooden partitions and screens into individual compartments or 'carrels', each complete with a seat and a desk or work bench. St. Joseph is shown in such a carrel. On the simply-made bench before him are an auger, a hammer and chisel, pincers, a paring knife, nails and a bird- or mouse-trap. On the downward-opening shutter of the window is a second trap, a weight-trap for birds actuated by a string. St. Joseph is using a breast-drill to make slanting holes in a piece of board on which the position of the hole is carefully marked. Detail from the Campin Altarpiece by the Master of Flémalle. Cloisters Collection, Metropolitan Museum of Art, New York

III GOTHIC

GOTHIC

Douglas Ash

It is impossible to discuss any of the arts of the Middle Ages without reference to contemporary architecture, which was the dominant influence in Gothic fine and applied art. It affected the forms and decoration of silverware, arms and armour, furniture and textiles. Even in medieval painting and sculpture, human beings were often depicted with slim, attenuated 'Gothic' figures. The origins of the fully-developed Gothic style are still uncertain although there is no doubt that one of its most important details, the pointed arch, was used by Islamic master builders for some centuries before it reached Europe.

In the 11th century, the most vigorous inhabitants of geographical France were the Normans, who, in the last forty years of the century had conquered England, Jerusalem, and Sicily. In Sicily they found the pointed arch already in use as a consequence of earlier Saracenic conquest. A further half-century, however, was to elapse before Gothic forms began to appear to any extent in new construction. Despite their military prowess, the Normans never managed to pursue a common or far-sighted political policy, and leadership soon passed to the more mature French kings. The increasing intellectual importance of Paris, where scholars came from far and wide to the schools of Notre Dame, ultimately established the French royal domain as the fountain-head of fully-developed Gothic art.

From about 1200, England began to evolve an indigenous style and even assisted in the development of Gothic in countries as far apart as Portugal and Norway. By the 13th century, Gothic had spread to northern Spain, the western parts of the heterogeneous Germanic Empire and the Low Countries and, constantly fanning out, had reached, in the late 13th century Poland, Finland, Scandinavia, Hungary and Italy. The vehicles of this expansion were political, religious, and commercial. Sweden, Denmark, and other northern European countries came under the artistic sway of Germany, chiefly owing to their close mercantile connections with the cities of the Hanseatic League, Hamburg, Lübeck, and Bremen, while pagan Lithuania received the Gothic style with the Christian faith, forced upon them by the Teutonic knights.

In Italy, source of so much artistic innovation, the Gothic spirit never found a happy resting place. Apart from the glaring sunlight, which limited the size of the windows and made large wall spaces inevitable, the persisting Classical influence watered down the imported northern conception and imposed compromise upon it. In order to temper the bleakness of the large bare areas of wall between or below the windows, artists were often commissioned to execute ambitious mural decorations. 61 These were necessary because architecture had really failed to achieve functional and decorative identity. The same half-hearted submission to the influence of northern Gothic is often evident in Italian medieval furniture, which was frequently painted rather than carved:

55 Detail from a 15th-century Bohemian painting of the Last Supper. The disciples are seated at a rectangular table, covered with a plain white cloth. On the left can be seen a simple three-legged stool with long slender legs. In the centre is a fine example of an X-chair. This detail comes from the wing of an altarpiece of 1494, originally in the parish church of Doudleby in South Bohemia, now in the Narodni Galerie, Prague

56 *Above right*: 13th-century French chest covered with ornate wrought iron scrollwork. Although the metalwork is highly decorative, its main purpose was to strengthen the chest which probably contained church muniments. Musée Carnavalet, Paris

57 *Right*: 13th-century English oak chest of simple construction, decorated with chip-carved roundels. Such chests were often enriched with colour, like the earlier Romanesque examples. Stoke d'Abernon Church, Surrey

58 Late 13th-century French chest with architectural arcading and elaborately carved knightly figures dressed in contemporary armour. They all bear swords or lances, and seem to be preparing for battle, for one is donning his helmet, another drawing his sword from its sheath. Musée de Cluny, Paris

59 14th-century English 'tilting' chest carved with a lively jousting scene. Such subjects were popular in a chivalric age. The lock plate is damaged, but the handle, in the form of a cusped arch, again reflects the preoccupation with architectural motifs. Victoria and Albert Museum, London

60 Late 14th-century English chest front carved with the legend of St George. The carving is more lively and naturalistic than in the previous example, and displays a typically Gothic love of detail—rabbits emerging from burrows, the king and queen peering from the windows of their castle. Victoria and Albert Museum, London

61 Bedroom in the Palazzo Davanzati, Florence. Although the furniture is 16th century, the mural decoration is typical of 15th-century Tuscany, where rooms had small windows and large areas of wall space. On the walls of the room, the scenes depicted are of courtship—couples embracing, or playing chess, or taking leave of one another. They stroll beneath a loggia upon a terrace, and ornamental trees and flowers can be seen in the background.

The Low Countries, which were later to achieve artistic supremacy under the great dukes of Burgundy, were initially subject to northern French influence, but with the passage of time this gave way to a Burgundian style, compounded of elements deriving from England, France, and western Germany, involving the use of a great deal of surface ornament. This ornament was admirably executed, and succeeded in avoiding an effect of vulgarity by the skilful way in which it was related to the scale of the buildings. Burgundian furniture-makers applied the same skill to their work.

The subject of medieval furniture has been bedevilled for many years by extravagant claims that the productions of one country can easily be distinguished from those of another. We have seen, however, that Gothic architecture spread fairly rapidly over most of Europe, and as furniture was always the satellite of architecture, the details of which, in any event, often lost much of their distinctiveness under the hands of the woodworker, such claims are generally invalid. They should, therefore, be discounted in a field of connoisseurship in which so little evidence remains. Certain styles and ornamental motifs were occasionally favoured in one country more than another, though this in itself does not provide conclusive evidence that they never occurred elsewhere. Indeed pieces are frequently encountered which, in the absence of information concerning their provenance, might quite well have been made in any one of several places as far apart as Flanders, Aragon and Suffolk.

In considering medieval domestic furniture it is necessary to remember two facts; first, that contemporary requirements were decidedly modest, and secondly, that very little has survived. The poorer classes either had no furniture at all, or at best had to be content with crude objects which they made themselves. A long-lived and international example of this peasant furniture is the three-legged stool, the origins of which are lost in antiquity. It was usually made by boring three holes in a circular piece of planking or section of tree trunk, and inserting three splayed legs with split tops. These were held firmly in place by wedges driven in from above. Stools of this type are still made to this day, and owing to the lack of evolutionary changes, it is quite impossible to date them. The most that can be said is that they appear to be either fairly old or fairly new.

Medieval manuscripts and paintings show that benches were often made in the same way. A long, stout plank was used, with two splayed legs fixed into each end. The detail of their construction gives no hint of their period, and they are usually devoid of decoration. They figure prominently, for example, in mid 16th-century paintings by Pieter Brueghel the Elder, and are still made in country districts today, but as dirt and hard wear soon give them a very respectable appearance of antiquity, they are mostly as undateable as the three-legged stools.

In 1254, the energetic Provost of Paris, Etienne Boileau, reorganised the guild system of the city, and as a result the carpenters and coffer-makers (or arkwrights) parted company. That the second of these groups should have attained such importance as to have a guild of its own gives some indication of the extent to which their respective activities had prospered in the first half of the 13th century, and suggests that secular patronage had begun to rival that of the Church.

The earliest, most important and widely distributed article of furniture in the Middle Ages was the chest or coffer. It was used for storage, and if the top was flat, as a seat, a table, and sometimes even a bed.

One of the earliest kinds of chest was of a form which explains the derivation of the word *trunk*. It was made from a length of thick tree trunk hollowed out, and sometimes strengthened with iron bands to prevent splitting. A slice cut from the top served as a lid. Chests of this type continued to be made far into the 17th century, though the later ones usually had tops made of planking. They were used in churches for the preservation of muniments but although they were also found in domestic surroundings, they were probably never very popular, as their curved tops made it impossible to use them for anything but storage. Whenever they are mentioned in medieval domestic inventories it is evident that the household concerned was a wealthy one, and was accordingly not obliged to use items of furniture for more than one purpose.

55

62 *Above*: Panel from a 15th-century Italian chest painted with a wedding scene. On the left is a splendid bed, and on the first floor of the central building *amorini* are bearing garlands. Although the dress is still medieval, the return to Classical example is indicated by the pedimented doorway on the right beside which wedding guests engage in conversation. Victoria and Albert Museum, London

63 *Below*: Detail from an altarpiece, *The Whim of the Young St Francis to become a Soldier* by Stefano di Giovanni called Sassetta 1392(?)–1450. St Francis sleeps in a bed with a simple half-tester, and beside the bed are plain chests entirely devoid of ornament. National Gallery, London

64 15th-century Italian *cassone* decorated with carved gesso ornament, painted and gilt. In the three lozenges are groups of figures; the remainder of the surface is occupied with fabulous animals with human heads enclosed in trellis spaces, combined with coronets. The regularity of the design which can be compared with the wall decoration in illustration 69 has more in common with Byzantium than Northern Gothic. Victoria and Albert Museum, London

65 Late 15th-century Italian *cassone* of Classical sarcophagus shape. Renaissance ornament has now entirely supplanted Gothic motifs. Entwined flowers frame Classical urns surmounted by griffins, and in the centre is a coat-of-arms. Victoria and Albert Museum, London

66 *Below*: Late 15th-century Italian *Cassone delle Torri* decorated with an intarsia of various woods. Such chests remained popular in Italy well into the 16th century. This fine example was made in Lombardy, probably Milan. Museo Civico d'Arte del Castello Sforzesco, Milan

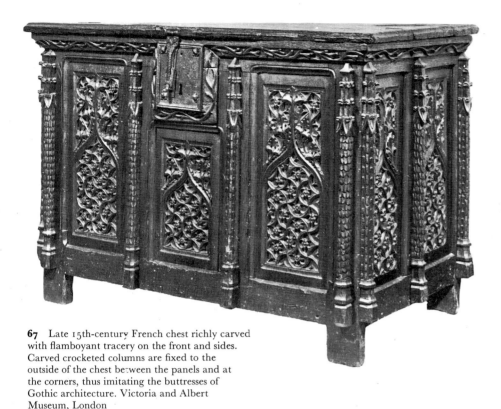

67 Late 15th-century French chest richly carved with flamboyant tracery on the front and sides. Carved crocketed columns are fixed to the outside of the chest between the panels and at the corners, thus imitating the buttresses of Gothic architecture. Victoria and Albert Museum, London

68 Late 15th-century chest carved with a type of foliage which is purely English in character. The use of decorative lettering is a late Gothic feature. In this case Lombardic script is used and the name FARES was probably that of the owner. Victoria and Albert Museum, London

69 14th-century folding X-stool, *c.* 1400. The seat would have consisted of leather or cloth slung between the top rails. At the intersection of the members is a boss carved as a rosette, and lion heads and feet decorate the terminals. Although this example will fold, many were fixed by the addition of a permanent back. Städtisches Museum, Wiesbaden

Quite early in the 13th century, French chests began to display signs of the elaboration characteristic of contemporary architecture, which was to make them to some extent a pattern for the rest of Europe. Coffers of the period, simply and stoutly constructed from broad planks of oak, were covered with wrought iron scrolls, which served not only to increase the strength and security of the chest, but also to relieve the plainness of its surface. Chests of this type were made in various places, and a good many have survived. The connection between their wrought iron volutes and those which often embellished cathedral doors of the same period, can clearly be seen. 56

Some chests were constructed with internal vertical stiles at the corners which emerged into view by being prolonged downwards to form feet. In this way the receptacle was raised above the damp floor and preserved from rot. Chests of this sort, with horizontal planks extending all along the front, existed concurrently with another kind in which all the components were fully visible. The stiles were of great width, and enclosed between them a horizontal panel often made from a single piece of timber. An example is in Stoke d'Abernon Church, Surrey. 57 Sometimes the surface was quite plain, at other times it was relieved by three or four chip-carved roundels or roundels combined with early Gothic arcading of simple type. Such chests were often coloured as well as carved. Perhaps the circular motifs derived from rose windows in cathedrals, though oddly enough the style was more prevalent in northern France and England than in the Ile-de-France. These chests were equipped with hinges of a type that did not outlast the 13th century, and were known as pin hinges. They consisted of a short horizontal pivot passing through a flange at each end of the lid and into the sides and back. The end of the pivot was covered with a small metal plate to prevent withdrawal.

The components of these chests were fixed together by mortice and tenon joints secured with wooden pegs or iron nails. No glue was used, except for the occasional application to uncarved surfaces of canvas or leather, which sometimes covered the whole surface, and was painted with small scale conventional ornamental designs or figure subjects.

Skilled woodcarvers, who were responsible for the splendid sculptures on choirstalls and other furniture in medieval churches and cathedrals, also applied their talents to secular objects. The late 13th-century coffer in the Musée de Cluny, Paris, bears not only boldly carved arcading across the front, but also a series of twelve knightly figures in high relief. These 58 figures are wearing armour of the late 13th century: mail hauberks with rectangular ailettes on the shoulders, and various headpieces typical of the period. The decoration extends to the back and sides, on one of which are depicted ten mounted knights at the foot of a steep hill, apparently protesting at the gradient to a peasant whom they have pressed into their service as a guide. These details, which are entirely secular, indicate that this chest was not part of the equipment of a church, but belonged to a rich private person. The architectural character of much of the decoration hardly needs stressing.

In the 14th century, when architecture itself assumed a more decorative character, chests with arcaded fronts became fairly common. Others were more elaborate, the analogy with the parent art being pursued so far that rows of buttresses were 67 spaced along the fronts as though they were supporting the walls of buildings. The majority were conceived in an architectural spirit, but some chests were more pictorial, and the relief ornament was of a kind often found carved in stone. In this category the most popular were carved with chivalric scenes such as the legend of St George, or two mounted knights jousting with lances. 60 The latter are generally known as *tilting* chests, though the description is not strictly accurate, for this term can be properly 59 applied only to the type of joust in which the contestants were separated by a barrier, or tilt. These chests continued to be made in the early 15th century. In the St George type, the method of continuous representation, often found in contemporary painting, in which successive events in the story are depicted at the same time, is sometimes used. The period of the fine example illustrated can be deduced from the armour worn by St George, 60 which includes a typical 14th-century bascinet. A number of episodes from the legend are shown, carved with characteristic Gothic vivacity.

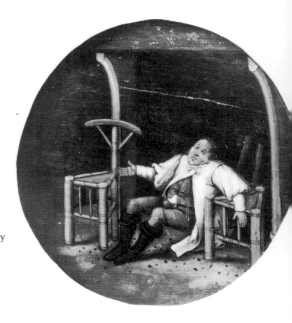

70 *The Virgin and Child before a fire-screen* by Robert Campin, 1378/9–1444. The Virgin is seated on an open-backed settle. Beneath the window is a triangular stool of turned elements, common throughout most of Europe during the 15th century. Behind the Virgin's head a halo is formed by a circular fire-screen of plaited cane. It has a vertical hinge down the centre allowing it to fold. The right-hand side of the picture which includes the chest and the chalice, is a modern addition. National Gallery, London

71 Circular panel painting by Pieter Brueghel the Younger, (c. 1564–1638) illustrating the proverb 'falling between two stools'. The left-hand stool has one leg prolonged upwards to form a back. Schloss Pommersfelden, Germany

Italian coffers were more often painted than carved, though the two techniques were occasionally combined. A mid-14th-century painted *cassone* which probably came from Florence, has a slightly curved top reminiscent of the primitive trunk. This example shows little evidence of architectural influence either in its construction or its decoration. The painted figures on the sides wear 14th-century costume. In the following century, when the skill of Italian painters became more highly developed, and their drawing as good as that of the Flemings, the panels of chests were often decorated with splendid figure compositions of such high quality that the chests were subsequently dismantled, the detached panels being treated as pictures and framed. Numbers of them are to be seen in various public collections. In 15th-century Italy, many chests were painted in one or two flat colours, and were often quite plain.

While English architecture and furniture became rather simpler in the 15th century, that of France and much of Europe displayed increasing elaboration in the use of repetitive, curvilinear forms. In Italy, however, Gothic influence remained generally slight, and the only concession to the northern style in the chest illustrated is to be found in the lozenge-shaped cartouches which relieve the surface. This chest is covered with

gesso, painted and gilt, which could be easily manipulated and carved, while the underlying wood was either perfunctorily carved to support the gesso, or left plain. This technique was much used in Italy, where wood carving was not yet highly developed, and those who employed decorative plasterwork in this manner may perhaps be regarded as the technical ancestors of the later stuccoists.

The Classical tradition had never really loosened its hold in Italy, and in the 15th century, the Renaissance style had no difficulty in putting the Gothic to flight altogether. The late 15th-century *cassone* illustrated is entirely Renaissance in both form and decoration, while another less magnificent specimen of the same period is inlaid with various woods in a manner which probably derived from Venetian and Genoese contacts with the Islamic world. Decoration of a generically similar kind was used by the Moors in Spain.

Many influences were at work in Spain: French, Flemish, Moorish, and even English to some extent. In the 15th century, the considerable number of Moors who remained after the fall of Granada were obliged either to leave the country, or abandon their faith and embrace Christianity. These Moorish apostates, who were known as *moriscos* and *mudéjares*, gave their name to the

72 Central panel of a polyptych by Dirk Bouts (c. 1415–75), the *Five Mystic Meals* (1464–8) showing two slab-ended stools and a dormant table. The long benches, of the same basic construction as the stools were particularly popular in England and the Low Countries. On the right of the picture can be seen a dresser standing on long legs and carved with linenfold panelling. Church of St Peter, Louvain

73 15th-century slab-ended stool, the edges of the supports shaped like buttresses. Victoria and Albert Museum, London

late Hispano-Mauresque style in architecture and furniture, an example of which will be examined later.

In northern Europe, architecture still provided the main inspiration, and late 15th-century chests bearing not only architectural panels, but also buttresses, survive.

Coffers made in one country often found their way to others, sometimes, no doubt, filled with goods purchased locally. So many from the duchy of Burgundy were reaching England in the second half of the 15th century, that English arkwrights considered their livelihood to be in danger, and the traffic was prohibited by an Act of 1483. It seems unlikely, however, that this measure was very effective, for we hear of 'Flaunders chests' far into the 16th century.

The various kinds of wood used for furniture depended on what was readily available in any particular district. Oak was the chief timber in northern Europe and England, not only because it was highly esteemed, but also because there was a great deal of it to be had. In the more southerly parts of France, in Spain, and in Italy, many other woods were employed, including lime, apple and pear, walnut, and cypress, while in the Alpine regions pine and fir were the most important. The fact that far more furniture was made in France from the late 15th

74 *Above left*: The Coronation Chair in Westminster Abbey is a famous example of furniture at its most architectural. It was made by Master Walter of Durham to the order of Edward I to hold the Stone of Scone which he had brought from Scotland in 1296. It was originally brightly painted, and later gessoed and gilt—during restoration seven layers of paint have been found. The four lions were added to the base in 1509, possibly for the coronation of Henry VIII. The present lions are copies made in 1727.

75 *Above centre*: Elaborately carved ceremonial chair traditionally called the throne of D. Afonso V. It dates from 1470, and is a good example of ornate Portuguese Gothic furniture. Museu Nacional de Arte Antiga, Lisbon

76 *Above right*: The Silver Throne of King Martin of Aragon, given after the death of the King in 1410 to the Cathedral of Barcelona. The throne is in fine condition, retaining all its gilt decoration. It is thought to have been made in the mid-14th century. Barcelona Cathedral

77 *Below left*: 15th-century Spanish tub-chair of carved walnut, bearing the coat-of-arms of the Enriquez family. Barrel chairs of this kind were often shown in manuscripts, the cruder type being made by cutting away parts of a large barrel. Instituto de Valencia de don Juan, Madrid

78 15th-century manuscript illustration showing a box settle with hinged lid and footboard, carved with linenfold panelling. A canopied cup board, partly enclosed, can be seen on the left. The players are using a large chest as a support for their chess-board. Cotton MS Aug V. fol. 334B. British Museum, London

79 15th-century German woodcarving of the Virgin and Child with St Anne. They are seated on a settle carved with an early form of linenfold decoration. The corners of the projecting seat are carved with Gothic brackets. Victoria and Albert Museum, London

80 Detail from a 15th-century altarpiece showing the Blessed St Agnes attending a sick man. Known as the altarpiece of the Grand Master Puchner, it was painted by a Bohemian artist in 1482. A plain box bed with headboard of simple plank construction can be seen, but the pillow cases are gaily striped and strikingly modern in appearance. Narodni Galerie, Prague

century than ever before may be partly due to the Hundred Years' War with England, which did not cease until the middle of the century. The plight of the peasants during the long period of hostilities had caused arable land to be encroached upon by forests owing to the neglect of tillage, and in the second half of the 15th century the quantity of well-grown timber available had increased. There is some truth in the old French saying: 'Forests came to France with the English.'

The Renaissance made very little impression on English styles 68 until well into the 16th century. Early Tudor chests displayed Gothic features such as cusping, decorative lettering or linenfold panelling. Later examples from the second quarter of the 16th century, however, sometimes form the battleground for an inconclusive struggle between both Gothic and Renaissance elements.

After the chest or coffer, the most important class of furniture was that used for seating. The type of chair or stool which probably had a longer history than any other had curved or straight 69 legs which crossed in the centre like a letter X. Those of early date had seats of textile or hide attached to horizontal rails, which, if high enough, might serve as armrests. They could be folded when not in use. Judging from medieval illuminated manuscripts, they were especially popular in the 14th and 15th centuries all over western Europe, by which time they had generally become of fixed construction with high, permanent backs, and could no longer be folded. These are usually known simply as X-chairs.

Many kinds of stool existed throughout the medieval period, 70 one international type consisting of three stout legs, either turned or cut, united by seat rails and stretchers, and topped by a wooden or rush seat, the triangular shape of which displayed a complete indifference to human anatomy. Sometimes one of the legs might be prolonged upwards with a bracketed cross-71 piece at the top to serve as a backrest, so that the whole formed what would now be called a chair, though quite normal chairs without arms were still known as *backstools* in England as late as the 17th century.

72 In the 15th century a type of stool known as slab-ended made what was probably its first appearance. The flat top consisted of a length of plank, supported at each end by another short length of which the edges were frequently shaped in a manner strongly suggestive of architectural buttresses. A piece of wood was cut out of the base leaving a space in the form of a trefoil, ogival, or 73 cusped Gothic arch, though the rounded, Romanesque arch was sometimes used, particularly in Italy. Seat rails, below the

projecting top, were either nailed to the end supports or slotted into them. Sometimes the supports were united by a stretcher, and if the ends emerged on the outer surface, they were secured by wedges—a device much favoured in modern times by the makers of reproduction oak furniture. Long benches were made in the same style, and were virtually elongated versions of the 74 stools.

Apart from seat furniture of a reasonably portable kind, manuscript illustrations, paintings, and a few actual examples bear witness to the existence, in the houses or castles of the wealthy, of more elaborate, throne-like structures which were probably seldom moved owing to their weight. Perhaps one of the best known in this category is the 14th-century Coronation Chair in Westminster Abbey. It would be difficult to imagine a 74 piece of furniture conceived with more regard to contemporary architecture; even the cresting of the back is in the form of a pointed gable. The same principle underlies the elaborately carved ceremonial chair, traditionally called the throne of D. Afonso V, dating from 1470, now in the National Museum 75 in Lisbon. It is a good example of ornate Portuguese Gothic furniture.

Even more sumptuous and equally architectural is the silver

Illustration from the Codex Amiatinus (A.D. 689-716), showing the Prophet Ezra writing. He is seated on a stool bench with square legs, painted with a decorative frieze. His footstool is of slab construction with a pegged stretcher, and nailed top. The small table has turned legs and a crossed stretcher with a fifth leg in the centre. The cupboard has panelled doors and base, the four shelves holding books. The pediment top and base are painted with birds and animals. Dividers and an erasing knife lie upon the floor, and the receptacle on the table is divided into two sections for different inks. Biblioteca Laurenziana, Florence

Romanesque carved figure of the Virgin, Rhenish, second half of the 12th century. The Virgin as *Sedes Sapientiae*, is seated in a chair with rectangular uprights and facetted knob terminals. The uprights are brilliantly painted with alternating triangles and the sides of the chair with Romanesque foliage on a yellow ground. Private Collection

Detail from a 13th-century mosaic lunette in St Mark's, Venice, from the fourth cupola of the narthex, illustrating Pharaoh's Dream. Pharaoh lies on a bed of box type with panelled and decorated sides and foot, and with a curved headrest. The bed has short moulded legs. The tester is supported on twisted and moulded columns with elaborate caps and bases.

81 Detail from the 15th-century German altarpiece in the parish church Tiefenbronn, showing Christ at the House of the Pharisee with Mary Magdalen drying his feet with her hair. The table has inverted V-trestles of turned members. The back of the bench on which Christ is seated is roughly made of rustic branches. The chair, on the other hand, is a sophisticated piece of turning.

82 *Above right*: Painted bed of 1337 from Tuscany. Panel paintings replace the Gothic carving that would be found north of the Alps. The bed has apparently been restored and perhaps altered. The barrel chair on the left is similar to the Enriquez chair in illustration 77. Ospedale del Ceppo, Pistoia

83 *Right*: Scene from a 15th-century French illuminated manuscript showing a royal party seated at a table supported on A-trestles. On the left is a partly enclosed cup board with cups, beakers and livery pots placed upon a cloth. Royal MS 20BXX. fol. 88b. British Museum, London

76 throne of King Martin of Aragon dating from the end of the 14th century, and still preserved in Barcelona. Other ceremonial chairs of the medieval period were mostly made of wood, and were sometimes furnished with high backs, curving forward at 78 the top to form a canopy, while others had a cloth of estate suspended over them like the tester of a bed.

In addition to these monumental examples, which are often to be seen in illuminated manuscripts, another type, very widely distributed throughout Europe, was shaped rather like part of a tub. Most were evidently plain, but the mid-15th-century 77 Spanish example illustrated is richly carved with Gothic tracery. It was quite possibly decorated in Spain by a Flemish carver, and is made of walnut instead of the more usual oak.

Wooden settles, consisting of benches or chests with backs and arms, provided seating accommodation for several persons. Some were built into recesses and usually had panelled backs; 78 others, of a lighter construction, were designed to be moved at will. The seat was sometimes covered with a long cushion known in England as a *banker*, and a footboard might also be provided to avoid draughts.

Late in the 15th century, what is usually known as the linen-fold pattern was introduced to England and other countries from the Netherlands, and began to be used on many objects of panelled construction, its incidence increasing markedly in the

16th century. A German medieval woodcarving illustrated shows St Anne, Mary, and Jesus on a settle with linenfold panel- 79 ling.

Several kinds of bed existed in the Middle Ages, some being of simple box-like construction. Others, especially in western Europe and England, stood permanently beneath draped testers suspended from the ceiling by cords. Contemporary illustrations show that bed chambers were commonly used as living rooms during the day, curtains at the foot of the bed being looped up in a pear-shaped bundle to enable it more conveniently to fulfil *Plate opposite* the function of a couch. Some beds had half-testers which were frequently an outward extension of the headboards. Italian 63 specimens were often without canopies, possibly because of the climate, and were more often painted than carved. 82

While contemporary sources attest the occasional existence of fixed, or dormant tables in the Middle Ages, there is no doubt that the majority were trestle tables, which could be dismantled and stowed away at the end of a meal. Even carpenters, who needed a flat surface for their work, made use of such tables. In *Ill. facing* manuscript illustrations depicting festive scenes, the invariable *page 24* presence of a large table-cloth makes it difficult to see the details 72 of the construction, but it is evident that the trestles were gener-ally in the form of an inverted V, or, if they were strengthened by 81 the addition of a cross-piece, like a letter A. Dormant tables 83 might sometimes have rectangular frames, with the upright members making a series of T-joints with the bottom rails resting on the floor. In well-equipped houses, what we should now call occasional tables were sometimes to be found in rooms other than those used for meals, and might have circular or 84 polygonal tops supported on central pillars. In rare instances they were large enough to be used for meals instead of the more *Plate opposite* usual trestle tables.

Most writing desks of the late Middle Ages were in the form of shallow boxes with sloping lids. They had the advantage of being portable, and could be placed on any flat surface. Others stood on their own supports, the earlier examples being similar to ecclesiastical lecterns, but by the end of the 15th century they were often of panelled construction, decorated with architec-tural arcading. Desks of this kind would have been used in scholastic establishments and in the counting houses of wealthy merchants. The one illustrated is English, the arcading on the 85 sides being in the prevailing Perpendicular style of architecture, but European examples often had more elaborate decoration with flamboyant tracery.

In medieval Europe, all who could afford to do so, accumu-lated large quantities of plate. In the Middle Ages, and for long

The Campin Altarpiece by the Master of Flémalle, (1375-1444), Cloisters Collection, Metropolitan Museum of Art, New York. In the central panel of the triptych illustrating the Annunciation, the Virgin sits against an open-backed settle, the side pieces decorated with carved lions. A ledge is fixed to the settle so that the feet can be raised off the cold floor. The polygonal table rests on a pair of carved supports on sturdy bases. In a recess on the left a vessel containing water is suspended and close by a towel hangs from a wall fitment. It is a warm spring day, for the window shutters are thrown open, and the bench is placed across the empty fireplace.

The Birth of the Virgin by the Master of the Life of the Virgin, Alte Pinakothek, Munich. The bed, which is raised upon a dais has a carved linenfold headboard. The curtains which would be dropped and drawn at night are raised up into pear-shaped bundles at the corners of the tester. A chest beside the bed holds linen and is carved, like the dresser on the left, with typical Gothic ornament. At this period the great bed often occupied the corner of the main living-room, and we can see that the bedroom area is curtained off for this event by a length of material hanging from a metal rail.

after, this usually took the form of silver drinking vessels, and vessels designed for serving wine and ale known in England as livery pots. Furniture makers soon provided wooden structures to display these cups and kindred objects, and as they consisted of simple arrangements of shelves or boards, they were known as cup boards. To begin with they were not enclosed, and this type persisted into the 17th century as the court cupboard. With the passage of time, parts of the structure began to be enclosed to form an aumbry, or what we should now corruptly call a cupboard. One type is sometimes called a *credence*; this had an open space below, and a compartment above fitted with a central door. The origin of the term is obscure, and is variously derived from the fact that such pieces were sometimes used to contain the reserved sacrament in churches, or as sideboards at which a lord's food and drink would first be tasted by a loyal servant as a precaution against poisoning.

Enclosed presses occurred in France in the late 12th century, all those recorded having been used in churches to contain vestments, but little is known of their use in domestic surroundings until the latter part of the medieval period. There seems little doubt that clothes were commonly stored in chests. A late 15th-century press from southern Germany is illustrated, decorated here and there with the elaborate architectural detail prevalent

in much of Europe at the time, and with a cornice embellished with crenellations like the battlements of a castle.

Mention was made earlier of Moorish craftsmen working in Spain. Their skill seems to have been highly esteemed, and they excelled in a form of surface decoration produced by inlaying numerous small pieces of wood in geometric patterns. A late medieval cabinet, with the doors treated in this manner, is illustrated. Much the same effect was achieved with mosaic by Moorish builders.

Eastern influences of this kind were not destined to find even a muted echo in the more northerly parts of Europe until considerably later, and the late 15th-century English livery cupboard illustrated, shows affinities with the Tudor-Gothic style of architecture then in favour. These pieces were evidently intended as containers for food, their fronts being pierced to permit the circulation of air. Gothic architectural details were eminently suitable for this purpose.

The artistic craftsmanship of the Middle Ages was expressed in a stylistic language with which we are no longer familiar in our daily lives, but their furniture was often conceived and executed with the same painstaking devotion as was lavished, on a grander scale, upon the churches and cathedrals which were the glory of medieval Europe.

84 *Above left*: 15th-century French illustration of the Last Supper. The disciples are seated at a circular table on a stout centre pedestal, the stand of which forms a foot rest. On the left is a folding X-chair apparently covered with a cushion. Royal MS 20BIV. fol. 105b. British Museum, London

85 *Above centre*: Late 15th-century English desk with hinged lid, decorated with Perpendicular arcading. Books and documents could be stored inside. Victoria and Albert Museum, London

86 *Above right*: Late 15th-century German press made of various woods, carved with architectural ornament and crowned by battlements. Bayerisches Nationalmuseum, Munich

87 *Right*: Late 15th-century cabinet made by a Moorish craftsman in Spain. The decoration is wholly geometric in character, in accordance with the Muslim principle—frequently evaded— that living forms should not be depicted. The ornament is similar to Moorish architectural mosaic. Museo de Artes Decorativas, Madrid

88 *Far right*: Late medieval English livery cupboard probably designed for the storage of food, the pierced openings permitting the circulation of air. The low arch on the underframing clearly derives from Tudor-Gothic architecture. Traditionally known as 'Prince Arthur's Cupboard', the piece came from a farmhouse in Shropshire, close to Tickenhall Manor, where Arthur, Prince of Wales, eldest son of Henry VII, lived with his bride, Katherine of Aragon, until his death in 1502. Victoria and Albert Museum, London

Engraved designs for chairs and tables from *Differents pourtraicts de menuiserie* by Hans Vredeman de Vries, published *c.* 1580

IV RENAISSANCE

ITALY

Hugh Honour

To the visitor from England or even France, the great palaces of 16th-century Florence, Venice, Genoa, Milan and Rome must have seemed almost unbelievably rich and luxurious. The walls of the main rooms were often frescoed by the greatest artists; ceilings were boldly carved and nearly always gilded; floors were inlaid with marble. There was an abundance of opulent fabrics—carpets from the Near East, the finest ormesin damasks from Persia, Genoese velvet and Lucchese silk brocade. Sideboards were decked with massive, intricately wrought silver and silver gilt ewers, basins and cups. In the smaller rooms there might be oil paintings on the walls, exquisite little bronze statuettes on tables and brackets, and hardly less finely worked bronze andirons in the fireplace. Yet, to modern eyes, the effect would have been distinctly sparse. It is indeed difficult to appreciate how bare the interiors shown in many 16th-century paintings would look if the gaily-clad throng of figures were suddenly to sweep out of them. These pictures show that in the early part of the century furniture was usually limited to the few essentials, and individual pieces seem to have been of the simplest construction.

Inventories reveal the surprisingly short supply of furniture even in the greater houses. That of Palazzo Badoer in Venice, drawn up in 1521, lists no more than four beds, two down cushions, one walnut table and eight chairs, a large sideboard, and four benches for the *portego*—the formal reception room— but a large number of chests of various size, several carpets including one to be draped over a table, many cloths and counter-panes. When Henry III of France visited Venice in 1574 an apartment was specially furnished for him in the Palazzo Foscari and contemporary sources describe the rooms in minute detail. The grandest of the bedrooms had a gilt bed with curtains of crimson silk and sheets hemmed with gold thread, which must have been uncomfortably scratchy, one gilt armchair under a cloth of gold canopy and a black marble table with a green velvet cloth. Despite their richness, these three objects of furniture would hardly have filled one of the vast rooms of a Venetian palace. Yet, at this date, Venice was a byword for luxurious living. An Italian contemporary remarked that her palaces were magnificent outside 'but within they are so richly and beautifully decorated that they astonish the visitor, and whoever seeks to describe them will be accused of lying.'

Much of this effect of richness was obtained by the use of opulent fabrics. Brilliantly coloured and boldly patterned Turkish carpets were very popular, especially in Venice which was the main European market for them. They were used to drape over tables and were sometimes hung on walls but rarely placed on the floor. Tables might alternatively be covered with velvet cloths, sometimes loose but otherwise fixed to the surface with brass nails. The woodwork of the more elaborate chairs might also be concealed in this way. Dining tables were, of course, covered with damask cloths; so also were the *credenze* or sideboards in the earlier part of the century. Paintings of this period suggest that beneath these covers the furniture was often of a very rough and ready type. Even in the grandest palaces the larger form of dining table seems to have been a very simple affair of boards and trestles. At the table, the seats were usually stools with three or four splayed legs, though Paolo Veronese allowed the guests at the *Marriage Feast at Cana* the rare comfort of upholstered chairs—to stress, no doubt, the magnificence of the occasion. It should be mentioned in this context that Italian houses did not have special dining rooms at this period. The furniture, being of an easily movable type, could be set up in whatever room was found most convenient—and this practice persisted until the 19th century. Indeed, the Sicilian Prince

89 *Studiolo* of Francesco I de' Medici. This room, designed by Giorgio Vasari in 1570–2, provides the perfect example of the setting in which a High Renaissance prince and patron of the arts wished to live. But like most Italian rooms of the period it owes its effect of great richness to the exquisite works of art— paintings by Bronzino and various pupils of Vasari, bronze statuettes by Giovanni Bologna and others—rather than to its few pieces of furniture. Palazzo Vecchio, Florence

90 *Above*: *The Vision of St Augustine*, 1502–8, by Vittore Carpaccio. This painting of St Augustine's room may well have been inspired by the study of some Venetian abbot. The chair and *prie-dieu* on the left—of a type used by high ecclesiastics—is the only piece of movable furniture; the cupboards, table and bench are either 'built in' or fixtures. All the woodwork is covered with cloth or leather. Scuola di S. Giorgio degli Schiavoni, Venice

91 *Below*: *The Marriage of Alexander and Roxana*, 1512, by Giovanni Antonio Bazzi, called Sodoma. Paintings suggest that Classically-inspired beds such as this were made in early 16th-century Rome, though none has survived. Palazzo della Farnesina, Rome

93 *Above*: *Cassone* of carved walnut, mid-16th century. The vogue for carved wood furniture, neither painted nor gilded, was a 16th-century innovation in Italy. This example, with its rather roughly carved decorations, is typical of many made in central Italy, especially Florence. Museo Horne, Florence

94, 95 *Above*: *Cassone* of walnut, mid-16th century. This magnificent *cassone* forms part of a group, two of which are in the Frick Collection, one in the Victoria and Albert Museum and one formerly in Palazzo Lancellotti, Rome. They were probably carved in Rome. The contorted male nudes on either side of the central coat-of-arms and the very overcrowded Roman triumph scenes strongly reflect the influence of Mannerist painters and sculptors. Frick Collection, New York. *Below*: detail of the same *cassone*.

92 *Above*: *Cassone* of carved wood and gesso, gilded and painted, *c.* 1500. The circular panels at either end, by the Veronese painter Bartolomeo Montagna, represent two scenes from Roman history (Duilius and Bilia on the left, the Vestal Tuccia on the right). The *cassone* was made for a member of the Buri family of Verona whose coat-of-arms appears in the central panel. The painting of the Holy Family, *c.* 1490–5, above the *cassone* is by Andrea Solario, in a frame which is a 19th-century imitation of a 15th-century type. Museo Poldi-Pezzoli, Milan

Giuseppe di Lampedusa remarked in his memoirs that a dining room was a rarity even in 19th-century Sicily—it was his own practice to dine in whatever room he fancied until his death in 1957.

The most elaborately furnished apartment in a palace seems to have been the *studio*, the sanctum of the master of the house who kept there his collection of manuscripts and books and perhaps statuettes, coins, medals and other objects of *virtù*. Studies like that in the Palazzo Ducale at Urbino, surrounded with intarsia panelling probably remained popular in the 16th century. The *studiolo* of Francesco I dei' Medici in the Palazzo Vecchio, Florence, and the adjoining *tesoretto* are both decorated above their many built-in cupboards with paintings and bronze statuettes by the greatest artists in Florence of the 1570s. A fair idea of a somewhat simpler *studio* in Venice at the beginning of the 16th century may be obtained from Carpaccio's painting of *The Vision of St Augustine*. The room makes a rich impression but there is very little movable furniture in it—the cupboards are built into the walls, the writing table and bench are also fixtures attached at one end to the wall, and the bookshelf is a very simple contrivance. The only notable piece of furniture, indeed, is a combined chair and *prie-dieu* of a type used by high ecclesiastics on ceremonial occasions and of which no example has survived. The woodwork of such a chair, as of the writing table and bench, would be covered with fabric.

Another painting by Carpaccio, *The Dream of St Ursula* sug- *Plate facing* gests how the bedroom of a great Venetian palace in the 1490s *page* 48 would have looked. No such bed as this is known to survive but it was probably a fairly common type. The furnishings in the room are so austerely simple that the crown at the foot of the bed looks a little out of place. Apart from the bed, the room contains only a somewhat old-fashioned armchair with a Gothic back, a three-legged stool, a table covered with a cloth, a small cupboard and a *cassone*. Yet there can be no doubt that Carpaccio intended it to be a bedroom fit for a princess. Florentine paintings of *The Birth of the Virgin* and similar subjects, executed at the beginning of the 16th century show bedrooms equally bare of furniture. The most popular type of bed appears to have been of a box-like form, mounted on a dais with a curtained tester above, either projecting from the wall or supported on posts. A particularly fine bed, probably of a type to be found in Rome early in the century, appears in Sodoma's *Marriage of Alexander* 91 *and Roxana*—the woodwork is delicately painted with grotesques, the posts are in the form of Corinthian columns. It is one of the surprisingly few pieces of furniture, other than *cassoni*, which reflect the archaeological interests of the period.

Beds were occasionally decorated with paintings. An early 16th-century Venetian example, said to be painted in the manner of Giovanni Bellini, survived into the 19th century. It is possible that such examples were broken up so that the paintings

96 *Cassapanca* of carved wood, *c.* 1550. The *cassapanca* was used both as a chest and a seat and is thus the descendant of the *cassone* and the ancestor of the sofa. This very large example was probably made for one of the Florentine palaces. Museo Nazionale, Florence

97 Centre table of carved wood, mid-16th century. The boldly sculptured supports of this table, bulging with grotesque sphinx-like creatures, reveal the influence of Mannerism, though the form of the table derives from ancient Rome. Palazzo Davanzati, Florence

might be framed as pictures. A similar fate overtook other pieces of furniture. Vincenzo Catena owned a *restrello*—a peculiarly Venetian piece of furniture for holding loose papers—painted by Giovanni Bellini. A series of paintings of allegories by Bellini, probably executed as decorations for a mirror or *restrello*, is preserved in the Accademia at Venice. Numerous little Giorgionesque pictures appear to have been executed as decorative panels for cupboards or cabinets, but few such pieces survive in any form from this period. And, of course, the famous painting of *Apollo and Daphne*, now in the Pinacoteca Manfrediana, Venice, generally attributed to Giorgione himself, once graced the front of a Venetian *cassone*.

Cassoni were the most elaborate pieces of furniture to be found in an Italian palace in the early 16th century, and for that reason they have survived in considerable quantity—they were probably the only things thought worthy of preservation from one generation to another. Their makers were craftsmen who seem to have held themselves rather above the common *falegnami* or household carpenters and joiners responsible for the rougher objects of furniture, and belonged to a separate guild. These *cassoni* were made, usually in pairs, to hold a bride's trousseau, and in armigerous families, one would be decorated with her coat-of-arms and the other with that of her husband. There is reason to suppose that they were also made as useful and

98 *Left*: The Farnese table, with carved marble supports and inlaid marble top, *c.* 1570. Tables such as this, inspired by ancient Roman examples were made only for the greatest palaces in 16th-century Italy. This one was made for the Palazzo Farnese, Rome, and possibly designed by the architect Vignola. The same type became popular once again in the Neo-Classical period. Metropolitan Museum of Art, New York. Dick Fund, 1958

99 *Above*: Cupboard with intarsia decorations, 1502, perhaps by Fra Giovanni da Verona, the greatest intarsia artist of his day. He devoted himself mainly to the decoration of choirstalls. This cupboard was made for a monastic library, but it is probable that similar ones were made for private houses. Abbazia di Monte Oliveto Maggiore, near Siena

100 Sideboard of carved walnut, mid-16th century. Probably made in Rome, this monumental piece of furniture reflects the Renaissance passion for the orders of Classical architecture. Pieces such as this came into fashion in the 16th century, replacing the simple tables draped with fabrics which had hitherto been usual. Museo di Palazzo Venezia, Rome

ornamental furnishings without any nuptial significance. Inventories reveal that they were used as containers for all manner of clothes, fabrics and other objects besides the bridal supply of linen and dresses. They might also serve as seats and some were fitted with backboards which converted them into *cassapanche*.

The greatest ingenuity was applied to the decoration of *cassoni*. At the beginning of the century the type set with paintings in a Classical architectural framework seems to have been most popular. In Florence, battle scenes and the triumphs of Roman generals were the vogue but further north paintings of religious subjects were more popular. Some were decorated with relief ornaments—friezes of *putti*, swags of fruit or flowers and so on—in gilt gesso. Others were embellished with panels of exquisitely worked intarsia in which buildings or still life subjects were rendered in a mosaic of different coloured woods. Intarsia decorations were also applied to large cupboards or wardrobes, usually for ecclesiastical use.

As the century proceeded the earlier types of *cassoni* went out of fashion in favour of those of carved and polished wood, neither painted nor gilt. Some of the new *cassoni* emulated the design of antique sarcophagi, supported on lion-paw feet, with crisp acanthus leaf foliage spreading over the surface or with carved scenes from Classical history and mythology on the front. In the style of the carving the influence of Mannerism is usually obvious—nudes are contorted into elegant attitudes, attenuated sphinxes sit at the corners, and there are panels of ornamental carving imitating leather strapwork of the type which later became so popular in northern Europe. A group of *cassoni* decorated in this way, now divided between the Frick Collection, New York, and the Victoria and Albert Museum, London, is among the minor masterpieces of Mannerist sculpture. The majority are, or course, much simpler than these magnificent pieces. But many are no less obvious products of Mannerism, with their free use of Classical ornament and figure carvings.

The addition of a back and arms could convert a *cassone* of this type into a primitive sofa—still rather angular but less uncomfortable than the earlier form of *cassapanca*. The new vogue for carved and polished wood was also manifested in other types of furniture. Massive tables on richly carved supports with satyrs and full-bosomed nymphs or sphinxes staring out of jungles of foliage became popular. For the very great palaces, tables of this pattern were also made in marble. Similar carved decorations were applied to cupboards. The *credenza* or sideboard which had hitherto been a rough table draped with a linen cloth now assumed a far more elaborate form, with pilasters or half-columns and a bold architectural cornice. Paintings reveal that in Venice, and probably elsewhere beds with posts in the form of caryatids or terms became fashionable in the 1570s. Other beds had posts of baluster form with richly carved testers. Smaller objects of furniture such as caskets, mirror and picture frames, candlesticks, lamps and bellows were wrought with the greatest fantasy and ingenuity. So small an object as the Farnese casket, for example, intricately adorned with human figures and mythological beings, is a notable piece of Mannerist artistry.

In the course of the century chairs began to assume more elaborate forms. The simple benches, stools and rush-seated ladderback chairs usual at the beginning of the century survived only in the poorer houses, for which they continued to be made to much the same design until very recently. It is, for this reason, very difficult to date pieces of furniture of this rustic type. Stools were made with elegantly shaped supports; the splats at backs of chairs were ingeniously carved. Padded chairs with arms and high backs terminating in knobs—which, at the beginning of the century seem to have been reserved for the master and mistress of a palace—gradually became numerous in all large houses.

Such developments reflected a general need for greater comfort, the result, no doubt, of a period of relative political stability after the turbulence of the 1520s. But it was the grandeur of these Italian Renaissance interiors and furnishings which was so keenly admired throughout Europe. Italian craftsmen were sought after and Renaissance forms and ornament were studiously imitated north of the Alps. In the meantime in Italy itself, taste was moving towards a greater elaboration which foreshadowed the bold richness of Baroque.

101 *The Birth of the Seventh Child, c.* 1550, by Lamberto Sustris, (detail). The bed with its curious Mannerist caryatid posts appears in more than one painting and is probably similar to a type popular in Venice, though no examples have survived. Despite the architectural richness of the room, the rest of the furniture is simple. Inventories reveal that bedrooms even in the greatest 16th-century palaces were as sparsely furnished. Galleria Borghese, Rome

102 The Farnese casket of silver gilt, by Manno di Bastiano Sbarri, with engraved rock-crystal panels by Giovanni Bernardi, made 1548-61. The casket was made to hold rare manuscripts and printed books. It reveals the influence of Michelangelo in its general design and numerous figures. Museo di Capodimonte, Naples

103 *Below left*: Design for a picture frame, *c.* 1540, by Girolamo da Carpi. Designs such as this, usually made by painters, first began to circulate in the 16th century and hastened the dissemination of stylistic changes throughout Europe. So far as can be gathered from surviving pieces of furniture the designs were rarely copied in their entirety but were used as sources of decorative details. Victoria and Albert Museum, London

104 *Below right*: A pair of bellows, of carved walnut, mid-16th century. With their amusing grotesque masks, these bellows show how the Mannerist style affected even the less important pieces of household furniture. Wallace Collection, London

FRANCE

Laurence Buffet-Challié

The taste for Italian ideas had come to France well before the beginning of the 16th century, mostly through the encouragement of royal houses. René of Anjou, also King of Naples and Sicily, poet and patron of the arts, attracted to his Court artists from the other side of the Alps. Two sculptors, the Dalmatian Francesco di Laurana and Pietro di Milano produced the first work in France to be influenced by the Italian Renaissance. Louis XI and the Dukes of Burgundy also showed an awareness of the new trends. But the real confrontation between the medieval world and the new humanism did not come about until the time of the wars with Milan and the Kingdom of Naples. On February 22nd 1495, the French, led by the 24 year-old Charles VIII, entered Naples in dazzling splendour. This campaign had been undertaken in the hope of reclaiming the lost Angevin possessions. It had all the glamorous air of a military progress passing through such stimulating centres as Florence, Lucca, Pisa, Rome and Naples. The Italian princes were reluctant to open their sumptuous palaces to these invaders for whom plunder was the better part of conquest, yet the French nobility was to learn much from their contact with this new society, a society already accustomed to literature, art and science. Such a taste for luxury and refinement was unknown in the Gothic world, and Charles dreamed of re-creating at Amboise the splendours of an Italian court. Besides a rich booty of works of art, he brought back with him twenty-two craftsmen 'to practise their craft in the Italian manner'. There were architects, sculptors, goldsmiths, dressmakers, gardeners, woodworkers and two notable intarsia workers, Domenico da Cortona and Bernardo da Brescia. Thus it was that the Renaissance sowed its first seeds in that stronghold of French tradition, the Loire Valley.

Italian influence at first produced nothing more than the application of the new style of decoration to Gothic structures. Architecture was the first to show signs of change, and furniture followed soon afterwards. Until now political instability had created a society in which complete households would move from castle to castle, carrying with them their portable goods. This explains the prevalence of folding chairs and collapsible beds, and the use of textiles, so much lighter and easier to transport than furniture made of solid wood. (The French word *meuble* meant mobile.) In the 16th century, life became more stable. A bourgeois class arose, enamoured of comfort and sensitive to the new artistic movement. This emergent clientele encouraged the new designs in order to satisfy a desire for a more refined way of life.

The French Renaissance was a complex movement. Not only were there divergent, even contradictory forces within it, but many medieval features were to persist for some time. Moreover, surviving examples of furniture are rare, and any division into styles must necessarily be arbitrary. For the sake of clarity the generally accepted classification is adopted here, namely: the First Renaissance or François I Style, which covers the reign of Charles VIII (1483–98), Louis XII (1498–1515) and François I (1515–47): the High Renaissance or Henri II Style (1547–89) which embraces the reigns of Charles IX and Henri III.

105 *Left*: The chest continued to be an important piece of furniture during the first half of the 16th century, but its construction was modified. The façade, instead of being sometimes divided into a series of small panels, now often had one single panel which allowed for a greater freedom of decoration. This early 16th-century example of carved walnut, which came from Azay-le-Rideau, one of the most perfect Renaissance châteaux of the Loire, is of high quality. Carved pilasters mask the joints. The decorative motifs are inspired by Classical 'grotesques', mythical animals, masks and delicate scrolls. Musée des Arts Décoratifs, Paris

106 *Below left*: This chest, dated 1546, is carved with scenes of the Labours of Hercules and derives from the celebrated sarcophagus in the Torlonia Museum in Rome. The artist had, of course, no direct knowledge of Classical sculpture but his carving is modelled on Italian Renaissance bronze plaquettes, and the fight with the Nemean lion is after Moderno. The architectural framework is very Italianate in manner. But the disproportionately heavy pilasters at the corners and the rudimentary treatment of the capitals suggest that the carver was copying fashionable forms without fully comprehending them. Musée des Arts Décoratifs, Paris

107 *Above right*: Detail from a mid-16th-century chest, showing a fine network of white arabesques on a dark ground. This type of decoration, known as Mauresque, derives from Arabic sources via Italy. Musée des Arts Décoratifs, Paris

108 *Right*: Detail from the panel of a chest of the 1560s. Strapwork decoration deriving from engraved designs was very fashionable in the 16th century. In 1563 Androuet Ducerceau had published his collection of engraved patterns: *Livre contenant passementerie de moresque.* Musée des Arts Décoratifs, Paris

109 *The Wedding Feast*, a painted miniature from 'The Art of Love'. As in the Middle Ages, the guests are seated on benches at a trestle table. In the background the *buffet* is still carved with ogival arches in the Gothic style although flanked by Classical pilasters and capitals and with a Classical cornice. The wall panelling is of the Italian type. Louvre, Paris

110 At the beginning of the 16th century the dresser retained its 15th-century form: a rectangular or hexagonal enclosed section on an open base, the supports linked by arcading. This example is divided horizontally into two stages. The upper section has two doors, the lower a central door flanked by fixed panels. The elaborate lock plates serve the same decorative function as they did on earlier Gothic chests. The carving is still flamboyantly Gothic, including crockets and pinnacles, but Renaissance features are also present such as the rounded arch, the shell, the fleur-de-lis. Musée de Cluny, Paris

111 Identical in form to the previous example, this early 16th-century dresser is more advanced in the character of the decoration. The carved heads within medallions are borrowed from Italy. They are realistically treated in vigorous high relief, as if they were portraits. The carver, while conforming to fashionable taste has lost none of his native vivacity. The linenfold panelling at the base, still Gothic in manner, would have been growing old-fashioned at the time, and has been relegated to a comparatively unimportant position. Philadelphia Museum of Art, Foulc Collection

112 The above engraving shows a dresser similar to that on the right; the same reeded pilasters, the same strapwork. Dressers appear in kitchen, hall, and living room alike. Notice the pewter vessels on the dresser and shelves, and the foliate decorative frieze above the fireplace. Bibliothèque Nationale, Paris

113 French 16th-century cabinet pieces are seldom without carved decoration. This somewhat heavy dresser from the Dauphiné region relies for its formal lines solely upon a number of architectural elements: reeded columns and pilasters, cornice and entablature. The only ornament consists of inlaid strapwork in the panels. The piece recalls Swiss examples of this type. Musée des Arts Décoratifs, Paris

The François I Style
(1483-1547)

The structure of furniture remained somewhat medieval and its
109 decoration evolved slowly. Under Charles VIII and Louis XII,
Italianate motifs like foliate scrolls and arabesques were com-
110 bined with such traditional Gothic features as pinnacles, pointed
111 arches and linenfold panelling. While woodcarving continued
to be in Franco-Flemish style, it is quite clear that in adding
foreign-inspired ornamentation, the craftsman was bowing to
the prevailing fashion. All traces of the Gothic had disappeared
by the reign of François I, giving way to a new repertoire of ideas
borrowed from Italian architecture. Notable among these were
grotesques, pilasters decorated with arabesques, composite
105 capitals, candelabra, dolphins and heads carved in high relief.
    François I was twenty when he came to the throne in 1515. He
had a Rabelaisian love of life, but was equally attracted to the
arts and the budding humanism. As early as 1517 we find him
discussing with Erasmus the founding of the *Collège de France*.
The French now had a king who was bent upon educating their
taste. At his castle at Amboise he tried to emulate Italian courtly
life, drawing around him, like a Florentine Renaissance prince,
a great body of artists, many of whom came from Italy, and no
less a person than Leonardo da Vinci was to spend the last three
years of his life there.
    In 1525 the King returned from captivity after the disastrous
battle of Pavia. This was the signal for a veritable flowering of
life in all its aspects. Literature, the arts, poetry and social life
came into their own. The Court had been frivolously given up
to balls, hunting, tournaments and conversation. It travelled
from one castle to another according to the season and to its own
whims. It had therefore lacked the roots from which an intellectual life might grow. Fontainebleau, not far from Paris, was
to provide the necessary stability, for it was this castle, built by
Louis VI in the heart of an immense forest, that François decided
to make 'the true abode of Kings'. He wanted its decoration to be
as sumptuous as possible and with this in mind he summoned
two distinguished Italians to work for him, Rosso in 1530 and
Primaticcio in 1532. These two artists who were painters, sculptors and stuccoists as well as architects brought about an unparalleled advance in the field of decoration. From these beginnings the great School of Fontainebleau was to grow, upsetting
all the existing ideas in French art.
    These two pioneers created a dramatic setting for the House
of Valois. In close collaboration with French and Flemish artists, they transformed this modest medieval castle into 'a new
Rome', covering the walls of the royal apartments with lively
frescoes in the style of the great contemporary Italian masters.
Dividing and framing these frescoes was the stucco work of
Rosso and Primaticcio, which displayed some surprising inno-
Plate facing vations. There were slender nymphs in the manner of Parmi-
page 49 gianino, graceful *putti*, heavy garlands, masks, chimerae, draped
117, 118 human figures and stylised scrolls, motifs which were adopted
in the decoration of furniture.
119

The Henri II Style
(1547-89)

With the new reign came a reaction, led by the architects and
decorators, Philibert Delorme, Pierre Lescot, Jean Bullant,
Jacques Androuet Ducerceau and the sculptor Jean Goujon,
all of whom had worked at Fontainebleau with the Italians.
Against the *bella maniera* imposed by François I they set up a
counter-reform proposing a style which was more specifically
French. In 1548, Philibert Delorme was appointed *Surintendant des Bastiments du Roi*. In 1550, Ducerceau published a collection of engravings which showed examples of furniture of
every kind. Although this work was based upon the Classical
canons of proportion and motifs drawn from antiquity, his own
highly personal interpretation of them is undeniable. The human figure played an increasingly important role in the decora-

114 The influence of Hugues Sambin and of Androuet Ducerceau are
reflected in this astonishing piece made in the last quarter of the 16th
century. Caryatids, harpies, strapwork, polished bosses, masks, arabesques—
here is the full range of Mannerist motifs. Nor are the mouldings left
unnoticed, for they are carved with palmettes and acanthus leaves. Four
long-necked chimerae link the upper stage with the moulded base. Their
bodies terminate in plumed scrolls from which dangle horses' tails. The
creatures stand upon a single lion's foot. Frick Collection, New York

115 *Below left*: By placing a square upon a rectangle, the designer has
lightened the overall effect. The decoration of this walnut cupboard dating
from the second half of the 16th century again stems from Ducerceau and
Sambin. Upon the upper door a helmeted Minerva is enclosed in a heavy
oval frame of fruit. On either side are ringed columns supporting a carved
pediment, broken at the centre and set with a mask. In the spandrels are
sea-horses, while winged horses decorate the doors of the lower half. A pair
of smiling terms flank each stage, and although in higher relief, they
harmonise perfectly with the whole ensemble. Philadelphia Museum of Art,
Foulc Collection

116 *Below right*: In his collection of engraved designs for furniture, published
in 1550, Ducerceau gives an example of a dresser of this type with flanking
columns extending to the full height of the piece. Light mouldings frame
the doors, and the base stands upon ball feet. Anticipating the cupboard
proper this is a fine example of the '*façon de Paris*', the description applied
to a similar walnut dresser listed in the inventory of Gauthiot d'Ancier in
1596. Musée des Arts Décoratifs, Paris

117, 118 The elegantly attenuated figures of the sculptor Jean Goujon derive straight from Italy. One has only to compare a drawing by Parmigianino, *(left)* with a nymph from the Fountain of the Innocents in Paris by Goujon *(right)* to see this. In their decorative schemes at Fontainebleau, Primaticcio and Rosso had introduced the Mannerist style of Parmigianino, and Goujon in his turn assimilated these influences. 'Spring' by Parmigianino, Louvre, Paris. Nymph from the Fountain of the Innocents (1574-9) by Jean Goujon

119 The name of Jean Goujon is linked with this type of furniture, so prevalent in the Ile de France. Yet it is at Fontainebleau one must seek for the source of its inspiration. Joiners and carvers did not solely rely on pattern books; the leading artists of the time also influenced their work. The four mythological figures carved in low relief on the doors of this dresser represent Jupiter and Juno (above) and Mercury and Venus (below). Musée de Lyon

tive arts, which were also invaded by such exotic creatures as sphinxes, chimerae and griffins, and by eagles, lions and rams. There also developed a trend towards geometric patterns such as strapwork. But towards the end of the century the approach to design became more scholarly and purely architectural. Among the conflicting streams a certain coolness can be discerned in sharp contrast to the earlier exuberance.

Numerous local variations make it difficult to gain a general picture of the Henri II style. The art of the Court, publicised by the ornamental engravings, spread throughout the whole of France, but this did not prevent a distortion or even a debasement of the new designs where regional tradition was strong. Thus Hugues Sambin, architect, sculptor and cabinet-maker, who worked at Dijon and Besançon, has been considered to be over-rich in his carving, yet this lively Burgundian was quite conversant with 'official' art. In his collection of engravings entitled *Oeuvre de la diversité des termes dont on use en architecture*, published at Lyon in 1572, we find illustrations similar to those produced by Ducerceau. If certain variations can be distinguished between the methods and attitude of craftsmen in the Ile de France, the Loire Valley, the Auvergne, Provence, the Lyon region and Burgundy, it would still be dangerous to conclude that there was any systematic division into 'schools'.

Types of Furniture

In the Middle Ages the construction of furniture was very simple. The mortice and tenon, dovetailing, and the groove and tongue constituted the sum total of the joiner's techniques. More subtle methods appeared in the 16th century—sunken dovetailing or mitred joints concealed the tenons within the thickness of the wood, leaving the carver free to decorate the entire surface. The sturdy oak of the Middle Ages was used less and less and was supplanted by walnut. The oiliness of this wood renders it smooth and dark so that it looks like bronze. With a finer grain than other woods it lent itself more easily to the carver's chisel and allowed him to attain the greater suppleness demanded by the new decorative repertoire.

If the furniture of the Italian Renaissance was indebted to the work of the painter, that of the French Renaissance was indebted rather to the architect and the sculptor. Low relief, high relief, and sculpture in the round achieved a mastery that stemmed directly from the sculptural tradition of the Gothic workshop. Italian influence revealed itself above all through the introduction of colour by means of intarsia, marquetry or gilding.

There is no better way to acquaint oneself with the furniture of a period than by referring to the contemporary inventories. To take just two examples, the inventories of the Constable of Montmorency (1568) and of Catherine de' Medici (1589) provide evidence that in the highest ranks of society there was an abundance of furniture covered in fabric but scarcely any carved and decorated pieces.

In 1539 Gilles Corrozet published in Lyon a curious little book (still preserved in the Bibliothèque Nationale in Paris) which gives us a vivid picture of 'the furnishing of a gentleman's house' in the first part of the 16th century. The amusing lines of verse accompanying each illustration are themselves a useful source of information on the different categories of furniture.

The chest, essential to the Middle Ages, was still used for the storing of 'adornments, finery and clothing'. The structure was now modified, however. The narrow panels of the façade were now superseded by a single panel decorated with carving, sometimes with small columns and caryatids set against the uprights. These were often marriage chests. A chest covered in leather, with iron fittings, and having a convex lid, could be used as a travelling trunk as well as a piece of furniture.

The dresser, 'firmly closed by two doors each bearing a medallion' was introduced in the first thirty years of the century and corresponds to the *buffet* or sideboard of medieval times. The upper part of the dresser was closed by two or more doors decorated in low relief with ornamental foliage round a raised portrait medallion. Below this, two drawers were sometimes placed. The whole structure rested on supports in the form of columns or pilasters, or on a solid base also provided with doors. From the reign of Henri II onwards, the structure of the dresser became more architectural in character. The verticals consisted of pilasters or columns or carved figures. The figures might be human or in the form of fabulous beasts, for which Androuet Ducerceau and especially Hugues Sambin provided many designs. The upper structure was usually separate, and placed slightly back in relation to the lower supporting part. It was often surmounted by a pediment sometimes broken in the centre to accommodate another carved figure. The separation of the upper and lower parts of the dresser was emphasised by a central frieze into which one or two carved drawers were fitted. The doors were decorated with allegorical scenes, mythological figures or architectural vistas. The decoration was further enhanced by inlays of marble, mother-of-pearl, ivory or precious woods. Another type of dresser, frequently encountered in the second half of the 16th century, consisted only of the upper structure with two doors. It rested on fluted pilasters or balusters or indeed on long-necked chimerae carved in high relief.

The term *armoire* (wardrobe) did not appear in Gilles Corrozet's book. Some examples did however appear towards the end of the century. They had one large door and the main structure was framed in four long thin columns. A design for a piece of this type is attributed to Androuet Ducerceau. It foreshadowed the wardrobe proper, which was to appear in the next century. The term *armoire* was sometimes applied to a cupboard fitted into the panelling of a room.

The cabinet, like the *armoire*, is a term that has given rise to some confusion. Gilles Corrozet applied it to a chest with many drawers, placed upon a stand. It was an elegant piece lined with silk or velvet, and served as a container for 'beautiful jewels, rings, chains and buttons'. The cabinet was not to take its final monumental form until the early 17th century.

The table, as in the Middle Ages, was often nothing more than a simple wooden top resting on trestles, easy to move about. At this period a table would not have a permanent place of its own, since a nobleman would dine in whichever room he chose. The table would be covered with a carpet or with material matching

Pourtrait du 1. Terme.

120 *Left*: Hugues Sambin, received as a master carpenter of the Dijon Guild in 1549 was the author of a collection of architectural designs called *Oeuvre de la diversité des termes dont on use en architecture*, published in Lyon in 1572. The plate illustrated here demonstrates not only his skill as an engraver, but also his vivid imagination. Bibliothèque Nationale, Paris

121, 122 Towards the middle of the 16th century the table ceased to be a single board placed upon stretchers, and acquired, like the dresser, an architectural form. Ducerceau, who had studied Classical architecture, is the author of this design *(above right)* which suggests a little Corinthian building. But when the joiners set about interpreting such designs, they added native touches and their work was consequently less archaeologically correct. The table below, in the Musée des Arts Décoratifs, Paris, has a heavy base, the paired piers forming a simple arcade. Beneath the four corners of the apron are turned pendant motifs in the shape of spinning tops.

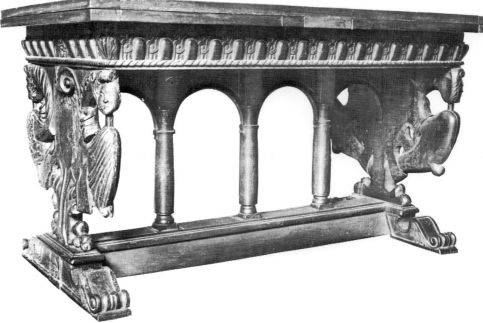

123 *Right*: In the second half of the 16th century the dining table differed very little from late Renaissance Italian examples based upon Roman prototypes. The supports are carved as griffins, rams, eagles or caryatids, fanning out from the base towards the top. They rest upon scrolled bases linked by a broad stretcher. Further supports also spring from the stretcher itself. These are sometimes arcaded columns, as in this example, sometimes of pedestal shape, and sometimes in the form of richly carved masks and foliage. The frieze might be decorated with palmettes, reeding, gadrooning or shells. The table top is sometimes supplied with a draw-leaf at either end. Musée des Arts Décoratifs, Paris

124 The ecclesiastical throne of the Gothic period was in the form of a chest with a high back extending forward to form a canopy, the side panels rising above the level of the seat as armrests. As time went on the chest disappeared, being replaced by a flat seat over an open structure supported on piers or columns. This imposing chair still echoes the earlier form with its high back, but now the reeded pilasters and the cornice replacing the earlier canopy reveal Classical influence. Collection: Nicolas Landau, Paris

125 Towards the end of the century a new type of chair developed, lighter and easier to move, with a low back and open arm pieces. This example dating from about 1590 is of carved walnut, enriched with inlaid panels of ebony. The curved arms have ram's head terminals. Stretchers form an H to link the square-sectioned back legs with the turned front ones. Sometimes these chairs have padded seats and back rests and are covered in velvet or silk. The fringes are of silk or wool, or, on very rich examples, of gold thread. Frick Collection, New York

126 The so-called 'gossiping' chair or *chaise caquetoire* has a trapezoidal seat to accommodate the wide skirts of the sitter. The back, in contrast to the armchair, is tall and narrow, sometimes pierced and always carved—this example is decorated with quills and strapwork. The arms, curving outwards towards the front, rest on turned balusters. Heavy stretchers brace the legs. Museum of Decorative Art, Oslo

127 *Left*: This engraving, dated 1587, shows the Duke of Nemours, one of Henri III's favourites, dressed as a *mignon* and seated on an elegant armchair. The back is carved, and the scrolled arms terminate in masks. As was the custom, a square cushion softens the wooden seat. The tapestry in the background anticipates the decorative style of Louis XIII. Bibliothèque Nationale, Paris

128 *Right*: Upholstered furniture was not uncommon in the 16th century and although few examples survive it is often shown in the paintings and engravings of the period. This portrait of Charles IX, painted by François Clouet in 1563 shows a chair entirely upholstered in velvet held in place by brass studs, and decorated with gold braid. This type of chair continued in use well into the 17th century. Kunsthistorisches Museum, Vienna

129 This engraving of Henri II lying mortally wounded in his bed, is from Perrissin et Tortorel's *Guerres, Massacres et Troubles adevenus en France les dernières années du règne d'Henri II*, published in Lyon in 1569-70. The canopy of the great bed is supported by caryatids, and the frame is carved with gadroons. Bibliothèque Nationale, Paris

130, 131 Surviving examples of Renaissance beds are rare. It is therefore revealing to compare a bed in the Musée de Cluny *(below)* with an engraved design by Ducerceau *(above)*. The construction is identical although the decoration differs in detail. In both cases the bed posts are partly columnar—and partly baluster-shaped and are carved with arabesques, masks, gadroons and acanthus leaves. The supports are different, but the carver rarely copied a design faithfully. The headboard suggests that the bed underwent certain modifications in later years.

the curtains and the chair coverings, a practice which lasted until the 18th century.

The table *à l'italienne* was widely adopted in France. It was first and foremost an ornamental piece, richly decorated with carvings. The rectangular top had a frieze round the edge, with ornaments of strapwork, gadrooning, palmettes, or other typical motifs. It rested on a very complicated support. The engravings of Ducerceau and Sambin give us examples: the supports at each end were made in the form of human figures, griffins, eagles or chimerae, placed back to back, which spread outwards as they approached the table top. The bases were connected by 123 stretchers. In the space between the stretcher and the table top were caryatids or other figural motifs carved in relief. Columns and arches, inspired by Italian architecture also appeared. We 121, 122 know, too, despite the absence of surviving examples, that square or round tables with one central leg appeared during this period. Most Renaissance tables were provided with sliding leaves which 123 could be extended. In the second part of the century such tables were often enriched with marquetry or with marble or gilding. Table tops in marble mosaic were also known, but were less common. Towards the end of the century there appeared a table with six or eight legs connected by intersecting transverse bars. Sometimes a turned pendant ornament was placed beneath each corner of the table top. 122

The bed had not changed its form since the end of the 15th century. It consisted of a wooden frame with four corner-posts supporting a canopy from which curtains were drawn to keep out the draughts at night. The fabrics used for the counterpane, 129 the curtains and the drapery of the bed posts were of costly material worked in embroidery, often depicting love scenes. This bed, 'encumbered with silk', thus owed its ornate appearance to the fabrics on and around it, but in Henri II's time, it was the structure of the bed itself that provided the decoration. Sturdy caryatids replaced the posts; headboards were heavily carved with strange, new motifs. Although very few of these beds 131 survive today, they are known to us from drawings and en- 130 gravings of the period. The *lit de repos* or day-bed was also very lavish in appearance, even though it had no posts or curtains.

The importance of chairs grew in keeping with the changes in social conventions. There were two distinct categories; those that were portable, and the heavier kind whose origins were those throne-like Gothic seats set against the walls.

The *chaire* usually placed beside the bed, was at first nothing more than a chest with three projecting sides acting as arms and a backrest. Then the arms opened out and the chest underneath 124 disappeared. The terms armchair and chair seem to have been used indiscriminately to describe a seat with a backrest, with or without arms, and resting on four legs joined by stretchers. It was either carved or upholstered. The inventory of Gabrielle 125, 128 d'Estrées mentions 'Two large chairs with backs, one with arms, the other without, decorated in gold and silver *passementerie*, with a three-inch fringe, and crimson silk covering the legs.' 127 This was the true ancestor of the armchair proper. The *caque-* 128 *toire* was a seat of trapezoid form. Its arms bow out in order to 126 accommodate the voluminous skirts of the sitter.

The bench was provided with arms and a back and could be fixed to the wall or placed beside the fire. The backless form of bench, like its smaller version, the *sgabello* or stool, was in use in country districts until the 19th century.

The *placet*, covered with tapestry and standing on four legs, was in effect a stool. It was closely related to the hassock, a simple cushion which allowed people to sit virtually on the floor. This type of seating prevailed at the Court throughout the 17th century.

As we have seen, the Renaissance made an immense contribution to the art of furniture, not only to its decoration, but also to its shape and form. But this great outburst of inventiveness diminished towards the end of the century. Delorme and Primaticcio died in 1570, Lescot and Bullant in 1578. The Wars of Religion weakened the creative faculty and there was no leading spirit to stimulate it. Furniture followed in the train of the general decadence; a few remaining examples of doubtful taste do not constitute a style. There was to be a long gap between the sparkling vigour which marked the height of the Renaissance and the rich flowering of the arts under Louis XIV.

GERMANY AND SCANDINAVIA

Hans Huth

The first signs of an understanding of the Italian Renaissance appeared in the German-speaking countries late in the first decade of the 16th century. Both Albrecht Dürer and probably Hans Holbein the Younger visited Italy and each brought back across the Alps a vision freshened by contact with the new ideals of Italian painters, philosophers and writers. But the artists whose work more closely influenced the decorative treatment of interiors and furniture in contemporary houses were the designers of ornament. These 'little masters' *(Kleinmeister)*, who worked mainly in Nuremberg, Westphalia and the Low Countries, had discarded the outmoded medieval preoccupation with religious subjects. Instead they turned their attention to ornamental themes derived from Classical antiquity and inspired by Italian example. Their designs were composed of running floral motifs entwined round naked figures, birds or animals, urns, masks, or trophies of arms. Either engraved or reproduced in woodcut, these ornamental patterns provided guidance for craftsmen such as goldsmiths, sculptors, stonemasons or woodcarvers who lacked the opportunity of studying Renaissance fashions at first hand. Cabinet-makers, too, adopted the new mode and before the mid-16th century, wholly abandoned Gothic ornament in decorating their pieces.

This change in decorative treatment, did not, however, lead to the introduction of new types of furniture. In those cities in which powerful guilds exercised authority, the approved patterns that apprentices were required to execute in order to become master craftsmen, were rarely changed. For example, in Berlin only three such changes took place in the course of two hundred years: in 1553, 1681 and 1768. A more progressive approach to design existed in commercial cities, such as Augsburg or Nuremberg, where the arts thrived. Craftsmen also enjoyed a measure of freedom in smaller cities where no guild regulations inhibited them; their situation was comparably advantageous when they were in the employ of a prince or abbot.

Peter Flötner of Nuremberg, a sculptor, carver and designer (d. 1546), was one of the first German artists to introduce Renaissance designs. Flötner had been to Italy and his woodcuts showing furniture and panels of engraved ornament reflect his impressions of Renaissance taste.

132

133
134

135
136

132 *Far left*: Engraved design by Heinrich Aldegrever bearing his monogram and dated 1535. Aldegrever was born at Paderborn in Westphalia and worked at Soest as an engraver and a designer of ornamental motifs until his death shortly before 1561. Engravings of this kind were used as patterns in the workshops of goldsmiths and carvers. They were much in demand, for craftsmen north of the Alps were unfamiliar with these decorative features derived from Italian Renaissance sources. Aldegrever, who was familiar with similar designs by Hans Holbein, introduced scrolling leaves, grotesque mythological creatures, masks and naked children.

133 *Above left*: Oak cupboard, *c.* 1540, Westphalia. The front of this cupboard, divided into panels of irregular size, betrays the uncertain sense of proportion familiar in pieces of the first half of the 16th century. The side panels are carved with linenfold panelling—a vanishing fashion of the Gothic world—while the front panels reveal a masterly command of the new Renaissance designs of scrolling leaves surrounding portrait heads in roundels. The rather tight, curled leaves recall those in the Aldegrever engraving in the previous illustration. Staatliche Museen, Berlin

134 *Left*: Oak dresser, *c.* 1550, Lower Rhine. The form of this piece is still medieval and indeed, the metal hinges on the central door are pierced with a Gothic quatrefoil and flamboyant tracery. The carved panels, on the other hand, are Renaissance in character, introducing scrolling leaves, cornucopiae, masks and naked half-figures. The carver was using an engraved design as his model, such as the example shown in the next illustration. Bayerisches Nationalmuseum, Munich

135 Woodcut by Peter Flötner, bearing his initials and dated 1533. Flötner settled in Nuremberg in 1522 where he worked principally as a carver and designer. He died in 1546. His woodcuts, intended for use as patterns by builders, carvers and joiners, include designs for architectural features such as columns, capitals and doorways and also for beds. Ornamental fillings for pilasters or panels, as in this example, draw upon Renaissance sources. The particular feature, shown here, of the female figure springing from a basket of leaves, was inspired by the stucco decoration in the Villa Madama, Rome. Thus, designs of this kind, drawing so confidently upon Italian example, helped to spread an understanding of the new style in the joiners' and carvers' workshops.

136 Cupboard of oak and ash, dated 1541, made from a design by Peter Flötner for the Nuremberg patrician family, Holzschuher. The logical design of this piece and the formal cornice bear witness to Flötner's grasp of Renaissance forms and decorative motifs. Germanisches Nationalmuseum, Nuremberg

137 Woodcut by the Master H. S. *c.* 1530. A group of some twenty-five woodcuts survive by a joiner and carver of whom only the initials are known, showing cupboards, beds and wall panelling. They were executed perhaps for the guidance of the craftsmen in the master's own workshop which was probably in Augsburg or even in Nuremberg. The cupboard shown in this woodcut is architectural in character, succumbing to the new Renaissance fashion for such features as columns and capitals.

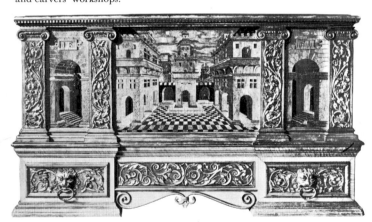

138 Walnut chest dated 1551. This example by the Master H. S., is decorated with carved scrolls, leaves and animal heads in the Renaissance manner. The three central panels are elaborately inlaid in coloured woods with architectural views in perspective. Staatliche Museen, Berlin

139 *Below*: Chest of limewood and ash, dated 1539. Known as the 'Erasmus chest', this piece is traditionally said to have been made in Basle in memory of Erasmus to the order of his heir, Dr. Bonifazius Amerbach. A portrait of Erasmus appears on the left and of Aristotle on the right. Historisches Museum, Basle

Another artist, who was also a cabinet-maker, is known only by his initials, H.S. He is thought to have come from Thurgau in Switzerland and worked in his youth in Augsburg where he produced woodcuts of a very professional type showing ceilings, wall panelling, doors and cupboards in a clear and forthright Renaissance manner. The influence of such prints, however, was limited for there existed between the north and south a marked difference in taste and mode of expression. This arose not only from a divergence of character but because the craftsmen had different materials with which to work. In the south there was also a readier acceptance of new ideas and a more imaginative approach. The north was conservative and less inclined to change. The use of softwood in the south made it desirable and necessary either to paint the surface or decorate it by means of inlay. In the north, oak was the accepted material. Sometimes, however, carved figures and other details were of walnut or lime. Oak lent itself well to sturdy construction as well as to carving and often the whole surface of a cupboard or chest was ornamented with carving, including panels in relief, the subjects being drawn from the scriptures or secular history. Colour was seldom used.

By the middle of the 16th century the principal decorative motifs, both in the north and south, were those adopted from Italy. But in mastering this new vocabulary, the traditional characteristics of the countries north of the Alps were by no means lost. In southern Germany as well as in Switzerland and Austria, they formed the basis for a definite national style which differed considerably from that of Italy as well as from the independent manner developing in northern regions. There was, for example, the popular so-called 'façade' cupboard of which the makers proudly called themselves 'architectural cabinet-makers'. These cabinets were constructed in an architectural manner, making full use of the classical orders and details such as mouldings, broken pediments and volutes. These moulded sections were applied to the surface of the piece. There was, however, much overcrowding and often a lack of clarity, characteristics which marked the later Mannerist phase and continued even into the Baroque age.

137, 138

154

150

The Dream of St Ursula by Vittore Carpaccio, *c*.1495. This painting probably gives an accurate impression of the type of bedroom to be found in the larger palaces in Venice in the late 15th and early 16th centuries.

The furniture is sparse and, apart from the bed and curious Gothic chair beside it, very simply made. Accademia, Venice

The Gallery of Francis I at Fontainebleau was built between 1534–9, and is the most striking example of the new kind of interior decoration which had been introduced into France by Rosso and Primaticcio. The lower stage of the walls is decorated with traditional oak panelling carved with cartouches displaying the emblems of Francis I. Above, stucco decoration in high relief alternates with allegorical frescoes by Rosso celebrating the great deeds of the king. The gallery was to upset all the traditional French ideas of decoration and ushered in the School of Fontainebleau. Here the crowds of courtiers would have strolled and here, too, the craftsmen, bookbinders, glove makers, embroiderers and silversmiths were permitted to ply their trade.

Sixteenth-century Burgundian *armoire à deux corps*. For many years any piece of 16th-century furniture carved in vigorous high relief tended to be attributed to one master— Hugues Sambin of Dijon. A closer study reveals the equally strong influence of Ducerceau, whose engraved designs were consulted all over France. In the 16th century, Dijon was the great centre for cupboards of this type, and the Burgundian woodcarvers were highly influential. This is a fine example of their work. The caryatids, half-human, half-animal sometimes have tormented faces reminding one of the designs by the Dutch engraver, Hendrik Goltzius—a further source of inspiration. The upper doors are decorated with convex mirror-like panels flanked by eagles. Below are swags of flowers and fruit and, upon the drawers, lion masks. The carved motifs of the friezes such as palmettes and acanthus leaves, derive from Classical sources. Philadelphia Museum of Art

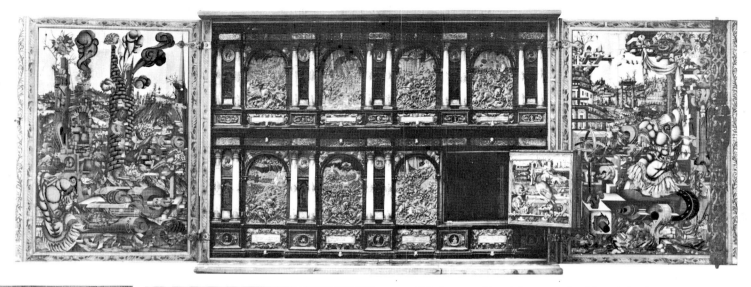

140 This famous cabinet is known as the '*Wrangelschrank*' because it was taken as booty in the Thirty Years' War by the Swedish commander, Count Wrangel. It is Augsburg work and is dated 1566. The doors are shown open, revealing the inner cupboard, arranged in two stages. Small doors, divided by coupled alabaster columns, and ornamented with boxwood carvings on a black ground representing historical scenes, enclose drawers and shelves. The capitals surmounting the alabaster columns and the portrait roundels between the columns are of boxwood. Cabinets of this splendour were, in themselves, works of art. Landesmuseum, Munster

141 *Far left*: Detail of the so-called '*Wrangelschrank*' shown in the previous illustration. This is the right-hand, side elevation of the cabinet, showing the outstanding quality of the intarsia. An imaginary scene, in which strapwork combines with monkeys and birds in surrealist encounters with architectural ruins, exhibits the unknown maker's skill. Back, front, sides and top of the cupboard are decorated in this way and also the inner surfaces both of the two main outer doors and of the smaller doors within.

142 *Left*: Woodcut by Lorenz Stöer from his *Geometria et Perspectiva*, 1567. The Augsburg intarsia workers drew their inspiration from engraved designs of this type by Stöer and other artists. But as Stöer did not introduce figures or animals into his architectural vistas it seems improbable that the unknown maker of the '*Wrangelschrank*' shown in illustrations 140 and 141, actually worked directly to his designs.

143 Living room showing cupboard and bed from the house of a wealthy farmer and magistrate, Markus Svyn at Lehe. The room is panelled in oak and has a heavy, cassetted ceiling, while the bed, which is hung with curtains, is built into the corner of the room. An appreciation of the new Renaissance fashions developed slowly in these northern provinces. While there are certain decorative features deriving from a Classical source, such as the bedposts in the form of columns and capitals, conservatism is reflected in the carved panels of the cupboard which all represent religious scenes. The carvings in the headboard of the bed are also medieval in spirit with the Crucifixion in the central panel. Heavily carved furniture of this type remained popular in Schleswig and Holstein well into the 17th century. Dithmarscher Landesmuseum, Meldorf, Holstein

In northern Germany the new style developed somewhat differently. Woodcuts and engravings by west German masters illustrate furniture of simple rectangular shape and unbroken outline, carved in solid wood with sober and somewhat unimaginative Renaissance designs. Severe forms, sometimes relieved by carved ornament are characteristic of mid-16th-century pieces.

As the standard of living rose, houses became more comfortable and new types of furniture were evolved. German Gothic beds had been simple. Even when they had canopies these were little more than hoods extended over the headboard. In the Renaissance period the canopy was enlarged and carried on four posts. Depending on the status of the owner, the bed was decorated more or less profusely. A splendid example of a late Renaissance bed, showing some Dutch influence, survives from the house of a magistrate in Holstein, built in 1568. Richly carved in the north German manner, the bed is an integral part of the magnificently panelled room which was clearly the focal point of the house. The prominence given to the bed is characteristic of the later development of the bedroom as a reception room both in middle-class houses and in palaces. In the Holstein house, the bed is built into the wall and the woodwork is carved with the same type of ornament as that on the surrounding wall panelling. At a later date, beds acquired a more independent character and were no longer built into the wall. In Gripsholm, Sweden, for example a mid-17th-century bed in the Dutch manner stands free in the room although the decorative features of the woodwork are architectural in character and still reflect those found on wall panelling. An elegantly shaped late 17th-century bed in the Bavarian National Museum in Munich, on the other hand, no longer clings to the earlier ornamental treatment or appears to need a position close to the wall.

143

152

144

The chest had changed little in shape in the course of its long history prior to the Renaissance. One of the most elegant chests of the period is that made in 1539, and once owned by the Swiss scholar Bonifacius von Amorbach. Perhaps designed by Holbein the Younger as a memorial to Erasmus of Rotterdam, the piece is unique and is totally unlike traditional examples in the shape of the front panel and the stand. While the design is definitely northern, it shows a sophistication that proclaims a knowledge of Italian example. Another chest made in 1561 and signed by the Master HS is decorated with inlay representing an architectural scene, a feature often found in Italian examples, and a clear indication of this artist's close ties with Italy.

The south German cupboard probably originated by placing one chest on top of another and then opening each from the front. For a long time, cupboards were divided into two, horizontally, and handles were attached to the sides of both compartments for convenience in moving. The two 'chests', fitted with drawers and a cresting above, had a frieze between the upper and lower sections and were mounted on a stand. In a cupboard made in 1541 from a design by Flötner, this old plan is used but the decoration is in the new Renaissance manner.

Towards the end of the century a more useful cupboard was developed. The central frieze was abandoned and the two sections united into one big compartment, large enough for the garments which were becoming more bulky and needed to be hung instead of laid flat. Nevertheless, tradition was so strong that the old type composed of two partitions was still being made even after 1600. In the north the more modern, single compartment cupboard did not appear before 1600. The front of the cupboard was often divided into a number of rectangular compartments. A central section was composed of a fall-front which could be let down and was supported by an iron rod. This arrangement is seen in a cupboard built into the wall in a room in Neumarkt, although for Austria it is somewhat unusual. Cupboards or chests on sledge-like stands were peculiar to the north. Most of these pieces appear to modern eyes to be overcrowded with decoration. It should be remembered, however, that they were part of the ensemble of a heavily panelled room in which the decorative features were repeated around doors and windows and both in proportion and ornament they were suited to their background.

In southern Germany, the great commercial and artistic centres of Augsburg and Nuremberg were famous for their furniture makers. Peter Flötner was active in both cities and the painter, Lorenz Stöer, had published a set of woodcuts containing suggested designs for intarsia panels popular in Augsburg for the decoration of furniture. Augsburg was also noted for the elaborate writing desks or cabinets produced there. One of the most famous of these pieces was a desk made to the order of the Emperor Charles V in 1554 by Lienhart Strohmeier. This desk is combined with a cabinet containing a great many drawers and compartments. The façade, of architectural form, shows little unity of purpose with its many columns, reliefs, friezes, and carved figures. Certainly it was the work of a highly skilled cabinet-maker and a gifted woodcarver. It was originally ad-

144 *Below*: Four-poster bed of purplewood, with applied ornamental strapwork of ebony and set with contrasting panels of ivory inlaid in ebony and ebony inlaid in ivory, *c.* 1580. The silk canopy is modern. The bed comes from Schloss Amberg and illustrates the late 16th-century passion for precious and exotic materials. Bayerisches Nationalmuseum, Munich

145 *Right*: Chair of chiselled steel, dated 1574, and given by the City of Augsburg to the Emperor Rudolf II in 1577. It was made by Thomas Rucker (*c.* 1532–1606) of Augsburg. This chair remained in Prague until 1648 when it was taken by the Swedes as booty at the time of the Thirty Years' War. In the 18th century it was acquired by an Englishman of Swedish descent, Gustavus Brander. He lived at Christchurch in Hampshire and fearing that the sea air might damage the steel he sold it in 1799. It is now in the possession of the Earl of Radnor, Longford Castle, Nr. Salisbury.

147 *Below right*: Detail of the back of the chiselled steel chair shown in illustration 145. The scenes illustrate the four great monarchies of the world: Babylonian, Persian, Greek and Roman, and since the chair was a gift to Rudolf II, the choice of subject was intended as a compliment to the Holy Roman Emperor. In the centre is Nebuchadnezzar's Dream.

146 *Far right*: One of a set of pearwood chairs, set with serpentine, made for Christian V of Saxony, *c.* 1590. These chairs were designed by an Italian, Giovanni Maria Nosseni, who came to Dresden in 1575, and worked there until his death in Dresden in 1620. Historisches Museum, Dresden

mired not for any aesthetic quality but on account of the brilliant ingenuity of its construction and of the erudite allusions in its decoration to literature, history and mythology which the scholar and the connoisseur could appreciate.

Once the city of Augsburg had established a reputation for this type of furniture, its craftsmen continued for more than a century to produce such show pieces. An outstanding and historically important example, in which intarsia or marquetry is the dominant feature, is the so-called *Wrangelschrank*, similar to some designs by Lorenz Stöer. Count Wrangel, commander of the Swedish Army in the Thirty Years' War, took the cabinet from Augsburg as war loot. In this piece the conception of the desk is abandoned. Instead it is a cabinet in which curios could be kept. If the result was a sacrifice of convenience to art, as the Augsburg historian, Paul von Stetten remarked in 1779, this was of no consequence, but rather added to the curiosity of the piece. The marquetry, composed of woods of various colours, sometimes stained green or shaded by means of burning, is of exceptional brilliance and vitality.

Nuremberg was also known for cupboards of many types. The ornamental details on these accorded with the prevailing fashions which followed each other rapidly at the end of the 16th century. Engraved patterns were appearing in increasing number and included new themes such as romantic ruins combined with roll-work, strapwork and auricular patterns. In the south, especially, these patterns were interpreted in terms of woodwork for the decoration of cabinet-pieces and chests. In Switzerland, because of its geographical location, a number of cross-

currents met. In Basle, Franz Pergo worked in a manner that recalls the imaginative and sometime fantastic designs of Hugues Sambin of Dijon. In a buffet made in 1607, Pergo adhered more closely to the Swiss style nurtured by influences from Italy. From the Italian *credenza*, the Swiss developed a type of buffet which, eventually, came to have an entirely Swiss character. It was well suited to the background of a sumptuously panelled room either in a patrician or a prosperous farmer's house.

On the western border of Germany, French and Dutch influences were strong. In Cologne and the adjacent Westphalian territory, the Gothic *dressoir* or dresser of French inspiration kept its traditional shape for a long period, though disguised with Renaissance ornament. Later it developed into the dresser with superstructure (*Überbauschrank*) with either elaborately carved ornament or rich inlay work, such as the examples made by Melchior von Rheydt around 1600. The popularity of inlay work spread in the 17th century throughout Germany, the Tyrol and Austria. As cupboards grew in favour, chests slowly went out of fashion. Only in the north, where the sense of tradition was strong were these elaborately carved pieces held in esteem.

The big dining table usually consisted of a board on trestles which was removed after a meal. As the 16th century advanced and expecially in the 17th century, these long tables were often made on fixed supports. Small elaborate tables came into general use during the Renaissance period. The square desk or counter-table of small dimensions was usually on an X-shaped stand and was fitted with an elaborate set of small drawers under the lid.

148 *Left*: This type of dresser, consisting of a cupboard enclosed by two doors below and a recessed upper stage above with a projecting frieze resting upon two lateral supports, replaced, in the second half of the 16th century, the earlier form of dresser shown in illustration 134. This example, elaborately decorated with inlay was made by Melchior von Rheydt of Cologne in about 1605.

149 *Right*: Panelled room from a house in Neumarkt, 1607. The panelling is simple and a fixed bench runs round the walls. On the right is a built-in cupboard, with shelves, and the fall-front is open, forming a table. The chair in the foreground is typical of the South and is modelled upon Italian examples while the two upholstered chairs are of a type common in Europe in the early 17th century. Landesmuseum Joanneum, Graz, Austria

150 *Left*: The so-called 'Last Supper cupboard', formerly at Thaulow, *c.* 1625. These elaborately carved cupboards retained an almost medieval spirit in Schleswig-Holstein, when such vast structures had long been superseded further south. The form is characteristic. So are the three carved figures of Faith, Hope and Charity in the niches, dividing the biblical scenes. Schloss Gottorf Schleswig, Schleswig Holsteinisches Landesmuseum

151 *Below*: Panel illustrating the Last Supper from the cupboard, shown left.

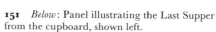

152 *Right*: The *Vasasal* from Gripsholm Castle, Sweden. Mid-17th century. The walls are painted with formal strapwork designs of a type found throughout Northern Europe in the first half of the 17th century. The furniture is elegantly simple, the chairs recalling the English 'Farthingale' chairs of the period and the bed canopy supported on plain turned columns. The table, with its baluster legs, straight stretchers and ball feet, is later in date, belonging to the third quarter of the 17th century. Nordiska Museet, Stockholm

153 Cabinet of ebony mounted with semi-precious stones, given by the City of Augsburg to King Gustavus Adolphus of Sweden in 1612. The practice of making a collection of works of art or science, which illustrated particular skills on the part of the craftsmen who made them, or were composed of exotic or precious materials to form what was known as a *Kunst and Wunderkammer*, was familiar in princely and noble households in the late 16th and early 17th centuries. This Augsburg cabinet is in itself a work of art worthy of a collector's pride. It not only uses what at the time were strange and magnificent materials, but it is designed according to an intellectual theme, symbolising a microcosm of the world. Upsala University, Sweden

154 Panelled room from the *Bärenfelserhof* (Martinsgasse 18), Basle. The walls are lined with panelling and concealed cupboards in contrasting inlays of oak, walnut, elm and ash. The built-in buffet on the left is a clearly defined architectural structure with wash-basin in the centre supported on two elegant fluted and tapered front legs, while the doors are flanked by fluted columns with Corinthian capitals, the bases carved with masks surrounded by strapwork. There is an air of rational clarity which might be expected of so famous a humanist centre as Basle. Historisches Museum, Basle

155 Panelled room from the *Alter Seidenhof* in Zurich, *c.* 1620. Less restrained than the Basle room shown in the previous illustration, there is already here a suggestion of Baroque. Again contrasting woods are used in the panelling and the insistence upon architectural features, such as columns and pediments and arches is apparent also in the design of the vast tiled stove on the right, dated 1620. Tiled steps lead up to a seat at the side of the stove. The draw-top table, supported on a square pedestal with bracket corners ending in lion-paw feet, is of a form typical of Switzerland and South Germany. The chair, on tapering turned legs, united by a curved stretcher dates from the latter half of the century. Schweizerische Landesmuseum, Zurich

This was a legacy from the Gothic period, though ornamented in the new manner. Later this type of table was developed into a larger square or into a round table which, by dropping segments of leaves, could be altered into a square table. The legs were ornamented with volutes, figures, or masks and were placed on a square platform, occasionally in such a way that the centre enclosed a small cupboard or open niches. Ivory, bone, ebony or mother-of-pearl were among the luxurious materials used for decorative inlay on such pieces and sometimes the table top was made of carved stone or marble. 149, 155

No great variety of chairs has come down to us. Some chairs from the Saxon court in Dresden, bearing the date 1590, are elaborate show pieces with stone incrustations, which were undoubtedly curiosities even in their own day. One of the strangest chairs ever to be made was of forged steel, completely covered with chiselled reliefs, to which were added chiselled steel sculptured figures. The chair was made for the Emperor Rudolf II by Thomas Rucker of Augsburg (1532–1606). Rucker was well known as a sword-hilt maker and also as a maker of scientific apparatus, such as an instrument to be installed on a carriage to measure distance. He even made ornamental stamps for tooling book bindings. During the Thirty Years' War, the chair went to Sweden as war loot; later it became privately owned in England. Shaped like a folding chair with a fixed back, the structural parts of the chair serve as a background for the reliefs and figures. 146 145, 147

The chairs favoured in the 16th century were sturdy and mostly without armrests. If more comfort was desired this was provided by cushions. The folding chair, adopted from Italy, went through many transformations until it became popular in church, palace and house and, according to need, was either simple or elegant. The bench continued to be in common use, as it had been in the Gothic period, often built into the walls of a panelled room, or fitted around a towering stove in the corner of a room. As an independent piece of furniture, however, the bench lost favour rapidly as more individual and convenient chairs were produced. Tables, chests, and chairs used in the church vestry or in front of the high altar as bishops' seats, followed the general pattern: they were, however, larger in order to accommodate the huge copes of the priests. 149
155

The early 17th century was a period of transition. The exaggerated Mannerist style, under the influence of which panelled cupboards were decorated with a confusion of ornament, was frowned upon in Nuremberg after the turn of the century. A greater sobriety was preferred and fine walnut surfaces were allowed to speak for themselves, unadorned by inlay. But in spite of this tendency towards restraint, the air was full of eccentric ideas as an essential expression of Mannerist art.

It was during this period that a particular type of cabinet was produced in southern Germany which was to make German craftsmanship and scholarship famous at home and abroad and examples were commissioned for the famous collections of many European princes. These cabinets constituted works of art rather than straightforward pieces of furniture. Elaborate constructions, composed of exotic materials, including ebony, tortoiseshell, ivory, lacquer, precious metal or semi-precious stones, they contained useful objects, such as writing materials, cutlery, toilet requisites, even tongue scrapers, as well as scientific instruments and curiosities. The product not only of the cabinet-maker but of the turner, the goldsmith, the ivory carver and the sculptor, these pieces were carefully planned by the scholar in accordance with an intellectual theme, to represent a microcosm of scholastic and scientific knowledge. Cabinets of this type rank among the triumphs of Mannerist art. An example, planned by the Augsburg scholar and antiquarian Philip Hainhofer, was given by the city of Augsburg to Gustavus Adolphus in 1612 and is still preserved at Upsala in Sweden. As far as cabinet-making is concerned, this cabinet unquestionably represents one of the glories of the craft but it also marks the end of an era. Other ideas were needed to give new life and force to the crafts as well as to the arts. This rejuvenation might have come about in Germany during the second quarter of the 17th century but it was crushed by the outbreak of the Thirty Years' War in 1618. When the war was over, Germany was exhausted. Living conditions had changed drastically and the continuity of artistic evolution was broken. 153

THE LOW COUNTRIES 1500-1630

Th. H. Lunsingh Scheurleer

156 *The Spectacle Vendor*, by the Flemish painter Jacob Cornelisz (*c.* 1477–1533). The bourgeois interior is oak panelled, and painted with Classical grotesques, indicating that Classical influence was already widespread by the early 16th century. The title is symbolic, and the spectacles represent illusion, for the young girl is being bribed to entertain an old man, and behind them a young man embraces an old crone while with his left hand he fingers a bowl of gold coins. Formerly Private Collection: Berlin

157 Oak chest, from the North Netherlands, *c.* 1550, carved with Renaissance ornament. The four panels, flanked by Classical columns, contain grotesques composed of trailing leaves, masks and figures surrounding portrait medallions. Unfortunately the portrait heads have been defaced in the course of time. Beneath the large lockplate, two figures support a crowned lion holding a coat-of-arms. Rijksmuseum, Amsterdam

158 *Below*: Oak cupboard of Gothic form from the *hospices civils* at Liège, first half of the 16th century. As well as having linenfold panelling on the sides, the cupboard bears carved mouldings on the front panels of the so-called X-shape, which is characteristic of Flanders. Gothic quatrefoils surround vine motifs of a type which often appear in English furniture of the period. Such cupboards sometimes have as many as fifteen panels in each door. Musée Curtius, Liège

In the course of the 15th century the feudal states of the Netherlands had gradually come under the sway of the Dukes of Burgundy. The richest communes of Flanders, Ghent, Bruges and Ypres, were centres of the weaving industry and its dependent activities. The textile industry was also largely responsible for supporting thriving communities in the cities of Antwerp, Louvain and Brussels in Brabant, and Namur and Cambrai in Hainaut. In the North, where the initial growth of civic life was slower, Dordrecht, Leiden, Haarlem, Delft and Rotterdam in Holland and Middelburg in Zeeland were all rich cities governed by municipal charter. It was the wealth of these centres of industry which sustained the glories of the Burgundian Court, famous throughout the Continent for its luxury and splendour. Not only was Burgundian Court etiquette a model for other royal households but the collections of Philip the Good (1419–67) and Charles the Bold (1467–77) included tapestries, gold, silver, jewels, embroideries, illuminated manuscripts and printed books which excited the travellers and chroniclers of the age.

In this sophisticated milieu the Gothic tradition achieved, towards the latter half of the 15th and into the 16th century, its final flourish, while side by side with this medieval world new trends of thought and modes of expression, deriving from the Italian Renaissance made themselves felt. Indeed, at the turn of the century, during the last days of the House of Burgundy, a change was apparent, for the exuberant vitality of the School of the Loire under Charles VIII was not to be confined to France. Flanders, too, was invigorated by Italian example and in these years of transition into the modern world, Classical columns and pilasters were combined in a Gothic framework, and grotesques and arabesques decorated available surfaces.

In 1508 the painter Mabuse left for Italy, returning to Flanders with fresh ideas. It was he who first introduced the nude Classical figure, as well as architectural vistas and Italianate poses into Flemish painting. These developments encouraged patrons in the Netherlands to give commissions to Italian architects, and in this way Vincidor de Bologna was closely associated with the rebuilding of the Palace of Henry III at Breda in 1536. But it was mainly the engravers who spread the new motifs of the Renaissance on a large scale. Lucas van Leyden shared the ability of German masters such as Barthel Beham, Hans Sebald Beham and H. Aldegrever, and in the 1520s was publishing engraved designs for decorative panels of grotesques, both for goldsmiths and wood carvers. Towards the middle of the century the Netherlanders, Cornelis Bos and especially Cornelis Floris, combined designs of grotesques with a new type of ornamental strapwork which had first appeared at Fontainebleau.

It cannot have been easy for joiners and carvers to apply these new decorative features to traditional forms, although examples such as chests show grotesques carved upon panels between Classical columns. The principle elements of Classical architecture were the Five Orders, and a knowledge of these was essential to Renaissance builders. By 1539 a Flemish translation of the Italian architect Serlio's *Fourth Book of Architecture* had appeared in Antwerp. Such works were indispensable to furniture makers and carvers, and they inspired the preparation of another publication, also on the Five Orders, this time by a Flemish designer, Hans Vredeman de Vries. It was followed in about 1580 by further designs by de Vries for ornamental motifs and for furniture. These were the first of their kind to appear in the Netherlands and were of immense importance, for the influence of this versatile artist, who was also painter, architect and military engineer, penetrated as far afield as England and Sweden. In 1630 two similar volumes were published by his son and collaborator, Paul Vredeman de Vries, in which the father's

159 *Left*: 'Caquetoire' chair of carved oak, second half of the 16th century. The tall panelled back and the apron are inlaid with contrasting woods in geometric designs. The arms rest on elegant, turned, fluted supports of Classical inspiration, but the curving outline of the apron is a Gothic feature. Rijksmuseum, Amsterdam

160 *Right*: Plate 8 of Hans Vredeman de Vries's *Differents pourtraicts de menuiserie*, *c.* 1580, showing designs for beds. This publication provided designs for various types of furniture for the benefit of joiners and their customers. De Vries's designs were used not only in the Netherlands, but in Germany, England and Sweden.

161 *Below left*: Oak bed from Dordrecht bearing the date 1626. This fine example is built into the corner of a panelled room and is ornamented with carved mouldings and inlaid panels containing arabesques. The arcades at the foot rest upon elegant, turned ebony columns. Rijksmuseum, Amsterdam

162 *Below*: Draw-top table of oak inlaid with ebony panels, North Netherlands, first half of the 17th century. The strapwork brackets beneath the apron and the turned bulbous legs recall the designs of Vredeman de Vries. Private Collection

influence is apparent. They contained designs for buffets, bedsteads, chairs, benches, chests, tables, and even for towel-horses, in which strapwork, masks and caryatids replace the earlier grotesques, and they were to become the main inspiration of the furniture makers of the Netherlands until well into the 17th century.

The marriage of Mary of Burgundy to Maximilian of Austria, elected Holy Roman Emperor in 1494, brought the Netherlands at first under Austrian and later, Spanish dominion. Torn by religious strife during the 16th century, the country reached a solution to these bitter struggles in 1579, when the southern provinces formed themselves into a league to defend the Catholic faith, while those of the north, already virtually independent, were to retain their freedom and ultimately, in 1609, to become a republic.

In the first half of the 17th century, furniture in the northern Netherlands began to acquire national characteristics. The Guild system encouraged the development of local styles and the main Provinces all developed their individual interpretations of late Renaissance motifs. The cupboard gradually assumed the role of the chest and became the most important creation of the cabinet-maker. In the Province of Holland, where the leadership of the Republic lay, several characteristic types were made. The most spectacular is the so-called '*Beeldenkast*', which derives its name from the intricate carved figures which are placed upon the panels of the doors. These cupboards are divided into

two stages, and on rich examples both parts have carved caryatid supports. The example illustrated bears upon the upper stage the figures of the Christian virtues, Faith, Hope and Charity. Charity, represented by a woman with children, occupies the position of honour in the centre. Since this is a marriage press, the doors are carved with stories of maidenly virtues, while upon the frieze scenes of manly valour are depicted. The carver would base his reliefs on contemporary engravings, among which those of Maarten van Heemskerk were popular. It should be noted that the rich carving on these cabinets belonged not to the domain of the cabinet-maker, but was the responsibility of the carver. The cabinet-maker was concerned solely with the construction of the basic piece, while the elaborate figures were the work of a specialist. This division of labour is confirmed in surviving accounts of Guild regulations in which the part played by each craftsman is laid down. In many cases, the cabinet-maker did not have to call on the carver. This would not have been necessary, for example, where the cupboards were only ornamented with pilasters or columns, and decorative carving was limited to the panels. Such cabinets were in general demand in Holland and were much less expensive than the '*Beeldenkast*' which was intended for a wealthier clientele.

The typical Zeeland chests are also divided like the *Beeldenkast*, into an upper and lower stage. The doors, however, are broader in relation to the height, so that they are practically square. Here, too, caryatids have their place. This characteristic

158
165
165

163 *Left*: Oak cupboard mounted with panels of intarsia representing architectural *trompe l'oeil* perspectives and vases of flowers, probably made in Antwerp *c*. 1620. The technique of intarsia reached South Germany and the Netherlands from Italy, and the scenes often include buildings in ruins. Museum Boymans-van-Beuningen, Rotterdam

164 *Right*: Carved oak buffet, made in Antwerp *c*. 1620. Of outstanding quality, this piece represents Antwerp Mannerist carving at its height. The heavily ringed Tuscan columns are of the type which appeared in the paintings of Rubens. The friezes are carved with exquisite Renaissance grotesques. Another interesting feature is the carved shell motif within the arched panels. The curved petal-like forms would seem to have inspired a similar feature on Newport furniture in America in the 18th century. Rijksmuseum, Amsterdam

165 *Left*: '*Beeldenkast*' or cabinet decorated with carved scenes, inlaid with ebony panels, made in the North Netherlands *c*. 1630. Such cupboards derive their generic name from the carved figures which decorate them. This rich example bears the figures of Faith, Hope and Charity, with Charity placed in the centre. It is undoubtedly a marriage press, and the panels are appropriately carved with scenes depicting womanly modesty and manly valour; Susanna and the Elders, St. George and the Dragon, etc. Along the central frieze a boar hunt in a forest is illustrated. Rijksmuseum, Amsterdam

166 *Right*: Cupboard of oak and ebony, made in Zeeland *c*. 1640. The type of geometrical moulding employed here was perhaps introduced into the Netherlands by Spanish craftsmen familiar with Arabic designs. Centraal Museum, Utrecht

Renaissance feature is also found in Brabant, where the low Zeeland-type chest seems to have been readily accepted. Generally speaking, the decoration of the Northern examples is simple and severe. In the South, on the other hand, the doors were ornamented with carved and applied mouldings arranged in geometrical shapes. These angular patterns recall Arabic motifs which were brought to Spain by the Moors and were probably introduced into the Netherlands by the Spaniards. In Zeeland, cupboards bore little decoration although the door panels were sometimes carved in the form of an arch.

Middelburg, the capital city of the Province of Zeeland, must have had important furniture workshops in the 17th century. Jean Macé, the French cabinet-maker, who was later to enter the service of the Queen-Regent, when he had a workshop assigned to him in the *Galeries du Louvre*, worked in Middelburg for two years round about 1620. During this period in Zeeland, he must have learnt the technique of intarsia and marquetry. Many Zeeland chests and cupboards are ornamented in this manner. In addition to carved features they also have intarsia panels representing architectural scenes in perspective, which are interesting to compare with those produced in South Germany. One specimen, decorated in this style, made in Diest and dated 1580, bears the inscription 'The eye of God sees all'. This inscription suggests that the imaginary scenes symbolise the divine vision. The Diest piece also indicates that the intarsia technique was not limited to Middelburg. In paintings of Ant-

werp interiors, cupboards and chests related in style to this example are often found, the friezes carved with griffins and trailing leaves. Another Antwerp chest with similar carved friezes is ornamented at the corners with free-standing ringed columns in the Tuscan style.

Antwerp enjoyed international renown as a centre for the production of fine veneered and painted cabinets intended as works of art in themselves. Like those made at Augsburg, they contained a number of small drawers in which precious stones, jewels and perhaps collections of shells or other natural objects could be preserved. As in Amsterdam, these early 17th-century Antwerp craftsmen worked in ebony and formed a distinct group amongst the makers of furniture. Ebony veneers were particularly suited for the decoration of the numerous little drawers, and sometimes both these and the insides of the cabinet doors were painted. The Forchoudt family specialised in selling such pieces, and played a notable part in establishing this type of furniture. Business letters preserved in the files of the family firm show how important it became, for ebony cabinets were exported to London, Paris, The Hague, Vienna and Lisbon. The purchaser was free to choose the subjects he wished to have illustrated in the paintings. Often the choice fell upon scenes from mythology, or was based on the writings of Classical authors. A preference was shown for subjects from the Old and New Testaments. A number of painters, such as Th. van Kessel, and various members of the Francken family specialised in this

branch of art. Often the ebony veneer on these pieces of furniture was combined with tortoiseshell mounted against red foil, so that the colour of the tortoiseshell was enhanced, and contrasted with the black of the ebony. Sometimes the entire piece of furniture would be veneered with tortoiseshell. The grouping of the drawers and small doors was sharply defined by the introduction of ivory fillets, which produced a disciplined effect. When cabinets were made for foreign patrons, stands were not provided, for these would be made locally in the country of destination. This is one of the reasons why the Antwerp cabinets found in most European collections, often remain unidentified.

Chairs also acquired their own specific Netherlandish character early in the 17th century. They were constructed on a rectangular plan, and have a high or low back of the same shape. No doubt the shape goes back to Spanish and Italian prototypes, but the details of the construction are original. The legs are of vase-shaped section, while the back of the chair is crowned by heads of lions or by lions bearing shields. This type was also known in Antwerp, and Rubens himself owned such a chair. They were usually made of walnut, those of ebony being rarer and more expensive. They were upholstered in leather, velvet or cloth which was attached by means of large brass studs. Ebony, which is extremely hard, allowed for the use of very slender members without weakening the chair. Frans Hals shows us that they were capable of bearing great strain for his picture of Willem van Heythuyzen, portrays the sitter tipping back his chair, leaning all his weight on the back legs alone. Fine quality chairs were also made of rosewood. Chair legs, following the Italian and Spanish style, are linked by carved and pierced stretchers. Armrests sometimes terminate in volutes or in animal heads. In emulation of Classical architecture, the back is sometimes composed of two carved arcades placed one above the other. Folding chairs also acquired a characteristic shape in the first half of the 17th century and these are repeatedly shown in portraits by Rembrandt and van der Helst.

Like the cupboards and the sideboards, tables are solid and sturdy. They were usually of oak, enlivened by small fillets of ebony. Some were made on the draw-top principle, by means of which they could be almost doubled in length. Their construction was strengthened by iron screws introduced above and under the legs.

We can learn a good deal about the interiors of Netherlandish burghers' houses from contemporary paintings and engravings. It is clear, for example, that the bed was an important piece of furniture. The cupboard- or closet-bed would be built into the corner of a room, the panelling of the bed echoing that of the walls. The rest of the furniture was made to harmonize with the wall panelling. Compared with contemporary Italian palatial interiors, those of the Low Countries were modest—in spite of the rich woods used—but suggest a high degree of solid comfort.

(Margin references: 171; 167; 167-70; 167; 168; 170; 168; 169; 162; 161)

167 *Far left*: Ebony chair with its original upholstery. North Netherlands, first half of the 17th century. Such chairs would normally be made of walnut, and ebony examples are rare, allowing for greater attenuation because of the hardness and strength of the wood. This example, with its finely tooled leather attached by heavy brass nails, recalls chairs made in both Spain and Portugal. Rijksmuseum. Amsterdam

168 *Centre left*: Chair of ebony and rosewood, North Netherlands, first half of the 17th century. This elegant chair has similar baluster turned legs, and double row of carved stretchers as those on the previous example. The arcaded back

derives from Italy and also appears as far afield as Spain and Northern England. Rijksmuseum, Amsterdam

169 *Centre right*: Folding X-chair of carved walnut, with leather back and seat, first half of the 17th century. This particular form of chair is an Italian type adopted in the North in the 16th century. Although this one clearly folds, northern examples which appear to fold were often fixed by a rigid back rail. Rijksmuseum, Amsterdam

170 *Right*: Armchair of rosewood, first half of the 17th century. The legs and arm supports are of turned baluster shape and the lower stretchers, with their attractive curved outline, are typical of Netherlandish work. The upper stretcher is composed of a broad frieze of pierced strapwork. It is interesting to note that all four chairs illustrated in this sequence have heraldic lions as finials. Rijksmuseum, Amsterdam

171 *Left*: Cabinet-on-stand, veneered in tortoiseshell and ivory, made in Antwerp, first half of the 17th century. The tortoiseshell is laid upon red foil which gives it a full glowing colour. The piece owes its distinction to the careful disposition of its small drawers and doors, with the restrained inlay of ivory. It is unusual in still possessing its original stand. Rijksmuseum, Amsterdam

172 *Below*: Cabinet, veneered in tortoiseshell with painted panels, made in Antwerp, first half of the 17th century. These cabinets were a speciality of the Antwerp workshops and were exported to rich patrons all over Europe. They were designed to house collections of jewels, shells, or other precious objects. This example is decorated with Classical scenes in which the goddess Diana is depicted with nymphs and fauns in woodland settings. The elegant ebony moulding to the drawers is typically Flemish. Rijksmuseum, Amsterdam

ENGLAND 1500-1630

E. T. Joy

In early Tudor manor houses the communal life of the household still centred in the great hall, although there were now more private rooms for the family—parlour, closets and bedrooms. These were often panelled in wainscot oak, while the ceilings and sometimes the friezes round the walls were decorated with stucco, perhaps painted and gilt. Contemporary paintings show how brilliantly coloured were the interiors of these great houses, with their splendid wall hangings and richly embroidered upholstery and table carpets. But despite the air of grandeur created by such sumptuous and costly textiles, early Tudor furniture was simple and kept closely to the medieval pattern.

The chief craftsman was the joiner, whose substantial and durable joined furniture, usually of oak but also of native woods such as walnut, ash or elm, developed on traditional lines until 1660, and to an even later date in provincial areas. Some of the best furniture, however, was imported, or made in England by immigrant foreign joiners, often Dutch or Flemish.

Henry VIII, whose tastes were neither insular nor conservative, encouraged Italian artists and craftsmen to come to England. These fruitful contacts ceased at the Reformation but, on a limited scale, decorative motifs from the repertoire of contemporary Italian ornament were introduced in English houses. This influence of the Renaissance on the decoration of furniture is seen in the appearance of carved medallion heads known at the time as *Romayne* work and other pseudo-Classical motifs. They were often incongruously mixed with Tudor roses and traditional Gothic ornament such as tracery, linenfold panelling and foliage. Following medieval custom, much furniture was gilt or painted in order to protect the wood and brighten the house.

On the dais in the hall a chair of estate, reserved for the master, occupied a conspicuous position. It was a heavy joined chair of box-like form, with framed and panelled back, sides and seat. A lighter chair, the *caquetoire* or *caqueteuse*, for parlours and bedrooms, was based on French models. It had a narrow panelled back and splayed arms, and was open under the seat. Two other types of chair of great antiquity were the X-chair and the turned or 'thrown' chair. The latter had arms, legs back and supports of turned members and a triangular seat. But in spite of their variety, chairs were very scarce. The inventory of The Vyne, Hampshire, drawn up in 1542, showed that its fifty-two rooms contained only nineteen chairs of which seven were imported and were described as *Flanders chairs*. Forms or benches and stools with solid splayed supports were more usual, the term *stool* being the accepted description of a seat for one person. Settles with backs and arms and sometimes with box seats were also common. Both settles and forms were often fixed to walls and around window recesses. A particular type of furniture which could fulfil two functions was the table-bench or chair-bench, the hinged back falling down to form a table top.

Chests remained very important pieces, used as seats as well as for storage. The ancient type, built up entirely of boards, was made until the 17th century. But after 1500 the panelled chest, carved with fashionable decoration, was much more usual.

The high table, known as the *table dormant,* stood on the dais in the hall. As its name suggests, it was on fixed supports. Trestle tables, which were boards (the usual term for tables), set on trestle supports, were used by retainers in the body of the hall. But already standing joined tables were in general use under which forms and stools could be kept when not required. One variety had trestles connected by stretchers and rails

(marginal references: 174 · 126, 159 · 187 · 180 · 175 · 178)

173 The craft of the cofferer, who was still considered in the early Tudor period to be the most skilled of the furniture craftsmen, is exemplified in this travelling coffer, of oak covered with leather, tooled and gilt with the Tudor royal arms and cypher, probably those of Edward VI (1547-53). The upper part of this coffer is a chest with a hinged lid; the lower has two long and two short drawers. The chest and the drawers are lined with silk. Victoria and Albert Museum, London

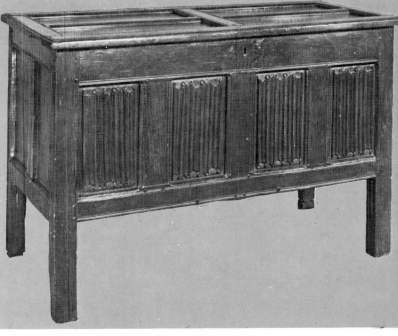

174 *Left*: This oak joined chair of the early 16th century shows the panel and frame construction employed by the joiner. The panels of the back and of the incomplete seat have linenfold carving. Early chairs of this type usually had panels beneath the arms. S. W. Wolsey Ltd., London

175 *Above*: The joiner's use of the panel and frame greatly improved the construction and design of furniture, as is seen in this early Tudor chest, with carved linenfold decoration. S. W. Wolsey Ltd., London

176 *Above*: An early 17th-century side table with folding top and drawer and arcaded decoration. The unfolded top rests on a pivoted leg. S. W. Wolsey Ltd., London

177 *Above right*: In early Tudor times 'cupboards' were still essentially open shelves for display. Many, however, began to incorporate doored compartments, as illustrated in this early 16th-century example. The carved medallioned head on the central panel (Romayne work) is an attempt at Renaissance decoration of Italian inspiration. H. W. Keil, Broadway

178 *Right*: The oak joined table with fixed underframing was the usual type of high table in great Tudor and Jacobean houses. This example of the early 17th century has fluted decoration on the frieze. S. W. Wolsey Ltd., London

179 *Left*: By 1600 the joined chair had achieved a lighter appearance by discarding the panels beneath both seat and arms, now scrolled beyond their turned uprights. These changes can be seen in this chair of the early 17th century. S. W. Wolsey Ltd., London·

180 *Below*: After 1550 the trestle stool was gradually replaced by the joined stool with four turned legs. These two examples illustrate the different types of turning, decoration and underframing found on stools of about 1600. S. W. Wolsey Ltd., London

181 *Left*: The court cupboard was introduced in England in Elizabeth's reign, and had open shelves to display plate. This Jacobean example of bulletwood and satinwood encrusted with panels of semi-precious stones shows the diversity of carved ornament on outstanding pieces—heraldic beasts and pseudo-Classical supports, dentil moulding and geometrical patterns on the upper, and strapwork and shell ornament on the central shelf. The bottom shelf and square feet are modern reconstructions. Victoria and Albert Museum, London

182 *Right*: The great bed, when complete with its costly hangings, was the most magnificent piece of furniture of the Tudor period. This bed, which is made of walnut, bears the date 1585 on a panel in the tester. The headboard displays the arms of John Sebright of Blackshall in Wolverley, Worcestershire and the frieze of the tester is inlaid with arabesques in box and holly. The moulded panels, inlaid decoration and turned footposts show Elizabethan joinery and turnery at their best. H. W. Keil, Broadway

183 *Below*: This fine oak table in the Guard Room at Lambeth Palace is an outstanding example of the joiner's and carver's craft in the early 17th century. The Church Commissioners, London

184 *Below right*: Detail showing one of the carved lion supports and strapwork frieze of the table in the previous illustration.

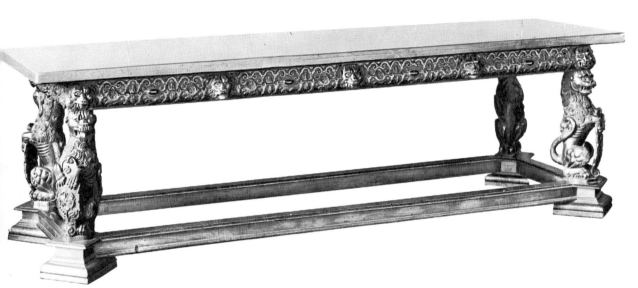

fastened by pegs on the outer side of the uprights. Various small tables stood about the house, including *faldyn* tables with folding tops, supported on pivoted legs, and games tables with a compartment beneath for dice.

The exact nature of the many kinds of cupboard mentioned in Tudor inventories is not always clear. The cupboard was basically an open structure with shelves to display the family plate. It was, in fact, a board upon which the cups were set. Part at least of some shelved pieces was enclosed by doors, for references occur to *close cupboards* and *cupboards with aumbries*. An aumbry (or almery, ambry, armory, armoire) was originally a wall recess, then any space enclosed by a door, or any small doored compartment in a larger piece of furniture. It was also a receptacle with doors in which broken meats were kept under the almoner's control for distribution to the poor. The livery cupboard was used for storing the allowance of food and drink given daily to members of the household, but it is uncertain whether it had doors. There were also food cupboards with doors pierced with tracery for ventilation. Hall and parlour cupboards in two stages had either the upper stage alone, or both stages enclosed, while the completely enclosed types are sometimes known as press cupboards. A press was a term loosely used to describe a tall doored piece with shelves and occasionally drawers for linen, or pegs for clothes. Another term of wide meaning was the hutch, now taken to apply to the hutch table, a long side table on short legs, with one or more doors. The celebrated *Sudbury's Hutch* at Louth Parish Church, Lincolnshire, is of this type and is so described in the churchwardens' accounts. It was made about 1490 and donated by the Vicar, Thomas Sudbury (c. 1504).

Owing to the cost of the hangings, the great bed was the most valuable piece of furniture. The early Tudor type had a canopy suspended from the ceiling in the medieval manner, but shortly after 1500 four corner posts were introduced, together with a panelled headboard. A low truckle bed was sometimes kept under the great bed for servants' use.

The growth of industry and foreign trade under Elizabeth and the rise of a new propertied class led to distinct advances in standards of luxury. Many old houses were renovated and vast and splendid mansions were built. In these the great chamber took the place of the great hall, while the long gallery, the dining parlour and numerous private rooms were essential features. There were now close cultural ties with Protestant Germany and the Netherlands. Flemish and German pattern books, containing engraved designs for architecture and furniture were imported. With their northern interpretation of Italian Renaissance forms and ornament, they exercised a powerful influence on the products of the joiners' workshops. The three most distinctive ornamental features which appeared, in consequence, on Elizabethan furniture were strapwork, an intricate arabesque ornament carved in low relief, usually in repeated patterns, *bulbs* on table legs and bed posts, and inlay in floral and chequer patterns composed of such woods as ebony, holly, bog oak, sycamore, box and poplar. Joiners also made more use of walnut, chestnut, beech, cedar and fir. Painted furniture was going out of fashion and plain surfaces were waxed or varnished.

In the latter part of the century a number of so-called *Nonesuch* chests were made, inlaid with designs representing formal architectural views, wrongly supposed in the 19th century to resemble Henry VIII's Palace of Nonesuch in Surrey, pulled down in the 17th century. Richly upholstered chairs were fashionable—in 1590 Lord Lumley's three residences had '76 chares of clothe of gold, velvet and sylke'. But these chairs were of beech and only a few, such as those at Knole in Kent, have survived. Their scrolled arms now extended beyond the uprights. The panelled back joined chair also had over-reaching arms. It was lighter in structure than the early Tudor type for it no longer had panelled sides beneath the arms and by 1600 the boxed-in seat had been discarded. It often had a carved scrolled cresting at the top, and brackets at each side. By 1600 the four-legged joined stool was replacing the older type.

After 1550 the draw-table, extendible to almost double its length by two leaves beneath the top, was found in dining parlours. The older joined and trestle tables, however, continued in use. The earliest mention of a draw-table appears to be the *drawing table* in the Duke of Somerset's inventory of 1552. The Great Chamber at Lumley Castle in 1609 contained 'two long drawing tables of Walnottree one folding table of wainscott and a little table of wainscott . . . one merketree (i.e. inlaid) table'.

The court cupboard is first named in late Elizabethan inventories, and continued in use well into the Stuart period. It was an open, three-tiered structure, said to have been so named on account of its low height (French *court*, short) as few are more than four feet high: drawers were often contained within the upper and lower friezes. A closely related type had an enclosed straight- or splay-fronted compartment in the upper stage. The larger press cupboards remained fashionable until the late Stuart period. Food cupboards were now often made to hang against the wall, with turned spindles in the doors. By 1600 *cupboard* was acquiring its modern sense of doored furniture.

Elizabethan beds were very large and often lavishly decorated. After 1550 the heavy wooden tester rested on a carved and inlaid headboard and on two foot posts standing clear of the bedstock, the two rear posts being discarded.

During the reigns of James I and Charles I, furniture was slow to show any significant changes. Progress was hampered by the Civil War while in the Commonwealth period, money was short and the Puritans did not favour displays of luxury. But after 1600 decoration was less exuberant and more stylised. *Bulbs* became flatter, and there was more emphasis on turning and on carved lozenges, lunettes, fluting, arcading and guilloches. Split balusters were often glued to surfaces.

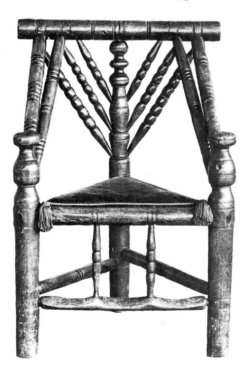

Chairs without arms, described at the time as back stools, first emerged at this time. They are now popularly called farthingale chairs and were so named in the 19th century because they were said to have been made for the comfort of women wearing the fashionable hooped skirts. These chairs had padded backs and seats, and their legs were often turned in columnar form. Two types of lighter chairs were known about 1650. One, the Yorkshire-Derbyshire, had a back formed either of turned balusters under an arcading, or of two broad and flat hooped rails; the other had a half back and seat covered with leather, fastened with rows of brass studs, and knob-turned legs and stretchers.

Gate-leg tables were now in increasing use. The older folding type had one leg halved vertically to form a swing support. The new type had two hinged flaps and a gate on each side; the fixed centre sections had either solid trestle uprights and feet linked by stretchers, or, more usually, turned legs.

Before 1650 a rudimentary chest-of-drawers appeared. Drawers, known as tills or drawing boxes, had been built into travelling coffers and larger furniture for some time, and before 1600 a chest with a single drawer at the bottom, known as a mule chest was in use. This convenient bottom drawer led to the development of a piece with two or more drawers in the lower section and a chest above. In about 1650 a true chest-of-drawers emerged—with a narrow drawer at the top, then a single deep drawer, and three long drawers at the bottom.

In general, surviving 17th-century furniture made in England before 1660 gives no hint of the Baroque splendours so rapidly gaining favour on the Continent. The original furnishings of a house such as Wilton in Wiltshire must have included many finely carved and gilt pieces of a more sophisticated type. But no trace remains of them and it was not until the restoration to the throne of Charles II that English furniture began to reflect the fashions of a new age.

185 *Above left*: The first chairs without arms, or back stools, were introduced into England in the 17th century. In this example of *c.* 1600 both the oak framework, with rare columnar legs, and the Turkey work upholstery (in imitation of 'Turkey' carpets), are of English manufacture. S. W. Wolsey Ltd., London

186 *Above*: A Yorkshire-Derbyshire chair, of carved and turned oak, *c.* 1640. The space between the uprights is filled with turned balusters beneath a broad arcading. In other chairs of this type the back contains a series of smaller arcades supported on turned balusters, or two broad arcades without balusters. S. W. Wolsey Ltd., London

187 *Left*: 'Thrown' (i.e. turned) chair; first half of the 17th century. This type of chair, of great antiquity, was made by turners, who fitted the ends of the supports into sockets in the framework. Victoria and Albert Museum, London

188 The Long Gallery at Aston Hall, Birmingham, was built early in the 17th century, and is an outstanding example of Jacobean splendour, with ornate fireplace, panelled walls with repeated arch motif, tapestries, and plaster ceiling moulded in intricate, flowing strapwork. Birmingham City Museum and Art Gallery

SPAIN AND PORTUGAL

Andrew Ciechanowiecki

The 16th century is, without any doubt, the greatest period in the history of the Iberian Peninsula. Both Spain and Portugal reached their apogee not only in political power and economic prosperity but also in their sense of historical mission and ideological purpose, then gratifyingly fulfilled. For Spain, finally united as a nation under Ferdinand of Aragon (1479-1516) and Isabella of Castille (1474-1504), the Middle Ages closed with the *annus mirabilis* 1492. That year, suggesting the providential, but for which two decades of rule by the Catholic monarchs had prepared the country, brought with it the final victory over the Moors and the fall of Granada, as well as the discovery of America, with all the wealth that accrued to Spain after Cortez conquered Mexico (1519-22) and Pizarro took possession of Peru (1531-4).

Spanish presence in the Netherlands and Italy and her involvement in Europe through her Hapsburg king, who was soon also to become Emperor of the Holy Roman Empire, both strengthened her cultural ties with other countries and gave her a new mission: the defence of Catholicism. That the Spanish and Austrian realms should be united in the person of a hispanicised monarch brought Spanish influence to bear on Europe far beyond the field of politics. A new philosophy, which can be summed up as the spirit of Counter Reformation, and the art it evolved, resulted from Spain's emergence on the European scene. '*Il n'y a plus de Pyrénées*' was, in fact, a reality for the rest of Europe a century and a half earlier than it was for France.

The 16th century has been called Spain's Golden Age. It was certainly so in the field of arts and letters. Even if the close of the century saw black clouds threatening the 'empire on which the sun never sets', with the realm thrice declared bankrupt as the result of mercantile theories absurdly applied, with penury despite the Indies, heavy military defeats and demoralising inroads into the mentality of the people—the greatness of Spanish artistic and literary achievements remained impressive for much longer than her political power. The two long reigns of Charles V (1516-66) and Philip II (1566-98) virtually

spanning the century which witnessed the pinnacle of Spain's power and her incipient decline are the frame for this artistic development centred upon a Court which had infused an austere Castillian tradition with a Burgundian love of ostentation. Every form of artistic endeavour was fostered by the Court and quickly copied by the Church and the nobility, already gathered into the Royal orbit during the previous reign. Architecture, both sacred and secular, came first, but the applied arts shared this general flowering.

Late Gothic and *mudéjar* mingled at the beginning of the century with Italian Renaissance influences, which soon gained the upper hand. As in nearly all European countries, the initial victory of the Renaissance in Spain was in the field of ornamentation. The structure of a building or of an object remained fundamentally medieval, while the exuberant decorative features which were now introduced derived from the Renaissance. This style, in which early Renaissance motifs such as antique heads with wreaths, cherubs, urns, trophies, masks, birds and grotesque half figures fill characteristically atectonic flat surfaces belongs to the reign of Charles V. It is known as plateresque because it was first applied to silver. It gave place to a purer, more classical and incidentally more Italianate style, culminating in the monumental severity of the architect, Juan de Herrera's work, epitomising the spirit of his patron Philip II.

The furniture of the Spanish *cinquecento* follows the same trend. It is much more numerous than in the preceding periods. The building of many town mansions by the nobility and the great rise in the standard of living of the middle classes during the first half of the century, created an unprecedented need for it. Although the wealth of furnishings in the old Royal Palace in Madrid was destroyed by fire in 1734, and the rooms at the Escorial give only a marginal comment on the best furniture of the period, inventories and many surviving pieces provide a clear picture of what was made and used in Spain at that time.

As in the preceding era, the abundance of walnut rendered it the most usual wood for furniture. But chestnut, poplar, oak,

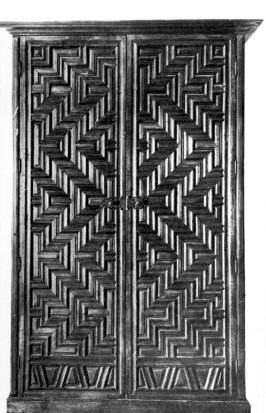

189 *Left*: Tall cupboard of pine, 16th-century Spanish. The two doors are carved with geometric mouldings which clearly derive from the *mudéjar* style. Fundación Tavera-Lerma, Toledo

190 *Right*: Mid-16th-century Spanish chest with severely architectural ornament. The treatment of the acanthus leaf motif anticipates the type of decoration which was to be very popular in the 17th century. Museo de Artes Decorativas, Madrid

189 orangewood and pine were also frequently employed. Imported woods such as ebony and mahogany, were soon to play an increasing part in the production of luxury pieces. The discovery of the silver mountain Potosi in Peru in 1545, as well as other abundant sources of this metal, allowed it to be much used for furniture or at least to enrich it until the sumptuary laws of 1593 and 1600 put an end to this growing fashion. The inventory of the possessions of the ill-fated minister of Philip II, Antonio Perez—the Fouquet of his times—describes beds, chairs, braziers, coffers and tables made of, or ornamented with silver, sometimes also using gold and precious stones.

The more modest, and more prudent, had their furniture enriched with elaborate reliefs, the panels sometimes decorated in the manner of Siloe or Berruguete, with marquetry and
201 mudéjar work (so close in feeling to the fashionable Italian certosina style) and with gilding and brass nails.

Notwithstanding the development of new types of furniture the chest continued to be the most popular and valued object in the Spanish home. As the last flowering of Gothic furniture, Catalonia produced in the early 16th century an elaborate type of chest, with an ornate lid, painted inside. These richly carved chests have a door at one side of the façade, concealing a set of
190 drawers for small articles. Renaissance chests, on the other hand, reveal a marked Italian influence, which entered the country through Aragon and the Levante. These either bear severely architectural decoration or they copy the cassone, with caryatids at the corners and ornate pediments. A certain coarseness and heaviness distinguishes them, nevertheless, from their prototype. Trunks covered in velvet or leather, with elaborate, pierced metal lockplates and numerous bosses and nails were also much used.

Probably the greatest change occurred in seat furniture. Benches continued to be used but chairs were much more common, even if ladies still usually sat on a dais strewn with cushions in the Moorish fashion. In the first part of the century
191 the hip-joint chair was introduced, under obvious Italian influence and usually elaborately decorated in mudéjar style. The ceremonial chair, with richly carved panels was also made, but more rarely. Towards the middle of the century a new type of chair appeared, this time under Flemish influence. It was plain and sturdy, relying only upon upholstery for its decoration. Rectangular in shape, of medium height, with the back rails finishing in metal balls or carved leaf finials and simple armrests, it had square legs terminating in bracket feet. The legs were joined by low and narrow stretchers at the sides and back
192 and by a wide one, fretted or carved, usually with armorial
193 bearings, in front. This type of chair was either hung with leather, attached by large ornamental nails or with velvet or brocade bordered with fringes. The upholstery either covers the
193 rails or is attached at the back (a madeiras vistas). The tooled and often coloured leather (guadamecil) was originally a Moorish speciality. Produced in many centres apart from Cordova, which gave guadamecil the name by which it was to become known in other countries, it was a distinctive Spanish invention, highly prized all over Europe.

These chairs, known today as sillones de fraileros, are the most characteristic of all Spanish seat furniture. They often had hinges in the stretchers so that they could be folded for easier transport, when the owner set forth on a journey, accompanied by his valuables. At a later stage, when chairs were more common, they usually ceased to be hinged. Chairs of this type, but without arms were also produced towards the end of the century.
194 They were mainly for women whose fashionable hooped skirts (verdugardes) made the use of armchairs impossible.

Tables continued to be very primitive. They were usually covered with rich table-cloths, which disguised their simple structure, but in the second half of the century refectory type tables appeared. Italian in origin, they were supported on columnar legs, with low stretchers. Later in the century, the legs became lighter and more ornate, while the stretchers were
196 of wrought iron, similar to those joining the legs of benches.

Beds also relied on rich hangings for their decorative effect. They were now four-posters, instead of the medieval two-poster, the hangings of which were raised during the day. But the posts are seldom decorated. They were usually dressed in fabric, the carved ornamentation being reserved for the headboard.

191 *Above*: This fine example of a hip-joint chair *(sillón de cadera)* is richly decorated with elaborate *mudéjar* inlay, and hung with late Gothic brocade, bordered with a fringe. It dates from the first half of the 16th century. Museo de Artes Decorativas, Madrid

192 *Above*: Late 16th-century chair of the type known as *sillón de fraileros*, or monk's chair, with a fretted front splat. The brocade hangings are attached by large ornamental nails. Museo de Artes Decorativas, Madrid

193 *Below*: Another variant of the *sillón de fraileros*. This late 16th-century example has a front splat with heraldic carving and the plain leather is attached *a madeiras vistas*, that is, attached to the frame, leaving the wood visible. Museo de Artes Decorativas, Madrid

194 *Below*: Late 16th-century Spanish walnut chair. The form evolved from the *sillón de fraileros* or monk's chair, while the back includes typical Renaissance arcading. Ordinary peasant seat furniture was later to develop from this type of chair. Hispanic Society of America, New York

195 The Dining Hall of the Fundacion Tavera-Lerma in Toledo. This room gives one a good idea of Spanish interiors in the second half of the 16th century. The table at the back of the room and the various types of chair, hung with textiles or with leather, are typical. (The chairs on either side of the large equestrian portrait of Charles V are 17th century.)

196 *Below*: This Spanish walnut table dates from about 1600. The removable, morticed trestle-type legs are linked by an iron stretcher, anticipating the characteristic tables of the later 17th century. Hispanic Society of America, New York

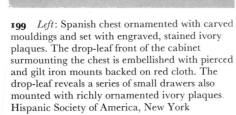

197 *Left*: A *vargueño* could be placed upon a stand *(pie de puente)* with pulls to support the drop front. This Spanish example is decorated with rich plateresque marquetry, and dates from the middle of the 16th century. Museo de Artes Decorativas, Barcelona

198 *Below*: This *vargueño* of walnut with marquetry side panels and drop front is remarkable for its fine carved boxwood reliefs on a velvet ground decorating the small doors and drawers. It is one of a notable group of cabinets in the plateresque style, probably of Catalan origin, and dates from the first half of the 16th century. Victoria and Albert Museum, London

199 *Left*: Spanish chest ornamented with carved mouldings and set with engraved, stained ivory plaques. The drop-leaf front of the cabinet surmounting the chest is embellished with pierced and gilt iron mounts backed on red cloth. The drop-leaf reveals a series of small drawers also mounted with richly ornamented ivory plaques. Hispanic Society of America, New York

200 *Left*: Detail showing a carved portrait head within a roundel, of boxwood on a red velvet ground. The architectural frame, with cornice and turned colonettes, reflects the Renaissance style of decoration. Victoria and Albert Museum.

Apart from the chair, the cabinet is the greatest and most original achievement of the Spanish Renaissance. It evolved from a piece of furniture used in church sacristies to house vessels and ornaments. This ecclesiastical type, architectural in shape and usually very ornate, developed into the cabinet with a drop-leaf front known since the 19th century as the *vargueño* and into a second type, without the drop-leaf front called the *papeleira*. Consisting of a rectangular case divided into drawers, usually with a small central cupboard, such cabinets rest either on a panelled chest *(taquillon)* or on a trestle stand *(pie de puente)* with pulls, usually terminating in the shell of St James, to support the drop lid. The decoration of the interiors of *vargueños* can differ widely from piece to piece, while their exteriors, usually very plain and only enriched with perforated metal plates and nails, are very similar. The finest belong to a presumably Catalan group, with delicate boxwood reliefs in plateresque style on a velvet ground. Others, early in date, are inlaid in wood and ivory in the *mudéjar* style, or are richly decorated with small ivory panels and gilding. These are the most typical and are usually associated with the name *vargueño*. Those influenced by Tuscan models of the late 16th century are more architectural in appearance, with arched panels, pediments and tiers of figures carved in the round. Others again have marquetry interiors varying in elaboration from the simple to the delicate, multi-

coloured marquetry, with *trompe l'oeil* views and landscapes, obviously copied from contemporary German examples. Finally, at the end of the century we find cabinets of which the interiors combine ebony with gilt bronze plaques and reliefs, copying thus in base metal the magnificent pieces which were the combined achievements of the Augsburg cabinet-makers and goldsmiths.

If Spain found the fulfillment of her historic mission as a self-appointed interpreter of the divine will in Europe, Portugal found hers in spreading Christianity overseas. After the 15th century, which had been the century of discoveries, the 16th followed to reap their harvest. Under Manuel I (1495-1521) and John III (1521-57) wealth flowed in, making Lisbon the richest capital of Europe, and settlements were built in the Far East from the Persian Gulf (1509) through Goa (1510), the Moluccas and Siam, to Japan (1542). But this fantastic effort was too great for a small country, precipitating a crisis of population. In the wake of unearned wealth, financial ruin, moral decline and corruption crept in. The stage was set for a dramatic change and the tragic defeat and death of King Sebastian at the battle of Alcacer Kebir (1578), opened the way for Philip II of Spain, the closest relative of the extinct Portuguese dynasty, to claim the crown and unite the two Iberian kingdoms (1580). The union, never more than a personal one, did not penetrate

358

199, 197
199

198

201
199
202

359

201 *Above*: This early 16th-century cabinet is decorated in typical *mudéjar* style, with elaborate and intricate geometric marquetry of coloured woods and ivory. Museo Arqueologico, Madrid

202 *Below*: Late 16th-century Spanish *vargueño* on stand shown with the drop-leaf lowered. The numerous small drawers are mounted with ivory plaques, engraved, gilded and coloured. Hispanic Society of America, New York

203 Detail of a cupboard door, dating from the late 16th century and reflecting clearly the French influence on Portuguese sculpture at the period. Municipal Museum, Portalegre, Portugal

204 *Below*: Portrait of D. Sebastian, King of Portugal, by Cristóvão de Morais, *c.* 1565. The Portuguese chair is clearly Spanish-influenced. Enriched with *mudéjar* marquetry, it is hung with velvet *a madeiras vistas* in the current fashion. Museo des Descalzas Reales, Madrid

into the soul and sinews of the country—but culturally it was to be of great significance. Portugal, where the Gothic style had flowered finally in the elaborate sea-influenced fantasies of the Manueline style, received its early Renaissance forms from Italy and France, but those of the mature Renaissance from Spain. The architecture of Terzi is close to that of Herrera, whose role he took over in Portugal.

It is more difficult to gauge the Spanish influence in the evolution of Portuguese furniture. Earthquakes and wars have taken their toll to such an extent, that virtually nothing has survived from the 16th century. There is no doubt that early 16th-century Renaissance furniture of a ceremonial character had panels with rich carvings, strongly influenced by France, as was all Portuguese sculpture of the period. We also know from documents that in 1549 the Lisbon guild of carpenters produced, amongst other things, folding hip-joint chairs. These must have been fairly common for they figure in numerous paintings and statues of the time, while the rectangular chair, anachronistically decorated in *mudéjar* marquetry which appears in a portrait of D. Sebastian dating from as early as 1565, shows Spanish influence even before the union. This type of chair usually hung with rich brocade or velvet must have been very popular—as witnessed by the chairs sent to the Sultan of Morocco in 1579.

The furniture of Portugal was from the very start subjected to another powerful influence: that of the Orient, her principal trading partner. During the 16th century, documents often speak of beds lacquered and gilt, which were imported from the Far East, or painted in Lisbon to resemble the Oriental ones. They differed from the normal model with the wooden structure hidden under rich hangings, and the bed sold from Portugal to François I of France, which was 'inlaid with scrolls in mother-of-pearl' must certainly have been either imported from the East or made under Eastern influence.

However rare and valuable furniture continued to be in Portugal at that period, quite large numbers of pieces must have been produced, for a census of the middle of the century in Lisbon lists no less than sixty-four cabinet-makers, forty-four turners, sixty painters and gilders and forty-seven carvers. The material used was mainly walnut and chestnut, but exotic woods soon appeared and the lavish use of ivory, silver and precious stones made it imperative to apply the Spanish sumptuary laws of 1593 with great severity.

The evolution of Spanish and Portuguese furniture was not only confined to the respective mother countries. Having by the treaty of Tordesillas in 1494, divided the whole of the unknown West between them in a magnificent gesture of self-confidence, both countries, albeit with different aims in view, settled colonies and far flung outposts, which were organised on the pattern of the homeland. In the early stages, everything was imported from Europe but soon copies of European products were made. The organisation of guilds of August 30, 1568, in Mexico for instance, required a cabinet-maker to be able to make a *vargueño*, a French type chair, an inlaid hip-joint chair, a turned bed and a table. This list shows not only how quickly the new colonies had become self-sufficient, an added explanation for the industrial downfall of the homeland, but also that their demands were considerable and were well in proportion to the wealth of the new territories. These early products were naturally just copies of Spanish models with no native influence. The descriptions give us some idea of the styles copied: the *mudéjar* and plateresque of Andalusia, whence, from Seville and Cadiz, craftsmen followed the conquistadors to El Dorado. There, having destroyed two great civilisations, they were to build on their ruins a New Spain.

Pietre dure table top designed by Jacopo Ligozzi and Bernardino Poccetti and made at the Opificio delle Pietre Dure, Florence, 1633–49, for Ferdinando II de' Medici. Perhaps the finest piece of *pietre dure* furniture in existence, this table top is composed of a mosaic of semi-precious 'hard' stones—agates, jaspers, lapis lazuli and chalcedonies on a ground of black Flanders marble. Museo dell' Opificio delle Pietre Dure, Florence

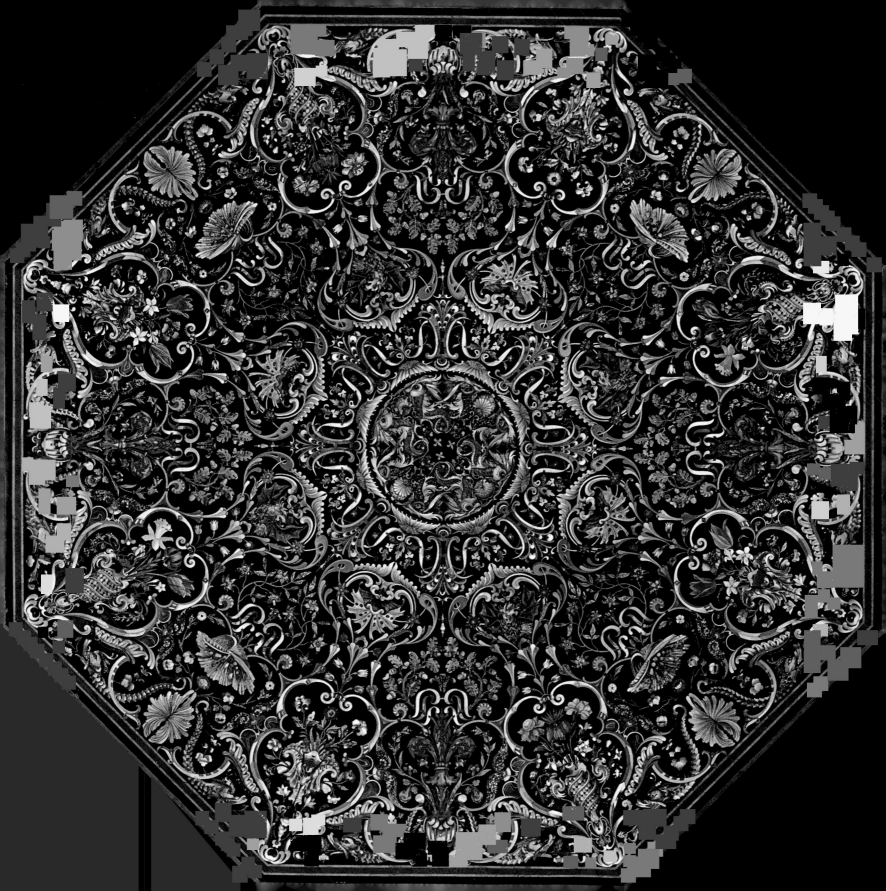

'Queen Elizabeth's virginal'. This fine virginal may possibly have been used by Elizabeth I (who played 'excellently well'), for it bears the queen's arms and the Boleyn badge. Although it is an Italian instrument, in a cypress case covered on the outside with crimson Genoa velvet and on the inside with yellow silk, it may have been decorated in England by an immigrant foreign craftsman. Victoria and Albert Museum, London

Table desk, c.1525, fitted with tills (i.e. drawers) and decorated with painted and gilt leather. It bears the royal arms of Henry VIII surrounded by the Garter, supported by *putti* blowing trumpets and, on either side, figures of Mars and Venus after woodcuts by Hans Burkmayer, the German engraver. Other decoration includes the head of Christ in a roundel, St George, profile heads of Helen of Troy and Paris, and the heraldic badges of Henry VIII and Katherine of Aragon, on backgrounds of arabesques or strapwork. This desk may be the work of an English craftsman or of a foreigner working in England. Victoria and Albert Museum, London

Carved oak griffin supporting the upper stage of a court cupboard. The decorative use of the griffin, a fabulous creature bearing usually the head and wings of an eagle on a lion's body, was popularised in post-Reformation England through its wide employment in the pattern books of Flemish and Dutch designers. Victoria and Albert Museum, London

V THE SEVENTEENTH CENTURY

The *Salon de la Guerre*, Versailles, begun in 1678 by Mansart and Lebrun. The decoration is carried out largely in terms of sculpture, and the central feature is the oval relief by Coysevox of the triumphant Louis XIV, heralded by Victory and Fame.

ITALY

Hugh Honour

The tendency towards greater comfort and elaboration in furniture design, which became notable in the late 16th century, was still more strongly marked in the 17th. Towards the end of the century, however, comfort and utility were more and more frequently sacrificed to opulence and fantasy of design. The desire for more commodious and imposing furniture seems to have permeated all but the lowest ranks of society. At the same time, the contrast between the furniture in the state apartments of a palace and that in the ordinary rooms grew more evident. For the greater part of the 16th century most of the utilitarian furniture to be found in houses of various types differed less in design than in the richness of the fabrics used to cover it or the paintings applied to it. Some idea of the simpler 17th-century furniture may be obtained from Daniele Crespi's painting of *St Charles Borromeo Fasting*. Tables and chairs like those shown in the painting had been made since the mid-16th century and they were to be made until the 18th. In the case of the table, the same design has been used even in the present century. It is unlikely that many examples of furniture as simple as this have survived from the 17th century, whereas numerous pieces of the richest types of furniture have been very carefully preserved.

In the social history of Italy the 17th century is marked by the emergence of many extremely wealthy new families. A succession of nepotistic Popes created a new Roman aristocracy of immense riches and sometimes great taste in the arts. Their names are commemorated in several of the grandest Roman palaces and villas—Aldobrandini, Barberini, Borghese, Chigi, Ludovisi, Pamfili—which were among the most opulent of their time, not merely in Italy but in all Europe. In Venice, newly enriched bankers, like the Rezzonico, bought their way into the patriciate at vast expense. Although the various states were impoverished, individual families continued to grow wealthier. In Genoa, for example, the great trading families prospered as never before. This considerable access of riches created a spirit

of competition. New and old families vied with each other in the decoration of their houses and the churches with which they were associated. Ostentation became the order of the day—and this was nowhere more obvious than in the choice of furniture.

The taste for splendour was most notably expressed in the state apartments of palaces—rooms intended for show rather than habitation. Among these, pride of place was given to galleries of a type which had hitherto appeared only in the palaces of ruling princes. The gallery with its frescoed ceiling and walls lined with antique statues contained furniture of a purely decorative character—mainly great carved and gilt console tables with marble tops, like those in the Palazzo Colonna, Rome. Similar tables appeared in the other state rooms where there were vast, richly carved and gilt thrones which would dwarf the figures of any who dared to sit in them. Intricately wrought cabinets were intended less as receptacles than as excuses for the display of semi-precious stones, rare woods, and, of course, more gilding.

In the design of the larger pieces of furniture the influence of Baroque architecture and sculpture was strongly marked. The characteristic Mannerist device of conceiving an object, whether a palace façade or a *cassone*, as a series of individual units, was abandoned in favour of the bold unifying conception of the Baroque. Such Mannerist architectural motifs as the reversed pediment and panels of strapwork relief slipped out of favour. Italian furniture of the 17th century tends to have an architectural boldness and solidity, with much use of massive foliage and carved human figures reflecting the style of contemporary sculpture.

Several new types of furniture came into use in the course of the century. The *cassone* was gradually superseded in the greater houses by the wardrobe and later by the chest-of-drawers. The former was frequently treated in an architectural manner with pilasters at the corners and a straight cornice or a pediment on

205 *Above*: *St Charles Borromeo Fasting*, *c.* 1625, by Daniele Crespi. This painting affords a rare glimpse of an ordinary early 17th-century Italian interior. The furnishings are very simple. The table is of a type which was popular in Italy from the 16th century until very recently. Church of Sta Maria della Passione, Milan

206 *Right*: *The Practical Joke of the Priest Arlotto*, *c.* 1640–50, by Baldassare Franceschini called Il Volterrano. Stools and chairs of this type appear to have provided the normal form of seat furniture in all but the greatest 17th-century Italian houses. They were also made in the 18th and 19th centuries and it is thus difficult to assign surviving examples to a particular period. Palazzo Pitti, Florence

205
210
216, 217
225
214
218

207 *Below*: Centre table of carved walnut, dated 1630, made in Piedmont. An early Baroque version of a type of table which had become popular in the 16th century. Museo Civico d'Arte Antica, Turin

208 *Left*: Chair of carved walnut, the back inlaid, 17th century. Rather uncomfortable chairs of this type, slightly more elaborate in decoration than those made in the 16th century, were popular throughout Italy during the 17th century, and were much imitated in the 19th. Wallace Collection, London

210 *Below, top*: Side table, carved and gilt wood with marble top, Roman *c.* 1675. One of a group of decorative side tables made for the opulent gallery of the Palazzo Colonna. It was certainly made by a carver rather than a cabinet-maker and should indeed be regarded as sculpture. Galleria Colonna, Rome

212 *Below, centre*: Side table of carved and gilt wood with marble top, *c.* 1680. This table was made for a room with a ceiling painted by Daniele Seiter who may also have designed it. The carver was clearly an accomplished sculptor and may have been Piedmontese or Roman. Palazzo Reale, Turin

213 *Below, bottom*: Side table of carved and gilt wood with marble top, made in Rome *c.* 1680–1700. The very thick marble top is characteristic of Roman furniture of this period. Palazzo Spada, Rome

209 *Above*: Centre table of carved and gilt lime-wood with a stone top veneered with red Egyptian porphyry, early 17th century. In design this table is transitional, still owing a great deal to 16th-century Mannerist patterns yet clearly a product of the 17th century. Wallace Collection, London

211 *Above*: Side table of carved and gilt wood with marble top *c.* 1675–1700. The very heavily sculptured console and side tables previously popular for palatial furnishing began to go out of fashion towards the end of the 17th century. This table obviously owes much to Louis XIV furniture, but the French motifs are handled in a characteristically broad Italian manner. Palazzo Reale, Turin

top. Handsome built-in bookcases with pilasters or columns and sometimes statues or carved urns on the cornice began to make their appearance in private houses. A great library surrounded by such cases might also contain a pair of terrestial and celestial globes, often supported by carved figures with some allegorical significance. Similar figures came into vogue as supports for vases or for candelabra, though one suspects that their practical purpose was subsidiary to their decorative value in furnishing a great state room.

Perhaps the most conspicuous innovation was the decorative table. Tables with richly carved supports and sometimes intricately inlaid wood or marble tops had appeared in the 16th century. But it was not until the 17th that the magnificent, and purely ornamental side or console table came into vogue. Great ingenuity was exercised in the design of their carved, and usually gilt, supports. Sometimes the marble tops rested on jungles of gigantic, flamboyant foliage, but vast shells and dolphins and human figures were probably more popular. In the Gallery of the Palazzo Colonna, Rome, there is a set of such tables supported by kneeling figures of Turkish slaves—with curious drooping moustaches and tufts of hair—accompanied by tritons and mermaids. Others incorporate proud eagles. And, of course, tumbles of wriggling, giggling *putti* were also much used.

Tables of this type were the work of sculptors rather than cabinet-makers, though surprisingly few can be assigned to the hands of known artists. In Genoa, Domenico Parodi (1668–1740) and Anton Maria Maragliano (1664–1739) are both known to have undertaken work of this kind. It seems probable that in other cities, especially Turin, Florence, Venice and Rome, sculptors who were usually responsible for ecclesiastical work in wood or marble occasionally turned their attention to the construction of elaborate furniture.

By far the greatest of these sculptor-furniture makers was Andrea Brustolon. Born in Belluno in 1662, he was trained in the woodcarving tradition of that district. In 1684 he settled in Venice where, in the course of the next twelve years, he carved eight chairs for the Correr family and a magnificent suite of twelve armchairs and several *guéridons* or vase stands for the Venier family, all of which are now in the Palazzo Rezzonico, Venice. In about 1700 he carved another set of twelve chairs, each one adorned with foliage, flowers or fruit emblematic of a different month of the year, for the Pisani villa at Stra: these are now in the Palazzo Quirinale, Rome. He is also known to have carved some very elaborate picture and mirror frames for which there are several designs among his drawings in the Museo Civico, Belluno. His style was richly sculptural. One of his designs for a mirror frame incorporates a flight of more than a dozen *putti* bearing emblems and representing, so Brustolon's annotations reveal, the triumph of Love over Valour and Virtue. His masterpiece is the set of furniture carved for the Venier family—chairs with arms and legs in the form of gnarled tree trunks and branches supported by little negro boys with ebony

214   *Above*: Cupboard of carved walnut, made in Piedmont *c*. 1650–75. Massive furniture of this type remained popular outside the main centres of fashion throughout the 17th century. Only in its superficial decoration does this piece differ from many 16th-century cupboards. Museo Civico d'Arte Antica, Turin

215, 216   *Above right and right*: Cabinet set with Florentine mosaic panels, 1645, by Domenico Benotti, and detail. John Evelyn bought the *pietre dure* panels in Florence and had them set in this cabinet on his return to England. In the 17th century many other travellers bought similar panels of Florentine mosaic. Collection: C. J. A. Evelyn Esq heads and arms and patches of ebony flesh glinting through the slashes in their boxwood breeches; *guéridons* held by tall, lithe, nude negro slaves with boxwood chains hanging around their necks; other *guéridons* in the form of tumbles of *putti* representing the Four Seasons; and a fantastic vase stand which incorporates the figures of Hercules, Cerberus, the Hydra, Classical river gods and three athletic young negroes. These exquisitely carved pieces of furniture reveal that Brustolon had far greater technical ability than any of his contemporaries Yet he was not primarily a furniture maker but a sculptor who was largely employed carving statues, low relief altar-pieces, crucifixes and tabernacles for the churches in and around Belluno. His chairs, *guéridons* and vase stands seem to have been designed less as pieces of furniture than as decorative sculptures which happen to have a practical use.

Few 17th-century chairs are as elaborate, or as elegantly sophisticated, as those carved by Brustolon. But throughout Italy, thrones which incorporated carving of rank foliage and human figures—usually *putti*—were made in the late 17th century. Elaborate carved and gilded mirror and picture frames were also very popular. One of the finest is the vast late 17th- or early 18th-century mirror and console table by Domenico Parodi in the Palazzo Reale, Genoa—embellished with lions and *putti* and shells and an abundance of fruit and flowers.

Cabinets, though fewer in number even in the greatest palaces, were often the richest objects of furniture. They were usually of an architectural form, often with little columns or pilasters, entablatures and central pediments like miniature Baroque palaces. Indeed, on at least one occasion an architect was responsible for the design. Carlo Fontana designed the magnificent cabinet in the Gallery of the Palazzo Colonna, Rome—made of ebony encrusted with ivory carvings by Francesco and Domenico Stainhart and resting on two figures kneeling on either side of a trophy of arms. This is a rare instance of the use of ivory reliefs on 17th-century Italian furniture. Rare woods, such as lignum vitae and ebony, and *pietre dure* or semi-precious stones were much more extensively employed, especially for the decoration of cabinets.

As in previous centuries, Italian fabrics, especially the silks of Lucca and the rich cut velvets of Genoa were in demand throughout Europe. In Italian palaces the lavish use of these materials added greatly to the impression of luxurious opulence. They were, of course, extensively used for covering chairs. The standard pattern of a chair had a high square padded back, padded seat, carved arms and either turned or carved legs and stretcher. Though rather cumbrous, such chairs are both imposing and comfortable and their manufacture continued well into the 18th century. But their craftsmanship tends to be rather coarse and they derive their effects largely from their upholstery.

The magnificence of Italian 17th-century beds also depends mainly upon the richness of the fabrics with which they were

217 *Above left*: Cabinet 1678–80, designed by the architect Carlo Fontana and set with ivory carvings by the brothers Domenico and Francesco Stainhart. This cabinet seems to have been made less as a receptacle than as a setting for the Stainharts' ivory carvings after famous paintings. The Stainharts also carved the kneeling figures and the trophy of arms. Palazzo Colonna, Rome

218 *Above*: Cupboard of carved walnut, late 17th century. This imposing cupboard is probably of Bolognese origin. Like so much of the furniture of this period it may equally well have been made for a house or the sacristy of a church. Fondazione Giorgio Cini, Venice

219 *Left*: Table top in Florentine mosaic *(commesso di pietre dure)* c. 1630–40, by Domenico Benotti, depicting sailing ships in the harbour of Leghorn. John Evelyn, the diarist, much admired this table top when he was in Florence in 1645, sought out the craftsman who made it and bought a number of panels of Florentine mosaic from him. (See 215, 216.) Museo degli Argenti, Palazzo Pitti, Florence covered and hung. Except in Sicily where iron bedsteads were usual, the four-poster bed seems to have been little employed. The finest beds of the later part of the century have a tester supported from above the head and covered in a rich silk, usually with appliqué decorations, which is also used on the panels surrounding the mattress so that no woodwork is visible. Any woodwork left uncovered was gilt. Beds of this type remained popular until the end of the 18th century and it is now difficult to date surviving examples precisely.

For the decoration of smaller pieces of furniture—especially tables, chairs and harpsichord cases—lacquer was used increasingly as the century proceeded. A form of lacquer painting had been adopted in Italy during the 16th century. Early in the 17th century it seems to have become particularly popular in Rome. Writing to Lord Arundel from Rome in 1616 an Englishman called William Smith listed among his several accomplishments that he had 'been much emploied for the Cardinalles and other Princes of these parts, in workes after the China fashion wch. is much affected heere'. No Roman *chinoiserie* furniture of this period is recorded but tables covered with an imitation lacquer of a single colour have survived. In the second half of the century Venice became renowned for its lacquer furniture and in 1688 Maximilian Misson reported: '*La Lacque de Venise est comme on sçait en réputation; il y en a à toute sorte de prix*'. The popularity of lacquer in Venice was no doubt partly due to the expense of even moderately good quality wood. Of the relatively few pieces of 17th-century Venetian lacquer furniture that have survived, nearly all are decorated with raised gilt *chinoiserie* figures. Furniture was very occasionally decorated with figure or landscape paintings by leading artists. In the 1660s, for example, Francesco Trevisani, who is known mainly for his large altar-pieces in Roman churches, painted a miniature *Flight into Egypt* as the decoration for a clock now in the Museo di Roma.

The materials favoured for the decoration of the most elaborate case furniture produced in 17th-century Italy were semi-precious hard stones or *pietre dure*—chalcedony, agate, sardonyx, lapis lazuli, porphyry and rare marbles. The vogue for objects wrought out of these valuable and intractible materials was well established throughout Europe long before the 16th century. But it was not until then that princes began to demand and craftsmen to make large pieces of furniture encrusted with mosaics composed of such materials. In the mid-16th century the main centre for this type of work was Milan, whence a number of craftsmen were lured to Florence by the Grand Duke Francesco I de'Medici in about 1588. The workshop he established in his palace flourished. In 1599 his successor, Ferdinando I, founded the *Opificio delle Pietre Dure*, housed in the Uffizi, as part of the Grand Ducal Office of Works.

The *Opificio* provided the Medici family with a supply of vases, ornaments and mosaic panels in semi-precious stones to enrich their palaces and to provide them with suitable presents for foreign monarchs. Towards the end of the century, for example, a table with an inlaid *pietre dure* top was sent by the Grand Duke to Queen Elizabeth I in London. Unfortunately it has not survived. In 1604 the *Opificio* began work on its major undertaking—the decoration of the whole wall surface of the Medici mausoleum with a mosaic of *pietre dure*. This costly project was never completed as originally planned, but as work on it slowed down, the Medici converted the *Opificio* into a new source of revenue. Cunningly they arranged in the Uffizi gallery a display of the exquisite figures and inlaid panels made for the altar of the mausoleum—in order to tempt the grandest of grand tourists to commission similar works to take home with them. Many succumbed, including John Evelyn, who was so impressed by the exhibition that he bought nineteen panels of *pietre dure* mosaic which he took back to England and had made up into a cabinet, now at Christ Church, Oxford. Many others, from all parts of Europe, acquired a dozen or so panels to make a casket or cabinet, and some bought whole table tops of these rich and glowing materials.

One of the finest products of the *Opificio* in the 17th century was a table made to the order of Ferdinando II mainly, one suspects, as a proof of the ability of the craftsmen. It consists of a large octagonal slab of black Flanders marble inlaid with tiny laminae of agates, jasper, lapis lazuli and chalcedony. The

220 *Above*: Globe stand of carved and painted wood, Venetian late 17th or early 18th century. The map on the globe was published by Vincenzo Coronelli in 1699. Most globe stands were of turned wood but here the Italian desire to treat furniture as sculpture prevailed. Collection: Francis Stonor Esq

222 *Below*: Vase stand of carved ebony and boxwood, *c.* 1684–96, by Andrea Brustolon. A piece of 'furniture' from the suite which Brustolon carved for the Palazzo Venier (see next illustration). The idea of filling rooms with realistic carvings of nude blackamoors was one that appealed strongly to sophisticated Venetians in the late 17th and 18th centuries. Palazzo Rezzonico, Venice

221 *Above*: Armchair of carved walnut, *c.* 1675–1700 (the upholstery modern). This chair reminds us that a desire for greater comfort as well as for opulence manifested itself in 17th-century Italy. Chairs of this type became popular towards the end of the century. Fondazione Giorgio Cini, Venice

223 *Below*: Armchair of carved boxwood and ebony, *c.* 1684–96, by Andrea Brustolon. Like many of the greatest Italian furniture makers Andrea Brustolon was primarily a sculptor. This chair forms part of a suite he carved for the Venier family soon after he settled in Venice in 1684. Palazzo Rezzonico, Venice

219

215, 216

Plate facing page 63

224 *Above*: Design for a looking-glass frame by Andrea Brustolon, *c.* 1690. Brustolon executed numerous designs for intricately carved looking-glass frames. He annotated this one to explain its symbolism—the left side is devoted to the Arts and Sciences, the right side to Valour, and it is crowned with an allegory of Love. Museo Civico, Belluno

225 *Above*: Combined pier-glass and table of carved and gilt wood, *c.* 1690–1710, by Domenico Parodi. Parodi was a sculptor who worked mainly in marble and few pieces of furniture have been attributed to him. This opulent fantasy perfectly catches the tone of the rich Genoese oligarchy in the late 17th century. Palazzo Brignole, Genoa

226 *Left*: Carved ebony and gilt frame made in late 17th-century Rome. The frame encloses a painting on looking-glass, probably by Lodovico Gemignani. Together they reflect the exuberance of late Baroque art. Palazzo Sacchetti, Rome

227 *Right*: *Prie-dieu* in ebony and *pietre dure*, designed by Giovanni Battista Foggini and made at the Florentine *Opificio delle pietre dure*, finished in 1706. Foggini was the leading Florentine sculptor of his day. Italian 17th-century palace furniture aspired towards work as bold, as precious and opulent as this. Palazzo Pitti, Florence

design, by the Florentine painters Bernardino Poccetti and Jacopo Ligozzi, was charged with symbolism: it incorporates numerous Florentine lilies, the oak leaves of the Della Rovere family, dragons for the Grand Duke, shells with pearls in them for the Grand Duchess and, in the centre, the Medici coat-of-arms. It took the craftsmen fifteen years of cutting and grinding the hard stones to make this elaborate piece. Table tops or panels sold to the public were, of course, much simpler and usually made up of larger laminae of stone. Rather stiff, formalised flowers and little chaffinch-like birds were the most popular motifs for the decoration of such panels: they were employed before the mid-17th century—as for the Evelyn cabinet—and seem to have been made also in the 18th. Port scenes with little boats rocking on a lapis lazuli sea were also created—there is a table top of this type in Palazzo Pitti, Florence.

The cabinets in which *pietre dure* panels were set were sometimes made in Florence—like that commissioned by the 3rd Duke of Beaufort in 1726 and still at Badminton House. But as few Florentines were rich, or perhaps one should say extravagant enough to indulge in such luxuries, and as the problems of transport were great, the more usual practice was to have the panels mounted elsewhere. Towards the end of the 17th century the *Opificio* seems to have carried on a brisk trade with France where finely wrought mosaic panels were much in demand for the decoration of furniture, especially for the royal palaces. Many of these panels originally commissioned for Louis XIV furniture were re-used in the 18th century for new pieces of less heavy proportions.

Although most panels of *commesso di pietre dure* are flat, reliefs were also made, decorated with festoons of flowers or, more usually, juicy fruits. These were particularly popular in France. Hard stones were also used in the round for columns and capitals on furniture. The leading Florentine sculptor of the late 17th and early 18th centuries, G.B. Foggini, designed several very rich furnishings which made great play with *pietre dure* carved into fruits, flowers and cherub heads—notably an octagonal frame for a painting of the Virgin and Child by Carlo Dolci, a holy water basin and a *prie-dieu* bulging with agates and chalcedonies which seem hardly suited to fix a worshipper's attention on the other world.

Table tops and panels of *commesso di pietre dure* were made in several Italian cities besides Florence. An inventory of Palazzo Malipiero, Venice, drawn up in 1660, lists a number of *pietre dure* tables, but fails to state whether they were of Florentine or Venetian origin. Some Florentine craftsmen appear to have gone to Paris to work in the royal workshops. But Florence remained the principal centre for such work throughout the 17th and 18th centuries. Elsewhere in Italy variously coloured marbles were used for similar purposes instead of true hard stones which were both expensive and very laborious to cut. Surprisingly enough, table tops made of a marble mosaic were usually in simple geometrical patterns. Before the end of the 17th century imitations of *pietre dure* work were made in *scagliola*, a special plaster or gesso made of powdered selinite. But the full possibilities of this material remained undeveloped until the mid-18th century.

Sir Osbert Sitwell remarked of the magnificent *pietre dure* cabinet at Badminton that it will have little appeal for the lover of old oak. The same could be said of nearly all the richest furniture made in 17th-century Italy. The virtues of Italian Baroque furniture lie in boldness and elaboration of design, in the use of precious materials, whether hard stones, rare woods or opulent fabrics, and in the sculptural excellence of the figures which are so often incorporated in cabinets and console tables. These qualities were transmitted from Italy to other countries. The use of large sculptured figures and of *pietre dure* embellishments on Louis XIV furniture derived from Italy. In the furniture designed by William Kent in England one may often see the reflection of the great carved and gilt tables and the magnificently hung beds which he saw in Italy in the early years of the 18th century. Curiously enough, despite the high quality of the decorative features of Italian furniture, the actual carpentry is almost invariably shoddy, the work of Brustolon being the most notable exception. It would have horrified the abler, if less exuberant cabinet-makers of London and the highly skilled *ébénistes* of Paris.

THE LOW COUNTRIES

Th. H. Lunsingh Scheurleer

In the course of the 17th century, the Republic of the United Netherlands, which comprised the Northern Provinces, was to become a maritime world power. It was a period of unparalleled prosperity and with the increase of wealth the arts flourished. Not only did architects and painters achieve international fame, but Dutch silversmiths, too, enjoyed a high reputation. Paul van Vianen, for example, was employed in Prague early in the century as Court Goldsmith to the Emperor Rudolf II, while his nephew, Christiaen, was persuaded by the Earl of Arundel in 1635 to settle in London for a period.

In the Southern Netherlands traditional manufactures continued to flourish. Flemish tapestries were still renowned and Flemish weavers were much sought after abroad. It was indeed upon their skill that Charles II's newly founded factory at Mortlake depended. The Low Countries were also famous for their fine leather wall hangings and Cardinal Mazarin's wealthy Finance Minister, Fouquet, possessed eight such hangings at his château, Vaux-le-Vicomte, in France.

Both Dutch and Flemish cabinet-makers were masters of the new techniques of veneering, and the commercial enterprise and control of the seas which enabled Dutch merchantmen to bring porcelain, lacquer and exotic woods to Europe not only aroused a lively interest in the East but also stimulated the cabinet-maker, providing him with means of creating new visual effects. Lacquered and painted furniture and marquetry pieces of contrasting woods, sometimes also incorporating veneers of tortoise-shell and mother-of-pearl, were among the sophisticated products of Netherlandish workshops. This newly flowering art was eagerly adopted in France and later in England. Thus the Baroque age came into being with the Low Countries at the height of their power, and if in the latter part of the century they, in turn, were to receive new ideas from France, in the first fifty years it was their achievements which aroused the admiration of Europe.

Although in furniture there was to be a gradual tendency towards refinement of ornament and a clearer definition of form, the Renaissance two-stage cupboard was not immediately abandoned. In the North, the typical Zeeland cupboards, now veneered with expensive rosewood, were still composed of an upper and lower stage. In the Province of Holland a popular type known as an 'arched' cupboard, was enclosed by long panelled doors, decorated with applied ornament in the form of an arch, the plain surfaces of the doors contrasting with applied mouldings of oak and ebony. This 'arched' chest enjoyed a certain international status, and appears several times in the paintings of Pieter de Hooch. Sometimes the arched mouldings on these pieces are replaced by carved ornament in the so-called auricular style. This ornament was first used by the Dutch silversmith Paul van Vianen who, while working in Prague, was inspired by the anatomy lectures of the famous Johann van Jessen to introduce strange cartilaginous forms into his work. Under the influence of Paul and his brother, Adam van Vianen, this whimsical ornament, reminding us sometimes of the soft flesh of marine creatures and at other times of the bones of a skeleton, found its way into the workshops of cabinet-makers and carvers.

228 Cupboard in two stages, of exotic wood with ebony *c.* 1650. Low cupboards like this were typical of the Province of Zeeland in the Northern Netherlands, where simple decorative features, often introducing arches, were favoured. Rijksmuseum, Amsterdam

229 *The Linen Cupboard* by Pieter de Hooch (1629–after 1684) This painting is dated 1663 when the artist was working mainly in Delft and produced many charming interiors. Here the housewife is handing the clean linen to her maid from a tall two-doored oak cupboard, characteristic of the Northern Netherlands, with applied mouldings in the form of an arch in contrasting oak and ebony. Rijksmuseum, Amsterdam

230 *Far left*: Tall, two-doored early Baroque cupboard of oak, with applied carving and mouldings in contrasting oak and ebony, *c.* 1650. This type of cupboard was made in the Northern Netherlands and is similar to that shown in the painting by de Hooch in the previous illustration. The carving on the door panels, in this case, is more adventurous, for it represents the strangely fleshy forms and masks of the auricular style, first introduced by the Dutch silversmith Paul van Vianen, and inspired by his studies of anatomy. Rijksmuseum, Amsterdam

231 *Left*: Cupboard in two stages, veneered with ebony, Northern Netherlands, *c.* 1660. Although this example is divided into an upper and a lower section, with two doors to each, the tall, two-doored cupboard of one stage only was more usual after the middle of the century. The twisted columns at the corners, the rich mouldings, and raised panels, carved with winged heads and floral swags, are characteristic of the Baroque style. Rijksmuseum, Amsterdam

232 *Above*: Side table of walnut, Northern Netherlands, *c.* 1670. The carved supports of this table suggest the fleshy, boneless forms of the auricular style. The central stretcher is carved with a bird amid foliage and flowers treated in a vividly naturalistic manner. The stand was originally painted and the present marble top is modern. Rijksmuseum, Amsterdam

233, 235 Carved and gilt table with marquetry top, signed by Pieter de Loose and Michel Verbiest, and dated 1689. Antwerp. The base is carved with splendid exuberance and suggests the influence of French Baroque. The marquetry top is composed of an elaborate arabesque of vines, foliage and flowers, interspersed with nude figures, birds and monkeys, in finely engraved brass against a tortoiseshell ground. Rijksmuseum, Amsterdam

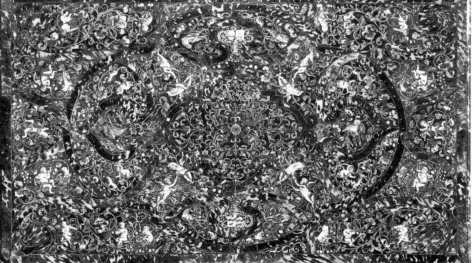

234 *Left*: Carved and gilt centre table, *c.* 1700, Holland. This table probably derives from designs by the Huguenot, Daniel Marot, architect to the Stadtholder of the United Provinces of the Northern Netherlands, later to become King William III of England. The design reflects the disciplined restraint of French Baroque, while the heads of the caryatids express a new sense of pathos. Twickel Castle, Holland

236 *Above*: Four-poster bed, the carved bedhead covered with velvet and the curtains of cut Genoa velvet in red, blue and yellow on a white ground. The floral motifs on the textile hangings reflect the Baroque delight in rich colours and luscious foliate scrolls. The marquetry frame of the mirror on the right, in which brilliantly coloured woods are combined with ivory flowers, is an expression of the same taste. Rijksmuseum, Amsterdam

237 *Above right*: Cabinet-on-stand veneered with acacia and other woods, *c.* 1690, Northern Netherlands. The veneer has been cut from branches of small diameter and the pieces have been laid in such a way as to create a geometrical pattern of star shapes. This concentration on surface decoration, using the natural figure of the woods to best advantage, is a feature of late 17th-century cabinet-making. Rijksmuseum, Amsterdam

238 *Right*: Detail showing the drawing room in a dolls' house, *c.* 1700, Northern Netherlands. In Holland, as in Germany, these dolls' houses were not toys for children but were proud records of family property. The walls of this room were painted by Nicolaes Piemont. The walnut chairs and tables all have twist-turned supports typical of the second half of the 17th century. Rijksmuseum, Amsterdam

In the Northern Netherlands, the demands of the Baroque style for sculptural features were met by the use on cabinet pieces of heavily moulded and raised panels, the central fields carved with such motifs as winged heads or swags of flowers and leaves, recalling the work of the sculptor, Artur Quellinus, in the Town Hall in Amsterdam. Cupboards of this type, veneered with ebony, were sometimes in two stages, but after the middle of the century, were usually only of one stage enclosed by two long doors. Pilasters of the same height as the doors, together with a very prominent cornice and base, contribute to the architectural character of these typical Dutch Baroque pieces. Reflecting the architectural style of the school of Jacob van Campen, these cupboards must have originated in the Province of Holland, but as wealth spread so local characteristics tended to disappear.

The influence of the Baroque style also found expression in the side table on four scrolled supports which was entirely the creation of the carver. The flowers, fruit and birds, already familiar in the carved reliefs upon the cupboards also decorated such tables with equal exuberance. Sometimes the carving suggests the loose, fleshy features of the auricular style.

In the 17th century the splendid Antwerp cabinets-on-stands looked like impressive miniature edifices, surmounted by balustrades and sculptured figures. They were veneered with ebony or with tortoiseshell and ivory, or were even mounted with inlaid marble plaques, depicting scenes from the Old Testament. The Baroque character of these pieces was sometimes heightened by the use of caryatids on the supports to the stands.

Antwerp was also the centre for marquetry of brass, tortoiseshell and mother-of-pearl. A carved and gilt table, with an incredibly intricate top is signed by the Antwerp craftsman Peter de Loose and dated 1689. In spite of such sophistication, however, the masterpiece which the Antwerp Guild regulations still demanded of their members in 1694 was a two-stage cabinet of conservative design. An example, veneered with walnut and tortoiseshell and ornamented with four large figures, representing Paris with the goddesses Venus, Juno and Minerva, is preserved in the Vleeshuis Museum in Amsterdam.

These heavy Baroque cabinets, of imposing scale, decorated with moulded panels, columns or pilasters, and with an important cornice and base, soon ceased to be fashionable in the Northern Netherlands. By the end of the 17th century the cabinet had a barely discernible cornice, and the doors and sides had plain flat surfaces. The cabinet-maker now concentrated all his efforts upon the careful selection of attractive, brightly coloured veneers, sometimes contrasted with ivory and ebony, with which to adorn these surfaces. But outstanding skill was required in the use of floral marquetry, and this type of ornament must have appealed particularly to Netherlandish craftsmen, for still-life paintings of flowers had long enjoyed favour. Towards the middle of the 17th century, the Amsterdam artist, Dirk van Rijswijk, perfected a technique of inlaying floral designs of mother-of-pearl in black marble. Then in about 1660, Pierre Golle, the cabinet-maker from the Netherlands who settled in Paris, where he became '*ébéniste du roi*', made a cabinet

231

231

230

233
234

232

Plate
facing page
80

233, 235

237

239 *Right*: Carved walnut chair, *c.* 1700, Northern Netherlands. Although the turned legs and stretchers are very close to contemporary French examples, the high caned back in a frame composed of long volutes terminating in leafy scrolls is typically Dutch. The practice of caning derives from the Orient. Rijksmuseum, Amsterdam

240 *Below*: Bureau-bookcase veneered in a star pattern with walnut, amboyna, thuya and other woods, *c.* 1720, Northern Netherlands. The quality of this elaborate parquetry is superb and supports the attribution of this piece to Dutch craftsmanship, although the form of the bureau is peculiarly English. Rijksmuseum, Amsterdam

241 Carved walnut chair, *c.* 1700, Northern Netherlands. Like the chair shown above, this example also has a perfectly straight back, although the curved back was soon to be introduced, which would allow the sitter a less rigid pose. The front stretcher echoes, with its arched curve, the cresting of the back. Rijksmuseum, Amsterdam

242 *Left*: Commode veneered with burr-walnut, *c.* 1730, Netherlands. Early Dutch commodes retain the bun feet found on 17th-century cupboards. The complicated concave and convex profile recalls the arched outline of contemporary crested mirrors. Rijksmuseum, Amsterdam

for Cardinal Mazarin, decorated with floral marquetry. By the end of the century, certain leading cabinet-makers of Amsterdam and the Hague specialised in the art: Philippus van Santwijk worked at the Hague, whilst Jan van Mekeren had an important workshop in Amsterdam and the inventory of his possessions drawn up in 1733 shows how prosperous he was. To him may be ascribed a cabinet, now in the Rijksmuseum, decorated with marquetry panels representing vases of flowers on tables similar to a pair of cabinets *en suite* with tables and *guéridons* in Amerongen Castle. In comparison with the marquetry of the great French cabinet-maker, André-Charles Boulle, van Mekeren's touch is broader—his marquetry vases almost give the impression of having been painted. They appeal far more strongly to the eye than do the decorative motifs of his great Parisian contemporary, who never allowed an interest in detail to detract from the overall effect of his pieces. Van Mekeren's cabinets show no such discipline, for the floral marquetry strays up to the cornice, and even down the legs of the stand.

As Louis XIV became more powerful, the Court at Versailles was to set the standard for Europe and the Dutch Republic now accepted the French as arbiters of taste. The influence of France was heightened by the arrival in the Northern Netherlands of Protestant refugees after the Revocation of the Edict of Nantes. Adriaan Golle, a younger brother of Pierre, and also a cabinet-maker, worked among others in Holland for Princess Mary, the wife of the Stadtholder William of Orange, later William III of England. Jean Pelletier, the French sculptor, also sought refuge in Holland until he established himself in England, where he was to receive commissions from King William.

But the most important émigré of all was undoubtedly Daniel Marot. He became architect and designer to the Stadholder, and his work strongly influenced the art of cabinet-making in the Netherlands. Son of the French architect Jean Marot, and nephew of Pierre and Adriaan Golle, Daniel Marot was brought up in Paris. In Holland he quickly developed into a gifted designer, commanding the entire field of the decorative arts. His engraved designs include projects for interiors and furniture, but his most spectacular creations are his great four-poster state beds, introducing the characteristic symmetrical volutes, with their acanthus and scallop motifs in ever-varying forms. These bedsteads were covered with costly materials embroidered in gold or silver with curtains *en suite*.

Marot also provided designs for carved tables and *guéridons*. A gilt table at Twickel Castle, supported on carved figures, so strongly suggests the work of an artist trained in France that we may certainly credit the design to Marot. Naturally not all the furniture to be found in the Marot style can be ascribed directly to him, for his designs widely influenced contemporary cabinet-makers. A particular type of chair with a high back, has carved motifs which strongly recall Marot's work. Similar chairs were made in the Netherlands in about 1700 in many variations, the backs sometimes being decorated with pierced carving. It was customary in the 17th century to place these chairs close together in a row against the wall, just as Marot's engravings indicate.

In Marot's work there was a positive effort to give furniture a more sculptural character and to break away from the outdated rectangular shapes. The new attitude is apparent in the development of the cabinet, which became the typical, and almost one could say, the national piece of furniture of the Netherlands in the 18th century. Early in this century the stand, which had previously been in the form of a table, now contained drawers and assumed the form of a chest upon which the upper stage was placed. The pediment above the doors enclosing the upper section was composed of two arches or was of single arched form. Chinese porcelain or Delft earthenware would be placed on plinths on the pediment.

By such means the silhouettes of these cabinets acquired a certain mobility. The corner-stiles were set diagonally, so that the sculptural and spatial qualities of the pieces were more firmly emphasised. Surfaces were veneered with walnut or burr-walnut, whilst the very rich cabinets were decorated in the traditional manner with floral marquetry. Thus concentration on form and mass became the main feature of late Baroque furniture in the Netherlands.

Plate facing page 81

256, 257
260

234

317

236

239

241

240

242

FRANCE

Laurence Buffet-Challié

Henri IV (1589–1610), Louis XIII (1610–43) and the Government of Mazarin (1643–61)

In France the spirit of the Renaissance died long before the end of the 16th century, for the political and religious wars of the last decades had paralysed all creative activity. Foreign influences which then infiltrated into a devastated France checked the development of any initiative at home, so that while the workshops in Paris and the provinces remained idle, the Court and a few rich patrons turned to Germany, the Low Countries, Italy and Spain for the provision of furniture and costly fabrics.

Henri IV's first aim was to re-establish order and to restore national industry. In 1608, he installed workshops in the Louvre where craftsmen were placed under royal protection. The majority of these craftsmen were of Flemish or Italian origin, and French craftsmen went in turn to the Low Countries to complete their apprenticeship. These developments brought about a gradual revival of the decorative arts, although the effects of the King's policy were not felt until after his death. When he was assassinated in 1610, it would have been difficult to imagine how glittering and influential the arts were to become under Louis XIV.

The Minority of Louis XIII delivered the kingdom into the power of Marie de Médicis. Although a Florentine, she had a taste for Flemish art, and while her Palais du Luxembourg was built in the Tuscan style, it was to Rubens that she turned for the greater part of its decoration. Indeed French art was inspired with new vigour by the vast numbers of Flemish immigrants who settled both in Paris and the provinces. From the time of her regency, there was a vast increase in private building. Magnificent mansions sprang up in Paris around the Luxembourg, on the Ile Saint-Louis and in the Marais. The structure of society was changing: a newly created nobility enriched by hereditary offices, and a flourishing bourgeoisie were adorning their houses luxuriously. Many interiors were modelled upon the Hôtel de Rambouillet, designed for the famous Marquise. A great staircase led up to the state apartments where a splendid vista opened out through a whole suite of rooms and ante-rooms. A *galerie des fêtes*, or Long Gallery, was sometimes added or substituted for the hall of former times. But these state apartments were devised to dazzle the eye rather than for practical living, and it was the bedroom which became the centre of private life. It contained an alcove reserved for the bed, the most outstanding piece of furniture, and it was quite usual for a lady to receive guests while in bed. The space around the bed was known as *la ruelle*, and here the guests were crowded on folding stools or merely on square cushions upon the floor. The *ruelle* in which Madame de Rambouillet held her receptions, was hung with blue silk, a startling novelty at the time.

Louis XIII was not a flamboyant character, and it was the royal family and the ministers of state who set the example in the arts. Cardinal Richelieu made every effort to organise artistic activity around the person of the King. On his own estate at Richelieu, he gathered together rare furniture, pictures, sculptures and *objets d'art*. This was the first attempt to develop a national style. The taste of the Queen, Anne of Austria, was influenced by Cardinal de Mazarin, an enterprising patron of the arts with a passion for 'curiosities'. But in his eyes everything beautiful came from Italy, and as an Italian, it was to his com-

Plate facing page 97

243 *Top*: This piece which comes from the Carthusian monastery at Villeneuve-les-Avignon, resembles in form the cupboards produced in the Low Countries. It has a heavy cornice and large bun feet, and great turned balusters in place of the pilasters of Renaissance times. The moulded panels are inlaid with flower decoration in ivory and coloured woods, a feature which was to be highly developed later in the century.

244 *Above*: This engraving by Abraham Bosse (1602–76) symbolising Winter, gives one a clear picture of bourgeois life during the reign of Louis XIII. Here we can see preparations being made for the *Mardi Gras* celebrations in a room which is at once kitchen, dining room and bedroom. The curtained bed is surmounted by vase-shaped finials known as '*pommes*' or '*panaches*'. Between the bed and the chimney piece a table has been erected consisting of a simple piece of wood placed upon trestles and covered with a cloth, which will be dismantled and put away after use. The chairs are covered with material, the walls with tapestries. A simple stool with turned legs and upholstered top is placed beside the fire. Bibliothèque Nationale, Paris

245 *Right*: The characteristic cupboard of the Henri IV period continued in use under Louis XIII but the decoration changed. Carving now covers all available surfaces. Instead of stylised Renaissance motifs there are trophies of arms, flowers and fruit carved with lively naturalism. The valorous knights whose exploits decorate the lower panels have given such cupboards the name '*armoire à cavaliers*'. They originated in Southern France. Musée des Arts Décoratifs, Paris

246 *Above left*: The technique of a marquetry of pewter and tortoiseshell on a palisander ground derives from Italy, but was practised in the Low Countries and in France by the beginning of the 17th century. It was later to be highly developed by André-Charles Boulle. This piece which marks a transition between the buffet and the cabinet is an excellent example of the type of decoration which anticipates Boulle. Arabesques of pewter are laid on a palisander ground, and it is interesting to note that the gilt bronze mounts now perform a decorative as well as a protective function. Collection: Nicolas Landau, Paris

247, 248 *Top and above*: The inlaid cabinets which were the speciality of Antwerp and South Germany in the mid-17th century were the prized possessions of rich collectors all over Europe. Anne of Austria and Cardinal Mazarin showed a particular interest in them, commissioning examples from foreign craftsmen working in France. The shining dark wood is set off by the richness of the sculptured decoration which in this case represents mythological scenes. Alternating caryatids and columns support the upper stage. The two doors, carved on both sides, reveal a rich, architectural *trompe l'oeil* interior with tiled 'floors' and mirrors enhancing the effects of perspective. The little turned columns have gilt bronze capitals through which can be seen arcaded perspectives in the Italian style. Private Collection

249 *Left*: Cabinets like this were used by rich patrons to house their collections of stones, shells, and other precious objects. This example, dating from the middle of the century, is strictly architectural in form, consisting of a central niche flanked by two tiers of drawers. It is entirely covered in floral marquetry of coloured woods, pewter and ivory on an ebony ground. Carved and gilt terms, representing the Four Seasons, form the base. Musée des Arts Décoratifs, Paris

250 *Right*: In the reign of Louis XIII tables were nearly always covered with a heavy cloth edged with fringes which allowed only the base to be seen. Smaller tables, however, which were easier to move about, became more numerous. They were of various shapes, square, rectangular or triangular and they had turned legs and stretchers. Walnut stools of similar form to the table illustrated, were also widely used. Collection: Nicolas Landau, Paris

patriots that he turned for the decoration of his palace and of the apartments of the Queen at the Louvre. Sculptors and stuccoists, such as Romanelli, Grimaldi and Borzoni introduced the ornate Italian style into France, decorating the rooms with great stucco

255 figures within niches and painted *trompe l'oeil* ceilings. Such apartments would be filled with the canvases of Italian masters, costly furniture, fine examples of the goldsmith's art and tapestries from Brussels and Mortlake, creating an imposing atmosphere of sumptuous grandeur. Ceilings equalled in magnificence

254 the splendour of the wall decorations. Beams were embellished with armorial bearings, garlands and cartouches, great coffered ceilings framed paintings of mythological scenes, while high coved ceilings were adorned with stucco enclosing a central

255 painting. Floors inlaid with costly woods, marble or Delft tiles were no less striking. Carpets, extremely rare, were found only in royal palaces or in the mansions of the wealthy.

At the beginning of the century, the bourgeoisie and the country gentry were still furnishing their houses in the style of the Second School of Fontainebleau. But Court fashions were to affect even the remote châteaux and later walls were covered with panelling painted with landscapes, mythological scenes, or vases of flowers, often in bright colours. More modest interiors were hung with tapestry—*verdures d' Auvergne*—or with fabrics ranging from plain 'tawny' serge to widths of velvet and damask in alternate bands, or even with embossed and gilt leather.

Turning was an essential feature of Louis XIII furniture both at Court and in the provinces. It was used for the legs and

252 stretchers of tables and chairs and for the uprights of cupboards

247 and cabinets. Many varieties of turning were introduced including bead, spiral, baluster and other forms, sometimes combined on the same piece. Mouldings were used with more variety

247 and originality. They not only outlined panels, but occasionally occupied the whole surface, employing various geometrical combinations of which the diamond shape is the most common.

251, 253 The role of the upholsterer acquired added importance, for seats, beds and tables were now encased in materials either fixed with brass-headed nails or as loose covers edged with fringing.

It was, of course, in the field of fashionable furniture that innovations occurred. The art of veneering in ebony, practised in Germany and the Low Countries, was introduced into France by Jean Macé, whom Marie de Médicis had recalled from the Netherlands. The use of this technique marks the birth of *ébenisterie* or cabinet-making. The decorative features were carved in

247 low relief, and are not easily distinguishable, but the light, playing on the polished surface of the ebony, creates a mysterious sheen. Sometimes pearwood was ebonised, so fashionable had the dark woods become. They were occasionally enlivened with a marquetry of *bois de violette*, purple-wood or cedar. The tech-

246 nique of inlaying pewter, silver, copper, gold, or *pietre dure*, tortoiseshell, mother-of-pearl, ivory, bone and even pearls was also introduced by Italian craftsmen.

Types of Furniture

Contemporary inventories indicate that the Court, with the exception of the king, enjoyed a taste for foreign luxuries. Mazarin's inventory, drawn up in 1653, lists: twenty-two cabinets of ebony or tortoiseshell made in Germany, Italy or the Low Countries, furniture in '*bois de la Chine*', Italian tables 'with marble tops enriched with semi-precious stones', five Venetian mirrors . . . The bedroom contained no less than fourteen seats, 'to wit, two armchairs, six chairs, six folding seats . . . the wood of the armchairs entirely covered with velvet nailed to the said wood'. The details of the bed furnishings are impressive: valances, bed-curtains, draperies for bases of the beds, for the posts, etc., were more important than the piece of furniture itself.

Cabinets, at first imported from Italy, Germany and the Low Countries and before long also made by French craftsmen, are

247 the most sumptuous pieces of furniture. The upper section con-

248 sisting of a series of drawers on either side of a central recess enclosed by two doors served as a pretext for a profusion of carving, marquetry and inlaid work.

245 The buffet in its traditional form, a two-tiered piece with four doors, surmounted by a pediment, was still popular at the be-

251 This bed, hung with '*point de Hongrie*', a material which is typically Louis XIII, is shown here in a contemporary setting. The walls are divided into small panels with simple mouldings.

The chairs are also covered in *point de Hongrie* and, with their crossed stretchers and curved armpieces, they mark the transition between Louis XIII and Louis XIV. Château de Talcy, France

252 *Above*: The influence of earlier styles persists in this carved armchair with its open back. But the spirally turned members are typical of the Louis XIII period. A square cushion softens the seat. Collection: Nicolas Landau, Paris

253 *Above right*: By the beginning of Louis XIV's reign the armchair had assumed more generous proportions. The gently curving arm supports, carved with acanthus leaves, contrast with the straight legs and turned stretchers, forming an H. Musée des Arts Décoratifs, Paris

254 *Right*: A fashion for painted ceilings with Renaissance motifs developed under Louis XIII. The beams and joists are decorated with flowers, ribbons and cartouches painted in brilliant colours. After the middle of the century the wall panelling would also be brightly painted with still-lifes of flowers and fruit, a practice which spread all over France. Château de la Roche-Pichemer, France

255 At the beginning of the 17th century the great Parisian houses nearly always possessed a long gallery in the Italian style. The Hôtel Lambert on the Ile St-Louis was built between 1645–50 under the direction of Le Brun, who painted the coved ceiling illustrating the legend of Hercules. Opposite the windows there are landscapes alternating with reliefs framed by stucco figures.

ginning of the century. Little by little it lost this architectural character and became a tall cupboard or *armoire* with two long doors. Extravagant carved ornament of Flemish derivation was gradually replaced by geometrical designs or mouldings in high relief. Spirally turned uprights replaced the pilasters and columns of the previous century. 243

Small easily movable tables were numerous. They are of solid wood, the turned legs joined by stretchers in H or X form. The frieze is sometimes decorated with gadrooning, while the top may be carved with a border of leaf ornament or rosettes in low relief. The marble-topped table of Italian origin enjoyed a certain vogue among the courtiers. 250

The bureau appeared at the beginning of the century. At first it is no more than a table fitted with drawers, but a more developed form can be seen in the later examples illustrated on page 81.

The bed is the main article of furniture, the masterpiece of the upholsterer, who lavished upon it many lengths of cloth, enriched with braid, embroidery, fringes and tassels. It is usually surmounted at the four corners by finials or plumed *panaches*. 251 244

The most usual seats have a framework of plain wood, the leather or textile upholstery being fixed to the frame with brass-headed nails. The armchair became the *fauteuil* with a straight back, the arms often terminating in the head of a lion, a ram or a female bust. The chair was distinguished from the *fauteuil* only by the absence of arms. At first the backs were low and rectangular: only the state chair had the higher back which was more generally used as the century advanced. *Tabourets* and X-shaped stools figure in all the lists of furnishings from the *petite bourgeoisie* to the Court. 244 253

Thus, from austerity to extreme opulence, new trends slowly develop during this part of the century. Foreign styles, once assimilated, will give birth to new techniques, destined to be brought by French craftsmen to a high degree of perfection.

256 The great cupboards of André-Charles Boulle were the showpieces of the age. Boulle is known to have modelled the mounts himself and to have carefully supervised their casting and chasing. Sometimes he combined a marquetry of pewter, brass and tortoiseshell with marquetry panels of contrasting woods, as in this example, which belonged to the Marquise de Piré (1698–1727) the mistress of Philippe d'Orléans, nephew of Louis XIV. Musée des Arts Décoratifs, Paris

257 This cupboard which came from the Royal Collection (*Mobilier de la Couronne*) is after a Boulle design. In spite of its complicated marquetry in *contre-partie*, the detail in no way detracts from the monumentality of the piece. *Putti* and trophies of arms stand out from a ground of glittering brass, creating an incredibly rich effect, altogether in keeping with the grand palatial interiors. Louvre, Paris

Louis XIV

Louis XIV was twenty-three when his minister Cardinal Mazarin, died in 1661. The time for the young king's personal rule had arrived. He resolved to restore the power of the throne and the brilliance of the Court, which had lapsed since the days of the Valois. In developing this policy he found a good administrator in Colbert, who in 1664 was appointed *Surintendant des Bâtiments*, the equivalent in modern terms of a 'Minister of the Arts'. Henceforth, architecture, painting and sculpture were to be consecrated to the glory of His Majesty.

Strangely enough, it was not the monarch but the *Surintendant des Finances*, Nicolas Fouquet, who first introduced a centralised system for the development of the decorative arts. His workshops at Maincy set up to furnish his own château at Vaux-le-Vicomte represented a new departure. It was he who discovered the exceptional qualities of the painter, Charles Le Brun, and put him in charge of the work at Vaux. If the costly excellence of Vaux-le-Vicomte ('*ce Versailles anticipé*', as Sainte-Beuve called it) brought about the arrest of Fouquet in 1661 on charges of peculation, it at least had the merit of bringing the young Le Brun to the fore to set the stage for the great reign. 284

258 *Left*: The *Compagnie des Indes* created by Colbert in 1664 encouraged a taste for Oriental works of art. Lacquer cabinets like this Japanese example were particularly popular. Chinese porcelain vases would be placed upon a base formed by the crossed stretchers of the stand. Bibliothèque de l'Arsenal, Paris

259 *Above*: Detail from a painting by Henri Gascard entitled '*Mme de Montespan dans la Galerie du Château de Clagny*' which demonstrates the rage for lacquer cabinets in the 17th century. The tops are stacked with Chinese porcelain. On the floor are silver vases containing orange trees, and the silver *jardinière* is filled with flowers. Otherwise the furniture is all placed against the wall. Private Collection

260 *Far left*: This cabinet, which is attributed to André-Charles Boulle, was given by Louis XIV to his grandson Philip V whose portrait decorates the central panel. The façade is decorated with a rich marquetry '*en première partie*' of pewter, brass and mother-of-pearl on a tortoiseshell ground, illustrating scenes of military life taken from the engravings of Martin de Batailles, Parrocel, and Van der Meulen. The companion piece in '*contre-partie*' still exists. Private Collection

261, 262 *Left and below*: This splendid jewel cabinet has come to be known as the '*toilette of Mme de Maintenon*'. A rich inlay of birds and flowers in *pietre dure* decorates the drawer panels. The cabinet rests on a stand with carved and gilt figures representing the Four Seasons, and it is crowned by a relief in gilt bronze illustrating the myth of Apollo and Marsyas. The central niche is flanked by columns with composite capitals, the shafts covered with a climbing vine motif. Musée de Strasbourg

Cabinet-on-stand made in Antwerp *c*. 1650. Pieces like this were works of art in their own right and were the speciality of Antwerp, being much sought after by foreign patrons. This rich example in the Baroque style is veneered in tortoiseshell and ebony, and the drawers are inset with marble panels painted with Biblical scenes. The four gilt negro supports of the stand are masterfully carved. The architectural character of the piece is emphasised by the pierced galley surmounting it. Rijksmuseum, Amsterdam

Cabinet-on-stand of floral marquetry, *c.* 1690, by the Amsterdam cabinet-maker Jan van Mekeren. Cabinet-makers in Amsterdam and the Hague were famous for their technique of floral marquetry. In the inventory of the furniture of Louis XIV particular mention is made of a piece with panels showing a vase of flowers 'placed at the end of a table', as is the case with the superb cabinet illustrated. The influence of Dutch still-life painting is very apparent and the quality of the workmanship is outstanding. Rijksmuseum, Amsterdam

Le Brun and the
Manufacture Royale des Meubles de la Couronne des Gobelins

Colbert began by creating an Academy of Architecture. Every official project had to be submitted to the Academy for its approval. In 1662 he bought up the *hôtel* of the brothers Gobelins, on the outskirts of Paris, grouped there several workshops, and transformed the place into a manufactory to deal with all the branches of the decorative arts. In 1667 the status of this establishment was raised to that of *Manufacture Royale des Meubles de la Couronne,* charged with the dual function of furnishing the royal residences and of developing a national style. It was placed under the control of Le Brun, by then chief painter to the King, whose duty it was not only to supervise the administration and to co-ordinate the work executed, but also to provide all the designs used in the Manufactory. Very wisely, Le Brun, in his new position, did not try to eliminate the influence of foreign artists. This is clear from the continuing presence at the Gobelins of Flemish and Italian craftsmen. It was, in fact, by collaborating with immigrants that French craftsmen acquired their unrivalled mastery of the arts of tapestry-weaving, cabinet-making and metalwork. At the same time Le Brun's own preference for Classical forms made for a majesty of style which appealed directly to the King.

Versailles

The furniture and works of art produced by the Manufactory of the Gobelins had one aim in view—that of glorifying the Palace of Versailles. For this superb and ambitious scheme Louis' expenditure knew no bounds. Jules-Hardouin Mansart transformed the façades, Le Nôtre planned the impressive gardens, while Le Brun devoted himself to the interior decoration. Although he was directly responsible only for the *Grande Galerie,* today the *Galerie des Glaces,* for the *Escalier des Ambassadeurs* (later destroyed) and for the *Salons de la Guerre et de la Paix,* it is to him that the entire palace owes its special character. Subtly harmonised marble panelling, tall mirrors, gilt stucco, immense allegorical paintings and decorative architectural features *en trompe l'oeil,* all served to evoke the Baroque manner of Roman palaces, which Le Brun cleverly adapted to create a French national style. Versailles became the temple of official art. The Court, which had taken so much from abroad, now set the tone for the whole of Europe in art, in philosophy, and in social life.

270
page 65

Among the King's innovations was the *Trianon de porcelaine,* built between 1670 and 1672 and reflecting the new vogue for Chinese porcelain and Delft blue and white earthenware. The walls of this garden palace were covered with blue and white motifs on a white stucco ground. The Trianon, later destroyed, was an early manifestation of the taste for the exotic, encouraged by the foundation by Colbert in 1664 of the *Compagnie des Indes,* though the fanciful variations were a long way from true Chinese art.

Jean Bérain and the Designers

Engraved designs were published from the late 17th century onwards, spreading the latest fashions adopted at Versailles to the provinces and even abroad. Those of Jean Le Pautre (1618–82), the leading exponent of Le Brun, were the first to appear. But even before the death of Le Brun in 1690, a new trend had emerged in the work of the architect, designer and engraver Jean Bérain (1638-1711). The influence of Bérain soon became predominant. He developed a style of linear arabesques peculiarly his own. He also took the grotesques of antiquity used by Raphael at the Vatican and by Primaticcio at Fontainebleau, and combined them in decorative designs, with draperies, lambrequins and vine trails, and in his world of strange divinities he even portrayed monkeys and Chinamen. These compositions are light-hearted and gay and they quickly invaded the whole

271

266
265

263 The *bureau* or writing table came into being in the second half of the 17th century. But it was not used only as a writing table as this engraving indicates. Bibliothèque Nationale, Paris

264 *Above:* This piece, which closely resembles the writing table in the previous illustration is decorated with marquetry of pewter and palisander, a technique which Boulle developed intensively at the Gobelins. Collection: Nicolas Landau, Paris

265 *Below:* Towards the end of the century furniture began to assume curved forms. The scroll-shaped legs are linked by crossed stretchers. The glittering marquetry is of brass and tortoise-shell, the colour of the latter heightened by the red foil beneath. Mother-of-pearl and ivory are also included. The design derives from Jean Bérain. Private Collection

266 *Right*: The influence of Bérain was apparent in France even before the death of Le Brun in 1690. His early manner is Baroque in its regard for symmetry and balance, but later his line was to soften, and instead of decoration in relief he tended towards a flat pattern of light graceful arabesques following the technique of Boulle. The shape of this *commode-tombeau* derives from the Classical sarcophagus and was to gain favour at the beginning of the 18th century. Bibliothèque Nationale, Paris

267 *Far right*: A Music Room at Versailles. The turned legs of the chairs and table in this engraving look back to the Louis XIII period. But the backs to the chairs are much higher, giving dignity to the sitter. On the table is a branched candlestick hung with little pendant drops, a form of lighting used throughout Versailles. *Cinquième Chambre des Apartemens du Roi* by Antoine Trouvain. Bibliothèque Nationale, Paris

269 The austere lines of this table, with baluster legs on bun feet goes back to the beginning of the century, but the apron with its carved feature imitating a fringed hanging is typically Louis XIV. Collection: Nicolas Landau, Paris

268· The solid form of this table contrasts with the virtuosity of the decoration. Here again the marquetry of tortoiseshell, brass, mother-of-pearl and lapis lazuli echoes the figures and arabesques in the designs of Bérain. The motif below the apron is flanked by gilt bronze ornaments imitating draped material, fringed and tasselled. The tapering piers of the legs are surmounted by further gilt bronze features in the form of Corinthian capitals. Collection: Mme Lopez-Willshaw, Paris

270 *Right*: The *Grande Galerie* at Versailles, now the *Galerie des Glaces* is shown here in its original state, just as it was designed by Charles Le Brun. Console tables alternate with tall mirrors, and the chandeliers are doubtless part of the fabulous collection of silver furniture designed by Le Brun for the royal apartments. Not a detail has been spared to attain the degree of magnificence which the King desired. Engraving by Sebastien Le Clerc (1637-1714) for the frontispiece of *Conversations* by Melle de Scudéry. Bibliothèque Nationale, Paris

271 *Far right*: Jean Le Pautre (1618-82) was Le Brun's greatest disciple. This design for a console table reflects the master's taste for sober magnificence. The table is flanked by *torchères* and surmounted by a mirror. Such an ensemble would have been carved and gilt, and would have looked very rich against the painted wall decoration. Bibliothèque Nationale, Paris

273 In the 17th century the domestic life of a household still centred around the bedroom. This is clearly the house of a lady of quality, who is receiving a visitor while her maidservant dresses her hair. Tapestries or hangings cover the walls, and on the chimney piece are porcelain vases. The dressing table is covered with a rich embroidered cloth. The armchair has a high back, slightly outward-curving. Bibliothèque Nationale, Paris

272 This fine table of carved and gilt wood represents the Louis XIV style at its purest. Its architectural lines reflect the influence of Le Brun, but the style of decoration is already a little more exuberant, with the pierced balusters and the flowing scrolls and leaves of the apron. Musée des Arts Décoratifs, Paris

274 *Far left*: The Louis XIV chair has a high back and ample seat. This example which dates from the end of the century has carved and gilt legs joined by diagonally crossed stretchers. It is upholstered in Utrecht velvet which covers the entire seat and back and suggests a greater degree of comfort than hitherto. Musée des Arts Décoratifs, Paris

275 *Left*: Around 1673 another type of armchair developed which was known as '*en confessionnal*' because the wings could hide the face of the sitter. It anticipates the *bergère* of the 18th century. This example has upholstered arms and graceful scrolled supports in a form known as '*os de mouton*' or ram's horns. Collection: Nicolas Landau, Paris

276 *Below*: The stool developed similarly to the chair. The seat was softened by a cushion and decorated with fringes; the legs were richly carved. Court etiquette laid down strict rules as to who might sit upon what, and folding stools were reserved for duchesses. In this case the cushion could lift off, but other stools had fixed upholstery. Salle du Conseil du Roi, Château de Versailles

field of decorative art. In particular, they inspired the cabinet-maker, André-Charles Boulle in many of his most intricate and splendid pieces.

From 1694 to 1697 the Manufactory of the Gobelins was bedevilled by financial troubles and it had to be closed for a time. Its failure saw the rise of the great André-Charles Boulle (1642–1732). In the workshops at the Louvre he produced furniture for the King as well as for members of the Court and an important private clientele. He collaborated so closely with Jean Bérain that it is often difficult to distinguish the part played by each in the design of furniture.

Louis XIV furniture has a monumentality in keeping with the majesty of the age. The repertoire of decorative motifs still derived from Classical antiquity but was less imaginatively exploited than it had been in the Renaissance. Terms and caryatids continued in favour, but columns had disappeared, leaving only pilasters. Classical flora and fauna were represented by lotus, laurel, oak and acanthus leaves, fruit and flowers, lions' heads and paws, rams' heads, griffins, dolphins and sea-horses, and the hooves of horses and goats. The insignia of the monarchy were even more frequently used: the two interlaced L's (the cypher of Louis XIV), the *fleur-de-lis*, and the sunburst motif, the emblem of the *Roi-Soleil*. Masks, symmetrical shells, trophies of arms and allegorical emblems were frequently portrayed, while

260, 261

282, 285

272, 278

rosettes, tasselled fringes and pelmets also appeared towards the end of the century. Carving in high relief gradually lost popularity. Instead, wood was carved in low relief and sometimes small flowers appear on a reticulated ground.

Under the influence of Le Brun, furniture became an integral part of the decoration of a room, together with the panelling, the hangings and the *objets d'art*. Gilding and silvering became more and more fashionable, in spite of the fact that the use of gold on furniture and in fabrics was, for reasons of economy, constantly forbidden.

The Court was installed at Versailles in 1682, and an account in the '*Mercure Galant*' tells us that the furniture in the *Grande Galerie*, in the *Salon de la Guerre*, and in the *Chambre du Roi* was almost exclusively of silver. It was a luxury that only Louis XIV could afford. His throne was also of silver, adorned with crimson velvet. This is to say nothing of other objects of silver such as the tubs for orange-trees, ewers, braziers, fire-dogs, fire-irons, chandeliers, candelabra and wall-lights hung with cut-glass pendants. But the financial strains of frequent war resulted in the first sumptuary edict of 1689 which consigned the greater part of these grandiose pieces to the melting-pot.

Veneering with precious woods now replaced the ebony veneers of Louis XIII's time. Marquetry of variously coloured woods was executed with marked virtuosity although the tech-

269

259

256

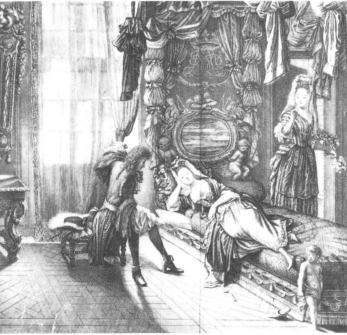

277 *Above left*: At the turn of the century, curved backs replaced those of rectangular shape, and chairs became more graceful. Musée des Arts Décoratifs, Paris

278, 279 *Above and above right*: The woodwork of this armchair *c.* 1700 is carved almost as if it were the work of a goldsmith. The curved frame to the back and seat, and the absence of stretchers anticipate the style of the 18th century. Collection: Mme Lopez-Willshaw, Paris

280 *Left*: The decoration of the bed was the upholsterer's chief task in the 17th century. Here we can see the lengths to which decoration could be taken, with fringes, braids, ribbons and ruching. Bibliothèque Nationale, Paris

281 *Right*: The *'lit à l'ange'* has a canopy which is slightly shorter than the bed itself, whereas the canopy of the *lit à la duchesse* extends to the full length of the bed. This engraving shows the design for the bed *à l'ange* in the *Chambre des Amours* of the Trianon de Porcelaine at Versailles which was built in 1672, but destroyed in 1687. At the head, two *putti* support a cartouche surmounted by a vase of flowers, and this graceful feature anticipates the more light-hearted style of the 18th century. But the splendid hangings of the bed are pure Louis XIV. Nationalmuseum, Stockholm

nique did not reach its zenith until the 18th century. The particular triumph of the 17th century was marquetry employing tortoiseshell pewter and brass. These materials had been used in the first half of the century. But the technique was so successfully developed by André-Charles Boulle that his name is now used to describe all furniture decorated in this way, regardless of its date or authorship.

Lacquer was introduced into France through contact with the Far East. Mazarin's inventory of furniture mentions beds in *bois de la Chine*, but the first pieces of furniture imported from China and Japan appear to have been lacquer cabinets which were mounted in France on gilt wood stands. Such was the enthusiasm for furniture and textiles *'façon Chine'* that imitations of oriental lacquer were produced, although little from the 17th century has been preserved.

From 1685 onwards, all furniture brought into the royal collections was entered in the *'Journal du Garde-Meubles'*, in accordance with an order issued by Louis XIV 'to avoid a repetition of the events of past centuries, when a stupendous waste occurred in our furniture depositories'. Imitated and simplified, the style of the royal furniture spread throughout France. The *armoire* or cupboard is a monumental display piece, sumptuously decorated. Apart from the great Boulle cupboards, there are also simpler examples of solid wood, decorated with carvings and mouldings, which were used as wardrobes. The *armoire-bibliothèque* or bookcase appeared at this period, the doors of the upper part being panelled in glass instead of wood.

During the early part of the reign, the cabinet provided an opportunity for a display of exceptional virtuosity on the part of the craftsman, as witnessed in the examples by Domenico Cucci at the Gobelins and by André-Charles Boulle at the Louvre. But by the end of the century, the cabinet had fallen completely out of fashion and was replaced in favour of the commode, or chest-of-drawers.

Although the *commode* originated in the 17th century, the term does not appear to have been used to describe this piece of furniture until 1708. In inventories earlier than 1700 the term *bureau* was used as well. Boulle was the inventor of this new article of furniture, which in its earlier form resembles a sarcophagus resting on heavy feet; hence the name *commode-tombeau*.

The bureau, on the other hand, evolved into a piece of furniture of rectilinear or *bombé* form, supported on eight legs of baluster or scroll shape with two series of drawers at each side. Sometimes the bureau is surmounted by a tier of drawers.

There were many kinds of table and some are particularly splendid. The massive silver tables designed by Le Brun and made at the Gobelins received rich ornamentation, while those in carved and gilt wood were hardly less magnificent. The profusion of carved ornament virtually conceals the structural form. The table top is usually rectangular in shape, but there are square and round tables, as well as games tables on pedestal supports. The materials include marquetry of tortoiseshell and

256
257
260
264
265

258

256, 257

Plate facing page 97

266

265

270

272

268
267

282 *Far left:* A Classical figure on an ornate scrolled base supports the tray of this *torchère* with its valanced edge, *c.* 1670. The candelabrum with crystal drops is contemporary with the piece which is one of a pair, and would have stood in a state apartment. Collection: Mme Lopez-Willshaw, Paris

283 *Below left:* This carved and gilt *torchère* with its acanthus leaves, volutes and flowers is typical of the second half of the 17th century. Musée des Arts Décoratifs, Paris

284 *Left:* Drawing by Le Brun for a *guéridon* or candlestand, destined for the Château of Vaux-le-Vicomte. Pieces very similar to this were made at the workshops at Maincy under his direction. Three eagles form the base; above, intertwined dolphins support *putti* which in turn hold aloft a vase forming the top of the stand. Nationalmuseum, Stockholm

285 Wall brackets were an important part of interior decoration. They were designed to fit in with the wall panelling and would be carved with the same motifs. Musée des Arts Décoratifs, Paris

brass or of marble in the manner of the Royal furniture produced at the Gobelins, as well as wood.

Plate facing page 97

The console table, richly carved, had a purely decorative function. The carved and gilt wood was manipulated with astonishing freedom, the apron often enriched with masks, shells and scrolls. The legs of baluster shape, or carved as caryatids, are joined by crossed stretchers. Towards the end of the century the supports were reduced to two curved legs linked by a light stretcher, supporting a marble top. A splendid effect was created by surmounting these console tables with tall mirrors.

The bed, as in the reign of Louis XIII, was the work of the upholsterer. The woodwork is wholly concealed by the textile hangings. There are a number of types: the four-poster; the *duchesse* bed, lacking the two front posts but surmounted by a canopy of the same dimensions as the couch beneath; the *280, 281* *lit à l'arge* with its shorter tester and gracefully gathered curtains, of which a delightful example is shown in a design by Le Brun, made as early as 1672 for the *Trianon de Porcelaine*. The day-bed, already known in Louis XIII's time, was now more widely used—there were about fifty at Versailles. It was the forerunner of the *canapé* or settee, large enough to seat two or three people.

The shape and the actual use of seats accorded with the demands of etiquette. At Court, indeed, they were the subject of constant bickerings which are mentioned in the writings of Saint-Simon, the Marquis de Dangeau and Madame de

Sévigné. The use of stools and folding seats for example, was a *276* privilege much disputed. There were as many as 1,323 at Versailles, the majority of gilt wood, softened by the addition of a cushion.

Chairs gradually became more comfortable. The seat became fairly low and spacious, the back being raised to form a tall rectangle. The armrests are curved, sometimes covered with an *274, 267* upholstered pad. The legs, in the form of balusters or half-figures, *277* are linked together by a stretcher carved in the style of Le Pautre. The wood is gilt, or painted in fashionable colours—red, green or gold. Upholstery of damask, velvet, gros-point, gold brocade *278* or embroidered tapestry, is completed by the addition of a woollen or silk fringe. The winged armchair, which appeared at the end of the century, was the ancestor of the *bergère*. *275*

This furniture reflected the taste of the Court and society. There is no doubt that a more modest type was used by less privileged classes, although little is known of the details of bourgeois interiors. Provincial workshops employed local woods and they probably still followed the style of Louis XIII right up to the 18th century.

In his old age the King lost his love of ostentation. After his marriage to Mme de Maintenon the Court resided more at Marly than at Versailles, and an atmosphere of austerity reigned. A more intimate way of life foreshadowed a more personal and less ceremonial style, in keeping with the aims of the new society.

ENGLAND 1660-1715

Anthony Coleridge

This section is primarily concerned with English furniture in the Baroque style. The period covered can be divided into two distinct phases in which the grandiose and opulent manner of Continental Baroque was assimilated and adapted to English taste. The first phase covers the reigns of Charles II and James II; the second those of William and Mary and Queen Anne. It can never be an entirely successful practice to label the various phases in the evolution of furniture with the names of reigning monarchs. Although styles were always changing, these changes did not necessarily coincide with the death or accession of a monarch, while it was often many years before a new style in the capital was taken up in country districts. It is interesting to compare the Baroque extravagance of the Restoration with the elegant and restrained good taste inherent in the simple furniture made during the early decades of the 18th century. Evelyn, after the Restoration, wrote in his diary: 'the king brought in a politer way of living which soon passed to luxury and intolerable expense'. The study of the domestic furniture which formed the background to this 'politer way of living' is the subject of the first part of this essay.

The Restoration of the monarchy revived patronage and gave craftsmen an opportunity to free themselves from the stolid dictates of Puritanism. The arts in England made little progress during the Civil War and the Commonwealth. At the Restoration, the prevalent Italian styles, Baroque and exuberant in conception and exaggerated in execution, were introduced via France and Holland to London where they were immediately adapted to England's more insular tastes. France, at this date, was accepted as the *arbiter elegantiae* in Europe, and Louis XIV had collected around him a brilliant team of cabinet-makers and craftsmen, such as Du Tel, Loir, Bonnemer, Cucci, Golle and, of course, André-Charles Boulle, to decorate and furnish Versailles and the other Royal residences. It was to Aubertin Gaudron, however, whose importance as a royal cabinet-maker was almost unknown until the recent publication of M. Pierre Verlet's *French Royal Furniture*, that the English probably owe their greatest debt, as it was he who influenced, and possibly taught, many Huguenot cabinet-makers later working in England and the Netherlands. He had perfected the technique of laying such motifs as urns, bouquets and vases of flowers in polychrome marquetry. It was to France, therefore, that England primarily looked for a lead and contemporary interest in French culture is apparent from a pamphlet published in 1663 entitled *England's Interest and Improvement*. The French, we are

286 *Left*: Ebony silver-mounted table, *c.* 1670, on unusual supports modelled as caryatids, or female figures. In the centre of the top, which has been renewed, the silver plaque bears the initials E.D. for Elizabeth, Countess of Dysart, who became Duchess of Lauderdale in 1672. It is described in the 1679 Ham House inventory as 'one ebony table garnished with silver'. Victoria and Albert Museum; Ham House

288 *Left*: Ebonised table mounted with silver plaques, 1675-80. The central oval plaque is chased with floral and foliate ornament enclosing the applied cypher FC and M reversed, and an Earl's coronet, for Frances Cranfield, daughter and heiress of Lionel, Earl of Middlesex, who married the 5th Earl of Dorset (1622-73). Collection: Lord Sackville, Knole, Sevenoaks

287 *Above*: Set of silver furniture bearing the royal crown and cypher of Charles II, and presented to the King by the City of London, *c.* 1670. The embossed and chased sheets of silver are mounted on oak. It was not unusual for silver furniture to be made, particularly as presentation pieces, in the late 17th century although most examples have long since been melted down. Reproduced by Gracious Permission of Her Majesty the Queen told, 'had introduced new modes and new tastes and set us all agog, and having increased among us considerable trades, witness the vast multitude of broad and narrow silk weavers, makers of looking glasses, paper, fringes and gilded leather'. But the Revocation of the Edict of Nantes in 1685, bringing numbers of Huguenot craftsmen to seek refuge in England, really popularised Continental styles and techniques, for during Charles II's reign the benefit of these had been primarily enjoyed by the King, the Court and a few rich magnates and landowners. The names of many Dutch and French Huguenot craftsmen appear in the Royal accounts—Richard Vanhuissen, John Guillibandie, Peter Pavie, Cornelius Gole and Gerreit Jensen. The strong Dutch influence was partly due to the normal exchange of ideas between the two countries and partly to the residence of the Stuart Court in Holland. The accession to the throne of William of Orange was also an important factor. Charles' Queen, Catherine of Braganza, came from Portugal and it is possible that she brought some of her native furniture with her, together with examples from Goa, as part of her dowry. There had for many years been close trading links between England and Portugal.

Italian carved and gilt furniture which suited the splendid proportions of Baroque *palazzi* was too exuberant for English taste. Whitehall Palace, and fine houses such as Knole, Ham House, Drayton or Petworth, were furnished with less panache although they were luxurious by English standards. Descriptions of the Duchess of Portsmouth's apartments at Whitehall give us some idea of their splendour, although the rooms were not as sumptuously furnished as those of Versailles. The Duchess's apartments were 'luxuriously furnished with ten times the richnesse and glory beyond the Queene's' and they contained 'Japan cabinets, skreens, pendule clocks, great vases of wrought plate, tables, stands, chimney furniture, sconces, branches, brasseras, etc., all of massy silver and out of number'. Much of the grandest furniture in the State apartments at Versailles was of silver, all of which was melted down in the early 18th century. Many of the larger pieces of English silver furniture were also melted, because they were outmoded and too large and the metal was needed for the making of other pieces. Some of the furniture was of solid cast silver, some in 287 wood encased in thin silver sheets and some was of ebony, or 288 ebonised wood, mounted with silver plaques. Mirrors, candle 289 sconces, tables, chairs, chandeliers, candlestands, andirons and fire irons were sometimes made either of cast silver or were mounted with silver plaques. Perhaps the most important set of silver furniture in the country was that presented to William III by the Corporation of the City of London and now preserved at Windsor Castle. It is mostly made of heavy cast silver and the form and decoration of the table and mirror are entirely in the tradition of late 17th-century veneered furniture. A second set in the Royal Collection dates from Charles II's reign. There are also two sets still at Knole which are earlier in date. One consists of a table, a mirror and a pair of *torchères* entirely encased in repoussé sheet silver. The other is of ebonised 288 wood mounted with silver plaques. Several pairs of silver andirons have survived. A pair at Knole with male terminal figures can be dated to *c*. 1660, and another pair in the royal plate bears the mark of Andrew Moore, who made the suite of silver furniture for William III. Sets of wall sconces were also made, usually incorporating in their design the arms and cyphers of their owners. The finest silver chandelier extant is that in the King's Presence Chamber at Hampton Court, made for William III, but there are other examples at Chatsworth in Derbyshire and Drumlanrig Castle in Scotland.

The Duchess of Portsmouth's apartments also contained 'Japan cabinets (and) skreens . . .', and this is but one example of rooms containing lacquer furniture. The word *japan* was used in a very loose sense during the 17th and 18th centuries, for it was employed both to describe true *lacquer* from the Orient and the European imitation. The popularity of lacquer grew after the Restoration parallel with the increase in European trade with the East. The East India Company was not slow to realise the importance of the growing craze for *chinoiserie* and an early reference to lacquered wares appears in the Company's Court minutes for the year 1683. Lacquered panels, usually imported

289 One of a pair of silver sconces, 1668, the plate embossed with a crowned C II R framed in fish ornament. Embossed silver sconces remained in fashion well into the 18th century. Collection: the Duke of Buccleuch

290 *Above*: Side table, *c*. 1680, the rectangular top has been cut from a panel of a Chinese 'Coromandel' lacquer screen, but the scrolled supports and stretchers are decorated with English japanning simulating Chinese lacquer. Imported Chinese screens of this type were frequently cut up for use as mirror frames and table tops. Collection: the Earl of Pembroke, Wilton House, Salisbury

291 *Below*: Gilt side table, *c*. 1685, the rectangular top and frieze decorated with 'Bantam Work' or 'Coromandel' lacquer, the scrolled supports carved as foliated cherubs. Stalker and Parker in *A Treatise of Japanning* (1688), state that 'Bantam Work' was then 'almost obsolete and out of fashion' but later examples are extant. Collection: Colonel N. R. Colville

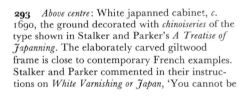

292 Black japanned chair decorated with gilt *chinoiseries, c.* 1680. One of seven similar chairs, probably those described in the 1683 Ham House inventory as '12 back Stooles with cane bottoms, japaned'. They were made for Elizabeth, Countess of Dysart, whose initials they bear, and were evidently an imitation of an Oriental form. Victoria and Albert Museum; Ham House

293 *Above centre*: White japanned cabinet, *c.* 1690, the ground decorated with *chinoiseries* of the type shown in Stalker and Parker's *A Treatise of Japanning*. The elaborately carved giltwood frame is close to contemporary French examples. Stalker and Parker commented in their instructions on *White Varnishing or Japan*, 'You cannot be

over-nice and curious in making white Japan . . .' Christie, Manson & Woods Ltd., London

294 *Above right*: Black Japanese lacquer chest, *c.* 1685-90, decorated in shades of gold, the giltwood stand carved with foliage, *putti* and a female mask. Collection: Colonel N. V. Stopford-Sackville

296 *Below*: Carved and gilt candlestand, *c.* 1680, the shaft formed of infant bacchanals, the tripod carved with foliage and eagle masks. It was possibly carved by one of the Dutch immigrant craftsmen employed at the Palace of Holyroodhouse and it is typical of pieces produced jointly by carvers and gilders. Reproduced by Gracious Permission of Her Majesty the Queen, Palace of Holyroodhouse, Edinburgh

295 Carved gilt wood and painted polychrome suite, *c.* 1680, of elaborate design, consisting of a mirror, a pair of candlestands and a side table. This type of decoration is frequently found on Dutch furniture. Collection: the Marquess of Linlithgow, Hopetoun House, West Lothian

297 *Above*: Centre table, *c.* 1680, with ebony frieze and beechwood frame, the *scagliola* top bearing the arms of the 2nd Earl of Peterborough, surrounded by polychrome foliate decoration. This is an early example of the use of *scagliola* in England. This material is an artificial marble compound of cement, isinglass and colouring matter to which chips of marble were sometimes added. Collection: Colonel N. V. Stopford-Sackville

in the form of screens, were cut up and adapted to form mirror
290 frames, cabinets, tables and chests. The Earl of Bristol's expense
book records that in 1689 he bought twelve leaves of 'cutt
Jappan skreens'. John Van Colma, a Dutchman, sold to Queen
Mary in 1694 a 'fine right Japan chest,' and in 1662 John Evelyn
noted the rare quality of the 'Indian' cabinets brought from
Portugal by Catherine of Braganza. He also speaks of a house
of a neighbour in Kent 'whose whole house is a cabinet of all
elegancies, especially Indian'. Rooms were panelled with lacquer as at Hampton Court Palace, Chatsworth and Drayton,
and it was not long before the demand for lacquer began to
exceed the supply. In Pollexfen's *A Discourse of Trade, Coyn and
Paper Credit*, 1697, we read that in about 1670 some artisans
were sent out to introduce patterns which the Chinese craftsmen
could copy in order that their products should be more acceptable to the prevalent European taste, for, as Pollexfen also wrote,
'nothing was thought so fit . . . for the ornaments of chambers
like Indian screens, cabinets, beds and hangings'. A document,
dating from *c.* 1700, records that several artificers were sent out
by the East India Company with 'great quantities of English
patterns to teach the Indians how to manufacture goods to make
them vendible in England and the rest of the European

markets'. It was erroneously thought at this time by many that
lacquer came from India, not China, and thus it is often referred
to as *India* or Coromandel work—the Coromandel coast being
in South East India.

However, there was an easier and cheaper way to meet the
demand for lacquered furniture and that was to produce a substitute for it. The most important and one of the earliest documents that we have on the art of japanning is *A Treatise of
Japanning and Varnishing* published by John Stalker and George
Parker in 1688. It contains receipts for the preparation of
lacquer and instructions on technique and is illustrated with
twenty-four engraved ornamental designs composed of pseudo-
Oriental motifs which form the basis of much of the *chinoiserie*
decoration depicted on japanned furniture. This information
is probably based on the study of Chinese originals and from
technical knowledge perfected by the Dutch who were ahead
of the rest of Europe in this field. The art of japanning quickly
became a fashion and a social accomplishment so that vast
quantities of indifferent japanned work were turned out by
amateurs. Sir Ralph Verney, in a letter of 1689, agrees to pay
'a guinay entrance and 40/- more' to buy materials for his
daughter Molly to be taught at school, and in 1694 there is an

298 *Above left:* Rectangular centre table, *c.* 1680,
the cedarwood top inlaid with ebony strings, the
walnut supports and stretchers elaborately carved.
The spiral supports tend to look forward to the
furniture produced towards the close of the
century and the basket of flowers in the centre of
the stretchers, unfortunately slightly damaged,
shows strong French influence. Collection:
Colonel N. V. Stopford-Sackville

299 *Above right:* Centre table, *c.* 1685, carved and
veneered with maplewood and parcel gilt, the
rectangular top inlaid with silver strapwork. This
table shows strong French influence. It was
probably made to the order of the 1st Duke of
Devonshire, who rebuilt Chatsworth. Devonshire
Collection, Chatsworth, Derbyshire. Reproduced
by Permission of the Trustees of the Chatsworth
Settlement

300 *Left:* Mirror in a gilt frame, *c.* 1680, carved
with *putti*, flowers and acanthus foliage in the
style of Grinling Gibbons. The *putti* on the cresting
support an Earl's coronet. A typical example of
the rich Baroque style of the period. Collection:
the Marquess of Exeter

301 *Right:* Detail of the Grinling Gibbons
room at Petworth, Sussex. The portrait of Henry
VIII after Holbein is framed in limewood carving
by Gibbons, executed between 1689 and 1692
when he was working on the Library at Trinity
College, Cambridge. It is a triumph of technique
and was described by Horace Walpole as 'the
most superb monument to Grinling Gibbons'
skill'.

entry in Lady Grisell Baillie's household book 'to materials to japan £3 . . .'. However, the art of japanning was very inferior to the true lacquer from the East, even when made by professionals.

Plate facing p. 112 293 294

One of the most popular types of furniture made from lacquer or *japan* was the chest or cabinet with a series of small drawers enclosed by two doors. These were often supported on a carved and gilt stand of Baroque design. The legs were sometimes in the form of carved *putti* or caryatids and were often united by an exuberantly designed apron carved with scrolls, foliage, strapwork, masks and other typical motifs. These stands, many of which were silvered and not gilt, were made by carvers and gilders who were specialist craftsmen. The carver was originally a member of the Joiners' company, but he had gained semi-independence at an early date and, by about 1670, his work had become so specialised that the carver who worked with the gilder was a different type of craftsman from the carver who worked with the cabinet-maker and chair-maker. The former worked in softwoods such as deal, lime and pearwood whilst the latter carved the harder woods which were used for case and some seat furniture. The carver, who was either in partnership with a gilder, or employed one, specialised in carving the

intricate detail and decoration on wall sconces, mirror and picture frames, candlestands, cabinet stands and the elaborate tables which were often surmounted by *scagliola*, or inlaid marble slabs or lacquered panels. Several craftsmen, such as Philip Brumfield and John Poictevin, are described as 'Guilders' in the Royal Accounts of Charles II's reign, and they were responsible for gilding the furniture carved by their colleagues either with oil or water gilding. The water gilding was of higher quality but the oil gilding, which was cheaper, was more durable. The differences between these two kinds of gilding and the technical methods of preparing them are also described by Stalker and Parker in their *Treatise of Japanning and Varnishing.*

The school of specialist carvers founded by Grinling Gibbons (1648–1720) is of the greatest importance and their softwood carvings, usually in lime, were highly naturalistic, representing swags and garlands of fruit, flowers, birds, game and vegetables. Sometimes such testing subjects were portrayed in wood as biblical scenes in an architectural setting, and an important set of carvings at Sudbury Hall are of particular interest as the original account for the work survives, which reads 'Mr Gibbond had for ye carved work on ye drawing room chimney . . . £40'. Examples of the work of Grinling Gibbons and his school

300 296 291

301

302 *Above left*: Set of walnut and marquetry furniture, *c.* 1670, inset with engraved ivory. The mirror cresting which was originally attached to the piece is missing. The marquetry shows strong Dutch influence but the construction and spiral supports are typically English. Collection: the Earl of Pembroke, Wilton House, Salisbury

303 *Above*: Interior showing a walnut veneered cabinet with unusual key pattern bandings, *c.* 1690, and a pair of open armchairs with spiral supports and stretchers, the seats and backs in embossed leather, *c.* 1660. Collection: Michael Dormer Esq

304 *Left*: One of a pair of cabinets, *c.* 1665, mounted with embossed silver and veneered in 'oyster' laburnam. It bears the monogram of Queen Henrietta Maria and formed part of the furnishings of Somerset House, Strand, where the Queen Mother was living from soon after the Restoration until 1665. Reproduced by Gracious Permission of Her Majesty the Queen

305 *Right*: Writing cabinet, or scriptor, *c.* 1675, veneered with 'oyster' princewood, the name applied to kingwood during this period, and with silver mounts. This, and another of similar type, are both mentioned in the 1679 Ham House inventory where they are described as 'scriptors garnished with silver'. Victoria and Albert Museum; Ham House

306 *Above*: Cabinet-on-stand, veneered with floral marquetry of variously coloured woods and white and stained ivory, *c.* 1690. The brilliance of these marquetry pieces contributed to the splendour of a Baroque interior while the interest in naturalistic ornament was a feature of the period. Jas. A. Lewis & Son, London

307 *Above*: Writing table, *c.* 1690, attributed to Gerreit Jensen, veneered with a marquetry of tortoiseshell, brass and pewter in the manner of André-Charles Boulle. Jensen made another writing table in 1695 for the Crown which is now at Windsor Castle. Collection: the Earl of Pembroke, Wilton House, Salisbury

308 *Below*: Writing table veneered with arabesque marquetry, 1690. It has a folding top bearing a crown and cypher. This is probably the piece referred to in Gerreit Jensen's account of 1690 'For her Ma^ts service at Kensington. For a folding writing table fine markatre with a crowne and cypher . . . £22.10.' The supports of the stand have been renewed. Reproduced by Gracious Permission of Her Majesty the Queen

309 *Below*: Carved oak bookcase with glazed doors, *c.* 1675. Similar bookcases made for Samuel Pepys are now in the Bibliotheca Pepysiana at Magdalene College, Cambridge. Oak furniture of high quality was still being made at this date. The National Trust; Dyrham Park, Gloucestershire

survive at Windsor Castle, Hampton Court Palace, Belton and Petworth, to cite but a few.

Cabinet-making is a craft which depends largely upon the technique of veneering and this involves the selection and laying down of veneer-cut wood upon a solid base. This technique was not widely known in England prior to the Restoration, when it was developed by immigrant Dutch and Huguenot craftsmen, many of whom were given Royal patronage. During this period indigenous woods were still being used, and, as oak was becoming outmoded, the cabinet-makers turned to walnut, yew, mulberry, laburnum, chestnut, olive, holly, beech and various fruit woods.

The most rich and decorative type of veneered treatment is known as *marquetry*. This process consists of laying veneers of contrasting light- and dark-coloured woods on to a solid carcase. It was the work of another specialist craftsman, called a *marqueteur*, and the technique reached England via France and Holland. It was widely used to decorate the surfaces of clockcases, cabinets, secretaires, or *scriptors*, chests, tables and mirror frames. The types of marquetry favoured in England are known as *seaweed*, *arabesque* and *floral*. In each case the design was first drawn out on paper and then clamped on to the layers of veneer. The patterns were then cut out and the pieces of light wood were fitted together and *married* into the ground wood. The marquetry panel, thus formed, was then placed on to the furniture carcase. Mother-of-pearl and ivory, often engraved and stained green, were sometimes used to make the designs more elaborate and craftsmen of foreign origin, such as Gerreit Jensen, on occasions employed a marquetry of tortoiseshell, brass and pewter similar to the technique which was being perfected by André-Charles Boulle in Paris. *Seaweed* or *endive* marquetry is composed of small-scale motifs resembling seaweed or endive leaves: *arabesque* marquetry is a type of inlaid decoration based on the intricate interweaving of flowing lines in the Near Eastern tradition. *Floral* marquetry, on the other hand, consists of designs, often of a complex nature, formed of bouquets, sprays and urns or baskets of flowers, sometimes with birds and other forms of wild life intermingled with the flowers and foliage. The human figure, landscape scenes, utensils and architectural motifs, so much favoured on the Continent at a later date are rarely, if ever, used during this period. Veneers were also selected from the boles and roots of olive, walnut or laburnum, and, after they had been sliced into panels of about two inches in diameter, about six to eight pieces to each inch of wood, were stuck together and formed into geometric patterns. The resultant designs were often referred to as being of *oyster* pattern and, if they were of cube or geometric form, were later called *parquetry*. The decoration of veneered furniture was often further enhanced by glueing strips of wood, with the grain running across the width, as a cross-banding or framework to the veneered surface. Bandings are sometimes cut and laid in such a way as to simulate a feather—hence the name given to this particular type of *feather* or *herringbone* banding. Another form of inlaid decoration, usually found in conjunction with banding, is *stringing*. This is a wire-like, linear inlay formed of very thin strips of coloured wood, square in section, which is often used as a framework to the borders or marquetry panels on veneered furniture. The lines of stringing, or *strings*, are found up to one-eighth inch square and the smallest are little thicker than cartridge paper. The commonest designs are of rectilinear or radiating form, often stemming from a central sunburst medallion, and the strings are cut from satinwood, boxwood, holly, purplewood, olivewood and ebony. A rather more striking form of stringing is known as *porcupine-quill* and is formed as an interlaced design of ivory and ebony strips.

Although veneered, lacquered, silver and gessoed and gilt furniture was fashionable, oak pieces in the Jacobean style were still being made in country districts well into the 18th century. The English craftsman appears quickly to have adapted himself to the new designs and techniques from the Continent, and Evelyn, writing in this connection, tells us that 'Locksmiths, Joyners and Cabinetmakers and the like from very vulger and pitiful artists are now come to produce works as curious for the fitting and admirable for their dexterity in contriving as any we meet with abroad.'

301

302

306, 308

307

308

306

304

305

328

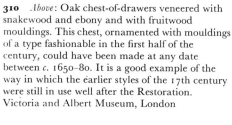

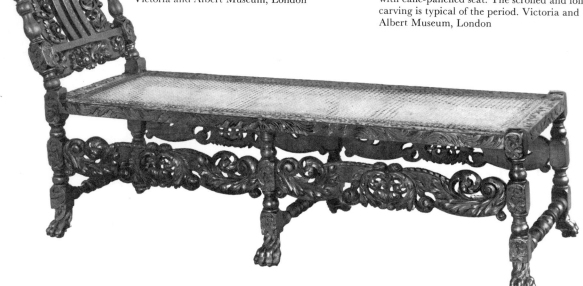

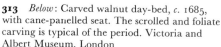

310 *Above*: Oak chest-of-drawers veneered with snakewood and ebony and with fruitwood mouldings. This chest, ornamented with mouldings of a type fashionable in the first half of the century, could have been made at any date between *c*. 1650–80. It is a good example of the way in which the earlier styles of the 17th century were still in use well after the Restoration. Victoria and Albert Museum, London

311 *Above*: Walnut armchair, the top rail carved with the Pembroke arms, *c*. 1680—the back and seat in canework. This is one of the finest examples of the cane chair-makers' craft. The Burrell Collection; Glasgow Art Gallery and Museum

313 *Below*: Carved walnut day-bed, *c*. 1685, with cane-panelled seat. The scrolled and foliate carving is typical of the period. Victoria and Albert Museum, London

312 *Above*: Walnut winged armchair, *c*. 1680, upholstered in velvet, the supports and stretchers carved with scrolls and foliage. This is an early example of a type of upholstered armchair introduced towards the end of Charles II's reign. Collection: the Duke of Buccleuch

314 *Above*: Rectangular stool, *c*. 1685, on typical carved beechwood supports and stretchers, the upholstery of later date. In comparison with the number of extant chairs from this period, relatively few stools have survived. Victoria and Albert Museum, London

315 *Left*: View of the Duchess of Lauderdale's Bedchamber at Ham House, Surrey, showing a contemporary bedstead. The wall hangings are a modern copy of a damask at Hampton Court woven for William III. A silver-mounted walnut scriptor stands on the right; the chair is one of a set mentioned in the inventories as 'with carved and gilt frames covered with rich brocade'. Victoria and Albert Museum; Ham House

316 View of the North Drawing Room at Ham House. The plaster frieze and ceiling were made in 1637 for the Earl of Dysart. The walls are hung with a set of Soho tapestries woven between 1699 and 1715. On the floor is a 17th-century Persian carpet while the fire-irons are silver mounted. The room contains three chairs from a splendid gilt set *c.* 1675 carved with dolphins and covered with the original brocaded satin; and the partly gilded walnut table may have been made by immigrant Dutch craftsmen, employed at Ham House between 1673 and 1679, as the caryatid supports are unusual in English furniture at this period. A further three chairs from a second set are of beechwood painted black and partly gilt, upholstered in contemporary red velvet. Victoria and Albert Museum; Ham House

317 *Above*: Engraved design for a State Bed by Daniel Marot, from the set of designs entitled '*Second Livre d' Appartements' c.* 1700.

318 *Right*: State Bedstead, *c.* 1695, the pinewood frame covered in crimson velvet with white silk trimmed with red braid. The headboard has the *appliqué* cypher and Earl's coronet of George Melville (1636-1707), created 1st Earl Melville in 1690, a Minister of William III. It is similar to two engravings for State Bedsteads in the first collected edition of Daniel Marot's designs published in 1702, (see previous illustration). Victoria and Albert Museum, London

During the closing years of the 17th century, chair-making became a specialist craft but the chair-maker, with the exception of cane chair-makers, was always either in partnership with, or employed by, a joiner. The cane chair-makers set up their own shops as, towards the end of the century, there was an increased demand for high-back chairs, their panelled backs and seats filled with a mesh of split cane.

Furniture design in the last decade of the 17th and in the early 18th centuries was much influenced by the work of William III's leading architect, Daniel Marot (1663-1752). Marot was born in Paris and was already launched on a promising career in the arts there, having studied under Le Pautre and worked in the *atelier* of André-Charles Boulle, when he was compelled to leave by the Revocation of the Edict of Nantes in 1685. He fled to Holland where he entered the service of William, Prince of Orange. There are few records of his activities in England, but it is known that he made designs for some of the gardens at Hampton Court Palace and was also probably employed in the decoration of some of the rooms there. His influence on the decorative arts was considerable at the turn of the century and this was primarily due to the publication of a large number of his engraved designs, covering all branches of the arts, including furniture. The first collected edition of these appeared in 1702. Among them were two designs for state bedsteads similar to the Melville bed in the Victoria and Albert Museum. This upholstered bedstead, which was made for a Minister of William III, has a highly elaborate cornice and hangings which are typical of Marot's fantastic designs. Other designs show tables, chests-on-stands, wall-glasses, chairs, and stools carved with masks, strapwork, coats of arms and scrolls, often supported by caryatids. The engraved patterns of other French designers, such as Jean Bérain or Marot's master, Pierre Le Pautre, were doubtless also studied.

Much more is known about the history and work of some of the cabinet-makers who flourished during the reigns of William and Mary and Queen Anne than about those of the Restoration. The Royal Accounts and the muniment rooms of some of the great houses have yielded up much information in the form of letters, accounts and bill-heads, and some pieces have been found that still retain cabinet-makers' labels stuck to the backs or drawer bottoms.

Jean Pelletier (active *c.* 1690-1710) was a specialist carver and gilder, probably of French origin, who supplied some fine furniture to the Crown during William III's reign. Two sets of carved and gilt tripod *torchères* of Louis XIV design at Hampton Court Palace can be attributed to him as his accounts survive:

'1699-1700   For carving and guilding six pairs of
                    large stands at £30 per pair   ...   £180
1701   For carving and guilding two pairs of
                    large stands   ...   .   £70'

There are also tables and firescreens of similar design at Hampton Court which have been attributed to him.

Gerreit Jensen, whose name was sometimes anglicised to Johnson, had been working for the Crown since at least 1680, as is shown by his first surviving account, and it can be deduced from his earlier Royal accounts that his furniture at this date was decorated with marquetry and japan, sometimes inlaid with metal. Examples in these media have survived at Windsor Castle, Wilton and Boughton House which may be attributed to him. Jensen must have been a considerable rival to Pelletier during the early years of the 18th century for he was also supplying furniture and mirrors to Hampton Court. He appears at this period to have specialised in the sale of mirrors and he is referred to as 'cabinett-maker and glasse-seller' in a document reappointing him cabinet-maker to the Crown. However, Jensen will be remembered rather for his marquetry work, both in wood and metal, than for his mirror glass, and it is John Gumley (active *c.* 1694-1729), another rival, whose name has survived as one

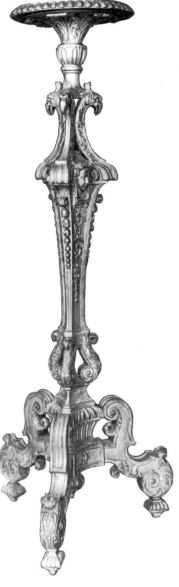

319 *Left*: Carved giltwood candlestand, *c.* 1700–1, made by Jean Pelletier for Hampton Court Palace, perhaps provided in accordance with a warrant dated October 25, 1701 'for the New Gallery' (Queen's Gallery). He made various sets and this is an example from one of them—they cost £30 a pair. Reproduced by Gracious Permission of Her Majesty the Queen, Hampton Court Palace

320 *Below*: Carved giltwood table with marble top, *c.* 1700, which can be attributed to Jean Pelletier on stylistic grounds—also at Hampton Court Palace. Pelletier's name appears in the Royal Accounts as early as 1690. Reproduced by Gracious Permission of Her Majesty the Queen

321 *Right*: Pier-glass of rather earlier date, *c.* 1695, in a carved and silvered frame within a blue glass border painted and gilded on the reverse *(verre églomisé)*, the hand-bevelled plate engraved with a thistle design and divided, as at this date plates of sufficient size to fill the frame were not cast. Victoria and Albert Museum, London

322 *Below*: Gilt gesso side table by Gumley's partner, James Moore (active *c.* 1708–26), the apron and top bearing the crowned cypher of George I. The rectangular top has a typical design of interlaced strapwork and the maker's name is incised above the crown. The style of design on the top is found on many gesso tables of simpler form dating from this period. Reproduced by Gracious Permission of Her Majesty the Queen

323 *Right*: Walnut bureau cabinet, the interior japanned red, *c.* 1710, which has the trade label of Hugh Granger pasted beneath a drawer. The label states that Hugh Granger 'at the Carved Angell in Aldermanbury' makes 'all sorts of fashionable household goods at reasonable rate'. Christie, Manson & Woods Ltd., London

324 *Far right*: Walnut veneered double-dome bureau-cabinet, *c.* 1710, with two bevelled mirrored panels in the upper section. The bun feet in this example should be compared with the later bracket feet in illustration 326. Collection: Sir Hugh Dawson, Bart

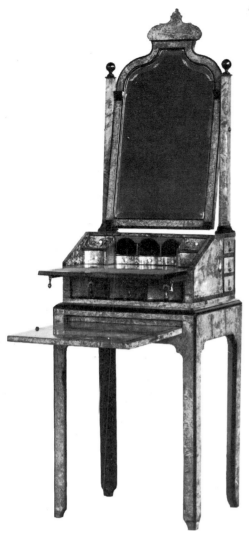

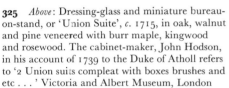

325 *Above*: Dressing-glass and miniature bureau-on-stand, or 'Union Suite', *c.* 1715, in oak, walnut and pine veneered with burr maple, kingwood and rosewood. The cabinet-maker, John Hodson, in his account of 1739 to the Duke of Atholl refers to '2 Union suits compleat with boxes brushes and etc . . .' Victoria and Albert Museum, London

327 *Below*: Bachelor's chest of unusual design, *c.* 1715, veneered with figured walnut. The folding top, which is found on all true bachelor's chests, is backed by a built-up tier of three small drawers. Chests, from this period, the short and long drawers often surmounted by a brushing slide, are commonly found—their design being similar to the lower part of this example. Christie, Manson & Woods Ltd., London

328 *Right*: Walnut veneered cabinet, with cross and feather bandings and with two glass doors above and two panelled doors below, *c.* 1710. The simplicity of this piece is typical of the furniture made during the early years of the 18th century. Collection: Sir Hugh Dawson, Bart

326 *Above*: Small walnut veneered bureau-cabinet, *c.* 1715, the upper section with the original mirror plate. Bureau and secretaire-cabinets of this size are rare. This example has cross and feather bandings. Christie, Manson & Woods Ltd., London

of the leading glass manufacturers of the period. He had set up a glass house at Lambeth in 1705 and was immediately involved in litigation with a rival firm, the Bear Garden House, Bank Side, Southwark, which had recently eclipsed in importance the celebrated glass house at Vauxhall. Gumley, who was successful in this case, rapidly made a fortune and married his daughter to the Earl of Bath. He supplied to Chatsworth and Hampton Court Palace, pier-glasses surmounted by scrolled and engraved crestings and contained within coloured glass borders. At this time borders were also decorated in *verre eglomisé* on a blue, green, red or black ground, the gold designs often being of an intricate nature. By 1700 it was evidently possible to make glass plates of considerable size, for the *Postman* of that year reported that Vauxhall offered for sale 'large looking-glass plates, the like never made in England before' which were 'six foot in length and proportionable breadth.' However, there was also healthy rivalry in this field for, two years later, the Bear Garden advertised 90-inch plates 'of lively colour, free from bladders, veins and foulness incident to the large plates hitherto sold.'

Gumley was in partnership with a cabinet-maker named James Moore (active *c.* 1708–26) who appears to have specialised in the making of gesso furniture. Gesso consists of a composition of whiting, linseed oil and glue, and from the Middle Ages was used as a foundation for painted and gilt decoration on woodwork. It was highly popular during the period under discussion as a form of surface decoration. A pattern in low relief, usually an intricate design of scrolls and strapwork, was carved in the thickness of the ground, the background was then stamped to give it a mat and even surface, and finally the gilding or silvering was applied. The technique was revived in about 1690 and began to decline in about 1730 although it was still used later in the century. It was employed to decorate tables, cabinets, stands, *torchères* and even, in one instance, a *scriptor*. It was sometimes used in conjunction with lacquered panels and during the early 18th century it was far commoner to find it in silver, although little has survived. Moore often signed his name in the intricate strapwork designs which decorated the surfaces of his creations in gilt gesso—an example is found on a set of a table and stands in the Queen's Audience Chamber at Hampton Court Palace. He supplied many other pieces in this medium to the Royal Palaces and a table at Buckingham Palace, originally at Kensington Palace, bears the cypher of George I and the rose and thistle on both the top and apron, and Moore's name is incised above the crown on the top. Many of his pieces include the crest and cypher of his clients and a table in the Victoria and Albert Museum, which was originally at Stowe House, bears the crest and coronet of Lord Cobham. He seems to have had many other influential clients and worked for, amongst others, the Duke of Montagu at Boughton, for the Duchess of Marlborough at Blenheim and for John Meller at Erthig in Denbighshire. Moore was not the only exponent of this technique for he must have had many rivals whose names are lost to posterity.

By about 1690 the cane panelled seat furniture of the Restoration period had become unfashionable and had been replaced by the so-called 'French' chairs with their stuffed and upholstered high backs and seats. Simon de Lobell, a Parisian upholsterer, supplied James II with a crimson velvet bed with gold and silver appliqué and 'two elbow chairs, six stools, the frames carved and gilt, all suitable to the bedde,' at a total cost of £1,515, and the elbow chairs were doubtless 'French' in design. Thomas Roberts (active *c.* 1685–1714), who succeeded Richard Price as Royal 'Joiner' during the reign of James II, supplied the Crown with seat furniture of a similar nature from about 1685 to 1714 when we find him still delivering chairs, bedsteads and firescreens to Queen Anne. In 1686 he made a couch, two armchairs and four stools for Whitehall Palace 'richly carved with figures gilt all over with gold', and it is probable that these are the chairs and stools which are now in the Venetian Ambassador's suite at Knole. It is known that they were sent there from Whitehall and they exactly conform to the description. He supplied chairs and stools to Hampton Court Palace in 1701 and was employed at Chatsworth in the following year.

The cabinet-makers whose work has been so briefly outlined above, are primarily remembered for the fine and grandiose furniture commissioned for the State Rooms of the Royal Palaces

322

319

322

312
316

329 *Left*: One of a pair of walnut candlestands, *c.* 1700. A typical example of a simple piece of early 18th-century walnut furniture. Collection: Sir Hugh Dawson, Bart.   **330** *Right*: Winged armchair covered in floral needlework, *c.* 1715, the plain walnut seat rail supported by scrolled cabriole legs carved at the knees with shell medallions. Collection: Sir Hugh Dawson, Bart.   **331** *Far right*: Walnut armchair, *c.* 1720, with scrolled down-curved arms, plain cabriole legs and pad feet, the waisted back and seat covered in floral needlework. Collection: Sir Hugh Dawson, Bart.   **332** *Below left*: One of a pair of walnut stools, the legs carved with shells and foliage, *c.* 1715. Many stools of similar design are extant. Collection: Sir Hugh Dawson, Bart.   **333** *Below centre*: One of a pair of walnut veneered side tables, *c.* 1715, with wide cross and feather bandings. The curve of the cabriole supports is pronounced and the knees are carved with shell medallions. This example is typical of the pieces being produced at the end of Queen Anne's reign. Collection: Sir Hugh Dawson, Bart.   **334** *Below right*: Walnut veneered gaming table, *c.* 1720, the rectangular top, when lifted off, reveals a back-gammon board. The brass swivel candle brackets are a sign of the high quality of this example. Collection: the Earl of Pembroke, Wilton House, Salisbury.

and the London and country houses of the great Whig and Tory magnates. However, many craftsmen of equal competence were producing furniture during the early 18th century for the city merchants and squirearchy who could not afford to pay the high prices charged by the fashionable cabinet-makers—and it is furniture of this nature that truly reflects the inherent good taste of the craftsman. Case and seat furniture alike were veneered and cross-banded with matched walnut veneers, and mulberry, yew and other 'burr' woods were sometimes used if a particularly rich and striking effect was desired. The sheets of veneer were often laid so that the figuring in the wood formed a symmetrical pattern. This was not difficult as each strip of veneer cut from the same log had the same figuring. When four pieces of identically marked veneer were used a more decorative effect resulted and this method known as 'quartering' was often employed for table tops. Chairs, stools and settees were also veneered. The spiral, baluster and bobbin turned supports of the earlier period slowly gave way towards the end of Queen Anne's reign to the serpentine or 'cabriole' leg. This distinctive form, which had originated in China, was probably suggested by the lower part of a quadruped's leg and it usually terminated in the early 18th century in a goat's or pad foot. Stretchers were used with the early cabriole form but became incongruous when the cabriole was fully developed as they interrupted the line of the curve.

The craftsmen producing this plain walnut veneered furniture were working in a vastly different medium from those of the previous generation, but their creations reflect the epitome of good taste in the history of cabinet-making in England. Their workmanship, selection of woods and sense of proportion have certainly never been surpassed, and the custom, practised by all too few, of sticking trade labels to their pieces or more rarely of

inlaying their names, has enabled us to rescue a few of them from obscurity. Samuel Bennett (active *c.* 1700–41) inlaid his name into the upper sections of at least three extant bureau-cabinets and Hugh Granger's trade label has been found on various pieces of case furniture. The label of the partners, G. Coxed and T. Woster, has been discovered on two bureau-cabinets. These are veneered with mulberry and burr-elm, stained to simulate tortoiseshell, and inlaid with pewter stringing, and this distinctive form of decoration has made it possible to attribute other pieces of similar design to the firm. The names of many more could be cited and others remain to be discovered, but it is the quality of the craftsmanship rather than the label of the maker that is the true hallmark of authenticity.

Probably the most important development in the history of furniture in the Restoration period was the emergence of the master cabinet-maker, who gathered around him specialists in every branch of the trade. It was this intense degree of specialisation and attention to detail and design which resulted in the high standards inherent in the furniture created during the 18th century.

The Hôtel Lauzun was built between 1650-8 on the Ile St-Louis by the architect Le Vau, and is a fine example of the sumptuous style which came into being when Louis XIV assumed the throne. The interior is flooded with gold and with paintings by the greatest decorators of the age—Le Sueur and Le Brun. For such interiors every piece of furniture was planned in advance for its particular place. Mirrors and paintings are framed by carved and gilt mouldings. The frieze beneath the cornice is carved with stucco figures from the workshops of Jacques Sarrazin. The ceiling is by Le Brun. The doors are ornamented equally richly, yet the detail in no way distracts the eye from the magnificence of the architectural framework.

GERMANY AND SCANDINAVIA

Hans Huth

When Germany emerged in 1648 from the destruction and chaos of the Thirty Years' War, an entirely new social order had come into being which fundamentally changed the relationship between patrons and artists and craftsmen. In the south, the power and wealth of the cities had weakened. The fortunes of the aristocracy, on the other hand, were in the ascendant. New buildings were needed and many of the ruling nobles employed their own architects, while others were themselves capable, as architects, of directing their own work. Court workshops were set up, giving craftsmen opportunities which the city guilds could never have provided. Furniture of hitherto unparalleled splendour was now to be commissioned by princes and noblemen whose status and dignity called for finely appointed palaces and costly works of art. Courtly taste, as we shall see, reflected the refinements of Italian, and later, of French fashions.

The houses of wealthy burghers, on the other hand, were less spacious and the furniture, of a practical nature, did not aspire to dazzling artistic quality. The tall cupboards of walnut or fruitwood, over six foot in height, were as vast as those of the previous century. On account of their size, such pieces could most conveniently be housed in a hall or on a landing. By the second half of the 17th century, they were constructed with two tall doors, underneath which was a shallow lower section containing two drawers side by side. In both proportion and line, these cupboards achieved a new elegance and discipline. Sometimes they were carved with decorative motifs of a strangely fleshy character, derived from engraved ornamental designs in what is known as the auricular style *(Knorpelwerk)*. Among the designers and cabinet-makers to publish pattern books in this manner was Friedrich Unteutsch of Frankfurt-am-Main. Similar motifs, relying on curvaceous forms, appeared on the carved backs of the simply constructed walnut chairs, in which the four turned and splayed legs were pegged into a plain seat. These chairs derive from Italian 16th-century prototypes, but the use of auricular ornament in their decoration points to a familiarity with contemporary design on the part of their makers and a certain prosperity in the way of life of their eventual owners.

The exceptional decoration on this writing desk is in the style of Domenico Cucci, the sculptor, metalworker and *marqueteur* attached to the Gobelins factory. A staggering combination of hard stones, mother-of-pearl, cornelian and lapis lazuli is set in a ground of glittering brass. Picturesque subjects are depicted with virtuosity and sensitivity. Gilt bronze mounts protect the corners and divide the panels. Late 17th century, the desk probably reconstructed later. Collection: Madame Lopez-Willshaw, Paris.

This bedroom furniture at the Hôtel de Sully in Paris has recently been assembled to show what a bedroom from the first half of the 17th century would have looked like. The bed, table and chair are covered with matching material, and the walls are also lined with material, for it was considered unhealthy to sleep in a room with bare wooden panelling. The bed was placed in an alcove leading off the great room, and the space around it was called the *'ruelle'*. Here intimate friends would assemble to entertain the occupant of the bed with witty conversation, a custom which went out of fashion later in the century.

The sculptor had an important part to play in the decorative arts during the reign of Louis XIV. This carved and gilt side table, *c.*1680, is designed to harmonise with the panelling of the room. The treatment is broad and open, the volutes, acanthus leaves and garlands being treated quite naturalistically. The supple caryatids add to the Baroque spirit of the piece. Hôtel Lauzun, Paris.

Armchairs provided the carver with a more rewarding opportunity to use the new motifs. Upholstered with damask or sometimes with leather, these conferred a certain dignity on the sitter and were reserved for the head of a household or important guests. Chairs without arms, or stools were in general use in comfortable middle-class houses, where the living rooms might be partly panelled. They often included a four-poster bed, for sometimes the functions of bedroom and living room were combined.

In the meantime, fine houses and palaces were being planned on more sophisticated lines. During the course of the Thirty Years' War, architects had begun to publish books on house design and a basic change had taken place in the arrangement of interiors. The first of these architects was Joseph Furttenbach (1591–1667) of Ulm, who had gone to Italy as a merchant but had become instead an expert architect. After his return he published a series of books on architecture, based on his Italian experience and on his knowledge of practical requirements. Furttenbach worked both for princes and wealthy citizens. His *Architectura Privata* (1640–41) also containing a detailed description of his own house, demanded considerable systematising in the planning of the rooms. This prepared the way for a new arrangement by which all rooms were accessible from a central hall and doors leading from room to room would permit a view through an entire suite. This plan, already usual in France, became general in fine houses in Germany from the end of the 17th century. The number of rooms in these suites depended upon the rank of owner. Each room had a special function, with an anteroom at the entrance of the suite and a cabinet or studio at the end.

Furttenbach's books were later followed by others in which the decorative motifs on ceilings and wall panelling were largely derived from French ornamental designs such as those of Jean Le Pautre, Daniel Marot and Jean Bérain. At the height of the Baroque style, when Versailles had long been the model for every princely household in Europe, Paul Decker (d. 1713) published his *Princely Architect (Fürstlicher Baumeister,* 1711) containing engravings of palaces. Decker had gained practical experience when he had worked in Berlin in the workshop of Andreas Schlüter and later had assisted in building the palaces of Erlangen and Bayreuth. Decker's publication illustrates interiors, showing the new fashionable stuccoed and painted ceilings and carved and painted wall panelling. Floors of wood marquetry or inlaid marble stressed the importance of a festive atmosphere. This mood of glamorous magnificence inherent in the Baroque style was heightened by the inclusion of great mirrors surmounting carved and gilt pier and console tables. In the first half of the 18th century it became an established practice for engravings to be published showing such interiors. These views often included figures and groups and they provide us with some idea of the harmony existing between costume, furniture and interiors. Engravings survive of the interior of the palace of Charlottenburg, Berlin (*c.* 1706), Favorite near Mainz (*c.* 1700–10), Pommersfelden near Bamberg (*c.* 1720), the Zwinger, Dresden (*c.* 1720) and of the Belvedere and Schönborn palaces, Vienna (*c.* 1714–24) among others. Other pattern books, such as those published by Johannes Indau, Vienna (1690–1710), Christian Senckeisen, Leipzig (*c.* 1700), and J. J. Schübler, Augsburg (1720s), contain designs for furniture. The majority of these ornamental engravings printed in ever increasing quantities from the late 17th and throughout the 18th century were published in Augsburg and Nuremberg. They contained both original and pirated designs which helped to spread ideas derived from all over Europe and so they made it possible for any cabinet-maker to follow the latest fashion.

337 *Right*: Engraved design by the Frankfurt
cabinet-maker, Friedrich Unteutsch, *c.* 1650. This
design is intended to offer a suitable motif for the
decorative carving applied to panelling on walls
or cupboards (see previous illustration). It was
probably the frontispiece to the pattern-book,
Neues Zieratenbuch published by Unteutsch, for in
the centre is a trophy composed of the woodworker's tools. These sinister, gristly forms are
known as *Knorpelwerk* or auricular designs.

336 Detail of the Strohmersches Dolls' House
showing the vestibule on the principal floor. In
well-to-do middle-class houses, which were
comfortable rather than fashionable, it was the
practice for the vestibule, or landing to be used as
a living room. In this case it contains a tall, inlaid,
cupboard, used for storing linen. There is a
second, smaller cupboard against the side wall,
upon which a helmet and breast-plate are
displayed. Germanisches Nationalmuseum,
Nuremberg

335 *Strohmersches Puppenhaus.* This so-called dolls' house, made in Nuremberg
and dated 1639 is an exact replica of a rich patrician's house, made, not as a
child's toy, but as a proud record of family possessions. Below are the stables,
wine-cellar, office and wash-room and above these, servants' bedrooms, a
store room and a small room where the lady of the house could sew and the
children play. On the main floor, the kitchen and one living room, which has
a bed in one corner and the dining-table in the centre, flank the vestibule.
Above are more living rooms. The more important rooms are partly panelled
up to two-thirds of the height of the wall, leaving space for pictures above.
Germanisches Nationalmuseum, Nuremberg

338 *Below*: Cupboard in fruit wood, *c.* 1660. Such large, architectural
pieces, with heavy cornices were often kept in the vestibule of rich, middle-
class houses as they took up too much space in the living rooms. The carved
scroll ornament on the door panels and on the three pilasters, representing
strangely fleshy, grotesque masks, amidst sinuous flabby forms, suggests the
influence of the Mannerist designer, Friedrich Unteutsch of Frankfurt, (see
illustration 337). Burg Eltz, Moselle

339 This Swiss chair, *c.* 1650–60, supported on
plain, splayed legs, derives from the medieval
stool. The back is carved and pierced with
auricular designs, introducing a grotesque mask
and strange birds' heads among glutinous scrolls.
Schweizerisches Landesmuseum, Zürich

340 Upholstered armchair, perhaps from Ulm
c. 1650–60. The back is carved in the auricular
style, with flabby, flesh-like forms, echoing the
designs of Friedrich Unteutsch. But in this case
the craftsman has fully exploited the strange
effects and possibilities of surprise which Mannerist
art countenanced; the sudden curve of the feet at
the bottom of the rigidly straight legs which
descend through the arm supports in a continuous
line, presents an unexpected paradox and lends
an air of uncertainty, as though the piece were
about to roll away. Bayerisches Nationalmuseum,
Munich

341 *Left*: Cembalo, *c*. 1710. This cembalo case belongs to a group of japanned cabinet pieces made in Berlin by Gerard Dagly between 1696 and 1713. Dagly was employed at the Court of Frederick I of Prussia as a maker of lacquer and held the appointment of *intendant der ornamente* which gave him control of the furnishing of the Royal Palaces. This piece, like many others in this group is japanned on a white ground, thus imitating porcelain. Schloss Charlottenburg, Berlin

342 *Above*: Engraved design by the Nuremberg architect, Paul Decker (1677–1713) showing a State Bedroom, from his *Fürstlicher Baumeister*, published in 1711. In this work, the author provided plans and interior designs for a hypothetical princely residence. The State Bedroom is lavishly draped with textile hangings while the bed itself, supported on winged half-figures at the foot, rises in a crescendo of Baroque exuberance. The high-backed chairs placed formally against the wall recall the designs of the Huguenot architect, Daniel Marot.

343 Detail showing the top of the table in the illustration below, by the late 17th-century Augsburg craftsmen, Esser and Wolfhauer. The central section of marble mosaic shows the figure of Diana surrounded by panels containing flowers and birds. The outer borders, representing vases of flowers and trailing leaves interspersed with peacocks, birds of Paradise, monkeys and *putti*, are in marquetry of tortoiseshell, brass, engraved silver and mother-of-pearl in *première-partie* and *contre-partie*. This superb table is in the bedroom of the Papal apartments in the *Residenz* at Munich.

344 *Below*: Centre table with carved and gilt supports in the form of four caryatids festooned with flowers. Late 17th century. The Y-shaped stretcher has a central finial composed of two intertwining dolphins, and stands upon four lion-paw feet. This vigorous Baroque composition, introducing sculpture in the round, combines a lively sense of movement with daring lightness.

In southern Germany in the third quarter of the 17th century, Munich became the most important centre of artistic activity. The marriage of the Prince Elector of Bavaria, Ferdinand Maria, to a princess of the house of Savoy, brought the Court into close contact with Italy. Thus architects and artists from Turin introduced the Baroque style which by this time had reached its most confident and robust stage. Tables with richly inlaid marble tops and legs in the form of caryatids enriched with carved acanthus foliage are typical of this style. The contrasts of colour which such pieces afforded were characteristic of the splendour of Baroque taste. After the turn of the century, however, the Court at Munich was to become much more aware of the artistic standards set by the royal workshops in France. The Elector Max Emanuel had been in exile at the Court of Louis XIV, and on his return in 1715, he established his own workshop which produced furniture in the manner fashionable at Versailles and particularly in the Boulle style. Among these is a writing desk made for the Elector, veneered with tortoiseshell, brass, silver and ivory. Still more important was the fact that the architect and designer, Joseph Effner, was sent to Paris to study under the famous French architect, Germain Boffrand. This was a step of real significance for the style of Effner and of other architects who had been nurtured on the most advanced French ideas was later to become a dominant influence in Munich.

Skilled cabinet-makers who catered for the aristocracy found it more convenient to set up workshops in the smaller cities where they were not bothered by the guild authorities. One of these was H. D. Sommer who settled in Künzelsau in Swabia, where he worked from around 1666–84. Sommer must have learned his trade in Paris from André-Charles Boulle, or some master close to Boulle, for he specialised in fine inlays of tortoiseshell, coloured horn or mother-of-pearl set in a frame of pewter. In shape, these richly coloured marquetry pieces adhered to the plain and disciplined outline of the Italian Renaissance and both cabinets and tables are mounted on rectangular tapering legs. A table by Sommer made for Prince Hohenlohe is still in existence and in pristine condition. Sommer also provided a group of furniture for Charles II, Count Palatine, and worked for other nobility in the region.

A speciality of the city of Eger in Bohemia were the cabinets and boxes mounted with intarsia panels carved in relief with mythological or biblical scenes, or with designs composed of leafy scrolls entwining animals or birds, inspired by engraved pattern-books.

Much 17th-century furniture in western Germany was scattered and lost during the wars which devastated this borderland. Cologne, which like many large cities, had created a wealth of magnificent furniture during the 16th century, now lost its initiative but its craftsmen maintained their competence and produced furniture especially for the ecclesiastical authorities of this region who were very powerful and possessed palaces as fine as those of the secular princes.

In northern Germany the situation differed from that of the south and the west. Here city states like Hamburg, Lübeck, Bremen, and Danzig were still powerful, and their influence reached beyond their own city walls into the Scandinavian countries. The same cultural ties linked the countries along the shores of the Baltic Sea. Since 1654, Sweden had been ruled by German princes. Denmark had been united with Norway since 1523 and was also under the rule of German princes. Throughout the north the great cupboards already described had been the most prominent pieces in the house. Gradually the front panels of these cupboards, which in the Renaissance and well into the 17th century, had been divided into many small sections, became simpler. The door panels would have centre-pieces framed by deep-set mouldings forming a polygon. The cresting of these cupboards varied according to region; Danzig liked a broken pediment, Hamburg favoured a straight cornice, and at Lübeck the cresting was arched. In the early 17th century, oak was used for these cupboards and later we find walnut veneer sometimes alternating with ebony. A cupboard of a very special type veneered throughout with walnut was developed in Frankfurt-am-Main, at that time an independent city. The decoration consisted of upright panels with mouldings set in frames one beside the other, and even across the corners. The

345 *Left*: Writing desk made in about 1700 for the Elector Max Emmanuel of Bavaria in the Boulle style. The piece is decorated with elaborate marquetry of tortoiseshell, brass and engraved silver in *contre-partie*, while the drawers are mounted with ivory panels decorated with *chinoiserie* scenes. Not only the marquetry technique but also the turned and fluted, tapering legs on bun feet with gilt-bronze acanthus leaf mounts, follow fashionable Parisian taste. Bayerische National museum, Munich

346 *Above*: Centre table decorated with marquetry of ebony, brass, tortoiseshell, pewter and ivory, signed by H. D. Sommer of Kunzelsau, Swabia and dated 1666. Both the use of exotic materials and the formal lines of this piece, with its square tapering legs and angular, interlaced stretcher, reflect the contemporary desire to imitate French example. Collection: Prince Hohenlohe, Hohenlohe Museum, Schloss Neuerstein

348 *Below*: Cabinet ornamented with intarsia panels carved in relief. This type of decoration, often combining a variety of different woods, was developed in the mid-17th century in the city of Eger on the frontiers of Bohemia. The doors open to reveal carved intarsia panels on the inside, while the cabinet itself contains a series of small drawers and a central niche. The carved figures on the panels represent the four seasons, Summer and Autumn appearing on the front, while inside are figures of Faith and Wisdom. Although such cabinets doubtless housed collections of curiosities and works of art, they really were works of art in themselves rather than functional pieces. Collection: Eric Pasold Esq

347 Detail showing the marquetry top of the table in the above illustration. The signature of the maker, H. D. Sommer, and the date appear just inside the inner border immediately below

the central roundel in which two half-figures support a heart inscribed with the motto of the Princes of Hohenlohe and again the date 1666.

349 *Above right*: Detail showing carved decoration on a small drawer of the cabinet shown in the previous illustration. The Eger carvers drew their inspiration from contemporary engravings. Sometimes they carved figures taken from engravings by Wenceslaus Hollar, for example, and set them against a background in relief of their own invention. The panels on these drawers, in which animals and birds peer through scrolling leaves, carved with astonishing freedom and vitality, were probably based upon the designs of Virgil Solis of which an example is shown below.

350 *Right*: Engraved design by Virgil Solis (1514–62), designer and engraver, whose workshop in Nuremberg was extraordinarily prolific, turning out some 600 engravings and woodcuts for the use of stuccoists, metalworkers or carvers. This design for a frieze or panel filling could equally well have served the needs of a goldsmith and may have inspired the carving in low relief on the door panel of the Eger cabinet.

352 *Above*: The bedroom of Count Wrangel in his castle of Skokloster, Sweden. Mid-17th century. Count Wrangel (1613-1676) was Commander of the Swedish troops in Germany in the Thirty Years' War before the Peace of Münster. Apart from his fame as a military leader, his name has been perpetuated by the so-called 'Wrangelschrank' (see illustration 140), an elaborate south German 16th-century intarsia cupboard which he took to Sweden as booty. Intarsia of the quality of that cupboard was unknown in the North and the door and panelling of the Count's bedroom are painted and stained. Warmth and splendour are provided by the tapestry hangings and the chimney-piece, carved with military trophies and coats-of-arms.

351 *Above left*: Walnut cupboard, known as a 'Hamburger Schapp'. It bears the date, 1682, in applied carving at the base of the three pilasters immediately above the turned feet. The moulding round the panels projects boldly. Museum für Kunst und Gewerbe, Hamburg

353 *Left*: Silver throne, the embroidered cover bearing the cypher of King Frederick IV of Denmark, surmounted by the Danish royal arms, including both Sweden and Norway. This piece is one of a suite made in about 1715 at Augsburg. Although it is unmarked, it was perhaps made at the Augsburg workshops of Hieronymus Mitnacht and J. Bartermann by whom a silver table, also made for King Frederick IV, is marked. Reproduced by Gracious Permission of H.M. the King of Denmark, Rosenborg Castle, Copenhagen

354 *Right*: Silver table, Augsburg, *c.* 1720. Since the palaces of Louis XIV were richly equipped with silver furniture, the fashion was followed by other European courts. This piece belongs to a suite of silver furniture made for the House of Hanover and was subsequently purchased by George II of England, Duke of Hanover. It returned to Germany in 1837 when the Kingdom of Hanover was separated from England on Queen Victoria's accession. Collection: the Duke of Brunswick

simplicity of these cupboards and the absence of any ornament gives them an air of distinction readily acceptable to modern eyes. At first three massive columns divided the façade, two flanking and one placed centrally. These columns were later replaced by pilasters with carved ornament.

In Sweden, German and Dutch influence lasted only into the third quarter of the 17th century. Count Wrangel's castle of Skokloster was the work of architects who were familiar with French fashions. The bedrooms have painted and grained wall panelling and tapestry hangings. Tall, veneered cupboards are included in the furnishing and straight-backed carved chairs, with cresting and stretchers composed of leaf motifs and crowns, which recall English chairs of the period.

The Prussian Court at Berlin began to achieve a tone of international elegance during the reign of the Elector Frederick William (1640-88). The Elector had strong ties with Holland and brought Dutch artists to his capital city although he was not really prepared to spend large sums of money as a patron of the arts. His successor, on the other hand, King Frederick I, was more sensitive to the importance of fashionable taste. He loved splendour and believed that it was a necessary support for his newly-won royal dignity. In 1702 he engaged Andreas Schlüter to be his architect. Schlüter, who built the palaces of Berlin and Charlottenburg, borrowed much from Roman Baroque but had enough creative spirit to blend these elements with his own ideas.

He evolved an individual style which influenced his successors for a very long period. No designs for furniture from Schlüter's hands are known. But those pieces which once formed part of the high, richly stuccoed state rooms of the Royal Palace at Berlin must have been created if not by him at least under his close supervision. Unfortunately, the palace at Berlin was damaged in the last war, and the ruins were later destroyed.

A feature of the Baroque age was a delight in silver furniture, ornamented by means of engraving and embossing. Much of this came from Augsburg which did an important export trade in it. In time of need such furniture was melted down and some of the pieces belonging to the Court at Berlin were sacrificed in this way by Frederick the Great. Outside Berlin one of the few surviving sets of silver furniture is in the possession of the Duke of Brunswick.

Another late 17th-century interest was in the products of the Far East which were both collected and imitated. Frederick I of Prussia boasted an entire room with walls decorated with porcelain. To this he added lacquer furniture of the first quality made in Berlin by Gerard Dagly, a native of Spa who since 1687, had produced lacquer pieces in emulation of oriental example, for the Great Elector. Dagly made lacquer cabinets, tables, *guéridons*, and cases for keyboard instruments decorated in black and gold, white or other colours. One piece was decorated in blue on white especially to accompany the blue and white

352

353

354

341

355 *Above*: State Bed of Prince Eugene of Savoy, early 18th century. For the convenience of Imperial progresses, it was the practice to maintain State Apartments for royal visitors in the principal Austrian monasteries. In these superb Baroque buildings, such as the Monastery of St Florian on the Danube panelled, painted and stuccoed rooms were magnificently furnished for this purpose. The State Bedroom of Prince Eugene at St Florian includes a vast stove in the form of a Temple of Fame and this bed, which recalls with its bound Turkish prisoners, trophies of arms and emblems of victory, the part played by the famous military leader in the defeat of the Turks before the walls of Vienna. Monastery of St Florian, Austria

356 *Above right*: The Mirror Room at Schloss Pommersfelden was completed for the Prince Bishop Lothar Franz von Schönborn by his Court cabinet-maker, Ferdinand Plitzner, in 1718. A number of princely palaces were furnished at the time with a *Spiegelkabinett* of this kind in which the rarity of the materials and the magnificence of the decoration enhanced the prestige of the Court. This octagonal room is panelled in walnut and the stucco ceiling by Daniel Schenk is set with mirrors. The walls are also set with mirrors overlaid with carved and gilt lattice work. Large mirrors surmount the console tables and both these and the candlestands have marble mosaic tops in which the colourful decoration echoes the elaboration of the marquetry floor. Count von Schönborn-Wiesentheid, Schloss Pommersfelden, Germany

357 *Below*: Cabinet-on-stand made for the Prince Bishop Lothar Franz von Schönborn by Ferdinand Plitzner, *c.* 1715–20. Although in form this magnificent cabinet is still essentially Baroque, the details suggest the spirit of Rococo. The exterior combines veneer of walnut, cedar, mahogany and rosewood with panels inset with ivory. Plitzner was the foremost Franconian cabinet-maker whose achievements rivalled those of contemporary Parisian workshops. Collection: Count von Schönborn-Wiesentheid, Schloss Pommersfelden, Germany

porcelain of the period. An apprentice of Dagly's, Martin Schnell, went to Dresden and established a workshop where he made similar fine furniture for Augustus II of Saxony. When Frederick I died in 1713, Dagly retired to the Rhineland. His brother, Jacques, on the other hand, who had worked with him, went to Paris and brought new life to the *manufacture des ouvrages de la chine* at the Louvre. The latter was sufficiently important to be visited by Peter the Great when he came to Paris in 1717.

The earlier part of the 18th century witnessed the building of a number of magnificent Baroque palaces in and around Vienna, although very little of their furnishing survives. One of the most splendid of these palaces was the Belvedere built for Prince Eugene of Savoy between 1714 and 1724, by Johann Lucas von Hildebrandt. Among the few pieces of furniture typical of this period is an enormous bed with carvings depicting the deeds of Prince Eugene, now preserved at the monastery of St Florian near Vienna. Though this bed owes its existence to the fancy of an enthusiastic provincial carver, it reflects the spirit of the high Baroque style.

During this period, Switzerland continued under the influence of its German, Italian and French neighbours. Panelled rooms remained in favour and were often decorated in an astonishingly rich manner, with characteristic regional features. Berne and Geneva were dependent on their French neighbour and at a very early period produced furniture close to French prototypes.

It was in Franconia, towards the end of the first quarter of the 18th century, that a powerful patron of the arts was to sponsor the erection of one of the most splendid Baroque palaces in southern Germany. He was Lothar Franz von Schönborn, Prince Bishop of Bamberg. He came of a family of churchmen, all of whom occupied high positions and were interested in furthering the arts and in building churches and palaces. Fortunately the palace of Pommersfelden, the summer residence of Lothar Franz, has survived intact. Here, the Mirror Room, by Ferdinand Plitzner, was completed in 1718. The walnut panelling, with carved and gilt ornament is inset with mirrors which also embellish the blue stucco ceiling. The brilliance and sparkle of the gilt mirrors and the astonishing variety of the ornamental treatment is staggering. The console tables and pedestals are also the work of Ferdinand Plitzner of Bamberg.

Pommersfelden represents the final achievement of the Baroque style. Among the furniture made for the palace is a writing cabinet-on-stand left unfinished on Plitzner's death in 1724. It was completed by Johann Matusch of Ansbach and the lighter mood of the decorative features, such as the scrolled motifs and the diaper carving on the apron of the stand, already suggest the coming change in which the rich splendours of Baroque were to give way to the charming fantasies of Rococo.

SPAIN AND PORTUGAL

Andrew Ciechanowiecki

Spain

The 17th century dawned with Spain still nominally a great power, full of imperial ambitions. It closed with the death of the last Spanish Hapsburg monarch, and with the dwindling importance of the country itself, now a mere pawn on the European chessboard. The three reigns covering the period, those of Philip III (1598–1621), Philip IV (1621–65) and Charles II (1665–1700) witnessed a mounting crisis of kingship, internal revolt and growing profligacy of the Court in the face of dire poverty in the country, while the final defeat of Spain, both in the Thirty Years' War and in the great duel with France, shattered any remaining illusion of power.

But the political, moral and economic downfall of Spain did not prevent the arts from flourishing. The reign of Philip IV was artistically the most fruitful of the century. It also marks the beginning of that colourful and rich Baroque style known as Churrigueresque (named after one of the leading architects of the period), which with its literary counterpart, gongorism, characterises Iberian *seicento*.

The evolution from the simple early Baroque forms of the first decades of the 17th century, to the rich and often picturesquely charming ones of its latter half is also reflected in furniture. The new artistic impulses came from Italy and France and found an extravagant Spanish Court to welcome them. In the face of growing economic crisis, the Court and, following its lead, the nobility and even the lower orders strove to present to the world a more and more luxurious façade.

An example of this passion for display can be seen in the proliferation of *vargueños*, previously possessed only by people of high rank, and now by everybody with pretensions to wealth or position. The most popular were still those of walnut or chestnut, their interiors designed with architectural features and decorated with faceted small ivory plaques, enlivened with gilding and sometimes engraved to resemble jewels. Other interiors have larger ivory plaques, engraved with Baroque foliage and mythological or religious scenes. An Asturian variant shows interiors delicately inlaid with stylised vases of flowers, scrolls and foliage of a charming, but slightly primitive nature. Foreign influence however, encouraged a taste for ostentation and another type of cabinet became prevalent. Veneered in ebony, tortoiseshell and ivory, always delicately engraved, it is enriched with plaques, gilt bronze mounts and figures in relief, topped with a pierced gilt gallery and figures. It usually does not have a drop-leaf front and therefore comes closer to the analogously changing *papeleira*. Both types rest on supports with turned legs.

The chest went out of fashion in the 17th century. Made of inferior wood such as poplar or pine and decorated with stylised, traditional carving, it remained in use for two more centuries in very modest households. It was generally replaced by a trunk with a domed top, usually covered in velvet or leather, with rich, pierced metal mounts, and placed on an elaborate stand.

Instead of the chest, the cupboard made its appearance. The doors are usually covered with geometrical patterns, but towards the end of the century they were often carved with an exuberant acanthus leaf decoration.

The heavily draped beds of the previous period now became lighter and more elaborate. The woodwork is usually visible and the coverings are less voluminous, which lightens their appearance. The posts are turned or carved and gilt, and exotic woods were used for the carved Baroque headboards. At the same time a Portuguese type of bed also became popular in Spain. This has either the so-called 'Herrera' architectonic headpiece with tiers of arcades, enriched with metal mounts and often topped by

358 *Left*: A typical example of a mid-17th-century cabinet of the *papeleira* type veneered in ebony, tortoiseshell and ivory. The door of the central cupboard is veneered with a carved ivory plaque. Gilt bronze mounts add to the splendour of the piece, which has drawn on many sources of inspiration for its final, unmistakably Spanish character. Museo de Artes Decorativas, Madrid

359 *Right*: This Spanish cabinet, more soberly decorated with pierced gilt bronze mounts on an ebonised ground, is strongly influenced by southern Germany, and dates from the first half of the 17th century. Museo de Artes Decorativas, Madrid

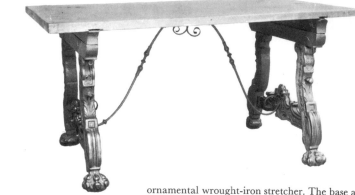

367 bronze religious figures, or a headboard composed of tiers of turned elements and flame-like finials.

361 Although plain trestle tables covered with textiles were still in use, there were now other types. The long table on columnar legs with low box stretchers was common. But new elements appear: turned legs and stretchers and drawers in the frieze, placed beneath an outward flared moulding, which is typically Spanish. These drawers are geometrically panelled or decorated with carved foliage; scroll brackets separate them and they have either knobs or iron drop handles. The tops of tables are also often supported by open lyre-scrolled trestles or splayed legs braced with decorative stretchers of wrought iron. The

360 joining of tops and legs by hinging or morticing is another characteristically Spanish device, which allows the tables to be folded. Small side tables were also made; these are usually squat with two rows of deep drawers.

Important changes occurred in seat furniture. The chair was still a seat of honour, but many more were made. In the first half of the century the dignified and elegant *sillón de fraileros* was predominantly used. Its great popularity can best be gauged by its appearance in so many portraits of the period. It became more comfortable by widening the back and sometimes the arms, turning them thus into small tables to support heavy books or possibly drinking vessels. Towards the middle of the century under the influence of France, the legs and stretchers changed their appearance: they were now turned and blocked or just

362 spirally turned. The arms are either turned or scrolled, the chairs being hung with velvet or leather. These chairs, closely connected with Louis XIII prototypes, developed towards the end of the century into Spanish counterparts of the Louis XIV

363 *fauteuils* with high, shaped backs and elaborately and richly carved stretchers or turned legs. They are upholstered and covered in fabric or leather, while caning, introduced from the Orient by the Portuguese, was favoured for the similar tall-backed side chairs of the period.

Spain also took over from Portugal another type of chair, evolved in that country in the second half of the century. High-backed, with an arched top decorated with brass finials, it has turned legs and side stretchers and a wide carved front stretcher usually composed of interlaced scrolls. The Spanish version of this chair usually has scrolled feet *(pe de pincel)* and differs from its prototype only by the profile of the back and the type of embossed leather used to cover it.

Simple wooden chairs were also made, closely following Renaissance patterns, and decorated with traditional flat carving. Similarly to chests and tables, they slowly degenerate into peasant furniture.

Portugal

The recovery of independence by Portugal (1640) under the new Braganza dynasty opened an era of much needed peace after the disastrous Spanish rule. Brazil was recaptured from the Dutch (1654) as well as some remnants of her former empire in the Far East, and this laid the foundations for the prosperity of the next century. In the meantime, frugality both at Court and in the country generally during the reigns of John IV (1640–56) and Pedro II (1683–1706) helped to promote economic stability. Poverty made the country self-contained. Few foreign artists could be employed, and as a consequence the 17th century was artistically Portugal's most original period.

If the first half of the century was marked by the use of the rectangular, Spanish-inspired Renaissance chair, the latter half produced a national chair, which influences Spain. It stemmed from the previous model and is equally simple and sturdy, with the decoration concentrated on the rich scrolls of the front stretcher. Made at first of walnut or oak, Brazilian wood such as jacaranda and pausanto were used later. Such chairs have high, curvilinear arched backs with brass finials, turned legs and

364 side stretchers. The feet are either bulbous *(pied d'oignon)*, scrolled *(pe de pincel)* or double-scrolled *(pe enrolada)*—the last under Far-Eastern influence. This type of chair is always hung with richly tooled, embossed and incised leather, fastened to the frame by large brass nails. The leather itself, Moorish in origin, was developed in many centres of the Iberian peninsula. But its

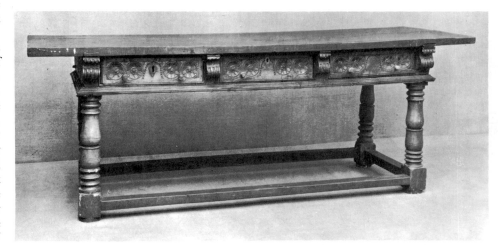

360 *Above*: Late 17th-century Spanish table with boldly carved scrolled trestles linked by an ornamental wrought-iron stretcher. The base and top are united by a morticed joint. Hispanic Society of America, New York

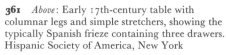

361 *Above*: Early 17th-century table with columnar legs and simple stretchers, showing the typically Spanish frieze containing three drawers. Hispanic Society of America, New York

362 *Left*: This Spanish chair clearly shows the evolution from the original 'monk's chair' *(sillón de fraileros)* towards a more Baroque form familiar in Europe in the first half of the 17th century. The rectangular wooden frame is now composed of spirally turned members, but the shape has not altered and leather is still used for the upholstery. Museo de Artes Decorativas, Madrid

363 *Below left*: Late 17th-century Spanish chair close to Louis XIV prototypes and to similar chairs in other European countries. This and many other examples were, however, upholstered in richly embossed leather, a characteristic Spanish feature. Museo de Artes Decorativas, Madrid

364 *Below*: A typical Portuguese late 17th-century chair. The front legs have ball feet and the beautifully embossed leather coverings should be noted. Museu Nacional de Arte Antiga, Lisbon

365 The cabinet *(contador)* is one of the most characteristic pieces of furniture produced in 17th-century Portugal. The drawers are faced with raised panels decorated with plaques of pierced brass, and the cabinet rests on a stand with elaborately turned legs. Museu Guerra Junqueira, Oporto

366 This late 17th-century cupboard in two stages has raised panels, surrounded by the characteristic wave pattern, and pierced brass mounts. The richly carved friezes denote a northern Portuguese origin. Museu Soares dos Reis, Oporto

367 *Above:* Portuguese bed of the *cama de bilros* type revealing the 17th-century delight in elaborate and varied turning, the more remarkable in this case as the material is Brazilian hardwood. Collection: D. Celesta Cabral, Evora

368 *Below:* Elaborately turned legs, raised panels on drawers, wave ornament and rich, pierced brass mounts are all characteristic of Portuguese 17th-century furniture. Museu Nacional de Arte Antiga, Lisbon

369 *Right:* The Fundação Ricardo do Espírito Santo Silva has recreated in this typical Portuguese setting, a room of the late 17th century. (The two side tables are of later date.) Museu Escola de Artes Decorativas, Lisbon

ornamentation in Portugal acquires during the 17th century a national flavour all its own, even if it often combines anachronistic features, such as the Imperial eagle of Charles V with *putti*, flowers and foliage. The use of tooled leather went out of fashion completely in the early 18th century, and the guild of workers producing it was dissolved in 1771.

This was the most usual Portuguese chair, but French-inspired Louis XIII chairs on turned legs with square backs, and later with Baroque curvilinear high backs and elaborate stretchers, also occur. They were introduced most probably via Spain. Benches, covered in leather, were also in great demand.

The importance of the Portuguese bed has already been mentioned. In the 17th century the draperies become less conspicuous as the result of the sumptuary laws of 1600 and 1611, prohibiting the use of gold and silver in textiles. Simpler beds are of walnut or chestnut and more elaborate examples of ebony and pausanto, sometimes decorated with brass or silver mounts. There are two main types of beds: One, the so-called 'Herrera' type has an architectural headpiece consisting of a superimposed series of arches and scrolls, decorated with inlaid ivory and metal mounts. The other, the Classical *cama de bilros*, of Oriental inspiration resorts to superimposed turned elements and carvings for its headpiece. Towards the end of the century massive headboards, vigorously carved, make their appearance. All have elaborately turned posts, supporting pagoda-shaped or plain testers.

The cabinet or *contador*, developed in Portugal in the middle of the 17th century, is supported by elaborately turned legs. It evolved from the Spanish *papeleira* and never has a drop-leaf front. But the characteristic wave mouldings *(tremidos)* surrounding raised geometrical panels are of Dutch derivation.

They were adopted in Portugal probably after the recapture of Brazil from the Dutch. Cupboards combine these wave mouldings with richly carved friezes and the heavy pierced brass mounts that are so typically Portuguese. Sometimes stylised lions couchant, instead of feet, support these cupboards. The chest, obsolete in Spain, was still much used in Portugal during this whole period.

The Oriental influence which always played an important part in the evolution of Portuguese furniture is clearly visible in the examples of lacquer furniture which have survived. The earliest pieces date from the late 17th century. Black, red and even green lacquer was used, usually embellished with gold—the oldest pieces known being cupboards and cabinets.

Tables are either very simple and covered with rich cloths or stand on elaborately turned legs, with turned stretchers and drawers in the frieze. The drawers are decorated with wave mouldings and have rich brass mounts and drop handles. Dutch influence is again visible in the decoration although the imaginative quality of the turning, which is characteristically Portuguese, the use of Brazilian wood and the pierced brass enrichments create a national and highly original style.

In the northern provinces of Portugal, much of the furniture was the product of carvers rather than cabinet-makers. Figural supports, a bold acanthus decoration and heraldic crestings can be found on many examples of this style of the borderland between Portugal and Spanish Galicia. The tradition of this carved northern furniture persists in the much simpler decoration of the popular furniture of Minho, usually made of chestnut, which is stylistically very close to that of northern Spain. Although following the traditions of the 17th century, it dates from the 18th and even sometimes from the 19th century.

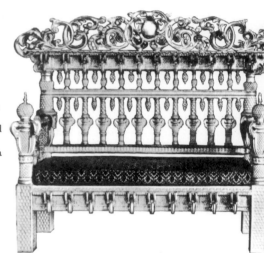

370 This remarkable carved cabinet is characteristic of a group of furniture of the late 17th and early 18th centuries found in the north of Portugal. Cabinets, tables, and cupboards, made by carvers rather than cabinet-makers, belong to this group which is closely connected with the exuberant Baroque carving in contemporary churches. Museu Guerra Junqueira, Oporto

371 *Above*: This splendid example of a cabinet piece encrusted with shell, or *mueble enconchado,* dates from the first years of the 17th century. It was a wedding gift to the grand-daughter of one of the Viceroys of Peru. The dark ebony ground contrasts with the rich mother-of-pearl inlay framed in silver; the feet, the bases and the capitals of the columns, and the mounts are of gilt bronze. It was made in the Philippines and imported into Peru, where similar pieces were later made. Collection: Celedonio Pereda, Lima

372 *Above right*: This table top, perhaps made for the Jesuit chapel of Lahore as a Mass or credence table, is a good example of the mingling of Portuguese religious iconography with traditional Indian decorative features. It dates from *c.* 1610 and is made of rosewood, inlaid with ivory, ebony and horn. The ivory inlay later became more intricate, often introducing coloured elements. The form of Indo-Portuguese furniture is usually influenced by Europe, while the decoration nearly always remains purely Oriental. Victoria and Albert Museum, London

373 *Right*: Late 17th-century carved bench from Cuzco. Made of cedar wood, gilded and painted in pastel tones, it combines the rich motifs of the Spanish Baroque goldsmiths' craft with a native sculptural tradition, and reflects the luxury of Latin American houses of the period. Collection: La Torre Lastres, Lima

Spanish and Portuguese Colonial Furniture

The growing prosperity of Peninsular colonial possessions both in Latin America and in the East was partly due to Government organisation, partly to church settlements. The latter were not only centres of civilisation but sometimes established influential schools of art, such as the Colegio San Andres in Quito. They naturally tended to produce richly carved church furnishings in which various European influences mingled with local aboriginal tradition. But rich secular furniture was also made.

In towns also, particularly the seats of government, sophisticated furniture appeared in keeping with the wealth of the local grandees, who like the Velazco family, dined only off gold and silver plate. In the capital of the Viceroyalty of New Granada, Santa Fé de Bogota, Miguel de Acuña was producing in about 1650, cabinets of ebony and fine woods, veneered with ivory and tortoiseshell and engraved with animals, leaves and flowers. In Peru, chairs were often sheeted with repoussé silver, and in Lima, the *mueble enconchado* was evolved—large pieces of elaborate furniture entirely covered with mother-of-pearl veneer joined by thin fillets of silver or ivory. This decoration, originating in the Philippines became characteristic of Peruvian furniture. But the craftsmen of the New World excelled above all in carving. Centres like Cuzco (despite the earthquakes of 1687, 1747), Quito, Santiago de Chile, Recolete, La Paz, still have many examples of splendid wood sculpture in the rich Spanish-Peruvian Baroque style, exuberant and fantastic, linking European elements with Indian mythology and with traditional Inca craftsmanship.

In the second half of the century the chair, which developed from the simple rectangular *sillón de fraileros*, covered in leather, acquired richly curved Baroque legs and exaggerated stretchers. A similar evolution can be observed in chests, cupboards and particularly in benches—amongst them those of Cuzco are the most original, with enormous carved crestings and balustraded backs, painted and richly gilt.

The furniture of Brazil developed differently and with it that of the Rio de Plata, where most of the craftsmen were of Portuguese origin (they were expelled from Buenos Aires in 1697). Here Portuguese influences mingled with Dutch, creating an indigenous style, which in turn was to influence the mother country. Splendid turning and the Dutch-inspired wave mouldings appear on tables, beds, cabinets and other furniture of the period. The chairs, like those of Portugal, are covered in tooled leather, locally produced since the 16th century.

The so-called 'Indo-Portuguese' furniture was produced on the West Coast of India at Diu, Daman, Goa and Calicut for the Portuguese living in India and also by Indian craftsmen working in Portugal, mainly in Lisbon. At the end of the 16th century Goa became one of the richest towns in the world. Graced with the same civic privileges as that of Lisbon, its population wanted good furniture, not only imported from home, but made locally from fine wood such as teak, ebony and rosewood. The shape of these pieces is usually European while the decoration is Oriental. Most of the chests, tables, rare chairs and many cabinets are of teak inlaid with ebony, imported Brazilian dark wood and sometimes with bone and ivory. The earlier pieces usually rely only on a leaf scroll decoration. The later ones are covered with an intricate inlay of circles, studded with ivory and ebony. Sometimes purely Indian decorations appear. The legs of the stands or tables are shaped like mermaids, crude figures of natives, birds or scrolls with stylised birds' heads. Indo-Portuguese furniture is also recognisable by its large elaborately pierced lock plates and other brass mounts. This furniture, impervious to European stylistic changes can only be dated on the basis of the inlay and the decorative mounts. Both become increasingly colourful and elaborate, with a loosening of formal discipline. Among all the Colonial furniture, it was the products of Goa, brought back by trading ships, which became most familiar in Europe.

371

372

373

AMERICA

Robert C. Smith

The earliest surviving American-made furniture, all of which seems to date from the second half of the 17th century, is based on English middle-class Jacobean models. It is therefore a mixture of medieval and Anglo-Flemish Renaissance forms and decoration. Some richly ornamented beds and press cupboards were brought to America by colonists and these might have served as models for 'joyners' like Thomas Dennis and William Searle and turners like Edward Dear and Joseph Brown, who settled in Ipswich, Massachusetts. In their massive furniture they used a combination of oak and pine with ash, elm, poplar and other sturdy local woods.

To Dennis (active after 1668), are attributed more than a dozen pieces of carved furniture, including the Boston Museum's cupboard of oak and pine which displays many decorative devices associated with the American Jacobean style. These include turned split spindles, bulbous supports and bun feet, as well as ornament carved to represent an arch or geometric patterns taken from late 16th-century Flemish models.

Closely related, though cruder, is the Staniford family chest-of-drawers of 1678, one of the oldest surviving pieces of furniture with painted decoration. This one has geometric designs in red, white and green, as well as black sprig motifs, suggestive of inlay, which were to be developed further in the areas around Guildford, Connecticut, and Taunton, Massachusetts, in the early 18th century.

Even before this time regional characteristics had appeared in the furniture of New England, the locality best represented in what has come down from the 17th century. Some of these traits can be seen in the different types of chest made in the Connecticut River Valley. One group, thought to have been constructed

374 *Far left*: Press cupboard, Massachusetts, 1660–1700. Oak and pine. This elaborate example of an American adaptation of an Anglo-Flemish Renaissance form, is attributed to Thomas Dennis of Ipswich, Massachusetts, with whose work the carved strapwork of the central section is associated, a familiar motif on English late 16th- and early 17th-century furniture. Museum of Fine Arts, Boston

375 *Left*: Chest-of-drawers, Ipswich, Massachusetts, 1678. Painted oak and other woods. An early example of American furniture with painted as well as carved designs, the dated Staniford family chest-of-drawers is ornamented with the same type of strapwork as that on the Massachusetts cupboard in the previous illustration, and is thought also to have been made at Ipswich. H. F. du Pont Winterthur Museum, Delaware

376 *Far left*: Tulip and sunflower chest, Connecticut River Valley, 1675–1700. Oak and pine. A type of furniture, developed from English chests in the Jacobean style, probably made by Peter Blin of Wethersfield, Connecticut, which takes its name from the low relief carving of stylised flowers on the front. Brooklyn Museum, New York

377 *Left*: Hadley chest, Connecticut River Valley, *c*. 1710–15. Oak and other woods. Chests with very flat carving of leaves and vines spread over the entire front surface were made in the Massachusetts towns of Hadley and Hatfield by John Allis and Samuel Belding and their followers between 1675 and 1740. This one bears the initials of Martha Bridgeman, who married Hezekiah Root in 1713. New York State Historical Association, Cooperstown, New York

378 *Right*: Oak wainscot armchair, New York, 1680–1700. Found at Southampton, Long Island in 1875, this is an extremely rare American example of the Jacobean wainscot chair with turned columnar supports and carved cresting in the form of foliate scrolls. H. F. du Pont Winterthur Museum, Delaware

379 *Far right*: Brewster type oak armchair, New England, 1650–75. Named in honour of an elder of the Massachusetts Colony, this is the most elaborate type of 'stick' furniture made in British America in the 17th century. The heaviness of the component parts suggests that this chair is a very early example. Henry Ford Museum, Dearborn, Michigan

by Peter Blin of Wethersfield, Connecticut, between about 1675 and 1725, has stylised sunflowers and tulips carved on the three front panels of the chest. These crisp flat patterns, taken from English Jacobean chests and press cupboards of the early 17th century, contrast in form and colour with the applied ebonised split spindle ornaments and the 'turtle-back' handles of the drawers to produce a rich effect evoking the spirit of Flemish Renaissance furniture.

Another group of chests is attributed to John Allis and Samuel Belding, who, with other members of their families worked in the Massachusetts towns of Hadley and Hatfield on the Connecticut River during the period 1675 and 1740. These Hadley chests, which lack applied decoration, are ornamented with flat carving representing entwined flowers, leaves and geometric forms much looser in their design than the tight panels of the Connecticut chests of the 'sunflower and tulip' variety. This carving covers the entire front surface of the Hadley chest in a style suggestive of early medieval illumination.

The exuberant decorations of both types of Connecticut River Valley chest offer a strong contrast with the austere geometric carving in panelled lozenges and friezes of overlapping lunettes which appears to have been common along the Massachusetts coast at the close of the 17th century. Some of these chests, as well as tables and stands, were originally painted red, green, or black in imitation of ebony, indeed the process of ebonising remained popular until the mid-18th century.

The turned supports of some 17th-century tables and joined stools are suggested in the handsome frame of a wainscot armchair from Long Island, New York, based on an English Jacobean prototype. Here the vigorous carving is limited to the cresting; in others the decoration includes rosettes or even dolphins, and in two examples attributed to Thomas Dennis the entire back is filled with a carved arch and textile or strapwork ornament.

A few Anglo-Flemish leather upholstered turned chairs of the 'Cromwellian' type appear to have been made at the end of the 17th century, but all existing evidence indicates that the most popular chairs were those of the so-called 'stick' variety. These were made in ash, hickory, maple or elm as simpler versions of English 'thrown' chair, fashioned entirely of turned bars. They are classified as either Brewster or Carver, being named after a contemporary elder and a governor of the Massachusetts Bay Colony. Brewster chairs have upright spindles beneath both arms and seats; Carvers have only stretchers in these places.

Both Brewsters and Carvers go back through English turned furniture of the Middle Ages to the stalwart Scandinavian chairs of the 11th and 12th centuries. The two pieces illustrated here show a wide variety of differently turned spindles and balusters as well as the popular 17th-century 'mushroom' finials of the front stiles of the Carver armchair and 'sausage' turning seen in its slightly sloping armrests.

Several of these elements as well as handsome 'bobbin' finials on the rear stiles distinguish another example of contemporary armchair, the back having three wide slats of crested profile. This slat-back type was eventually refined into the 18th-century slat or ladderback chair and armchair, in which all the parts are thinner, the back higher and narrower, the turning more pronounced. Within this category, pieces made in the Delaware River Valley have a distinctive back composed of four, five, and occasionally six graduated arched slats. The seats of Brewster, Carver and slat-back chairs are almost invariably of rush. Some 17th-century cradles, firescreens and other furniture were made of wicker.

(margin numbers: 376, 377, 378, 187, 379, 380, 381, 382)

380 *Left*: Carver type armchair, New England, 1660–1700, of maple. A simpler form of 'stick' chair, named after a governor of Massachusetts, the Carver has no spindles beneath the seat or arms. Henry Ford Museum, Dearborn, Michigan

381 *Below left*: Slat-back armchair, New England, 1680–1710. Maple, ash and oak. A notable example of sensitive turning with exceptionally fine ovoid and mushroom-shaped finials. H. F. du Pont Winterthur Museum, Delaware

382 *Below*: Graduated slat-back chair, New Jersey, *c.* 1710. Maple. This chair is of a type developed in the Delaware River Valley in the early 18th century, which seems to have evolved from the earlier form shown in the previous illustration. Both the lambrequin of the curving motifs below the seat, and the turned stretcher are typical of the period. H. F. du Pont Winterthur Museum, Delaware

Right: Beauvais tapestry showing a scene from Molière's comedy '*Le Malade Imaginaire*' after a design by J. B. Oudry, dated 1732. The furnishing of the room is rather old-fashioned for the 1730s but the decorative frame, with its *rocaille* forms is typical of the Louis XV style.

VI THE EIGHTEENTH CENTURY

LE MALADE IMAGINAIRE

FRANCE

Yvonne Brunhammer

At the opening of the 18th century Louis XIV still reigned over the political destinies of France, but as far as art was concerned, the Louis XIV style already belonged to the past. Dominated by a monarch who was uncompromising even in the smallest details, the Court had been the centre of social life. This autonomy in matters of taste was to be replaced, from the beginning of the century, by an era in which Parisian society was to give the lead. The aristocracy now resided in Paris, rather than at Versailles, and the enriched bourgeoisie profited by their proximity to copy their way of life and, eventually, to assume the lead themselves. So it was that a new way of life was to extend even to the provinces and ultimately influence, in turn, the Court itself. In fact the revolutionary spirit of the 18th century had its roots in this change in the pattern of life.

Both Louis XV and Louis XVI transformed the official residences they had inherited. At Versailles, Fontainebleau, Marly and Compiègne, small intimate rooms were planned, decorated and furnished to satisfy contemporary taste for informality. In the neighbourhood of these royal palaces, the small châteaux increased in number. Among them were the abodes of the mistresses of Louis XV; Choisy, where he visited Madame de Mailly, Louveciennes, the home of Madame du Barry and Bellevue, that of Madame de Pompadour, who was also refurnishing the Château de Champs, built at the beginning of the century, and establishing herself at La Celle, at Aunay and at

Compiègne. Under Louis XVI the need for intimate surroundings led Marie-Antoinette to prefer Le Trianon and Le Hameau to the palace of Versailles and the Comte d'Artois to occupy Bagatelle, away from the Court. Princes and nobles constructed or restored and furnished their châteaux in the provinces and their Parisian houses, in which the state rooms fulfilled a very different need from the small, private apartments. Although the old, traditional furniture could be placed in the state rooms on the first floor, new types, reduced in size, were needed for the small salons, boudoirs and bedrooms where the daily life of 18th-century society was spent.

The modernising of old houses and the new conception of informal living in intimate surroundings, gave rise to an astonishing increase in the variety and importance of furniture. Fashion demanded different suites, appropriately upholstered, to suit the seasons of the year. Towards the end of the *Régence*, as a result of these luxurious practices, the cost of wood became so high that loose covers were introduced so that the upholstery could be varied without the need of having several sets of chairs. But prompted by a fastidious clientèle, joiners and cabinet-makers still created various new types of furniture suited to the size and purpose of the new small rooms.

The desire for informality engendered a concern for comfort, and here perhaps is one of the determining influences of the century. In addition to the formal seats or *sièges meublants* which con-

383 *Above*: This commode which combines the technique of Boulle with the designs of Bérain dates from the very beginning of the 18th century. The frame is massive, with four long serpentine drawers, the short legs terminating in goats' hooves. The marquetry in *contre-partie* on an ebony ground is enriched with chased and gilt bronze mounts, including the keyhole escutcheons in the form of masks and shells. The top is in marquetry, with designs of animals, birds, grotesques and a fountain set in a group of exotic figures with two Eastern musicians. Wallace Collection, London

384 *Above right*: The large *bureau plat* or writing table of the 18th century is already foreshadowed in this design in pen-and-ink, heightened with red chalk, by André-Charles Boulle. The tall sinuous legs are no longer joined by stretchers as in the 17th century. In the frieze there are seven drawers only, of which the centre one is slightly recessed. The bronze mounts play a significant part in outlining the form and emphasising the rhythm. Musée des Arts Décoratifs, Paris

385 *Right*: On this *bureau plat,* or writing table attributed to Boulle, bronze mounts, similar to those in the preceding design include the richly scrolled corner pieces and the mask bordered by palms and surmounted by a shell on the central drawer. It has a lighter appearance as it is without the sets of side drawers, but the central drawer is still clearly defined and recessed. This piece which dates from about 1710-15, combines severity with supple grace. Louvre, Paris tinued to line the walls of reception rooms and served only a decorative purpose, the seats in practical use or *sièges courants* became attractive and intimate, often padded with deep cushions. Little tables appeared, which were so constructed that they could be made to serve for reading, writing or powdering; and any number of charming pieces, unknown to previous generations, were there to meet each momentary need. A great many of these were for the use of women, who were the pivots of this society of the *Ancien Régime*.

The Revolution was a social upheaval which affected the evolution of furniture less profoundly than has frequently been claimed. The clientele was indeed no longer the cultured and informed nobility. But the new patrons, the wealthy bourgeoisie, were nevertheless content with the Louis XVI furniture of former days and thus the spirit of the *Ancien Régime* was to survive until the end of the 18th century. The Revolution was rather a period of arrested development. It was not until the Empire that craftsmanship in furniture-making took on a new lease of life, but by then the social atmosphere had changed; the 19th century of Napoleon I was to turn its back on the carefree elegance of the past.

The Furniture Craftsmen

In spite of the extreme rigour of the Guild system, possibly even thanks to it, French furniture achieved, in the 18th century, such a state of perfection that it was sought after throughout Europe. The Guild regulations, encouraged specialisation and incited the sons of master craftsmen to continue in their fathers' trade by the prospect of economic advantages. The result was exceptional professional skill, and the rise of veritable dynasties of joiners and cabinet-makers, handing down the secrets of their craft from father to son.

In the year 1743 the revised Statutes of the Guild made it obligatory that every master craftsman should stamp his work. This was necessary in order to resist the competition of the 'free craftsmen' who set up their workshops in those parts of Paris where the ancient medieval rights of asylum still held good, such as around the Abbaye Saint-Antoine des Champs. These craftsmen, for the most part of German extraction, were not bound to the long apprenticeship imposed on Guild members before they could become masters of their craft, nor did they pay admission fees. For this reason they could sell at a low price. They were not, however, alone in being exempted from the regulations of the Guilds. Since the days of Henri IV and Louis XIV, the king reserved to himself the right to appoint master craftsmen and to set up his own workshops outside the control of the Guilds. The great advantage of this was that the craftsmen in royal employ were not hampered by regulations which demanded that each should confine himself to his specialised trade.

The Guild system did, in fact, rigidly separate the crafts. The *menuisier*, or joiner, worked the solid wood, cutting, shaping, carving the mouldings and joining. The carver contributed any decoration in relief, while the painter and gilder added colour when required. The piece was finally waxed and polished by the *menuisier*. This method was used for cupboards and simple commodes of walnut or beech, for walnut seats, and increasingly in the second half of the century, for pieces of solid mahogany. The upholsterer was responsible for the furnishings of seats and beds and even acted as a salesman. In this way a piece originally conceived and signed by the *menuisier* was in reality a collective work. One can imagine the rivalries which divided these different guilds. The *menuisiers* resented, above all, the prerogatives of the carvers, and, according to André Roubo, a practising *menuisier*, whose book *L'Art du Menuisier* appeared between 1769 and 1775, they often carved small decorative motifs themselves, such as a Louis XV Rococo scroll, or a Louis XVI patera.

As the art of veneering was developed in the 17th century by the so-called *menuisiers en ébène*, a term later shortened to *ébénistes*, or cabinet-makers, these craftsmen also became part of the Guild of the *menuisiers*. The new title of the Guild, the *Corporation des Menuisiers-Ebénistes* first appears in the Statutes of 1743. But the custom of decorating their furniture with gilt bronze mounts

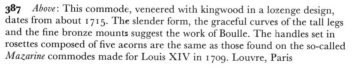

386 The influence of Boulle and Bérain is again evident in this design for a clock in red chalk, attributed to Gilles-Marie Oppenord; but the type of clock, with a long pendulum enclosed in a tall case, is new. The Baroque form and original arrangement of the feet point to a date around 1720. Musée des Arts Décoratifs, Paris

387 *Above*: This commode, veneered with kingwood in a lozenge design, dates from about 1715. The slender form, the graceful curves of the tall legs and the fine bronze mounts suggest the work of Boulle. The handles set in rosettes composed of five acorns are the same as those found on the so-called *Mazarine* commodes made for Louis XIV in 1709. Louvre, Paris

388 *Above right*: Attributed to Cressent, this commode is comparatively austere beside the many sumptuous examples by the same cabinet-maker preserved in the Residenzmuseum at Munich, the Musée du Louvre, the Wallace Collection, London and in private collections. The body, though raised on tall legs, is still heavy. The marquetry outlines and emphasises the bold curves of the gilt bronze mounts made by Cressent himself. The Rococo handles, and the contrasting scrolls of the corner mounts suggest a date of *c*. 1735-40. Rijksmuseum, Amsterdam

389 *Right*: Detail of a large *bureau plat* or writing table, attributed to Cressent. The frieze is lively and varied, accommodating three drawers with gilt bronze mounts. The top is more severe and is framed in a rectilinear bronze ovolo moulding. The bronzes, especially the masks of fauns and the female busts in the style of Watteau, known as *espagnolettes*, are typical of Cressent. They evoke a mood of fantasy characteristic of the years 1730-5. Louvre, Paris obliged the *ébénistes* to call in the services of two different and rival guilds, the *fondeurs-ciseleurs* who cast and chased the bronze and the *ciseleurs-doreurs* who gilded the metal. Others might be called upon before the piece was eventually completed. There were the craftsmen who specialised in lacquering and whose importance grew with the cult for *chinoiserie*, the glaziers, the plate-glass makers, an amazing variety of specialists. The *ébénistes* were for the most part new men, whose recruitment differed greatly from that of the *menuisiers*. The latter were often *menuisiers* from father to son, by tradition, like Tilliard, Foliot, Lebas, Lelarge, Sené, and all, without exception, were French. Although the majority of *ébénistes* were French and pre-eminently Parisian, there were also many foreigners—Flemings like Bernard Van Risen Burgh, Dautriche, Criaerd and Roger Vandercruse, and Germans, whose numbers were increasing on the eve of the Revolution, among whom were Oeben, Riesener, Weisweiler, Beneman and Stöckel. The legend, according to which Marie-Antoinette brought in many Germans, is without foundation. These expert craftsmen were attracted by the exceptional demand for furniture in 18th-century Paris. Marriages were frequent among the families of the *ébénistes*, the most celebrated example being that of the Fleming, Franz van der Cruse. His eldest son became the *ébéniste* Roger Vandercruse, known as Lacroix (R.V.L.C.), two of his daughters married the *ébénistes* Simon Oeben and Simon Guillaume, the third was the wife first of J. F. Oeben and then of J. H. Riesener. The widows, in fact, were glad to marry *ébénistes* who could take over the *atelier* of the deceased husband.

The *marchand-merciers* were furniture dealers, as their name implies. But they were men of stature who played an important part in the development of furniture, for they were in close touch with the purchasers whose taste they understood and whose eager interest they fostered. These men influenced the *ébénistes* by the orders they placed with them and they were often called upon, in fact, to co-ordinate the work of the various craftsmen belonging to different Guilds, who found it difficult to act in concert. A *marchand-mercier* such as Lazare-Duvaux, or his successors, Simon-Philippe Poirier and Dominique Daguerre wielded considerable power in matters of taste. A few *ébénistes* were themselves also dealers and therefore put their stamp to pieces they had ordered from the workshops of their colleagues.

Relentlessly criticised, an unsuccessful attempt to suppress the Guilds was made by Turgot in 1776, and they were finally abolished in 1791. It would not be correct to infer that the quality of the furniture was immediately affected by the disappearance of the Guilds. Most of the craftsmen working at the end of the century had been trained under the *Ancien Régime*. In retaining their high standards, they strove to enrich their work by the use of techniques which the Guild regulations had withheld from them. For example, the best *menuisier* of the Louis XVI period, Georges Jacob, now showed himself to be also an *ébéniste* of outstanding merit. But if the meticulous separation of the crafts favoured specialisation, it also had some surprising results: it is by no means unusual to find identical bronze mounts on the work of different *ébénistes* and to see the same ornament carved on chairs by different *menuisiers*. The carver Valois worked for Sené as well as for Boulard and had no hesitation in repeating a favourite motif.

The *Régence* Style

The first thirty-five years of the 18th century were decisive in the evolution of furniture. Both form and decoration became noticeably more free and reflected the new enthusiasm for life and pleasure in entertainment which had so long been curbed during the reign of Louis XIV. The Regent himself encouraged this tendency by creating a sophisticated atmosphere at Court in place of pompous formality. The transitional style which marks this passing of Baroque grandeur and the birth of a new age of elegance is known as *Régence*. It extends beyond the eight years in which Philippe d'Orléans acted as Regent for the young king, and covers the old age of Louis XIV as well as the youth of Louis XV.

The imagination and exuberance which can be seen in the interior decoration and furniture was introduced by the men of

390, 391 *Above and above right*: This giltwood screen is typical of the *Régence* style. The uprights are enriched with pierced and carved foliage which enlivens the contour, the cresting and the base are each ornamented with a stylised shell. The female busts at the upper corners recall the

espagnolettes on the writing table by Cressent in the previous illustration. The delicate ornament of lattice-work and flowers, treated as though in metal, was of a type inherited from the end of the 17th century. The Beauvais tapestry, *La Musique*, after Boucher, is later than the frame, which dates from *c.* 1715. Louvre, Paris

392 This early Louis XV table of carved and gilt wood, with a marble top is still rectangular. The curving contours of the frieze are strictly symmetrical and, with the heavy festoons of flowers round the legs, derive from the Louis XIV tradition. The four legs have swelling curves and are ornamented at each corner with a symmetrical shell. The delicate lattice-work and stylised flowers are typical of the years 1715-20. Louvre, Paris

393 This walnut armchair has a dignity inherited from the Louis XIV style. Although the high rectangular back is entirely upholstered in Savonnerie, the wood of the seat rails is exposed and carved with scrolls around a shell. The sinuous arms are splayed and their supports answer the curvaceous form of the front legs which end in scroll feet; very supple X-form stretchers are still retained. *c.* 1715-20. Musée des Arts Décoratifs, Paris

Late 17th-century English cabinet-on-stand
in gold and silver on a ground painted to
imitate tortoiseshell. The interior contains
drawers japanned with *chinoiserie* subjects.
The stand and cresting are of carved and
silvered wood. Victoria and Albert Museum,
London

394 *Left*: Three designs in red chalk for commodes by Nicolas Pineau. While the one in the middle still retains the sober aspect of *Régence* furniture, the other two are outspokenly Rococo, with their bounding contours and lively decoration. *c.* 1730-40. Musée des Arts Décoratifs, Paris

395 *Right*: Carved and gilt Rococo console table; the two graceful scrolled legs are united by a stretcher with a central carved motif in the form of a dragon's head emerging from a pierced asymmetrical cartouche. The marble top rests on an undulating frieze which is pierced and carved with leaves and flowers. *c.* 1735-40. Louvre, Paris

the late 17th century, the architect Robert de Cotte who influenced the *menuisiers* and sculptors, and the ornamentalists Gillot, Bérain and Audran. But it was above all, the ornamental designs of Jean Bérain, who rediscovered the grotesques of the Italian Renaissance and combined them with graceful arabesques and fanciful linear decorations that were in particular demand in the field of decoration. Bérain's designs were used, for example, by André-Charles Boulle for his cabinet pieces veneered in brass and tortoiseshell and made from the last decades of the century until his death in 1732. Boulle adapted himself very quickly to the new lighter and less rigid forms: the two commodes he made for the Trianon, delivered in 1709, are curved and supported on sinuous legs. His many designs for furniture, through which his 384 work can sometimes be identified, also introduced curved lines.

The fashion for *chinoiseries* in the Louis XIV period still prevailed in the early years of the 18th century. A whole literature was created around this passion for the Orient—Montesquieu's 'Les Lettres Persanes', appeared in 1721.

The change in style was accelerated by artists such as Oppenord and Charles Cressent who were employed by the Regent. The architect Oppenord designed the interiors and the 386 furniture for the Palais-Royal. He soon broke away from the grand manner of the first years of the century and his work already reveals a sensuality and exuberance which foreshadows the spirit of Rococo. Cressent became *ébéniste* to the Regent on the death of Joseph Poitou, whose widow he married. He was as 388 much a sculptor as an *ébéniste* and the gilt bronze mounts which are freely introduced on his furniture suggest the influence of Robert de Cotte, and later even the lively and supple designs of 389 Watteau. It was the grace and gentle, symmetrical curves of his *Régence* style which were to lead to the more robust charms of Louis XV Rococo.

This study at the Château de Champs was redecorated during the reign of Louis XV with carved Rococo panelling by Verberckt. The commode with geometric marquetry is attributed to Cressent and was made between 1720-5. The caned armchairs are also *Régence*.

A Louis XV bedroom at the Château de Champs, near Paris. The bed has a carved and gilt head- and foot-board, and is placed in an alcove which takes the place of a canopy. The two-drawer commode on the left is decorated with floral marquetry, and with gilt bronze mounts. The two carved and gilt armchairs are covered with yellow silk damask to match the bed hangings.

The *grand salon* at the Château de Champs was decorated in the reign of Louis XV by Christophe Huet. The pale fresh colours are typical of the period, as is the *chinoiserie* decoration of exotic birds and woodland scenes.

In general, the shape of cabinet furniture at the beginning of the century remained heavy, despite the adoption of curving outlines. Essentially an invention of the 18th century, the first commodes, *à la Régence* or *en tombeau*, have three tiers of drawers and stand on very short legs. The front is serpentine and the legs continue the curve of the stiles. In about 1715, Boulle invented a lighter commode with only two tiers of drawers supported on 387 slender legs. It was, however, probably the Cressent commode with two drawers separated by a fixed rail, tall cabriole legs, and a serpentine front with a shaped apron which inspired the typical Louis XV commode. The *commode Cressent* is infinitely richer 388 than the *commode à la Régence*, with its sumptuous gilt bronze mounts and costly veneer. *Plate left, above*

The large *bureau plat* or writing table replaced the 17th-century bureau with eight legs. The finest came from Cressent's workshop and were mounted with superb bronzes. The *Régence* 389 cabinet-makers were fond of plain veneer and marquetry of purplewood and tulipwood in geometrical lozenge designs.

By contrast the *menuisiers* were slow to abandon the type of ornament they had inherited from the preceding century: rosettes, gadroons, shells and stylised flowers, carved in flat relief with a precision that recalls engraving on metal. They only 390 gradually introduced more deeply cut mouldings and figures carved in relief inspired by Watteau. They also retained from 397 the age of Louis XIV a taste for rich colours and gilding and silvering, although oak and above all walnut were still used for chairs and for the more massive cupboards and *buffets*.

The centre table was no longer the richly carved and gilded piece it had been under Louis XIV. It was reduced in size and the wooden top with moulded edges rested on four graceful 392 cabriole legs. The console table, on the contrary, remained in the luxurious tradition of the 17th century. In oak or in natural walnut, but more often gilt, it formed part of the interior decoration and was placed beneath a high mirror fitted into the panelling. The pedestal, designed to carry the heavy marble top, often consisted only of the front legs curved back against the wall and joined by a stretcher with a central ornamental feature 395 carved in high relief.

Chairs were no longer all set against the wall but were adapted to the needs of conversation. The cabriole legs were enlivened by 393 feet in the form of goats' hooves, while stretchers became supple in shape before disappearing altogether. The fashion for wearing hooped dresses which was introduced about 1720 caused the arms of chairs to be set back by a quarter of the length of the side rails. At the end of the *Régence* period, a new method of upholstering had come into use, which enabled chair seats to be changed according to the season. Textile materials were sumptuous, but cane-work too, banished under Louis XIV, returned to fashion, *Plate left,* to record an intimate and domestic note. *above*

The Louis XV Style

The age of Louis XV accepted the innovations of the *Régence* style and brought them to superb fruition. For the first time since the Middle Ages, Antiquity and the Italian Renaissance ceased to be the inspiration for both form and ornament. Although architecture continued to draw upon Classical example, painting, interior decoration, furniture and all the decorative arts shook off the memory of it to explore a profoundly original and voluptuous art which was ultimately to captivate the whole of Europe. The Louis XV style cannot be confined within the rigid time limits of the sovereign's reign. When the Regent died in 1723, it was not yet fully developed, but by the death of Louis XV in 1774, Neo-Classicism had already dispossessed it, although the king himself always preferred it.

The Rococo style triumphed in its spirited opposition to Classical severity. It derived some of its characteristic motifs from the grottoes which had long been fashionable features of garden landscapes; fanciful constructions of rocks and shells, set with enamelled tiles among cascading waterfalls. The ornamental designs of Meissonnier (1695–1750) introduce these features and depend upon the subtle play of curves to achieve their provocative charm. His designs for furniture introduce swirling, asymmetrical forms and echo the free-flowing lines of the wall panelling. Meissonnier's Piedmontese origin may account for his passionate delight in contrasting shapes and sweeping contours. But the designs of Nicolas Pineau (1684–1754) reflect the true character of French *rocaille*, which, in comparison with the frenzied zest of Continental Rococo, always retained harmonious proportions. In Pineau's work the lines are supple and graceful, and the ornament of shells, flowers and palms is clearly defined on curving surfaces. His influence on furniture was profound for his designs were engraved by Mariette and were much used in mid-18th-century workshops. But while it is unusual to find a piece of furniture wholly based on one of his designs, it is in the shaping of a shell or a flower or in the contour of a moulding that his style can be traced.

Although furniture in general adopted Rococo features, the pieces most directly affected were those planned as part of the interior decoration of a room and designed with the panelling. These were the console tables, the *sièges meublants* or chairs which stood against the walls, and the beds, all made by *menuisiers*. A panelled room, including the gilt or painted console tables and the chairs, with their backs carved to match the curves of the wall-panelling rarely survives. It is also exceptional to find a bed in its original setting, with the wooden frame painted in harmony with the walls and the hangings matching the window curtains and the covers of the seats. Carved Rococo ornament included scallop shells amid asymmetrical scrolls and curves evoking in their restless forms the continuous movement of waves. Strange animals, masks, trophies and emblems mingle in this voluble, tumbling world of intertwined foliage and unexpected forms.

The dealers fostered this taste in their clients and encouraged the *ébénistes*. Criaerd, Jacques Dubois and Bernard van Risen Burgh (B.V.R.B.) made use of all the resources of their splendid craft to lend their furniture grace and elegance. Cabinet-pieces rely on elongated and supple curves and the legs are of cabriole type. Veneer and marquetry throw into relief the lively, sparkling forms of the bronze mounts, the handles composed of curling foliage, cartouches, volutes.

The sinuous shape of the armchair 'en cabriolet' of the Louis XV period perfectly reflected the new desire for informal living. A variety of new forms were also developed which allowed for comfortable relaxation: the *fauteuil de bureau* with a curved front seat rail and a supplementary leg, the *fauteuil de toilette* and the *bergère*, furnished with a thick cushion and with closed upholstered sides, and the *duchesse brisée*, a type of day-bed in two or three separate parts. A compromise between the day-bed and the *canapé*, or settee, are the deep armchairs with undulating backs known as *veilleuses*. These were generally made in pairs and were placed on either side of the fire-place, balancing each other in the answering curves of their backs. This variety of chairs suited the requirements of the new small apartments and they were in

(margin references: 394, 397, 395, 396 Plate facing page 113, 395, 396, 398, 399, 399, 462, 401, 403)

396 *Above*: This very beautiful armchair of carved and gilt wood is upholstered in Gobelins tapestry. Carved ornament, consisting of rosettes, leafy scrolls and shells, covers the entire framework. It has a shaped back, while the curving arms are set back, their gently sweeping supports repeating the bend of the cabriole legs. *c*. 1740. Musée des Arts Décoratifs, Paris

397 *Right*: In this design in red chalk for an *encoignure* or corner cabinet by Nicolas Pineau, the lively bronze mounts and curving lines of the clock case contribute to the Rococo character of the piece. An *encoignure* by Jacques Dubois, of an even more animated character, was inspired by this example. *c*. 1740. Musée des Arts Décoratifs, Paris

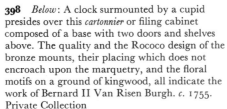

398 *Below*: A clock surmounted by a cupid presides over this *cartonnier* or filing cabinet composed of a base with two doors and shelves above. The quality and the Rococo design of the bronze mounts, their placing which does not encroach upon the marquetry, and the floral motifs on a ground of kingwood, all indicate the work of Bernard II Van Risen Burgh. *c*. 1755. Private Collection

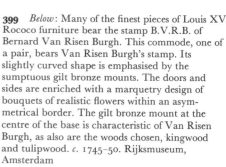

399 *Below*: Many of the finest pieces of Louis XV Rococo furniture bear the stamp B.V.R.B. of Bernard Van Risen Burgh. This commode, one of a pair, bears Van Risen Burgh's stamp. Its slightly curved shape is emphasised by the sumptuous gilt bronze mounts. The doors and sides are enriched with a marquetry design of bouquets of realistic flowers within an asymmetrical border. The gilt bronze mount at the centre of the base is characteristic of Van Risen Burgh, as also are the woods chosen, kingwood and tulipwood. *c*. 1745–50. Rijksmuseum, Amsterdam

400 This portrait by the Swedish painter, Alexandre Roslin, shows Madame de Pompadour seated before a *coquiller*, a cabinet of small drawers designed to house a collection of shells, a fashionable piece of Rococo furniture between 1730–50. She is seated in a Louis XV armchair, comfortably upholstered, while the carved frame is painted in two colours. The man standing is perhaps her brother, the Marquis de Marigny. Musée de Goteberg, Belgium

401 *Above*: A demand for comfort resulted in a fashion for deep, wide armchairs like this winged *bergère* by Jean-Baptiste Tilliard (1685–1766). The frame is of beech, carved with Rococo cartouches, foliage and scrolls. The undulating line of the splayed arm-posts which are set back, flows into the curve of the seat rail. *c.* 1750. Private Collection

402 *Above*: The rounded form of this small, cane-backed armchair is a variation of the Louis XV cabriole shape. Concern for comfort is the basic reason for the pronounced semi-circular design of the front seat rail, necessitating the support of a leg in the centre. Bearing the stamp of E. Meunier, it is a rare example of a chair veneered in tulipwood and kingwood, enriched with gilt bronze mounts. *c.* 1755. Rijksmuseum, Amsterdam

403 *Left*: This kind of day-bed known as a *duchesse-brisée* is essentially an armchair which could be converted into a sofa by adding the separate foot-piece against the seat rail. It was made by Jean-Baptiste Lebas, who became master in 1756, and was *menuisier* to Madame du Barry and the Comte d'Artois. The frame is carved with scrolled mouldings and flowers. *c.* 1760. Private Collection

404 *Right*: This armchair bears the stamp of a provincial *menuisier*, Pierre Nogaret of Lyon. It shows how close his work was to that of the Parisian craftsmen, although the contours are more relaxed and the ornament is more florid. Musée Nissim de Camondo, Paris

405 *Below left*: This kind of *canapé* or sofa with closed ends was known as a 'sultane', a name which reflects the contemporary taste for the exotic. It was usually placed against the wall and its comfort relied upon the upholstered seat and bolsters, and often also the cushions with which it was furnished. Here the frame is carved with flowers and is painted grey. The charming curves are characteristic of Jean Avisse, who became master in 1745 and whose mark it bears. *c.* 1760. Musée Nissim de Camondo, Paris

406 *Left*: Pronounced curves and the bowed shape of the base of this commode are characteristic of Pierre Roussel, who became master in 1745, and whose stamp it bears. The bronze mounts are restrained but the marquetry includes a luxuriant bouquet of flowers in polychrome woods on a veneer of tulipwood and kingwood. 1750–5. Musée des Arts Décoratifs, Paris

407 *La Sultane*, by Carle Van Loo, 1755. The taste for the exotic included an interest in both the Near and the Far East. Madame de Pompadour commissioned the painter, Van Loo, to decorate her bedroom at Bellevue in the Turkish manner. This overdoor panel represents the favourite herself in the costume of a Sultana. Musée des Arts Décoratifs, Paris

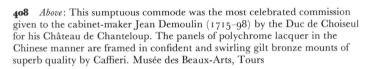

408 *Above*: This sumptuous commode was the most celebrated commission given to the cabinet-maker Jean Demoulin (1715–98) by the Duc de Choiseul for his Château de Chanteloup. The panels of polychrome lacquer in the Chinese manner are framed in confident and swirling gilt bronze mounts of superb quality by Caffieri. Musée des Beaux-Arts, Tours

409 *Above centre*: This small commode with two drawers, lacquered in the Oriental manner and with Japanese lacquer on the side panels, was made by Nicolas-Jean Marchand, who became master in 1738. It is one of a pair made for Queen Marie Lesczynska at the Château de Fontainebleau, made to match another pair in the king's bedroom. Wallace Collection, London

410 *Above right*: This *encoignure* or corner cabinet of oak stained black and veneered on the front with a panel of Chinese lacquer, representing a landscape with human figures in it. An invention of the 18th century, this piece is supported on four short curved legs. The contours are curved and it is enriched with finely chased and gilt bronze Rococo mounts in the style of Cressent. Mid-18th century. Wallace Collection, London

411 *Right*: The fall-front and door of this small writing desk in tulipwood and kingwood are veneered with panels of Japanese lacquer with human figures in red and gold on a black ground. Secretaires of this type are compara tively rare. This example, which has an air of suave assurance, bears the stamp of Jean-François Leleu, who became master in 1764. He is known chiefly for furniture of architectural design in transitional and Louis XVI styles. *c*. 1770. Musée des Arts Décoratifs, Paris

412 *Far right*: This *chiffonière* or small table with a single drawer is painted in *Vernis Martin* with a lattice pattern in imitation of the lozenge design on the Sèvres porcelain top. It is signed by Roger Vandercruse, who became master in 1755. The colour, originally white, has acquired, with the passage of time, a very pronounced yellow tint. Other small tables are known in this technique which was very fashionable under Louis XV: one, for example, is in the Louvre and another in the Metropolitan Museum, both signed B.V.R.B. *c*. 1760–5. Musée Nissim de Camondo, Paris

regular use, fulfilling quite a different purpose from the formal, square-backed, traditional *fauteuils à la reine* which were inten-

393

ded to be set against the walls.

Several types of seat owed something to the *fauteuil à la reine*: certain winged *bergères* which recall older models, the *marquise*, more often called 'confidante' or 'tête-à-tête', seating two people, the very fashionable *canapé* or settee with its high unbroken back and undulating arms, and the *canapé à confidante*, closed at either

405

end with a corner seat. The *sultane*, with two rolled-over ends, and the sofa, which consisted mainly of a mass of cushions and brocaded materials, placed in a niche frequently lined with mirrors, did not need backs, but they were attached to the wall in the same way as were the *canapés*, although some of the latter were movable. A great many stools and benches were crowded into the interiors, again most often placed against the wall. Although the traditional bed 'à la française', crowned with a canopy, continued to be used, a preference was shown for the more secluded

Plate facing page 113

bed 'à la polonaise', which was placed with one side against the wall, in an alcove. Screens and fire-screens, indispensable for intimacy and comfort, were carved in the same manner as the chair frames and were upholstered *en suite*.

The reign of Louis XV sanctioned vivid and harmonious colours. Panelling was pale blue, sea-green, lilac, jonquil, or white enriched with gold. The woodwork of chairs and beds were usually in two contrasting colours: blue and white, green and white, pink and green, pink and white, yellow and silver.

Gilding continued to be used on richly carved woods. Upholstery shared in the harmony: it was of silk and, less frequently, of tapestry. Cane and Morocco leather were reserved for the

402, 404

simpler chairs and those in common use.

Today we have little conception of the vivid and varied colours of Louis XV furniture. The painted wood is faded and worn, and sometimes the natural wood shows through. The colours of the marquetry have lost their brilliant, contrasting sharpness and now only faintly echo their former splendour. The rare, exotic timber from which they were cut was highly prized by the *ébénistes*, who virtually composed pictures in marquetry upon their commodes, secretaires and table tops in rosewood, tulipwood, kingwood, purplewood and satinwood, set off with indigenous woods, such as wild cherry, maple and holly.

The favourite motif of the *menuisiers* and the *ébénistes* was the flower, which was constantly introduced into their Rococo orna-

403, 404, 405

ment. It was carved on the cresting of chairs, on the front seat rails and on the knees of cabriole legs. It appears in bouquets, in festoons, on flowering branches and in baskets, or on fine pieces of marquetry, in isolated sprigs. In search of realism the woods which represented leaves were tinted green with dye while those which composed the heart of a rose were darkened with hot sand. Flowers were the feminine emblems of the Louis XV period; not until the reign of Louis-Philippe would Frenchmen once again appreciate this charming symbol and take it as a favourite ornament.

413, 414 *Left and above*: This writing table by Pierre Roussel carries the Louis XIV tradition into the mid-18th century. It is veneered with ebony inlaid with brass stringing; the top is covered with red Morocco leather. The absence of drawers, the proportions, the high quality of the bronze mounts representing emblems of Neptune and the sea make it an exceptional piece. Louvre, Paris

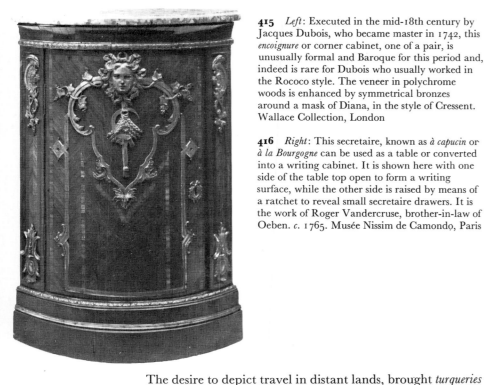

415 *Left*: Executed in the mid-18th century by Jacques Dubois, who became master in 1742, this *encoignure* or corner cabinet, one of a pair, is unusually formal and Baroque for this period and, indeed is rare for Dubois who usually worked in the Rococo style. The veneer in polychrome woods is enhanced by symmetrical bronzes around a mask of Diana, in the style of Cressent. Wallace Collection, London

416 *Right*: This secretaire, known as *à capucin* or *à la Bourgogne* can be used as a table or converted into a writing cabinet. It is shown here with one side of the table top open to form a writing surface, while the other side is raised by means of a ratchet to reveal small secretaire drawers. It is the work of Roger Vandercruse, brother-in-law of Oeben. *c.* 1765. Musée Nissim de Camondo, Paris

The desire to depict travel in distant lands, brought *turqueries* and *chinoiseries* more and more into fashion. Madame de Pompadour commissioned from Carle Van Loo decorations 'à la turque' for her bedroom at the Château Bellevue. This new fashion led to certain types of settee becoming known as, for example, *turquoises, paphoses, ottomanes* and sofas. The passion for the Far East was not new, but the *chinoiseries* painted by Boucher and Christophe Huet provided a gay and romantic note unknown to the 17th century. Fantastic animals and dragons lent their tortuous shapes to Rococo ornament. Panels of Chinese and Japanese lacquer were cut out from cabinets and screens and mounted onto cabinet pieces. The fashion was so enthusiastically adopted that the supply was insufficient and panels were imitated in French lacquer. *Ebénistes* like van Risen Burgh, Mathieu Criaerd and Jacques Dubois made a speciality of lacquered furniture. Oriental lacquer is usually on a dark ground but some *ébénistes*, encouraged by the *marchands-merciers*, preferred panels of French lacquer on a white or coloured ground. These harmonised with the Sèvres porcelain plaques which were beginning to be used as an ornament for furniture.

The Louis XV commode had evolved its final shape with two contiguous drawers, standing on tall cabriole legs. Commodes with doors began to appear, often made as companion pieces to the first type, and others with one drawer only, mounted on very slender legs, doubtless intended to be placed beneath a pierglass. *Encoignures*, fitting into the corner of a room, were usually made in pairs, but few examples survive complete with the shelves with which they were originally surmounted.

The large writing table was still popular, but the top is now of serpentine shape. It was accompanied by a filing-cabinet which was either joined to one end of the table or was an independent piece. Among other types of writing tables, those with marquetry tops contained a drawer concealing the writing-slide. Desks included the slant-front and fall-front secretaire.

The small writing tables could readily be adapted to other uses. They sometimes served as toilet tables in which case the writing-board had a mirror on the reverse side. There were countless other small tables, each fulfilling a precise function in the house: coffee or breakfast tables, work tables, enclosed bedside tables, serving tables with compartments for bottles and for silver and cutlery, and games tables.

The triumph of the Louis XV style did not, however, wholly banish tradition. Some cabinet-makers remained attached to the balanced and formal expression of their art, inherited from the late 17th century; others like Migeon, continued to use the simple, geometrical marquetry of the *Régence*. A number of other *menuisiers*, especially those established in Paris for several generations were also conservative in their work. Such persistent traditions remained very much alive in the mid-18th century and it is not surprising that the instigators of the Neo-Classical movement had little difficulty in recapturing the themes of the Louis XIV period.

407

Plate facing page 113
395

409, 410, 411

412

406, 408, 409
399

410, 415
397

398

416

413, 414,
415

The Transitional Style

In the mid-18th century there came a reaction to the excesses of Rococo art. In his '*Supplication aux Orfèvres, Ciseleurs et Sculpteurs sur bois*', published in the '*Mercure*' in 1754, the engraver, Nicolas Cochin (1713–90) pleaded for a return to the 'way of good taste of the preceding century'. It was this arch-enemy of Rococo who was chosen, together with the Abbé de Blanc and the architect Soufflot, to accompany Madame de Pompadour's brother on his travels to Italy between 1749 and 1751. This young man, the future Marquis de Marigny, was sent to prepare himself for his duties as *Directeur-Général des Bâtiments* and to absorb the essence of Classical culture.

It was an important journey for it reflected and, indeed, was part of a new interest in Antiquity felt throughout Europe. In France, the Comte de Caylus published, between 1752 and 1757, seven volumes of his '*Recueil d'antiquités égyptiennes, étrusques, grecques et romaines*', while in 1764 another Classical scholar, Lalive de Jully edited a '*Catalogue Historique*' of his collection of which the most important item was a small room decorated and furnished '*à la grecque*'. In 1763, Baron Grimm declared that the fashion was so widespread that '*tout est à Paris à la grecque*'.

A very different world from that of the first half of the century was about to be born. The Court began only gradually to adopt the new ideas, following the example of Madame de Pompadour and particularly that of Madame du Barry, who had given large orders for new furniture for the Pavillon de Louveciennes although the king remained totally indifferent to them. But the decoration and furniture which welcomed him at Louveciennes on the occasion of the reception given in his honour in 1771, was in a fully Neo-Classical style with not a trace of Louis XV Rococo.

Two collections of engraved designs in the new Louis XVI manner were to have considerable influence. Roubo's '*Art du Menuisier*' issued between 1769 and 1775, included designs for Rococo and Neo-Classical chairs. In his collection of two hundred engravings, published about 1771–2, Delafosse was more of an innovator. The rather heavy, massive forms which he favoured often feature garlands and laurel swags, but at the same time they retain curving profiles. It is this combination of Rococo tendencies with Classical elements which represents the

transitional style of the decade 1760–70.

The cabinet-maker, Jean-François Oeben (d. 1763), himself a pupil of the sons of Boulle, exercised a determining influence on the period through his own work, that of his pupils Riesener and Leleu, and through the members of his own family: his brother Simon Oeben and his brother-in-law, Vandercruse. His pieces are of full, ample form with gently contrasting curves, while the marquetry is either of geometrical design in cubes, lozenges and rosettes, or represents flowers. He was especially interested in mechanical devices such as those which released or raised drawers by an apparently magical process. The writing desk, known as a *bureau à capucin* is an example of this type of cabinet piece, while the roll-top desk was to be Oeben's invention.

420
416

417, 418

419

Furniture of this transitional period tended to become more restrained. The break-front commode is characteristic, the projecting panel in the centre echoing in more severe form the *bombé* shape of the old Louis XV version. Both the new arrangement of the drawers in three tiers and the somewhat heavy form recall the *Régence* commode. Chairs sometimes combined Rococo and Neo-Classical features. The most pleasing are those conceived in the manner of Delafosse, in which carved motifs inspired by Antiquity appear on elegantly curved chair frames. The tapering legs are surmounted, at the juncture with the seat rail, with a square member carved with a flower, a feature possibly invented by Georges Jacob, or Delanois. Michel Gourdin made some very fine chairs in which the undulating framework is carved with interlaced bands and acanthus leaves; the linking members uniting the front legs to the seat rail are present but do not break the flowing line.

420

425

The study of drawings and paintings of this period, when fashionable design was hesitating between two extremes, reveals the presence in interiors of both Louis XV and Louis XVI furniture. Undoubtedly among the earliest pieces in the new style were those made by René Dubois in about 1765 to 1768 and offered by Louis XV to Catherine II of Russia. But the time limits which divide one style from another are always difficult to fix even though this particular transitional phase was expressed only in terms of Parisian taste and was almost unknown in the provinces. For example, cabinet-makers like Topino and Martin Carlin continued to use cabriole legs until the eve of the Revolution while Louis XV furniture was made throughout the century, chiefly in the provinces.

422

437

417, 418 *Left and below left*: Jean-François Oeben made several tables similar to this, serving equally for the toilet or for writing. A drawer, released by the sliding top, is divided into partitions over which a slide which can be drawn for writing or raised to form a book-rest. The bronze mounts and the floral marquetry are still fully Louis XV, but the rather stiff curves reveal the development of the transitional style. *c.* 1760–5. The marquetry top represents an actual picture in polychrome woods: a basket of flowers in a symmetrical cartouche between two bouquets. Surrounded by a raised border of gilt bronze, it relies on the convex and concave curves characteristic of Oeben. Rijksmuseum, Amsterdam

419 *Right*: The same slightly contrasting curves exist in this small *secrétaire à cylindre* or cylinder-top desk which is certainly the work of Oeben, and presents a less ostentatious version of the large roll-top desk of the Louis XV period. Here Oeben uses his talents both as mechanic and a cabinet-maker. The roll-top composed of separate slats, the superb floral marquetry, and the bronze gallery round the shelf place this charming piece at about 1765. Musée Nissim de Camondo, Paris

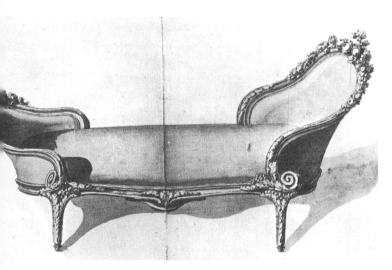

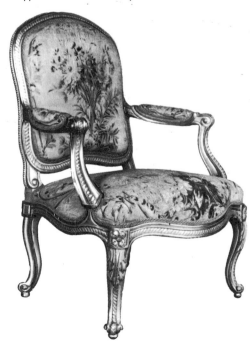

420 *Top left*: This commode, stamped by J. F. Leleu, one of the best pupils of Oeben, represents the commode of the transitional period. It preserves the typical Louis XV cabriole legs and a central projection dividing the façade into three panels. On the other hand, the rectangular form, the seven drawers of which three are in the frieze, the marquetry design and the gilt bronze mounts of Classical inspiration belong to the Louis XVI style. *c.* 1770. Musée Nissim de Camondo, Paris

421 *Above left*: This commode, one of a pair, is also transitional in style, and is signed by Pierre Garnier. Its outline is still curvaceous and the legs are of the cabriole type. The door panels of black and gold lacquer witness a persistent taste for the exotic. The gilt bronze mounts in the style of Delafosse and the small galleries which border the corner shelves were new features. Musée Nissim de Camondo, Paris

423 *Left*: This design for a day-bed, in pen-and-ink and wash, is by Jean-Charles Delafosse, whose manner so successfully lent amplitude and dignity to his chair designs in the transitional period. The straight tapering legs are carved with foliage while the curve of the apron answers the bold swirls of the two ends. Musée des Arts Décoratifs, Paris

424 *Below left*: This *canapé* or settee, one of a pair, the other being in the Louvre, is a very elegant example of the work of Lebas in the transitional style. (See illustration 403.) The curved legs and the undulating supports to the arms are still Louis XV; the well-defined seat rail and the formal framework of the upholstered back, carved with acanthus leaves and interlaced bands, belong to the new Neo-Classical manner. *c.* 1770. Musée des Arts Décoratifs, Paris

422 *Above: La Lecture*, (detail), by Baudouin (1723-69). Louis XV furniture and some pieces already entirely in the Louis XVI style are found together in this bedroom where a young woman sits reading and dreaming; a screen partially obscures the door and protects her from draughts. Before 1769. Musée des Arts Décoratifs, Paris

425 *Below*: This beautiful walnut gilt armchair, one of a set of six, bears the stamp of Michel Gourdin, who became master in 1752. In the 19th century the set was in the possession of King Louis-Philippe at the Château d'Eu. The chair is typical of the transitional style. The ornament of interlaced bands and acanthus leaves on the flat curves of the members is of Classical inspiration. *c.* 1770. Wallace Collection, London

The Louis XVI Style

The completion of the Pavillon de Louveciennes for Madame du Barry, in 1771, celebrated by the famous supper-party shown in a pen and ink and water-colour drawing by Moreau le Jeune in the Louvre, marks the final evolution of the Louis XVI style, which remains linked with the name of a monarch who had not yet ascended the throne—Louis XV was to reign for another four years.

Louis XVI was only interested in furniture from a technical point of view, in the mechanical devices, in the details of the marquetry or in the chiselled bronze mounts, but Marie-Antoinette welcomed the Neo-Classical style; she placed some large orders for furniture from which it is clear that her taste favoured mother-of-pearl and rich, fastidious pieces. The Court, the Comte d'Artois and the Comte de Provence, who frequently employed the *ébénistes* Stöckel and Beneman, shared her love of extravagant grandeur. The rich and heavy character of some Louis XVI pieces reflects the taste for ostentation which prevailed right up to the Revolution.

Parisian society, no less than the Court, was set on a frenzied course of sumptuous living which was to lead straight to catastrophe. For the French cabinet-makers it was a prosperous period. Their fame was international: the sovereigns of Russia, Spain and Portugal, and the princes of Germany, Scandinavia and Poland came to buy in Paris. The English nobility and landed gentry who had their own eminent cabinet-makers at home, did not disdain to choose a few pieces from the fashionable Parisian *marchands-merciers* in the neighbourhood of the Faubourg Saint-Honoré. This European demand for French furniture followed by the dispersion abroad of many fine pieces during the Revolution and Napoleonic Wars, accounts for the fact that the most important collections of Louis XVI furniture, with the exception of the Louvre, are to be found in the Wallace Collection and in private collections in England and in the Residenzmuseum in Munich.

The most representative *ébéniste* of the Louis XVI period is undoubtedly Jean-Henri Riesener (1734–1806). His work betrays an intensely personal manner although in it the evolution of the Louis XVI style can be followed. Trained by Oeben, his early work provides a link between the mid-century and the transitional style. For his commodes, he long retained the breakfront form with a central panel of trapezoidal shape. This latter feature was then abandoned in favour of rectangular panels. Until about 1775, his furniture remained comparatively supple in outline; both scroll feet and straight legs, canted or fluted were used. After that date, his style became more settled; the forms are heavier and the marquetry he constantly employed until the Revolution consisted either of lozenges sometimes containing stylised flowers, or it represents what can best be described as a still life in the form of baskets and bouquets of flowers. Riesener's great period came after 1780 when he was producing furniture ranging from the most luxurious for Marie-Antoinette to the most sober but infinitely delicate pieces; beside the marquetry of mother-of-pearl destined for the boudoir at Fontainebleau, we now perhaps prefer his plain veneers of satinwood or kingwood and especially those of mahogany, enriched with delicate festoons of flowers in gilt bronze. Both in form and ornament Riesener made an original and valuable contribution to the art of cabinet-making and new types of furniture, such as a travelling-desk with detachable legs, now in the Louvre, may have been his invention.

But Riesener, the greatest cabinet-maker of the period, was not the only one to benefit by Oeben's teaching. Leleu too, acquired much from his master, including an admiration for the technique and the designs of André-Charles Boulle. Among his pieces, he made a console table in marquetry of brass and tortoiseshell after a Boulle design. Other cabinet-makers such as Levasseur and Montigny, also used ebony with brass inlay, and copied Boulle's designs.

While at first Louis XVI pieces betrayed a conservative pleasure in supple shapes, rectangular forms and straight legs ultimately prevailed. Marquetry of geometrical design with lozenges and trellis-work in light-coloured woods, such as satinwood, was

(margin references: 428, 430; 432; 435; 429)

426 *Above:* This chiffonier containing narrow drawers behind sliding doors bears the stamp of Oeben. If it is indeed by his hand, it must be earlier than 1763, the year of his death. Because of its decided Louis XVI character, it is often ascribed to Riesener who directed Oeben's workshop after his death, using his stamp. When Riesener finally married Oeben's widow in 1767 he carried on the workshop in his own name. The marquetry of cubes within an interlaced border is, however, typical of Oeben who may well have introduced designs in advance of his period. Louvre, Paris

427 *La Coupe Enchantée,* by Fragonard (1732–1806), shows one of the characters in this illustration of La Fontaine's fable, seated in an armchair which is decidedly in the Louis XVI style, with spirally fluted, straight legs. Musée des Arts Décoratifs, Paris

428 *Right:* This beautiful Louis XVI commode, with three drawers in the frieze and four below, hidden by sliding panels, is a characteristic work by Jean-Henri Riesener, who became master in 1768. His style is recognisable in the three panels in the façade, a reminder of the transitional style, in the tulipwood marquetry in lozenge design, in the large bouquet of flowers and in the gilt bronze mounts. Less magnificent than the royal commodes, the quality of the craftsmanship is just as high. *c.* 1775. Musée Nissim de Camondo, Paris

429 *Below:* This charming little work table, with a drawer containing a writing slide, was made by Riesener in 1788 for the private apartments of Queen Marie-Antoinette at the Château de Saint-Cloud. The tulipwood marquetry is of lozenge design, and is contained within a double border in black and white, an idea borrowed from Oeben. It can be compared with the richer and grander table made by Riesener for the Queen's boudoir at Fontainebleau, in which the lozenge marquetry is in mother-of-pearl. Musée Nissim de Camondo, Paris

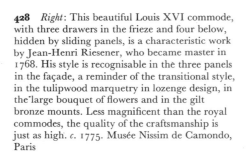

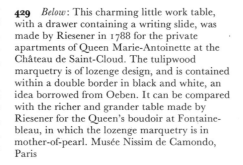

430 *Left*: This chiffonnier bears the cypher of the Biron family. It belongs to the period in which Riesener reached his highest achievement. Its lines are perfectly straight and the short pedestal legs continue the canted stiles. The marquetry has a purely pictorial effect on this exceptional piece which unites sober lines with superb quality. *c.* 1780. Musée des Arts Décoratifs, Paris

431, 432 *Above and above right*: Riesener made many small writing tables. On these the central panel of each side almost always projects. This desk is in mahogany, the frieze mounted with gilt bronze. The tall, tapering legs are set with vertical bronze fillets, terminating in foot mounts in the form of acanthus leaves. The top is surrounded on three sides by a fret gallery attached by exposed screws. *c.* 1780–9. Like Boulle and Cressent before him, Riesener often modelled his bronze mounts himself. The corner mount in the form of flowers, marvellously chased, is typical of the years 1780–9. So also are the interlaced acanthus leaves surrounding a central flower and wreath motif, a detail which occurs often in Riesener's marquetry design. Louvre, Paris

433 *Left*: Riesener's stamp is also found on pieces veneered with mahogany, in which the effect is one of extreme simplicity. The only decoration on this roll-top desk is the fluting of the straight legs continuing up the sides of the cylinder top, the triglyphs between the drawers, and the keyhole escutcheons set in foliate ring handles. *c.* 1780–9. Musée des Arts Décoratifs, Paris

434 *Above right*: Possibly invented by Oeben, this type of heart-shaped toilet table is comparatively rare. Signed by Charles Topino, who became master in 1773, this piece still has the curved legs which indicate the transition between the Louis XV and Louis XVI styles. Serving equally for writing, it is decorated with marquetry in the Louis XVI manner. *c.* 1775. Musée Nissim de Camondo, Paris

435 *Below*: Etienne Levasseur, who became master in 1767 was a pupil of Boulle's sons. He copied the furniture of the great cabinet-maker to Louis XIV, as one can see in this ebony bookcase decorated with marquetry of brass on a tortoise-shell ground. The oval medallion in gilt bronze represents the *Rape of the Sabine Women*. A similar piece in the Wallace Collection, in *contre-partie* adorned with a medallion illustrating the *Abduction of Helen*, and also signed by Levasseur, is perhaps the companion piece. Private Collection

436 *Below*: Ascribed to David Roentgen who became master in 1780, this roll-top desk veneered with purplewood and decorated with marquetry of polychrome woods is enriched with gilt bronze mounts *à l'antique*, regularly disposed. The contours are severely straight and angular. This piece, given by Louis XVI to Catherine II of Russia, was made in about 1785. Louvre, Paris

fashionable. Flowers and trophies were also used and David Roentgen and his school introduced landscapes, architecture and human figures in marquetry. The demand for colour brought into fashion furniture mounted with Sèvres porcelain plaques painted in floral designs, or set with panels of *verre églomisé*. The vogue for Oriental lacquer and *Vernis Martin* in bright reds, blues or greens, continued, matching the panelling against which the furniture was placed. Oriental lacquer and *Vernis Martin* panels were incorporated in pieces veneered in tulipwood, kingwood and particularly in ebony. Weisweiler specialised in such sombre compositions. When he used ebony alone he enlivened it with bronze mounts, with marquetry of brass and pewter, and with metal fillets set in fluted columns and feet.

One of the most striking features of Louis XVI cabinet pieces are the large panels of plain mahogany veneer cut from parts of the tree where the branches or roots join the trunk to reveal 'mottle' or 'curl' figurings. These simple veneers were set off by luxurious and finely chiselled gilt bronze mounts in the form of Vitruvian scrolls, trailing leaves, key patterns, interlaced bands and palmettes, plaques with Classical scenes, columns and

caryatids, garlands of flowers, and laurel wreaths. Bronzes of such ravishing finesse and variety had not been used hitherto. Mounts in the form of draped material were favoured by Martin Carlin, and plaques with Classical scenes in relief or with simple chased borders by Weisweiler. Gradually new features were introduced. Gouthière invented a process by which part of a mount could be left mat to contrast with the burnished elements. A good deal of mahogany furniture was merely embellished with plain brass or bronze mouldings outlining the profile or the panels, while practical ring handles, shoes and castors now made their appearance.

Fashionable furniture remained the prerogative of the cabinet-makers. The Louis XVI commode became more distinctive in about 1770. Supported on short, circular, tapering legs, sometimes terminating in metal mounts, the arrangement of the drawers remains the same, although after 1780 the breakfront disappears. The uprights are straight, canted or rounded and are often fluted. Shortly before the Revolution columns or caryatids were added. Some commodes are enclosed by two or three doors, or by sliding panels disclosing drawers. Among the new types to appear were the *demi-lune* commode, the side cup-

437 *Above*: The taste for colourful pieces is illustrated by this remarkable *bureau plat* or writing table stamped I. Dubois and doubtless the work of René Dubois, who became master in 1755 and used the stamp of his father Jacques Dubois. It is lacquered green and gold on an oak carcase and embellished with gilt bronze mounts which include the sirens surmounting the legs. This latter feature is also found on the famous commode by the same cabinet-maker made for Marie Antoinette and now in the Wallace Collection. The form and ornament of this piece are entirely in the Louis XVI Classical style. Since it is said to have been offered together with a *cartonnier* or filing cabinet and an ink-stand to Catherine II of Russia by Louis XV, it cannot be later than the years 1765–8 and must be one of the earliest pieces in the fully-developed Louis XVI style. According to tradition, the Treaty of Tilsit was signed upon this table in 1807. The ceremony took place on a raft on the River Niemen, the signatories being the Emperors Napoleon I and Alexander I of Russia and King Frederick William III of Prussia. Wallace Collection, London

440 *Below*: Japanese black and gold lacquer panels are mounted in the doors of this commode veneered with ebony. It was commissioned from Martin Carlin by the dealer Darnault *en suite* with two corner cabinets and delivered to *Mesdames* (the daughters of Louis XV) in 1785 for the Château de Bellevue. This type of commode with three doors was very common in the Louis XVI period. The feet in the shape of a spinning top and the gilt bronze mounts in the form of wreaths and garlands are characteristic of the Louis XVI style. Louvre, Paris

438 *Above*: The dealers Poirier and Daguerre made a speciality of furniture decorated with Sèvres porcelain plaques. They had several cabinet-makers producing pieces of this type for them, among whom was Martin Carlin, who became master in 1766, and was the maker of this *bonheur-du-jour* or small secretaire. Similar pieces are at Waddesdon Manor, Bucks, and in the collection of the Duke of Buccleuch. This piece is veneered with tulipwood. The porcelain plaques are dated 1766. Musée Nissim de Camondo, Paris

439 *Above right*: Leaves taken from a Coramandel lacquer screen have been mounted on the fall-front and doors of this veneered secretaire in the Louis XVI style. It bears the stamp of Charles Topino, who is chiefly known for his small tables and cabinet-pieces often mounted with gilt bronzes in the Louis XV style in spite of their advanced date (see illustration 434). *c.* 1780. Collection: Princesse A. de Broglie

441 *Right*: The upper part of this unsigned secretaire is veneered with ebony and mounted with Japanese lacquer panels in gold on a black ground. The fall-front is flanked by slender uprights in the form of caryatids in gilt bronze—possibly the work of Gouthière. Similar bronzes also recur on the table by Weisweiler delivered in 1784 by the dealer, Daguerre to Marie-Antoinette for the Château de Saint-Cloud, and on several other works by the same cabinet-maker. The interlaced stretchers are characteristic of Weisweiler, to whom this piece can be attributed. *c.* 1788–90. Rijksmuseum, Amsterdam.

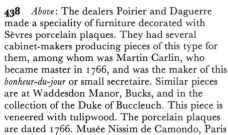

421 boards enclosed by curved doors and the *encoignure* or corner *commode*. Similar to the corner commode were the very popular low cabinets or *meubles d'appui*, usually made in pairs and close in appearance to the early 18th-century chests-of-drawers. The
430 chiffonnier, a variant of the commode, adopted the same proportions as the *secrétaire à abattant* or fall-front desk, with which it was often *en suite*. The fall-front desk was an important piece and was
439, 443 architectural in character. Sometimes it was supported on tall
441 legs instead of surmounting a cupboard base, in which case the
436, 433 effect was much lighter. The roll-top desk replaced the slant-front desk and was often surmounted by a set of drawers or small cupboard. It was very often the same size as the large writing
427, 437 table, inherited from the first half of the century. In addition to these a lady's writing table with a small cabinet or shelves at the back of the top became so fashionable that it was named *bonheur-du-jour*. The *secrétaire debout* enabled the writer to stand, but the
438 table *à la tronchin* which included mechanical fittings enabling the writing-board to be raised when required became more popular. Writing desks were often made *en suite* with bookcases with latticed or plain glass doors which could also be used for the display of *objets d'art*.

Generally speaking, small tables were the same as those of the Louis XV period. A few new types occur: heart-shaped toilet 434 tables, possibly invented by Oeben and perhaps intended for men, *tricoteuses* or work tables, the top surrounded by a raised 429 border to contain balls of wool and silk, coffee and tea-tables, *tables en chiffonnière* containing drawers of square, rectangular, round or oval shape, tables with tops containing metal receptacles for plants and *tables servantes* with one or two shelves which avoided the need for servants at an intimate meal. The mahogany dining-table made its appearance, and a new version of the 18th-century *guéridon* or candlestand, with a round top set on a pedestal base was destined to enjoy great success at the end of the century and under the Empire.

While Riesener was the leading *ébéniste* of the Louis XVI period, Georges Jacob (1739-1814) was the dominant *menuisier*. After working for a short time in the Louis XV style, he had gradually introduced Neo-Classical features into the design of his chairs. Between 1770 and the Revolution he was constantly inventing new forms and ornaments and introducing new ideas such as chairs of mahogany for instance. He collaborated with the best architects of the time, including Bélanger, who was in

442 This design for a commode is signed by Julliot *fils* and dated 1784. It is very close to the work of the designer J. D. Ducourg (1749-1825). In execution, the piece is intended to be mounted with panels of *pietre dure*—a revival of a 17th-century technique. The caryatids recall those on some of Weisweiler's pieces, (see the next illustration). Musée des Arts Décoratifs, Paris

444 *Left*: This little Neo-Classical ebony table with a *verde antico* marble top, is in the manner of Weisweiler, who became master in 1778. It is one of a pair. The typical crossed stretchers support an antique ewer in green bronze while the straight legs are set with vertical fillets in pewter. c. 1785. Musée Nissim de Camondo, Paris

445 *Right*: This commode, veneered with mahogany and stamped by Joseph Stöckel, (master in 1755), was hitherto ascribed to Guillaume Beneman. Stöckel's originality is apparent in the heavy columns, the narrow drawer in the frieze, the very thick marble top and in the austere fillets of metal. c. 1785. Musée des Arts Décoratifs, Paris

443 *Above*: This dignified *secrétaire à abattant*, or fall-front desk, is a superb example of the Louis XVI style. Veneered in mahogany it is formal without being severe. The decoration relies on the finely-chased gilt bronze mounts which include the vertical supports in the form of caryatids identical with those of Weisweiler's furniture, and may be the work of Gouthière (see illustration 441). Ascribed to Levasseur and commissioned for the apartments of Madame Adelaïde at the Château de Bellevue, of which it bears the mark B.V., this secretaire dates from the last years of the *Ancien Régime*. Louvre, Paris

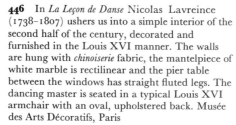

446 In *La Leçon de Danse* Nicolas Lavreince (1738-1807) ushers us into a simple interior of the second half of the century, decorated and furnished in the Louis XVI manner. The walls are hung with *chinoiserie* fabric, the mantelpiece of white marble is rectilinear and the pier table between the windows has straight fluted legs. The dancing master is seated in a typical Louis XVI armchair with an oval, upholstered back. Musée des Arts Décoratifs, Paris

447 *Right*: This armchair is one of a pair. It is painted in grey, blue and pink and is carved with delicate motifs, including a frieze of rosettes which often appears on chairs by Georges Jacob, by whom the chair is signed. The arm-rests join the square back in an elegant curve, characteristic of Jacob, while the arm supports are carried through to the front legs by scrolled members carved as acanthus foliage. *c.* 1780-5. Musée Nissim de Camondo, Paris

448, 449 *Left and below*: This armchair is part of a notable set comprising a *canapé*, two *bergères*, and eight armchairs. It is signed by Jean Baptiste Sené, (master in 1769). Although influenced by Jacob, he possessed an individual style, noticeable here in the spirally fluted legs, the wide foliate scroll that joins the seat to the back, the wreath of roses and the palms forming the cresting and finally the scroll ornament terminating the juncture of the arms with the back. *c.* 1780-5. Musée Nissim de Camondo, Paris

450 *Below*: This *voyeuse* is a chair with a low seat and a padded cresting across the back, used for watching card-playing. The back of white painted wood is carved in the shape of a lyre, flanked by uprights in the form of columns. The back legs assume a new form and are curved in sabre shape. The chair bears the stamp of Georges Jacob, *c.* 1785. Formerly in the collection of Christian Dior

451 *Below left*: Georges Jacob was possibly the first to adopt mahogany for the construction of chairs, following the English practice. The back of this chair is pierced and carved in a strapwork design between uprights in the form of columns. The straight legs are fluted and the seat rail is carved with a marguerite, a characteristic Jacob feature. Chairs to this design were later also made by his sons. *c.* 1785-9. Château de Fontainebleau

452 *Below centre*: An example of the whimsical taste of Jacob who did not hesitate to adopt all the varying fashions of the period. The rage for the exotic inspired this armchair. The wooden frame simulates the texture and colour of bamboo and even in the construction the Chinese manner is imitated. The chair anticipates those in the Royal Pavilion at Brighton and dates from the last years of the *Ancien Régime*. Formerly in the collection of Christian Dior

453 *Above*: A pen-and-ink drawing by Richard de Lalonde which illustrates the constant concern of the designers in the Louis XVI period to incorporate seat furniture—here a sofa—into the planned decoration of an interior. The back of the sofa is designed to accord with the decoration of the panelling behind it. *c.* 1780. Musée des Arts Décoratifs, Paris

454 Design for a bed in pen-and-ink and sepia wash, by J. C. Delafosse. This canopied bed in the traditional style is placed in an alcove. The wall-panelling is composed of coupled pilasters flanking scenes of *putti* playing around tripod stands upon which lamps are burning. The fanciful draperies and plumes on the canopy, surmounted by a pair of billing doves are in the prevailing fashion. Musée des Arts Décoratifs, Paris

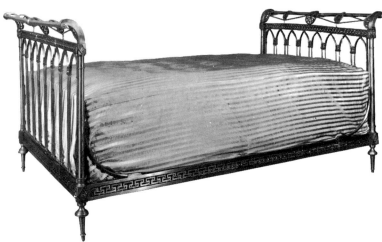

455 At the end of the century beds were made with iron, steel or gilt bronze frames. In this example of steel and gilt bronze the head- and foot-piece are scrolled back in the Etruscan manner while strictly formal Classical motifs suggest the coming severity of the *Directoire* style. *c.* 1790-5. Musée Nissim de Camondo, Paris

456 Much of the finest furniture in the *Directoire* style was made by Georges Jacob, who had worked as a *menuisier* or joiner under the *Ancien Régime* and became a cabinet-maker after the Revolution as a consequence of the suppression of the Guilds. This veneered mahogany commode with four drawers separated by horizontals is an unusual design. The uprights are in the form of monopodia, patinated to resemble antique bronzes, and the drawers are ornamented with marquetry in which swans in purplewood are set on a citruswood ground. The elliptical curves of the base also occur on other pieces by Jacob. *c.* 1795. Collection: Lefuel, Paris

charge of the work at Bagatelle, while in 1787 he made the chairs for the *Laiterie* at Rambouillet designed by Hubert Robert, in an Etruscan style that already foreshadowed the *Directoire*. His rival, Jean-Baptiste Sené (1740-1803), received important orders from the Crown although he was less fortunate than Jacob. The designs of Richard de Lalonde also helped to spread the taste for Neo-Classicism while J-D. Dugourc's Neo-Pompeian designs attracted the attention of influential patrons and both Madame Elisabeth and the Comte de Provence commissioned from him interior designs in this style in the last year of the reign.

Although Louis XVI chairs abandoned curves in favour of straight lines, they successfully avoid an appearance of cold severity. They have upholstered medallion-shaped, square or rectangular backs, occasionally with an elliptical top rail. Octagonal, and, less frequently, shield-shaped backs, as in the set of chairs by Sené in the Musée Camondo, also occur. The front seat-rail is often rounded, while the turned legs are straight and tapering, carved with straight or spiral flutings. In about 1785 the form changes. The back legs were set at a slight angle or curved in 'sabre' form. The armrests spring from the back in an elegant curve, at first sweeping forward to about two-thirds of the length of the side rail and then later reaching forward to join the seat rail immediately above the front legs. Pale tones such as grey, or lilac replace the vivid colours of the days of Louis XV; plain gold or plain white were the most popular. Much attention was given to upholstery, introducing elaborate draperies, cushions and bolsters.

It was Jacob who introduced chairs with carved and pierced splats with such motifs as a lyre, a wheat-sheaf, or a wicker basket. He was the first to use solid mahogany, a fashion he adopted from England, while such was the influence of Chippendale's designs upon him that his chairs in the Chinese taste closely reflect the manner of the *Director*. Although mahogany was the wood preferred for chairs with pierced splats, it was occasionally replaced by beech stained in imitation or painted in fashionable colours.

The types of chairs had not changed since the reign of Louis XV. The *sultane* is now perhaps more in favour. In about 1785, the armchair *en gondole*, of embracing form, the curve of the arms continuing the tall, rounded back, is used at the writing table. Screens and fire-screens followed the fashion and modified their contours. Beds *à la française* or *à la polonaise*, conformed to the interior decoration while the alcove bed with a back and two ends was also popular. At the end of the reign, the first beds in mahogany and metal made their appearance.

The *Directoire* Style

The last decade of the 18th century was much too disturbed to encourage fresh invention. The style known as *Directoire*, in honour of the only stable government of the period, was in fact the expression of a taste for 'Etruscan' decorative features which had already developed several years before the Revolution. The furniture designed by the painter David for his studio and which can be seen in his painting '*Les Amours de Paris et Hélène*' of 1788, was austerely Classical and reflected an academic approach to design which was to become more marked at the end of the century and to triumph under the Empire in the work of Percier and Fontaine. The art of the 18th century, however, still aroused nostalgic admiration. Engravings published by La Mésangère in the '*Journal des Dames et des Modes*' advertised furniture which owes much to the Louis XVI style stripped of its former splendour. Angular pilasters replace columns at the corners of heavy pieces, handles are semi-rectangular rather than circular while the gallery surrounding the tops of tables and commodes is now pierced in a lozenge design. As a general rule, the rounded contours which so often softened the effect of straight lines have disappeared while the materials used are of poorer quality; mahogany veneer is now embellished with brass rather than bronze mounts.

The 'Etruscan' style, at first confined to a few aesthetes, now prevailed in Paris. In about 1795, La Mésangère published engravings of chairs with scrolled backs and 'sabre' legs, inspired by the work of Georges Jacob who dominated the Revolutionary period until 1796, when he handed over his workshop to his two

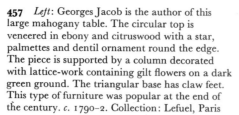

457 *Left*: Georges Jacob is the author of this large mahogany table. The circular top is veneered in ebony and citruswood with a star, palmettes and dentil ornament round the edge. The piece is supported by a column decorated with lattice-work containing gilt flowers on a dark green ground. The triangular base has claw feet. This type of furniture was popular at the end of the century. *c*. 1790–2. Collection: Lefuel, Paris

458 *Right*: Mahogany armchair, stamped by Jacob *frères* (1796–1803). The sons of Georges Jacob have borrowed from their father certain details: the marguerite carved on the apron (see illustration 451), and the lattice-work back carved with palmettes recalling the 'Etruscan' furniture made in 1787 for the *Laiterie* at Rambouillet. Collection: Lefuel, Paris

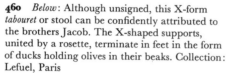

460 *Below*: Although unsigned, this X-form *tabouret* or stool can be confidently attributed to the brothers Jacob. The X-shaped supports, united by a rosette, terminate in feet in the form of ducks holding olives in their beaks. Collection: Lefuel, Paris

461 *Below right*: This purplewood armchair of gondola shape dates from the very first years of the 19th century. In spite of the graceful presence of the carved swans, patinated and gilt, it has a severity and a certain massiveness far removed from the spirit of the 18th century. Collection: Lefuel, Paris

459 *Below*: The two scrolled ends of this day-bed are in solid mahogany, carved at the junction of the frame with a lion's head surmounted by an acanthus leaf. The design of the six legs terminating in feet in the shape of spinning tops, occurs in a slightly modified form in an engraving published by *La Mésangère* and dates between the years 1796–9. Collection: Lefuel, Paris

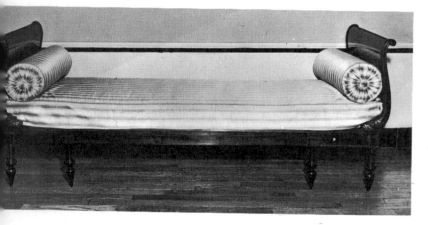

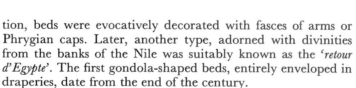

sons. Trained in the fastidious atmosphere of the *Ancien Régime*, he understood the subtleties of cabinet-making and employed marquetries of ebony, satinwood and pewter. He also used mahogany veneer and solid mahogany, which he sometimes patinated to imitate bronze. The brothers Jacob, who were to be the chief furnishers of the Consulate period, revived some of the decorative features used by their father, for example, the inclusion of a marguerite at the junction of chair legs and seat rail.

Mahogany chairs with pierced splats inspired by English examples were more popular than ever. The top rail was scrolled over and carved, inlaid or painted, while the splat was pierced and carved in various ways. The back legs were curved in 'sabre' shape to counterbalance the scrolled back; the front legs usually remained straight and fluted. The first chairs with X-shaped supports appeared at the end of the century, when stools of this same form also came into use. The armrests of chairs are nearly always straight, supported by the Louis XVI baluster or slender column and later by a griffin, a winged lion, a sphinx or female bust. Comfortable deep armchairs and settees fitted with cushions were no longer made. They were replaced by a day-bed called a *méridienne*, which had either one or two curled-over ends, either upholstered or of solid, pierced and carved wood.

Concerning beds, the *'Journal des Dames et des Modes'* is illuminating. These appear to reflect, more than other furniture, the successive fashions born of political life. During the Revolu-

tion, beds were evocatively decorated with fasces of arms or Phrygian caps. Later, another type, adorned with divinities from the banks of the Nile was suitably known as the *'retour d'Egypte'*. The first gondola-shaped beds, entirely enveloped in draperies, date from the end of the century.

The types of furniture were fewer under the *Directoire*. The most popular commode had three or four drawers. It was often made *en suite* with a fall-front secretaire, which now tended to supplant other types of writing furniture. A few writing tables were still to be seen, but pedestal desks were now usual. As for the *bonheur-du-jour*, it now rivalled the secretaire in size and had no longer anything but a distant connection with the charming piece conceived in the mid-18th century. Among many tables were two original types: the *guéridon* with a round top on a central pillar, and the *somno*, a bedside pedestal table.

Jacob and his sons were not the only cabinet-makers of the period. Men of the *Ancien Régime* were still working, such as Beneman and Molitor. Jacob, however, is the more important figure. Like Oeben in the mid-century, he represents the link between the *Ancien Régime* and the Empire. The last furniture he made before retiring in 1796 was already in the Empire style.

The 18th century ended, as it had begun, in a period of transition. The *Directoire* style reflects the dilemma of a generation which recalled the grace and delicacy of the *Ancien Régime* but boldly turned to the military future of the Empire.

456, 457

458

458

460

461

459

457

ENGLAND 1715-1765

Helena Hayward

In the 18th century, architecture was the most important of the arts and for a man of wealth his house and furniture presented a spectacular means of exhibiting good taste. The interiors and furnishings of the many splendid mansions built in the course of the century and particularly in the 1720s and 1730s, became the direct concern of architects, professional and amateur. Never before had English architects seriously devoted themselves to furniture design or exerted so strong an influence on the products of the cabinet-makers' and carvers' workshops as they were now to do. But it was the taste of the owners of these fine houses which created the demand and set the standard. How this taste developed and what was the atmosphere it evoked deserves particular attention if we are to understand and appreciate the furniture of the period.

The accession to the throne in 1714 of George I, Elector of Hanover, was more than a political triumph for the Whig magnates whose policy had brought him the crown. The king could speak no English and isolated from his court and people, had neither the ability nor the interest to create around himself a lively artistic circle. At once the Whigs established themselves as the new directors of taste—a taste audacious enough to claim moral righteousness as its justification. 'He who aspires to the character of a man of breeding and politeness is careful to form his judgments of arts and sciences upon the right models of perfection', Lord Shaftesbury had declared. The 'right models of perfection' were, of course, to be found only in Rome, or at least in Italy. Baroque was condemned as being over-emotional and undisciplined. Instead the virtues of Classical proportion claimed the devotion of the new era. They were ardently admired by the supporters of the Palladian movement whose influence firmly moulded English taste between 1715 and 1765.

George I

The new movement was concerned to revive the precepts of Classical art by taking as model the work of the great Italian Renaissance architect, Andrea Palladio. Two publications appeared in 1715 which presented a clear picture of the new ideals. Both were dedicated to George I and represented a statement of Whig policy in matters of taste. The first, Colin Campbell's *Vitruvius Britannicus*, surveyed the growth of the English country house. Among a series of engravings of fine mansions were included, as a focal point, the architect's own designs for Wanstead House, Essex, then being built for Sir Richard Child. A vast mansion, of strikingly formal appearance, it was revolutionary in spirit. The second, an English translation of Palladio's own *Four Books of Architecture*, was of even greater importance. It was not only a contemporary source of inspiration but also the work upon which the English architect Inigo Jones (1573-1652) had drawn, some hundred years earlier, when the ideals of Classical form and harmony had first been understood in England. As a student of Palladio, Inigo Jones was admired in the early 18th century. His designs for interior features, such as overmantels, panelling and doorways were shortly to be used as models by the architects of the new Palladian movement. In consulting these two publications, English noblemen and country gentlemen could acquire scholarship and taste to enable them to build 'correctly' and furnish 'politely'. And behind this earnest endeavour lay the devotion to reason and good sense for which the poet Alexander Pope pleaded:

> Something there is more needful than expense
> And something previous ev'n to taste—'tis sense.

462 Carved and gilt walnut chair with original caning in the back and seat, *c*. 1725. It is one of a set of twelve. Although caning first became fashionable in the reign of Charles II, it continued occasionally to be used, even for chairs of fine quality throughout the 18th century. The carved, interlaced strapwork on the splat derives from French engraved designs. Lady Lever Art Gallery, Port Sunlight, Cheshire

463 Portrait of Mr and Mrs William Atherton by Arthur Devis, *(detail)*, painted in the second quarter of the 18th century. The room is sparsely furnished, with no carpet, but the cabinet-on-stand, with straight top and cabriole legs, was highly fashionable at the time. The suite of seat furniture, from which two stools, two chairs and a settee are shown, reflects the taste for simple, elegant lines. Walker Art Gallery, Liverpool

464 Settee of walnut and walnut veneer, *c*. 1725. The drop-in seat is covered with the original olive-green cut Genoa velvet. The carved and applied shells on the splats and seat rails and the carved shell motifs on the knees of the cabriole legs are crisp and lively and lend distinction to the piece. Toledo Museum of Art, Ohio. Gift of Florence Scott Libbey, 1960

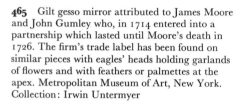

465 Gilt gesso mirror attributed to James Moore and John Gumley who, in 1714 entered into a partnership which lasted until Moore's death in 1726. The firm's trade label has been found on similar pieces with eagles' heads holding garlands of flowers and with feathers or palmettes at the apex. Metropolitan Museum of Art, New York. Collection: Irwin Untermyer

466 *Centre*: Bureau dressing table of walnut and burr walnut veneer, *c*. 1725. The bevelled mirror has a border of gilt gesso. Cabinet pieces of this period successfully avoid hard lines and harsh angles. Metropolitan Museum of Art, New York. Collection: Irwin Untermyer

467 *Above right*: The Saloon, Holkham Hall, Norfolk. The decoration and furniture were designed for Lord Leicester by William Kent. The walls of the Saloon are hung with crimson velvet and Kent's sumptuous gilt chairs have their original green velvet upholstery. Reproduced by permission of the Earl of Leicester

468 *Right*: The Painted Parlour, Rousham House. William Kent redesigned the Parlour in *c*. 1738 and painted the ceiling with grotesques. The splendid Palladian marble chimney-piece is surmounted by a carved and gilt overmantel. Kent's furniture includes the side table, chairs and stool in carved mahogany, partly gilt. Reproduced by permission of T. Cottrell-Dormer, Esq., Rousham, Oxfordshire

The English domestic interior at the outset of Hanoverian rule evoked just this atmosphere of rational calm which Pope demanded. The Palladian movement was in its infancy and was preoccupied at first with the establishment of new rules of taste. But this dawning vision of Classical correctness and an atmosphere of self-conscious good breeding required a background of elegant restraint. Contemporary paintings show that rooms in middle-class houses were often modestly furnished, suggesting a mood of cool primness. A carved overmantel, crowned by a broken pediment, carved overdoors or painted *sopraporti* represented quiet and formal features of interior design.

Much fine furniture of George I's reign was made of walnut and also veneered with walnut. On such pieces carved ornament was mainly confined to the shell on the knee of a chair—or table leg. Seaweed marquetry, still found on Queen Anne pieces, lost popularity and the beauty of the surface depended entirely on the natural figure of the veneer. Form and harmony were paramount, as befitted so rational an age. The dominant feature was the serpentine line. Most happily expressed in the gently flowing sweep of the chair back, it was answered in the curves of the seat and generous bend of the cabriole leg. These bold, full lines of the spoon-back, the cabriole leg of rounded section and the claw-and-ball foot were all features of George I chairs, although they are often erroneously ascribed to the Queen Anne period. This type of chair, with either a drop-in or stuffed-over seat, remained, in fact, in general use until the mid-century and constantly appeared in scenes of domestic life by contemporary painters such as Hogarth, Arthur Devis, or Joseph Highmore. It was also shown on mid-18th-century trade cards and clearly, at

this late date, satisfied conservative patrons when bolder taste demanded new designs. Sometimes, instead of the veneered splat, the chair back was upholstered. Settees for two people, with shepherd's crook arms of walnut, were usual and sets of stools were made *en suite* with chairs. Winged armchairs, already common in the 17th century, were made in the early Georgian period, sometimes with cabriole legs. The cost of textile coverings limited the use of fine upholstered seat furniture in middle-class houses. In noble mansions, on the other hand,

This little Louis XVI *ottomane* of *c*.1780 is carved with rope moulding around the curves of the back and with a key pattern along the seat rail. The legs are tapered and fluted. The work table was made by Riesener in 1788 for the *cabinet intérieur* of Marie Antoinette at Saint Cloud. The top is of lozenge marquetry, and the drawer has a slide which transforms it into a writing table. Musée Nissim de Camondo, Paris

The *grand salon* at the Musée Camondo is decorated with carved panelling painted white and gilt, *c*. 1775-80. The *meuble d'appui* beneath the oval painting is one of a pair with elaborate gilt bronze mounts and with a Japanese lacquer panel in the centre. It bears the stamp of Weisweiler and dates from 1780-90. The round table in the centre was made in about 1770 by Martin Carlin. The elaborate gallery is in imitation of basketwork and the drawer-fronts are mounted with Sèvres porcelain. The chairs which date from 1780-5 are covered with Aubusson tapestry and the *marquise* or small settee is stamped by Georges Jacob. The carpet is Savonnerie.

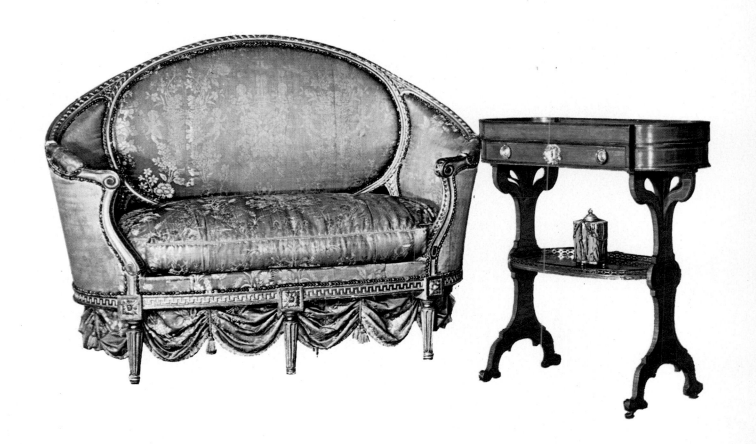

an upholstered suite of parcel gilt walnut chairs or a set of
462 carved and gilt gesso chairs might furnish a state room. The
sumptuous quality of gesso was suited to formal grandeur.
465 Carved gesso mirror frames, side tables and stands for lacquer
322 cabinets, lent a restrained magnificence to state rooms. Cabinet
323 furniture of veneered walnut included small pieces such as knee-
466 hole chests and dressing tables, as well as tallboys and bureau-
324 bookcases with domed crestings. The cabinet-on-stand, with
straight cornice, supported on cabriole legs was also a feature of
the early Georgian room and echoed with unassuming grace the
463 mood of the age.

Palladian Taste

By the accession of George II in 1727, the Palladian movement
was already established. Colin Campbell's work, *Vitruvius
Britannicus*, attracted the attention of Lord Burlington who had
returned from a journey to Italy to celebrate his twenty-first
birthday in 1715. An active and exceedingly rich young man
and a Whig, Burlington was ready to use his money and taste in
support of Palladian ideals. Both lent him, at so crucial a
moment, a quite exceptional power. But he needed experience
and scholarship if he were to achieve his aims. In 1719 he set off
again to Italy to study the work of Palladio. He returned in the
same year, wholly committed to Classical taste and as ardent as
Lord Shaftesbury had been in the previous generation in his
revolt against the indiscipline of Baroque. He brought with him
to England a young Yorkshireman, William Kent, whose work
as a designer of interiors and furniture was to be of unusual
brilliance.

Lacking in means and social position, Kent had been fortunate enough to be sent to Italy to study painting ten years
previously. His studies there had ranged beyond the strict con-
fines of painting. Among the distinguished English travellers
whom he met was Thomas Coke, later first Earl of Leicester, the
future builder of Holkham in Norfolk. He spent several months
with Coke in 1714 and again in 1716 and 1717, visiting Italian
cities and purchasing pictures and sculpture for the future Earl's
collection. Their days together must have been stimulating
since they involved rigorous sightseeing and Kent had the time
and enthusiasm to sketch details of the buildings which interested him.

Back in London with Lord Burlington, Kent at first set to
work as a painter, a field in which he was not to excel. But more
profitable for his future career was the task he undertook of
publishing the *Designs of Inigo Jones*. The close study of these
models of Palladian correctness, upon which he had been engaged for three years, appeared in 1727 and proved both a
discipline and a stimulant. In future, he was to direct all his
energies to the practice of architecture in which he included the
designing of interiors and furniture and the planning of landscape gardens.

In the meantime, Lord Burlington had become the most distinguished amateur architect in the country and his influence
was vital. The ideals of the Palladian movement had won the
support of enlightened patronage and many cultivated noblemen shared Lord Burlington's abilities. For the planning of
their new and severely correct houses there was precedent
enough in the designs of Palladio and Inigo Jones. But upon
what was the furniture to be based? There were no Classical or
readily available Italian Renaissance examples to offer guidance. For interiors, Inigo Jones's formal, pedimented overmantels were, of course, familiar to Kent. Indeed his own rooms

469 Carved and gilt console table with marble
top after a design by the architect, Henry
Flitcroft, c. 1735. Console tables were usually
designed in pairs and fulfilled a decorative rather
than a practical need. They were not, in fact,
'movable' furniture and as important features in
the plan of a room, were often designed by
architects. Temple Newsam House, Leeds

470 One of a pair of carved and gilt pedestals
in the form of terms supporting Ionic capitals
festooned with leaves, c. 1735. This design goes
back to William Kent, but a drawing by the
architect, John Vardy, shows scroll supports of
the same type as those on this piece. Victoria
and Albert Museum, London

471 Carved and partly gilt mahogany settee,
c. 1735. One of a pair made for Lord North at
Wroxton Abbey, Oxfordshire. Classical motifs,
such as the wave ornament carved on the apron,
the scale pattern which appears on the scroll legs
and the money pattern on the stretchers and on
the uprights of the back, are typical of Kent's
work and indeed of early Georgian pieces in the
second quarter of the 18th century. Victoria
and Albert Museum, London

The Green State Bedroom at Houghton Hall, Norfolk. The house
was begun in 1722 by Colin Campbell for Sir Robert Walpole, and
the interiors are thought to have been decorated and largely
furnished by William Kent. The great double shell, towering up to
the canopy achieves a sculptural importance which makes it the focal
point of the room. This motif may have been suggested by a design
for a State Bed by Daniel Marot. Reproduced by permission of
The Marquess of Cholmondely. Photograph: *Country Life*

468   included such features. But Kent was flamboyant and a man of exuberant spirits. His patrons were extremely wealthy and most of them much travelled. It would have been impossible for them, in spite of their rules of taste, to have been quite untouched by Continental fashions and the splendours they had seen in Roman or Genoese Baroque palaces. At Houghton Hall, Norfolk, where Sir Robert Walpole entrusted the interiors and furnishing to Kent, the state rooms reflect an altogether Baroque magnifi-

467   cence. Nearby, at Holkham, the hall and saloons evoke a stricter mood and perhaps Kent's natural verve was held in check by Lord Leicester. But in spite of this, a sense of dramatic grandeur overshadows any underlying deference to Palladian example. Stuccoed ceilings, sometimes gilt, Genoese velvet hangings, rich, smooth marble and overmantels boldly carved with scrolling brackets, masks and figures, give an air of magnificent opulence. It is as though the ordered theories of the ancient Classical world, of which Palladio's work was a symbol, were cherished by these 18th-century Palladians as a romantic ideal. In practice, sobriety and correctness stayed outside the front door, while Kent's feeling for drama brought new brilliance to the interior and furniture.

Plate facing page 129
467
    Kent thought of his rooms rather as he planned his landscape gardens. They offered him an irresistible opportunity for creating romantic vistas. He enjoyed the view across a great saloon or up a sweeping flight of stairs. Each room contained imposing features to catch the eye. A vast scallop shell presided with towering elegance over the green state bed at Houghton. Perhaps a pair of console tables of sculptural splendour presented a focal point, just as a garden statue stood out at the end of a shaded walk. Only furniture of noble proportions could maintain its presence in such splendid surroundings. With his memories of Italy and his debt to French ornamentalists, the furniture Kent designed achieved just that sense of startling grandeur which was needed. His own experience of French Baroque was limited, but he knew the engravings of the prolific

478
469   designer, Jean Le Pautre and those of the Huguenot, Daniel Marot. Both he and his contemporary architects, such as John Vardy and Henry Flitcroft, made use of them. They conceived of furniture as part of the design of a room. Carved and gilt mirrors hung *en suite* with pier tables. Their size and weight

Plate facing page 129
471
470   made it impractical to move them and they were virtually architectural features. Chairs inevitably fulfilled functional rather than decorative needs, but the large sets made for Palladian mansions, often with carved and gilt frames, cabriole legs and lion-paw feet, contributed to the formal plan of the room. Pedestals for the support of candelabra, marble busts or porcelain vases, flanked the pier walls. Their symmetrical disposition was

472   essential. Sconces, too, demanded ordered arrangement, but there were other wall fittings besides. Brackets were needed upon which busts and bronzes, brought back by travellers returning from the Grand Tour, could be shown to advantage. General Dormer's collection of bronzes was set out upon a series of wall

468   brackets in the Painted Parlour which Kent designed for him at Rousham in Oxfordshire.
    Gilt furniture and table tops of marble or porphyry suited the lofty halls and magnificent saloons of the wealthy. But by the 1730s and 1740s an increasingly prosperous middle-class was ready to share the ambitious ideals of the leaders of fashion. Carvers and cabinet-makers quickly followed the lead in furniture design given by fashionable architects. Cabinet-pieces re-

473
474
475   flected the cult of architecture. Bookcases were surmounted with heavy cornices or pediments and sometimes incorporated fluted pilasters. Chests and commodes with curving outlines, perhaps supported on heavy lion-paw feet, echoed the opulence of Baroque and particularly the manner of Louis XIV's cabinet-makers. These pieces were very often of Cuban mahogany, a rich, close-grained wood which only gradually replaced walnut in popularity as the century advanced. Chairs, in fact, were either of walnut or mahogany until the middle of the century and were often boldly carved with vigorous Baroque lion masks or eagle heads.
    Surveying these years, from 1715 to 1740, we can see that a furniture style had come into being in England which presented more than one strange paradox. In a society governed by ideals of Classical virtue and theories of logic and reason, the most fashionable furniture was yet magnificently Baroque, displayed

472 *Above*: One of a pair of wall-lights of carved mahogany intended to support a candle or lamp, *c.* 1740, and clearly inspired by an engraved design. The frame surrounding the mask, with its scrolls and leaves, recalls a design for a clock case included in Batty Langley's *Treasury of Designs* published in 1740. This, in turn, had been copied from a German pattern book by Johann Friedrich Lauch. It is interesting to see how the international use to which such designs were put led to the rapid interchange of ideas. Lady Lever Art Gallery, Port Sunlight, Cheshire

473 *Above right*: Carved mahogany bookcase, formerly at Rokeby Hall, Yorkshire, *c.* 1730-40. The formal, architectural character of this piece accords with Palladian taste. The carving of the egg-and-tongue mouldings is of extremely high quality, while the dignified proportions require the setting of a spacious library.

474 *Right*: Cabinet-on-stand, mahogany and mahogany veneer with engraved brass inlay and gilt bronze mounts, *c.* 1735. Compared with the modest cabinet-on-stand of some ten years earlier, shown in the Devis portrait (see illustration 463), this piece is of particular magnificence. The use of brass inlay in cabinet-making had been made fashionable in France in the late 17th century by Boulle and English pieces combining brass inlay with mahogany veneer reflected an interest in this technique, already exploited so successfully on the Continent. Victoria and Albert Museum, London

475 *Below*: Commode of carved mahogany and mahogany veneer, *c.* 1730. This is one of the earliest English commodes. The sarcophagus shape derives from French example. Although this early piece has a marble top, a feature of French commodes throughout the 18th century, English commodes of the mid-century usually have mahogany tops. Victoria and Albert Museum, London

in settings of imaginative splendour. Derived from Italian and French example, it had been conceived to suit the taste not of a royal Court but of noblemen and landed gentry, and it had become an essential expression of English living. Kent's designs for furniture have a panache which gives them a character of their own. But apart from his personal and original contribution, the work of both architects and cabinet-makers offered, for English taste of the time, an entirely new vision. And yet, in comparison with modern taste on the Continent, it was positively reactionary. Kent had found inspiration in the earlier achievements of the Baroque age. But in fact, his own contemporaries in France had already abandoned Baroque and were deeply involved in new decorative schemes at the Court of Louis XV. It was now the fresh charms of French *rocaille* which were to arouse admiration and encourage imitators in England.

The Rococo Style

Rococo provided a new freedom in comparison with the formal symmetrical grandeur of Baroque. Lively 'C' scrolls, interlaced with flowers, formed a decorative background for picturesque motifs. French architects, painters and designers had been responsible for the gradual development of the style. By 1730 it had reached maturity in France and the designs, in particular, of Juste Aurèle Meissonier were bringing him commissions not only from the French Court but from all over Europe. Architect, sculptor, painter, decorator and furniture designer, he must

have astonished conservative taste in England by his use of rich swirling curves and bold asymmetry. Among his first English patrons was the Duke of Kingston, for whom he designed, in 1735, Rococo silver tureens and a table-centre. English goldsmiths, especially those of Huguenot descent, were quick to follow the French lead and were the first among English craftsmen to handle the style with freedom. Engraved Rococo ornament on silver salvers, trays or bowls, composed of asymmetrical leafy scrolls and flowers, appeared shortly after 1730, at a moment when, in other fields, quite a different mood was dominant. English cabinet-makers, in fact, were not yet ready to follow the example of the goldsmiths and engravers. Nevertheless fine cabinet-pieces made in the early 1730s are sometimes found with both silver and brass lock-plates engraved with Rococo ornament.

This style, so much at variance with Classical ideals, was hardly pleasing to professional architects. As late as 1749 Lord Chesterfield's architect, Isaac Ware, acquiesced unwillingly in his demands for Rococo stucco decoration in the drawing room of his new house. But although the new Rococo style did not disturb architecturally the sober balance of English houses, it offered exciting possibilities to designers and craftsmen concerned with their interior decoration. English stuccoists and wood carvers acquired technical skill from Italian craftsmen working in England. They were among the first to exploit the new mode from France by introducing 'C' scrolls, combined with masks and floral motifs, and eventually free-flowing asym-

477 *Above:* Detail showing the engraved brass lock-plate on the mahogany bureau-bookcase in the previous illustration. The asymmetrical cartouche, composed of flame-like motifs and scrolling leaves, is fully Rococo and reflects the manner of French designers of the 1730s. In England, engravers and goldsmiths were among the first craftsmen to handle the Rococo style with ease.

479 *Below:* Detail of a stucco ceiling in Linley House, Bath. The house was built in 1742 and the plasterwork was undertaken by a certain John Hutchins. This detail represents *Summer* while the other three Seasons appear in the remaining three corners of the ceiling. The leaves breaking out from scrolls and the flowers surrounding the head of *Summer* have a Rococo flavour, although the design retains a certain formality.

478 *Above:* Design for a side table, plate 32 from William Jones's *The Gentlemens or Builders Companion*, published in 1739. Although the design is not wholly free of the Palladian manner of Kent and his contemporaries, it nevertheless suggests a new appreciation of lighter forms acquired from a knowledge of French fashions.

480 *Below:* Side table of carved mahogany with *verde antico* marble top, *c.* 1740. The carving on the apron and the legs of this piece displays the virtuosity of the best London carvers of the mid-18th century, while the heads have an individuality which distinguishes them from the earlier Classical masks. The piece may have been inspired by the design by William Jones shown above. Victoria and Albert Museum, London

476 *Above:* Bureau-bookcase veneered with mahogany and with engraved brass inlay, *c.* 1740. In this piece, a triangular broken pediment replaces the earlier domed pediment surmounting the cabinet shown in illustration 474. The pedestal in the centre is intended to support a bust. The figured veneers on the drawers and the door panels, carefully matched, are evidence of the high quality of the piece. Iveagh Bequest, Kenwood, London

483 Pen-and-ink drawing of a side table, *c.* 1750, by the carver, cabinet-maker and designer, John Linnell. Although Linnell later produced some charming Rococo designs, this is an early drawing, for the shaggy legs and lion's paws and the heavy mask in the apron seem to look back to Baroque rather than forward to Rococo. Victoria and Albert Museum, London

481 Engraved design for a chair from a set by Gaetano Brunetti, dated 1736 and entitled *Sixty Different Sorts of Ornaments*. Brunetti was an Italian working in England and his designs were among the earliest for Rococo furniture to be published in England

482 Carved mahogany chair, *c.* 1740. An early example of Rococo, perhaps inspired by the design of Gaetano Brunetti. The tall back recalls the shape of earlier chairs, but the ornament in the form of carved Rococo scrolls and leaves is new. These are rather formally dispersed as though they presented an unfamiliar problem to the chairmaker. Collection: J. F. Hayward, Esq

486 *Below*: Gilt gesso mirror, *c.* 1745. The long, gentle curves combined with conventional masks, and the cresting, in which the outlines of a broken pediment are hardly disguised, are all features of the first phase of Rococo in England. The piece was perhaps inspired by Lock's early designs for sconces, published in 1744.

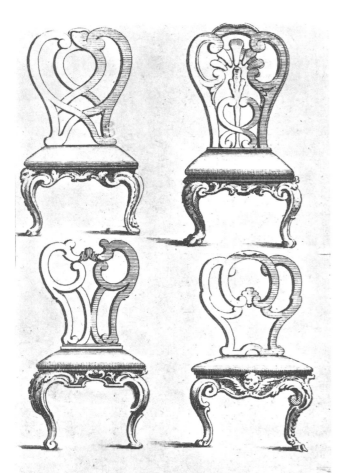

485 Carved walnut chair, *c.* 1745. The back is made of three separate layers, first a foundation of straight-grained walnut, then a veneer of figured walnut and finally the applied carved details. The pierced, shell-shaped design recalls De La Cour's designs. Victoria and Albert Museum, London

484 *Above*: Engraved designs for chairs, *c.* 1745, by De La Cour. As early examples of Rococo furniture, these chairs, with their heavy cabriole legs, are rather cumbersome. They retain many features of earlier Baroque fashions, such as the high back and the lion-paw foot.

487 *Right*: Carved and gilt figure of a dragon, *c.* 1755. Detail from a japanned *chinoiserie* bed made for Badminton House, Gloucestershire, probably by Chippendale's firm. Victoria and Albert Museum, London

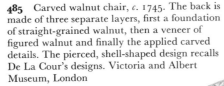

488 Ceiling decorated with stucco in the 'Gothick' style, c. 1765. Claydon House, Buckinghamshire; National Trust

489 Carved mahogany pedestal table, c. 1750. By releasing a pin beneath the supporting platform it is possible to turn the table top sideways. The carved ornament on the legs and the elegantly scrolled feet are evidence of a more confident approach towards the Rococo style on the part of cabinet-makers.

490 *Above*: One of a pair of writing desks of *bombé* form veneered with mahogany and inlaid with brass and with gilt bronze mounts, c. 1750. This desk is one of a group of several pieces, all lavishly mounted with gilt bronze or inlaid with brass and made by the London cabinet-maker J. Channon. Victoria and Albert Museum, London

491 *Right*: Armchair of carved mahogany, c. 1755. The chair is similar in manner to those described as 'French Chairs' in Chippendale's *Director*. The cabriole legs, carved with scrolls and leaf ornament, terminate in curl-over feet.

metrical ornament. Pattern books containing engraved designs for ceilings, doorways and chimney-pieces were issued by architects and builders and these began gradually to include the new devices. Some examples of carved furniture were contained in *The Gentlemens or Builders Companion*, published in 1739 by the architect William Jones. His designs for pier tables, intended to be executed either in mahogany or soft wood, gessoed and gilt, at once suggest a lighter touch than Kent's and caught something of the new spirit of French Rococo.

Pattern books offered a choice to the patron and a model to the craftsman which could be varied at will. This practice of publishing furniture designs was to grow in the course of the century and both drawings and engravings provide valuable evidence of the gradual development of the Rococo style in England. A few designs for chairs were included among the set of engraved ornamental motifs published in London in 1736 by an Italian, Gaetano Brunetti. They inspired some early Rococo carved mahogany chairs with tall backs and rich curves, which suggest an Italian ancestry. They are curiously heavy and the new Rococo style is handled a little uneasily, as though the carver were more accustomed to weighty Baroque forms than the curvaceous elegance of French example. Indeed, in these years of transition, Baroque features were not immediately abandoned. Both cabinets-on-stands and side tables made in about 1740 or soon after survive, virtually weighed down by heavy scrolls—the cabriole legs, finishing in lion paws, carved to represent the furry skin of an animal. In such pieces Kent's ponderous manner is strangely combined with new romantic themes.

A series of pattern books published in London between 1741 and 1746 containing lively Rococo ornamental motifs and including designs for chairs, were issued by a Frenchman working in England called De La Cour. His chair backs were composed of interlaced bands, a feature often used, with variations, a little later in the century by English designers such as Matthew Darly, Ince and Mayhew, Robert Manwaring and Copland. De La Cour's designs probably inspired a type of early Rococo chair in which the carved back consists of interlaced bands arranged in a fan shape. It was introduced soon after 1740 and was popular throughout the middle of the century. As yet the means of adapting Rococo motifs to furniture design had hardly been explored. Carvers' pieces, such as console tables and mirrors, intended as features of interior design, rather than practical furniture, were the first to reflect a more daring manner. Matthias Lock published in 1744 a set of designs for mirrors, entitled *Six Sconces*. This was followed, two years later, by *Six Tables*. Both these sets are of primary importance, for they interpreted French *rocaille* with a new freedom and provided a challenge to the carver. He now required not only skill but inventiveness. Lock's designs included 'C' scrolls, flowers and masks. Birds, winged dragons and leaping hounds were entwined in frothy, wave-like ornaments and dolphins slithered under cascades of water. Lock's workshop was in Tottenham Court Road in London but unfortunately little is known of his work as a carver. Notes written on his own surviving drawings have preserved for us the names of a few of his patrons such as Earl Poulett and Lord Holderness, and a number of the pieces he made for Earl Poulett have been identified. In general, though, it is seldom possible to attribute pieces to a particular hand or workshop. Many carved and gilt sconces and console tables survive, inspired by Lock's designs in these two publications. Among them, the mirror frames, composed of gently curving, almost flaccid scrolls, suggest a new confidence. Such pieces belong to the first phase of the Rococo in England in which there was real understanding of the need to combine form and ornament.

The use of picturesque themes in interior decoration and furniture design had come to stay and the revival in England of the Gothic style was an early expression of this romantic indulgence. Unlike Rococo, however, which in England appealed to decorators rather than architects, 18th-century Gothic first appeared as an architectural style, introduced in a spirit of mock medievalism. Encouraged by Batty Langley's *Gothic Architecture Improved*, published in 1742, which included engraved designs for Gothic chimney-pieces, it became a fashionable mode of interior decoration. Sanderson Miller, an amateur architect, designed Gothic furniture as a *jeu d'esprit*. In 1749 George Lyttelton wrote to him about the chairs to be designed for his house,

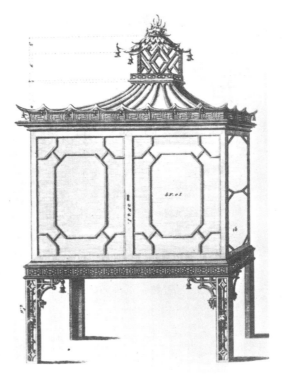

492 *Above left*: Mahogany chair with pierced and carved splat and cabriole legs carved with cabochons and leaf ornament *c.* 1755. Designs for chairs of this type were included in all the editions of Chippendale's *Director* and in other contemporary pattern books. Chairs were rarely executed precisely in accordance with any one design.

493 *Above centre*: Design for a china case. Plate CVIII in the 1754 edition of Chippendale's *Director*. Although this design seems so exotic it was, in fact, carried out, for Chippendale tells us 'This design I have executed with great satisfaction to the Purchaser'. The piece to which he referred may have been the padouk china cabinet probably made between 1748 and 1752 for Joseph Damer of Milton Abbey, Dorset, which still exists.

494 *Above right*: Design for a 'Gothick' bed. Plate XXIX of the 1754 edition of Chippendale's *Director*. 'This cornice will look extremely well if properly work'd', the author observed.

495 *Right*: Pedestal desk of mahogany and mahogany veneer, *c.* 1750. The carved ornament on this piece echoes similar features in Chippendale's design on Plate XLII of the *Director* (1754). Desks of this type stood in the centre of a library.

Hagley Hall in Worcestershire: 'You know they are not to be common chairs but in a Gothic form'. Horace Walpole, on the other hand, brought true antiquarian zeal to his plans for gothicising his villa at Strawberry Hill, Twickenham, upon which he started in that same year. After the middle of the century, Gothic features were incorporated in many fashionable houses, and by this time both cabinet-pieces and chairs sometimes included Gothic motifs, such as ogival or pointed arches, pinnacles and crockets.

More readily introduced into schemes of interior decoration and particularly into designs for carvers' pieces were the exotic *chinoiserie* motifs which presented another aspect of the taste for the picturesque. Oriental birds, imaginary pagoda-like structures, bells, lattice-work and Chinamen provided themes not only for porcelain decorators and goldsmiths, but also for stuccoists, woodcarvers and cabinet-makers. These romantic visions of the charms of the East were neither confined to English taste nor were they entirely new. They derived from the decoration on Oriental porcelain and on lacquer screens and cabinets which had long been popular in England. Chinese wallpaper also provided a source of inspiration. In England, Matthias Lock, with a collaborator named Copland, published in 1752 *A New Book of Ornaments*, a set of twelve designs for mirrors, console tables, wall lights, a candlestand and a chimney-piece. Here, for the first time in designs of this kind, *chinoiserie* played an important role. Carvers' pieces were suited to imaginative treatment and gilt mirrors and girandoles, in particular, often included pseudo-Oriental features and Chinamen poised in airy structures of scrolls and leafy branches. The decorative treatment of

stucco ceilings and wall panels also reflected the fascination of this theatrical vision of the East and many houses had rooms decorated and furnished in the Chinese taste.

By the mid-18th century, the freedom and originality which Rococo permitted was generally accepted. Cabinet-makers were now combining fluent lines with carved Rococo features on tables, chairs and case furniture. Mahogany was the most popular wood. Supplies were imported from Cuba and San Domingo, and, in the second half of the century, from Honduras. The last two varieties produced a fine figure for veneering. Cuban mahogany, in particular, was crisp for the carver. Large numbers of cabinet-making firms existed in London. Many were big undertakings, advertising themselves as upholsterers, cabinet-makers, valuers and sometimes also as funeral furnishers. It was the general practice for these firms to hold stocks of the cheaper varieties of furniture, while the fine pieces were made to special order and elaborate carvers' pieces were obtained from specialist carvers. Some firms had branches in provincial centres, but where a large order was concerned, it was quite normal for a leading cabinet-maker to travel to his customer's house to present designs and estimates. In London, the principal firms were centred round the northern boundary of the City of Westminster and particularly in and around St Martin's Lane.

It was to St Martin's Lane that Thomas Chippendale moved in 1753 when his success as a cabinet-maker enabled him to expand his workshop. Here he became the neighbour of the most eminent cabinet-makers of the day, William Vile and John Cobb, whose firm supplied furniture to the Crown. Although Chippendale's workshop appears to have been smaller than that

498 *Above*: China table of mahogany and mahogany veneer, *c.* 1755. The serpentine top is surrounded by a pierced fretwork gallery. An example shown in Plate XXXIIII of Chippendale's *Director* (1754) has stretchers of the same flowing form. Metropolitan Museum of Art, New York. Collection: Irwin Untermyer

496 *Above*: Design for a carved mirror, Plate CXLI in Chippendale's *Director* (1754). These designs often include *chinoiserie* motifs. Rococo mirrors of this type were made in pairs, *en suite* with console tables and candlestands.

499 *Below*: One of a pair of writing tables of carved and gilt mahogany, with marble top, *c.* 1750. This piece is one of a set of five of similar design formerly at Rokeby Hall, Yorkshire, attributed to William Vile. Reproduced by Gracious Permission of Her Majesty the Queen, Buckingham Palace

497 *Above*: One of a pair of commodes veneered with mahogany and with applied carving, *c.* 1755. While French Louis XV commodes often contain two deep drawers, English examples more usually have three drawers or perhaps combine a cupboard with a set of drawers. Designs for a number of such pieces, showing various combinations of cupboards and drawers appeared in Chippendale's *Director*. Lady Lever Art Gallery, Port Sunlight, Cheshire

500 *Below*: Card-table of carved mahogany, the top veneered with kingwood and boxwood, *c.* 1730-40. The Greek key pattern of the frieze is of boxwood. When the hinged top is opened the two rear legs slide back in the so-called 'concertina' action and the ugly gap which occurs in the frieze when there is only one swinging leg is avoided. Victoria and Albert Museum, London

of his neighbour, it was clearly an important establishment and he employed craftsmen for every branch of the trade. But as the head of a firm he was not himself wholly immersed in the technicalities of his craft. He moved in a circle of artists and designers and must have been very much aware of the possibilities which fashionable Rococo taste offered. He was probably at this time in close touch with Matthias Lock, who seems to have worked as a carver either with or for him in the coming years. Chippendale appreciated Lock's originality as a designer and was himself a man of ideas and energy. It was, in fact, his enterprise in publishing an extensive set of furniture designs in the new Rococo manner which brought him publicity in his lifetime and ensures his fame today. Architects' pattern books were, at the time, familiar. Indeed, as we have seen, engraved designs for Rococo ornament, for chairs, and in a more fluent vein, for carvers' pieces had already appeared. But no book, solely devoted to furniture, had hitherto been published in England.

Chippendale's *Gentleman and Cabinet-maker's Director* appeared in 1754. It contained 160 engraved plates and apart from the first few describing the five Classical orders, all were devoted to furniture. They illustrated the full range of furniture of the day and reflected an uninhibited delight in exotic motifs and sinuous curves. Some upholstered 'French Elbow Chairs' had light cabriole legs ending in scrolled feet, the knees carved with cartouches and leaves. Chairs without arms had backs pierced and carved with interlaced scrolls and leaves. Those in the 'Chinese taste' introduced carved pagoda-like shapes or lattice-work in the back, along the seat rails or on the stretchers. Some had legs carved in imitation of bamboo. Lattice-work also appeared on

tables or case furniture. The function of china cabinets suggested an occasion for *chinoiserie*, although designs for many other cabinet-pieces, such as wardrobes or bookcases, retained a certain architectural severity. Gothic idioms appeared in cabinet-pieces and on chairs and there was one design for a 'Gothick' bed. Commodes and tables were sometimes of *bombé* or serpentine form and introduced carved scrolls or flowers from the repertoire of Rococo ornament. The range of designs for carvers' pieces was small but mirrors, girandoles and candlestands include many *chinoiserie* features.

Dedicated to the Earl of Northumberland and subscribed to by the nobility and gentry and by a large number of builders, cabinet-makers and other craftsmen, the *Director* inevitably attracted attention. In preparing his publication, Chippendale had been able to draw upon existing Rococo ornamental designs and his own experience of contemporary fashions. In that sense he did not introduce a new style, but he was the first to issue engravings in which Rococo forms and motifs were applied with such freedom to cabinet furniture and chairs and his plates contributed some new and original ideas.

Of Chippendale's work as a cabinet-maker, little is known. Correspondence with clients and occasional bills survive to tell us something of the orders he fulfilled. The Duke of Atholl, the Duke of Portland, the Earl of Pembroke and the Earl of Dumfries were among his clients and surviving documents have made it possible to identify some of the pieces he made for them. They include both simple, inexpensive pieces and elaborate examples made to special order. Chippendale must have had many clients, although wealthy patrons often ordered upholstery and furni-

502 *Above*: Design for a girandole. From Plate 51 of Thomas Johnson's designs for carvers' pieces published in 1758.

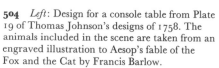

501 *Above*: Carved and gilt console table inspired by a design on Plate 19 of Thomas Johnson's designs of 1758, shown in illustration 504, although the fable scene is omitted. Collection: the Marquis of Waterford, Curraghmore, Co. Waterford

503 *Above*: Carved and gilt girandole, *c.* 1760. After Plate 51 in Thomas Johnson's designs of 1758. While numbers of pieces inspired by Johnson's designs can be found, girandoles have rarely survived on account of their fragility.

504 *Left*: Design for a console table from Plate 19 of Thomas Johnson's designs of 1758. The animals included in the scene are taken from an engraved illustration to Aesop's fable of the Fox and the Cat by Francis Barlow.

ture from several cabinet-makers and his firm was only one of many of high standing in London. Some of the finest pieces for which he is known to have been responsible are those made between 1766 and 1770 for Harewood House, Yorkshire. They are in the Neo-Classical style of those years, not in the traditional Rococo manner which Chippendale used in his *Director*. Pieces after those designs survive, but in the absence of other evidence, they can seldom with any confidence be attributed to Chippendale's workshop. The *Director* could indeed be used as a model by any cabinet-maker and, as a second edition was issued in 1755, a number of firms or individual craftsmen must have owned the publication. In general, the term 'Chippendale' is now loosely and inappropriately used to describe mid-18th century Rococo pieces which evoke the mood or broadly reflect the manner of the *Director* designs.

It was not the practice of English cabinet-makers to sign their pieces, although there are rare examples bearing a signature. The occasional presence of cabinet-makers' labels helps to identify the work of a particular firm. References in contemporary letters, literature, or newspapers throw light on the activities or standing of certain 18th-century craftsmen, while the survival of trade cards has rescued the names of others, of whom nothing else is known. Accounts preserved in the muniment rooms of country houses are of the greatest interest since the pieces described can sometimes be recognised. From these sources we learn of the work of leading cabinet-makers such as John Linnell, William Vile and John Cobb, Samuel Norman, William Hallett and Benjamin Goodison. Among these, examples by Vile and Cobb have attracted particular interest, since

cabinet-pieces supplied by their firm to George III and Queen Charlotte are still at Buckingham Palace today. The firm seems to have favoured a rather formal manner in which the carved detail often included such features as a key pattern, lion masks and a border composed of small flowers alternating with a running ribbon ornament. But particular decorative idioms are seldom peculiar to one firm and attributions without documentary support can only be made with reserve.

The publication of the first two editions of Chippendale's *Director* did more than stimulate a fashion. It immediately provoked competition and it is the appearance of subsequent designs by other carvers and cabinet-makers which provides us with the clearest picture of developing taste. In 1755 a new set of engravings appeared by a hitherto unknown designer and carver. *Twelve Gerandoles* by Thomas Johnson was published from his workshop at Queen Street, Seven Dials, London, and consisted of four sheets containing designs for wall lights to be executed in soft wood, gessoed and gilt. Unhampered by the demands of function, these pieces were particularly well suited to original treatment and to the romantic nature of Rococo. Johnson's designs, with their sharp and piercing outlines, expressed at once a new sense of creative energy. Features from Aesop's Fables, which Johnson knew from Francis Barlow's engraved illustrations to the text, appeared among spiky branches, wiry scrolls, fountains and dripping waterfalls. The designs presented a surrealist world of strange encounters and although the motifs themselves were part of the repertoire of Rococo ornament, they were combined in vital and fresh compositions.

In the course of 1756 and 1757 Johnson issued another series

510 511

499
500

504

505 *Left*: One of a pair of carved and gilt candlestands, *c.* 1760. Compared with the fanciful forms of more overtly Rococo pieces, this presents a modest and restrained appearance foreshadowing the Neo-Classical delight in clear outlines.

506 *Right*: The Library at Rousham House. William Kent was originally responsible for this room but of his work only the ceiling remains. The stuccoist, Roberts of Oxford, was called in in 1765 to redecorate the room, and the stucco overdoors and Rococo surrounds to the pictures are his work. Reproduced by permission of T. Cottrell-Dormer, Esq., Rousham, Oxfordshire

507 *Below right*: Design for a commode. Plate LXVIII of the 3rd Edition of Chippendale's *Director*, 1762. The formal lines of this piece, the use of masks, husk motifs, scale pattern and the shape of the supports all suggest a return to Classical inspiration.

of designs in monthly numbers. These included girandoles, console tables, mirrors, picture frames, chimney-pieces, candlestands and also designs for ceilings. In the next year the whole set appeared in book form, to be followed in 1761 by a second edition under the title *One Hundred and Fifty New Designs*. Both in range and size it was the most important set of designs for carvers' pieces to be published at that time in England. Many of the sheets were reprinted in the 19th century by an unscrupulous publisher who issued them falsely under the name of Chippendale. This was a most unfortunate deception for it destroyed the memory of Johnson's achievement and has caused confusion ever since.

Johnson's *One Hundred and Fifty New Designs* included a wealth of ornamental motifs. Rustic scenes, figures of peasants, jesters or Chinamen, animals and birds, masks, fountains, dolphins and *putti* appeared among the rhythmical scrolls and leafy branches of a mirror frame or entwined in unexpected union on a candlestand. They presented a bold and sparkling approach which was far removed from the gentle manner and flaccid curves of early Rococo. Their vitality inspired the last phase of Rococo in England and was reflected in such animated schemes of interior decoration as that undertaken at Claydon soon after 1760. Of Johnson's own work as a carver we have no documented evidence. Many pieces after his designs survive and the finer examples were probably executed in his workshop. Others must have been the work of contemporary carvers using his designs. They confirm the success of his publications and suggest how widespread was his influence.

Among other cabinet-makers to publish designs for furniture

at about the same time was the firm of Ince and Mayhew. *The Universal System of Household Furniture* appeared as a book probably in 1762, although it was, in fact, undated. Intended to compete with Chippendale's and Thomas Johnson's publications, it included a wide range of Rococo furniture and of carvers' pieces but it was less original than either. The appearance in the same year of the third edition of Chippendale's *Director* provided with 105 new plates, confirmed the popularity of bounding rhythmical lines and writhing forms. In this edition some prominence was given to carved overmantels, mirrors and console tables, in emulation of Johnson's example. But Chippendale also included in this latest work some new designs for cabinet and other pieces which hint at a coming change of taste. Among them were designs for pedestals and, in particular, for a commode which included features of Classical derivation such as rams' heads, key patterns and lion paws. These few designs in a new manner suggest that Chippendale's experiment may have been encouraged by James Stuart's Neo-Classical designs for the furnishing and decoration of Kedleston in Derbyshire and for Spencer House in London which had been prepared in 1757 and 1759.

Neo-Classicism was now, indeed, to advance relentlessly. The year 1762 was crucial. It was then that Robert Adam, succeeding Stuart at Kedleston, turned his attention to furniture design and his influence was to hasten a revolution in fashionable taste. Rococo had flourished for less than thirty years. But against a background of English Palladianism, it had provided an atmosphere of grace and wit. Superseded by the rational elegance of Neo-Classical designs, its airy fantasy was one of the most entrancing contributions of the 18th century to English furniture.

502
504

*Plate
facing page* 144
506
501, 503

507

505

ENGLAND 1765-1800

Clifford Musgrave

In the early 18th century fashions in furniture design were not subject to rapid change. In fact it is often difficult to distinguish the difference in date between an article made in 1715 and one made in 1735. From this latter time onward changes in furniture style followed one upon the other more rapidly. During the years between 1754 and 1762, when the first and third editions of Thomas Chippendale's *The Gentleman and Cabinet-Maker's Director* were published, fashionable patrons became accustomed to Chippendale's fantastic novelties in the French, Chinese and Gothic tastes.

In 1765 hardly any patrons, however much in the vanguard of fashion, suspected what innovations of style lay in store for them. They were barely realised even by the little group of connoisseurs who were then commissioning a promising new architect, Robert Adam, to remodel their houses.

Soon after his return in 1758 from four years' architectural study in Rome, Adam was making a sensation in the fashionable world with interiors created in a novel decorative style. Instead of being based on the lively naturalistic motifs of the Rococo taste of a few years earlier, with its profusion of swirling branches of foliage, rockwork, shell-work and effects of falling water and icicles, or on the solemn and ponderous Classical architecture favoured by the Palladian architects of the first half of the century, the decorations of Robert Adam were in the manner of the delicate stucco reliefs in the baths, tombs and villas of ancient Rome. These decorations included Classical motifs such as strings and festoons of husks or bell-flowers, paterae, highly formalised shell-ornaments, honeysuckle, palm-leaves, and delicate formal running scrolls of foliage which he called the 'flowing *rainceau*' or branch.

Adam was also extremely fond of the brightly painted motifs known as 'grotesques', with which Raphael and his pupils had decorated the loggias of the Vatican and the walls of the Villa Madama in Rome. In 1777 he published with his brother the folio volume of engravings describing *The Works in Architecture of Robert and James Adam*. In the introduction they spoke of 'an almost total change' which they had by then brought about in the form, arrangement and variety of shapes of rooms, and in the decoration of the interiors. Nearly thirty years later, Sir John Soane, architect of the Bank of England, was to refer to the 'electric power' of this revolution in taste which the Adam brothers effected.

The most illuminating guide to the work of Robert Adam is the remarkable collection of over 9,000 drawings now preserved at the Soane Museum in Lincoln's Inn Fields, London, having been bought by Sir John Soane after Adam's death. Several hundred of the drawings are of furniture, and we may trace in them not only the development of Adam's furniture style, but various stages in the evolution of the design of various well-known pieces. Few of the drawings show the furniture as finally executed by the craftsman. It is assumed that those which survive were tentative designs and that mostly the final drawings were sent to the cabinet-makers, from whom they were rarely returned.

The domestic architecture and decorative work of Robert Adam falls into two main phases; the first from about 1760 to 1770, when he was engaged in the remodelling of large country houses, such as Harewood House and Nostell Priory in Yorkshire and Syon House in Middlesex. At this period his style is broad and bold. His ornament is in strong relief, large in scale, and given full effect by appearing in ample areas of undecorated space. Adam's second phase of domestic decoration is from about 1770 to 1780, when he was chiefly engaged in the building and decoration of town houses in London, such as 20 St James's Square, Home House (now The Courtauld Institute), Portman

508 This carved and gilt armchair, designed by Adam as one of a set of chairs and sofas for Sir Laurence Dundas in 1764, is early Georgian in form, with cabriole legs and crested lion-paw feet and bow-shaped back rail, but the carved ornament is of Classical character, consisting of honeysuckle, sphinxes, formal leaf and scroll designs and paterae. Victoria and Albert Museum, London

509 One of Robert Adam's most successful innovations was the dining-room sideboard, flanked by urns or pedestals. This engraving from *The Works in Architecture of Robert and James Adam* represents a group made for Osterley Park, Middlesex, designed in 1767. It shows not only the complete range of dining equipment which Adam devised for the house, but the perfection of fine detail in each article. The delicately shaped baluster legs of the sideboard mark an advance in elegance upon the more sturdy and robust, square legs of Adam's earlier tables.

510 The dining room group of sideboard with pedestals and urns at Harewood House, supplied in 1771, provides one of the most remarkable instances of the masterly interpretation of the Adam style by Thomas Chippendale. The urn and pedestal shown, one of a pair, reveal consummate craftsmanship. Reproduced by Gracious Permission of H.R.H. the Princess Royal, Harewood House, Yorkshire

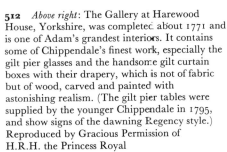

511 *Above*: When Robert Adam had devised a suitable Classical style for the furniture of his interiors, other craftsmen were quick to follow suit. Thomas Chippendale, in particular, rapidly adapted his productions to the prevailing fashion, and the furniture he supplied to Harewood House is the finest of his whole career. This side table provided for the Music Room in 1767 is a particularly magnificent piece. Reproduced by Gracious Permission of H.R.H. the Princess Royal, Harewood House, Yorkshire

512 *Above right*: The Gallery at Harewood House, Yorkshire, was completed about 1771 and is one of Adam's grandest interiors. It contains some of Chippendale's finest work, especially the gilt pier glasses and the handsome gilt curtain boxes with their drapery, which is not of fabric but of wood, carved and painted with astonishing realism. (The gilt pier tables were supplied by the younger Chippendale in 1795, and show signs of the dawning Regency style.) Reproduced by Gracious Permission of H.R.H. the Princess Royal

513 *Left*: This chair is one of a set made in the Adam style in about 1770 for the Drawing Room at Saltram House, Devonshire. Despite the straight, tapering legs and fluted moulding in the seat rail typical of Neo-Classical taste, they still retain the cartouche-shaped backs and curved arms of the Rococo style. The scrolled foliage ornament below the seat rail is unusual. Saltram House, Devonshire; The National Trust

514 *Below*: This fine bow-fronted commode is one of a pair made for Osterley Park in 1773, possibly by John Linnell. No Adam design for the entire commode exists, but there are a number of the various parts and one, inscribed 'Top of Commode for Robert Child Esq', is dated 1773. Victoria and Albert Museum; Osterley Park, Middlesex

Square, and Apsley House, Piccadilly. The rooms at Osterley Park, Middlesex, rebuilt between 1761 and 1780, show the progression from his early style to his last phase. Adam's decoration in this period is smaller in scale, less deeply modelled, and has become very smooth and sophisticated. Eventually it came to be looked upon as effeminate and trivial, and critics like Horace Walpole talked of Adam's 'snippets of embroidery and gingerbread', and Sir William Chambers of 'the harlequinades of Adam', and his 'filigraine toywork'.

From Adam's drawings we can see that the phases in the evolution of his furniture style correspond fairly closely to the two main periods of his architectural and decorative work, although with some irregularity. It is in fact possible to discern four phases of style in his furniture designs. Early (1762-4), Transitional (1765-8), Mature (1769-77) and Late (1778-92).[1] To distinguish between these periods, however, necessitates the detailed study of the drawings and of the furniture executed from them.

Adam's earliest essays in furniture design were based on designs of the early Georgian period. Such a piece is the handsome gilt armchair designed in 1764, now at the Victoria and Albert Museum. The surface decoration consists of honeysuckle, Classical sphinxes and delicate formalised scrolls of foliage from Adam's new repertoire of ornament, but the form of the chair with curved cabriole legs and bow-shaped back rail derives from an earlier period. However, by 1765 Adam had established a completely satisfying Classical style for the furniture of Syon House, with the series of magnificent side tables there. As early as 1762, he had already arrived at a bold simple formula for this furniture, with the sideboard tables he designed in that year for the dining room at Kedleston, Derbyshire. Instead of the curvilinear shapes of the earlier Rococo furniture, they were inspired by furniture in the Classical style, with straight tapering square-section legs, which had been provided by James Stuart in 1759 for Spencer House, St James's, London, and from an early drawing by Stuart for Kedleston. Furniture of this kind from Spencer House may be seen today at Althorp, Northamptonshire. Stuart was nicknamed 'Athenian' by Horace Walpole because he had revealed the beauties of Grecian architecture in his book, *The Antiquities of Athens*, published in 1762. For a time Adam laid aside the Stuart formula while he experimented with early Georgian forms. But he returned to it in his designs for side tables at Syon House. Indeed he expressed it with great confidence in his richly decorated gilt tables in the ante-room of that house with their friezes finely carved with Classical leaf ornament, and in those of the drawing room, where the capitals of the legs consist of ram's heads. All these early pieces, designed in 1765, are satisfyingly bold and masculine.

A delicate and more feminine manner, generally regarded as most typical of Adam's work, is found in the gilt sideboard designed for the Eating Room at Osterley Park, which has legs of delicate baluster shape. An even more marked tendency towards lightness and elegance is evident in the side tables at Saltram House, near Plymouth, Devonshire, designed between 1769 and 1771, with their slender, round tapering legs, and in the side table in the Tapestry Room at Osterley Park, made to Adam's design in 1775 (Soane Vol. 17 No. 8). Of the same date are the delightful pier tables at Nostell Priory, one pair of which has legs in the form of terminal figures holding festoons, while the other pair has oval medallions set in the square tapering legs, and shaped stretchers carrying urns borne by *putti*. Nearly all these tables have scagliola tops either in geometrical designs, as those at Syon House, or decorated with delicate patterns of festoons of

[1] E. Harris: *The Furniture of Robert Adam*, Tiranti, 1963.

515 *Left*: This side table and mirror belong to a pair in the earlier, still Rococo, Velvet Drawing Room at Saltram House, Devonshire, where they act as a prelude to the Adam decoration beyond. They were made by the craftsman Perfetti to a design of Adam, dated 1771. The mirror cresting, formed of sphinxes supporting a medallion, is typical of Adam's middle period. Saltram House, Devonshire; The National Trust

516 *Below*: This engraving of a pier glass is from *The Works in Architecture of Robert and James Adam* (plate VIII). With minor alterations, the design was executed in 1773 for the Dining-Parlour at Kenwood, London, the house enlarged by Adam for Lord Mansfield. This oval form is one of the most beautiful types of mirror designed by Adam; other fine examples are to be seen at Osterley Park and Harewood House. Sir John Soane's Museum, London

517 The State Bed at Osterley Park is probably the most spectacular article of furniture conceived by Robert Adam. The design is similar to that of a small Classical temple for a gentleman's park, with the dome upheld by four columns. Horace Walpole thought the dome 'too theatric and too like a modern head-dress' and asked 'What would Vitruvius have thought of a dome decorated by a milliner?' The posts are decorated with finely painted stripes and lines of minute bell-flowers, while the bed head and tester are ornamented with carved and gilt figures and sphinxes. Victoria and Albert Museum; Osterley Park, Middlesex

518 *Below*: The Etruscan Room at Osterley is a gay, informal little chamber intended as a dressing-room for the adjoining State Bedroom. Horace Walpole spoke of it as 'like a cold bath next to the bed-chamber'. The decorations are in what was believed to be the style of the Etruscans, forerunners of the Romans, but actually the Pompeiian colour scheme of red, green and black derived from late Greek vase decorations and wall-paintings, and Adam planned the various decorative motifs more in the manner of Italian Renaissance grotesques. Victoria and Albert Museum; Osterley Park, Middlesex

519 *Below*: The interior of the domed canopy of the State Bed at Osterley Park is no less magnificent than the exterior, and Robert Adam considered it of such importance that he made a special drawing for it in 1776.

520 The characteristic elegance and delicacy of the Adam period is well expressed in this group of furniture. The marble-topped side table is similar to one supplied by Chippendale to Harewood House, and shield-back chairs were greatly favoured by Hepplewhite. Mallett and Son, Ltd., London

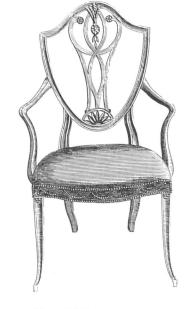

521 *Above*: Shield-back chairs are amongst the most beautiful included in the designs of George Hepplewhite, and the illustration shows two of the many designs he provided of this type in his *Cabinet-Maker and Upholsterer's Guide*, (Plate 4), of 1788 and 1794. In their extreme refinement Hepplewhite's designs closely followed the delicacy of the Adam style. They were devised for the use of any good craftsman and clearly indicate how the style introduced by Adam had spread before long through the middle classes.

522 *Left*: This armchair is remarkable in the way it makes striking use of the decorative motif of a Classical urn with flowers as an openwork device in an oval chair back. Usually such a motif appeared as flat inlay on a cabinet or commode. The chair is veneered in satinwood and kingwood with the fluting and rosettes inlaid in lighter woods. In many respects it resembles one of the Library chairs at Osterley, made by John Linnell, and this chair may well be from the workshop of the same craftsman. Collection: Eric Pasold Esq

husks or bell-flowers, medallions, paterae, shell-ornaments, grotesques and honeysuckle. These pieces of the early 1770s represent Adam's furniture style in its most mature phase, satisfying in form, yet combining refinement and elegance. After 1777 the forms tended to become more nerveless and spindly and the decoration sometimes trivial and niggling. From 1780 onwards painted furniture became increasingly popular, especially with decoration in the 'Etruscan' taste. This style, then believed to be that of the forerunners of the Romans as early as eight centuries B.C., was copied from mural decorations and vase paintings found in Rome, and at Pompeii and Herculaneum. They were in fact late Greek, especially the pottery with red figures on a black ground. The famous Etruscan Room at Osterley Park, much criticised by Walpole as being an anti-climax to the earlier apartments, contains a suite of furniture designed by Adam and painted in the 'Etruscan' style. 518

The range of Adam's furniture was very limited. Comparatively few of his designs for chairs survive, but those for side tables and pier tables are very numerous. These were important to him as part of the permanent unified decorative scheme of a room. Like William Kent earlier in the century, Adam's ideal was to design every detail of all the fittings, furniture and equipment of a room, even, as Soane remarked, 'down to the keyhole of a lady's secretaire'. Adam designed few beds, but the State Bed at Osterley Park for which his drawings survive is truly monumental, with its domed canopy, although Walpole scoffingly likened it to a lady's hat. 517 519

Among the most magnificent creations in Adam furniture are the splendid commodes which were made to his designs or under his inspiration. In the drawing room at Osterley Park are a pair of commodes which are probably the most superb of their kind in existence. Deriving from preliminary drawings by Adam, now in the Soane Museum, one of which is dated 1773, they are of bold semi-circular form, veneered with harewood and satinwood, and inlaid with circular and oval medallions containing figures of Venus and Cupid, Diana and her hounds, and nymphs. 514

One of the most important and far-reaching contributions by Robert Adam to furniture design, was the development of the dining room sideboard as an elaborate group consisting of a long table flanked by urns or pedestals, with a wine-cooler underneath. Such a rich composition was thought by Adam to be appropriate to the splendour of the dining rooms of great houses where, as he asserted, political decisions were made at the table over a bottle. Settings of this kind are to be seen at Harewood House, where the furniture is of rich golden mahogany ornamented with mounts of English ormolu of the greatest richness; and at Saltram House, where the various pieces are delicately painted, in a setting with a gently curving apse. 509 510

Designs for mirrors are probably the most numerous of any class of furniture that Adam produced. But they fall into three main types. One type, more favoured by Adam in the earlier stages of his career, up to about 1768, was the upright 'picture frame' shape, consisting of a broad flat moulding, with stylised foliage and classical ornament. During the 1770s an especially beautiful form of cresting developed, with female figures, fabulous sphinxes or griffins supporting an urn or a medallion. These are seen at Saltram House, Osterley Park and Kenwood House, Hampstead. A distinctive type, continuing into Adam's final period, was based on the design of a Venetian window, having a large centre glass, sometimes with an arched top, flanked by two narrow upright glasses, all in a frame consisting of delicate slender supports, usually in the form of attenuated terminal figures. A third and often very beautiful type was the oval mirror. Sometimes the main frame was broad and flat, but it was frequently surrounded by elaborate festoons. 515 516

The incessant demands made upon Adam prevented him from designing all the furniture for his interiors, but the great craftsmen of the day such as John Linnell, Samuel Norman and above all, Thomas Chippendale, were quick to grasp the principles of the Neo-Classic system of design that he had established. The first two cabinet-makers did in fact often work to Adam's drawings, but Chippendale seems always to have worked independently for Adam's clients, making Neo-Classical furniture for them to his own designs.

Beautiful as Chippendale's productions are in the style of the

523 *Left*: Like so many types of furniture now associated with the name of Hepplewhite, sofas of this design were originally developed by Adam. The long sweeping curve of the back and arms and the depth of the seat are especially pleasing. The shape derives from French models, but the coin-moulding and guilloche ornament are in the early Georgian Classical tradition. The casters are not original to the piece. Mallet and Son, Ltd., London

524 *Right*: The refinement and elegance of late 18th century design is manifest in this secretaire-cabinet, especially in the graceful vase-like shaping of the glazing bars. The curved and splayed feet and apron piece are also typical of the period. The drawer-front lets down to form a writing surface. Mallett and Son, Ltd., London

526 *Below*: The sideboard with pedestal cupboards and table drawer combined in one piece was developed by Hepplewhite about 1788 from the separate units introduced by Robert Adam some twenty years earlier, and became so successful as a piece of dining-room equipment that it was made in sizes small enough for the most modest household. Norman Adams, Ltd., London

525 *Below*: The window seat, upholstered stool, or small 'sopha' as it was often called in the Adam period was one of the most popular articles of furniture of this time. The form varied little from piece to piece, but the material and details of ornament differed greatly. In this example of *c.* 1785 the Classical motifs are painted, and the legs are round, tapering and fluted. Temple Williams Ltd., London

French, Gothic and Chinese taste shown in his book *The Gentleman and Cabinet-Maker's Director*, they are surpassed in excellence by the furniture he supplied in the severe and dignified Classical manner of the Adam movement.

At Nostell Priory, Yorkshire, some early examples of Chippendale's new style may be seen, such as the library writing table of 1767, which is boldly carved with Classical motifs, and the bedroom and dressing-room furniture which has superficial ornament only, in green and gold japanning.

One of the great masterpieces of Chippendale's latest style is the magnificent library table in the gallery at Harewood House, made about 1771. This noble piece is satisfyingly plain in form, while the decorative urns, vases, honeysuckle and festoons of husks and bell-flowers in harewood, rosewood and satinwood are inlaid in pale golden mahogany. Other splendid pieces of similar character are the pair of tall china cabinets that were once at Panshanger and are now to be seen at Firle Place, near Lewes in Sussex.

Many articles of Adam furniture possess features characteristic of French furniture of the late Louis XVI period, such as delicate round baluster-shaped chair legs, chair backs of oval and cartouche shape, and slender round tapering legs of side tables. These features were used by Adam as early as the 1760s, and it was long believed that they originated in Adam's work and were later adopted by the French, for they are not, in fact, found in the productions of that country until the late 1770s. However, it has now been established that certain basic Classical features were introduced by pioneer French designers between 1756 and 1763, and gave rise to the statement by Grimm in the latter year that 'tout est à Paris à la grecque'. Such furniture was found only in the houses of a few *avant-garde* Classical enthusiasts in

Paris, and it was not generally adopted in France until the late 1770s and '80s, years after Adam had been making full use of these elements in a more delicate and feminine way, which became characteristic of the later Louis XVI style.

Adam furniture was designed for a few great houses. Especial interest lies in the fact that it was inspired, if not always actually designed, by an exceptionally accomplished architect, and that much of it can still be seen in the great houses for which it was originally intended.

The revolution in the spirit of English furniture that was brought about by Robert Adam in the great houses quickly spread through the fashionable world generally, and before long throughout every class of the furniture trade. The principal craftsmen and cabinet-making firms which had worked for Adam and his clients, such as Samuel Norman, William France, William Beckwith, John Linnell, Ince and Mayhew, Thomas Cobb, and Thomas Chippendale, must have been the first to spread the influence, and soon the new system of Classical form and decorative motifs was adopted by the big furniture workshops such as Seddon and Sons, who employed over four hundred workmen, and the firm of Thomas Shearer.

The demand for furniture designs in the new style among smaller firms and individual craftsmen, not only in London, but in the provinces and the country, must have been enormous. This need was met in 1788 by the publication of a work entitled *The Cabinet-Maker and Upholsterer's Guide*, under the name of G. Hepplewhite and Co. George Hepplewhite had died in 1786, and it was his widow who published the *Guide*. It was the most useful and comprehensive book of furniture designs to appear since Chippendale's *Director*, and was such a success that a second edition was produced in the following year, and a third in

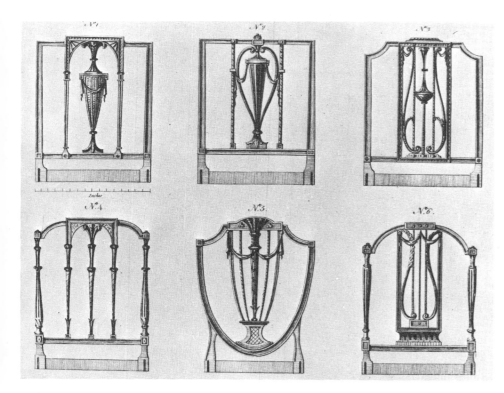

1794. The great merit of the book was that it showed designs for articles of domestic furniture, such as bedroom and dressing-room furniture. Except for beds, Robert Adam had not concerned himself with these.

Despite this wide range of different articles, certain types of furniture are especially associated with the name Hepplewhite, which has become a synonym of grace and elegance. First of all are the designs for chairs, which include a beautiful series with backs of oval-, heart- and shield-shape. The influence of Adam is seen in the shaping of the back-splats as urns or vases, festoons of husks or drapery, and wheat-ears, rosettes, and petals of flowers. The Prince of Wales's feathers was a favourite decoration, either carved or painted. The legs of Hepplewhite chairs were usually straight and tapering, either round or square, and with leaf ornament.

521 Plate facing page 145

Sofas were especially delicate in structure, although larger and more relaxing in character than Adam would have allowed—the seats were deeper from back to front. The legs were of slender baluster form, and the Gothic taste was becoming fashionable once again, causing legs to be shaped sometimes as a Gothic clustered column. The French types of sofa known as *confidante*, which had a chair-like section added at each end, and the *duchesse*, which was an armchair converted into a day-bed by means of a large matching upholstered stool, were also popular.

523

Hepplewhite perpetuated the formal type of sideboard group introduced by Robert Adam, having a central table flanked by urns. He also featured the newer type combining table and pedestals in one piece, which was especially popular in the smaller houses. The pedestal cupboards contained a wine cellaret on one side, and on the other, which was lined with sheet-iron, a rack for plates and a spirit lamp for heating them.

526

Pier tables, side tables and console tables formed a class of furniture for which Adam himself had made many drawings. Hepplewhite's designs owe a substantial debt to articles such as these. When made of satinwood or mahogany, they were inlaid with delicate Classical designs, but painted decoration in pale colours was also much used for this type of furniture. Card tables, Pembroke tables and other occasional furniture were also frequently treated in a highly decorative fashion, either by inlaying or by painting.

529

Library tables, bookcases and large cabinets were a class of furniture rarely designed by Adam. The inspiration came directly from Chippendale's *Director*, the basic forms remaining similar to those shown in that work, but with Classical ornament in place of Rococo, Gothic or Chinese decoration.

Another type of article which has become especially characteristic of Hepplewhite elegance is the secretaire-cabinet, in which the base is made like a chest-of-drawers, with the front of the top drawer opening downwards to form a writing surface. The upper stage has glazed doors, the glazing frames embodying either Classical vase-like shapes, designs of drapery, patterns of Gothic tracery, geometrical shapes of diamonds, octagons or other patterns. The tops of such pieces were often shaped as pediments with vases or urns as ornaments.

524

Although only one design for a drawing-room commode appears in the *Guide*, the Hepplewhite period was one in which great numbers were made in the form developed in the days of Robert Adam. The majority were of light mahogany or satinwood, inlaid more or less elaborately with contrasting woods in floral or Classical designs. In some, circular or oval medallions contained inlaid figure subjects, or merely inlays of richly grained woods. Some were painted with pictorial subjects on grounds of pale green or ivory.

Four-poster beds with slender posts also developed from the Chippendale tradition. The posts were usually fluted and with a vase-shaped lower portion carved with formal Classical leaf ornament. The cornices were sometimes straight, but the *Guide* also illustrated highly decorative fitments shaped as pediments with urns or vases at the centres and angles, or as formalised scrolls of foliage. Few of these seem to have survived, possibly because of their great fragility. Indeed, in the majority of existing Hepplewhite beds the cornice is absent, its place being taken by a valance of frilled material similar to the bed hangings.

The full range of bedroom and dressing-room furniture was illustrated in the *Guide*, and includes the distinctive Hepplewhite

527 The chairs shown by Thomas Sheraton in his *Cabinet-maker and Upholsterer's Drawing-book* of 1791-4 were almost all of square-back design, for the straight line in furniture was the distinguishing characteristic of furniture from 1790 onwards. He did however make one or two concessions to the continued popularity of the beautiful shield-shaped back. These designs are all for 'Parlour-chairs', that is for the dining-parlours. Chairs for the drawing room were more elaborate. Sheraton's designs are more complex in detail than Hepplewhite's and show a nervous intensity that contrasts with his rival's fluid elegance of line.

528 *Left*: French types of furniture were adopted in many of the designs of Adam, Hepplewhite and Sheraton, and here the *bonheur-du-jour* has acquired an English character, the beauty of the piece consisting not in applied ornament or carving, but in fine proportions, quality of craftsmanship, and in the lovely figure and colour of the woods used, including satinwood for the main surfaces, sycamore for the door-panels, and rosewood for the panel borders, with delicate inlaid fillets of ebony and boxwood. The oval drop-handles are finely chased. Norman Adams, Ltd., London

529 *Left*: George Hepplewhite was the first to illustrate a Pembroke table, in his *Cabinet-Maker and Upholsterer's Guide* of 1788. Later Sheraton developed the type, and innumerable charming examples were made by various craftsmen. The table illustrated is of about 1790, and the veneered ornament of shells, medallions, festoons and strings of husks owe their origin to Robert Adam's designs. Temple Williams, Ltd., London

530 *Above*: In this secretaire-cabinet of about 1795 the richness of the satinwood and golden Honduras mahogany combines with the delicacy of the carving of the leaf capitals and fluted columns, and with the urn finials, to create a piece of great elegance. Norman Adams, Ltd., London

531 *Above*: The appeal in modern times of furniture of the Sheraton period is due to the simple form of many of these pieces and to the restrained, unobtrusive ornament. In this satinwood card table the only ornament is some reticent inlay of medallions in the frieze and of a simple shell-pattern in the top. Temple Williams, Ltd., London

532 *Below*: The kidney-shape was developed by Sheraton and became extremely popular for pedestal writing tables and dressing-tables. The restrained Classical ornament of black inlay on mahogany is typical of the years 1800 to 1805. Temple Williams, Ltd., London

chest-of-drawers, often with a bowed or serpentine front, and with the base shaped with a drooping apron-piece forming a continuous curve with outward-splayed feet. Tallboys were double chests, the top having a cornice moulding.

Dressing-tables, both for men and for women, were often designed as deep tables with several drawers, and having a top hinged at the sides and divided in the middle so as to open, revealing inside receptacles for toilet articles. Much ingenuity was often lavished on mechanical fittings for such tables, including dressing mirrors that rose and fell in slots, or were pivoted at the sides on brackets.

A distinctive feature of the Hepplewhite period, evident more strongly in the furniture than in the illustrations of the *Guide*, was the persistence of French Rococo elements of design, especially in the survival of curved legs, arms, seat and back rails of chairs and sofas.

The success of Hepplewhite's *Guide* was probably one of the factors precipitating the publication of another of the great design books of the 18th century. This was the *Cabinet-Maker and Upholsterer's Drawing Book* issued by Thomas Sheraton in four parts between 1791 and 1794, and containing 113 plates.

The *Drawing Book* seems to have been an immediate success. The spirit of the designs in many respects remained the same as that of Hepplewhite; in many others it represented new departures. Sheraton retained the square tapered leg for chairs and 531 tables, but also made greater use of the round baluster leg. Sheraton continued to show one or two shield-back designs for chairs, but his square chair backs made the radical change from 527 the spirit of the 1780s to the new style of the 1790s. As well as vase, leaf and drapery motifs in chair backs, he illustrated new lattice and lozenge designs, deriving from France, all with a vertical emphasis.

The Neo-Classical ornament of husks, festoons, paterae, swags and grotesques was less used by Sheraton. On the other hand, he made greater use of painted figure subjects and naturalistic floral decoration, which Hepplewhite had also shown. The increased use of such decoration was also due to a renewal of French influence.

A Sheraton innovation were the domed tops given to the upper parts of ladies' writing tables, dressing-tables, and occasional furniture.

The extreme artificiality of manners before the Revolution gave place after that event to an increasing tendency to casualness and informality. Furniture was arranged less ceremonially, and a demand arose for a greater number of small pieces, such as Pembroke tables and 'quartetto' tables, in sets of four, to serve 529 people in their casual occupations of reading, playing games, tea-drinking, sewing and embroidery. In her novel *Persuasion* Jane Austen spoke of the young people using small articles of furniture to give 'the proper air of confusion'.

Hepplewhite continued to use the 'picture frame' and oval mirrors which Adam had introduced, but the mouldings of the former have a greater slenderness. Sheraton did not give any illustrations for mirrors in his first book.

It was the special delicacy and richness of the later Louis XVI period that Sheraton, more than any other designer, established in the tradition of his time. He expressed it notably in the shaping of break-front table tops with serpentine or straight fronts and with quadrant-shaped ends; and in the delicate scrolling of flower and leaf patterns combined with ribbon decoration that he indicated for the 'borders of pier-tables'. Most distinctively and perhaps most charmingly is this element expressed in his adaptation from the French of slender turned colonnettes with feet of 'spin- 530 ning-top' shape as supports for cabinets, commodes, dressing-tables and side tables.

Detail showing the wall decoration of the Eating Room (now the North Hall) at Claydon House, Buckinghamshire. The Rococo frames to the niches and the doors, carved in wood and painted white, *c*.1768, are by a certain Lightfoot of whom otherwise nothing is known. The carved motifs of birds and flowers suggest that Lightfoot may have worked to the designs of Thomas Johnson. The National Trust

GERMANY

P. W. Meister

Introduction

In the 18th century, the German Empire was composed of numerous territories, some under princely rule and others, such as the Free Cities and the Hanseatic towns, flourishing as mercantile centres of middle-class culture.

The Courts of the separate domains exercised a powerful influence on the development of furniture styles. Each prince sought to give his Court a particular renown and to impose his own individual taste. Some were conservative, while others were more adventurous in attracting artists and craftsmen from other territories within the Empire or even in bringing in foreign talent from abroad.

Vienna was the Emperor's official residence. As capital of the Holy Roman Empire and of the Hapsburg territories it was an important political centre and a focal point of artistic endeavour. Here, once the city had been freed from the threat of Turkish invasion in 1683, both the Emperor and the nobility had lost no time in building themselves some of the most superb Baroque palaces in Europe. Recalling the glories of Versailles, the walls of these new Viennese palatial interiors gleamed with the rich colours of marble or *stucco lustro*. Mirrors reflected the ambitious ceiling frescoes, in which mythological scenes were enacted in ethereal splendour. So rapid an expansion in the last decade of the 17th and in the early 18th century owed much to Italian architects, painters and stuccoists. But in Vienna, as elsewhere, native talent was quick to develop and the Bohemian city of Prague soon followed in becoming a flourishing Baroque centre. Further north, in Saxony, the Zwinger Palace at Dresden was begun in 1711 for Augustus the Strong, King of Poland and Elector of Saxony, while in the same year the foundations of another magnificent Baroque palace were laid, this time for the Elector of Mainz, Lothar Franz von Schönborn: Pommersfelden in Franconia. The new official *Residenz* of the Electors of Mainz, on the other hand, the palace of Würzburg, was begun nine years later, in 1720. Among the many ambitious princely and noble palaces which came into being in the first half of the century throughout the German territories, Würzburg was one of the finest and set a standard to be envied. It illustrates the changing tastes of the century, for it was conceived in Baroque terms and the long years in which it was slowly reaching completion brought the gayer delights of Rococo into the decoration of the interior. By the time the great Venetian painter, Giambattista Tiepolo had added the frescoes in the *Kaisersaal* and over the great staircase, shortly after 1750, the mood was one of sparkling brilliance. Well before the mid-century, Rococo decoration, sometimes in scintillating white and gold or blue and silver, had, in fact, become fashionable for the interiors of palatial residences and it is against such airy backgrounds that German Rococo furniture was set.

Beside this constant striving after prestige which stimulated cultural life both in the larger and in the less important terri-

The Dining Room at Saltram House in Devonshire is one of Robert Adam's finest interiors, designed in 1768 or soon after. The ceiling is decorated with delicate plasterwork and paintings by Antonio Zucchi. Its design of a circle and portions of a circle with a central shell-like ornament is repeated in the carpet, and the walls are set with pictures of Classical ruins. The chairs are of Hepplewhite design, the back splats being carved in a stylised 'wheatsheaf' pattern. The National Trust

533 This great Baroque double staircase at the Würzburg Residenz was built by Balthasar Neumann between 1737 and 1744. The frescoes by Giovanni Battista Tiepolo and his son, Domenico, were painted between 1750 and 1753, while the stucco decorations on the wall-panelling were added in 1764.

534 Cabinet on open stand, walnut veneer, Frankfurt-am-Main, *c.* 1700. This ungainly piece looks back in style to the mid-17th century, but the choice of figured walnut instead of ebony indicates its later date. Museum für Kunsthandwerk, Frankfurt-am-Main

tories, and which was so effectively fulfilled in grandiose building schemes, the wealth of the great merchants of the Free Cities buttressed a solid taste for expansive comfort rather than a flexible search for novelty.

German furniture of the 18th century presents, in consequence, an extraordinarily diverse picture. Frequently modelled upon French prototypes, it offers widely varied interpretations of fashionable Parisian taste. A knowledge of changing fashions was spread by the use of engraved designs. Apart from those by some well-known sculptors and architects, many sets of designs were published in Augsburg and Nuremberg. These were frequently re-issues of French ornamental engravings and of English and Italian designs. It is difficult to say how far they served as exact models, but they certainly provided basic examples upon which variations were made. German furniture is seldom signed and anonymity was encouraged by the strict Guild regulations. In recent years research into original documents, such as correspondence and accounts, has brought to light the names of a number of cabinet-makers. But little is known of their work, while their widely differing backgrounds and the varied tastes they served make it impossible to attribute many pieces to particular cabinet-makers. Bearing in mind stylistic changes in the course of the century, from Baroque of the early years to the compelling vivacity of Rococo and the final triumph of Neo-Classicism, it is on the basis of regional characteristics that German furniture must be discussed.

Furniture from the Free Cities and the Hanseatic towns retained Baroque forms when these had already lost favour in the South. The Frankfurt cupboard, for example, kept its late 17th-century shape far into the 18th century, although towards 1750 it became lighter and more elegant and heavy architectural features, such as columns and pilasters, were abandoned. This particular type of so-called Frankfurt cupboard was common throughout central Germany and in Switzerland in the early part of the century. Hamburg cupboards are closely related to those of the northern and eastern coastal regions. These, too, did not alter in shape until the second half of the 18th century, when they were influenced by English fashions. As a result, applied carving was less popular and heavy cornices were gradually replaced by broken pediments.

A new type of cupboard evolved in North Germany towards the middle of the century under both Dutch and English influence. It was constructed in two stages, the lower part as a chest-of-drawers and the upper composed of a cupboard with doors. Pilasters provide decorative features at the corners. Lübeck and Schleswig-Holstein cupboards in two stages, decorated with applied and gilt carving, belong to a small group made in North Germany. Brunswick cupboards, decorated with intarsia of various woods and of ivory and pewter, are examples of North German individuality and were popular middle-class pieces. Spectacular cupboards richly ornamented with gilt lattice-work in brass or wood were also made in Brunswick for the ducal *Residenz*, during the early years of the century.

In the first half of the century Baroque seat furniture of Dutch type was usual in the North and was then replaced by a series of styles suggesting a comparison with Chippendale, and later, Adam and Hepplewhite. The frequent use of mahogany in the second half of the century was also inspired by the popularity of this wood in England.

Oak furniture was favoured in the territories of the Lower Rhine, the decoration being carved in the solid wood and not applied. The quality of the carving in low relief is of surprising freedom and equals that of French *boiseries* of the period. Ornament varied from late Louis XIV to Louis XVI, following contemporary fashion. As well as the two-doored wardrobe, commodes and seat furniture, the china cabinet was very popular—the emergence of the latter piece probably being due to the fondness felt for it by the Dutch.

The cabinet-makers of Mainz were famous for their cupboards. The Joiners' Guild regulations required the presentation of a cupboard as a masterpiece and most of the master designs have been preserved. Writing cabinets, of which many examples still exist, were also popular pieces of Mainz furniture. Typical features are the corner volutes, *bombé* surfaces and asymmetrical

(margin numbers: 534, 536, 535, 537, 538, 539)

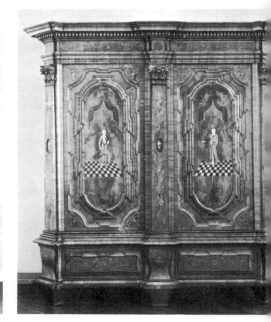

536 *Below*: Wardrobe, walnut veneer, the doors set with marquetry panels of various woods, ivory and pewter. Brunswick, *c.* 1740. The proportions, the layout of the door panels and the Corinthian columns are still Baroque; the static pose of the inlaid figures, with faces and hands of ivory, is another archaic feature that points to the provincial character of North German taste at this time. Museum für Kunsthandwerk, Frankfurt-am-Main

535 *Above*: Cabinet, walnut veneer, with panels of ash and strapwork of palisander. The doors of the upper and lower stages are filled with pierced and engraved gilt brass grilles introducing the crowned cypher, motto and devices of Duke August Wilhelm of Brunswick-Wolfenbüttel. With their attractive contrasts of light and dark woods and the superbly designed and executed metalwork, this series of cabinets ranks amongst the finest German cabinet-work of the late Baroque. Residenzschloss, Brunswick

537 *Left*: Chair, walnut with caned seat and back, North German, first half of the 18th century. This type of chair is found over a wide area including Holland, England and north-western Germany. The numerous curves in its design evolved easily into the even more curvaceous forms of Rococo. Museum für Kunsthandwerk, Frankfurt-am-Main

538 *Above*: Wardrobe, carved oak, Aachen, mid-18th century. The furniture of Aachen shows the same characteristics as that of Liège. Not even in France was the carving of the intractable oak brought to a higher pitch of delicacy. The influence of French *boiseries* on the design is evident. Stadtmuseum, Cologne

539 *Right*: Writing-cabinet, marquetry of walnut and other woods, constructed in three stages, Mainz, *c*. 1750–60. Although the maker has exploited every conceivable device in his effort to lighten the effect, he has not succeeded in reducing the weighty appearance of this piece and its legs sag almost to breaking point. An interesting and original feature is the repetition of the applied volutes on the exterior in the detail of the marquetry panels of the doors. Museum für Kunsthandwerk, Frankfurt-am-Main

540 *Far right*: Bed 'à la polonaise', soft wood carved and gilt against a brown stained background, made by P. A. Biarelle and J. G. Wörflein of Ansbach for the *Residenz* in 1741. In spite of the name, this type of bed was of French derivation: it provided an agreeable alternative to the vast 'lit de parade' which was reserved for formal occasions. Bed-chamber of the Markgraf Carl Wilhelm Friedrich, Residenz, Ansbach

541 *Below*: Bureau-cabinet, walnut veneer with marquetry of engraved ivory, the legs and cresting carved and gilt. Made by Carl Maximilian Mattern of Würzburg in 1744. In spite of the bulky form of the piece and the vastly heavy legs, an overall effect of lightness is achieved through the contrast between ivory inlay and walnut ground and the gaiety of the pierced cresting. The carving is attributed to G. H. Guthmann. Mainfränkisches Museum, Würzburg

542 *Below centre*: Bureau-cabinet, one of two made by Johann Georg Nestfell about 1750 for Schloss Bruchsal. The tricks of the fresco painter in devising perspectives in *trompe l'oeil* are here taken up by the *marqueteur* who has used the considerable space provided by the two doors of the upper stage to represent the interior of a vast Baroque palace. Badisches Landesmuseum, Karlsruhe.

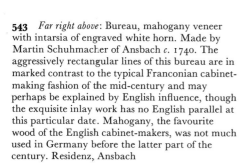

543 *Far right above*: Bureau, mahogany veneer with intarsia of engraved white horn. Made by Martin Schuhmacher of Ansbach *c*. 1740. The aggressively rectangular lines of this bureau are in marked contrast to the typical Franconian cabinet-making fashion of the mid-century and may perhaps be explained by English influence, though the exquisite inlay work has no English parallel at this particular date. Mahogany, the favourite wood of the English cabinet-makers, was not much used in Germany before the latter part of the century. Residenz, Ansbach

544 *Right*: Commode, walnut parquetry, attributed to Nicolaus Bauer of Bamberg, *c*. 1760. Some of these German commodes are of such grotesque form that one suspects the makers of being perfectly prepared to sacrifice both beauty and convenience in order to achieve originality. The extremely complex plan of this piece, with serpentine curves in both vertical and horizontal planes, called for the greatest skill and perseverance on the part of its maker, but it must be admitted that he has given birth to a monster. Residenz, Bamberg crestings. Especially characteristic are the ornamental mould-ings on the doors.

541 Franconian furniture, akin to that of Mainz, is often of high quality and the best examples were probably made for princely residences at Würzburg, Bamberg and Bayreuth. As one of the finest palaces in Germany, Würzburg was equipped with cabinet furniture of particular distinction and Franconian Court furni-ture enjoyed in the German territories much the same reputa-tion as Parisian furniture in France. There is hardly a district with so many well-known names as this and among them are artists of outstanding individuality and originality: Auvera, Mattern, Schumacher, Tietz and Spindler were all internation-ally known and their fame almost equalled that of the French cabinet-makers. The sculptors, Heiliger and Wagner, among others, were entrusted with the execution of carved pieces.

Würzburg and Ansbach, were the most important Franconian centres of early Rococo furniture. The *Residenz* at Würzburg was furnished in accordance with Parisian taste by the Prince Bishop, Johann Philipp Franz von Schönborn, and later by his successor, Friedrich Carl. At first, Parisian craftsmen were employed, but after the death of Johann Philipp in 1729, the greater part of the furniture was produced by the Court sculptor Franz Anton Schlott of Bamberg, the four brothers Guthmann of Munich and ultimately in the Würzburg Regency style by Ferdinand Hund. The well-known architect Johann Lucas von Hildebrandt, who was employed by Friedrich Carl von Schön-born at his palace in Vienna, also exercised a considerable influ-ence upon the development of Würzburg furniture. Hildebrandt was born in Genoa. His decorative schemes reflect the mood of North Italian Baroque, and the sumptuous appearance of the Würzburg furniture, for which Guthmann and Schlott were partly responsible was certainly due to his influence. The carved console tables, made for this palace by the Court sculptor Johann Wolfgang van der Auvera are among the most splendid crea-tions of the Rococo in Germany. Veneered and marquetry furni-ture from the Würzburg cabinet-makers' workshops was also of 541 high quality. Carl Maximilian Mattern and Johann Georg Nestfell were both outstanding cabinet-makers. Mattern worked at Würzburg from 1733 to 1770 and was known to be proud of his own skill in using marquetry in the French manner. He em-ployed ivory and variously coloured woods. In spite of his great gifts, Mattern was never appointed Court cabinet-maker. Per-haps the Prince Bishop, Friedrich Carl von Schönborn, found his pieces a little old-fashioned with their insistence upon heavy, Baroque forms. The Prince was indeed very conscious of the growing fashion for Rococo, and in the year 1744, he directed that a particular writing cabinet should be removed, as 'such objects are no longer suitable for princely Courts'. Johann Georg Nestfell had worked since 1720 for Count von Schönborn at Schloss Wiesentheid before he came to Würzburg in 1761. 542 Two writing cabinets from his hand, decorated with intarsia, were made for Schloss Bruchsal in about 1750.

Next in importance to Würzburg in the evolution of early Rococo furniture were the workshops of Ansbach. The redecora-tion of the Ansbach *Residenz* was undertaken between the years 1736 and 1744 under the supervision of the Italian architect, Leopold Retti. It is probably due to his influence and perhaps also to that of Paul Amadeus Biarelle of Liège, that Ansbach furniture is usually lighter in appearance than that of Würzburg. A marked English influence is also evident in some Ansbach 540 cabinet-pieces, particularly those veneered with mahogany. They were produced in the workshops of Martin Schumacher, 543 who probably spent some years in England. Schumacher may also have visited Paris on his travels, for a writing table from his hand is probably the earliest German example of a type which had first appeared in France.

Bamberg was another important Franconian centre. The 544, 546 sculptors, Johann Peter Wagner, Johann Köhler and perhaps 545 Ferdinand Tietz were responsible for carved furniture produced for the *Residenz* of the Prince Bishop, Adam Friedrich von Seinsheim. In 1764 Köhler also provided some of the finest Rococo furniture for the *Residenz* in Würzburg. F. M. Mutschele and the brothers J. H. and V. Schall worked at Bamberg from the middle of the century. Among their important pieces are the console tables made for Schloss Seehof near Bamberg. These are particularly lavish and include naturalistic features such as supports in the shape of tree trunks.

The art of combining scroll-work with naturalistic decoration is also characteristic of the furniture made at Bayreuth. This was a vital centre for the development of Franconian Rococo furni-ture particularly during the reign of the Markgraf Friedrich and his wife, Wilhelmine, the favourite sister of Frederick the Great, for their enthusiasm for building was naturally accompanied by a need for fine furniture. Court sculptors were employed in the production of carved console tables for the state rooms, in which the bold, fluid Rococo carving and, in particular, the flame-like motifs on the legs are typical of Bayreuth. Bayreuth chairs and tables are often of soft wood covered with gesso and stained to imitate walnut. Besides Matthäus Eberhard Müller, who pro-

545 *Right*: Sofa, carved and gilded wood, made by Johann Köhler of Würzburg for the *Residenz* in 1764. This sofa constitutes something of a *tour de force* of carving and may reasonably be criticised as a work of virtuosity rather than a piece of furniture. Residenz, Würzburg

546 *Below*: Cylinder-desk, marquetry of walnut and mahogany, made by Balthasar Herrmann of Bamberg, *c.* 1765–70 for Adam Friedrich von Seinsheim, Prince-Bishop of Bamberg. In this outstanding piece French fashion has clearly influenced the design. The desk can be used from either side by pushing back the slatted cover. Residenz, Bamberg

547 *Below*: Settee, carved wood, gilded against a stained ground. Made *c.* 1750–60 by the Spindler brothers for the Neues Schloss in Bayreuth. The restricted finances of a small Court did not allow the Spindlers to be as ambitious as so many of their German contemporaries, but they have here produced a comfortable and attractive piece. Neues Schloss, Bayreuth

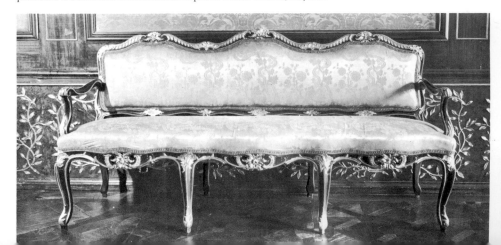

548 Interior of the Music Room in the Potsdam Stadtschloss, (now destroyed) the stucco by Johann August Nahl, *c.* 1745. The stucco decorations of the numerous palaces—constructed or reconstructed—for Frederick the Great show a spirit of fantasy and elegance that rival even Bavaria and quite overshadow their French prototypes. It was in this room that Bach played for Frederick the Great on a theme given to him by the King and which he later made up into *The Musical Offering*.

549 Armchair of softwood, carved and painted. Potsdam, mid-18th century. The pronounced curves of the frame lend a daringly provocative air to the piece and confirm the influence of Johann August Nahl, whose work as designer and carver at the Court of Frederick the Great at Berlin helped to inspire the vivacious manner of Frederican Rococo. Museum für Kunsthandwerk, Frankfurt-am-Main

550 *Below*: Commode veneered with palisander. Potsdam, *c.* 1740-50. The bold, contrasting curves are typical of Frederican Rococo. The sweeping, elegant gilt bronze mounts recall the designs of Hoppenhaupt but the composition as a whole owes much to the influence of von Knobelsdorff, architect to Frederick the Great. Schloss Charlottenburg, Berlin

551 *Below*: Commode, veneered with tortoiseshell and decorated with elaborate Rococo gilt bronze mounts, by Johann Melchior Kambli. Potsdam, *c.* 1765. Kambli was employed as a sculptor and cabinet-maker at the Court of Frederick the Great at Berlin. He had his own workshops for the production of bronzes and this commode exhibits the superb quality of his mounts. Sanssouci, Potsdam

vided marquetry commodes of *bombé* form for the palaces, the most important cabinet-makers in Bayreuth were the brothers Spindler, who later moved to Berlin.

Until the reign of Frederick the Great, the furnishing of the Berlin palaces had remained conservative and even old-fashioned. His father, Frederick William I, had not been fond of Berlin nor of the Palace of Charlottenburg. He had preferred his town palace of Potsdam which was modestly furnished. Immediately on his accession Frederick II began to make alterations and additions to his royal residences and he found in Georg Wenzeslaus von Knobelsdorff, who was soon appointed 'Surintendant' of the palaces, a brilliant organiser ready to carry out his wishes. Knobelsdorff was a good judge of craftsmanship and chose artists of exceptional skill to re-decorate and furnish the new state rooms. Under his leadership the so-called 'Frederican Rococo', relying on bold, contrasting curves, was evolved by such craftsmen as Johann Michael Hoppenhaupt, his brother Johann Christian, Johann August Nahl, and later, Johann Melchior Kambli.

Knobelsdorff remained nominally 'Surintendant' until his death in 1753 but in 1745 he had a disagreement with the King over the plans for the Summer palace of Sanssouci, which deprived him of any further direct influence. Yet he had so successfully united his artists and craftsmen that when he lost the royal favour, co-operation among them continued as before. In the decoration and furnishing of the palaces of Charlottenburg, Potsdam and Sanssouci there was no apparent break or change of manner.

The greatest of the three most important artists working for Knobelsdorff was the designer and carver, Johann August Nahl, who had been in Italy and in Paris. In 1735 we hear of his presence in Strasbourg where he worked at the Palais Rohan. Knobelsdorff invited him to Berlin, where he was appointed 'Directeur des Ornements' in 1741. The sculptural quality of his furniture, especially of his chairs and stools, is a clear indication that they are the work of a carver, and although they are of somewhat heavy appearance, the freely flowing scrolls and flowers lend them a certain liveliness. His most outstanding achievement was the Golden Gallery in the palace of Charlottenburg. He left Potsdam in 1746 and later worked in Kassel.

The brothers Hoppenhaupt succeeded Nahl at his post in Berlin. The furniture of each of the brothers is outstanding for the masterly way in which ornament and form are combined and for the effective contrast of plain surfaces and marquetry decoration. The designs of the elder brother, Johann Michael, were published between the years 1751 and 1755.

The fourth great craftsman to play an essential part in the evolution of Frederican furniture was the Swiss, Johann Melchior Kambli. He went to Potsdam in 1746 to work as an ornamental sculptor in wood and stone, but he was also responsible for some splendid furniture for the palaces ornamented with rich, gilt bronze mounts. In 1752 he was granted a Royal privilege allowing him to set up a workshop for the making of bronze mounts. His skill gained him the contract for the decoration of the '*Bronzezimmer*' or Bronze Room in the Berlin palace, carried out between 1754 and 1755, upon which his fame was founded. He later produced fine cabinet pieces veneered with dark tortoiseshell contrasting with light cedarwood and furnished with rich gilt bronze mounts. Although Kambli favoured conservative designs, perhaps inspired by Hoppenhaupt, he succeeded in giving his own furniture a personal character.

In 1764, two cabinet-makers who had made a name for themselves at the Court of Bayreuth, arrived in Berlin. The brothers Johann Friedrich and Heinrich Wilhelm Spindler worked predominantly for the Court, the elder at Potsdam and the younger in Berlin. Some of the commodes in the state rooms in the *Neues Palais* at Potsdam are certainly the work of the younger Spindler, and he was the more important cabinet-maker of the two. Until the Second World War, most of the pieces by the brothers were in the *Neues Palais*. For the most sumptuous examples marquetry of mother-of-pearl, silver and ivory was used. What a change it must have been for the Spindler brothers to work for a Court where there were no financial restrictions to limit technique, in contrast to Bayreuth, where they were often unable even to use veneer. The freedom they enjoyed is evident in their work at Potsdam. Here, in co-operation with Kambli, who provided the rich bronze mounts, they were able fully to exploit their skill, particularly in the lavish use of marquetry. Had their work not been confined to Potsdam and Berlin (apart from the years in Bayreuth) they would probably have achieved international repute among famous European cabinet-makers.

In Saxony, a typical Dresden Rococo cabinet-piece was the writing-cabinet in which the doors of the upper stage contain panels of looking-glass. The design is unified and less insistent upon the horizontal division between upper and lower stage. Lacquered pieces, particularly writing-cabinets are among the most sumptuous examples of Saxon furniture. In Dresden, Martin Schnell specialised in this technique and was appointed lacquer-maker to the Court in 1710. He provided the royal palaces and those of the nobility with richly lacquered pieces in the oriental manner. The decoration on his writing-cabinets is not only raised and painted but includes a new ornamental technique introducing figures, in relief, of lacquered and gilt copper. Engraved designs published by P. Shenk in 1702 in Amsterdam, entitled *Picturae Sinicae ac Surattenae, Vasis Tabellisque exhibitae, Admiranda* served as models for these relief figures. They also provided motifs for the decoration both of lacquered furniture and of porcelain in the first half of the century. In Dresden the commode enjoyed great popularity during the century and references to this particular piece of furniture occur in contemporary documents from 1727. It is, however, curious that none is listed in the two inventories of the Dresden and Moritzburg palaces made in 1720 and 1733, although examples are mentioned in the 1732 inventory of Schloss Pillnitz.

Most of the Saxon commodes of the first half of the century are rectangular in shape. Serpentine lines and *bombé* forms did not appear before 1730 or 1740 and then became more pronounced by the middle of the century. Commodes supported on rather longer legs and of lighter appearance, modelled on French examples, were also made in Saxony. But the bronze mounts were less lavish than those of their prototypes and fulfilled a practical rather than a decorative function. Among the furniture made for the Saxon palaces between 1720 and 1730, tables also are so similar to early 18th-century French pieces that one is inclined to attribute them to Frenchmen working in Dresden, such as Henry Hulot, although copies were, of course, made by local craftsmen.

Eighteenth-century seat furniture listed in contemporary Saxon inventories includes stools, described as *tabourets*; high- and low-backed chairs, settees and armchairs. As well as the carved examples there are also plainer *tabourets* made between 1720 and 1730 with *pieds de biche* in the French manner. The state rooms of the palace of Moritzburg were furnished in 1728 with 'English' caned-back chairs. In Dresden, English influence was particularly marked on the design of chairs and writing-cabinets. In 1710 Augustus the Strong had ordered twelve splat-backed chairs 'in the English style' but in 1739, as this fashion waned, the Court chair-maker, J. P. Schotte, was the only one in Dresden to produce 'English' chairs. Later, French influence spread, for an inventory of 1769 lists many pieces of seat furniture which 'had come from France and were used as models'.

The Seven Years' War (1756–63) caused severe losses to Saxony, and pieces of exceptional splendour were no longer ordered by the Court or the nobility. Workshops in Dresden, Leipzig and other towns in the province continued, of course, to provide for middle-class needs, but they confined themselves to less ambitious furniture based upon designs in French and English pattern-books. Towards the end of the century the simple shapes of English pieces were admired.

In Austria, Italian influence was strong from the late 17th until well into the 18th century. Italian architects and craftsmen had been employed, particularly in Vienna, since the 17th century. It was, in fact, an Italian architect, Niccolo Paccassi who was responsible for the alterations to the palace of Schönbrunn for the Empress Maria Theresa (1740–50) which included the re-decoration, in the 1760s, of many of the state rooms. Not until Maria Theresa's time is it possible to speak of a characteristic Austrian style of furniture, although this is not so much a Court as a middle-class style. The Court itself was so concerned to

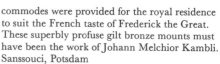

552 *Above*: Commode veneered with tortoiseshell, by Heinrich Wilhelm Spindler, Potsdam *c.* 1765. The Spindler brothers came to Berlin from Bayreuth in 1764 to take part in the furnishing of the *Neues Palais* at Potsdam. Magnificent commodes were provided for the royal residence to suit the French taste of Frederick the Great. These superbly profuse gilt bronze mounts must have been the work of Johann Melchior Kambli. Sanssouci, Potsdam

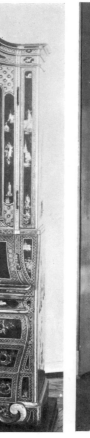

553 Lacquered writing-cabinet with gilt bronze mounts by Martin Schnell, Dresden, *c.* 1730–40. Schnell was appointed in 1710 as a specialist in lacquer to the Dresden Court of Augustus the Strong, Elector of Saxony and King of Poland. He provided lacquer furniture for the royal palaces and among them for the famous *Japanisches Palais* at Dresden. This piece is lacquered with gold and silver borders on a red ground; some of the figures are of gilt copper. Inside the desk and the upper stage, lacquer *chinoiserie* scenes are in gold on a blue ground, so that when open the cabinet presents a brilliant spectacle. Museum für Kunsthandwerk, Frankfurt-am-Main

554 Bureau-cabinet, walnut veneer with numerous panels of looking-glass, and gilt bronze mounts. Made by Erich Nicolas Noor of Dresden in 1727. English influence was very marked in Saxon cabinet-making of the early 18th century: this piece shows a compromise between English and local styles. A common feature of the Saxon furniture of this period was the use of mirror glass in the pilasters. This exceptional piece, made for the Saxon Court, has the lower stage set with glass panels engraved with *Régence* ornament. Museum für Kunsthandwerk, Dresden

555 Stool of beech, the carved mouldings and decorative motifs gilt. Saxon, *c.* 1720–30. The influence of France is apparent in the character of the carved decoration and in the hoof feet, while the curving stretchers are an earlier feature still surviving in this pleasing design. Museum für Kunsthandwerk, Dresden

552

554

553

555

557

556 *Left*: The Mirror Room in the Amalienburg, 1735, is the central feature in the garden palace built in the park of Nymphenburg for the Elector Carl Albrecht of Bavaria, the future Emperor Charles VI. Designed by François Cuvilliés, it is among the finest Rococo rooms in existence and the stucco by Johann Baptist Zimmerman achieves an astonishing virtuosity.

557 *Right*: The *Millionenzimmer* in Schloss Schönbrunn, Vienna. This room, panelled with marquetry, set with Indian miniatures in carved and gilt frames, is among a number decorated for the Empress Maria Theresa in the 1760s.

558 *Below*: Console table of carved and gilt wood in the manner of Joseph Effner. The heraldic cartouche supported by two *putti* over the stretcher is charged with the crowned lion rampant of Bohemia. Museum für Kunsthandwerk, Frankfurt

559 *Below right*: Commode, carved and gilt wood against a white painted ground, designed by François Cuvilliés and carved by Johann Adam Pichler of Munich in 1761 for the *Kurfürstenzimmer* in the *Residenz*. Residenzmuseum, Munich

imitate Parisian fashions that it is often difficult to decide whether a piece was made in Austria or France.

As the Court of the Elector of Bavaria resided at Munich, the city took the lead in south Germany in matters of taste. Two architects were particularly concerned with the planning, decoration and furnishing of the princely residences. Firstly, Joseph Effner, who was appointed chief Court architect in Munich in 1724 and was concerned in all the most important undertakings. His designs for furniture, although very much akin to those of the French School, in which the influence of Boulle and Cressent is clear, reflect nevertheless his own originality; they introduce very lively and quite unacademic ornamental motifs, the marquetry representing freely composed scenes with figures, in a manner which was quite his own. His designs for carved side and console tables are splendid expressions of Bavarian Rococo, which was to reach its epitome in the designs of the second great architect of the time, François Cuvilliés the elder. Cuvilliés was a Walloon in the service of the Elector Max Emanuel of Bavaria, by whom he was sent to Paris to study between 1720 and 1724. Upon his return he worked on the planning and particularly on the interior designs and furnishings of the *Residenz* in Munich and of the palace of Nymphenburg. He published a number of designs for ornament, interior panelling and for furniture, through which he exercised a powerful influence in South Germany and, indeed, beyond the frontiers of the German territories. The designer and carver, Johann Michael Schmidt, worked under him between the years 1760–63 on the decoration of the rooms of the Munich *Residenz*.

In contrast to Franconian Rococo furniture, the designs of Effner and Cuvilliés are crisp, elegant and sophisticated. The French schooling these architects had both received was responsible for the easy freedom of their work, which avoids clumsy or vulgar extremes without becoming dry and academic.

For the development of middle-class furniture in South Germany, two artists were of special importance. The first was Franz Xaver Habermann, a draughtsman and ornamental engraver of Augsburg, who had published many designs for interior decoration, tables, seat furniture and commodes; they dis-

play elegant, rhythmically flowing lines and a restrained use of ornamentation. The second artist was the cabinet-maker and draughtsman Johann Rumpp of Augsburg, whose many designs published by Martin Engelbrecht, illustrate south German middle-class furniture in the Rococo taste.

Another South-west German Court, which was of importance was that of the Elector Palatine at Mannheim. Until recently only the work of the court cabinet-maker, Jakob Kieser, who produced furniture for the Mannheim *Residenz* between 1764 and 1780, was known. But before Kieser's time a carpenter, Johann Georg Wahl of Osthofen, had apparently executed large orders for the Elector Carl Theodor. A number of pieces by Wahl in a pronounced and original Rococo style, have now been recognised and they represent the individual contribution of the Palatinate to mid-18th-century German furniture design. His writing-cabinets are lavishly inlaid with ivory, brass and mother-of-pearl. He made a practice of putting his signature, with the exact place and date, on the inside of a door on the upper stage of these pieces. He also made tables and clocks. But with the exception of Nahl, Spindler, Kambli, Effner and Cuvilliés, no cabinet-makers attained the international repute of the two Roentgens.

The father, Abraham Roentgen (1711–93) spent his years as an apprentice and journeyman in Holland and England and opened the workshop in Neuwied in 1750. His son, David worked there from 1761, at which time furniture was already being sent abroad and there were many orders from royal customers.

David Roentgen was one of the most important cabinet-makers of the century. The lighter appearance of furniture made at the end of the 60s was certainly due to his influence. In 1772 the management of the workshop was finally handed over to him, although his father continued to work there until his 80th year. As a result of his travels, the young David Roentgen made many international contacts. While in Paris in 1779 he was introduced at Court and received many commissions. In 1780 he was registered as '*maître ébéniste*' by the Paris Guild. He also visited Berlin, Brussels and St. Petersburg. The success of these

560 *Left*: Writing bureau, walnut veneer with marquetry of ivory and various woods, made by Johann Georg Wahl of Osthofen for the Elector Palatine, Carl Theodor, in 1750. This piece of furniture serves as a background for the display of a large number of marquetry figure scenes. Schloss Berchtesgaden, Germany

561 *Right*: Settee, carved walnut, by Abraham Roentgen, founder of the Neuwied workshop which was to gain a European reputation under his son in the later years of the 18th century. Abraham Roentgen had worked in England and described himself as an 'English' cabinet-maker, but there is little English influence here, except perhaps for the simple profile of splats, arms and legs. Schloss Pommersfelden, Germany

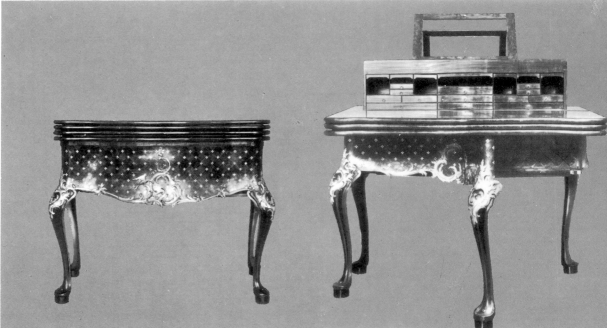

562 *Left*: Desk made in 1773 by David Roentgen, son of Abraham Roentgen, for the Munich *Residenz*. The restrained lines of this desk announce the approach of the Neo-Classical style. The delicacy of the marquetry, carried out mostly in light-coloured woods is typical of Roentgen's later style. Residenzmuseum, Munich

563, 564 *Above, centre and right*: Writing and games table, marquetry of rosewood, walnut, brass, mother-of-pearl and ivory, the mounts of gilt bronze. Made by Abraham Roentgen of Neuwied in about 1765 for Johann Philipp von Walderdorf, Elector of Trier. The construction with hinged flaps one on top of the other was a usual English one. The gilt bronze mounts display a daring asymmetry. Museum für Kunsthandwerk, Frankfurt-am-Main

565 *Far left*: Writing cabinet by J. C. Fiedler, cabinet-maker to Frederick the Great, Berlin 1775. Turned legs, rectangular outlines of the lower stage, and gilt bronze mounts announce the Neo-Classical style, but the curving pediment and marquetry decoration retain their Rococo character. Museum für Künst und Gewerbe, Hamburg

566 *Left*: This chair of painted softwood, of Neo-Classical design, the silk upholstery painted with *chinoiserie* scenes, was made for one of the rooms in Schloss Charlottenburg, Berlin, decorated in the Chinese style for Friedrich Wilhelm II of Prussia in 1790.

567 *Below*: Settee, carved and gilt, made, *en suite* with a set of armchairs, for the Palace of Nymphenburg, Munich, *c*. 1775. The bracket legs of slightly curved shape betray an unwillingness wholly to abandon Rococo features.

568 Watercolour drawing by the Weimar artist, G. M. Kraus (1737–1806), of Frau von Fritsch and Fräulein von Imhof drawing, c. 1790. These rectangular-backed chairs reflect the fashion for English furniture which was widespread in Weimar and was encouraged by the widowed Duchess, Anna Amalia. Wittumspalais, Weimar

569 *Below*: Commode of carved walnut. Rhineland, c. 1775–80. This modest Neo-Classical piece, with its reticent decoration of carved husks, ribbons and trailing leaves, achieves a sense of elegance in spite of its evident provincial character. Museum für Kunsthandwerk, Frankfurt-am-Main

570 *Below*: Pier table of carved softwood, gessoed and gilt, the details painted white. North German, c. 1780. The influence of English designs was particularly marked in the late 18th century in Germany, especially in the Hanseatic towns and in the North in general. Museum für Kunsthandwerk, Frankfurt-am-Main

571 *Below*: *Bonheur-du-jour* veneered with mahogany, inlaid with borders of silver wire, and mounted with Wedgwood blue and white medallions. Vienna, c. 1780–90. The elegant restraint of this piece, in which both French and English features are adopted, is characteristic of Viennese furniture under the Emperor Joseph II. Museum für Kunsthandwerk, Frankfurt-am-Main

visits led to the founding of workshops in these towns. Frederick William II appointed him as his diplomatic agent for the Lower Rhineland. After 1795 the Neuwied workshop came to a standstill as a result of the French occupation, but Roentgen was able to save a large part of the stock in Kassel, Gotha and Altenkirchen. He died in Wiesbaden while on his travels in 1807.

David Roentgen's pieces, more elegant than those of his father, are distinguished by the superb composition of the marquetry decoration, in which flowers and leaves, festoons of ribbons and sometimes writing- and musical-instruments are included. After 1770 delicate pictorial marquetry became a speciality of his workshop, the designs for which were frequently taken from paintings by Januarius Zick. Towards the end of the 70s, Roentgen was producing furniture in the Louis XVI style. An original feature of the splendid writing desks made in the later years of the Neuwied workshops is the complicated built-in mechanism which can be operated by moving a section of the piece. Long-case clocks, usually made in co-operation with the clockmaker, Peter Kinzing, were also among their products.

Although, as an international figure, David Roentgen was outstanding for his cabinet-making in the Neo-Classical style, his orders were largely for reigning or princely houses or for foreign Courts. His example was to be followed by other cabinet-makers but at first the German territories were reluctant to accept the Louis XVI style. In Berlin, for example, the Court cabinet-maker to Frederick the Great, Johann Christian Fiedler, was producing cabinet-pieces in 1775 in which the decorative features still retained a Rococo character. The furnishings of the Neues Palais in Potsdam supplied in the 1770s were, in fact, still fully Rococo. The Neo-Classical style was first expressed in terms of ornament: bead mouldings, paterae, garlands and festoons, urns and other motifs derived from Classical antiquity. Sometimes such features were combined with *chinoiseries* but gradually the new manner gained general favour, although there was no leading architect whose designs were to encourage its development, or whose role could be compared with that of Robert Adam in England.

A series of designs for furniture in a transitional Neo-Classical style were published by Franz Heissig in Augsburg in about 1780, while a journal, illustrating fashion in furniture and dress was established at Weimar in 1787 under the title of '*Journal des Luxus und der Moden*'. Here the furniture illustrated had finally abandoned Rococo and was modelled on contemporary English examples fashionable at the time.

The surviving designs of the Mainz Joiners' Guild show a new, and indeed, advanced understanding of the Louis XVI style. Those of the 1780s include a cylinder-top bureau, in which the roll-top to the desk derived from French example while the heavy lower part enclosing drawers was still typically German. This type of cylinder bureau remained popular until the second decade of the 19th century.

In northern Germany, particularly in the coastal districts, furniture began to adopt a more Classical manner. In the Lower Rhine and Moselle districts both cabinet and seat furniture included Louis XVI decorative features, but the Neo-Classical style was never as fully developed as it was in France.

In Austria during the last years of the Empress Maria Theresa's reign there were signs of a revulsion from Rococo forms, and these were clearly expressed in the Neo-Classical pieces of the time of the Emperor Joseph II (1780–90). Towards the end of this decade English influence was already discernible in a number of pieces of middle-class furniture, particularly in seat furniture. Simple shapes and practical construction exemplified the renewed interest in Classical antiquity.

The china cabinet of Rococo form was now gradually losing its curves and becoming rectangular in shape. Writing-tables with slender legs now superseded the two stage writing-cabinets. They were furnished with a centre drawer with two smaller drawers on each side; the cylinder-shaped writing table was also popular. Veneers of walnut and of light-coloured fruitwoods, such as pear or cherry were favoured. A feature of most Viennese furniture is the quality of the craftsmanship, encouraged by the high standards of the Guild. Indeed into the early 19th century, Vienna was to remain a centre at which craftsmanship, allied to simplicity of form, continued to earn the city international renown.

ITALY

Hugh Honour

No sharp line divides the late 17th century from the early 18th in the history of Italian furniture. The grandiose palace furniture, especially console tables, made in the first three decades of the new century seem to have differed little from those which had become popular in the 1660s. Very few pieces can be dated from documentary sources, for the study of Italian Baroque furniture is still in its infancy, and one cannot even be sure that the lighter and more elegant pieces are later than others.

The desire for splendour continued unabated in the new century. The great frescoed gallery became a commonplace in nearly all the larger palaces outside Venetia where a certain conservatism in planning did not allow sufficient room. Indeed, several of the most handsome Italian galleries date from the 18th century. Some are in royal residences—like the Veneria Reale, outside Turin. But the wonderful gallery of the Accademia Filarmonica, Turin with its elegant paintings, mirrors, exquisite stucco work and profuse gilding, was created for a wealthy nobleman. So also was that in the Palazzo Balbi-Durazzo, Genoa, which dates from the 1730s and has as its only furnishings, stools of an elegance which announces the Rococo style. Galleries scarcely less rich were built for palaces even in small provincial towns. There is a very handsome gallery with great carved and gilt console tables in the Palazzo Buonaccorsi at Macerata, dating from 1707. But the gallery was only one of several state apartments. Opulent Baroque furniture, richly carved and gilt, maintained its place in the several reception rooms of a great palace. In state bedrooms the beds were still hung with glowing Lucchese silks or Genoese velvets. Indeed, this type of 'show' furniture was so intimately connected with the Italian idea of palatial splendour that it survived changes in fashion from the Baroque to the Rococo and even to Neo-Classicism. By the end of the 18th century the state apartments of most Italian palaces looked hopelessly out of date. Visiting the Palazzo Borghese, Rome, in 1804, Kozebue remarked that the elegant and modern furniture revealed that the mistress of the house was French and not Italian. For it was conservatism, rather than poverty, which prevented Italians from turning out their Baroque furniture to make way for Neo-Classical pieces.

When President de Brosses called at Palazzo Foscari, Venice, in 1739 he complained that there was nowhere to sit because of the delicacy of the carving on the chairs. He was, of course, referring to the state rooms which were the only ones normally shown to visitors. One might indeed hesitate to sit on the magnificent armchairs, like those carved by Antonio Corradini and now in the Palazzo Rezzonico, Venice, just as one would hesitate to lean against the console tables by the same sculptor. As in the previous century, the furniture of the state apartments was intended to cut a *bella figura* or make a show—to be admired rather than used.

In the smaller rooms, usually on the floors above and below the *piano nobile*, the furniture was simpler and more comfortable. And it was, of course, in these rooms rather than in the vast *saloni*, which are still almost impossible to heat in winter, that even the grandest Italian families spent most of their time. Sometimes these little rooms were very elegantly furnished, with comfortable chairs, rather French in appearance, and little *bombé* commodes painted or lacquered in gay colours with patterns of flowers blossoming all over them. The existence of such furniture has led many to believe that the small room was an invention of the 18th century. This is, however, as untrue in Italy as it is elsewhere. Small rooms had been used for normal habitation at earlier periods, but the chairs and tables with which they were furnished were usually of such simplicity that they were cast out when in need of serious repair and relatively few have survived. The innovation of the 18th century was the greater attention paid to furnishing and decorating the smaller rooms.

margin notes: 572
Plate facing page 161
575
578
573
584
582

572 *Left*: Vitrine in carved and gilt wood, Roman *c.* 1725. The absence of documented pieces makes it difficult to date examples of Italian 18th-century furniture. In this vitrine the Baroque curve seems to be on the point of breaking into Rococo froth. Collection: Signor Fabrizio Apolloni, Rome

573 *Below*: Pair of carved and gilt chairs from a set made in Florence in the early 18th century. The somewhat angular design of these chairs is reminiscent of much early 18th-century Florentine architecture. Palazzo Serristori, Florence

574 *Below*: Design for a console table, *c.* 1730, by Filippo Juvarra. Several pieces of furniture in the Palazzo Reale, Turin, show the influence of the great architect Juvarra who may well have designed some of them. Biblioteca Nazionale, Turin

At the same time the professional and middle classes began to pay more attention to the furnishing of their homes. The Italian social system, like that of England, was fairly fluid and could absorb the successful businessman into the ranks of the aristocracy. Even in the closed oligarchy of Venice, it was possible for enriched members of the bourgeoisie to buy their way into the patriciate—and in the course of the 18th century the price of admission declined steadily. Naturally enough, the middle and professional classes profited greatly from the long reign of peace in 18th-century Italy, even as the fortunes of the ancient aristocratic families declined. It became quite usual for prosperous members of the bourgeoisie to own both a town house and an elegant small villa, sometimes no more than an hour's carriage drive away. As far as one can judge, these houses were furnished in much the same way as the unofficial apartments in the great palaces. But unfortunately they have suffered still more than the great palaces from the Italian law which rules that a man's property must be divided equally between his children. Few, if any, of these small city houses and trim country villas have preserved the full complement of their 18th-century furniture.

579 The genre pictures of Pietro Longhi and his imitators reveal that in Venice the furnishing of the smaller rooms was still rather sparse. There were a few upholstered chairs and stools with carved cabriole legs. In nearly every room there seems to have been a Murano glass mirror engraved with a figure in the centre. Solid and sensible chests-of-drawers frequently appear. Four main types of table were in use. Low four-legged tables, no more than about 18 inches high, were popular. Tall and rather spindly *trespoli*, generally used to support dressing mirrors, formed a normal item of bedroom furniture. Card tables were usually supported on a central pier. The larger tables were almost invariably draped with carpets or velvet, and were probably rather rough-and-ready underneath. The great formal portraits of 18th-century Venice reveal that similar draped tables were also to be found in the state apartments.

579

Several new types of furniture came into common use in 18th-century Italy. The largest and most imposing was the bureau-bookcase, similar in design to those popular in the England of Queen Anne, with a chest of three drawers, sloping fall-front desk and cupboard above. Chests-of-drawers introduced into Italian houses in the 17th century came into more widespread use. At first they were made on very simple designs but gradually developed into exuberantly decorative though no less useful objects. Another 18th-century novelty was the long sofa with an upholstered seat and back or sometimes with a rush seat and elegantly carved back.

577

These new types of furniture were, of course, derived from north of the Alps. England and Holland provided the designs of the great bureaux which were extensively imitated in Italy. Indeed, it is often difficult to decide whether a lacquered bureau is

575 *Left*: Carved and gilt chair, *c.* 1730, probably by Antonio Corradini, Venice. Like many of the finest pieces of Italian furniture this throne is the work of a sculptor, not a cabinet-maker. Palazzo Rezzonico, Venice

577 *Right*: Japanned bureau, probably Venetian, early 18th century. Japanned furniture was produced in many Italian cities during the 18th century and it is seldom possible to be certain about the place of origin of a particular piece. This bureau is of a type which was popular in Venice. Palazzo Sacchetti, Rome

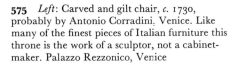

576 *Right*: Bureau inlaid with ivory and various rare woods by Pietro Piffetti, 1738. This piece was made for the Palazzo Reale, Turin, by the leading cabinet-maker in the city. The large inlaid medallion on the upper part represents the Arts and Sciences paying homage to the statue of Minerva. Palazzo del Quirinale, Rome

578 *Far right*: Side table, carved and gilt wood, *c.* 1730, probably by the sculptor Antonio Corradini, Venice. The table is *en suite* with the magnificent chair in illustration 575. Both are fine examples of the type of showy furniture used to decorate the state apartments of great palaces. Palazzo Rezzonico, Venice

of English, Dutch, German or Italian make. Generally, Italian pieces can be distinguished by the greater vitality of the decoration, the poorer and less 'oriental' quality of the lacquer varnishes and the often shockingly bad carpentry. In the middle of the century French influence was strong, if not quite as strong as some historians have suggested. Piedmont and Liguria were the states most open to French influence, but the furniture made there was distinguished from Parisian and even provincial French prototypes by greater exuberance but poorer craftsmanship. French patterns for armchairs seem to have been copied fairly faithfully in all parts of Italy. But most other French designs for cabinet pieces were interpreted in a manner which would have caused the raising of horrified eyebrows at the headquarters of the Guild of *menuisiers-ébénistes* in Paris.

The Venetians absorbed the French Rococo style of furniture and determined even to improve upon it. They developed the elegantly swelling *bombé* commode into a riot of bulging curves which gave it a distinctly full-bosomed appearance. Sofas were extended to preposterous lengths, especially for the furnishing of ball-rooms or the long *porteghi* which run from front to back of a Venetian palace. The carved backs of these pieces were fashioned in a complex pattern of intersecting curves. In Piedmont, French designs were treated with rather more respect. The furniture made for the Palazzo Caraglio (now the Accademia Filarmonica) Turin, in the 1760s is of a striking elegance and would not have looked out of place in a Parisian *hôtel* a decade earlier. Indeed, many of the artists and craftsmen employed here had been trained or had worked in France. But generally in Piedmont, the curves are slightly bolder, the decoration slightly richer than in France. Italians tended to exaggerate the most conspicuous qualities of French furniture, making the elegant boudoir trifles more bizarrely spindly and the solid pieces more emphatically ponderous. Rococo furniture lost its reticence, its sense of *bienséance*, as well as its superb craftsmanship on the journey across the Alps.

For the decoration of Italian furniture, lacquer—or japanning —remained popular throughout the greater part of the 18th century. Lacquer painting was practised in most Italian cities and not, as is commonly supposed, only in Venice. Indeed, Roman and Piedmontese lacquer seems to have been of higher quality than Venetian. Until after the middle of the century *chinoiserie* designs were extensively used for the decoration of lacquer. Lacquer varnishes were also applied to pieces of carved furniture, like the delightfully fantastic cradle made for some sprig of the Venetian nobility in the 1750s.

Italian *lacca* was a varnish of much thinner substance than the lacquer—or japan—employed in England and northern Europe. Even so, a still cheaper imitation called *lacca contrafatta* was produced by Italian craftsmen, especially the Venetians. Furniture to be treated with *lacca contrafatta* was first painted the desired colour; little paper cut-outs of rustic or chinoiserie figures, painted in bright colours, were then glued to it and the whole surface was varnished. Cut-outs were printed for this purpose by the Remondini firm of Bassano del Grappa. *Lacca contrafatta* was especially popular for the decoration of cupboards and bureaux made for the smaller town houses and country villas. Its effect is distinctly rustic, though sometimes attractive.

Furniture such as this added further notes of lively colour to the *settecento* interior. Painted furniture, also described by the Italian word *lacca*, was very popular too, cupboards with landscapes on their doors, commodes adorned with festoons of flowers sometimes in relief, harpsichord cases sprinkled with little bunches of roses, bed-heads with Rococo curlicues framing a Virgin and Child or other religious subjects. On Venetian furniture these decorations so strongly reflect the styles of contemporary painters that attempts have been made to attribute them to artists as famous as Tiepolo or Guardi. Although it is highly improbable that painters of such standing would have turned their attention to the embellishment of furniture at this period, for the painters of pictures and the painters of furniture belonged to different guilds, it is more than likely that they sometimes provided designs for the chairs, tables and candlestands in the rooms they frescoed. Among the drawings from the Tiepolo studio in the Victoria and Albert Museum there are designs for commodes and for a console table.

Margin references: 582, 583, *Plate facing page 161*, 580, 577, 581, 588, 587

579 *The Toilet* by Pietro Longhi, c. 1760. A glimpse of a mid-18th-century Venetian interior. The furnishings are handsome but, as in earlier periods, rather sparse. Many chairs, stools, looking glasses and *trespoli*, or three-legged tables, like those shown in the picture have survived. Museo Correr, Venice

580 *Above:* Green and gold japanned commode, Venetian, c. 1740. This commode forms part of a complete suite of japanned furniture. Palazzo Rezzonico, Venice

581 *Below left:* Cradle, carved and painted in *lacca*. One of the most endearingly preposterous pieces of Venetian furniture, dating from about 1750. Private Collection: Venice

582 *Below right:* Painted commode, mid-18th-century Venetian. The high-bosomed form is characteristically Venetian, so too is the lively painted decoration of a type called *lacca* in Italy. But the somewhat shoddy craftsmanship is evident even in a photograph. Palazzo Rezzonico, Venice

583 *Above*: Sofa of carved walnut, Venetian mid-18th century. Sofas like this were made for ballrooms and also to stand in the *portego*—a room running from front to back of a Venetian palace. Palazzo Rezzonico, Venice

585 *Below*: *Charles 7th Earl of Northampton in Rome*, 1758, by Pompeo Batoni. One of Batoni's numerous portraits of young Englishmen on the Grand Tour. The chair is of a type that had been popular since the late 17th century but the curious altar-like table suggests the tendency towards Neo-Classicism evident in Batoni's pictorial style. Fitzwilliam Museum, Cambridge

584 *Above*: A small room in the Palazzo Balbi-Durazzo, Genoa. The chairs, stools and console are Genoese and date from the mid-18th century. Much greater care was devoted to the furnishing of small rooms such as this in the 18th century than in earlier periods.

586 *Below*: *Scagliola* table top made for an English grand tourist, Mr. East, by Lamberto Cristiano Gori in Florence in 1758. An improved method of working *scagliola*, invented by Gori's master, Ignazio Hugford, made this slightly cheaper imitation of *pietre dure* very popular in the 18th century, especially among visitors to Italy. Collection: John Fleming, Esq

Designs for furniture were also provided by architects. In the larger 18th-century palaces much of the more impressive furniture was, so to speak, 'built in' or very carefully designed to form part of the decoration of a room. In the great galleries, console tables and seats formed part of the wall decoration and complimented the designs of the frames of the mirrors above them. Filippo Juvarra, the great Sicilian architect who worked mainly for the Savoy court in Turin, provided numerous drawings for console tables and very probably drew up rough designs for all the furnishings in the magnificent palaces and villas he built. As might be expected, the decorations on this furniture repeat the motifs of the stucco work and *boiseries*. Juvarra's example seems to have been followed by Conte Benedetto Alfieri: the built-in seats and console tables in the gallery of the Accademia Filarmonica, Turin, built to his design in the 1760s are so carefully integrated in the general scheme that they can hardly have been designed by anyone else.

Juvarra was responsible for assembling in Turin a group of highly-skilled craftsmen capable of carrying out his designs. They included Francesco Ladatte, a bronze sculptor who had been trained in France and became the only Italian *ciseleur* of note; Carlo Giuseppe Plura, a talented woodcarver; and Pietro Piffetti, one of the very few Italian cabinet-makers worthy to be called an *ébéniste*. A craftsman of rare ability, Piffetti indulged a *mauvaise passion* for exceedingly intricate, sometimes fussy, marquetry of

Plate facing page 161

574

ivory, mother-of-pearl and rare woods. Some of his finest works appear to have been designed by Juvarra—the writing desks in the Palazzo Reale, Turin, and the Quirinale, Rome, for example. Among his simpler productions, the marquetry tables decorated with *trompe l'oeil* playing cards are perhaps the most attractive.

Table tops and panels for the decoration of cabinets were made of *pietre dure* in Florence throughout the 18th century. But these very expensive *objets de luxe* were beyond the pockets of nearly all Italians and even the majority of grand tourists. Thus, imitations made in *scagliola* paste became increasingly popular. Enrico Hugford, the Abbot of Vallombrosa, developed a new technique which enabled him to use scagliola pastes as paints capable of great delicacy of tone. He and his pupils, Lamberto Cristiano Gori and Pietro Belloni, produced numerous pictures and tabletops in this substance, especially for export to England. The table top illustrated reveals the potentialities of the medium—at first sight it appears to be a painted table on which a number of flowers have been strewn, on closer inspection it looks as it if were made of a very fine inlay of semi-precious stones. The eye is thus twice deceived before the true nature of the substance is appreciated.

Scagliola table tops made in the second half of the 18th century follow the gradual change in style from the late Baroque or Rococo to Neo-Classicism. The wayward cartouches, the flowers carelessly strewn over the surface, the little landscapes, gradually

576

596

586

587 *Left*: Design for a side table, *c.* 1760, by Domenico Tiepolo. The drawings from the Tiepolo studio include a few designs for corner cupboards and tables. Victoria and Albert Museum, London

589 *Right*: A bedroom in Palazzo Balbi-Durazzo, Genoa. The very fine Louis XVI-style bed and tester were probably made in Genoa in the 1770s under French influence. The other furnishings, also influenced by France, are some twenty years earlier. Nevertheless, the room is strongly Italianate in feeling, due largely to the rich red silk hangings, the painted ceiling and *terrazza* marble floor.

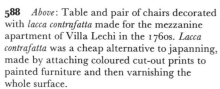

588 *Above*: Table and pair of chairs decorated with *lacca contrafatta* made for the mezzanine apartment of Villa Lechi in the 1760s. *Lacca contrafatta* was a cheap alternative to japanning, made by attaching coloured cut-out prints to painted furniture and then varnishing the whole surface.

592 *Below*: Painted bureau of carved wood by Giuseppe Maria Bonzanigo, Turin, *c.* 1780. The exquisite relief carvings are picked out in white on a pale turquoise ground. Bonzanigo made numerous pieces of furniture for the House of Savoy though he was mainly employed as a wood carver. Palazzo di Stupinigi, Turin

591 *Below*: Painted and gilt firescreen made in Turin in 1775 by Giuseppe Maria Bonzanigo. The painted decorations are by Michele Rapous. The carving is executed with a meticulous precision rarely found on furniture outside France. In design the firescreen owes something to Louis XVI furniture, but its rich exuberance is characteristically Italian. Palazzo Reale, Turin

590 *Above*: Centre table with white marble supports and a porphyry top. Rome *c.* 1775–85. Probably designed by the architect Antonio Asprucci who redecorated the interior of Villa Borghese 1775–85. This form of table is inspired by an ancient Roman type which had been copied also in the 16th century. Galleria Borghese, Rome

593 *Below*: Bedroom in the Villa Bianchi-Bandinelli, near Siena. The furniture appears to have been made in Siena in the late 18th century—the silk hangings on the bed are original.

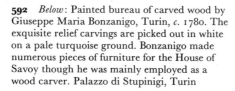

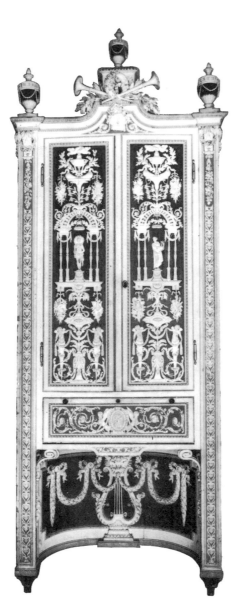

594 *Above*: Bronze table designed by Giuseppe Valadier, 1789-90. The figures of Hercules were cast from models by the sculptor, Vincenzo Pacetti. Vatican Library

595 *Left*: Commode, inlaid with palisander, ebony, mahogany, and other woods by Giuseppe Maggiolini, Milan, 1790. This commode is signed and dated by Maggiolini, the most famous of 18th-century Italian cabinet-makers to whom all pieces of furniture in this style tend to be attributed. Museo Civico d'Arte del Castello Sforzesco, Milan

596 *Below*: *Pietre dure* table top made in Florence towards the end of the 18th century. Table tops such as this, made of a mosaic of semi-precious hard stones were among the most costly pieces of furniture made in 18th-century Italy. Museo del' Opificio delle Pietre Dure, Florence

597 *Below*: The Romulus Room in Palazzo Altieri, Rome, 1791. This room with a ceiling by Stefano Tofanelli and a dado carved in marble by Vincenzo Pacetti provides a good example of Roman Neo-Classicism. With the exception of the pier table and the writing table, which are earlier, the furniture is of the same date as the decorations.

give way to correct architectural motifs, still-lifes of 'Etruscan' vases and other antiquities, and upright figures of Grecians and Romans. At the same time every trace of frivolity or fussiness is banished from the carved wood bases on which the scagliola panels rest.

A shortage of well documented and dated pieces of *settecento* furniture makes it very difficult to trace the early development of Neo-Classicism. In the 1750s, for example, there was a vogue for 'ruin rooms' furnished with stools in the form of broken columns or upturned capitals and sofas resembling antique sarcophagi—but none are known to survive. They reflect the feeling for romantic archaeology expressed in the engravings of Roman ruins by J-B Piranesi, who became a close friend while he was in Rome of the young Scottish architect, Robert Adam. Piranesi's *Diverse Maniere d'adornare i Camini*, published in 1769, included some intricate Neo-Classical designs for tables. By the 1770s a few *avant-garde* spirits had decorated their rooms with whole-heartedly Neo-Classical furniture of a type which anticipates the Empire style—console tables resting on the heads of Egyptian statues, little tables supported by lion-headed terms and so on. But strangely enough no one seems to have been directly inspired by the chairs shown on antique sculptured reliefs or statues (like that of Agrippina) or by the tables illustrated in the paintings from Herculaneum and Pompeii.

The vogue for sculptured furniture persisted in 18th-century Rome. When the Villa Borghese was redecorated by Antonio Aspruccì in the 1770s, the galleries were furnished with great tables on marble supports in the form of winged lions. Perhaps the finest, certainly the most monumental, piece of Roman furniture of this period is a table in the Vatican library supported on eight bronze statues of Hercules modelled by Vincenzo Pacetti in 1789 and cast by Giuseppe Valadier. Furniture such as this was, of course, reserved for the state apartments of the greatest palaces.

Marquetry furniture remained popular throughout the 18th century. A fine Roman example of this type of work is provided by the writing desk made for Pope Pius VI in the 1770s or 1780s. But the most famous centre for marquetry pieces was Milan. Here the outstanding cabinet-maker was Giuseppe Maggiolini, who signed a number of cabinets and commodes elegantly decorated with marquetry featuring Neo-Classical motifs. His name is, in fact, now used by the antique trade to describe virtually all such pieces made in Italy. His furniture is closer in feeling to that produced in the France of Louis XVI than to the Neo-Classical furniture made in Rome.

In Piedmont an elaborate variation of Louis XVI furniture became popular in the last decades of the century. But despite the free use of Classical motifs and rectilinear designs, it usually retained some trace of Rococo frivolity. The leading craftsman was an exquisite sculptor in wood, Giuseppe Maria Bonzanigo, who was responsible for carving some very delicate objects for the royal palaces in and near Turin and a bedroom suite of exquisite fragility.

The influence of English furniture styles was also evident in the second half of the 18th century. Designs from the pattern books of Chippendale, Hepplewhite and Sheraton were copied, especially those for chairs. So far as may be judged, however, they were employed mainly by less expert craftsmen and for smaller houses. The general outlines of the English pieces were imitated but the carved decorations tend to be rather clumsy and are generally much simplified. Patterns popular in the 18th century remained in use for much of the 19th. There is, for instance, reason to believe that Venetian Rococo commodes of an exuberantly *bombé* outline were made in the 19th century not as 'reproductions' but simply as furnishings of a pleasing design.

The writer on Italian furniture of the 18th century must inevitably concentrate his attention on the finest pieces which, with the notable exception of those by Piffetti and Maggiolini, are more often the work of sculptors than cabinet-makers. It should not, however, be forgotten that the majority of the furniture of this period was made by household carpenters. The Italian word *falegname* was and is still applied to the carpenter and the cabinet-maker. Such pieces are, of course, undocumented and the complete absence of Italian furniture pattern-books prevents one from dating them with any precision. Though they may seem crude in comparison with French or English provincial furniture of the same period, they often have considerable rustic charm.

589 590 594 595 591 592 576, 594

SPAIN AND PORTUGAL

Andrew Ciechanowiecki

Spain

The will of the last Hapsburg ruler had bequeathed the crown of Spain, in the face of international intrigues, to a Bourbon, the grandson of Louis XIV, thus precipitating a protracted and onerous war. The Treaty of Utrecht (1713) finally confirmed Philip V (1700–46) in his domains, diminished by the loss of Gibraltar, Minorca and the Spanish possessions in Italy. These last were, however, to be recovered through the scheming diplomacy of Isabella Farnese, Philip's consort, for her children: Parma in 1731, Naples and Sicily in 1735. With French influences in politics and at Court, the new dynasty introduced a spirit of enlightened reform, which under Philip's successors, Ferdinand VI (1746–59) and Charles III (1759–88) allowed Spain to stage a remarkable but, unfortunately, brief recovery. It can be seen in the field of industry and commerce, public life and the secularised education which brought new intellectual vitality to the country. Unfortunately under Charles IV (1788–1808) misrule undid much of what had been achieved and Spain became ripe for Napoleon's invasion.

In the 18th century, France and Italy were again Spain's principal sources of artistic inspiration. The close family connection between the two lines of Bourbons, as well as the artistic dominance of Versailles, explains the former. On the other hand, both the wives of Philip V were Italian, and Charles III, before succeeding to the throne of Spain, had ruled in Naples for over twenty years in a cultural ambience which suited him perfectly and which he tried to transplant to Spain. If the earlier part of the century and its finest product, La Granja, are completely influenced by France, the latter part, with artists such as the architect Juvarra, the painter Tiepolo and the decorator Gasparini, testifies to a resurgence of Italian taste which was to blend with that of France in the Neo-Classical period. English influences,

entering Spain through Galicia and Portugal must also be taken into consideration.

Although Spanish houses, with their very large rooms, still remained poorly furnished, new types of furniture were introduced and the new pieces were simpler and lighter than before. Carved and gilt console tables, fastened to the walls, or side tables with marble tops, *en suite* with large mirrors in ornate frames, which had long been an integral part of French palatial interiors, became so popular in Spain during the first decades of the 18th century, that in 1736 Philip V established a mirror manufactory at S. Ildefonso, which copied French designs interpreting them in a local fashion.

The occasional table, veneered or carved and parcel gilded on a coloured ground, already known in Rococo examples, came into its own in the so-called style of Charles IV, the equivalent of the French Louis XVI. Together with games tables and small desks they were produced in large numbers. Their elaborate marquetry, characteristic of Spanish late 18th-century furniture, is similar to Italian inlay of the period.

With the disappearance of the ornate cabinet or *vargueño*, of which only a few provincial examples can now be found, a French-inspired piece of furniture, the commode, came to take its place. The early examples made of solid wood, with simple, carved decoration, sometimes gilt, present little interest but the *Manufactura Real* or Royal workshops, since 1768 under the direction of the great Neapolitan decorator, Gasparini, encouraged the production of much more ambitious pieces. An example can be seen in a Neo-Classical commode from the Royal Palace in Madrid, which is strongly Italianate in feeling. It is made of mahogany with fine quality gilt bronze mounts, painted 'Pompeian' panels and small engraved mirrors. In other cases Buen Retiro and Wedgwood plaques were inserted, or the piece of furniture was enriched with gilt bronze reliefs shown against a background of inset white marble. Marquetry of an elaborate

598

599

601

598 This small writing table, dating from the reign of Charles IV, is an excellent example of the Italian-influenced, rich Neo-Classical marquetry then fashionable in Spain. No mounts appear on this and similar pieces. Palacio Nacional, Madrid

599 Commode *en tombeau* made at the Royal Workshops in Madrid shortly after the Neapolitan decorator, Gasparini, had become director. The design derives from André-Charles Boulle, but the marquetry and mounts clearly show the Neapolitan background of the artist. Palacio Nacional, Madrid

The Mirror Room or *Spiegelkabinett*, in the Residenzschloss at Fulda in Germany. The redecoration of the wing of which the *Spiegelkabinett* forms a part, was undertaken for Adalbert von Walderdorff, Prince Bishop of Fulda in 1757. The walls are set with small mirrors in Rococo stucco frames, and the mirrors in the ceiling reflect the elaborate parquetry of the floor.

600 *Above*: Part of the set of seat furniture designed by Gasparini for the rooms which still bear his name at the Royal Palace in Madrid.

602 *Below*: This chair is based on an English prototype, although the carved and gilded decoration is peculiarly Spanish and is characteristic of the mid-18th century. Museo de Artes Decorativas, Madrid

603 *Below*: Late 18th-century Spanish chair in white and gold. The traditional Neo-Classical form has undergone substantial modifications in a purely national spirit. Palacio Nacional, Madrid

604 *Below right*: This armchair from a set furnishing the Yellow Room in the Royal Palace, Madrid, is a good example of the late 18th-century, Italian-influenced chair. The back *en gondole*, delicately pierced and veneered, derives from Italian sources. Palacio Nacional, Madrid

601 *Above*: Late 18th-century commode of mahogany and amboyna wood, with rich ormolu mounts, decorated with painted Pompeian panels and engraved mirrors. It clearly derives from Italian Neo-Classical prototypes, although the final result is Spanish in feeling. Palacio Nacional, Madrid

605 *Below, far right*: This Spanish chair derives from a Renaissance type, but the unmistakably Neo-Classical character of the decorations is typical of the late 18th century. Private Collection, Madrid

trompe l'oeil character was also very popular, while as in Italy bronze mounts were not in demand until the very end of the century, and then only for important pieces.

At the beginning of the century, the heavy Louis XIV *fauteuil*, sometimes covered in leather, and the Portuguese-type chair with an old-fashioned high back were still much used. Ceremonial, carved and gilt chairs, however, were inspired by Italian Baroque example. On the other hand, Louis XV *fauteuils* were also copied by Spanish craftsmen, sometimes faithfully, and sometimes with the addition of a native touch, usually resulting in something more ponderous, but also more picturesque than the original. These tendencies can be seen in the splendid set of seat furniture designed by Gasparini for the Royal Palace in Madrid. Veneered in rosewood and inlaid with ebony, they have exaggeratedly curved Baroque arms and are richly decorated with gilt bronzes. Although Louis XV in conception, they are more Italian than French in feeling.

English influence from Queen Anne to Chippendale is also clearly visible in some Spanish chairs. In spite of the long period of wars, much English furniture was exported to Spain in the early 18th century. Contemporary documents refer to chairs,

The gallery of Palazzo dell' Accademia Filarmonica, Turin, *c*. 1760–70. The interior appears to have been designed by the architects, Benedetto Allieri and Giovanni Battista Borra. Decorative carvings in wood, including the built-in furniture have been attributed to Francesco Bolgieri who was trained in Paris. This magnificent interior was created for the Marchese di Caraglio.

mirrors, clocks, joinery and upholstered furniture, much of it lacquered in red and caned. These imported pieces, as well as impulses from Portugal produced a typically Spanish chair which is Queen Anne, George I or Chippendale in inspiration and generally in shape, but the richly carved and usually gilt decoration is Baroque or Rococo and has nothing in common with the prototype. Similarly the cabriole legs with claw-and-ball feet are usually connected by a stretcher of French influence long adopted in Spain. These chairs are made of walnut or poplar.

In the Neo-Classical period, the English-inspired chair does not disappear. From Minorca, (English until 1782) and Galicia as well as from Portugal, Sheraton designs entered Spain and were copied—but not so much as before. On the whole Charles IV chairs follow two trends: the first is purely French, copying with various degrees of fidelity the Louis XVI originals, which continued to be imported into the country, at their best achieving a delicacy and lightness associated with their French prototypes. But the Italian tendency persists and we find that much late 18th-century seat furniture in Spain is an adaptation of Italian, particularly Neapolitan, designs. These are usually much bolder and more picturesque, if sometimes slightly exaggerated. Chair backs pierced with interlaced geometric patterns or floral motifs, arms sometimes set at a sharp angle to the seat and not connected with the back, disproportionately large seats compared to the backs, are all features of this fashion which can well be studied in the Royal Palace in Madrid and at the former Summer Palace of Aranjuez. All these chairs are painted white or cream and are parcel gilt. But in the last decade of the 18th century, chairs

602

603

604 veneered in mahogany, such as those in the Yellow Room of the Royal Palace, with their backs *en gondole*, delicately pierced and decorated with an inlaid frieze, were also made. They have no analogy in Europe, but their Italian source of inspiration is clear, showing also a knowledge of Sheraton and Hepplewhite designs. Around the turn of the century heavy mahogany furniture in the manner of the French *Directoire* was made, but this group belongs more to the 19th century, which it ushers in, than to the 18th century which dies amidst the orange trees and the delicate Pompeian tracery of Aranjuez furniture.

Together with the whole of Spanish 18th-century furniture, the bed undergoes a process of simplification, becoming lighter and less ceremonial. The tester disappears and the headboard is now usually painted in light colours and parcel gilded. Beds of French type were also in use. This elegant furniture influenced by the Court was of course not adopted immediately by the whole country and never, in fact, by the poorer classes. They had to be content either with following obsolete traditional patterns or adapting modern ones, or finally with the addition of a fashionable Rococo or Neo-Classical touch to pieces belonging structurally to a past age. So for instance many chairs were made which followed a 16th-century model, but were japanned in red, parcel gilded and decorated with *rocaille* ornaments. Thus, as in many countries, a borderline type of furniture appears in Spain, which tries to bridge the gap between solid tradition and the sophisticated fashions of a glamorous, if decadent Court.

Portugal

While for Spain the early 18th century was a period of war and disaster, in Portugal it opened with the glorious reign of John V (1706–50) the Portuguese counterpart to Louis XIV. An enlightened despot, John was also a notable patron of the arts, whose greatest achievement was the Portuguese equivalent of the Escorial, the Mafra Palace near Lisbon. The apparently inexhaustible wealth in gold and diamonds coming in from Brazil allowed the reappearance of luxury at Court and in the capital, but sapped the vitality of the people. In 1703, the Treaty of Methuen with England not only provided for the future a defence, when needed, but also created strong economic ties and in consequence artistic bonds between the two countries. Under Joseph I, (1750–77), in spite of the terrible destruction of Lisbon and other cities in the earthquake of 1755, an enlightened programme of political and economic reform was carried through, to be almost completely abrogated in the next reign, that of Maria I, (1777–1816), paving the way for the conquest of Portugal by Napoleon and the new ideas for which the revolution stood.

John V looked towards Italy and Austria for his architects, but the minor arts and in particular furniture came under the sway of England. There were many reasons for this. Bitter relations with Holland, Spain and France, particularly during the war years with the ensuing severance of all contact with Paris, drew Portugal closer to England. The simplicity and utilitarian qualities of English furniture, of which much was then imported, must have appealed to the Portuguese unsophisticated way of life. The return to Portugal in 1693 of the widowed Catherine of Braganza, who brought with her large quantities of English furniture, helped to create a fashion in this respect and the heavy Baroque turning and carving of the previous century soon vanished in favour of simpler forms. The next change occurred towards the middle of the century when French influences again reached Lisbon both directly and via Madrid.

Of all types of furniture, these influences and their Portuguese adaptation can best be studied in seat furniture. The 17th-century high-backed chair covered with tooled leather remains the ceremonial seat, together with Louis XIV *fauteuils*, sometimes enriched with carved crestings and stretchers, suggesting the

606 coming fashion for Rococo. In some cases these chairs are quite plain and rely on a brocaded slip cover for their decorative effect *(cadeiras de vestir)*. The English cabriole leg with three types of foot was adopted: the club foot, the *pe de sapata* and the claw-and-ball, which was particularly popular. Towards 1730 their seats

606 *Above left*: Mid-18th-century Portuguese mahogany chair in which the mouldings and the flowing lines reflect the Rococo taste. The members uniting the back legs with the carved frame of the back betray a certain provincial awkwardness. Museu Nacional de Arte Antiga, Lisbon

607 *Above*: This Portuguese chair is an early example of those influenced by English taste. Deriving from a Queen Anne prototype it is decorated with Rococo carving and dates from the second quarter of the 18th century. Museu Nacional de Arte Antiga, Lisbon

608 *Left*: Portuguese chair of the second quarter of the 18th century. Although deriving from English prototypes, the exaggerated curves, thin legs and beautifully crisp carving give it an unmistakably national style. Museu Nacional de Arte Antiga, Lisbon

609 *Below left*: This charming, low-backed armchair shows how French influences were merged with English styles in Portugal. Basically a Louis XV armchair, of French inspiration, the splat is adorned with tracery in the English 'Gothick' taste. Mid-18th century. Museu Nacional de Arte Antiga, Lisbon

610 *Below*: Mid-18th-century Portuguese chair illustrating the adaptation by Portuguese craftsmen of English fashions. The pierced splat back is of a type popular in England. Museu Nacional de Arte Antiga, Lisbon

611 *Above left*: Settee and a chair from a set of painted furniture, (so-called *doiradinhas*), inspired by English examples and belonging to a popular late 18th-century type. Museu Escola de Artes Decorativas, Lisbon

612 *Above*: Mid-18th-century Portuguese bed in which posts no longer feature, while the headboard has developed into a richly carved frame, surrounding a panel covered in crimson damask. Nothwithstanding stylistic changes the Portuguese bed remains a wholly original achievement. Collection: Russell de Sousa, Oporto

613 *Left*: This late 18th-century interior in the Fundação Ricardo do Espírito Santo Silva in Lisbon admirably re-creates the atmosphere of a Portuguese *salon* of the period. Museu Escola de Artes Decorativas, Lisbon

became wider and the arms were curved outwards to enable ladies in the new pannier dresses to use them.

But the most characteristic chair of the period was based upon the English Queen Anne type with a pierced baluster splat, cabriole leg, curved stretchers and crested back. In Portugal it was usually made of hard Brazilian wood (jacaranda, pausanto) instead of walnut, which allowed a much crisper finish to the carving, a substantial thinning of the legs and the omission of stretchers. If early examples follow their English prototype fairly closely, the later ones acquire a movement of their own, higher cresting often terminating in a windswept plume of Baroque feathers, an elaborate apron and carvings on the knees. A mastery of execution, allied to a great originality of design, gives them a completely personal style. In the North of the country, the carvings on these chairs are sometimes gilded—an added touch of magnificence. Having thus adapted the Queen Anne chair, the same was done with Chippendale models. The elaborately designed splats, with vases, scrolls, Gothic tracery or of the ribbon type and even Chinese Chippendale become in the hands of the gifted Portuguese carvers even more elaborate but never lose a sense of proportion and beauty. In the North simpler examples exist, usually polychromed and gilt, in which the local craftsmen translate Chippendale's vocabulary into the idiom of the prevailing Rococo. English late 18th-century chairs after the design of Hepplewhite and Sheraton were also skilfully adapted but the later the period the more faithful the copy, which suggests that English pattern-books were widely known.

The French influence prevalent during the reign of King Joseph produces some exact copies of Louis XV chairs and armchairs. But this fashion which introduced more delicate ornament quickly adapted itself to Portuguese traditions, and one can therefore safely say that nearly all the purely Louis XV pieces of furniture found today in Portugal were imported. Portuguese Rococo chairs often introduce the French *violonné* back, but with an English splat, sometimes even decorated with Gothic tracery,

thus showing a characteristic mixture of both formative influences, typical of their national style.

During the French Revolution English influence grew. It can be noticed in the chairs mentioned earlier but also in an English-inspired group of painted furniture, mostly after Hepplewhite designs. These so-called *doiradinhas* painted cream, white or black, with a touch of gold or gilt carving, were beautifully decorated *en grisaille* or with polychromed 'Pompeian' subjects. Their seats were usually caned.

The settees followed the evolution of the chair, their backs formed by three, four or five chair backs. This is even the case with the Louis XV type of settee, while the upholstered, French inspired *canapé* is as rare as the comfortable French *bergère*, or *marquise*, 'easy' chairs such as these seeming never to have been adopted in Portugal.

The Portuguese bed continued to be a completely original achievement, not influenced in any way from abroad. In the early 18th century turned columns are still in use, but soon they were to be dropped. The legs become cabriole ones with claw-and-ball feet. The headboard, similarly to the carving on chairs, adopts Baroque and later Rococo decorative motifs sometimes surrounding an oval panel upholstered in material, usually crimson, to match the bed covers. Day-beds of the same type but with slanting headboards, sometimes mounted on trestles so that they could be folded, were also made. In the second half of the century the headboards are bigger, more architectural, and with a simpler outline and less carving. Instead, elaborate inlays appear on some of them, already Neo-Classical in feeling. In the last quarter of the century the headboard was either rectangular or oval with a Louis XVI cresting flanked by small finials on the side and filled with inlaid decoration. Another popular type was the *leito a inglesa*, a bed folded into the seat of a settee. This ingenious idea, of English inspiration, has survived in numerous examples.

The great increase in wealth of both the nobility and the middle classes in the 18th century led to the appearance of new types of furniture: the console and mirror, the commode, and the *papeleira* (commode-bureau) and various occasional and games tables. The decorative ensemble of a carved and gilt console and a large framed mirror, was popular from the middle of the century onwards. Late Louis XV or transitional in style, elaborately carved and slightly heavy in design, the earlier ones had large oval mirrors with an intricately carved cresting. The later ones, purely Neo-Classical, had the mirror framed in tall panels like the French *trumeau* (but of larger dimensions) decorated with carved motifs and often containing a framed painting above the mirror. They were usually used in pairs. Portuguese commodes seem to have evolved from the sacristy chests in use since the 15th century. Always taller than the average continental commode, they contain four long drawers and in the 18th century have a serpentine fronts, often *bombé* sides, low richly-carved bracket feet and similarly decorated corners. They never have marble tops, and the elaborate brass or silver mounts are sometimes close to contemporary Dutch designs. Another type of commode is an adaptation of the French *Régence* and Louis XV *bombé* shapes. On the whole faithful to its prototype it shows nevertheless its Portuguese origin in the exaggerated design of the apron, the mounts and an indifferent marquetry on a background of Brazilian wood. The tops are of marble. This type of commode undergoes a stylistic transformation in the last quarter of the century to become the Neo-Classical commode of the reign of Queen Maria. Veneered now in rosewood, in simple marquetry

and with a marble top, it has characteristic enamelled Louis XVI mounts, again strongly reminiscent of Dutch furniture of the same period. Good craftsmanship is characteristic of these attractive pieces of furniture. At the close of the century many small Neo-Classical commodes were made, often semi-circular, with delicate inlay and tall, tapering legs.

Occasional tables of the earlier part of the century again follow English models: gate-leg tables, pie-crust tables, and small tables with one or two drawers, all beautifully made in Brazilian wood enriched with carving, with delicate spidery cabriole legs showing the craftsman's delight in his mastery of the material. In the North the shapes appear heavier, less graceful; local materials are often used, and the carving is gilded. Later, with the victory of Neo-Classicism, tables are usually veneered with rosewood or mahogany and elaborately inlaid, their shape reflecting the prevailing taste. We also find beautiful and complicated games tables, the finest dating from the 1750s with an intricate system of adjustable tops for the various games. The delicate carving and the beautiful inlay in ivory show Portuguese craftsmanship at its best. Neo-Classical games tables are much simpler and often semi-circular.

Another type of furniture much in demand was the commode-bureau *(papeleira)*. Built on similar lines to the normal commode and similarly decorated, it has a slanting desk top deriving from English Queen Anne prototypes. Later, under French influence a type of *bureau à cylindre* was also introduced.

615 *Above*: Late 18th-century Portuguese commode in the style known as 'D. Maria'. The marquetry of exotic woods continues on the heavy apron below. The piece has a marble top and the handles are mounted with enamel roundels. Museu Escola de Artes Decorativas, Lisbon

614 *Above*: Mid-18th-century Portuguese commode. The richly scrolled bracket feet, the carved motifs and the substantial height of the piece lend it originality. Museu Nacional de Arte Antiga, Lisbon

616 *Below*: This splendid games table of the mid-18th century, shows Portuguese craftsmanship at its best; graceful proportions are combined with superlative carving. The several reversible tops inlaid with ivory reveal various games' boards. The mounts are of silver. Fundação Ricardo do Espírito Santo Silva. Museu Escola de Artes Decorativas, Lisbon

617 *Below*: Cylinder-top bureau, ornamented with marquetry made in Lisbon by Domingos Tenuta in 1790. Although of so late a date the keyhole, escutcheons and handles are somewhat old-fashioned in design. Tenuta is one of the few Portuguese cabinet-makers who signed his work, and sometimes his signature appears in secret drawers, embossed on leather panels. Collection: Vasconcelos Porto, Oporto

Spanish and Portuguese Colonial Furniture

For the colonies of Latin America the 18th century was a period of economic and cultural development, during which ties with the mother country slowly loosened. The viceregal courts and the elegant life of the upper classes testify to a high level of civilisation. In Brazil, the capital was moved from Bahia to Rio de Janeiro, a town which developed rapidly, and was to enchant the Portuguese court and royal family when they arrived there in 1808. Changes in the pattern of development were also influenced by the expulsion from the colonies of the Jesuits, who had previously been evicted from Portugal in 1759 and Spain in 1767.

True colonial furniture only evolved in the 18th century. Although the models were still European, (often not only Spanish or Portuguese, but German or Flemish, depending on the country of origin of the ecclesiastic or artisan), the native craftsmen added local elements more and more often. Oriental influence was also felt in Mexico, Chinese wallpapers and other products being copied. Both Mexico and Peru still used silver to decorate their furniture. Rectangular chairs echoed Spanish prototypes while English models were also adapted. The lighter, Rococo style was reputedly introduced by the viceroy Don Manuel Afat and his Peruvian mistress La Perricholi, while the first pieces of Neo-Classical furniture are thought to have been made under the influence of Father Josef Schmid, a Bavarian working in Belem, and of Martin Maestro. But undoubtedly the Baroque colonial furniture was the most popular and it was only replaced by Neo-Classicism at a very late date, in Brazil in fact only with the arrival of the Portuguese Court in 1808. Even then it had a special flavour to it, using no bronzes but only a rich inlay of wood, ivory and mother-of-pearl. The wealth of Brazil in the 18th century led to much furniture being produced, which in a rather heavy manner repeated Portuguese designs. In Bahia for instance, the richly carved chairs and tables have particularly large aprons, while in Minas Gerais conservative tables with heavy turned legs were still popular. Beds were either carved like Portuguese examples or were painted, but they never had testers. In Peru and Ecuador, in spite of the earthquakes of 1747 and 1755, many heavily carved pieces of furniture have survived. In these, flat carving covering the whole surface was in keeping with a massive shape and heavy aprons. A special type is the tiny low table of similar structure known as a *ratona*.

Spanish and Portuguese fashions, adapted to local taste, dominated colonial furniture of the 18th century, but at the close of the period the Latin American countries, in keeping with their rapid political evolution, were turning more towards England and other European countries for artistic leadership.

621
618
619

621

620

618 *Above*: This splendid chair dating from c. 1770 derives from Portuguese models of thirty years earlier—but its exaggerated line points to a Brazilian provenance. Palacio Itamaraty, Rio de Janeiro

619 *Above centre*: Mexican chair of the early 18th century, combining Spanish Baroque motifs with local traditional features and creating a highly original effect. Hispanic Society of America, New York

620 *Above right*: Carved wood table painted white and partly gilded, made for a sacristy of a Paraguayan church in the mid-18th century. In form it derives from European examples to which a typical native exuberance in execution is united. Private Collection, Asunción

621 *Right*: Even in the Neo-Classical period, the severe form of this desk, made for the Bishop of Buenos Aires, D. Manuel de Azamor y Ramirez (1788–96), is relieved by the exuberant, and still wholly Baroque, inlaid decoration. Museo Historico Nacional, Buenos Aires

THE LOW COUNTRIES

Th. H. Lunsingh Scheurleer

Close connections between Holland and England in the last decades of the 17th century were fostered by personal contacts developed when the future Charles II was in exile and later by the presence of a Dutch King on the English throne. These links brought Dutch cabinet-makers to London and enabled English craftsmen to benefit from a closer knowledge of the new techniques of veneering. Meanwhile, a flood of Huguenot refugees, forced to leave France by the Revocation of the Edict of Nantes in 1685, had streamed into Holland and to England, bringing with them the disciplined sophistication of French taste. The rich cities of the Netherlands, already accustomed to a high standard of craftsmanship, had therefore also begun to benefit from foreign example and by the early years of the 18th century, not only French but English furniture too was much admired.

Among cabinet-pieces, the bureau-bookcase with a lower stage composed of a slant-front desk on a chest-of-drawers and the upper enclosed by two doors with looking-glass panels, was of English origin. Dutch cabinet-makers were quick to imitate their English colleagues and did their utmost to surpass them in the use of skilfully matched veneers. Bureau-bookcases of the first quarter of the century, surmounted by two arched pediments, are strongly reminiscent of English work.

It is significant that between 1711 and 1762 the cabinet-makers of The Hague were required by their Guild regulations to submit what was described as an 'English cabinet' as their masterpiece. The Guild records survive and include the names of two Englishmen, John Lywood and J. Simney, who thus presented their masterpieces in the years 1722 and 1723 respectively. They were probably young men trying their luck abroad as, indeed, many Dutchmen had done before them in England. But such was the popularity of English furniture that it doubtless suited even the Dutch to be described as English cabinet-makers. For this reason it is often difficult to distinguish English work from Dutch.

In the case of chairs, the connection with England is often equally unmistakable. The English type, with the pierced splat and cabriole legs, must very frequently have been made in the Netherlands, as it is repeatedly mentioned in contemporary inventories. The shape and decoration varied according to individual taste or requirements. Sometimes the cresting suggested a Chinese source of inspiration while the veneered splat might contain a marquetry panel, a characteristically Dutch feature. Also essentially Dutch are the sharp convex and concave curves of the seat rail on many chairs of the first half of the century. Many varieties of chairs with upholstered backs, inspired by French influence, were also produced.

Shortly before the middle of the century Rococo features began to appear. The curved profiles and *bombé* shapes of cabinet-pieces are now accentuated and so contribute a new sense of movement. The door panels of bureau-bookcases or corner cupboards are outlined at first by gently curving applied mouldings, sometimes breaking into scrolling leaves; while carved ornament might include a diaper pattern or husk motifs. As the century advanced panels of cabinets or cupboards became freely asymmetrical, sometimes including shell motifs. When the doors are mounted with looking-glass panels, these might be painted with Chinese birds, reminders of the Dutch trade with the Far East.

622 Armchair of elm, the cabriole legs terminating in hoof feet. Dutch, first half of the 18th century. Like the English chairs of the period, this example relies not upon surface ornament but upon suavely flowing lines. Rijksmuseum, Amsterdam

623 Chair veneered with burr-walnut and decorated with marquetry panels. First half of the 18th century. The pronounced curves of the seat rail and the deep marquetry panel in the centre of the apron are characteristic Dutch features. Rijksmuseum, Amsterdam

624 Walnut chair. Dutch, mid-18th century. The curving lines of the back and seat rail pay deference to Louis XV chairs but the claw-and-ball feet are familiar features of English chairs. The upholstery is later. Rijksmuseum, Amsterdam

625 *Above*: Bureau-bookcase veneered with burr-walnut, *c*. 1740. Like many cabinets from the Low Countries, this piece has chamfered corners both on the upper and lower stages. Dutch trade with the East created a particular interest in Chinese porcelain and a garniture of vases was displayed on the cornice which was specially designed for this purpose. Rijksmuseum, Amsterdam

626 *Above*: Commode veneered with burr-walnut and ornamented with marquetry panels, *c*. 1740. The complex, curving profile and the deep apron piece with turned pendant finial are Dutch characteristics. The scrolled 'Spanish' foot is an earlier feature, still persisting in Holland. Rijksmuseum, Amsterdam

628 *Below left*: Corner cabinet veneered with burr-walnut, *c*. 1750–60. Dutch cabinet-makers, accustomed to the pictorial character of marquetry decoration, were also sensitive to the decorative quality of burr veneers and in this example the natural figure of the wood provides the most striking feature. Rijksmuseum, Amsterdam

629 *Below*: Tea table veneered with walnut, *c*. 1750. Porcelain tea cups were rare and highly valued at this period and the 'tray' top protected them against mishap. The *bombé* form of the drawer is a feature of Dutch tables of the mid-18th century. Rijksmuseum, Amsterdam

630 *Right*: Oak cupboard ornamented with Rococo carving in relief, *c*. 1745. This type of cupboard, more usually rectangular in shape, carved with lively scrollwork and flame-like motifs, came from Liège and towns in the neighbourhood. Musées Royaux d'Art et d'Histoire, Brussels

627 *Above*: Cabinet-on-chest veneered with burr-walnut. Dutch, *c*. 1750–60. The serpentine and *bombé* profile and the choice of a burr veneer for the sides as well as for the front proclaim the high quality of this piece. The cornice, now Rococo in form, still provides for the garniture of vases; other Rococo features include the carved, plume-like motif in the centre of the pediment, the swirling leaves on the apron, the meandering scrolled mouldings round the door panels, and the asymmetrical handles and key-hole escutcheons. Rijksmuseum, Amsterdam

631 *Above left*: Commode veneered with tulipwood and decorated with marquetry, *c*. 1760. Signed, on the base of the plinth upon which the marquetry vase of flowers stands, by the cabinet-maker A. Bongen of Amsterdam. This piece closely follows French example, but the awkward placing of the key-hole escutcheon would hardly have been countenanced by a Parisian cabinet-maker. Private Collection, Holland

632 *Above right*: Cupboard veneered with rosewood and satinwood, Dutch, *c*. 1780. The straight lines and clearly defined proportions defer to Neo-Classical taste. Private Collection, Holland

633 *Left*: Fall-front secretaire veneered with satinwood, ebony and other exotic woods and mounted with panels of Chinese lacquer, *c*. 1780. Dutch pieces of this type were based upon Louis XVI secretaires but they have fewer gilt bronze mounts than their French prototypes. Rijksmuseum, Amsterdam

634 *Right*: Table decorated with marquetry of harewood, satinwood and other exotic woods, contrasting with ebony borders, and mounted on the top with a panel of Chinese lacquer, Dutch, *c*. 1780. Private Collection, Holland

Many 18th-century cabinets have chamfered or rounded corners. Perhaps this feature may have contributed towards the development and growing popularity of corner cupboards. They were usually intended for the display of porcelain and glass and although they had panelled doors, these were often decorated on the inside with lacquer so that the cabinet could be left open for the contents to be admired. Some were veneered with burr walnut producing a mottled effect almost as though it were marble. Other china cabinets had glass doors and the fashion in the Netherlands for collecting earthenware and porcelain explains the popularity of these pieces.

An important type of cupboard in a Netherland's household, which appears to have originated in the region of the River Zaan, is that which contains a linen press in the upper stage. In the 18th century it was apparently not always considered desirable for this useful piece of furniture to retain too domestic an appearance so it was disguised as a respectable writing cabinet or bureau-bookcase.

Early in the century the habit of taking tea at certain fixed times became a fashionable practice in Holland as elsewhere. Tea tables of the English type, with a tray top supported on four cabriole legs, were popular, although the *bombé* surfaces and curvaceous forms of the Dutch examples give them a more florid appearance than their English prototypes. Oval folding tables on a pedestal support were even more in demand. These were of deal painted with flowers and leaves, and were so constructed that the top could be tipped forwards into a vertical position.

The large-sized wardrobes executed in oak, which originated in Liège and its environs in the Southern Netherlands, are wholly different from those of the Northern Netherlands. They have two or more doors, decorated in the French manner with carving in relief of asymmetrical scrolls and flowers. The corners of these cupboards are rounded. Sometimes the front is of bow-shape although they are usually rectangular.

The Dutch commode closely imitated French examples. Often of *bombé* shape, the finest are veneered in burr walnut. But to save expense the burr veneer was frequently confined to the front of the commode, leaving the sides with plain veneer.

The great popularity which both French and English furniture thus enjoyed in the 18th century often brought the Dutch cabinet-makers into difficulties. Imports—especially from France—became so numerous that the Amsterdam Guild felt compelled to protest. As a result, in 1771 the importation of all furniture made outside the Netherlands was prohibited. Only the annual fairs were exempt from these regulations, but in order not to victimise traders, those in possession of foreign furniture were allowed to sell what was already in Amsterdam during the following three months. After that period, however, they were compelled to brand every piece of furniture with the mark of the Amsterdam Joseph's Guild (the letters J.G. on either side of the Arms of Amsterdam). To satisfy the taste for French furniture, Dutch cabinet-makers produced work in the French style, using marquetry decoration. The Amsterdam Master cabinet-maker, Andries Bongen was particularly known for this type of work.

It is not possible to determine whether the action of the

635 *Above left*: Commode veneered with exotic woods and set with panels of lacquer and of marquetry, Dutch, *c.* 1790. This piece is *en suite* with a fall-front secretaire. The hinged top opens to reveal a cistern and basin and is similar in design to that shown in illustration 638. Frans Hals Museum, Haarlem

636 *Above right*: Drawing room from a Haarlem house, by the architect Abraham van der Hart, now preserved in the Rijksmuseum in Amsterdam. *c.* 1780. The wall hangings of embroidered silk, the curtains and the carpet are original. The Louis XVI furniture was ordered from Paris.

637 *Left*: Mahogany chair, *c.* 1780. Dutch chairs of this period imitated French Louis XVI designs although the choice of wood, the manner of the carving and the set of the arms combine to give this example a peculiarly Dutch character. Rijksmuseum, Amsterdam

638 *Right*: Commode decorated with marquetry panels, *c.* 1780. It is shown with the hinged top open and fitted inside the lid is a cistern. One of the two flaps is also open, providing additional space, and revealing the basin in the centre. This type of commode could thus be used as a serving table, allowing glassware to be washed in the drawing room. Rijksmuseum, Amsterdam

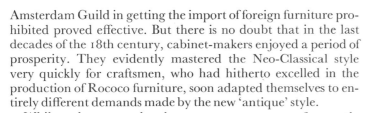

Amsterdam Guild in getting the import of foreign furniture prohibited proved effective. But there is no doubt that in the last decades of the 18th century, cabinet-makers enjoyed a period of prosperity. They evidently mastered the Neo-Classical style very quickly for craftsmen, who had hitherto excelled in the production of Rococo furniture, soon adapted themselves to entirely different demands made by the new 'antique' style.

While mahogany and mahogany veneer were now frequently used, especially for wardrobes and cupboards, the earlier *bombé* shapes gave way to rectangular forms and straight lines. But the cabinet-makers of the Netherlands continued to distinguish themselves in the art of marquetry, using exotic woods such as rosewood, satinwood or ebony. Sometimes panels of Oriental lacquer were mounted in these Neo-Classical pieces and it is possible that this practice in the late 18th century of including lacquer panels as a decorative feature may have been introduced by the Dutch. Even in the early 18th century they had used Canton enamel plaques as decorative mounts and by 1780 the use of lacquer panels to enliven a veneered surface was as usual in the Netherlands as it was in France. Despite the delicacy of the material, lacquer panels were even used on table tops, the dark ground foiled by the use of harewood or satinwood. A more refined sense of proportion is apparent in the late 18th century. Cabinet-makers adopted the form of the French drop-front secretaire, sometimes introducing Oriental lacquer panels, contrasted with a marquetry of satinwood, bordered with dark woods such as rosewood, mahogany or ebony. But in spite of their kinship with French work, the somewhat angular, contrasting geometrical shapes of the marquetry on such pieces and the infrequent use of ormolu mounts, with the exception of keyhole escutcheons and handles, lends them a specific Dutch character.

Secretaires were sometimes made *en suite* with commodes, the latter being usually rectangular in shape, with canted corners. These commodes could combine the function of a buffet with that of a low cupboard, for the top could be raised to reveal a pewter cistern attached to the lid, and by lifting two horizontal flaps, the basin beneath could be conveniently used for washing porcelain or glass while the flaps provided additional space. Shelves within the lid, on either side of the cistern, could be used for the display of glasses or cups.

As in France, the chair of this period had an oval or rectangular back, with many variations. But in the Netherlands mahogany was preferred for the frame while the carved decoration and the way in which the arms are set lend these chairs a specifically Netherlandish character. Chairs painted in light colours after the French fashion were not unknown in the Netherlands. Sometimes they were bought in France and indeed Willem Kops of Haarlem, ordered a French suite for his drawing-room consisting of a sofa, 4 armchairs, 12 ordinary chairs and 2 firescreens, all covered in embroidered silk on a blue ground. This entire room with its furniture is now in the Rijksmuseum, Amsterdam and with the original silk curtains and wall hangings, the carpet and cut-glass chandelier and candelabra, the apartment provides an admirable example of a late 18th-century interior.

SCANDINAVIA

Peter Thornton

A whole new chapter in the history of Scandinavian taste opened when the Great Fire destroyed large parts of London in 1666. Suddenly enormous quantities of timber were needed for rebuilding the damaged areas of the English capital, and the already well-established timber trade with England now became an extremely profitable business for the Scandinavian countries. Most of the timber came from Norway, but Norwegian prosperity quickly came to be reflected in Denmark because Norway was politically and culturally joined to Denmark at this period and remained so until 1814. The Court and the seat of government of the two nations were in Copenhagen. Sweden, too, was engaged in this timber trade although her share was smaller than that of Norway. On the other hand, Sweden also exported iron ore to England and the total volume of her trade with this country was considerable. These commercial links brought Scandinavia increasing prosperity, accentuated by England's spectacular expansion during the 18th century which of course resulted in an even greater demand for timber and iron ore. In return English goods were imported in large quantity, with the result that the people of Scandinavia soon became quite familiar with English taste in a number of fields, notably in that of furniture.

The English Influence

A great deal of English furniture had already reached the Scandinavian countries during the last decades of the 17th century. For instance, English high-backed chairs, so typical of that period, are found in some numbers in each of the three countries —Norway, Denmark and Sweden. These importations served as models for indigenous craftsmen who, in turn, started to produce imitations that were more or less faithful copies of the originals.

Having once adopted this style, however, the Scandinavian craftsmen were reluctant to give it up, and chairs obviously derived from the English high-backed formula continued to be made in this old-fashioned style until well into the 18th century.

It is indeed in the chair-maker's craft that English influence is most obvious throughout the 18th century in all the Scandinavian countries. Until quite late in the century, the craft of chair-making was entirely separate from that of cabinet-making. The cabinet-makers were comparatively receptive to new ideas whereas the chair-makers were remarkable for their conservatism. Long after their English counterparts had adopted the graceful, unbraced cabriole leg so typical of late Queen Anne and early-Georgian chairs, their Scandinavian makers continued to furnish such legs with a complete set of stretchers, neatly turned on a lathe—for the chair-makers were an offshoot of the Turners' Guilds—but none the less incongruous. The conservatism of the Scandinavian chair-makers is also to be seen in the way they retained English forms long after they had gone out of fashion in England; early Georgian backs still appearing on mid-century chairs.

In Denmark, this conservatism was accentuated by the prohibition, introduced in 1746, on the importation of foreign chairs. While this measure helped the native chair-makers to sell more of their own wares, it effectively prevented them from seeing examples of the latest English styles. The result was that their art became stagnant and they continued to turn out versions of the early-Georgian fiddleback chair until after the embargo was lifted in 1768. Naturally they tried to keep up with the fashion of the times but their efforts are reflected, not in the forms of their chairs, but in the decoration. Realising that the symmetrical shell ornament so common on the cresting and front seat rails of early-Georgian chairs was out of date, they gave these motifs a

639 *Above left*: In Sweden a maker of cane-seated chairs was already known as an *engelsk stolmakar* early in the 18th century. The English derivation of this chair form, with its high back and cane seat, is unmistakable. Such chairs were popular in Norway, but this Swedish specimen of oak bears the cypher of Charles XII (1697–1718). A form with a lower back is more common in Sweden and Denmark. Nordiska Museet, Stockholm

640 *Above*: Norwegian oak armchair in the English style, c. 1715, with gilt leather upholstery. The form of the front legs, the fan-like motif and birds on the cresting and stretcher are characteristic of a group of chairs thought to come from the Bergen area, although similar forms are to be seen on Danish chairs of the period. Kunstindustrimuseet, Oslo

641 *Left*: One of a pair of carved and gilt *guéridons* probably made early in the 18th century in Stockholm by Burchardt Precht. Precht was a German who had settled in Sweden in the 1670s. At the height of his career he worked in the French Baroque idiom introduced into Sweden by the architect Nicodemus Tessin, but he tended to impart a Germanic flavour to his work. Later, the principal Swedish craftsmen assimilated the French taste more fully. From Precht's workshop came carved and gilt mirrors, console tables, sconces and candelabra, always of high quality and in this late Baroque style, often with details derived from Jean Bérain. Nordiska Museet, Stockholm

642 *Left*: Danish clock in a simplified version of the English style, by the Copenhagen clock-maker Peter Mathiesen, who flourished during the second quarter of the 18th century. English and Dutch japanned furniture was much admired at this time in Scandinavia. Long case clocks decorated in this medium were imitated and they were sometimes even deceitfully furnished with a spurious London maker's name. Nationalmuseet, Copenhagen

643 *Below*: Danish chest-of-drawers *c.* 1720–40, of characteristic form but unusually high quality. Richly mounted and brightly painted chests or coffers were still far from rare at the beginning of the 18th century, even in the grandest Scandinavian houses. They then often had separate, and perhaps gilt stands. The newly invented chests-of-drawers were frequently to retain their stands (still apparently, if not in fact, separate) in Denmark and Norway for several decades. Nationalmuseet, Copenhagen

644 *Right*: This handsome cabinet was made in about 1751 by Mathias Ortmann, one of the principal mid-18th-century Copenhagen cabinet-makers. Displaying Anglo-Dutch features, it is an early piece and not typical of his work, which mostly has a Germanic Rococo bias, with *bombé* forms. Ortmann was the only Danish maker with sufficient capital to keep a stock of furniture in a shop ready for sale; his rivals all relied on commissions from their customers. He numbered his products in ink on a printed trade plate pasted inside each article, and he occasionally held lotteries with furniture as prizes. This cabinet was apparently won by the King himself. Fredensborg Palace, Denmark. Reproduced by Gracious Permission of H.M. the King of Denmark

twist and contorted them into a *rocaille* form in the new Rococo taste. This ornament is usually rather naïvely carved and is generally quite large. It gives a lop-sided look to these otherwise essentially upright and symmetrical chairs. A mild form of this *réchauffé* early-Georgian type is found in the Lübeck area, whence it may have sprung. But this curious exaggeration, often underlined by the fact that the *rocaille* ornament is picked out with gilding, is characteristically Danish and thus also Norwegian. It is not found in Sweden.

Unfortunately it is otherwise very difficult to point to any peculiarly Scandinavian characteristics in Scandinavian imitations of English furniture. Features such as a certain form of crown in the cresting of their high-backed chairs, a particular form of leg, an identifiable royal monogram, a detail in the construction, or the kind of wood used—may help one to recognise a Scandinavian product. The best imitations are very faithful indeed and might mislead even the expert. But the average Scandinavian copy tends to be simplified and to display a certain change in the proportions; some of the features become emphasised, curves and scrolls lose the tension which characterises a really good design, and there is often a disjointedness about the composition. This is most noticeable in the chair backs. In cabinet work the forms are usually much better integrated. Walnut, beechwood, and sometimes oak were certainly used for the

manufacture of the best Scandinavian chairs of the period, but stained and painted imitations made of birchwood, ash or deal were more common. Deal chairs tend to have members of somewhat thicker section and any carving will usually be simpler and less crisp than that in the harder sorts of wood. Scandinavian birchwood and deal chairs are usually painted, often a reddish-brown, in imitation of the rarer woods, but also in shades of grey, olive green and even in a bamboo colour or in dark blue. The paint is fairly matt. Such chairs were found in the best houses of the time, at any rate in the less important rooms, but are more characteristic of the smaller country houses and of peasant furnishings. The peasantry was, of course, a large and numerous class and some of its members were comparatively rich. They had their own traditions and, for the most part, felt proudly independent of the middle and upper classes—although they ultimately adopted the successive upper-class fashions, one after the other. This led to some curious juxtapositions; debased Viking and Gothic carving is found alongside Renaissance and Baroque forms and the whole may then be decorated with wild Rococo ornament. Peasant furniture is almost entirely of deal but occasionally oak was used, notably in the south of Jutland.

Walnut continued in use as the standard wood for high-class Scandinavian cabinet furniture until well into the second half of the 18th century, when it began to be supplanted by mahogany

645 It is not certain whether this is a French gilt beechwood armchair or a good Danish copy. It is probably the latter, since it is dated 1740, and few French specimens are dated. It bears a mark showing that it was part of the furnishings of the new Danish royal palace, built in the 1730s and subsequently burnt down. Fredensborg Palace, Denmark. Reproduced by Gracious Permission of H.M. the King of Denmark

646 Carved and gilt console table, *c*. 1750, made in Stockholm. Probably carved by a Frenchman but designed by the Swedish Court architect, Carl Harleman (1700–53), who had studied in Paris under Vassé. This piece must have been made after Harleman's return from his third visit to Paris in 1745 where he had fully assimilated the latest fashion. It is in a pure French High Rococo style. Royal Palace, Stockholm. Reproduced by Gracious Permission of H.M. the King of Sweden

647 *Below*: The Blue Drawing Room at Näs i Ro, a charming Swedish country house built largely in the 1770s. Typical are the low ceilings, largely bare floors and painted canvas wall covering. Swedish country houses from about 1730 onwards normally have this *enfilade* of rooms, based on French models. Painted chairs in the Anglo-Dutch and the French styles may be seen. The former have a 'keyhole' cut-out in the splat, characteristic of Swedish chairs derived from the Early Georgian fiddle-back form.

which, however, never won quite the same widespread favour it acquired in England. Mahogany was regarded as much too expensive for such general use, and it was rarely used for chairs at all until late in the century. The hidden structure of carcase furniture is mostly of deal, except in the very finest pieces, when oak was sometimes employed. Again, much was made of deal throughout, painted or stained.

Scandinavian cabinet-makers adopted certain English forms with great enthusiasm and continued to produce these over a long period. Most noticeable are the typical fall-front desks of the early decades of the century. These were much imitated and were still being made late in the century. English long-case clocks were also copied, while the imitations were usually of deal and not oak. So great was the demand for English clocks in Scandinavia during the middle of the century that at least one London clock-maker found it worth his while to have his trade plate printed in English and Danish.

The common English type of brass loop-handle with a shaped back-plate, so often found on English carcase furniture of the first half of the century, was copied and used on Danish furniture of many varied styles until the end of the century.

The continual opportunities afforded Scandinavian cabinet-makers to become familiar with English importations ensured that their productions were for the most part sturdy, rarely over-ornate, and of a design well suited for their purpose. However, other influences were at work that counteracted this fondness for the simple line.

664

642

643

The Dutch Influence

Large numbers of Netherlandish artists and craftsmen had already gone to work in Scandinavia in the 16th century, mostly on commissions for the Danish and Swedish courts, and Netherlandish styles in architecture, sculpture, metalwork and furniture soon became familiar throughout the three Northern countries. A general identity of interests and outlook further ensured that the artistic tastes of the Low Countries found special favour in Scandinavian eyes. This predilection was particularly strong during the 17th century, when Holland became a great power and Dutch maritime trade flourished; it survived deep into the 18th century, long after the Dutch sea-going trade had dwindled almost solely to coastal commerce with her nearest neighbours.

The great similarity between English and Dutch furniture, which lasted from about 1665 until 1730 or so, is well known; at first it was Holland which influenced England in this field, while, after about 1700, the reverse was the case and a great deal of Dutch furniture made during the 18th century displays many features derived from England. Since English and Dutch furniture was reaching Scandinavia in some quantity during the first half of the century, both direct English influence and English influence transmitted through Holland was being brought to bear on the Scandinavian furniture makers. For this reason, Scandinavian scholars prefer to talk of 'the Anglo-Dutch style' and do not attempt to unravel the tangle.

However, actual Dutch influence is also to be found in some Scandinavian furniture, notably in the work of the Danish cabinet-makers during the first half of the century. For instance, the tall Danish late Baroque chests-of-drawers, with undulating 'broken' fronts, and usually with separate stands possess definite Dutch or north German features. The same may be said of a whole range of Danish long-case clocks which have rather a *bombé* base and bevelled sides to the hoods. The more ambitious Danish and Swedish cabinet-makers also emulated the Dutch style of floral marquetry, sometimes with pleasing effect.

It is possible that many Scandinavian chairs in the early-Georgian manner may, in fact, have been inspired more by Dutch versions of this style than by the English originals. The depth and curvature of the front seat rails of many Swedish chairs of this type, together with the greater thickness of the top half of the legs, would seem to be closer to the Dutch than the English form. In the same way, that 'disjointedness' so apparent to those familiar with English furniture, which one finds in the backs of certain groups of Danish and Norwegian chairs in the same general style, may have originated in Holland, where a rather similar disjointed version of the English style occurs. On the other hand, this feature could simply be due to the inability or disinclination of the Scandinavian craftsmen to copy the English form faithfully. Whatever the case, the taste for chairs in this Anglo-Dutch 'Early Georgian' style was widespread in Scandinavia and lasted until after the middle of the century. When the Copenhagen Chairmakers' Guild had a strong-box made for their own official use in 1744, they chose two chairs of this type to be represented in marquetry on the outside. And when the Stockholm Chairmakers decided in 1765 to mark their products with a stamped label, the stamp used bore a representation of a similar chair. By that time this form had been out of fashion in England for about thirty years.

The French Style

It has only been possible to make rather general statements about the Anglo-Dutch influence in Scandinavian furniture because it was brought to bear on such a wide front through everyday commercial contacts. Sober in form and decoration, it found favour with a middle-class clientele—to such an extent that furniture in the Anglo-Dutch style came to form an essential part of characteristic middle-class interiors in Scandinavia. The French style, on the other hand, reached Scandinavia via the Courts of the Danish and the Swedish kings; it remained principally a Court style, although towards the end of the century it was filtering down to influence middle-class furniture as well.

It is far easier to trace the history of French influence in this field because most of the principal commissions marking the various steps in the introduction of the French style into Scandinavia are well known and datable. Moreover, the French taste was brought in under the guidance of a mere handful of influential men—chiefly a series of Court architects, supported by a few enlightened noblemen—whose activities in this direction are well documented.

As far as furniture is concerned, the French taste only began seriously to affect the work of Scandinavian craftsmen during the Rococo period—that is, during the 1730s and, for the most part, not really until the middle of the century—although a few ripples of French influence had reached the three Northern countries earlier.

Like their cousins on thrones elsewhere in Europe, the Danish and Swedish monarchs had taken note of the glories with which Louis XIV was surrounding himself at Versailles, and they set out to emulate the Grand Monarch as best they could. The last decades of the 17th century found both the King of Sweden and the King of Denmark tinkering with the medieval castles which served as their residences—the old castles of Stockholm and

643

644

647

650

645, 646

660

641

648 A handsome Rococo bureau of marked Germanic form but probably the work of a Danish cabinet-maker. The 'breaks' in the front are typical of German late Baroque and Rococo case furniture. While the handles and keyhole escutcheons are of gilt brass, the gilt scrollwork of the legs and apron, and the flamboyant Rococo cresting, are of carved wood. The parquetry lattice pattern is often found on high-class Scandinavian furniture of the period. Collection: Baron Jens Wedell-Meergaard. Svenstrup Castle, Denmark

649 *Above*: This unpainted beechwood chair was made in 1767-8 for the Town Hall of Altona (Holstein), then a Danish city and a centre of furniture production. The cypher of King Christian VII (1766-1808) has been incorporated into an adaptation of an English mid-century chair back. The legs are of an up-to-date pattern but the curvature seems to sag, the apex of the outward curve coming lower on the leg than on English chairs. The same sagging character may be seen on the Swedish chairs in the Anglo-Dutch style shown in illustration 647. Kunstindustrimuseet, Copenhagen

650 *Right*: Norwegian chair of walnut, perhaps from the Bergen area, c. 1770. The Rococo ornament is intended to lend the chair a fashionable air. This is a rather incoherent design but the chair is a well-made example of a type found both in Norway and Denmark. The embellishment of the Danish versions is usually less wild. Historisk Museum, University of Bergen

651 *Right*: This clock could easily be mistaken for the product of a Parisian workshop—except that the lively Rococo casing is entirely of wood and not of gilt bronze. It is a good example of the faithful reproduction of fashionable French forms in Sweden from about 1730 onwards. The movement is by the Stockholm clockmaker Erik Lundstrom. Nordiska Museet, Stockholm

652 *Below*: A tallboy of this kind had to be submitted by a Stockholm journeyman cabinet-maker when seeking admission as a master of his Guild. Until late in the 18th century, they derived from the North German Baroque wardrobe form, but the details tend to be relatively up-to-date, and the lower section of this example takes the form of a typical Stockholm mid-century commode, with its vase-like break in the centre. Made in 1763-4 by a journeyman in the workshops of Lorenz Nordin, an important Stockholm cabinet-maker. Nordiska Museet, (Svindersvik), Stockholm

653 *Below*: A filing cabinet which, with its pendant writing desk, was made in 1771 for Queen Lovisa Ulrika of Sweden, sister of Frederick the Great, by one of the most outstanding Stockholm cabinet-makers, Nils Dahlin (master, 1761-87). Little is known about his early career but one suspects that he must have worked for a while in Paris. Furniture veneered with Oriental lacquer like this is very rare in Sweden. The splendid gilt-bronze mounts are probably Swedish and that at the top centre bears the Three Crowns of Sweden. Tullgarn Palace, Sweden. Reproduced by Gracious Permission of H.M. the King of Sweden

Copenhagen—in order to bring some degree of coherence and classical order into these piles of heterogeneous architecture. The results were far from pleasing and when the Stockholm Castle was burnt down in 1697 the Swedes, under the energetic guidance of Nicodemus Tessin the Younger, took the opportunity of starting afresh. They built an imposing new palace in an idiom that effectively captures the spirit, if not quite the scale and magnificence, of Versailles. The Danes followed suit and pulled down their old castle-palace to build a fine new palace, Christiansborg, in the centre of their capital. This was unfortunately destroyed by fire in 1794.

These two important enterprises created work for a large number of artists and craftsmen, and a great quantity of furniture now came to be needed. With this requirement very much in mind, both the Danes and the Swedes imported a considerable number of important pieces of high-class furniture which, apart from adding greatly to the magnificence of the palace interiors, also served as models for indigenous craftsmen.

During the Rococo period, this kind of French influence had little effect in Denmark, however, whereas it was of great significance in Sweden. This was largely because each of the successive Swedish Court architects of the time had received his training in Paris. The result was that Swedish Rococo art produced in the shadow of the Court is very strongly influenced by the current French taste. Moreover, the Court architects and designers made sure that some of the most capable Swedish craftsmen—including a number of cabinet-makers—went to Paris to become conversant with the new taste and techniques.

The Danish Court architects, on the other hand, had learned their trade in Germany, albeit at German Courts where French influence was strong. Danish Rococo art is therefore less assured and somewhat more turbulent than the Swedish, while Danish-Norwegian furniture in this style has a marked Germanic flavour and scarcely exhibits any French influence at all.

The position changed greatly during the Louis XVI phase. Both Sweden and Denmark received early notice of the new classicising style. A room in a Swedish country house (Åkerö), based on drawings sent from Paris as early as 1754, is in an advanced Neo-Classical idiom although this manifestation seems to have had little effect on Swedish taste at the time. Only a year later, the Danes invited the French architect Nicolas Jardin, who was an early exponent of the revived Classical taste, to come to Copenhagen where he decorated a room in a thorough-going Neo-Classical style. This room already completed in 1757, was in the palace of an important nobleman and soon came to influence Danish taste. This development received further encouragement from the French sculptor Jacques-François Saly, who had come over in 1753, ostensibly to produce an equestrian statue of

646, 653, 651

648

659

645
646

655

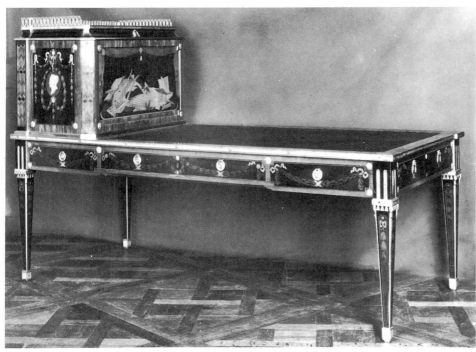

654 *Above*: This is the 'masterpiece' of the most important Swedish cabinet-maker, Georg Haupt, made in 1770, shortly after his return from Paris and London. The royal patronage Haupt enjoyed enabled him to secure from the Stockholm Guild a dispensation from making the traditional tallboy (see illustration 652). Instead he produced this handsome desk with which he demonstrated his mastery of the fully developed Louis XVI style. Royal Palace, Stockholm. Reproduced by Gracious Permission of H.M. the King of Sweden

655 *Above*: Swedish Rococo commode, made in 1771 by Gustaf Foltiern, a competent Stockholm cabinet-maker. The chubby form, which came in about 1760, is characteristic; so are the gilt channels between drawers, the parquetry decoration in walnut, and the insubstantial handles. Sometimes the corner members are not knife-edged like this, but are of rounded section, skilfully veneered. The earlier form of Swedish commode had a horizontal ridge differentiating the top section, containing one drawer, from the bottom part with its two drawers—Swedish commodes all have three drawers. This form, which is based on French *Régence* models, can be seen forming the lower part of the tallboy in illustration 652.

656 *Left*: A fine commode, *c.* 1779, by Georg Haupt (see illustration 654). Haupt had worked in Paris, probably under Riesener. There is little in this example to show that he also stayed for about a year in London. Panels with semi-circular ends often feature in the decoration of Haupt's work; so do Vitruvian scrolls in the frieze. Victoria and Albert Museum, London

657 *Below left*: Turned chairs were, of course, made all over Europe and were probably even found in quite grand houses. This specimen is in the Cavalier's Wing of Gripsholm Castle in Sweden. Note the checked linen covers and hangings and the simplicity of this interior. When these rooms were 'discovered' intact during the early years of this century, they had a profound effect on the Swedish Arts and Crafts revival movement and it may be said that the character of such interiors lies behind the modern idiom in Scandinavian interior decoration.

658 *Below*: Carved and gilt armchair in the Louis XVI style made in Denmark *c.* 1775–85. Chairs of this general type were also made in Sweden. The forms are somewhat simpler than on the equivalent French chairs. The members that join the medallion back to the seat rail would normally be curved on a French chair; here they are straight and rather thick. Nationalmuseet, Copenhagen

659 Small mahogany commode, *c.* 1780, made in Denmark. The treatment is strictly Classical, although the metal keyhole escutcheons are still Rococo. This piece is reminiscent of furniture designed by the architect C. F. Harsdorff (1735-99), who was a pupil of Nicolas Jardin, the French architect responsible for introducing Neo-Classicism to Denmark at a very early date. The quality of this commode is outstanding, but the general form—including the overhanging frieze and flanking columns—is characteristic of many Danish commodes made during the last decades of the 18th century. Kunstindustrimuseet, Copenhagen

660 Room from a small manor house, Lille Haesbjerg, on the island of Funen, now re-erected in the National Museum in Copenhagen. The proportions of this room are typical of the smaller Danish country house and rectory. So is the bare floor with its wide deal boards. The room is painted pink, white and gold. The mirror, of an English-inspired form, is painted green and white. The stretchers are fitted somewhat incongruously to the Louis XVI-type legs of the chair, which is also painted.

the reigning monarch. He became, in fact, Director of the newly-formed Academy, the focal point of Neo-Classical influence in Denmark for two decades. What is more, he ensured that the Academy not only moulded artists and architects but also a range of craftsmen: he insisted that all aspirants to the rank of master cabinet-maker should lay a drawing of the 'masterpiece' they intended to make, not only before the officers of their Guild, as they had long done, but also before the Academy, in order to make sure that these designs were well composed and in accordance with the best academic taste. The influence the Academy thus had on the work of all Copenhagen cabinet-makers, especially during their formative years, was considerable and was to have far-reaching—and, let it be said, beneficial—effects on Danish and Norwegian furniture until well into the 19th century.

A mild form of Louis XVI had made its appearance in Swedish interior decoration in the 1760s, but few traces of the style were to be seen in Swedish furniture until after the return of that highly skilled cabinet-maker, Georg Haupt, to his native land in 1769 after spending several years in Paris, where he is thought to have worked under the great Riesener himself and in London. He brought back a very thorough understanding of the fully developed *Louis Seize* style in furniture, indeed his work may easily be mistaken for that of one of the great French cabinet-makers of the day. What the other high-class cabinet-makers of Stockholm learned from Haupt enabled them to continue to make fine furniture in a very passable imitation of contemporary French taste. The French domination of the Swedish Court style was even maintained into the purer Neo-Classical phase of the late 18th century, chiefly under the guidance of the Masreliez brothers—Swedish by birth but of French extraction—who became the exponents of a charming and delicate version of this style, with its archeological bias.

The German Influence

Cultural influences had been reaching Scandinavia from her southern neighbour, Germany, since time immemorial. No sea separates Denmark from northern Germany. The rich lands of Holstein and Schleswig, including the city of Altona, on the Elbe, close to Hamburg, were for a long time Danish and were only lost in the middle of the 19th century. A large section of the Danish nobility was of German origin or had close links with German aristocracy. It is therefore not strange that Germanic influence runs as a strong undercurrent through Scandinavian art of all times, however misleading the superficial appearance may be. This is particularly so in the case of furniture. The tendency was somewhat artificially maintained in the 18th century by the craft guilds, which were modelled on their German counterparts and continued as a general rule to send their journeymen to one of the great German cities in order to learn the refinements of their trade. With close contacts so firmly established, it commonly happened that German craftsmen settled in one of the Scandinavian countries and then proceeded to turn out works in the current German style.

German forms and techniques were thus well understood by members of the craft guilds, who were therefore particularly ready to appreciate and adopt new styles coming from the south. Certain forms of Dutch, English and French origin came to be transmitted to Scandinavia at second hand through Germany. The most outstanding example of this is the strong Germanic twist given to the Rococo style on its way from France through Germany to Denmark and Norway in the middle of the century, at a time when Sweden, on the other hand, was obtaining her Rococo in a purer and less exuberant form direct from Paris. The Danish cabinet-makers preferred the German idiom; they derived much inspiration from the Franconian Baroque and Rococo styles and even seem to have taken note of styles current in the south, in Vienna and possibly even in Venice.

In 1777 the Danes set up a Royal Furniture Emporium *(Kongelige Meubel Magazin)* in order to encourage and sell the work of Danish furniture makers (by this time the distinction between cabinet-makers and chair-makers was becoming less marked).

659
661

654
656

652

648

The McIntire Room, H. F. du Pont Winterthur Museum, Delaware. In this room, which contains a chimney-piece attributed to Robert Wellford of Philadelphia, is exhibited the finest furniture of the Federal period (c. 1790–1810), influenced by the English design books of Hepplewhite and Sheraton. All the chairs reflect the style of Samuel McIntire of Salem, Mass., the night table with tambour front that of John Seymour of Boston, while the sewing table is in the manner of Ephraim Haines of Philadelphia. The bed is associated with a bill from the Pennsylvania cabinet-maker Jacob Wayne.

Drawing room from the Samuel Powel House, Philadelphia, as installed in the American Wing of the Metropolitan Museum of Art, New York City. The panelling, neo-Palladian with Rococo details, dates from about 1768, when Samuel Powel returned from Europe to occupy the house. A portrait of his wife, born Elizabeth Willing, by Cosmo Alexander hangs above the fireplace. The collection of outstanding Philadelphia Chippendale furniture (c.1760–75) includes a side chair with hairy paw feet, a speciality of local cabinet-making, two great pedestal tables and a related pole screen, a tall clock, and, at the far left, the Wister family desk, in which the Chinese flavour complements the wallpaper. The upholstered settee is from New England.

661 *Left*: The maker of this sturdy and pleasantly-proportioned Danish chair, which might easily be mistaken for a product of the 1950s although it was made in the late 18th century, was Jens Brøtterup who had learned his craft in London. He continued to make chairs in the English style, using English techniques, after his return to Copenhagen where he also helped to instruct his countrymen. Kunstindustrimuseet, Copenhagen

662 *Right*: From time to time the Scandinavians used various indigenous woods for the embellishment of their furniture. This very plain late 18th-century Swedish commode is veneered with alder-root burr. (So, apparently, is the lunette of the small Danish piece shown in illustration 997). Commodes of similar shape to this are also found in Denmark where they sometimes have fretted brackets between the front legs. Nordiska Museet, Stockholm

663 *Left*: Late 18th-century Swedish painted chair of common type, displaying a strange mixture of styles. The legs and medallion back derive from Louis XVI, the stretchers remind one of Hepplewhite forms, and the splat, with the 'keyhole', is by this time a traditional Swedish form originally borrowed from Early-Georgian fiddle-back chairs (note the vestigial scrolls), but here adapted to fit the medallion shape of the back. The channel in the front seat rail is a common feature of Swedish chairs of this period. They are mostly made of birch, sometimes of pine. Nordiska Museet, Stockholm

664 *Right*: Mahogany bureau made in 1792 by the important Stockholm cabinet-maker, Gottlob Iwersson. His early style was based on that of Georg Haupt, (illustrations 654, 656) but he later evolved his own style in which block-like components with little decoration, often perched on rather insubstantial legs, play a striking part. He was inspired by contemporary English furniture, although his work is not derivative, and had a considerable influence on Swedish cabinet-making at the turn of the century (see illustration 999). Nordiska Museet, Stockholm

Georg Roentgen, of the famous Roentgen family of German cabinet-makers, was invited to Copenhagen in order to take a leading part in this enterprise. He introduced certain new forms, notably a small oval, straight-legged table that is found rather frequently in Danish houses, and must have impressed his Danish colleagues with the floral marquetry with which he embellished his furniture; interest in this kind of ornament was anyway revived in Denmark towards the end of the century. Roentgen's stay was brief, however.

Anglomania

In 1781 the directorship of the Royal Furniture Emporium was put into the capable hands of Carsten Anker—statesman, man of affairs with wide interests, and member of an influential Norwegian family who greatly admired English taste in many fields, including that of furniture. In his new post, he made sure that several Danish furniture makers who had worked in London were brought home to instruct their countrymen in the latest English techniques; that the mahogany necessary for making furniture in the English style was imported in larger quantities and subjected to a proper seasoning process; that the design books of men like Hepplewhite and Sheraton became readily available to Danish craftsmen; and that a trained designer was attached to the Emporium in order to produce suitable designs for the furniture trade. By such means, and with a great deal of actual English furniture continuing to appear on the Danish market,

the late 18th century style of English furniture came to be fully assimilated in Denmark during the last decade or so of the century and continued to influence the shape of much Danish furniture—especially chairs—until well into the next century. A serious fire destroyed much of central Copenhagen in 1795 and further destruction was caused by the English bombardment of the city in 1807. A large quantity of new furniture was required to replace that lost in these disasters. This explains why a considerable amount of furniture from this period survives. It is generally of a very high quality, and it is noteworthy that a good deal of this Danish furniture was exported to southern Sweden.

As in the earlier phases of the history of Scandinavian furniture, the Norwegian taste in furniture followed the prevailing Danish styles. Again, certain features may help one to distinguish the Norwegian versions. A band of fluting along the lower edge of the front seat rail, for example, is said to be characteristic of many late 18th-century Norwegian chairs. But in general, Norwegian furniture of this period has a strong English flavour, like the Danish counterparts. While it could be of good quality, it is probably fair to say that it was rarely as elegant as the best Danish products. Indeed, a visitor to Norway in 1800 could not help remarking that '*Die Form der Möbel war plump*' ('Their furniture was ungainly.').

Anglomania also struck Sweden late in the century and its influence may be seen in much Swedish furniture of the period—again, particularly in the form of Swedish chair-backs—but one gets the impression that the preference so long shown for the French taste in fashionable Swedish circles was so strong that the English taste continued to be one chiefly favoured by the middle classes.

661

663

POLAND

Bozenna Maszkowska

665 *Left*: Cupboard-on-stand, *c.* 1750, made in the provinces of southern Poland (Little Poland) The marquetry pattern of elm, black oak, and walnut dyed green, includes many traditional folk motifs, such as flowers, and birds within geometric frames. National Museum, Warsaw

666 *Far left*: The Red Drawing Room, Nieborów Palace, 1766–71. The furniture in the French Rococo style was made for the owner, Michael Casimir Ogiński, probably in his own estate workshop. The chairs and settees, painted and gilt, are upholstered in red damask. The decorations on the coved ceiling are a later 19th-century addition.

667, 668 *Below left and below*: Designs for the boudoir of the Royal Palace in Warsaw by Victor Louis, a French architect recommended by Madame Geoffrin to the King, Stanislaw August Poniatowski. Louis provided many designs for the Palace in 1766. The seat furniture, which was made in France, is in the richest Neo-Classical manner.

The 18th century was an age of changing moods in Poland, as it was elsewhere in Europe, and these changes were reflected in the development of interior design and furniture. Poland's commercial and cultural ties with other European countries encouraged the adoption of new fashions. Furniture and furnishings were imported, for example, from France, England and Austria, while the work of immigrant craftsmen also acted as a stimulant to local taste.

In the first half of the century, the courts of two successive kings of the Saxon Wettin dynasty became the centres of artistic enterprise. Augustus II and III brought architects and artists to Poland from neighbouring Saxony. The work of these artists reveals the powerful influence of France which dominated European taste at the period. Rococo furniture, either imported from France, or manufactured locally on the manorial estates by Polish craftsmen, slowly began to replace in favour the heavier pieces hitherto so popular throughout the country. These included the ponderous cupboards in the so-called Danzig manner, and Renaissance or Baroque pieces based upon Italian, French or German examples. In country districts simple, uncarved furniture was still constructed in the medieval tradition. Textiles, used both as wall hangings and as coverings for furniture, remained traditional in Polish interiors right up to the 18th century and made them very colourful. Oriental textiles continued to be imported to Western Europe through Polish intermediaries throughout the 17th and 18th centuries.

Several cabinet-making centres took advantage of the growing interest in Rococo and Neo-Classical designs in the second half of the 18th century, to increase the output of their workshops.

During his reign (1764–95), Stanislaw August Poniatowski, the royal Maecenas and collector, was deeply concerned to encourage art in Poland. Above all, he admired the achievements of French architects and craftsmen, although English taste also attracted him. While he was king, Stanislaw August initiated many educational and economic reforms. Towns grew richer, particularly Warsaw. New banks and industries were founded, and attempts were made to reform the agrarian system. These promises of national prosperity were wrecked by a series of tragic political events. In the three successive partitions of 1772, 1793 and 1795, Austria, Russia and Prussia took over larger and larger tracts of Polish territory and in 1796 the Polish Commonwealth ceased to exist on the map of Europe.

By 1780 the new styles made fashionable in Europe first by the leading architects and designers of France and subsequently by those of England and Austria, were firmly established in Poland. The lead had been given by the king and the great aristocratic families whose households were so vast that they were, in effect, miniature courts. Designs for interiors in the Rococo style had earlier been provided by Juste-Aurèle Meissonier, and Jean Pillement, among others. Subsequently Charles-Pierre Coustou, Victor Louis, Vincenzo Brenna and finally Percier and Fontaine were among those who contributed designs in the Neo-Classical

665

666

667, 668

669 *Left*: Bureau made in Kolbuszowa (Little Poland) *c.* 1780. Although in the Neo-Classical style, the piece is typical of Kolbuszowa manufacture with its stylised floral marquetry. Rzeszów Museum, Poland

670 *Right*: The State Ballroom at Łańcut Castle, *c.* 1800. The splendid Neo-Classical decoration is the work of Christian-Peter Aigner, and the plasterwork is by Frederic Bauman. The ceiling is painted sky blue with white clouds *en trompe l'oeil*, the wall panels are in the fashionable yellowish orange and the white plaster details derive from Classical Roman example. The late 18th-century sofas and armchairs, painted white and gilt are of Polish workmanship.

672 *Below centre*: Neo-Classical chest-of-drawers made of mahogany with a marble top and gilt bronze mounts. A typical Warsaw production of the late 18th century inspired by French example. National Museum, Warsaw

671 *Below*: Roll-top desk made in Warsaw, *c.* 1780, probably by cne of the cabinet-makers brought to Warsaw from Neuwied in 1775. It is of course based on French example in the tradition of Oeben and Riesener. National Museum, Warsaw

673 *Below right*: Bonheur-du-jour, *c.* 1780. Pieces such as this were popular in Warsaw drawing rooms of the late 18th century. Veneered in rosewood with painted floral panels, and gilt bronze mounts, it demonstrates the fashion for lighter more feminine designs. National Museum, Warsaw

taste. Pattern-books published in Paris and London were also well known. Cabinet-making firms in the large towns such as Warsaw, Kielce, Lublin, Plock, Grodno or Dubno and the workshops on the great family estates began to displace the old craft guilds.

An example of an estate workshop was that at Kolbuszowa, near Rzeszów in southern Poland. It belonged to the Lubomirski family who were among the more powerful and enlightened of the great landowners. Very probably in existence in the early 18th century, it was certainly active until the beginning of the 19th century. The term 'Kolbuszowa' furniture dates back to the 18th century. It is now loosely used to describe that particular type of furniture which originated both at Kolbuszowa itself and at similar neighbouring estate workshops. 'Kolbuszowa' furniture consists mainly of writing desks, bureaux, commodes, sideboards, secretaires and boxes. These are usually veneered with walnut and decorated with marquetry and parquetry. The motifs include geometrical patterns, in which banding, stringing, stars, rosettes, circles and ovals with radiating lines, meanders, chequers, or rhomboids are introduced. Floral designs in local fruitwoods or pine veneers are also combined with coats-of-arms and monograms. Mid-18th-century Kolbuszowa pieces are in the Rococo style, but during the later years of the century they adhered to a Classical manner which was close to Austrian example.

The most important cabinet-makers' workshops, however, during the reign of Stanislaw August were in Warsaw. Besides those producing exquisite pieces for the royal palace (Warsaw Castle) and for Lazienki, the king's summer residence, there were a number of cabinet-makers previously employed in the workshops of Abraham and David Roentgen at Neuwied in Westphalia, who were brought in 1775 to Poland by Prince Adam Poniński. Among these, the following names are recorded, Duercks (or Diereks), Nenecke, Andreas Simmler, the founder of the Warsaw cabinet-making family famous in the first half of the 19th century, Stersing, Fries, Gersting, Johann Michael Rummer, who spent a year in London besides working for Roentgen for six years, and Dreistz.

In the late 18th century orders given for fine furniture were enormous. In the last three decades Warsaw was greatly enlarged and new residences were built both within the city and in the neighbouring countryside. The furniture produced for these houses is Classical in style, modelled on French and English taste. It is sometimes painted and gilt, and sometimes veneered and decorated with marquetry of local and exotic woods. Rosewood and mahogany are usual as veneers, while mahogany was also often used for carcases. Small Warsaw writing-tables, commodes, tables and chairs, sofas and armchairs of the last two decades of the 18th century often have inlaid panels, painted with floral or Classical motifs. Neo-Gothic features also appeared, reflecting the growing Romantic tendencies which captured the imagination of so much of Europe.

RUSSIA

Bozenna Maszkowska

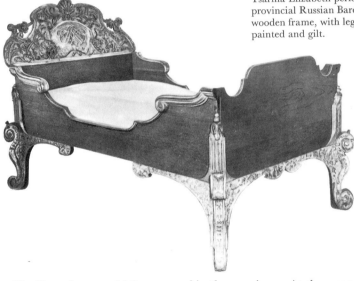

674 *Above*: The Red Drawing Room at Kuskovo Palace, designed by the architects Argunov and Mirionov, 1770–80, in the Neo-Classical style. Rococo armchairs of the so-called *Coiffeuse* type flank the richly carved console table beneath a tall Neo-Classical mirror. As is usual in Russia the large stove is designed as an integral piece of furniture, painted to fit in with the general decorative scheme.

675 *Far left*: Detail of a carved and gilt table, early 18th century. Still purely Baroque, with elaborate, heavy scrolls, the Russian carver probably drew inspiration from Dutch or German sources.

676 *Left*: Clock-case, dated 1794. The case is of curiously heavy proportions being rather broader than contemporary Western examples. State Historical Museum, Moscow

677 *Below*: Carved wooden bed, *c.* 1750. Tsarina Elizabeth period. A good example of provincial Russian Baroque, the bed has a plain wooden frame, with legs and crestings carved, painted and gilt.

The Russian Court and aristocracy of the 18th and 19th centuries looked to western Europe for direction in taste and fashion. Expensive furniture was imported from France and Germany and passed on to the indigenous cabinet-makers to be copied. In the early 18th century the influence of Dutch and German Baroque can be recognised while towards the middle of the century the influence was more distinctly German. The interiors of the Leningrad palaces, in particular those of the imperial palace of Tsarskoe Selo are of extraordinary splendour and in the wild profusion of their Rococo carving recall most closely the interiors erected by Cuvilliés at Nymphenburg and in the Munich *Residenz*. Most magnificent of all is the Amber Saloon which was installed for the Empress Elizabeth between 1750 and 1755. In spite of the predominantly German character of Russian Rococo, its main protagonist in Russia was Count Bartolommeo Francesco Rastrelli, who was born in Russia, the son of the Italian sculptor. In the execution of his schemes for the decoration of the interiors of Peterhof, Tsarskoe Selo and the Winter Palace in an exuberant and mature Rococo style, he evidently enjoyed the services of a team of highly skilled carvers, who were presumably of Russian birth.

Under Catherine the Great (1762–96), who was born a German princess, Russia became a major political power. In 1762 the landed gentry were released from compulsory military service and, provided now with both leisure and means, they built palaces, great houses and country villas in the two capital cities of St. Petersburg and Moscow and in the provinces. At the same time commercial development encouraged building activity in the provincial towns.

During the reign of Catherine the Great, the decorative styles of France and England were to dominate Russian taste, though not to the exclusion of Germany, whence a number of immigrant craftsmen came. The French architect, Vallin de la Mothe, was responsible for the Academy of Fine Arts at St. Petersburg, while the celebrated Scottish architect, Charles Cameron, designed the interiors of Pavlovsk and Tsarskoe Selo in a Pompeian style which owed much to his fellow countryman, Robert Adam. Like Adam, Cameron went to both Italy and France and came under the influence of Adam's mentor, Clérisseau. In his interior designs he not only drew upon these English and French sources but exploited the more colourful Russian traditions, using such semi-precious materials as agate, ivory, mother-of-pearl and jade.

Although Russian craftsmen continued throughout the century to find example and inspiration in imported western European furniture, they developed a native style, which, while it may sometimes seem heavy and ill-proportioned to western eyes, is not unsuited to the monumental scale of Russian palace interiors. The very circumstance, however, that Russian styles were usually derived at second hand from an external source meant that they lost something of the elegance and inspiration of the original. The Empress Catherine the Great imported

678 *Above*: Sofa, after a design by Count Bartolommeo Rastrelli, the architect who reconstructed the Peterhof (1747–52), and built the Palace of Tsarskoe Selo (1752–7), the Winter Palace at St Petersburg, and many other splendid residences. His grand Rococo interiors have a markedly individual character, the *boiseries* being exuberantly Rococo, and carved with sharpness and precision. But his love of violent colours is purely Russian. The sofa, like all Rastrelli's furniture, is massive and sumptuous.

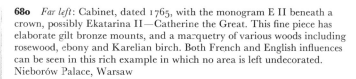

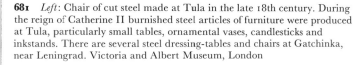

679 *Above*: Cut-steel fireplace made at Tula *c*. 1802. The intricate fender is made up of countless facetted beads. The fireplace may have been given by Princess Dashkova to a Miss Martha Wilmot, who visited Russia with her aunt, Mrs. Hamilton, an Anglo-Irish friend of the Princess. In a letter to her father written in 1806, Miss Wilmot writes: 'the curiosity from Tula is a Machine for perfuming the rooms . . . I suppose it will lie quietly on the steel chimney-piece'. Victoria and Albert Museum, London

680 *Far left*: Cabinet, dated 1765, with the monogram E II beneath a crown, possibly Ekatarina II—Catherine the Great. This fine piece has elaborate gilt bronze mounts, and a marquetry of various woods including rosewood, ebony and Karelian birch. Both French and English influences can be seen in this rich example in which no area is left undecorated. Nieborów Palace, Warsaw

681 *Left*: Chair of cut steel made at Tula in the late 18th century. During the reign of Catherine II burnished steel articles of furniture were produced at Tula, particularly small tables, ornamental vases, candlesticks and inkstands. There are several steel dressing-tables and chairs at Gatchinka, near Leningrad. Victoria and Albert Museum, London

French furniture by the leading Parisian cabinet-makers and German furniture of equal merit from the Roentgen establishment at Neuwied. These pieces in the Neo-Classical taste were followed by the Russian makers, not however, without a certain simplification of design and coarsening of detail.

A peculiar feature of Russian cabinet-making is that the craftsmen were themselves serfs bound to a particular property. Amongst the country houses to which cabinet-making workshops were attached may be mentioned Ostankino, near Moscow, Kursk and Viatka. Even a most celebrated Russian piece, such as the marquetry cylinder-top desk of the Empress Catherine the Great, was made outside St. Petersburg at Okhta. This desk follows the contemporary Parisian style but displays a richness of ornament which leaves no area undecorated.

A truly original Russian contribution is the furniture made in the town of Tula in central Russia. Since the beginning of the 18th century and perhaps earlier, the craftsmen of Tula specialised in the production of furniture constructed entirely of steel. It was a by-product of the important small arms industry of the town, which had been greatly enlarged in the early 18th century. An armchair in the Victoria and Albert Museum is in the early Tula style. Little of the earlier Tula furniture has survived, but during the reign of the Empress Catherine, steel furniture for the Imperial Palaces was provided by the Tula State Arsenal. Most of this furniture is still in the Hermitage in Leningrad but a few examples have come out of Russia, prob-

ably as gifts to foreign princes or diplomats.

The style of the later Tula furniture shows strong English influence and but for a lack of harmony in the proportions and a tendency to overdecorate it might well be attributed to the factory of Matthew Boulton in Birmingham. Both Catherine the Great and her favourite, Count Orloff, admired the work of the Boulton factory and it seems likely that one or more of the Birmingham craftsmen went to Russia to introduce at Tula Boulton's methods of steel cutting and polishing. This Tula furniture is designed in a somewhat attenuated version of the Adam style, the use of steel making it possible to reduce the thickness of the constructional members. The ornament consists mostly of steel beads, each cut with many facets and then riveted individually to the framework. In some examples many thousands of beads of various sizes and shapes were employed.

The Tula craftsmen developed another technique that was not practised at Birmingham—the incrustation of the hard steel with softer metals such as silver, pewter, brass and copper. By combining these metals in one piece—perhaps the apron or frieze of a tea-table—it was possible to achieve an effect similar to that produced when jewellery is enriched with multi-coloured gold incrustations.

The lack of surviving examples after 1796 suggests that the State Arsenal at Tula which had produced so much fine furniture in her lifetime, was closed at the death of Catherine the Great.

680

681

679

AMERICA

Robert C. Smith

American furniture of the period 1650–1810 can best be seen in four great collections open to the public—the American Wing of the Metropolitan Museum in New York City, the Henry Francis du Pont Winterthur Museum outside Wilmington, Delaware, the Mabel Brady Garvan Collection at Yale University, New Haven, Connecticut and the Henry Ford Museum and Greenfield Village at Dearborn, Michigan.

These collections, composed of furniture from various parts of the Atlantic coastal area first settled by the British, prove how consistently the fashions of the mother country were followed, though with an inevitable lag in time, through each successive style. They also show how widely the different regions varied in their interpretation of a given model, which is not surprising in so large a colonial territory without a central government. In British America, especially in the early 18th century, certain new types of furniture were produced, like the 'butterfly' table, while traditional pieces, such as the high chest-of-drawers and various kinds of chairs with turned frames, were modified.

Any study of colonial furniture made in the 18th century, before the Revolution of 1776, will establish the supremacy of three centres of production. One was Philadelphia, the metropolis of the middle colonies and by 1750 the second city of the English-speaking world; the other two were the New England seaports of Newport and Boston. In the Federal period, which followed the Revolution, these cities were joined by Baltimore, Maryland, New York, and Salem, Massachusetts, as the places where the most distinguished furniture was made in the south, the middle colonies and New England respectively.

In all of these places, as well as in the rural centres of the Connecticut River Valley and the Pennsylvania and New Jersey back-country, certain distinctly American qualities can be discovered, such as a scale and a use of ornament which seem modest by European standards. As with much Early American architecture and silver, however, there is a beauty of line, form and proportion and a feeling for the material which at least equals the finest European examples.

682 Fall-front secretary desk of walnut. This cabinet is stamped on the base of one of the small drawers, Edward Evans 1707, and is the earliest signed and dated Philadelphian piece. It displays the cushion frieze, fielded panelling and academic mouldings of the American William and Mary style. Colonial Williamsburg

683 Slant-front secretary desk of walnut, with mirrored doors, Pennsylvania, 1700–30. This piece is very close to English early 18th-century examples, while the feet and mouldings are related to those of the previous piece illustrated. Philadelphia Museum of Art

684 High chest-of-drawers of veneered walnut and maple, Pennsylvania, 1700–30. The high chest-of-drawers first appeared in the late 17th century and developed as a major showpiece of colonial cabinet-making. The turned legs, arched skirting and contrasting veneers are characteristic of the early 18th century. Philadelphia Museum of Art

The American William and Mary Style (1700–25)

685 The Hardenbergh Room at Winterthur includes an early 18th-century painted *kas*, in the Dutch style. All the rest of the furniture is of the same date except for the table in the left foreground which dates from the late 17th century: H. F. du Pont Winterthur Museum, Delaware

686 *Above*: Apparently an American invention, the 'butterfly' table owes its name to the shape of the moveable supports of its hinged leaves. This example of maple comes from New England and dates from 1700–30. Prentis Collection, New Hampshire Historical Society

687 *Right*: Wing chairs with rolled arms on vase-turned frames are the principal manifestations of the Baroque style in early American furniture. In the best examples the cresting of the back is vigorously shaped, continuing the handsome curves of the frame. New Hampshire, 1700–25. Prentis Collection, New Hampshire Historical Society

The first years of the 18th century saw a rapid growth of the American economy, the emergence of a wealthy merchant and landowning class and the construction of fine houses in the narrow area along the Atlantic coast. These houses were furnished with a degree of luxury and refinement hitherto unknown, in which the academic style of British upper-class furniture predominated, replacing the traditional popular taste. The new American furniture, following English fashion, was made of walnut in Pennsylvania, while in the North-East maple and pine were used, sometimes veneered. Based on English late 17th-century models it displayed the first features of the Baroque style.

A basic innovation was the chest-of-drawers with round or oval bun feet, drawn up in severe fashion with architectural base and cornice. Sometimes such a chest was combined with an upper section to form a secretary desk, and this was destined to remain one of the traditional showpieces of 18th-century American furniture. A writing cabinet, with fall-front on English late 17th-century lines, now at Williamsburg, is signed by the maker, Edward Evans of Pennsylvania, and dated 1707. It is of special 682 interest because of the similarity between its mouldings and panels and the cushion friezes and bevelled panelling of the finest contemporary American rooms.

A fine bureau-bookcase secretary desk, in the Philadelphia Museum with sloping fallboard and an upper section containing bookshelves has bun feet and mouldings like those of the Evans piece. The upper section, based on familiar Anglo-Dutch models, has a double arch cornice that dictates the pattern of the hand- 683 some beading surrounding the mirrored panels of the doors.

Chests-of-drawers were also set on low stands and, for greater height, upon a table-like base, fitted with drawers, which was also produced on a smaller scale as a separate piece of furniture. These dressing-tables (lowboys) and the accompanying high chests-of-drawers (highboys), which were sometimes made as 684 matching sets, constituted a second category of showpiece furniture throughout most of the 18th century. Carried on legs of Baroque cup or trumpet turning, with prominent stretchers repeating horizontally the vertical concave and convex curving of the skirting, the high chests preserve their architectural bases and cornices. The façades are often decorated in the Baroque taste which favoured colour contrasts. This was accomplished either by means of maple or walnut veneers or by using paint, varnish and gesso in imitation of oriental lacquer with vivid Chinese figures and landscape elements set against a black background. This technique of japanning, especially developed in Boston, stems from the importation from England of oriental porcelains and their imitations in Dutch faience, for the display of which some American William and Mary style highboys were given terminal pyramids of shelves.

The descendants of the Dutch settlers of New York preferred to store their possessions in a massive two-door wardrobe locally called a *kas*, which continued to be made in New York and northern New Jersey until the early 19th century. It is the American version of the Netherlands *kast*, one of the most effective inventions of Dutch furniture makers in the 17th century. In some New York and New Jersey pieces, usually made of fruitwood or gumwood, the entire front and sides were decorated with *grisaille* 685 paintings displaying large swags of fruits symbolising fertility, of a type also engraved upon early New York silver beakers. This kind of decoration represents one of the earliest types of still-life painting to be produced in British America.

Early 18th-century tables of the American William and Mary style, like their English 17th-century prototypes, have turned supports. But these are more delicately proportioned and intricately shaped than Anglo-Flemish examples. Most characteristic are the large gate-leg tables, which first came into favour in England in the mid-17th century. Here the straight turned legs are supplemented by one or more moveable 'gates' swinging out from the frame to support hinged leaves, usually of oval form.

In America a new type of table was created, probably in Con-

688 *Right*: Bannister-back armchair of ebonised pine, maple and oak, Rhode Island, 1700–25. An exceptionally rich example of an American William and Mary chair with columnar turning. Henry Ford Museum, Dearborn, Michigan

689 *Centre right*: Bended-back maple side chair upholstered in leather, 1700–70. This type of chair, with a back of Chinese derivation, was known in the 18th century as a 'Boston chair' because it was exported in quantity from that port. Connecticut Historical Society

690 *Far right*: Armchair of ebonised maple, 1710–30. This chair is transitional to the American Queen Anne style. The piercing and carving of the cresting is characteristic of the work of John Gaines II, of Portsmouth, New Hampshire. Metropolitan Museum of Art, New York. Bequest of Mrs J. Insley Blair, 1952

691 *Below*: Walnut tea table, Massachusetts or Connecticut, 1730–50. Perhaps the supreme expression of the New England aesthetic of lean proportions and plain surfaces is found in tea tables of the American Queen Anne style. American Museum in Britain, Claverton, Somerset

necticut, in which the legs are almost always slanted outward from a frame containing a single drawer. In place of the 'gate' a solid moveable wood support was provided for the leaves and the sweeping curves of the outer edge of this support have given the name 'butterfly' to this kind of table. More graceful than the conventional gate-leg, the slanted legs and 'butterfly' supports create that impression of vigorous movement which is inherent in all successful Baroque furniture and especially in fine American William and Mary style chairs.

The most spectacular are the high-back upholstered armchairs with rolled arms that exemplify the new luxury and comfort of the early 18th century. The best pieces have a flamboyantly shaped cresting and delicate vase turning on medial stretchers and legs, which end abruptly in 'paintbrush' feet, a Portuguese Baroque convention adopted in Restoration England, where it became known as the 'Spanish' foot. This type of foot, in which the diagonal grooves suggest the bristles of a brush, is found on various chairs, built principally of exposed wood, with caned or leather seats, which can be classified according to the form of their backs.

One type has flat vase-shaped balusters, like those used in the finest staircases of the period. These chairs were made of a combination of woods disguised by ebonizing, with Baroque scroll arms and 'explosive' ball-and-reel turning in the stretchers. Similar treatment of stretchers is seen in contemporary Delaware River ladderback chairs. A second type, usually upholstered in black or red leather, has a 'bended' back with a single broad splat gracefully curving in imitation of the much earlier Chinese chairs which obviously inspired them. Pieces like this were made with variations until late in the 18th century, and came to be known as 'Boston' chairs. The frame of this chair is essentially the same as that of a third category, with its vase-shaped splat and curved cresting, sometimes enriched with scroll and leaf carving. This last type of chair is associated particularly with John Gaines, who worked at Portsmouth, New Hampshire.

The American Queen Anne Style

American furniture, like its European forerunners, underwent a basic change in the first half of the 18th century through the introduction of the cabriole leg. This was a revolutionary event in the history of furniture, for it took the curving line, which had previously been an adjunct to Baroque designs, and made it the dominant feature. The curve of the cabriole leg was echoed in the skirting of tables, in the bonnets of high chests, in the outlines of all parts of the chair, thus producing a carefully co-ordinated effect of continuing movement.

686

687

688

689

690

691

693, 695

692 *Right*: Chest-of-drawers on frame, probably Connecticut River Valley, *c.* 1750. Cherry. Characteristic of the Connecticut Valley are the thin slipper feet and the projecting, richly scalloped top. The skirting is typical of Massachusetts. This chest-of-drawers was given by David Hoyt (1722–1814) of Deerfield to his daughter Mary. Old Deerfield

693 *Far left*: High chest-of-drawers of white walnut or butternut with inlaid decoration of birch and dyed sycamore. Massachusetts, 1725-40. An important American Queen Anne regional style, distinguished from its English prototype by lighter proportions and a scroll pediment. H. F. du Pont Winterthur Museum, Delaware

694 *Left*: High chest-of-drawers of mahogany lined with tulipwood attributed to Job Townsend of Newport, Rhode Island, 1750-60. Townsend is thought to have introduced this type of concave voluted shell ornament. H. F. du Pont Winterthur Museum, Delaware

695 Side chair of walnut, 1740-50. One of a number of regional American Queen Anne examples, this Newport chair has a characteristic shell ornament on the knee and cresting. H. F. du Pont Winterthur Museum, Delaware

696 Walnut side chair of the second quarter of the 18th century, a period when New York chair-makers abandoned traditional Dutch forms in favour of those influenced by neighbouring New England. The shape of the splat and carving on the cresting are typical of New York. H. F. du Pont Winterthur Museum, Delaware

697 Side chair of japanned wood, 1740-60. Built with the high 'Chinese' back of the Massachusetts-Connecticut area, this is one of a set made for the Winthrop family, whose arms it bears. Old Deerfield

In the second quarter of the 18th century, both turning and inlay were largely abandoned in favour of carving, and the cabriole leg was applied to all sorts of furniture along with a variety of feet, including eventually the claw-and-ball. At the same time strong local characteristics began to assert themselves. The most striking are the general tendencies toward attenuation, verticality and flat linear effects in the furniture of New England as opposed to the ampler proportions and more plastic concepts of the middle colonies and especially Philadelphia.

691   The results of the New England practice can be seen at their best in the tea table, introduced from England with tea itself, and the card table, both of which became popular at the time. Made generally of walnut, cherry or mahogany, a fine Massachusetts or Connecticut example will have long cabriole legs of great delicacy ending in pad feet, the commonest type in Queen Anne furniture, sometimes set on small circular plinths. The movement begins here, flowing smoothly upward to the undulating skirting which provides a contrast with the straight tray top of the table, although even this is softened by slightly rounded corners. The table depends for its effect entirely upon its pure lines and plain surfaces.

692   Similarly designed is a cherry chest-on-frame, probably made in the Connecticut River Valley in the mid-18th century. The pattern of the skirting, contrasting straight with curved lines, was widely used in Massachusetts. This feature appears in many high chests-of-drawers like one at Winterthur, where the tall

693   pilasters and flaming urns are characteristic of New England attenuation. Equally typical of local usage is the recessed semi-circular motif on the two drawer fronts of this piece. They are treated as stylised shells or 'scalups', to quote a cabinet-maker's bill of 1737, by means of an inlay of thin strips of birch and dyed sycamore. It was also used for the pair of stars inset at the top and sides of this highboy, which are a rare survival of a popular Dutch and English ornament of the late 17th century. The decorative skirting with its reversed finials of acorn-like form, recalls those on the oversailing of 17th-century clapboard houses, which survived in 18th-century staircases.

Almost identical skirting is found on one of the contemporary masterpieces of Boston cabinet-making, the Loring family high chest-of-drawers, made in about 1740-50 by John Pimm, who lived until 1773 in the metropolis of New England. This piece, made of pine and maple, is full of refinements such as the tiny strips of mahogany that edge the skirting. There is fine carving in the claws of the front feet, the finial urns and, above all, in the

Plate facing page 192   garlanded shells of the recessed areas at top and bottom. The great glory of the Loring piece, however, is the elaborate japanned decoration, attributed to Thomas Johnson, 'Japanner at the Golden Lyon in Anne Street, Boston.'

A similar cornice of arched or scroll form, recalling a popular type of New England doorway, appears in a fine piece from Newport, Rhode Island, after Boston the greatest centre of wealth in New England. This is a high chest-of-drawers the lower sec-

694   tion of which displays two typical Newport features. One is the elongated claw-and-ball foot with undercut talons, the other the concave shell with plume-like mouldings emerging from a tight volute in a design which recalls certain silver dishes of the time. This piece is made of mahogany, a West Indian wood which came to be preferred to all others on account of its warm and lustrous colour and its resistance to the attacks of insects.

A convex voluted shell with pendant flower decorates the

695   knee, and an identical shell ornaments the cresting of a walnut side chair that is equally characteristic of Newport. The back is a fully developed expression of the design seen in the Gaines-style

690   chair, in which the swelling form of the vase-shaped splat is reflected in the curving stiles.

These forms were frequently imitated in New York chairs, which were rather less elegant because of the over-rounded

696   splats and the partial detaching of the cresting shell over a passage of foliate carving. In Massachusetts and Connecticut, on

697   the other hand, the cult of verticality favoured higher, narrower

689   backs, closer to those of the earlier 'bended' chairs which continued to be made in and exported from Boston. The stout rear legs and stretchers of New England Queen Anne chairs, those of Newport and those of Massachusetts and Connecticut, contrast with the thinner forms ending in square pads employed without stretchers in New York City and the Hudson River area.

698   *Above*: This mahogany armchair of 1750-60 has all the qualities of the Philadelphia Queen Anne style—the generous proportions, naturalistic shells, paired scrolls and acanthus carving. It is said to have been in the Samuel Powel House, furnished in the 1760s. Philadelphia Museum of Art

699   *Above*: The presence of Rococo carving on this Philadelphian mahogany chair suggests a late date of about 1750-60. H. F. du Pont Winterthur Museum, Delaware

700   *Above*: Windsor settee, 1750-70, of painted hickory and other woods, an 18th-century version of the earlier 'stick' construction. American examples often have more delicate forms than the English. Metropolitan Museum of Art, New York, Gift of Mr and Mrs Paul Moore, 1946

701   *Below*: This walnut sofa was one of the first to be made in America and is unusual because of the absence of stretchers, which must have been considered a technical *tour de force* at the time. Delaware River Valley, 1750-60. H. F. du Pont Winterthur Museum, Delaware

702 *Below*: Walnut dressing table, New Jersey, 1720-35. This piece represents the transition from the American William and Mary to Queen Anne style. The 'paintbrush' feet are topped by mouldings called 'wristers', a local New Jersey characteristic. H. F. du Pont Winterthur Museum, Delaware

703 *Right*: Cabinet for an air pump, Philadelphia, 1739. Painted pine. An important example of 'architectural' furniture including Palladian features made by John Harrison for the rooms of the Library Company in the State House of Pennsylvania. Library Company of Philadelphia

704 High chest-of-drawers of mahogany, Philadelphia, 1740-50. Capt. Samuel Morris, founder of the First Troop of Philadelphia City Cavalry, is said to have owned this handsome piece, which is typical of the Delaware River Valley in its use of trifid feet and a high skirting. Philadelphia Museum of Art

Philadelphia chairs, usually of walnut, were also generally constructed without stretchers, but their most striking characteristic is the sculptural quality of the frames. The deeply carved concave and convex shells, the acanthus 'grasses', as they were called in 18th-century Philadelphia, spread over the knees and the delicate claws of the feet are much more realistic than the ornament of New England.

These elements were intensified after 1750 when the stiles became almost entirely convex and the now pierced splat was filled with acanthus carving, which like that of the knees, tends to obscure the typical Philadelphia paired volutes of the profile.

Among the new forms of furniture introduced from England in this period were the upholstered settee and the sofa, both of which found admirable expression in Philadelphia. The beautiful rolled arms and the elaborate shaping of the high and splendid back are related to the best easy chairs of the period. The unadorned Philadelphia sofa, derives its beauty entirely from its handsome lines and belongs, like the Massachusetts tea table, to an eminently American category of plain furniture that also includes the fine chairs and settees of 'stick' construction called Windsors. These were used not only in private houses but frequently in inns and public buildings like the State House of Pennsylvania, where the delegates to the Continental Congress held in 1778 were seated in Windsor armchairs made by Francis Trumble.

Chairs of this sort were produced as early as 1725 in Philadelphia, which became a great export centre, especially in the period after 1760, from which most of the surviving examples date. American Windsors, which were also made in other centres besides Philadelphia, have turned 'stick' legs set at a raked angle in a saddle-shaped seat, which is generally thicker than those of English examples. American backs, on the other hand, are lighter than the standard late 18th-century English type, which contains a wide pierced central splat. In the colonies, Windsor backs and arm supports were made exclusively of graduated spindles in a variety of designs, the most popular of which were the hoop or bent bow (framed in a continuous curve) and the

comb-back with horizontal cresting. Occasionally these two features were combined in a single piece.

Constructed of a combination of different woods, American Windsor furniture, which was frequently used out of doors, was traditionally painted green or black. Of all the American plain furniture, it was probably the most satisfactory because, in addition to being cheap and easy to build, it derived great strength from its form of construction and at the same time was light and elegant in appearance.

The same generous proportions exhibited in the seat furniture of the Delaware River Valley are found also in the mid-18th-century case pieces from this area. A mahogany high chest-of-drawers and a walnut dressing-table serve as examples. Both are lower than corresponding New England pieces and both have thicker legs, thus creating an impression of stability lacking in New England examples.

In English cabinet-making of the 18th century the so-called architectural pieces, with pilasters, entablature and Classical mouldings framing conventional drawers or bookshelves, played a great part, thanks in large measure to the long-lived vogue for Palladian building. It is therefore not surprising to find an American approximation to this kind of furniture in Philadelphia, which in the first half of the 18th century had become the colonial town closest to London in its tastes and resources.

An example of this kind of furniture is the 'press' cupboard, made to contain the air pump presented in 1738 by Governor John Penn to the Library Company of Philadelphia for scientific experiments. It was made in the following year by John Harrison, one of the carpenters who worked on the State House of Pennsylvania, whose Palladian revival woodwork it closely resembles. The single door, glazed with London glass, is flanked by fluted Doric pilasters carrying a broken pediment enriched by mouldings. This appears to be the earliest surviving example of such a motif in American furniture. Pilasters and pediment are combined with frieze blocks containing carvings of three fish-like husks, a motif which later reappears in Philadelphia where the Rococo style was most fully developed.

The American 'Chippendale' Style (*c.* 1760–80)

705 If we examine the frame of the trade card of Benjamin Randolph,
706 we can obtain a good idea of the decorative repertoire of Phila-
707 delphia cabinet-makers at the height of the Rococo fashions.
713 With Thomas Affleck, William Savery, James Gillingham,
Jonathan Shoemaker and others, Randolph continued the fine
tradition of Philadelphia furniture in the period just before the
Revolution. The Rococo style was to be found in Philadelphia in
about 1763, the year of Affleck's arrival from London, and continued until the 1780s, although the style was occasionally
practised as late as 1800. Mahogany, carved but rarely inlaid,
was usually employed for fine furniture. The secondary woods,
of which the carcases were made, continued to vary from region
to region, thus providing an important clue to their provenance.

The sample furniture which Benjamin Randolph had engraved on his trade card is based on combinations of scrolls and
pierced and flaring forms that were popular in both London and
Paris in the mid-18th century and which constitute what was
called in Philadelphia, in deference to its origin in Paris; the
'New French Style.' Today in America both the surviving richly
carved examples and the numerous simpler pieces are loosely
and somewhat ambiguously called Chippendale.

The new style, which succeeded the American Queen Anne
throughout all the colonies at about the same time as it appeared
in Philadelphia, that is to say from about 1760–5, is marked by
these three general characteristics: (1) a tendency to complex
curved forms; (2) the use of a 'cross bow' type of cresting in chair
backs, derived apparently from China; (3) the almost universal
use of the claw-and-ball foot with the cabriole leg. With these
went the use of blocked fronts in case pieces, a special characteristic of New England, and the *bombé* form of chest-of-drawers, a
725 splendid peculiarity of late 18th-century Boston.

In Philadelphia and the Delaware River Valley the local tradition of generous proportions continued into the new era.
Especially typical are the transitional side chairs. A few of these
706 bear the label of William Savery (1721–88) and a sketch of one
by Jonathan Shoemaker dated 1766 is now preserved in the
Philadelphia Museum. They have in common the use of trifid
feet, a broad plain splat which retains the Queen Anne scrolls,
and the rippling outline of the new bow cresting. Sometimes
scrolls also appear on the knees. A naturalistic shell was a
707 favourite ornament for the centre of the seat frame, as it had
been in the richest of the Philadelphia Queen Anne style chairs,
in comparison with which the transitional pieces seem, paradoxically, old-fashioned.

All traces of this transition disappear, however, once the splat
is pierced, the claw-and-ball foot is added, and the carving of the
'New French Style' is applied. This can be seen in a chair at
Winterthur in which the skirting is decorated with delicate carv-
708 ing of pierced forms emerging from scrolls. The centre of the
cresting is carved in the same low relief with ruffled leaf profiles
extending from an asymmetrical scroll, while leaf and flower
garlands, like those of the Randolph trade card, trickle down the
boldly curving stiles. This naturalistic ornament contrasts with
the conventional foliage on the seat frame and the base of the
splat, a fine London touch found only in Philadelphia chairs.
The ultimate sophistication was reached in one of the six sample
709 chairs attributed to Benjamin Randolph in which appear the
scroll feet, favoured by Chippendale, along with Gothic Revival
tracery in the splat, both of which figure prominently on the
trade card. The carving also includes gadrooning, applied
around the skirting of the chair.

Philadelphia case furniture of the American Chippendale
period is distinguished by the wide use of slender quarter colonnettes at the front angles. These are always of the Doric order,
like the columns and entablature in the background of Randolph's advertisement. They appear in the drawing for a chest-
on-chest or double chest-of-drawers in the Shoemaker design
book of 1766 in company with the broad ogee-curved bracket
feet constantly used with these heavy pieces. The cresting re-
peats the curving outline of the feet.

705 Trade card of the Philadelphian cabinet-
maker Benjamin Randolph, engraved by James
Smither *c.* 1770. The Rococo frame is similar to
those on London trade cards of rather earlier
date. The furniture illustrated is inspired by the

published designs of Chippendale, Manwaring,
Ince and Mayhew, Thomas Johnson and other
English cabinet-makers and woodcarvers.
Library Company of Philadelphia

706 One of a pair of Philadelphian mahogany
chairs bearing the label of William Savery,
1760–70. The back is typical of the transitional
style between the American Queen Anne and
the so-called Chippendale. The stretchers are
unusual. Colonial Williamsburg

707 Mahogany side chair, Philadelphia,
1760–70. A sketch for a chair very similar to this
appears in Jonathan Shoemaker's design book of
1766. Shoemaker was active in 1757 and died in
1793. H. F. du Pont Winterthur Museum,
Delaware

708 This mahogany chair was originally owned by the Lambert family. The profuse Rococo carving is in a manner found only on Philadelphian pieces. H. F. du Pont Winterthur Museum, Delaware

709 One of six so-called sample chairs of mahogany thought to have been made by Benjamin Randolph, *c.* 1765–80. The splat has pseudo-Gothic tracery and volute feet of the type recommended by Chippendale's *Director*. Feet like these are rare in American furniture. Colonial Williamsburg

710 *Right*: A celebrated mahogany high chest-of-drawers, carved in a flamboyant Rococo manner, made for William Turner of Walnut Grove, Philadelphia, between 1765–80. H. F. du Pont Winterthur Museum, Delaware

711 *Above*: Mahogany dressing table, Philadelphia, 1765–80. This piece, like the high chest-of-drawers in the previous illustration, displays ornament closely related to that on Benjamin Randolph's trade card (illustration 705). Museum of Fine Arts, Boston, M. & M. Karolik Collection

712 *Right*: Looking-glass of yellow pine painted white and gilt, Philadelphia, 1765–80, made by James Reynolds for General John Cadwalader. The painted and gilt frame is one of the most completely Rococo designs in surviving Philadelphia Chippendale furniture. H. F. du Pont Winterthur Museum, Delaware

713 *Right*: Upholstered armchair, with straight, so-called 'Marlboro' legs, associated with the cabinet-maker Thomas Affleck, who came from London to Philadelphia in 1763. The shape of the back is typical of Philadelphian pieces. Metropolitan Museum of Art, New York, Funds from Various Donors, 1959

714 *Far right*: Chairs of this type were made by German settlers who transported to Pennsylvania one of the richest folk cultures of Europe. This walnut peasant chair is dated 1770. H. F. du Pont Winterthur Museum, Delaware

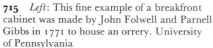

715 *Left*: This fine example of a breakfront cabinet was made by John Folwell and Parnell Gibbs in 1771 to house an orrery. University of Pennsylvania

716 *Right*: Armchair, New York, 1765–75. Mahogany. A typical New York Chippendale style chair made for Stephen van Rensselaer of Albany, in which several features of English chairs of the George II period, like the tassel in the splat, are retained. H. F. du Pont Winterthur Museum, Delaware

Similar in shape are the great high chests-of-drawers, the real showpieces of Philadelphia Chippendale furniture, although these, like their Queen Anne predecessors, are carried on sturdy cabriole legs. None can be positively associated with any known maker but a few bear the Rococo ornament used on Randolph's trade card. Thus the celebrated Turner-Van Pelt family highboy, which has a lower drawer covered with typical Philadelphia 'scallop and grass' carving, displays a skirt edged with the asymmetrical scrolls that frame Randolph's name on the engraved card. These are repeated beneath the terminal scrolls of the highboy, where they flank tiny relief piers with flared imposts that resemble the motif on which Randolph's eagle is posed and which is one of the most popular decorative devices of the English Rococo designers. The lower moulding of this bizarre perch seems to disintegrate like the rills of water carved beneath the scrolls of the top.

Equally redolent of Randolph's trade card ornament is the Philadelphia dressing-table in the Karolik Collection at the Boston Museum. Here the central drawer is carved with the same web of scrolls, piers and dripping water, over which glides a swan. Below this relief there is a vase with flowers very similar to the draped urn of Randolph's advertisement. The dressing-table is even more elaborately carved than the high chest-of-drawers, for the angle colonnettes are strewn with garlands and the handsome piece has a frieze of pseudo-Chinese fretwork alternating with Palladian rosettes.

A third member of this Randolph group, and indeed the most Rococo of all, is a superb gilt mirror of which the inner frame has the same elongated piers with flared imposts as in the two preceding chest pieces. They all seem to be the work of the same woodcarver.

If Randolph is associated with the extreme Rococo ornament of the Philadelphia school, the name of Thomas Affleck (1740–95) is just as firmly linked with the use of the straight or 'Marlboro' leg, which Chippendale had recommended as an alternative to the cabriole form. This was used in Philadelphia for chairs, sofas, beds, bookcases and tables, the surface decorated either with vertical mouldings or a succession of panels combined with pseudo-Gothic and Chinese or classical ornament, with or without small plinth-like feet.

Affleck made chairs and a sofa in this style for Governor Penn between 1763 and 1766, now in the possession of the Chew family of Cliveden, on the basis of which it is possible to attribute a few similar armchairs to this excellent London-trained craftsman. One such, at the Metropolitan Museum, has feet with panels of a shape used by Chippendale and arms carved in rounded forms overlaid with flat leaf carving. The same combination of formal outlines with Rococo ornament occurs in the carved bases of a number of well known Philadelphia pedestal tables.

The most important piece of architectural furniture made in Philadelphia at this time and one of the outstanding examples of the 'Marlboro' leg in case furniture is the great breakfront cabinet containing the orrery or planetarium made by David Rittenhouse for the University of Pennsylvania. This case was constructed in 1771 by John Folwell, who had just completed the pulpit of Christ Church and a few years later was to advertise his intention of publishing a *Cabinet-Maker's Director* of his own, although, apparently because of the Revolution, this plan was never carried out.

In its grand proportions the orrery conforms to the taste of the city. The upper section, in which the glazing bars are arranged

717 *Below*: Kneehole chest-of-drawers of mahogany, made in Newport, 1765–75. The kneehole form, popular in England, was seldom used outside Rhode Island, where it was splendidly interpreted. Rounded blocking was combined with the characteristic Newport stylised shell. H. F. du Pont Winterthur Museum, Delaware

718 *Right*: Secretary desk, 1765–75. This richly decorated mahogany showpiece of Newport Chippendale furniture was made by John Goddard for the merchant and financier John Brown of Providence, Rhode Island. Rhode Island Historical Society

in the same way as those in plate 67 in the 1754 edition of Chippendale's *Director* has the elegant entablature found in a group of Philadelphia high chests, double chests and tall clocks. Like these, the orrery case displays a delicate lattice between the serpentine scrolls ending in acanthus tufts. The stand on which the Rittenhouse orrery rests, a well proportioned composition of rectangular units, discreetly ornamented with gadrooning and fretwork, is closely related to a number of Philadelphia card, serving and tea tables of the period.

One of the last innovations in the colonial furniture of Philadelphia was the employment of the serpentine or 'sweep' front in large chests-of-drawers with canted front angles and massive polygonal ogee-curved feet, a simplified restatement of those made in London in the mid-18th century.

More than any other colony, Pennsylvania received settlers from the Continent of Europe. Among these were Germans from the Palatinate and elsewhere, who brought to America their traditional furniture and decorations, such as the richly ornamented wardrobes and chests, trestle tables, wainscot and banister-back armchairs and the characteristic German side chairs of the period. These were made principally of walnut with slanted 'stick' legs and octagonal seats and shaped backs which echo the form of Italian Renaissance chairs. The backs are pierced with popular heart-shaped designs, and one dated example has a prancing stag engraved upon it, a motif found on the late medieval furniture of Switzerland and the Tyrol.

The marriage chests of the Pennsylvania Germans, based on an ancient south German model, are decorated with inlay of wood or wax or with paintings, generally composed around three arched panels. These chests are frequently dated and some-

714

times bear the name of the original owner. The painted examples have formal flat designs in brilliant colours that can be related stylistically to the illuminated birth and baptismal certificates of the region. Typical ornament includes, in addition to geometric decoration, tulips, vines in vases and parrot-like birds. Rampant unicorns, symbolising virginity, help identify the chests of Berks Country, some of which have been attributed to the painter Johann Heinrich Otto, active in the 1780s. One such chest at Winterthur has picturesque horsemen in contemporary clothing recalling the decorations of Pennsylvania German pottery, while the strange figures above them holding tulips wear fantastic hats reminiscent of the high crowns inlaid in the wax technique on the doors of the wardrobe of Georg Hüber dated 1779, in the Philadelphia Museum. *Plate facing page* 192

The influence of the great Chippendale school of Philadelphia extended eastward across the Delaware River to the colony of New Jersey and southward into Maryland. To the north, New York had a style of its own. One peculiarity of this style was a tendency to retain old forms, like the rounded or compass chair seat; another was the use of extremely low relief carving.

The latter trait can be seen in the favourite New York Chippendale style chair back of the famous Van Rensselaer armchair. Here the head of the tassel forming the central motif is incised with diagonal cross hatching typical of the city. The cresting is also characteristic, with its very flat leaves, as is the gadrooning between the front legs. 716

Among the distinguished categories of furniture made in New York City in the years just before the Revolution were the card tables with cabriole legs, and serpentine frames. The complex continuous curving of the full Rococo style, and the scrolls

719 Tall clock, Newport, 1760–75. Mahogany. The cases of these Newport tall clocks are distinguished by long blocked doors with the typical shell ornament. This example is attributed to John Townsend or John Goddard on the basis of a similar clock case by Townsend now at the Metropolitan Museum, New York. Museum of Fine Arts, Boston, M. & M. Karolik Collection

carved in low relief are characteristic of that city. But New England Chippendale furniture was much more important and Newport and Boston each produced distinctive styles of their own. Both were deeply influenced by the linear traditions of their regions, although the earlier tendency towards thin proportions and vertical effects was held in abeyance for a time. In both towns the bureau-bookcase or secretary desk and the double chest-of-drawers became the great showpieces of the cabinet-makers, entirely eclipsing the high chest-of-drawers, which had been the ultimate expression of Queen Anne Boston, as it remained that of Chippendale Philadelphia.   718

In Newport, where some twenty-one members of the inter-related Quaker families of Goddard and Townsend entirely dominated the furniture craft between 1760 and 1780, the link with the local Queen Anne style was the stylised shell set in the centre of the skirting of dressing tables and high chests-of-drawers. In Newport furniture of Chippendale style this motif, which had previously been employed singly and always in concave form was now used in groups of three, with the shell in both concave and convex positions, glued to the surface of the case. In addition, the volutes at the base of the shells were enriched with a curving row of petals which vary from piece to piece. These shells are considerably more opulent than the earlier ones but they remain essentially stylised in comparison with those of Philadelphia.   717

The rounded panels, which John Goddard (1723–85) called 'sweld', perform an essential role in Newport case furniture by creating a marked contrast of planes. The technical process, known as blocking involved concave recessed compositions as well as convex, deriving from similar forms used in the designs of the French cabinet-maker, André-Charles Boulle in about 1700, which so influenced the case furniture of northern Germany and Holland. Never popular in England, blocked fronts were made in various parts of British America but especially in New England, where the technique was practised as early as 1738 in a secretary desk signed and dated by Job Coit, Jr of Boston, now in the Winterthur collection.

Blocking was given a strong local flavour in Newport by the   717 use of the shell forms at the top of a blocked area. This is demonstrated in a group of kneehole chests-of-drawers or bureau tables, one at the Boston Museum bearing the label of Edmund Townsend (1736–1811). These pieces, which are a speciality of Newport, also display in their front bracket feet the local spiral ornament that makes them look rather like cabriole legs.

Blocking was also applied to chests-of-drawers and double chests, to slant-front desks and to the grandiose secretary desks   717 which are related to them. The upper sections of these pieces, which like the Townsend-Goddard tall clocks, have fluted Doric   719 quarter colonnettes at their angles, contain three blocked doors which balance the drawer fronts and the fall-board below. In some pieces the complexity of the feet is repeated at the other extremity, where corniced parapets intercept the bonnet scrolls. These end in rosettes carved in flat linear patterns so different from the sculptural quality found in Philadelphia.

Various aspects of this powerful Newport style appear in the furniture of other parts of New England. Rhode Island blocking, for example, is found in some notable pieces from the coastal area of neighbouring Connecticut, where John Townsend (1732–1809) was once thought to have settled. There are, however, certain basic differences. One is the introduction of straight lines   720 into the shell-like ornaments, thus destroying the rhythm of the Newport pieces. Similarly the bracket feet of Connecticut furniture are simplified and the typical scrolls of Connecticut skirting   720 are flat and rather prim. In distant New Hampshire, where members of the Dunlap family worked somewhat later in a style, by then old-fashioned, variants on the Newport shell are found, sometimes fantastic in scale and always hard and flat in pattern.   721 They were arbitrarily used by the Dunlaps on high chests-of-drawers, on slant-front desks and on curious high-back chairs remotely related to designs in the *Director*.

In Newport, as in Philadelphia, Chippendale tables were made with straight legs as well as cabriole and the master craftsmen of Rhode Island, like their contemporaries of Pennsylvania, introduced a number of refinements to soften the resulting angularity. John Townsend, for example, used brackets of pseudo-

High chest-of-drawers, Boston, 1740–50.
Japanned maple and pine. This masterpiece
in the American Queen Anne style was built
by John Pimm for Commodore Joshua Loring
of Boston and painted in imitation of oriental
lacquer probably by Thomas Johnson. Both
craftsmen worked in the second quarter of
the 18th century. H.F. du Pont Winterthur
Museum, Delaware

Oval-back side chair, Philadelphia, 1796.
Painted beech. One of 24 chairs in the
Hepplewhite style ordered by Elias Hasket
Derby of Salem, Massachusetts, through his
agents Joseph Anthony and Co. of Phila-
delphia. These painted chairs were imitated
at Salem by the Scottish painter Robert
Cowan, some of whose pieces, inspired by this
example, are now at Deerfield, Massachusetts.
Museum of Fine Arts, Boston, M. & M.
Karolik Collection

Marriage chest, Pennsylvania, 1780–90.
Painted white pine. A Pennsylvania-German
chest with painted decoration, including the
confronted unicorns which were a favourite
device in Reading and the adjacent Berks Co.
This and a similar chest at the Metropolitan
Museum suggest the work of the painter
Johann Heinrich Otto. H.F. du Pont
Winterthur Museum, Delaware

Chinese fretwork and the same kind of ornament in the intersecting stretchers.

No characteristic Chippendale style chair was ever widely used in Newport, for the Queen Anne form seems to have persisted there until the end of the colonial period. In Massachusetts, on the other hand, the towns of Boston and Salem had versions of their own with easily distinguishable features. One is the frequent use of a seat upholstered over the frame rather than made to slip into it. Another is the type of back with a pierced scrolled splat taken from a design of the London cabinet-maker, Robert Manwaring. A third is the leanness of proportion, especially in the rear legs and seat frame, which sometimes led to the use of stretchers. A fourth trait is the local form of claw-and-ball foot in which one claw is drawn backward, as opposed to the elongated, rather drooping claws of Newport, the large squarish formation of New York and the claws firmly grasping a slightly flattened ball of Philadelphia. A fifth characteristic is the spare, very thin carving sometimes omitted altogether from the back or from the knees of a fine Massachusetts chair.

The same restraint is seen in most of the great blocked case pieces, which in Boston were less spectacular than in Newport and coastal Connecticut. Here the decoration was flatter and unaccompanied by shell forms. It was seldom applied to the upper section of a double chest or secretary desk, so as to form a contrast with the lower section. This contrast was achieved by emphasising the flatness in the upper portion and by framing the drawers with fluted pilasters. There is none of the naturalistic carving that would adorn a great Philadelphia piece of this era; instead the lower chest section displays the modest, flat lunette decoration found all over New England in the 18th century. This sober ornament suggests that Bostonians had no taste for the 'New French Style' of Philadelphia.

There were, however, some notable exceptions, especially the furniture made by and attributed to John Cogswell. A secretary desk thought to be the work of this Boston craftsman, who was first mentioned as a cabinet-maker in 1769 and died in 1818, has a ruffling of carved leaves beneath the pediment and realistic petals to the rosettes of the scrolls. The bookcase section is flanked by Ionic pilasters, which became fashionable in Boston as they never did in Philadelphia; yet the profiles of the panels have Palladian leaf mouldings like those of Philadelphia. The fretwork friezes at top and bottom of this section are apparently a mark of Cogswell's style. The Rococo ornament above is complemented by the form of the desk section below, with its *bombé* profile. The closest parallel in European furniture is found in the towering cabinets and desks made of veneered walnut in Holland in the mid-18th century, which may also have provided the precedent in Boston for combining the *bombé* case with broad claw-and-ball feet instead of the bracket type generally employed in American furniture. But Boston cabinet-makers like John Cogswell improved upon the Dutch model by raising the case higher from the floor and by shaping the drawers to fit the *bombé* form. Finally Cogswell's drawers, like those of the double chest attributed to Frothingham, have the cockbeaded edges found on such masterpieces of late 18th-century Philadelphia furniture as Jonathan Gostelowe's 'sweep front' chest-of-drawers.

The same serpentine form appeared in other regions at the close of the 18th century. It occurs in the lower section of a famous double chest made for Elias Hasket Derby of Salem, in 1791 by Stephen Badlam (1751–1815) of Boston and, at the other extremity of the colonial area, in a number of Charleston, South Carolina breakfront bookcases thought to have been made at this time. The character of the carving and design of the brasses in the Massachusetts 'sweep front' piece as well as the use of inlay in the South Carolina furniture marks them as transitional to the Neo-Classical style of the Federal period.

Marginal references: 722 723 / 725 694 716 698, 711 / 724 / 725 / 725 / 724 / 726 727

720 *Above*: Chest-of-drawers of cherry, made in coastal Connecticut, 1770–85. Newport blocking influenced the neighbouring area of Connecticut, where however it was significantly modified. This chest, with incised and punched ornament around the shells, has been attributed to Aaron Roberts of New Britain, Connecticut. Collection: Mr and Mrs Stanley Stone

721 *Below*: Slant-front desk, New Hampshire, 1770–90. Maple. Newport shells, although distorted in form and scale, can be recognised in this provincial desk which suggests the work of Samuel Dunlap II. H. F. du Pont Winterthur Museum, Delaware

The bedroom of the Empress Josephine in the Château de la Malmaison near Paris was re-furnished for her use in 1810. It is in the form of a Classical tent of red cloth embroidered with fine gold thread supported by slender gilt wood columns. Beside the state bed, executed by Jacob-Desmalter, is a mahogany '*saut de lit*' on three legs with basin and jug of Sèvres porcelain. On the left is a bronze *guéridon* with three winged lions at its base and a top of inlaid marble.

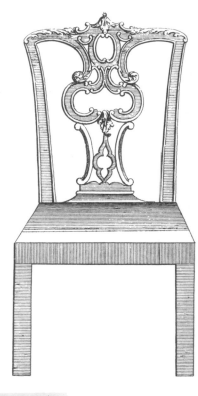

722, 723 *Right and far right*: Side chair of mahogany, Massachusetts, 1770–90, a type of Chippendale style chair popular in Boston and Salem. The back is directly inspired by plate 9 of Robert Manwaring's *The Cabinet and Chair-Maker's Real Friend and Companion* (London, 1765). Museum of Fine Arts, Boston

724 *Below*: Double chest-of-drawers, 1760–75. This mahogany piece, partially blocked in a manner characteristic of Massachusetts is attributed to Benjamin Frothingham of Boston, Massachusetts. Collection: Mr and Mrs Lansdell K. Christie

725 *Below right*: Secretary desk, Boston, 1770–85. Mahogany. A piece, attributed to John Cogswell, showing the *bombé* profile of the finest Boston Chippendale furniture with the unusual additional feature of decorative carving reminiscent of the Philadelphia Rococo style. H. F. du Pont Winterthur Museum, Delaware

The Federal Style
(*c.* 1790–1810)

During the 1760s, when the American Chippendale style was still developing, Robert Adam was establishing in England a new vocabulary of decoration based on antique Roman ornament. His innovations were not felt in America until after the Revolution, which ended in 1783, and no examples of the new style for furniture appear to have been made before 1790.

The furniture of that decade and the following is called Federal because this was the key word of that period. For the first time there was a federal government and federal political party and the federal city of Washington was then being constructed. This Federal furniture, which represents the first phase of the Classical Revival, was not based directly upon models by Robert Adam, which had lost their novelty during the Revolution when no new British fashions were followed in America. Instead, it conforms, sometimes literally, to designs in the pattern books of the late 18th-century London furniture designers, Thomas Shearer, George Hepplewhite, and Thomas Sheraton. American Federal style furniture makers took advantage, also, of Adam's example in using marquetry, painted decoration and caning and also satinwood and other exotic woods. Similarly, on the authority of the English pattern books, Federal cabinet-makers made constant use of Neo-Classical ornament.

In spite of federal government and the easier intercommunication at the turn of the century between the former colonies, a surprising amount of regional forms persisted. Particular types of furniture were created in certain areas, like New England. Others, like New York and Philadelphia, identified themselves with the use of a specific model from one of the London pattern-books. Still others distinguished themselves by special decorative techniques, such as Baltimore's panels of painted and gilt glass. New England's fondness for slender forms was not merely maintained in the Federal period, but became even more marked.

Massachusetts furniture was dominated by the personalities of Samuel McIntire (1757–1811) and John Seymour (*c.* 1738–1818). The latter, one of the few distinguished British cabinet-makers who emigrated to America of whom we have precise knowledge, came to Maine in 1785 with his son and future associate Thomas. In 1794 they settled in Boston, where they produced such elegant, superbly finished pieces as the semi-circular chest-of-drawers for Mrs Elizabeth Derby in 1809. Richly veneered in contrasting woods with painted shells on the top, the commode owes much to Sheraton. Its reeded colonnettes became a speciality of Boston and Salem, as well as a combination of two kinds of foot, the bulbous and the brass lion paw. Equally novel in its form and influential in its impact is the labelled Seymour lady's desk with straight tapering legs, this time inspired by a Hepplewhite design. The upper section has a tambour, or sliding reeded front, into which is inlaid a festoon of flowers. The striking pilaster motifs with satinwood shafts are as characteristic of the Seymours as the 'book' inlay of Federal style tables made in Rhode Island was of Holmes Weaver and John Townsend of Newport, who had previously worked in the Chippendale style. A labelled card table by Townsend has the fashionable semi-circular form of the Seymour commode and, in addition to the 'book' type, other typical inlay of the period.

The little seaport of Salem, situated a short distance above Boston, grew suddenly rich through the China trade at the close of the Revolution and great Salem merchants like Elias Hasket Derby (1733–1799), the leading American patron of the period, ordered furniture after designs by Samuel McIntire, a wood-carver who designed both houses and tables and chairs.

In its heyday before 1812 Salem supported half a dozen fine cabinet-makers working in the Federal style including Nehemiah Adams, Edmund Johnson, William Hook, William Lemmon and Elijah and Jacob Sanderson. These men introduced a piece of furniture combining the features of bookcase and cabinet called a 'Salem secretary'. One example shows three decorative elements typical of this period, thin bands of inlay, inlaid swags of bell-flowers, and veneered panels of oval form, contrasting in tone and grain with the wood around them.

728

729

730

731
732

736

726 One of four mahogany double chests-of-drawers made for Elias Hasket Derby of Salem at the workshop of Stephen Badlam of Boston, Massachusetts in 1791. This is one of the earliest examples of American furniture in which Neo-Classical ornament appears. The finial figures are by John Skillin (1746–1800) and his brother Simeon Jr. (1757–1806). Mabel Brady Garvan Collection, Yale University

727 Breakfront mahogany bookcase, Charleston, South Carolina, 1790–1800. A transitional piece showing characteristics of the Neo-Classical Federal style in the delicate pediment scrolls and in the revived use of inlay. Mabel Brady Garvan Collection, Yale University

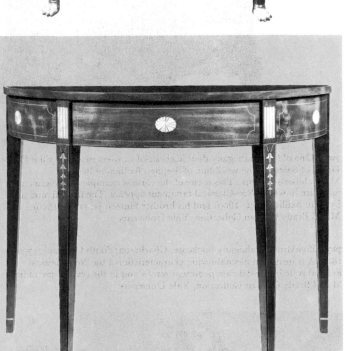

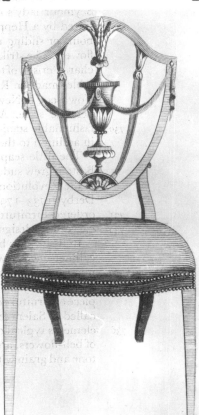

728 *Above left*: Commode of mahogany, satin-wood, rosewood, and other woods, made by John and Thomas Seymour of Boston for Miss Elisabeth Derby in 1809; the bill reveals that the carving is by Thomas Whitman and the painting of sea-shells on the top by John Penniman. Museum of Fine Arts, Boston, M. & M. Karolik Collection

729 *Above right*: Tambour desk, Boston, 1795–1800. Mahogany and satinwood. Labelled by John Seymour and Son, Creek Lane, Boston, the interior has the blue-green paint used by these English cabinet-makers. H. F. du Pont Winterthur Museum, Delaware

730 *Left*: Card-table of mahogany with satinwood inlay. This piece bears the label of Townsend of Newport, dated 1796. The Neo-Classical motifs include paterae and bell-flowers and above the legs the typical Rhode Island 'book' ornament. H. F. du Pont Winterthur Museum, Delaware

731, 733 *Right and below right*: One of a set of mahogany side chairs with ebony feet owned by Elias Hasket Derby and probably carved by Samuel McIntire, the foremost craftsman of Salem, *c.* 1795. The back is derived from plate 2 of George Hepplewhite's *The Cabinet-maker and Upholsterer's Guide* (London, 1788), but McIntire has added a delicately carved trail of vine-leaves to the front legs. Museum of Fine Arts, Boston, M. & M. Karolik Collection

732 Mahogany sofa, *c.* 1795, carved with the vine motif and cresting typical of Samuel McIntire of Salem to whom this piece is attributed. Museum of Fine Arts, Boston, M. & M. Karolik Collection

734 *Left*: Federal looking-glasses represent the closest approach in American furniture to the English style of Robert Adam. This example was made in New York or Connecticut, 1790–1800. Metropolitan Museum of Art, The Sylmaris Collection, Gift of George Coe Graves, 1931

735 *Below*: Upholstered armchair of mahogany with birch inlay, made in New Hampshire 1800–10. This kind of armchair, named after Martha Washington, is an adaptation of an earlier form (see illustration 713). Attenuated proportions persisted in New England furniture into the Federal period. Metropolitan Museum of Art, Gift of Mrs Russell Sage, 1909

736 *Below*: A 'Salem secretary' bearing the label of Nehemiah Adams of Salem, 1780–1805. This piece, veneered with mahogany, was shipped as 'venture cargo'. In the early 19th century some Salem cabinet-makers entrusted their furniture to sea captains, bound for the West Indies and Brazil. The captains undertook to sell it and invest the profit in rum, sugar, spices and other local products which could be sold advantageously in New England. In return the sea captains received a commission from the cabinet-makers. The piece illustrated was discovered in Capetown. H. F. du Pont Winterthur Museum, Delaware

The same colour contrast, absent from American furniture since the early 18th century, can be seen in an inlaid New Hampshire armchair of about 1800–10, which represents yet another local form called originally a 'Martha Washington' chair. An extreme example of regional elongation, the piece was developed from English models which themselves appear attenuated in comparison with Philadelphia Chippendale upholstered armchairs. In even stronger contrast are the rounded forms of a typical Philadelphia Rococo looking glass and the straight lines of the new Federal style. An attractive example dating from the last years of the 18th century has a frame surmounted by vases with flowers and wheat ears, made either in Connecticut or New York.

The city of New York, which in the colonial period had played a secondary role, assumed an important position in the Federal age as a centre of fine furniture making. With the rapid growth of the city between 1800 and the middle of the 19th century, the largest group of cabinet-makers in the nation was concentrated in New York and many were exporting their products to the rest of the country.

The great period for New York opened in 1789, when George Washington began his first term as president there. Such men as Michael Allison, Elbert Anderson and the firms of Stover and Taylor and Mills and Deming made furniture after Hepplewhite and Sheraton designs in the years between 1795 and 1805. A favourite New York chair has a square back displaying a pierced urn and drapery within an arch, taken from a Sheraton design. Sometimes the details are carved, occasionally they are carried out in shaded inlay, as in a fine mahogany chair in the Karolik Collection, where the drapery, Prince of Wales plumes and other details are worked out in satinwood.

The best known craftsman of the city and the only one to possess a great personal style was Duncan Phyfe (1768–1854), an immigrant from Scotland via Albany, New York, who maintained a shop in New York City from 1795 to 1847 and during this long period interpreted with great distinction and an unusual measure of originality a series of European styles. Phyfe's first manner, inspired by early Sheraton designs, can be seen in an armchair made in 1807. Characteristic reed moulding is applied to the arms, the stiles and the front legs. A strong continuous movement leads up to the frieze-like carving of the rolled cresting rail, filled with arrows and ribbons, which Phyfe also used for his sofas. The Greco-Roman 'sabre' form of the front legs and the diagonally crossed bars of the back of the Bayard chair, anticipate the master's development after 1810, when he used such features of the English Regency style as the lyre back and front legs of 'dog' and curule form.

Charles Honoré Lannuier, active in New York City from 1803 until 1819, was the first of a number of French cabinet-makers whose work enriched American furniture in the 19th century.

737 *Above*: Side chair of a type particularly popular in New York, 1790–1800. The design was taken from plate 36, fig. 1 of Sheraton's *Cabinet-maker and Upholsterer's Drawing Book* 1791–94. Museum of Fine Arts, Boston, M. & M. Karolik Collection

738 *Above*: This armchair is one of a set of mahogany chairs made in 1807 for William Bayard of New York by Duncan Phyfe. The bill is also preserved at Winterthur. H. F. du Pont Winterthur Museum, Delaware

739 *Above*: Pier table of mahogany and brass with white marble top, made in New York, 1805–10, and bearing the stamp of Charles Honoré Lannuier, who arrived from Paris in 1803. It was owned by James K. Paulding (1778–1860), Secretary of the Navy under President Van Buren and author of *Salmagundi Papers*. H. F. du Pont Winterthur Museum, Delaware

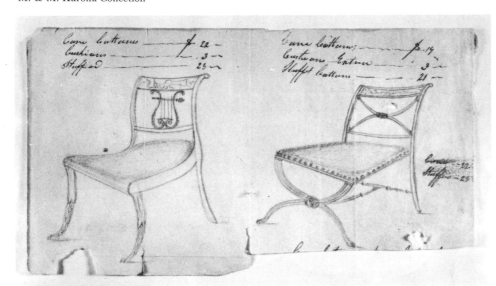

740 *Above*: These drawings of chairs accompanied an estimate sent by Phyfe to Charles N. Bancker of Philadelphia in 1816. They represent the second phase of his stylistic development, which corresponds to English Regency taste. Phyfe, unlike many Federal cabinet-makers, preferred carving to inlay. H. F. du Pont Winterthur Museum, Delaware

741 *Left*: One of a set of 'bar-back' ebony chairs with settee *en suite* made by Ephraim Haines in 1806–7 for Stephen Girard (1750–1831). The bill indicates that the carving was done by John R. Morris, the turning by Barney Schumo. Reproduced from the Girard Collection, Girard College by Courtesy of the Trustees of the Estate of Stephen Girard

742 *Right*: Secretary desk of mahogany and satinwood made in Philadelphia, 1795–1805. One of a number of elegant Hepplewhite pieces decorated with inlaid ovals in striking patterns, characteristic of Federal Philadelphia. John Davey, who signed this piece, was active in 1802. Metropolitan Museum of Art, Fletcher Fund, 1962

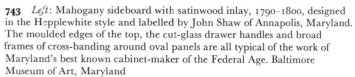

743 *Left*: Mahogany sideboard with satinwood inlay, 1790–1800, designed in the Hepplewhite style and labelled by John Shaw of Annapolis, Maryland. The moulded edges of the top, the cut-glass drawer handles and broad frames of cross-banding around oval panels are all typical of the work of Maryland's best known cabinet-maker of the Federal Age. Baltimore Museum of Art, Maryland

744 *Below left*: Mahogany sideboard with boxwood, ebony and satinwood inlay, silver and painted glass panels, made in Baltimore, *c.* 1795–1800. One of the most elaborate pieces of furniture executed in the United States during the Federal period, this Sheraton style sideboard was ordered by David van Ness for his country house Maizefield at Red Hook on the Hudson River. Metropolitan Museum of Art, Gift of Mitchell Taradash and Pulitzer Fund, 1945

745 *Below*: Card-console table of mahogany with satinwood and other inlays, 1790–1805. An outstanding example of the use of marquetry, another speciality of Federal Baltimore, where pendant tassels, shells and an unusual kind of bell-flower were favourite forms of decoration. Collection: Mrs Giles Whiting

Until about 1812 Lannuier followed the late 18th-century style of France, which he had learned in Paris. Subsequently, like Duncan Phyfe at the end of his career, he preferred heavier Empire forms. Outstanding among his early pieces is a stamped 739 pier table with brass decoration in the Louis XVI style.

In Federal Philadelphia, which during the 1790s was the national capital, there were no less than 101 cabinet-makers and 21 chair makers, 11 carvers and gilders and 17 men who specialised in Windsor chairs. Chippendale furniture continued to be made there by Thomas Affleck until his death in 1795 and one year later the great French-born merchant Stephen Girard purchased various pieces of furniture designed in this manner.

At the same time, however, Philadelphia had been acquiring a reputation for fine work in the Neo-Classical style, for no less a connoisseur than Elias Hasket Derby of Salem ordered in 1796 a set of 24 painted oval back Hepplewhite chairs, some of which *Plate* survive in various collections. The chairs are white, a colour *facing page 192* especially esteemed in Philadelphia, with gilt decorations. The oval backs have knots of ribbon in green and pink, depending on the chair, from which rise either pink ostrich plumes or peacock feathers, like those occasionally painted on contemporary English satinwood furniture.

Philadelphia cabinet-makers employed the same Sheraton urn and drapery design for square chair backs as was used in 737 New York but they also used other patterns. One of these was

republished in the *Philadelphia Journeyman Cabinet and Chairmakers' Book of Prices* in 1795. It is a rectangular design which 737 includes as a central motif an urn isolated within long loops of festooned drapery. Both Henry Connelly and Ephraim Haines made 'bar-back' Sheraton chairs, but those of the latter can sometimes be distinguished by a tapering foot with bulbous crown. In 1806–7 Haines designed a set of ten ebony side chairs, two armchairs and a settee for Stephen Girard, in which the richly carved columnar bars and foliated panels are charac- 741 teristic of Philadelphia Federal style seat furniture.

The finest Philadelphia case furniture of the 1790s, principally bookcases and fall-front secretary desks, was constructed with a minimum of carving and less figural inlay than was customary in certain other areas. Large ovals of contrasting veneers produced effects of great dignity. A desk by the little known maker John Davey, with the usual flaring bracket feet, has an 742 extremely simple parapet which projects in Neo-Classical fashion. This is typical of Federal taste in a city which was now losing to New York the leadership in furniture making it had enjoyed in the colonial period.

Similar veneered panels are found in the Federal furniture of Baltimore, the last of the great centres of production. Baltimore, which received its city charter only in 1797, saw its population double in the 1790s, thanks to Clipper shipping. In the pre-Federal era Maryland had imported its best furniture from

746 Lady's desk of mahogany with satinwood inlay and painted glass decoration, 1745-1805. Oval glass panels with reverse painting in black and gold were a speciality of the luxurious Federal furniture of Baltimore. H. F. du Pont Winterthur Museum, Delaware

747 Side chair of painted tulip and other woods, one of a set of six 'fancy' chairs probably made in New York *c.* 1810 and thought to have come from the Van Rensselaer family manor house at Albany, New York. The painted splats show scenes on the Hudson River, a favourite romantic site of the period popularised by the stories of Washington Irving. H. F. du Pont Winterthur Museum, Delaware

Philadelphia, some of which was imitated at Annapolis, the capital of the colony. It was there that John Shaw (1745-1829), a native of Glasgow, developed his personal version of the Hepplewhite style. This can be seen in the sideboard bearing his label, a piece of furniture invented in England in the late 18th century and first illustrated in Thomas Shearer's London pattern-book of 1788, and also in Hepplewhite's book of the same year.   743

Baltimore Federal furniture was often decorated with oval or lozenge-shaped glass panels with gold and black painting on the reverse side, generally representing allegorical figures. This technique of *verre églomisé* was practised almost exclusively in Baltimore and marquetry was used there more than anywhere else in America. A luxurious Sheraton style inlaid sideboard has panels of silver. The motif of confronted griffons in the central recess, recommended by Sheraton, is rare even for Baltimore and with the encircling acanthus plumage strongly recalls the technically finer compositions of Giuseppe Maggiolini of Milan.   744   595

A speciality of Baltimore was the delicately proportioned lady's writing desk, elaborately decorated, with a folding or roll top. An example of the first category has a variety of fine veneers on its case framed with triple bands of inlay. Its marquetry panels show vines rising from urns, a typical Baltimore feature. Typical too are the wide cross-banding of the oval looking-glass, the black and gold domed boxes that flank it, and the five black and gold panels of *verre églomisé*, representing allegorical figures set in satinwood veneer elegantly inlaid with thin ebony fillets. All are in Classical dress and the centre figure is seated on a *klismos* of the sort seen on imported European wallpapers and printed textiles of the 1790s but not found in American furniture until after 1810, when the vogue for furniture inspired by Greek models began.   746

Baltimore craftsmen also excelled at making card-console tables, comparable in line and finesse only to the great New England examples. Some have rich marquetry decoration. One charming table shows tiny bouquets of holly in oval panels above the front legs, which are decorated in typical Baltimore fashion with inlaid tassels and the most celebrated Baltimore ornament of all, a taut string of bell-flowers with enlarged central petals.   745

This delight in figural ornament made the new city a centre for the production of gaily painted 'fancy' chairs, designed on Sheraton lines, between approximately 1795 and 1825, in sets that often included a small settee. A New York chair with fancifully shaped 'carrot' legs has small painted panels on the maple frame and in the back a landscape of the Hudson River with a steamboat. This helps to date the chair, for the first steamboat, invented by Robert Fulton, was used there in 1807. It also provides a link with the furniture of the Romantic period of the 19th century, when the Hudson River became the most fashionable subject for American landscape painters.   747

The Furniture Section at the Great Exhibition, held at the Crystal Palace, London, in 1851.

VII THE NINETEENTH CENTURY

ENGLAND 1800-1830

Clifford Musgrave

There were many opportunities during the last decade of the 18th century for English craftsmen and designers to become familiar with French furniture in the latest vogue. Early in the 1780s French purveyors of furniture settled in London and were supplying articles to the Prince of Wales and other wealthy patrons. French craftsmen were also active in England, and English visitors to Paris bought large quantities of French furniture. After the Revolution the number of refugee craftsmen coming to take up work in England increased.

Thomas Sheraton was quick to sense the changes of taste that were taking place in the Royal palaces and the great houses like Southill and Althorp, and he was to forecast the trend of style for some years to come in his two later works, the *Cabinet Dictionary* published in 1803, and the *Cabinet-maker, Upholsterer and General Artists' Encyclopaedia* issued in parts from 1804 to 1806. The *Cabinet Dictionary*, in which Sheraton summed up so many of the newer tendencies, was the first crystallisation in an English publication of what was eventually to become famous as the Regency style.

The Classical inspiration was now being expressed with much greater historical exactitude. In the *Cabinet Dictionary* Sheraton illustrated for the first time in England the Grecian couch with scrolled ends and lion-paw feet, and chairs which 'follow the antique taste and introduce into their arms and legs various heads of animals'. In this work began to appear designs, such as those for the 'Sister's cylinder-bookcase', which seem almost pathological in their ugliness and complexity, and which seemed to foreshadow the mental infirmity to which Sheraton later succumbed. Designs of this sort were more numerous in the *Cabinet-*

maker, Upholsterer and General Artists' Encyclopaedia, which was Sheraton's last work, of which only 30 of the projected 125 parts were published, between 1804 and 1806. Fantastic designs for chairs with shaggy lion legs and with camels forming the backs, and the canopy bed with winged chimera supports, were quickly seized on by the critics as evidence of a disordered mind. But many of the designs spoke of the old characteristic refinement, like the corner washing-stands, shown with the newly fashionable reeded columns and curved legs, and what was to become especially distinctive of the Regency as the 'Trafalgar' chair, appeared in an early form with curved legs, rounded knees, and broad yoke-shaped Grecian back. Marine emblems of dolphins, and of anchors and cordage appeared profusely as Nelson's victories mounted.

The Battle of the Nile brought into English furniture the Egyptian element which the French had adopted at the time of Napoleon's Egyptian expedition. The *Encyclopaedia* was the first work to illustrate this taste, which inspired furniture decorated with ornaments of crocodiles and with supports in the form of terminal figures with sphinx heads. Although many of the designs in the *Encyclopaedia* as a whole were not attractive, the work was important as a source of many details and motifs that later became common in Regency furniture. It is fair to say, indeed, that it is in Sheraton's *Dictionary* and *Encyclopaedia* that the domestic style of the Regency, apart from its more scholarly and strictly antiquarian aspects, is chiefly represented.

In the midst of these fantasies, a need was felt amongst many patrons and collectors for a return to 'the pure spirit of antiquity'. What amounted to a codification of Classical styles was provided

748 *Above left*: The influence of Sheraton's *Cabinet Dictionary* of 1803 is apparent in this handsome writing table, embodying oval shapes in the form of the pedestals. The lion feet and the very restrained ebony stringing on the mahogany are also typical of Sheraton's designs. M. Harris and Son, Ltd., London

749 *Above*: This exquisite writing table of rosewood with supports of ebonised wood and gilt mouldings, represents one of the most beautiful types of furniture produced during the Regency. The crossed supports are imitated from ancient Classical models, and follow a Sheraton design in the *Cabinet Dictionary* of 1803. Royal Pavilion, Brighton

750 *Left*: A necessary adjunct of the sofa was the sofa table to hold needlework or writing materials. Until about 1810, the supports were plain uprights on splayed legs, and the decoration a simple pattern of boxwood, sometimes with ebony stringing set in mahogany or rosewood. Royal Pavilion, Brighton

751 *Above*: The elegant form of this writing table of about 1810 derives from the French *bonheur-du-jour* type of desk of the Louis XVI period. The ringed ornament of the legs is inspired by the jointing of bamboo which was simulated in furniture by the great French craftsman Georges Jacob. The Classical influence is represented in the lion mask drawer handles. With the brass grille-work the table has a lightness and grace that makes it eminently suitable for a lady's boudoir. Temple Williams, Ltd., London

752 *Above*: The increasing elaboration of furniture after 1815 is apparent in this dwarf cupboard, which expresses a number of the principal tendencies in Regency furniture—the pleated silk fronts with grilles to the cupboard door and side-panels, the use of mirror-glass, the lion head plaques, and the top painted to represent marble. Temple Williams, Ltd., London

753 *Left*: One of the supremely beautiful examples of Regency design was the 'Trafalgar' chair, so called because it reached the height of development in 1805, the year of Nelson's famous victory. The gilt cable-moulding of the back is a nautical emblem. The design derives from an ancient Greek model. Royal Pavilion, Brighton

754 *Below*: Decoration in the form of pen-work, consisting of designs drawn with a pen on light coloured wood such as sycamore, was a favourite treatment for furniture in the Regency age. The designs consisted not only of naturalistic leaf and flower motifs as in the cabinet shown, but also of Classical ornaments such as Greek figures, honeysuckle, palm, lotus, poppies, cornucopiae, and fret- or key-patterns. Sheets of printed designs for copying could be bought at Ackermann's print shop in the Strand, and at many bookshops and stationers. The form of this cabinet expresses French influence in the tapering, fluted supports and the 'spinning-top' feet. The inset panels are of embroidery. Temple Williams, Ltd., London

755 *Below centre*: When the Prince of Wales re-decorated his Pavilion at Brighton in the Chinese style, in 1802, he imported a great deal of bamboo furniture from China, but he also bought furniture in beechwood, carved and painted to simulate bamboo, from British craftsmen. The firm of Elward, Marsh and Tatham made the chair shown, which has been returned to the Pavilion from Buckingham Palace by H.M. The Queen.

756 *Below*: The circular mirror was one of the most distinctive types of the Regency. This example is unusual in having the frame formed as a serpent. Two snakes support the candle-holders, and the *caduceus*, or winged staff of Mercury, is entwined with snakes. Royal Pavilion, Brighton

757 The Entrance Hall at Buscot Park, Faringdon, Berkshire, recreates a room in Thomas Hope's London house of 1807, with the sofa and chairs that were designed by the famous connoisseur for the Egyptian Gallery there. The furniture is of remarkable quality in material and craftsmanship. The Egyptian lions on the sofa, and seated figures supporting the chair arms are modelled in bronze. The 'lion-monopodia' table to the left was made to a design of 1808 by George Smith, who was greatly influenced by Hope's innovations in the Classical and Egyptian styles. The painted wall decorations are modern. Lord Faringdon: Buscot Park, Berkshire; National Trust

758, 759 *Above and above right*: This magnificent bookcase-cabinet is a remarkable example of how closely actual pieces followed published designs. It corresponds in almost every detail with a design by Thomas Sheraton in his *Cabinet Encyclopaedia* of 1806. This piece has a handsome dignity, despite the elaborate details, because of the perfect proportions and the beauty of the wood and carving. The inlaid ornament of ebony is typical in character of the early years of the 19th century. The pediment with an antefix in the centre and acroters at the angles adds to the severely Classical air. The portrait busts represent Charles James Fox, leader of the Whig party, and William Pitt, Prime Minister. They were supplied by the sculptor J. D. Giannelli of No. 33 Cock Lane, Snow Hill, whose name is inscribed on the back of each. Jas. A. Lewis & Son, London

760 *Below*: During the late 18th century Neo-Classical furniture designs had been free interpretations, embodying the decorative motifs of the ancient world but bringing little change in traditional forms. The furniture designed in about 1807 by Thomas Hope, the banker-connoisseur, attempted on the other hand, to recreate the precise forms of ancient Greek and Roman furniture. The chair shown has the typical arc back and curving legs of Greek chairs as shown in ancient vase paintings, and the decoration in black and red was inspired by the same source. Victoria and Albert Museum, London

in *Household Furniture and Interior Decoration*. This was produced in 1807 for Thomas Hope, member of a wealthy banking family and a talented connoisseur, as a record of the interior decoration and furnishing of his house in Duchess Street, London.

Thomas Hope is believed to have designed the furniture himself, and in addition to articles in the Roman, Greek and Egyptian styles, he included furniture in the French Empire manner which had developed during the Revolutionary and *Directoire* periods. Thus, Hope's book represents what came to be known as the 'English Empire' style. Like its French prototypes, this consisted of articles severely rectilinear in shape, and with plain surfaces of mahogany veneer, sparsely relieved with small ornaments in ormolu of Classical motifs such as honeysuckle or palmette, lotus or acanthus leaves, wreaths, paterae and figures of chimerae or sphinxes. Articles of Thomas Hope's own furniture are to be seen in several public collections, such as the Victoria and Albert Museum, London and the Royal Pavilion, Brighton.

Motifs that were afterwards common in domestic furniture were such features as lion monopodia supports for tables; *torchères* or vase-stands shaped as Classical tripods; cross-framed chairs and stools; and column supports for tables and cabinets divided into symmetrical halves by a double lotus-leaf ornament.

Hope's Classical furniture was much more archaeologically correct in following antique models than earlier designs had been, and although somewhat severe in character, its significance lay in the fact that it was widely copied, and exercised a purifying influence. As it consisted of large plain surfaces and straight lengths of timber not requiring to be elaborately carved or shaped by hand and decorated only with applied metal orna-

ment, it was eminently suitable to factory production methods which were then coming increasingly into use.

Hope's ideas were popularised in a work bearing a similar title to his own book, entitled *Collection of Designs for Household Furniture and Interior Decoration*, published in 1808 by George Smith, a London cabinet-maker. His designs included many of fantastic and even bizarre character, especially those embodying animal forms of the lion, and of the fabulous sphinx and chimera. Gothic designs, which had not been profuse in pattern-books since the days of Chippendale, were once more fairly numerously represented in Smith's book. His work was chiefly important, however, in that like Hepplewhite or Sheraton, he provided a complete guide to the furnishings of all the principal rooms of a house.

From 1800 to about 1811 or 1812 Regency furniture was generally simple and elegant in form and decoration, despite the Classical and Egyptian, and even sometimes Gothic and Chinese details. These features were usually subordinate to the principal lines of a piece.

In the early years of the century, the backs of chairs were still made in lattice-patterns, but the lines now had a horizontal instead of a vertical emphasis. From about 1805 onwards a horizontal back-splat was more common. The arms at first swept in a curve downwards to an upright support, but later they were shaped in a bold downward-curving scroll.

One of the elements of design in Sheraton's *Drawing Book* which persisted into the new age was the use of reeding for the legs of tables and chairs and for the edges of shelves and uprights. Another was the use of splayed or 'claw' feet for table and tripod

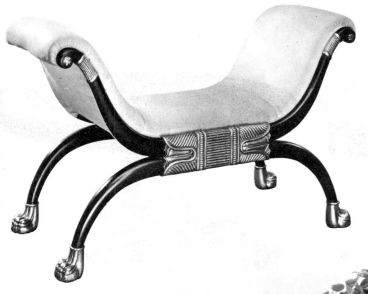

761 *Above*: Stools were common articles of furniture in Greek and Roman times, and became extremely popular in Regency days because the Classical models were easily adaptable to modern needs. This stool closely follows Classical example, with its lion-paw feet and lotus-leaf decoration, and similar designs appeared in the books of Thomas Hope and George Smith. The decoration of black and gold was a popular colour scheme in Regency rooms. Temple Williams, Ltd., London

762 This design for a sofa-table from George Smith's *Household Furniture* published in 1808, shows an example of table legs in the form of lion monopodia. This feature derived from ancient models, and was introduced in the designs of Thomas Sheraton and Thomas Hope.

764 *Below*: In his *Cabinet Dictionary* of 1803 Sheraton illustrated many examples of elaborate furniture to celebrate Nelson's victories. This amusing chair with dolphins acting as arm supports, and sea shells forming the legs, is part of a famous suite made by William Collins in 1813 and presented to Greenwich Naval Hospital in memory of Nelson. Admiralty House, London

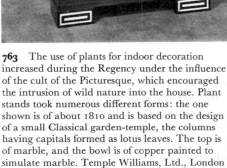

763 The use of plants for indoor decoration increased during the Regency under the influence of the cult of the Picturesque, which encouraged the intrusion of wild nature into the house. Plant stands took numerous different forms: the one shown is of about 1810 and is based on the design of a small Classical garden-temple, the columns having capitals formed as lotus leaves. The top is of marble, and the bowl is of copper painted to simulate marble. Temple Williams, Ltd., London

765 *Below*: The triumphant ending of the Napoleonic wars also created a need for ceremonial furniture to be used on great occasions. This state armchair was made about 1815 for a visit of the Prince Regent to Walmer Castle, Kent. Royal Pavilion, Brighton

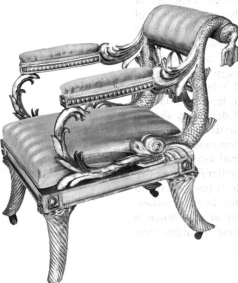

supports. These were used in the three forms of a concave, convex, or a double curve. Kidney-shaped table tops, and concave or convex fronts, and rounded ends for writing desks and chests-of-drawers, which Sheraton had developed, also lived on in the new century.   748

Among the most characteristic types of the Regency period, fully developed by 1805, is the 'Trafalgar' chair, so called not only because it appeared about the time of Nelson's victory in that year and often had a back rail incorporating cable- or rope-moulding, but because many of them were produced by the great firm of Morgan and Saunders, who renamed their establishment the 'Trafalgar workshops' in memory of the hero. With its elegant lines, flowing in a single curve from back rail through sides to the sweeping back legs, and again through curved seat rails to the scimitar-shaped front legs, the Trafalgar chair is one   753
of the loveliest types in all furniture, and it remained popular in slightly modified form until the 1820s and even later.

The backs of chairs usually had scroll-shaped sides with a flat or turned back-piece, but yoke-backs in a wide sweeping curve on Grecian lines were not uncommon. Chairs and other articles, made of beech, turned with rings and painted to simulate bamboo were popular as occasional and bedroom furniture after their important early appearance at the Prince of Wales's   755
Pavilion at Brighton in 1802, and continued to be made with few changes of design not only as late as the 1820s and 30s, but even up to the 1860s and after.

Sofas were usually on the Grecian model with outward curv-   769
ing ends and legs. A highly characteristic Regency invention was the sofa table, intended to carry needlework, books or writing materials for the fashionable ladies of the Regency. This was a   750
variant of the Pembroke table, with hinged flaps at the ends instead of at the sides, and there were small drawers at the sides. They were often made with a reversible sliding surface in the top, one side for writing, the other chequered for draughts or chess. A recess underneath the slide was marked for the game of backgammon. At first the supports were flat, sometimes vase-shaped, on curved feet. In the early 1800s the ends were often shaped as lyres, or simple turned supports were used. From 1812 onwards the end supports gave place to central pedestals on a more or less   766
elaborate claw base.

Dining tables were made with rounded ends, the edges of the top reeded, and at first the supports were usually in the form of a turned pedestal on a tripod claw or concave curving legs. These gradually became richer in form, but after 1812 the claw supports gave place to tablet bases, or triangular concave-sided plinths with tall turned pedestals. Large circular tables, called   767
loo tables or breakfast tables, were popular Regency types, and their supports underwent a similar evolution. When elaborately formed and decorated they were used as drawing room tables, and were often made with triangular tripod-shaped pedestals, or turned pillars as supports, or tablet bases with feet in the form of lion-paws or shaped as double scrolls.

Sideboards underwent a further transformation during the Regency. The centre part of the top, containing a long drawer, was depressed some inches below the level of the side pedestals, giving the whole piece the form of an ancient Greek or Egyptian pylon gateway. The pedestals themselves were often tapered in form, like ancient sarcophagi, and were supported on lion-paw feet.

The Regency period made its distinctive contribution to the variety of looking-glasses, which were in greater favour than ever because of the desire 'to extend the perspective of rooms'. Pier-glasses were made with a deep frieze panel at the top, or were framed in a reeded moulding with paterae at the corners. Overmantel mirrors were low and broad, with a large central glass and two narrow upright ones at the sides. They often had a deep frieze containing Classical figures in stucco, or occasionally a landscape decoration in *verre églomisé*. The most celebrated type   756
of Regency looking-glass, however, was the circular convex mirror. These usually had a black reeded fillet round the glass, and a gilt frame studded with balls and surmounted by an eagle. Some more fanciful examples embodied the forms of serpents.

The French Empire types of furniture that Hope had drawn in 1805 greatly increased in popularity from 1812 onwards, when English visitors were able to travel to France again after   765
the fall of Napoleon. Articles made in this style by Snell of Albe-

766 *Right*: After about 1812 the supports of sofa tables, or of writing tables, were made as a single pedestal on splayed legs. Ornament was beginning to become more elaborate, motifs of conventional flower design being used in a sparse, open pattern. Rosewood was now more popular than mahogany. Royal Pavilion, Brighton

767 *Far right*: From about 1815 onwards, furniture became more sumptuous and florid in character. This drawing-room table is veneered with dark rosewood and ornamented with marquetry of rosewood and brass in *contre-partie*. The revival of so-called 'buhl-work' was encouraged by the Prince Regent and was based on early 18th-century French furniture by the cabinet-maker André-Charles Boulle. Royal Pavilion, Brighton

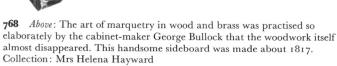

768 *Above*: The art of marquetry in wood and brass was practised so elaborately by the cabinet-maker George Bullock that the woodwork itself almost disappeared. This handsome sideboard was made about 1817. Collection: Mrs Helena Hayward

769 *Above right*: The absorption of Classical form into the English furniture tradition is well expressed in the dignified lines of this mahogany sofa, made about 1820. The Classical element exists in the curving lines of the ends, the back rail and the legs. Royal Pavilion, Brighton

770 *Right*: The decline in Regency design was expressed in the drawings of Michelangelo Nicholson in *The Practical Cabinet-maker* of 1826. Short stumpy feet took the place of the elegant curved Classical legs and the general lines became coarse and clumsy.

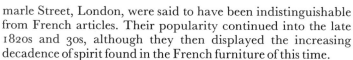

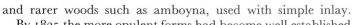

marle Street, London, were said to have been indistinguishable from French articles. Their popularity continued into the late 1820s and 30s, although they then displayed the increasing decadence of spirit found in the French furniture of this time.

From 1815 onwards a more florid tendency in furniture design became apparent, which, during the 1820s, developed into an opulence foreshadowing the fulsome shapes of early Victorian times. Many of the features which were now being adopted, such as bun feet, sometimes ornamented with gadrooning or ribbing, in cabinets and commodes, and plinth bases for cabinets, derived from French furniture of the Louis XIV period.

Remarkable changes in the decorative style took place during the Regency. In about 1805 ornament was often inlaid in ebony on pale mahogany, Classical designs of key-pattern and honeysuckle being popular. Then, towards 1812, under the influence of the Prince Regent, the art of brass inlay, in the manner first practised under Louis XIV by the French cabinet-maker André-Charles Boulle, was revived. Pieces made in this technique remained popular almost without a break until the Revolution. In England brass inlay was used sparingly at first, separate ornaments of flower or leaf shape being used in a string as a border round a table top. Later, the inlay became richer. Running floral scrolls were used and whole panels were covered with inlay in floral and grotesque forms until, in the work of Charles Bullock, about 1817, the whole of the furniture was said to present 'a brazen front'. The brass inlay certainly looked splendid on dark mahogany and rosewood, but late in the 1820s there was a movement towards the use of lighter woods like satinwood and maple,

and rarer woods such as amboyna, used with simple inlay.

By 1825 the more opulent forms had become well established in furniture design. In that year Henry Whitaker published a volume of *Designs of Cabinet and Upholsterer's Furniture* in which we see that the backs of chairs and sofas have acquired the coarsely carved scroll-work in leaf form that will later be found in articles of the Victorian era. Other design books of this date confirm the tendency, and the later phases of Regency taste were summed up in George Smith's last work *The Cabinet-maker and Upholsterer's Guide*, published in 1828.

Most of these designs have completely lost the elegance of earlier years. The legs of chairs are now usually turned instead of being gracefully scimitar-shaped, and the back-yokes have ends carved with outward scrolling volutes. Sofas also have stumpy turned legs in place of curved feet, and a boldly carved cresting of honeysuckle shape, or in a foliate scroll design, decorates the back rail. Bed posts, cabinet supports and table legs are elaborately turned, and the leaf ornaments which, from the days of Adam and Hepplewhite, had been long and delicately shaped are now more crudely cup-shaped. Despite this decline, many of the designs of this period for cabinets and commodes are well proportioned, and the abandonment of animal forms removed an element of the grotesque that made some earlier furniture distasteful to many patrons and connoisseurs. At its best, the furniture of the Regency embodied elements of grace, beauty, robustness and vigour of design, combined with great excellence of craftsmanship, and purity of ornament. These qualities were more rarely to be found in the succeeding age.

752

768

770

ENGLAND 1830-1901

Charles Handley-Read

Nothing in Victorian history is more stimulating than the recurring conflicts between tradition and reform. Divisions of opinion were not, however, confined to politics. The 'split between the progressive and the antiquarian elements that runs through all Victorian culture'[1] is a theme which is relevant to a discussion not only of Victorian literature, but also of the fine and industrial arts, furniture included.

From about 1835 onwards the largely uneducated tastes of the majority were satisfied by furniture produced in the factories. Popular, commercial furniture of this kind, almost always derivative, is by turn shoddy, vulgar, boring, spectacular, grandiloquent. Sometimes it embodies superb craftsmanship, an arresting scale, and an absolute conviction in a positive set of materialistic values; sometimes it embodies the essence of Victorianism, and could be described as 'Victorian-Victorian'. If the most poignant fault of much commercial furniture is the mis-application of labour and materials, a few good designers can always be found in whose furniture this fault is banished, for instance Barry and Salvin among the Early Victorians. But in their design for furniture neither of these men was an innovator or a reformer. The reform of furniture was in fact initiated by A. W. Pugin, but even his prophetic zeal had little immediate effect. Lesser men were no more successful when they tried to raise the standard of design just before and after the Great Exhibition. In fact it is only after the foundation of William Morris's firm in 1861 that the conflict between tradition and reform can be consistently traced throughout the rest of the century. Reformers' furniture was evolved chiefly by progressive architects who on aesthetic, rational, or moral grounds were reacting against commercial standards; and their designs were as a rule distinctly anti-Victorian in spirit.

Thus Victorian furniture falls broadly into two main but unequal groups, a fact which reflects the familiar conflict in Victorian culture and explains the arrangement of this article in two parts.

788, 796, 797, 817

797
774
773, 781

784-6
820-33

835, 836

829, 834
861, 864

Part I: Popular Furniture
The Early Victorian Period c. 1835-55

The most prominent element in Victorian furniture is a re-use of past styles. The four main styles in the Early Victorian period are: Classical (with an emphasis on Grecian), Louis XIV (merging with Rococo), Elizabethan (merging with Tudor, Jacobean and Stuart), and Gothic. In addition Italian Renaissance and *François Premier* styles occasionally appear in isolation, while a blend of several of these styles is sometimes seen in one piece of furniture. *François Premier* is the least easily recognised, and it was probably the least popular; literal-minded Victorians liked to be able to put a name to a style without difficulty. Most of these styles survived, obviously with changes of interpretation, until the end of the reign.

CLASSICAL, GRECIAN

Broadly speaking, furniture in the Classical (or Grecian or Antique) style was based on Regency patterns, and the sustained use of a style already popular calls for no special explanations. By Regency standards the purity of shapes and details became coarsened and the term 'sub-classical'[2] fairly describes some of the furniture designed by the architects Philip Hardwick, Charles Barry (later knighted) and Henry Whitaker, and by the firm of Gillow.

772
774, 771
773

[1] Graham Hough: *The Last Romantics*, 1947 (edition of 1961).
[2] Peter Floud: 'Furniture: The Early Victorian Period', *Connoisseur Period Guide*, 1958 (Eds. Ralph Edwards, L. G. G. Ramsay). I am also deeply indebted to the same author's 'Victorian Furniture', *Concise Encyclopaedia of Antiques*, III, 1957; to Elizabeth Aslin's *19th Century English Furniture*, 1962; and to *Victorian Furniture* by R. W. Symonds and B. B. Whinneray, 1962.

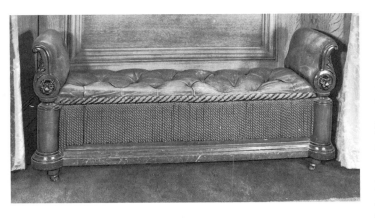

771 *Far left*: Carved and inlaid mahogany table designed by Henry Whitaker for the Conservative Club, 1844. Regency elements again survive in Early Victorian sub-classical form. The Bath Club, London

772 *Left*: Upholstered bench made under the supervision of the architect Philip Hardwick, 1834. Sub-classical forms in the Early Victorian period mark the sustained popularity of Regency 'Antique' styles. Goldsmiths' Hall, London, reproduced by permission of the Goldsmiths' Company.

773 *Right*: Satinwood music-stand, unstamped but almost identical to a design of 1839 in the Gillow records, No. 5263. Similar 'knulled' feet and balustrading were repeated in Gillow's furniture over a period of perhaps thirty years. Private Collection, London

774 *Left*: Carved and veneered table in light wood. Probably manufactured by Holland and Sons from a drawing (now in the Royal Institute of British Architects), dated 1840, by Charles Barry who also designed the building. Reform Club, London

LOUIS XIV, 'OLD FRENCH', ROCOCO

Louis XIV and 'Old French' are terms often used to describe furniture in Victorian pattern books, but the examples nearly always turn out to be Rococo, a term also widely used. The gilt chairs and settees which in the 1820s appeared at Tatton Park, Cheshire, may be among the earliest pieces of English furniture in this style. From about 1825 onwards, Rococo interiors appeared at Belvoir Castle, Leicestershire, and, in London, at York House, Crockford's Club and Apsley House.

What made the Louis XIV-Rococo style popular? In addition to their search for comfort, perhaps the Early Victorians also sought a frivolous style as a change from Greek, Elizabethan or Gothic. Certainly the scrolls and volutes of Rococo, with or without white paint or gold leaf, provided a curvilinear luxuriance which could be executed by indifferent craftsmen. Moreover, Rococo furniture had none of the lofty associations with the Classical past which furniture in the Antique styles suggested, nor any nationalistic associations evoked by the Gothic or Elizabethan styles. Partly because Rococo was a frivolous style it became a decorators' style, and architects disliked it. Yet the well-known white and gold drawing room furniture at Goldsmiths' Hall, London, was in fact made in 1834 under the supervision of the architect Philip Hardwick. Here and elsewhere in Victorian Rococo furniture, the sources were nearly always French in origin. Yet even at a time when English furniture of the 18th century was unfashionable, early Victorian cabinet-makers occasionally turned to mid-Georgian Rococo for inspiration.

ELIZABETHAN

If adequate explanations are not easily found to account for the rise to popularity of the Louis XIV-Rococo style, the Elizabethan style presents fewer difficulties. In 1835 a Parliamentary Select Committee recommended that the Palace of Westminster be rebuilt in the Gothic or Elizabethan style; both were part of the national heritage and as such received official approval. Walter Scott's novels of the 1820s (including *Kenilworth*, 1821) were partly responsible for his rising influence and popularity in the 30s. His home, Abbotsford, enlarged after 1819, became well known as an example of Scottish Baronial architecture; and the picturesque furnishing of the library probably encouraged the adoption of Tudor, Jacobean or Stuart styles in a fair number of English interiors.

Many castellated and manorial houses were built in the Early Victorian decades and, apart from Gothic, Elizabethan would have been the most suitable style in which to furnish some of their apartments. Who, then, designed good examples of furniture in this style, and where is it to be found? Anthony Salvin's 'Elizabethan' suites at Mamhead, in Devonshire and at Scotney Castle in Kent,[3] hitherto ignored by specialist writers on Victorian furniture, are important because they make up a large body of well-documented architect's furniture which is also consistently designed.

Did Salvin borrow from Henry Shaw's *Ancient Furniture* or had he actually seen some of the examples Shaw reproduced? We may never know. In any case there is mounting evidence that Shaw's book was widely influential, and so was Robert Bridgens' *Furniture with Candelabra and Interior Decoration* of 1838—in which 7 designs were 'Gothic', 25 'Grecian', and no fewer than 27 'Elizabethan'. It was borrowing from books of this kind which gave to many specimens of Victorian furniture its 'tepid eclecticism'. This phrase perfectly describes a carved satinwood chair, dating from about 1845, which bears a stencilled label of Holland and Sons (admittedly, eclecticism here makes stylistic attribution very difficult). More positive in style is a chair at Charlecote Park, Warwickshire. Both the chairs reproduced here might be compared with what was described in 1846 as a 'Scott' chair, once to be seen in a Pavilion-room decorated with frescoes from Scott's novels. The Pavilion,[4] destroyed in the 1930s, formerly stood in the grounds of Buckingham Palace. Better known as an example of Scott's influence on furniture design is the celebrated Kenilworth buffet of 1851.

776
775

778, 781

779

782

783
780

[3] Christopher Hussey: *Late Georgian Country Houses*, 1958.
[4] *The Decorations of the Garden Pavilion in the Grounds of Buckingham Palace*, 1846. Introduction by Mrs. Jameson, the publication supervised by L. Grüner.

775 *Right*: Pedestal cabinet carved and veneered in mahogany, *c.* 1850. The Rococo style could provide frivolous alternatives to the Grecian, Elizabethan or Gothic styles all of which evoked rather sober antiquarian associations. Collection: Michael Levi, Esq.

776 *Below*: Rococo sideboard from *The Cabinet Makers' Assistant*, 1853. Luxuriant, curvilinear, almost plastic designs of this kind probably satisfied an Early Victorian desire for opulence.

777 *Bottom of page*: The Library, Abbotsford, Scotland. Enlarged after 1819, Sir Walter Scott's home reflects, like his novels, a blend of historicism and romanticism. Both may have encouraged a taste for vaguely 'Elizabethan' furniture and furnishing.

778 *Above*: Oak bedroom furniture at Mamhead, Devonshire, designed by Anthony Salvin who was the architect of the house. The bedroom was 'prepared' for a visit from Queen Adelaide. Collection: Sir Ralph Newman, Bart. Copyright: *Country Life*

780 *Right*: The 'Scott' chair: plate 15 from *The Decorations of the Garden-Pavilion in the Grounds of Buckingham-Palace* by L. Grüner, 1846, (detail). One room in the now-demolished pavilion was decorated with scenes from Scott's novels.

779 *Above*: 'Bedsted of the time of James I': plate 38 from Shaw's *Specimens of Ancient Furniture*, 1836. Some of Salvin's furniture derives either from this bed, then at Goodrich Court, Herefordshire or from Shaw's engraving of it.

781 *Below*: Mahogany four-poster bed at Scotney Castle, Kent, *c.* 1843. Designed by Anthony Salvin, the architect of the house. Collection: Christopher Hussey, Esq. Copyright: *Country Life*

782 *Below*: Carved satinwood armchair bearing a stencilled label of Holland and Sons, *c.* 1845. In the 'Elizabethan' style—but tepid eclecticism here makes unequivocal categorisation very difficult. Private Collection, London

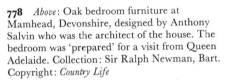

783 *Left*: 'Elizabethan' carved oak armchair *c.* 1855. Charlecote Park, Warwickshire

784 Drawing for an armchair by A. W. Pugin, perhaps of *c.* 1835. The Regency 'Gothick' tradition is plain to see. Royal Institute of British Architects, London

785 Writing table by J. G. Crace of Wigmore Street resembling sketches by Pugin, *c.* 1847. Advanced formalised patterns are overwhelmed by heavy archaeology: this table is an example of Early Victorian 'un-reformed' Gothic. Abney Hall, Cheadle, Cheadle and Gatley Urban District Council

786 Drawing by A.W. Pugin for a sideboard, *c.* 1850. 'Un-reformed' archaeological furniture of this kind was designed by Pugin for the Palace of Westminster. Commercial derivatives were numerous. Royal Institute of British Architects, London

GOTHIC

772, 774 The sub-Classical designs of Hardwick, Barry, Whitaker and
771 others, often unmistakeably Early Victorian in appearance, were as a rule based on Regency models. Many specimens of furniture of this type survive, most of them unidentified, and the style must have been popular. Less popular, by contrast, was the Gothic style. Yet if in the 30s and 40s designs based on antique sources were degenerating, the Gothic style was slowly being revitalised as the vehicle of reform. So in the Early Victorian period it would be reasonable to look for the Gothic equivalent of sub-Classical designs (a continuation of Regency 'Gothick'), for true Early Victorian versions of Gothic (equivalent to Early Victorian versions of Elizabethan), and for examples of reformers' Gothic.

A. W. Pugin provides examples of all three types. Like some of his early furniture for Windsor Castle, several of his unexecuted
784 designs are in the Regency 'Gothick' tradition. At the other end
826 of the scale there are the rational, reformed examples discussed
825, 829 in Part II. In between (but the dividing line may be a matter of opinion) there are some very fine if rather heavy designs which cannot be included in the category of reform since in them he relied too much on archaeology and too little on a rational
786 imagination. These true Early Victorian designs, which had an acknowledged influence on commercial production, are the exact equivalent of the Elizabethan designs of Anthony Salvin. To this category belongs most of the Crace-Pugin furniture at
785 Abney Hall, in Cheshire, certain examples exhibited in the Medieval Court at the Exhibition of 1851, and some of the furniture and fittings at the Palace of Westminster, London. L. N. Cottingham also designed furniture which probably fitted into the category of true Early Victorian Gothic.

THE EARLY VICTORIAN 'NAMELESS' STYLES; AND THE 'NATURALISTIC' STYLE

Not all Early Victorian commercial furniture was designed in the styles of the past, and as a result many examples find us at a loss for terms. Moreover the search for comfort in these years meant that shapes were sometimes dictated by the demands of the body rather than of the eye—for instance in chairs and sofas where the framework is smothered by billowing upholstery:
787 hence a new if dubious opulence. Furniture of this kind, unindebted to the past, at times almost amorphous, and very popular in the 40s and 50s, was an important commercial innovation.

Again by the substitution of curves for straight lines, the
788 separate parts even of wooden sideboards and chiffoniers are sometimes fused together in an overall unity; and the result is a new amplitude, opulent in its way, even a kind of plasticity. But curvilinear plasticity easily degenerates into bonelessness, and

papier mâché chairs, chiffoniers, and dressing-tables, sometimes
designed in quite new shapes, often seem about to melt.   790

What adds fluency to furniture of this period is just as likely to be sinuous tendrils and naturalistic flowers as it is to be Rococo   788, 789
scrolls; in fact the term 'Naturalistic Style' is now accepted as covering a whole category. In 'naturalistic' furniture the details often seem to be extruded rather than carved—as in the 'Repose'   791
armchair, where the plasticity is partly explained by the fact that it was executed from a sculptor's model. Naturalistic carving was to take a prominent place at the Great Exhibition of 1851. Spectacular naturalistic panels are to be seen on Cookes's sideboard now at Alscot Park (dated 1851 but not completed   796
until 1853).

Aside from items shown in 1851, comparatively little Early Victorian furniture is painted, elaborately inlaid, or made up of contrasting woods. Most of it, of mahogany, rosewood or oak, is left severely plain without carving or gilding. But there are of course exceptions—as may be seen in an attractive writing desk. This example also underlines the fact that the Early Victorians   792
could endow their furniture with strong character without recourse to historical styles.

THE EXHIBITIONS

Several national exhibitions of manufactures had been held in Europe between 1830 and 1850, but when in 1873 *The Art Journal* remarked that the second half of the 19th century would be known as the 'Age of Exhibitions', it had in mind the 'international' or 'universal' type inaugurated in 1851.

England at this date was in a position of unchallenged supremacy among the nations of Europe, and her robust self-confidence was reflected in the invitation to other nations to compete on home ground at the Crystal Palace. But she had paid little official attention to art. The Prince Consort and his associates knew this when they had promoted the exhibitions organised by the Society of Arts. Thus exhibits in 1851 provided massive evidence of Great Britain's material prosperity, but also of her backwardness in design.

Soon to be criticised in official reports, the shortcomings in the industrial arts were ascribed chiefly to a lack of education and discernment not only among manufacturers, designers and craftsmen, but also by implication among patrons. Partly as a result of the industrial revolution, we now know that the Georgian tradition had disintegrated in the first quarter of the century, that patronage, by 1851, was in the hands chiefly of a new uneducated middle class, and that furniture making, once a craft, had become an industry. Manufacturers, deprived of a sustaining tradition, made irresponsible use of a variety of styles, and perhaps shared only one aim: to outshine their competitors.

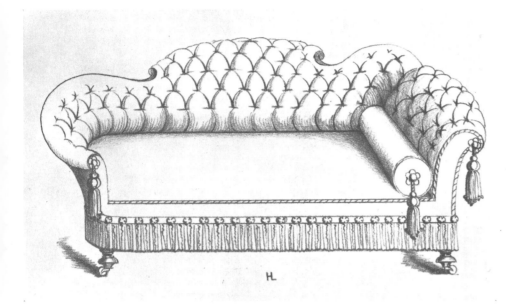

787 *Above*: Upholstered sofa from H. Lawford's. *Book of Designs*, probably of the mid-40s. All-over upholstery of this kind was a commercial innovation. Comfort comes before style; opulent, curvilinear shapes are dictated by the body rather than the eye.

788 *Right*: Carved walnut sideboard, probably of the late 40s. Curves on plan and in elevation provide a new overall unity, even a kind of plasticity. The details are a blend of Rococo and naturalism. Victoria and Albert Museum, London

789 *Left*: Carved firescreen, probably of walnut, *c.* 1845. The sinuous fluency of line is provided by semi-naturalistic tendrils, not by details with historical origins. Collection: Mrs G. H. M. Carfrae

790 *Below left*: Papier-mâché console table, probably before 1850. The Early Victorians could invent new shapes, but curvilinear plasticity often degenerates into bonelessness: papier-mâché furniture sometimes seems about to melt. Collection: Mrs Wallace Hughes

791 *Below*: Design for the 'Repose' armchair, modelled by the sculptor, John Thomas. From *The Illustrated London News*, 1848. The details in the 'Naturalistic' style—opulent, 'bossy', sinuous, plastic—here seem to be extruded rather than carved.

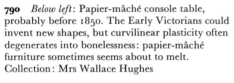

792 *Above*: Inlaid writing desk, *c.* 1837. Most Early Victorian furniture was plain: no inlay, carving, gilding or painting. But this exceptional example again proves that a pungent character did not always depend on historical styles. Victoria and Albert Museum, London

793 Design for a table shown by Morant of London at the Great Exhibition, 1851. It had a 'plate glass top, painted in imitation of Florentine mosaic'. Luxuriant naturalism shading into Rococo was a common feature of 1851 Exhibition furniture.

794, 795 *Above and below*: Carved wood table, finished in white paint and gold, probably by Morant of London, *c.* 1851. The top of the table is decorated with a naturalistic wreath of fruit and flowers, executed in real mosaic. Collection: Lady Ashton

In their attempts to win prestige and custom, most of them sought to catch the eye by sheer elaboration of decorative detail, but some of them also hit on the device of making certain kinds of furniture larger than it had ever been made before. From 1851 onwards, a new towering scale became a feature not only of items shown at the exhibitions held later in the High Victorian decades, but very often of furniture made for ordinary domestic purposes.

Exhibition furniture puts popular taste under a magnifying glass. The furniture may have been untypical of average commercial production, but everyday commercial furniture often reflects the tastes popularised by the exhibitions. This is one reason why exhibition furniture is worthy of attention.

In many showy and unpractical examples at the exhibitions of 1851 and 1855 (London and Paris), broken outlines are often combined with a wealth of naturalistic detail[5]—as in the design of a luxuriant table shown in 1851 of which a close variant in white and gold survives. In the Alscot Park sideboard, dated 1851, but not shown until the Manchester Art Treasures Exhibition of 1857, the broken outlines and naturalistic detail relate it to many other specimens shown at exhibitions of earlier and later date. 793 794 796

Of the French furniture shown at the Paris Exhibition of 1855 George Wallis wrote that the 'most striking lesson the English are likely to learn . . . is the extent to which artistic education has been carried amongst the workmen who execute the carvings and inlaid work'. In his opinion, a vast cabinet and mirror shown in Paris by Jackson and Graham marked the advance of British manufactures since 1851. From that date onwards, cabinet furniture often incorporates huge sheets of looking-glass—as in the present example. This was one of several popular devices responsible for a recurrent topheaviness of design. The Jackson and Graham cabinet was designed by a Frenchman, but no fewer than forty English craftsmen executed the supporting details. Adam Smith's 'division of labour'—seen as a mark of progress by others beside the Prince Consort—often enabled manufacturers to achieve astonishing complexity and ingenuity of construction and decoration. Also for the exhibition of 1855, Gottfried Semper, an exiled German architect in the Consort's circle, designed a small but elaborate standing cabinet which was sent to Paris by Holland and Sons. Of the cabinet itself, many commercial equivalents still survive. 797 798

Examples of furniture by the reformers at the exhibition of 1862 were designed to exhibition pitch in terms of scale, but several of their cabinets were decorated with paintings by rising young artists. The inclusion of serious paintings meant that these cabinets were probably in marked contrast to most of the other exhibits in which the recipes for popular success lay very often in the provision of gilding, elaborate inlay, carved figures and enormous sheets of looking-glass. *Plate facing p.* 224 · 799

Few aspects of Victorian taste over the years *c.* 1830–65 are now more striking than the widespread hatred of what was sometimes described as the 'Dark Ages of art'—that is, English architecture and furniture of the 18th century. In the 60s, however, with the stirrings of the so-called 'Queen Anne revival', Georgian design began to regain favour, and a well-known satinwood cabinet in the style of the Adam brothers, exhibited in Paris in 1867, is an early symptom of this change of taste. From now until the end of the century catalogues and journals are full of suggestions based on Chippendale, Adam, Sheraton and Hepplewhite. 801

At the South Kensington Exhibition of 1871, Collinson and Lock exhibited T. E. Collcutt's ebonised cabinet. But Gothic was not yet dead, even for exhibition purposes, and to the Exhibition of 1872, again held in London, Collier and Plucknett sent a monumental Gothic writing desk which suggests that the designer knew the work, among others, of William Burges. 800

Few examples from the later exhibitions have yet been traced and, from about 1874 onwards, as it happens, commercial firms seem rather to have lost interest in them. Efforts to locate examples sent to Philadelphia in 1876 and to Chicago in 1893 (some of which probably survive) have proved fruitless. At the Paris Exhibition of 1900, it seems that only seven British firms contributed.

[5] Nikolaus Pevsner: *High Victorian Design*, 1951.

796 *Above*: Sideboard designed by H. Protat and carved by W. Cookes of Warwick. Dated 1851, made in 1853, and exhibited at the Manchester Art Treasures Exhibition, 1867. The epitome of allegorical naturalism of the type frequently applied to mid-century dining room furniture. Collection: Mrs James West, Alscot Park, Warwickshire

797 *Right*: Cabinet and mirror by Jackson and Graham, shown at the Paris Exhibition, 1855. Nearly fourteen feet high, it embodies all the elements of a succesful exhibition entry: towering scale; carved, cast, chased and inlaid enrichments; human figures, lavish gilding, and a sheet of looking-glass. Victoria and Albert Museum, London

798 *Below*: Cabinet and stand in ebony with Wedgwood plaques and gilt mounts. Designed by Gottfried Semper and shown in Paris, 1855. Victoria and Albert Museum, London

799 *Below centre*: 'Sideboard' in oak, walnut, and ebony, relieved with gold, shown by James Lamb of Manchester at the London Exhibition, 1862.

800 *Bottom of page, centre*: 'English Modern Medieval' cabinet made by Collier and Plucknett of Warwick. Shown in London, 1872. The influence of Gothic reformers of the early 60s— Webb, Burges, Seddon—is still alive. (see 835, 836, 837)

801 *Above*: Satinwood cabinet in the Adam style. Shown by Wright and Mansfield at the Paris Exhibition, 1867. An early symptom of the return to favour of 18th-century models. Victoria and Albert Museum, London

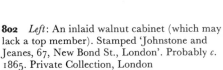

802 *Left*: An inlaid walnut cabinet (which may lack a top member). Stamped 'Johnstone and Jeanes, 67, New Bond St., London'. Probably *c.* 1865. Private Collection, London

804 *Below*: Veneered and inlaid games table, stamped 'Gillow' and entered in the firm's records in 1869, No. 7585. Basic cost to the retailer, £17 5s. Private Collection, London

803, 806   Carved and inlaid table designed by C. P. Slocombe. From 1854 onwards the work occupied several craftsmen for more than eleven years. The top of the table (below) is composed of pieces of ivory and mother-of-pearl and more than twenty different woods provide contrasting colours in this 'allegory of the senses'. The central face wears spectacles. Collection: The Duke of Northumberland, Alnwick Castle

805 *Below*: A 'Low Wardrobe' veneered in Hungarian ash and inlaid with purplewood. Stamped 'Gillow and Co., 850' (perhaps a stock number). At least five wardrobes of similar design were made by Gillow in the 1860s. Private Collection, London

The Mid-Victorian Period c. 1855–70

A suitable link between Early and Mid-Victorian furniture is provided by a magnificent table at Alnwick Castle, Northumberland, even if it is untypical of commercial production. Commissioned by the fourth Duke of Northumberland, it was probably designed in 1853 but not completed until 1866. Its distinction lies in the quality of carving and inlay, but the inlay is retardatory by comparison with the inlay on Pugin's table of *c.* 1850, and the curvilinear Rococo legs might by 1866 have appeared distinctly old fashioned.

The fact is that Early Victorian undulations and plasticity are often replaced, in the Mid-Victorian period, by crisper curves and more severe outlines—as in an inlaid walnut cabinet, perhaps of the mid-6os, stamped by the manufacturers Johnstone and Jeanes. Here, moreover, the inlay has been formalised into a flat pattern, thus perhaps reflecting the influence of Pugin or Owen Jones. From the later 5os until at least the early 8os, innumerable cabinets were designed which on plan include crisp quarter-circle curves at the ends.

Similar in some ways to the Johnstone and Jeanes cabinet is a Gillow low wardrobe veneered in Hungarian ash and inlaid with flat decoration in purplewood. In the third quarter of the century Gillow's made perhaps twenty or thirty wardrobes more or less to this design, at least five of them in the 6os. Crisply drawn

outlines are again to be seen in a small games table, also manufactured by Gillow's. Stamped with the number 7585, and recorded in the 'Order Books' as a 'Princess Table' on May 4, 1869, it was made by 'Jno' Hutton for the sum of £7 9s. 0d., the total basic cost being £17 5s. 0d. to the retailer. The design was repeated in walnut a year later, without the drawer, at a cost to the retailer of £13 2s. 3¾d; it was then called a 'Prince's Table', and the client was the Duke of Northumberland. The replacement, in these tables, of a single central support by a group of four slender colonettes is typical of the 6os. A plate in C. & R. Light's catalogue of 1880 suggests that similar designs, perhaps based ultimately on Regency prototypes, remained popular for at least twenty years.

From the point of view of style, the Johnstone and Jeanes cabinet and the Gillow wardrobe elude easy description, and might perhaps be included in a Mid-Victorian 'nameless' category. In a Wright and Mansfield satinwood cabinet, however, where the rather wide glazed door is typical of Mid-Victorian design, certain elements reveal debts both to the English Regency period and to 18th-century France. Yet in this cabinet historicism is not a prominent feature, whereas in a well-known group of furniture made by Holland and Sons in 1868, French 18th-century sources have been combed for every detail.

Nor in these years was the Gothic style ignored, and furniture based on Pugin's ideas was probably not uncommon. Bruce

807 *Above*: Cabinet veneered in satinwood with carved gilt enrichments. Stamped 'Wright and Mansfield', *c.* 1865–70. Private Collection, London

810 *Below*: A Royal Academy drawing of 1870 by Bruce Talbert: Pl. 44 in his *Examples of Ancient and Modern Furniture*, 1876. A retardatory 'Jacobean' style here replaces Talbert's earlier progressive ideas, (see illustration 845).

808 *Above centre*: Inlaid cabinet with gilt mounts by Holland and Sons, part of a suite of furniture made in 1868. Victoria and Albert Museum, London

811 *Below right*: Slate pedestal with enamelled 'marble' surfaces. The *trompe l'oeil* technique is probably imitated by the unknown manufacturer from specimens shown by G. E. Magnus at the Exhibition of 1851. Private Collection, London

809 *Above*: Carved and painted cabinet with gilt mounts, made for John Jones to the designs of a man called Hayward. Perhaps dating from after 1870, it embodies influences from Webb, Burges, and Bruce Talbert. The carving is in some ways 'Ruskinian'. Victoria and Albert Museum, London

Talbert's first book of 1867–8, *Gothic Forms Applied to Furniture*, includes some original designs that mark him as an innovator, and some that probably helped to popularise ideas which had their origins in furniture of about 1860 designed by Webb, Burges and Shaw (Part II). By about 1870, the ideas of these zealous Gothic reformers were sometimes adopted by commercial firms. Collier and Plucknett, for instance, could hardly have evolved the shape of their 'English Modern Medieval' cabinet, exhibited in 1872, without the examples of furniture say by Burges, Shaw or Talbert. Again, it could only have been the painted furniture of Webb, Burges and Seddon that prompted a man called Hayward to include paintings of Pre-Raphaelite type in a pair of cabinets now in the Victoria and Albert Museum. These cabinets also embody gilt metal mounts and reliefs which suggest a knowledge of Talbert's metalwork, but their most impressive feature is the carving: crisp, naturalistic, accurately observed, 'Gothic', it is in marked contrast to the sprawling Rococo excesses of the 40s and 50s. Moreover this carving, even if it is also indebted to Talbert, is the equivalent in furniture of innumerable stone cut details in the churches of the 50s and 60s—details which would probably have been called 'Ruskinian'. These cabinets in fact provide a remarkable summary of earlier innovations by 'Gothic' reformers, but if they date (as I suppose) from the 70s, they are too late and too derivative to be included as specimens of reformers' furniture. Bruce Talbert himself, in

839
837
838

800

835, 837, 836

809

845

Examples of Ancient and Modern Furniture (his second book, of 1876) reverted chiefly to a retardatory Jacobean style.

The Early and Mid Victorians had an immense respect for ingenuity—for '*trompe l'oeil*, the cute disguise, the surprising gadget',[6]; and perhaps in due course this aspect of Victorian taste will be the subject of an essay on 'simulations'. Besides furniture decorated with leather stamped to look like wood, or made out of gutta percha, the examples might include two well-known chairs, one made out of coal and the other, complete with upholstery and fringes, made entirely out of cast iron. Painted imitation inlay and artificial wood graining were also popular techniques which were not always mis-applied. If possible, the theme of simulation would also be illustrated by a specimen of Magnus's patent marbled slate furniture of the type exhibited in London in 1862. Certainly the marbled slate pedestal illustrated here, although of unknown manufacture, is so deceptively realistic that it is fairly included as a specimen of *trompe l'oeil*. But most of these tricks and deceits were probably evolved to capture attention at the exhibitions and were not widely applied in representative furniture. Simulation was after all a stunt, but it provides an interesting footnote to Victorian taste.

810

811

[6] Nikolaus Pevsner: *op. cit.*

812 *Left*: Frontispiece to Robert Edis's *Furniture and Decoration of Town Houses*, 1880. The 'bracket-and-overmantel style'—as the late Goodhart-Rendel described Free Renaissance architectural designs. The term often applies perfectly to Free Renaissance cabinet furniture.

813 *Right*: A prize-winning panel in the 'Free Renaissance' style carved by James Osmond, 1870. Victoria and Albert Museum, London

Late Victorian 1870–1901

ECLECTICISM: 'FREE RENAISSANCE' REVIVALS— THE 'BRACKET-AND-OVERMANTEL' STYLE

Journals covering the last thirty years of the reign suggest that in this period commercial furniture manufacturers were above all concerned to provide their readers with variety and novelty. Illustrations of designs based on Classical, Medieval and Renaissance prototypes are readily found; 'Jacobean' furniture was evidently popular, furniture based on 18th-century French models more popular still. Empire furniture was revived, there was even a renewed interest in the furniture of Thomas Hope, and, due to the 'Queen Anne' revival of these years, copies and adaptations from Chippendale, Adam, Sheraton and Hepplewhite were perhaps inevitable. Careful studies of infinitely varied historical examples from European museums, reproduced in the trade journals, were accompanied by suggestions for 'Anglo-Japanese' furniture, 'Art Furniture', 'Quaint' furniture, and 'aesthetic' furniture, the last four terms as a rule describing debasements of progressive designs discussed in the next section. Over the years 1870 to 1901, most commercial firms were prepared to revive almost any historical style, and, in their desperate search for novelty, to give their adaptations some new and often vicious twist.

One style stands out rather more prominently than the others. It was based ultimately on European Renaissance models. Cabinet furniture in this style is strictly comparable to contemporary English architecture in the style of the 'Free Renaissance'— whence the term; and the decorative details by which the furniture is typified can be seen not only in cabinets but in occasional pieces of all kinds.

The Italian Renaissance had been a source of inspiration before 1870, but its influence was stronger in the 50s and 60s than it had been in the 40s, and it became stronger still from about 1870 onwards. In the art and literature of Walter Pater's period, an 'idealised Renaissance supplanted an idealised Middle Ages'.[7] In 1890 *The Magazine of Art* noticed the 'gradual movement towards the Renaissance, as practised in this country during the last two decades'; and by 1893 *The Studio*, in an article about woodcarving, remarked that 'designs built more or less on the Renaissance seem alone to find favour today'. Free Renaissance architecture is as a rule urbane, fluently eclectic, and elegant in its detail to the point of daintiness; and the same may be said of the furniture. The 'bracket-and-overmantel style'—that is how one critic characterised Free Renaissance architecture[8]; and the phrase might have been invented to describe Free Renaissance cabinet furniture.

The cabinets, sideboards, wardrobes or chimney-pieces, however elaborately designed to include brackets, niches, shelves and cupboards, are usually dominated by architectural members. The carved or inlaid decorations are often based on north Italian models of around 1500, sometimes on the later models of Mannerism; but Elizabethan, *François Premier* and *Henri Deux* models were also used just as they were in architecture. Designers could have gathered their ideas from countless pattern-books.

The examples chosen for reproduction are suitably introduced by a medal-winning panel carved by James Osmond in 1870. With the same panel Osmond secured a prize at a Carpenters' Exhibition in 1884. The panel was sent to India where it gained orders for a firm then in Regent Street, London, and after 1884 it was shown at several exhibitions organised within the Arts and Crafts movement. While the details in this panel typify the decorative style of the Free Renaissance revivals, carving of this quality was rare in specimens of furniture.

By 1880 the Free Renaissance style was adopted by many architects, including the cautious Robert Edis, and by then too it must have been popular with most commercial furniture manufacturers. Gillow's exploited it for more than twenty years, a number of their 'Renaissance' designs being associated with T. E. Collcutt (but no drawings from Collcutt's hand survive among the firm's records now in London). Gillow's 'Collcutt' furniture includes a sideboard designed to be carved in oak. A Gillow mahogany sideboard, not to be associated with Collcutt, shows their interpretation of the style at its grandest, if we look for an emphasis on carving. A design for a cabinet made soon after 1887 shows what their craftsmen could do in the field of inlay.

Even more spectacular from the point of view of craftsmanship was the inlaid furniture executed for the firm of Collinson and Lock (absorbed by Gillow's in 1894). A rosewood cabinet, stamped with their name, was probably designed by Stephen Webb, who must certainly have executed the engraved ivory inlay. This craftsman was a member of the Art Workers' Guild from 1887 to 1902, and a member also of the Arts and Crafts Exhibition Society. The distinction of his work lies not so much in the adaptation of Renaissance details, but in the quality of the engraving. It is doubtful whether engraved detail of this kind has ever been more delicately executed.

Innumerable low-grade specimens of furniture in the 'bracket-and-overmantel' style survive. Its character can be judged by a typical commercial print of 1887.

[7] A. E. Rodway: 'The Last Phase', *From Dickens to Hardy*, Guide to English Literature, edited by Boris Ford, Vol. 6.
[8] H. S. Goodhart Rendel: 'Victorian Public Buildings', *Victorian Architecture*, 1963, edited by Peter Ferriday.

810

851

813

812

814

815

816, 819

818

817

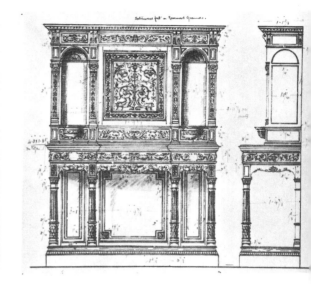

814 *Above*: An 'Oak "Collcutt" sideboard'. From a drawing among the Gillow records, No. 12349, 1881, probably based on a design by that architect. Waring and Gillow (Contracts) Ltd., London

815 *Above*: Carved mahogany sideboard in the 'bracket-and-overmantel' style. From a drawing among the Gillow records, No. 13379, 1884. Waring and Gillow (Contracts) Ltd., London

816 *Above*: Drawing from the Gillow records, No. 18578, Nov. 1889. At least three cabinets were made closely resembling this design. Waring and Gillow (Contracts) Ltd., London

817 *Below*: Drawing by H. V. Aspen from *The Furniture Gazette*, Oct. 1 1887. Commercial 'bracket-and-overmantel' furniture of this type survives in large quantities.

818 *Bottom of page, left*: Rosewood cabinet inlaid with engraved ivory, the decorations designed and executed by Stephen Webb. Stamped 'Collinson and Lock, London. 822', *c*. 1890. Victoria and Albert Museum, London

819 *Below*: Rosewood cabinet carved and inlaid with ivory and mother-of-pearl, stamped 'Gillows, 16575'. An almost identical design appears in *The Art Journal*, 1887 (p. 200). Private Collection, London

Part II:
Progressive Design:
Reformers and Innovators

The Early Victorian Period:
A. W. Pugin 1812–52

The first Victorian reformer of the applied arts was the architect A. W. Pugin.[9] When towards the end of his life he remarked, in a letter, 'My writings, much more than anything I have been able to do have revolutionised taste in England', he may have claimed too much, even for his theories. Yet the echo of these theories is to be found in the writings of Ruskin and Morris, while the influence of his furniture designs has in recent years perhaps been underestimated.

In 1835 he published *Gothic Furniture*, a book of designs which reveal his debt to late medieval prototypes. Augustus Charles Pugin, his father, had also published a book with the same title in which most of the Ackermann illustrations date from the 1820s. If the plates in these two books are compared, the contrast is inescapable. Those in the elder Pugin's book are picturesque, decorative, *Gothick*; in them the Regency interpretation of the style is still in many ways typified. Those in the younger Pugin's book appear archaeologically sound and they provide the basis, just before the reign began, for a new and serious interpretation of Gothic furniture.

[9] A. W. Pugin: *Contrasts*, 1836. *The True Principles of Gothic Architecture*, 1841.

820 *Above*: Frontispiece to A. C. Pugin's *Gothic Furniture*. The plates of the 1820s are picturesque, decorative, 'Gothick'; the furniture is constructionally unsound, archaeologically incorrect.

821 *Above*: Plate from A. W. Pugin's *True Principles of Christian Architecture*, 1841. An attempt to kill Regency 'Gothick'.

823 *Above*: Chair from A. C. Pugin's *Gothic Furniture* (plate of 1826).

824 *Above right*: Chair from A. W. Pugin's *Gothic Furniture*, 1835.

822, 825 *Above left and left*: Carved and inlaid table based on A. W. Pugin's designs, *c.* 1847. The legs reflect Pugin's antiquarian interests. Pugin wrote 'The real source of art is *nature*', but he could formalise naturalistic detail into superb flat patterns. At this date this table top is almost a reformer's manifesto. Victoria and Albert Museum, London

826 *Right*: Chair based on A. W. Pugin's designs, *c.* 1840. Sound archaeology and sound construction are combined with the vigour and realism of reformer's Gothic. Victoria and Albert Museum, London

Pugin loathed 'sham'—as witness many satirical etchings. He laid great emphasis on honest (i.e. revealed) construction, believed that detail should 'have a meaning and serve a purpose', and deplored 'sprawling Rococo' wherever it appeared. He remarked that the 'real source of art is *nature*' and was a true innovator in his translations of naturalistic detail into flat patterns. He complained that there was 'no repose, no solidity' in interiors designed by modern admirers of Gothic, that 'Glaring, showy, and meretricious ornament was never so much in vogue as at present', and that 'ordinary articles of furniture, which require to be simple and convenient, are not only made very expensive, but very uneasy'.

But Pugin's theories are not reflected in all his work, which, as we have seen, falls into three categories. There are his own Regency 'Gothick' designs, and the 'enormities' as he described them in 1841—the furniture of the kind which as a young man he had designed for Windsor Castle; there are the Early Victorian designs, also mentioned in Part I; and there are the designs which mark him as a reformer. But Pugin's furniture is not always easy to categorise unequivocally. In the case of the long table at Abney Hall, for instance (already compared with Salvin's furniture), we might say that the flat-pattern inlay is overwhelmed by archaeology—by 'period' elements which give it the look of a 'reproduction'. But while in the case of an octagonal table, also designed for Abney Hall, the base is similarly archaeological, the top with its superbly formalised inlay is almost a reformer's manifesto, quite free from 'period' flavour.

For rather different reasons a well-known chair must also be included in the category of reform: tough and resilient, where Salvin is apt to be academic, it displays all the 'vigour' and 'realism' of regenerated Gothic. Finally, there are the comparatively simple designs represented for instance by yet another

well-known table, and again by a table supplied in about 1852 to Horsted Place, Sussex. The Horsted table was reliably attributed to Pugin some years ago, and the attribution is strengthened since the design was forecast in Pugin's sketches of 1843 for furniture—never executed—intended for Balliol College, Oxford. The emphasis, in these tables, is on rational structure, not on elaborate decoration, and in progressive examples of this kind Pugin has all but emancipated himself from the trappings of Gothic.

It is the extent to which these simple designs were influential that may yet prove to have been underestimated in recent years. It is true that commercial manufacturers such as Morant and Crace usually borrowed from Pugin's most elaborate designs. Even the modest, but distinctly archaeological table design of 1835 was copied fairly often—I have seen six or seven examples of varying quality and complexity in as many months. But derivative commercial productions sometimes involved simplification, not elaboration, as may be seen in a design of 1853 from *The Cabinet Makers' Assistant*. Again, while Gillow's copied Pugin's elaborate linenfolds, colonettes, and brattishings, there are dressing-tables and other domestic pieces of the late 60s which repeat Puginian structure rather than Puginian decoration. This even applies to designs in Light's catalogue of 1880.

In fact, my own recent discoveries of cheap, rational furniture of Puginian type lead me to believe that examples must have been fairly numerous (which is not to say that they all merit a place in the category of reform). My tentative conclusion is that simple furniture, ultimately originating with Pugin, and produced over a very long period, may prove to have been at least as popular as furniture which betrays, say, the beneficial influence of Godwin's celebrated 'Anglo-Japanese' furniture of the 60s and 70s.

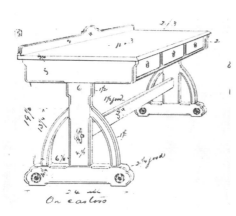

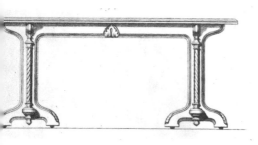

827 *Above left*: Design for a table from A. W. Pugin's *Gothic Furniture*, 1835.

828 *Above*: An oak dressing-table from the Gillow records, 1869 (No. 7632). A cheap commercial adaptation of Puginian structure.

830 *Left*: Design for a table from *The Cabinet Makers' Assistant*, Pl. XX, 1853. In the 50s, commercial adaptations of this type may have been fairly common.

831 *Below left*: Carved walnut table, perhaps of the mid-50s. Pugin's influence is unmistakable. Private Collection, London

829 *Above*: Contrasts: Regency 'Gothick' and rational Gothic. An oak table, *c.* 1850, and a chair by Morel and Seddon, *c.* 1828-30, made for Windsor Castle, both from designs by A. W. Pugin. The table: Collection: The Rev. Charles E. Steward. The chair: The Clermont Club, London

832 *Below centre*: Table from C. and R. Light's catalogue of 1880. It may yet be shown that Pugin's simpler designs fathered a considerable body of furniture produced over a long period.

833 *Below*: Oak table once at Horsted Place, Sussex, supplied by the London decorator John Webb in *c.* 1852. Almost certainly based on a design by A. W. Pugin. Private Collection, London

High Victorian Progressive Design

REFORMERS' GOTHIC AT THE LONDON EXHIBITION OF 1862

One of Pugin's most widely discussed achievements was the organisation of the Medieval Court at the Exhibition of 1851, an exhibition at which, from the point of view of the applied arts, the Early Victorian period may be said to culminate. The beginning of the High Victorian period could perhaps be said to coincide with the completion of Ruskin's *Stones of Venice* in 1853. This publication does much to explain why the Gothic style continued to provide the vehicle of reform. For the generation of reformers after Pugin, certainly, Ruskin's chapter on 'The Nature of Gothic' was a major source of inspiration and in the 60s Gothic became an 'almost irresistable force'.[10] But the leaders of the post-Pugin generation, most of them too young to contribute to the Paris exhibition of 1855, did not come before the public until the London International Exhibition of 1862. Meanwhile the architect William Butterfield had designed in *c.*

834   1855 some simple and attractive inlaid furniture which, like a few of Pugin's designs, shows the reformer's touch in that it is almost emancipated even from Gothic.

William Morris's firm was founded in 1861. Examples of

835, 836   furniture designed by Webb and Seddon were shown in the firm's name in 1862, but they were untypical of the furniture which the firm produced later on. Besides Webb and Seddon, progressive designers whose furniture first appeared publicly in 1862 in-

837, 838   cluded the architects Burges and Shaw. It was no longer Tudor
Plate   Gothic to which they turned for inspiration, but the sterner
facing p. 224   Gothic of the 13th century. Certain contributions from Morris's firm apart, only a few pieces of reformers' furniture were designed especially for the exhibition, but exhibitions, which were part of the background of the High Victorian decades, encouraged inflated ideas in unexpected quarters. A still small voice would have been inaudible in these years, nor is it uncommon for reformers, in their zeal, to overstate their case in private. In the design of furniture, this perhaps explains not only the almost caricatural overstatements of style but also the aggressive scale

836   in the enormous cabinets shown in 1862 by Burges, Seddon and

838   Shaw. But even in the painted decorations on several of the cabinets by Webb, Burges and Seddon, we again recognise the note of reform since the paintings were executed by progressive young artists; indeed painted cabinets of this kind, first designed by

837   Webb in 1857, and by Burges in 1858, mark an important innovation in Victorian Gothic Revival furniture. From the point of view strictly of eye-catching elaboration and sheer size, however, there is little to choose between some of the cabinets de-
Plate   signed by the reformers and the large and elaborate prestige
facing p. 224   pieces associated in these years with commerce and popular
796, 797   taste. Both sides caught the competitive spirit of the exhibitions
801   and although they spoke different languages, were apt to raise their voices to exhibition pitch. The differences lay in style. Voysey at a later date was to deplore the influence of the exhibitions.

Webb and other designers working for Morris's firm are due for attention presently. Very little of Shaw's furniture has so far been traced. Burges continued to design elaborate Gothic furniture until he died in 1881. J. P. Seddon has left several books of drawings for Gothic furniture (now in the Victoria and Albert

836   Museum) but apart from the cabinet shown in 1862, executed examples await discovery. He it was who first re-introduced

839, 840   diagonal panelling, a device often adopted by Talbert, Richard Charles and Eastlake—three designers who provide a link between Webb, Burges, Seddon and Shaw, and manufacturers

800   such as Collier and Plucknett.

WILLIAM MORRIS AND COMPANY, WEBB, MADOX BROWN

'Of William Morris it is not too much to say that he revolutionised the public taste in domestic art.' This assessment from *The Art Journal* obituary of 1896 has been echoed ever since. Yet Morris's own interest in the design of furniture was distinctly limited.

His theories are well known. The central dilemma in his

[10] Joseph Kinnard: 'G. E. Street, the Law Courts, and the 'Seventies', *Victorian Architecture, op. cit.*

834   *Above*: Inlaid furniture designed by William Butterfield, *c.* 1855. Rationally designed, it is almost emancipated even from the Gothic style. Collection: The Misses Drew

835   *Above*: The 'St George' cabinet designed by Philip Webb showing panels painted by William Morris. Exhibited in London, 1862. Painted panels of this kind mark an important innovation in High Victorian Gothic furniture. Victoria and Albert Museum, London

836   *Below*: Cabinet designed by J. P. Seddon and shown by Morris's firm in London, 1862. Madox Brown, Burne-Jones, and Rossetti contributed painted panels. Its massive, re-vitalised medievalism cries out against commercial brashness and vulgarity. Victoria and Albert Museum, London

837 Cabinet designed by William Burges, 1858, with paintings by E. J. Poynter. Shown in London, 1862. Burges's over-emphasis of the finials probably reflects his passion for 13th-century Gothic. Victoria and Albert Museum, London

838 A cabinet bookcase designed by Norman Shaw. Shown in London, 1862. The towering scale and plain-spoken joinery reflect the aggressive spirit of some of the Gothic reformers. Victoria and Albert Museum, London

839 A Dining Room from Bruce Talbert's *Gothic Forms Applied to Furniture,* 1867-8. In the 60s, Gothic became an 'almost irresistible force'. Talbert here seems to have caught the inflated scale of exhibition pieces.

840 A commercial Gothic sideboard designed by Richard Charles. From *The Cabinet Maker. A Journal of Designs,* 1868. The diagonal panelling, adopted by Talbert, Charles, and Eastlake, probably stems from Seddon's cabinet of 1862, (see illustration 836).

841 *Above*: Sideboard designed by Philip Webb with panels painted by William de Morgan, *c.* 1865. William Morris Gallery, Walthamstow

842 *Above right*: A 'Gothic' sideboard designed, according to a Morris catalogue of after 1896, by Philip Webb in '*c.* 1862'. A similar specimen is now in the Victoria and Albert Museum, London

843 *Left*: Oak table designed by Philip Webb, *c.* 1859. Sensitive, yet 'heavy as a rock', it is still faintly medieval in character. Collection: Dr D. C. Wren

844 *Above*: Rush-seated chairs of the type manufactured by Morris's firm from *c.* 1865 onwards. From a catalogue of after 1896.

philosophy, which was developed in large measure from Ruskin, is expressed in the household words 'What business have we with art at all unless all can share it?'. From 1861 onwards, although he had several assistants, Morris had the welfare of a business on his hands and his personal dilemma is expressed in its products. Some of the firm's furniture was cheap, some of it very expensive: nearly all the finest Morris interiors were evolved for rich patrons. As we should expect, furniture associated with Morris was from the first soundly constructed in 'conscious revolt' against the shoddy, everyday products of commerce; and in the 60s this was in itself a mark of reform. But striking originality was not as a rule the distinguishing feature of Morris's furniture designers. Progressive in so far as they gradually broke away from pedantic historicism, men such as Webb and Madox Brown, and later George Jack and W. R. Lethaby relied a good deal on traditional designs. Indeed, some of the firm's best cheap furniture was designed by adapting simple specimens which had been found in the country.

Some of Webb's early furniture designed for Morris's personal use is well documented, but no complete list survives of the items shown by the firm at the exhibition of 1862, and since nearly all their records were destroyed, while catalogues known to me are undated, it is often difficult to date the furniture with precision. Surviving examples of Webb's early unpainted furniture include a well-known table of *c.* 1859: sensitively designed, yet 'heavy as

a rock', it is still faintly medieval in character. The earliest specimens of Webb's painted furniture date from 1857; a celebrated wardrobe, decorated chiefly by Burne-Jones, survives from 1858; and the St. George cabinet of 1861 was exhibited in 1862. A cabinet of *c.* 1865, with panels painted by William de Morgan, is now in the Morris Gallery at Walthamstow. Besides painted decorations, Webb sometimes incorporated in his early furniture not only decorations in gesso but also leather panels which were tooled, coloured and gilded; and a recently discovered example, now in the Victoria and Albert Museum, is in many ways similar to a 'Gothic' sideboard which was made, according to a Morris catalogue, at Red Lion Square in *c.* 1862.

In about 1860 the painter Ford Madox Brown introduced a surface finish of green stain which was applied to cheap bedroom furniture produced by the Morris firm evidently in 'large quantities'. Ranges of furniture which were in production perhaps from about 1865 onwards include the rush-seated chairs of a type often copied by other firms, a variety of upholstered chairs, and also no doubt many pieces of furniture designed by Webb. But for the reasons given it is difficult to provide examples of the firm's furniture which can be reliably attributed to the 70s and 80s. The furniture of about 1890 onwards designed by Lethaby, Jack and Benson, all of them associates of Morris, is referred to again towards the end of the section on the Arts and Crafts movement. Meanwhile attention is claimed by reformers and innova-

835
841

842

844

872
869, 871

845 *Above left*: Inlaid walnut cabinet with metal enrichments designed by Bruce Talbert and made by Holland and Sons, 1867. Exhibited in Paris in that year. A progressive alternative to the High Victorian Gothic style. Victoria and Albert Museum, London

846 *Above*: Part of a design for a cabinet. From the frontispiece to Charles Eastlake's *Hints on Household Taste*, 1878 (first published ten years earlier).

847 *Left*: Carved oak sideboard manufactured by Gillow's, 1873. Probably based on a design supplied by Talbert. Bradford Town Hall, Yorkshire

tors such as Talbert, Godwin, and Collcutt who from about 1865 onwards broke away from Gothic as the vehicle of reform.

BRUCE TALBERT: 1838-81

Talbert was trained in the offices of Dundee and Edinburgh architects and employed for a time by Doveston, Bird and Hull, a well-known Manchester firm of cabinet-makers. He was later occupied with the full-size working drawings for George Gilbert Scott's metalwork on the Albert Memorial—a point worth remembering when looking at the metalwork on his cabinets.

839   His first book of 1867-8 helped to popularise several decorative devices which he perhaps adapted from the furniture of 837, 836, 838 Burges, Seddon or Shaw—specimens of which, shown in 1862, had been published. Moreover Talbert was one of many designers who was captured by 'exhibition scale', and the main horizontal divisions of the sideboards in one of his drawings are 839 at shoulder height of the figures. The weighty Gothic of these and other Talbert designs, several of which were executed, provides a link between Burges and Shaw and a few pieces of 800 commercial Gothic furniture produced in the 70s.

An innovator rather than a reformer, Talbert was perhaps the first to provide consistent and progressive alternatives to the furniture of High Victorian Gothic. Very often original, probably prolific, and certainly influential, as a designer his grasp of construction was accompanied by a flair for evolving attractive

details both in carving and inlay—as may be seen from drawings in his book, and in a celebrated cabinet shown in Paris in 1867. A 845 group of furniture supplied by Gillow's to Bradford Town Hall 847 in 1873 was probably based on his designs. Better known than the Bradford sideboard is the 'Pet' sideboard which embodies most of the design elements still being copied after his death in 1881. While several designs in the second book of 1876 echo his earlier ideas, most of them are in a derivative Jacobean style and 810 belong to the section on popular taste.

CHARLES LOCK EASTLAKE

In Eastlake's *Hints on Household Taste* of 1868, a quotation from Viollet-le-Duc prepares us for a common-sense attitude to design which is full of 'sane ideas'. If Eastlake was himself indebted perhaps to Webb, Burges and Talbert, it is always claimed that his own designs had a widespread influence, not only in England but also in America. His book was reprinted many times, yet not more than one or two pieces of furniture based on his designs have yet been traced. By contrast to the work of the earlier Gothic reformers, Eastlake's designs seem well suited to ordinary 846 domestic life. His book first came out in the early years of the 'domestic revival' and was a timely reminder that reformers and innovators should try to design simple, well made, cheap furniture of moderate scale which did not rely for effect on elaborate decoration. Morris's firm had then settled down to similar aims.

THE INFLUENCE OF JAPAN ON VICTORIAN TASTE: E. W. GODWIN AND 'ANGLO-JAPANESE' FURNITURE

848
854
In or about 1867 Godwin began to adapt Japanese elements of design to furniture that was at once elegant, sophisticated and original, and further examples of about 1876 had a considerable influence. In 1877 he made designs for an *Art Furniture* catalogue for William Watt in which the frontispiece shows a chair that

850
853
849
was soon copied. An actual example survives of an almost identical chair made by the firm of Collier and Plucknett, and a very similar is shown in the frontispiece to *Decoration and Furniture of Town Houses* by Robert Edis (1881). Edis also reproduces

852
a Jackson and Graham cabinet, again in Godwin's style.

Godwin's furniture designs are remarkable for their original overall shapes. In commercial 'Anglo-Japanese' furniture, Japanese details were usually applied to shapes which remain

855
traditionally European—as in H. W. Batley's upright piano.

In 1880 the Japanese 'mania' was at its height. Probably with the commercial appetite for novelty in mind, *The Cabinet Maker* in that year reproduced a 'Side of a Room—Chinese Style', thus encouraging vicious mixtures. Commercial productions, like

851
those advertised by T. Lawes in 1881, show the debasement of ideas for which Godwin was perhaps ultimately responsible.

The most spectacular examples of the cult of Japan include the Jeckell-Whistler Peacock Room of 1876-7, and the furniture and interiors imported from Japan by Mortimer Menpes in about 1900.

T. E. COLLCUTT

Collcutt's furniture was of at least three different kinds. Several simple oak tables of around 1870, still faintly Gothic, suggest a knowledge of designs by Webb and Talbert. Then, in the 80s, he

814
designed Free Renaissance furniture of the type already discussed. Meanwhile a celebrated ebonised cabinet, made to Collcutt's designs by Collinson and Lock, was shown at South Ken-

856
sington in 1871. It provides a landmark in the history of Victorian furniture.

Unfortunately no furniture drawings from Collcutt's hand have so far been traced, and it is therefore difficult to judge the exact extent of his responsibility for designs attributed to him (sometimes on documentary evidence). Moreover a knowledge of his architecture, which corresponds closely in style to his Free Renaissance furniture, does little to explain the apparently isolated stroke of inspiration which produced the cabinet of 1871. But even if he once again borrowed details from other designers, he synthesised them to produce a piece of furniture the like of which had never been seen before.

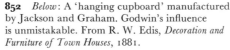

848 *Above*: Ebonised wood sideboard designed in about 1867 by E. W. Godwin. The style was copied in much 'Anglo-Japanese' commercial furniture. Victoria and Albert Museum, London

849 *Left*: Detail from the frontispiece to R. W Edis's *Decoration and Furniture of Town Houses* of 1881. In the text, the chair is ignored.

851 *Below left*: 'Anglo-Japanese' furniture advertised by T. Lawes in *The Cabinet Maker* of 1881. Godwin's ideas are here debased and perhaps blended with Chinese elements.

852 *Below*: A 'hanging cupboard' manufactured by Jackson and Graham. Godwin's influence is unmistakable. From R. W. Edis, *Decoration and Furniture of Town Houses*, 1881.

850, 853 Detail of a page in William Watt's 'Art Furniture' catalogue of 1877, *(above)*. The designs were by E. W. Godwin. Chair with a metal label of the manufacturers Collier and Plucknett, *c*. 1880, *(below)*, Victoria and Albert Museum, London. Plagiarism of this kind was common in the Victorian furniture trade.

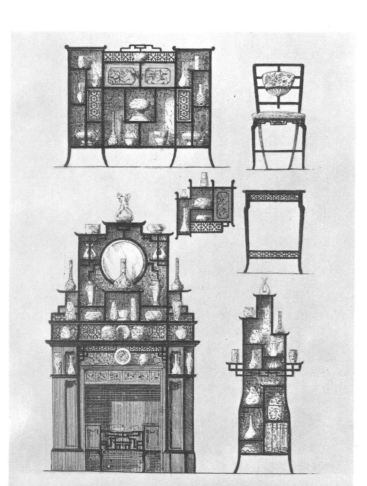

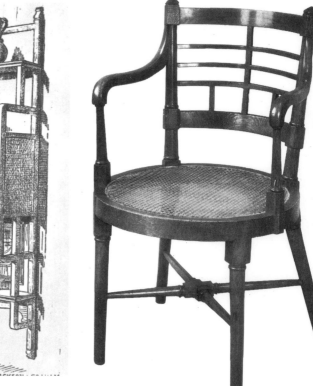

Painted and gilded bookcase, nearly eleven feet high, designed by William Burges. Executed between *c*.1859 and 1862 for his rooms in Buckingham Street, Strand, London, and later moved to Tower House, Kensington, the house designed by the architect for his own occupation. Artists who painted the pictures included E. Burne-Jones, E. J. Poynter, Simeon Solomon, Albert Moore and H. Stacy Marks. The pictures on the left-hand side are devoted to Christian art, those on the right to pagan art. Victoria and Albert Museum, London

Chinese lacquer throne, painted in red and gold on a d a r k ground, 17th century. The latticework back and sides, interspersed with leaves and flowers, are gently curved to produce an elongated serpentine line, while the supports also avoid any sense of rigid inflexibility. Victoria and Albert Museum, London

Corner of a Japanese house with the *shōji* drawn back. This detail from an anonymous painted scroll *c.* 1650 reveals the almost complete absence of furniture, the decorative and functional use of the screen, and the sense of the house being linked with the landscape. The *engawa* or balcony extends both towards the highway and the garden. Private Collection

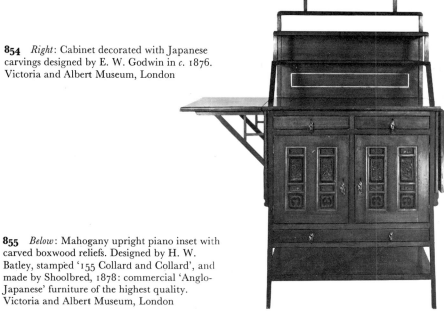

854 *Right*: Cabinet decorated with Japanese carvings designed by E. W. Godwin in *c.* 1876. Victoria and Albert Museum, London

The painted and coved panels, bevelled glass and turned supports subsequently reappear, with modifications, in ebonised 'Art Furniture' over a period of ten or fifteen years. Manufacturers who produced cabinet furniture incorporating several of these devices include Maddox, Gillow, Cooper and Holt, and C. and R. Light. The style can also be traced in tables, clocks and bookshelves, and especially in the design of over-mantels for chimney-pieces. Collcutt's cabinet was one of the most influential pieces of furniture ever designed by a Victorian architect.

858

855 *Below*: Mahogany upright piano inset with carved boxwood reliefs. Designed by H. W. Batley, stamped '155 Collard and Collard', and made by Shoolbred, 1878: commercial 'Anglo-Japanese' furniture of the highest quality. Victoria and Albert Museum, London

Late Victorian Progressive Design
The Arts and Crafts Movement

Several leading figures in this movement—Mackmurdo, Lethaby, E. S. Prior, Ashbee—have left evidence that Ruskin and Morris were the major sources of their inspiration. They were drawn together by a unanimous hatred of commercial standards and no doubt this helps to explain the emphasis on careful craftsmanship in Arts and Crafts furniture. They shared an eager desire to re-establish the status of the artist and craftsman, and for them, as for Ruskin and Morris, the 'creation of beauty' was a 'duty owed to society'.[11] They were determined to break down the barriers between the 'fine' and 'applied' arts, and to see to it that the arts were fertilised by free exchanges between artists, architects, and craftsmen of all kinds. They believed that little could be achieved by reformers working in isolation, hence the formation of societies and 'guilds'.

In 1882 the Century Guild was founded by Mackmurdo and Selwyn Image. In 1883 a small group of Norman Shaw's pupils formed themselves into the St George's Art Society, and out of this grew the Art-Workers' Guild founded in 1884. Also in 1884 the Home and Arts Industries was founded with a special interest in the rural crafts—a pointer to the rustic element which in this movement must be acknowledged but not exaggerated. In 1888 Ashbee founded his Guild of Handicraft. In that year the Arts and Crafts Exhibition Society held its first exhibition, and further exhibitions followed in 1889, 1890, 1893, 1896 and 1899. But guild societies were not confined to London: in 1886 an 'A·W·G' had been established in Liverpool; in 1900 the Bromsgrove Guild, in Worcestershire, sent well-received exhibits to the Paris Exhibition; and another 'A·W·G' was set up in Birmingham in 1902.

856 *Below*: Cabinet in ebonised wood designed by T. E. Collcutt and exhibited by Collinson and Lock, London, 1871. One of the most original, attractive, and influential pieces of furniture ever designed by a Victorian architect. Victoria and Albert Museum, London

857 *Below centre*: 'Art Furniture' cabinet in ebonised wood with saltglazed stoneware reliefs by George Tinworth. Exhibited by Doulton's of Lambeth, London International Exhibition, 1872. Victoria and Albert Museum, London

858 *Below right*: 'Art Furniture' cabinet in ebonised wood with a label of G. Maddox, manufacturer, 21, Baker Street, London, probably *c.* 1875. Pottery by Thackeray Turner, Christopher Dresser, Watcombe Terracotta Co., and the Martin brothers. Private Collection, London

[11] A. E. Rodway: *op. cit.*

THE ARTS AND CRAFTS MOVEMENT:
A. H. MACKMURDO (1851–1942)

Few reformers applied their talents exclusively to furniture design, and it is often difficult to find examples which consistently embody their most advanced theories.

By 1883 Mackmurdo had designed what is probably the first specimen of European Art Nouveau, and Art Nouveau elements appear in his wallpapers and textiles, and again in a fragment perhaps from a piece of furniture. But who would recognise, in the textiles the hand of the same designer as seen in a well-known writing table, or in a satinwood cabinet which was part of a group made for Mackmurdo's guild in 1886? They all merit the utmost respect, but they have nothing in common. Moreover the cabinet may embody the ideas of several guild members.

Further examples of his furniture may yet be re-discovered. Some of his designs, progressive and influential, are of international significance, and their variety alone enhances his reputation. But it is impossible to summarise his theories or his achievement from the inconsistent pieces of furniture at present associated with him. In this, Voysey presents a welcome contrast.

THE ARTS AND CRAFTS MOVEMENT: C. F. A. VOYSEY (1857–1941)

Outstanding in nearly all Voysey's furniture, designed from about 1886 onwards over a period of perhaps twenty years, and nearly always in oak, is evidence of keen deliberation over every line on the drawing board. For some of his ideas—for instance the 'attenuated shafts' in so many of his cabinets—he was indebted to Mackmurdo's exhibition stands. A hatred of ostentation did not prevent him, in the hinges of his cabinets, from exploiting his gifts as a flat-pattern designer. Although he loved bright heraldic colours, his furniture and interiors nearly always suggest a Quakerly moderation. But from his furniture all traces of a merely naive rusticity have been abolished, and he combined an eager and positive love of design with a craftsmanlike care over construction. But misapplied craftsmanship raised his ire. And he was insular. He detested those 'human apes' who lavished 'exquisite executional skill' on 'dead styles' of foreign origin. In his interiors he sought above all the element of 'repose'.

Reproductions in the trade journals of the later 90s show that his ideas were widely copied by commercial designers. His furniture was reproduced in French and German periodicals, and his influence acknowledged by certain designers of European Art Nouveau. Voysey loathed it.

THE ARTS AND CRAFTS MOVEMENT: C. R. ASHBEE (1863–1942)

The foundation in 1888 of Ashbee's Guild of Handicraft gave rise to productions that are not more important than the social experiment which lay behind them. In 1886 he had gone to live at Toynbee Hall, in London's East End, where he ran classes for young people. His idea of a guild grew out of these classes. Within limits, the 'working conditions of a medieval guild' was what he aimed to recreate, and this partly explains the character of the Guild's designs.

A walnut cabinet of about 1903 was designed by Ashbee, made by J. W. Pyment among others, and enriched with leather work by Statia Power. The cooperation of several craftsmen in one piece of work was typical of the Arts and Crafts Movement in general and particularly of Ashbee's own guild. Many specimens of Ashbee's Guild furniture remain to be re-discovered—for instance a writing cabinet reproduced from *The Studio* of 1900. Once again, it may have been designed for group production—hence, perhaps, a hint of over-elaboration. Ashbee's buildings need no vindication. But his furniture sometimes suggests that he put the claims of social therapy and a co-operative society before those of rational design.

THE ARTS AND CRAFTS MOVEMENT:
THE LATER FURNITURE OF MORRIS'S ASSOCIATES

Morris, Lethaby, Jack and Benson (but not Webb) were all members of the Art Worker's Guild. All of them, including Webb, sent examples of their work to the exhibitions run by the Arts and Crafts Exhibition Society. As a rule Morris and Benson appear in the catalogues representing their respective firms.

Webb's influence can still be traced in furniture designed in

859   *Above*: Satinwood screen, *c.* 1886 with an Art Nouveau textile design by A. H. Mackmurdo. William Morris Gallery, Walthamstow

860   *Above right*: Art Nouveau fragment, perhaps from a piece of furniture, associated with Mackmurdo. Probably of the mid-80s. William Morris Gallery, Walthamstow

861   *Right*: Oak desk designed by Mackmurdo in the mid-80s. William Morris Gallery, Walthamstow

862   *Below*: Carved and painted satinwood cabinet designed by Mackmurdo for the Century Guild. Made by Goodall and Co., Manchester, 1886. Victoria and Albert Museum, London

863   *Above left*: Oak writing desk with a pierced copper hinge, designed by C. F. A. Voysey, 1896. Victoria and Albert Museum, London

864   *Above*: A group of oak furniture designed by Voysey between *c.* 1895 and 1898. Photograph: Voysey documents, Royal Institute of British Architects, London

865   *Left*: Design by Voysey for the hinge in the illustration above it, (to be 'mounted on red leather') 1896. Quarto Imperial Club album, Royal Institute of British Architects, London

866   *Right*: Design for a cabinet and a chair by Reg. Audley from *The Cabinet Maker and Art Furnisher*, 1899. A commercial adaptation of Voysey's ideas.

867   *Below left*: 'Writing cabinet in grey oak'. Designed by Ashbee and executed by members of his guild. Reproduced from *The Studio* of 1900.

868   *Below*: Walnut cabinet of about 1903. Designed by C. R. Ashbee and executed by his Guild of Handicraft. Craftsmen included Statia Power (leather work) and J. W. Pyment. Victoria and Albert Museum, London

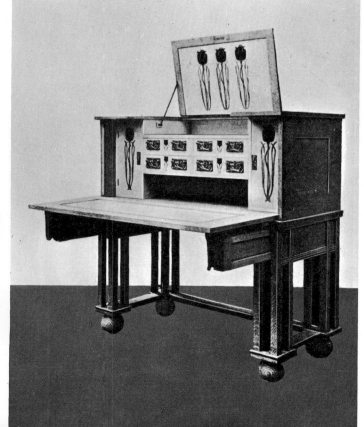

the 90s by his followers, George Jack and Lethaby. An imposing cabinet, now at the Norenfjeldske Kunstindustrimuseum, Norway, with features which suggest the hand of Webb or Lethaby, was it seems designed in about 1890 by George Jack. Nevertheless Lethaby and Jack soon evolved personal styles. Well known is Lethaby's large sideboard once in Melsetter House in the Orkneys, now in the Victoria and Albert Museum. A small table —by the same designer, in the same style, and from the same house—is here seen against a Morris fabric from the Melsetter Drawing Room. It is surmounted by a Benson mirror (Melsetter again) and a Voysey candlestick. George Jack's inlaid table, shown with a Voysey kettle, echoes designs in a late Morris catalogue. In Benson's two-tier cabinet, reproduced from the same catalogue, the emphasis on the mounts reminds us that his greatest achievement ultimately lay in the design of metalwork.

Included here for convenience is a Morris and Co. chair with its original upholstery. Again reproduced in the catalogue, it was ordered in the 1890s, but the designer has not yet been identified.

M. H. BAILLIE SCOTT (1865–1945)

Very little of Baillie Scott's decorative work has yet been rediscovered in the British Isles, but it is familiar from many publications. Between 1894 and 1902 *The Studio* alone devoted ten illustrated articles to his furniture and interiors, and the reproductions included four plates in colour. Baillie Scott was in fact one of the few Victorian designers endowed with a 'colour sense' —the capacity to evolve, at least on paper, very delicate colour harmonies. The gift has always been rare among architects.

His most widely publicised furniture was executed for the New Palace at Darmstadt. Prettily painted, and enriched with pewter, ivory, and repoussé copper, it was executed by the Guild of Handicraft and shows affinities with Ashbee's own furniture. Photographs suggest that in its setting it was overwhelmed by traditional furniture of little merit.

In several of his designs, for instance in those for the *House of an Art Lover*, Baillie Scott experimented with unified rooms incorporating built-in furniture and semi-enclosed inglenooks and 'bowers'. But if he screens off certain units from the main area, he also expands the space by providing glimpses through shutters and openings into galleries and staircases. His reputa-

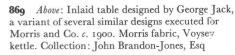

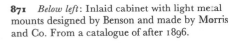

869 *Above*: Inlaid table designed by George Jack, a variant of several similar designs executed for Morris and Co. *c.* 1900. Morris fabric, Voysey kettle. Collection: John Brandon-Jones, Esq

870 *Left*: The 'Saville' easy chair covered in original 'Cherwell' velvet. Ordered from Morris and Co. in the 1890s. (Cost at that time £7 5s., upholstered.) Collection: Sir Colin Anderson

871 *Below left*: Inlaid cabinet with light metal mounts designed by Benson and made by Morris and Co. From a catalogue of after 1896.

872 *Below centre*: An oak table designed by W. R. Lethaby and an oak mirror designed by W. A. S. Benson, both from Melsetter House, Hoy, in the Orkneys, *c.* 1900. Morris fabric, Voysey candlestick. Collection: John Brandon-Jones, Esq

873 *Below*: Inlaid dressing table by Heal and Son, 1900. Designed by Ambrose Heal. With great credit to the designer, Arts and Crafts principles are here faithfully reflected in commercial furniture.

tion will always be enhanced by his attempts to incorporate in one large two-storey space the amenities of a house which at that time were usually provided in several separate rooms—dining room, music room, study, etc. Furniture embodies only a hint of this designer's worthiest achievements.

HEAL AND SON

Around 1900 several commercial firms successfully adopted Arts and Crafts ideals, for instance J. S. Henry, Wylie and Lockhead, and Heal and Son. Only the last can be represented here.

Instructive comparisons can be made between the catalogues published by this firm before and after 1897. In that year a catalogue of wooden bedsteads includes a quotation from Lethaby about 'that crawling slime ornament'. This prepares us for a series of simple designs in the Arts and Crafts tradition.

Typical of this firm's new approach to design are the bedroom suites they exhibited in Paris in 1900 and again in Glasgow in 873   1901. If at this time a few pieces of Heal's bedroom furniture were made of mahogany, the preferred materials were oak or ash, either stained or left plain. By 1900, certainly, the use of mahogany with a glossy finish was not approved in Arts and Crafts circles. Barry Parker, writing in 1901 about the 'smaller Middle Class House' comments disparagingly on 'This polished mahogany life of ours . . .'; and in a *Studio* special number of the same year we read: 'To detest the French polisher . . . may be looked upon as the beginning of wisdom . . . in household decoration'—a remark which could hardly have been made without the example of Morris, Webb, Voysey and Lethaby, and by which Arts and Crafts ideals are partly summed up.

CHARLES RENNIE MACKINTOSH (1868–1928)

After the sanity of the Arts and Crafts Movement, it is a shock to come upon a designer who often abandons common sense. Some 877   of Mackintosh's tall-backed chairs, for instance, are crazily unpractical, while a purely rational approach to design would never have permitted the inclusion of details which tease us into asking 'Why is it there?' or 'What is it for?'. There is also the evidence among his decorations of a curious neuroticism—the 'spook school' element evoked by weeping spirits, disconcerting 876   eyes, and tall figures caged among roses.

Many of Mackintosh's interiors included built-in furniture. The interiors were unified, conceived organically but not plastically, indeed in certain photographs everything looks brittle and unrelaxed. His 'white' rooms must have embodied a rare blend of sophistication and freshness, but even those immaculately 875   drawn curves in furniture and chimney-pieces can have done little to relieve an atmosphere of breathless tension.

Some of Mackintosh's furniture was uncomfortable, some of it was criticised for its shoddy finish. Yet a few of his chairs appear sturdy and hard-wearing, and several sober and rational in-   874 *centre* teriors reveal affinities with Voysey. But Mackintosh, by com-   878 parison with Voysey, was a more brilliant and original designer, and in spite of his faults he could manipulate his ideas not merely to shock but to endure—as in his masterpiece, the Glasgow School of Art. He was extremely influential, both at home and abroad, and his work has rightly been assessed[12] in the context of European achievement.

But Mackintosh was only the last of the Victorian designers whose work gains in significance when seen in a European context. From the time of Pugin onwards—and sooner, perhaps than any other European nation—England saw the need to reform the industrial arts. Pugin was followed by Owen Jones, Ruskin, Morris, Webb; then came Talbert, Godwin, Eastlake, Dresser; then Mackmurdo, Voysey, Ashbee, Baillie Scott; then Mackintosh and his Glasgow associates. Very often evolving personal theories which yet had much in common, all these men tried to combat degenerate commercial design with progressive alternatives, and for once their efforts were noticed abroad. With what effect?

It is not too much to say that if their theories and designs had been ignored, then three of the most substantial books on Art Nouveau[13] could not have been written. To put it another way, if European Art Nouveau had been deprived of influences from the British Isles, it would probably have been a rather different phenomenon. Not for many centuries had English and Scottish designers helped to shape a European movement.

[12] Thomas Howarth: *Charles Rennie Mackintosh and the Modern Movement*, 1952.
[13] Tschudi Madsen: *Sources of Art Nouveau*, 1956. Peter Selz and Mildred Constantine, Editors: *Art Nouveau*, New York, 1959. Robert Schmutzler: *Art Nouveau*, London, 1964.

874 *Above*: Drawing room at 78 Southpark Avenue, Glasgow, by C. R. Mackintosh, the house to which Mackintosh and his wife moved in 1906. His style oscillates between Arts and Crafts simplicity and the intoxicating exaggerations associated with European Art Nouveau. Chair, left: probably from 'Windyhill', Glasgow, 1899–1901. Chair, centre: perhaps from the Argyle Street Tea Rooms, Glasgow, 1897. Chair, right: a type which was included in the Wärndorfer Music Salon, Vienna, *c*. 1902. University of Glasgow Art Collections
875 *Right*: Armchair, toilet table and mirror, and tea table all in white enamelled wood, all designed by C. R. Mackintosh, *c*. 1900–2. University of Glasgow Art Collections

England
1901-1918

878 *Above*: Entrance Hall of Hill House, Helensburgh, designed by Charles Rennie Mackintosh for the publisher, Walter Blackie, in 1903. The furniture, carpets and all the decorations were also designed by the architect.

876 *Above left*: Cabinet of white enamelled and carved wood. The decoration on the inside of the doors is inlaid with opaque coloured glass. Designed by Charles Rennie Mackintosh about 1902 and shown in the Scottish Pavilion of the Turin Exhibition of that year. University of Glasgow Art Collections

877 *Above centre*: Oak dining chair designed by the architect, Charles Rennie Mackintosh. Made in about 1901, it is typical of his work of this period with its elongated forms and restrained ornament. Glasgow School of Art

879 *Left*: The dining room of the White House, Shiplake, designed by George Walton. The house was built between 1907 and 1910 and all the furniture, carpets and decorations were the work of the architect.

880 *Right*: Armchair of oak inlaid with ebony and with a rush seat. Designed by E. G. Punnett and made by William Birch Ltd of High Wycombe in 1901. Victoria and Albert Museum, London

881 *Below left*: A combined entrance hall and dining room, the work of Messrs Marsh, Jones and Cribb of Leeds about 1901. The furniture is typical of some of the best design of the date and so is the use of the rose motifs as an inlay on the chairs, as well as on the carpet, portiere and wallpaper.

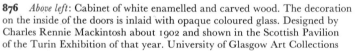

882 *Below*: A music room designed by M. H. Baillie Scott. This is one of a set of prize-winning designs for *The House of an Art Lover* published in Darmstadt in 1902 by Alexander Koch, and although the design was never carried out it is similar to numbers of rooms decorated by Baillie Scott in English country houses in the early part of the century. The architectural setting, stained glass, carpets and furniture were all designed by the architect.

883 *Above left*: Child's high chair of oak inlaid with coloured woods designed by M. H. Baillie Scott and made by J. P. White of Bedford, who made all his furniture. This is one of the pieces illustrated in a catalogue of Baillie Scott designs issued in 1901. Collection: Sir Andrew McTaggart

884 *Above centre*: Oak armchair with a rush seat designed by C. F. A. Voysey and made in about 1903 by C. F. Nielsen in London. Collection: Mrs Mary Francis

886 *Left*: Mahogany bookcase inlaid with ebony, pearwood and mother-of-pearl, designed by Sir Ambrose Heal (1872–1959) and made by Heal and Son *c*. 1905. Victoria and Albert Museum, London

885 *Above right*: Wardrobe of English oak designed by Ernest Gimson (1864–1919) and made at his Daneway House Workshops at Sapperton, Gloucestershire, in about 1906. Gimson, as the leader of 'The Cotswold School' has had a continuing influence on English furniture design through the first half of the 20th century. All his work was based on a respect for the materials used and on an intimate knowledge of craft processes.

887 *Right*: Cabinet and stand in brown ebony inlaid with mother-of-pearl and with bright iron handles designed by Ernest Gimson and made at his Daneway House Workshops, 1908.

888 *Below left*: Cabinet of cherry wood decorated with carved and coloured gesso designed by Frank Brangwyn (1867–1956) and made by Paul Turpin *c*. 1910. Now best known as a painter, Brangwyn designed rugs, textiles, stained glass and much furniture, including some particularly intended for the 'cheap' market. He was also responsible for several complete schemes of decoration. Victoria and Albert Museum, London

889 *Below centre*: Revolving bookcase in sanded walnut with a black and white inlay decoration designed by Sidney Barnsley (1865–1926) and made by the designer in 1913. Barnsley, also a member of 'The Cotswold School' was a close associate of Ernest Gimson. Victoria and Albert Museum, London

890 *Below right*: Dining chair painted red and with a cane seat and back designed in about 1914 by Roger Fry (1866–1934) for the Omega Workshops founded by Fry in the previous year.

FRANCE

Serge Grandjean

'. . . What delight it gives me every morning to draw up this little antique table on its three claw feet, at which I drink a delicious cup of tea with my dear Pauline, prepared by her own hand.'[1]

This comment made by a Parisian in 1800 perfectly evokes the contented and carefree atmosphere which pervaded middle-class homes at the outset of the last century. The decorative arts, and cabinet-making in particular, were in full flower again, despite the rumbling echoes of the French Revolution. During those desperate years of upheaval the venerable Guild of Joiners and Cabinet-makers *(Corporation des Menuisiers-Ebénistes)* had been suppressed, and the furnishings of the former royal palaces and the principal residences of the nobility had been sold by auction. Thus the greater part of Parisian furniture of the 18th century which had been the pride and glory of the age, was lost to posterity. The easing of tension brought about by the Directoire government was followed by a return to general stability and prosperity. The clear-sighted policy of the Consulate and, above all, the leadership of Bonaparte, the First Consul, helped to maintain the improvement. This new atmosphere of security and well-being brought a flood of orders for fine furniture and revitalised the cabinet-maker's craft. Fortunately at so crucial a moment the craft itself was not without support. A number of Parisian master cabinet-makers, who had flourished during the reign of Louis XVI, were still active after 1800. Reopening their workshops, these survivors of the *Ancien Régime* were able to hand on to their successors the fruits of their experience, nourished by tradition and respect for good craftsmanship.

There was no doubt, however, that with the exception of the Napoleonic period, French cabinet-making after the Revolution suffered profoundly from the absence of royal and private patron-age. The demands of a wider but less adventurous and exacting clientele no longer called for pieces of outstanding quality. This lowering of standards was accompanied by a new development.

In 1797 the first of a series of industrial exhibitions was held in the courtyard of the Louvre in Paris. Commercialism was thus frankly encouraged and while there were undoubtedly technical improvements in cabinet-making, art was sacrificed to technique. Since the suppression of the Guilds in 1791, cabinet-makers were free to reorganise the craft and to compete with each other on a commercial basis. As a result, craftsmen set up their own business concerns which brought together for the first time the various branches of the trade and created the new furniture industry.

As a result of this repudiation of tradition and indeed of good taste, the last three-quarters of the 19th century witnessed a period of fluctuating and trivial fashions which brought about the decline of the art. This unfortunate development in the field of cabinet-making presented a marked contrast with the creative vitality reflected in the other decorative arts, notably in gold-smiths' work or ceramics, which gave proof of originality and renewed vigour during this same period.

The 19th century in France was rich in experiments, new ventures and discoveries of all kinds. But as a modern critic has said, it also saw the opening of a closely contested 'battle between aestheticism and functionalism'.

1 '. . . *Avec quel plaisir je la fais rouler tous les matins, sur ses trois pieds de griffon, cette petite table antique, sur laquelle je bois avec ma Pauline un thé delicieux, préparé par elle-même.'* L.F.M.B.L. (Belin de Libordière), *Voyage dans le Boudoir de Pauline*, Paris, 1800, p. 183.

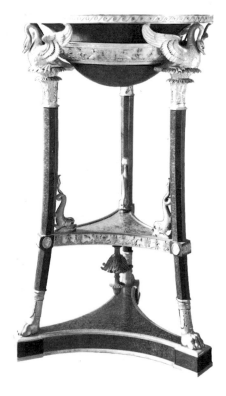

891 *Above*: *Athénienne* or tripod wash-hand stand made in Paris *c.* 1805, veneered in elm root, with gilt bronze mounts. After a design by the architect, Charles Percier, it was very probably executed by M-G. Biennais, who worked as a cabinet-maker before he became a celebrated goldsmith. This elegant piece, still purely Neo-Classical, is in Napoleon's bedroom in the Château de Fontainebleau (Petits Appartements)

892 The Music Room at Malmaison by Auguste Garneray painted in 1800. Musée de Malmaison, Paris

The Consulate (1799-1804)

893 *Above*: Settee of solid mahogany made in Paris, *c.* 1805. The front legs, with terminals in the form of female heads, are a survival from the late 18th century. The scrolled back is typical of the first quarter of the 19th century. The simple lines of this piece characterise much of the bourgeois furniture of the Napoleonic period. Musée des Arts Décoratfs, Paris

894 *Below*: Chair, *guéridon*, and armchair, a page from La Mésangère's *Collection de Meubles et Objets de goût*, published in 1807-18. Bibliothèque Nationale, Paris

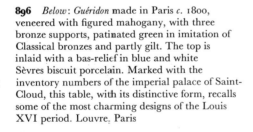

895 *Below*: Fall-front secretaire made in Paris *c.* 1804, veneered with mahogany, with white Carrara marble top. It was part of the furnishing of Saint-Cloud, ordered by Napoleon when the palace was newly furnished for his use. Apart from motifs borrowed from Classical antiquity and the mythological subject of the central mount depicting Apollo's chariot, the four gilt bronze ovals illustrate themes from the fables of La Fontaine. Louvre, Paris

896 *Below*: *Guéridon* made in Paris *c.* 1800, veneered with figured mahogany, with three bronze supports, patinated green in imitation of Classical bronzes and partly gilt. The top is inlaid with a bas-relief in blue and white Sèvres biscuit porcelain. Marked with the inventory numbers of the imperial palace of Saint-Cloud, this table, with its distinctive form, recalls some of the most charming designs of the Louis XVI period. Louvre, Paris

Let us go back to the year 1800. The prestige of Napoleon had increased since his Egyptian victory at the Battle of the Pyramids. In this period of transition, when the great principles of government which formed the foundation of the Empire were being elaborated, the decorative background of everyday life was noticeably modified though it retained a certain nostalgia for the splendid interiors of the closing 18th century. Furniture managed to adapt itself to the current taste, aiming as much at the lightness as at the severity of the Classical style.

The transitory nature of the *Consulat* style makes it difficult to define its particular characteristics. The Louis XVI style still lingered on, but the Empire style had not yet quite emerged. Neo-Classicism survived but Classical antiquity was no longer adapted and interpreted freely, as designers were fond of doing before 1800. Instead, it was revived in all its original purity, although sometimes, perhaps a little dryly, by the new architects, such as Percier and Fontaine, who had studied the originals on the spot in Italy. Contemporary interest in archaeology was widespread. It extended, of course, to the ancient Greek, Roman, Etruscan, Egyptian and even to the Oriental civilisations, and was to leave its imprint on the furniture of the time. The Jacob brothers were among the cabinet-makers who produced fine furniture in this manner. In maintaining a high standard of execution, they preserved both the refinement and above all the traditions of the *Ancien Régime*.

Generally speaking, *Consulat* armchairs have rectangular backs. The horizontal top rail is incurved while the arm is either open or the space between the arm and seat may contain a pierced motif in the form of a palmette, star, or other Classical features. Sometimes the back curves over at the top in scroll form. This latter shape was very widespread in France and was still popular at the beginning of the Empire period. The front legs were often turned in spindle, column or baluster forms, as in the Louis XVI period. But the back legs are of *sabre* type, in the Greek manner. Combining in this way features deriving from different styles, these chairs sometimes have a disconcerting appearance of instability, accentuated by an extraordinary lightness and delicacy, particularly as regards the upright chairs.

The beds, too, developed new forms. Before the middle of the century, the upholsterer was to play the triumphant role in their construction. Decorative curtains and hangings gained in importance while a variety of canopies was in use. Besides the bed of Classical inspiration with its single headboard, known as the *lit à l'antique*, there was also the *lit à la turque*, with curved head- and footboard of equal height. In particular, the *lit en bateau* earned tremendous popularity. It was already Romantic in spirit with its boat-shaped end-pieces, curved and flaring outwards in the form of swans' necks, and a famous example belonged to the beautiful Juliette Récamier. Of solid mahogany, the simple surface of the woodwork and elegant lines of this bed enhance the effect of the gilt bronze mounts. Besides such superlative pieces, which were sometimes set on raised platforms and carefully placed in relation to the architecture of the bedroom, simple bedsteads or *lits droits*, in natural or painted wood with triangular pediments still in the Louis XVI style, were usual in middle-class and rural houses.

904

Small, round *guéridons* and occasional tables were especially in favour, and continued to be so under Napoleonic rule. They were welcomed for their practical advantage in rooms where people had occasion to meet together. Commodes, so characteristic of the 18th century, lost their distinctive personality to become integrated with the surrounding furnishings, and in particular with the fire-place, from which they borrowed such ornamental motifs as caryatids, griffins, Egyptian busts, and swans. They became utilitarian rather than decorative, a weakness they betrayed throughout the century.

896

Among the greatest artistic achievements of the *Consulat* was the work done at the Château de la Malmaison, acquired in 1799 by Madame Bonaparte, the future Empress Josephine. The Château was made ready in record time under the supervision of the architects Percier and Fontaine. They designed the furniture, executed by the Jacob brothers, as well as the interior decora-

Plate facing page 193

898 *Below*: Writing-table made in Paris *c.* 1810, veneered with plain mahogany, supported on elegantly curved legs in the form of an X, with gilt bronze terminals and feet. Similar pieces were made by Jacob-Desmalter for the imperial palaces of Fontainebleau and Compiègne. Musée de Malmaison

897 *Left*: Large console table made in Paris *c.* 1804, veneered with figured mahogany. The two supports terminate in winged female busts with Egyptian-style heads in bronze, partly gilt and patinated in the manner of Classical bronzes. This impressive piece originally graced the Elysée Palace in Paris. Louvre, Paris

899 *Below*: *Grand Salon des Saisons* in the Rue de Lille, Paris, the private mansion of Prince Eugène de Beauharnais, Viceroy of Italy, decorated in about 1805. An exceptionally good example of the harmony that existed between furniture and architecture, the latter being wholly Neo-Classical in spirit. This superb residence is today the German Embassy.

tion for the music room and the library. With their columns and panelling of mahogany, these rooms are still intact today. There is no doubt that the interiors at Malmaison, immediately acclaimed for their elegance, decisively influenced the cabinet-maker's art during the years preceding and immediately following the opening of the Empire period.[2]

Empire (1804-15)

French furniture achieved exceptional brilliance in the Napoleonic era. Paris became once again the most important centre for fine cabinet-making and even set the tone for the rest of Europe. This supremacy was made possible by certain political and economic factors. Not only did Napoleon's creative understanding stimulate the activity of cabinet-makers by providing generous patronage, but his military conquests played a considerable part in spreading this art to all the corners of Europe and even as far afield as Russia.

Between the years 1800 and 1813, over ten thousand workmen earned their living in the furniture industry in Paris, while in 1807 there numbered no less than 88 employers among whom was the famous Jacob-Desmalter.[3] At this time, he employed as many as 350 workmen in his own workshops in the Rue Meslée, near the Porte Saint-Denis in Paris. 'His annual output reached the value of 700,000 francs, of which a third was for export; the stock in his warehouses was worth some 500,000 francs.'[4] Such evident prosperity in the industry continued until the end of the Empire, despite the continental blockade which, from 1806, prevented the importation into France of mahogany from the English colonies. This restrictive measure had the double effect of exaggerating the value of mahogany, the favourite wood of the Empire period, and of intensifying the use of indigenous woods, including walnut, oak, elm, ash, maple, plane, yew and beech. The last was admirably suited for gilding.

Before putting these various woods to use, cabinet-makers turned for guidance to the study of furniture designs either in the form of drawings or engraved patterns. These were supplied by architects, who thus continued to play a vital part in moulding taste in the domain of furniture and incidentally contributing to the survival of Neo-Classicism. Jacob-Desmalter, the most fashionable cabinet-maker in Paris, and his various rivals, drew

upon the designs of those brilliant collaborators, Percier and Fontaine, official architects to the Emperor and joint authors of the *Recueil de Décorations Intérieures*, published in Paris in 1801 and re-issued in 1812. In this pattern-book, which had a considerable influence in France and in most of Europe, furniture was given pride of place. Although it inspired an 'official art', to which heavy forms lend a slightly theatrical air, it evokes, too, a sense of majestic grandeur, reflecting Napoleon's genius for building and his nostalgia for the proud splendour of ancient Rome.

There were, of course, some furniture designers who were not architects, but they were in a minority. Notable among them was Vivant Denon, archaeologist and engraver, who became director of the *Musée Napoléon* in the Louvre. His famous *Voyage dans la Basse et Haute-Egypte*, published in Paris and London in 1802, inspired that touch of Orientalism which formed an essential feature of fashionable taste. The charm of his work pervades the furniture of the beginning of the Empire, for the engravings in his book were the source of decorative themes used by more than one French cabinet-maker bent on making a reputation. Painters also had a contribution to make, and Louis David and Lagrenée the Younger made the drawings for the suite of armchairs, chairs and stools intended for the *Grand Cabinet de l'Empereur* in the Palais des Tuileries, 1811. These were to be upholstered in Gobelins tapestry, on a purple and gold ground.[5]

For private or middle-class patrons, it was the ornamental designers who supplied the cabinet-makers with patterns in the form of engravings, usually colour prints. None of these ornamentalists enjoyed as much success and good fortune as Pierre de La Mésangère, whose famous book of designs, *Collection de Meubles et Objets de goût*, appeared between 1802 and 1835 in a magazine called *Journal des Dames et des Modes*. Approximately four hundred plates from this publication appeared during the Empire period; they played an effective role in making the many

891

[2] Serge Grandjean, *Inventaire après décès de l'Impératrice Joséphine à Malmaison*, Paris, 1964, pp. 90-98.
[3] Comte Chaptal, *De l'Industrie française*, Paris, 1819, Vol. II, p. 199.
[4] Hector Lefuel, *F. H. G. Jacob-Desmalter*, Paris, 1925.
[5] R., G., C., Ledoux-Lebard. *Le grand Cabinet de l'Empereur aux Tuileries*, in *Bulletin de la Société de l'Histoire de l'Art français*, Paris, 1941-47, p. 42 (re-printed).

900 *Above*: Armchair of carved and gilt wood made in Paris *c.* 1810, bearing the stamp of P. Brion, one of the best cabinet-makers supplying the *Garde-Meuble Impérial*. The pediment back shows obvious architectural affinities. The chair is part of a set of furniture matching the interior decoration of the salon, the set being completed by a folding screen and a fire screen. Château de Fontainebleau (2nd salon of the Petits Appartements de l'Empereur)

901 *Above right*: Armchair of carved mahogany, from the Palais des Tuileries, the principal official residence of the French Emperor. The chair bears the stamp of Jacob-Desmalter and has that military appearance already in existence in about 1800, when Napoleon was First Consul. Louvre, Paris

902 *Right*: Chair of highly polished mahogany made in Paris *c.* 1815, of standard pattern but good make. Although still Empire in spirit and general form, the lines tend to be softer and more supple. It bears the stamp of J. Louis. Louvre, Paris

903 *Below*: Square pianoforte made in Paris *c.* 1815, veneered with mahogany, with lyre-shaped pedal-board, by '*Pape, facteur de pianos, cour des Fontaines no. 1 à Paris*'. The four columnar legs recall Classical example in a manner characteristic of the beginning of the Napoleonic period. Musée des Arts Décoratifs, Paris

features of middle-class Napoleonic furniture familiar, and even helped to sustain their popularity beyond the chronological limits of the Empire. The delicious simplicity of La Mésangère makes a pleasing contrast with the splendid architectural severity of Percier and Fontaine, from whom La Mésangère borrowed, in a simplified form, certain designs, such as that for Josephine's jewel cabinet.

In La Mésangère's intentionally simple designs, brightened by the lively colouring of the woodwork and gleam of the gilt bronze mounts, there is already a shy hint of the coming vogue for Romanticism and a discreet suggestion of the revived Gothic taste. In as early as 1804, the cabinet-maker Mansion the Younger proposed a piece of furniture 'ornamented with Gothic attributes'[6] for Napoleon. This new style did not develop in any positive way until after the restoration of the Bourbons in 1815, despite the example of the great gallery in the Château de la Malmaison, conceived in 1808 in the Gothic manner by the architect Berthault. Similarly, the Chinese taste is conspicuous for its absence under the Empire, at a time when it was so much in evidence in England, at Carlton House, the Royal Pavilion, Brighton, and elsewhere. On the other hand, the Egyptian, Greek and Roman tastes were very much in favour, the first, as we have seen, owing more to Vivant Denon than to Piranesi or to other recognised promoters of Neo-Classicism.

In form and proportion alone, Empire furniture did not differ from that made under the Consulate, although it tended progressively to become heavier and more majestic. Novelty was expressed in the ornamental features of the veneering and marquetry and, above all, in the design of the gilt bronze mounts of which the delicacy and elegance gradually coarsened towards 1815. The console table, retaining its rectangular shape, became a specifically Napoleonic piece of furniture, with an interesting variety of supports usually in the form of Classical fauna motifs in place of the columns, pilasters and other architectural elements previously in vogue. Commodes on the other hand were designed in a number of different ways depending upon the arrangement of the vertical side panels and the horizontal drawers, as we can see from La Mésangère's engravings. In comfortably furnished rooms, the commode was faithfully accompanied by the indispensable fall-front secretaire. In bedroom furniture, this period endorsed the success of the arch-shaped or rectangular *psyché* or cheval-glass, with its mirror mounted on pivots, in which the coquettes of the day could admire themselves from top to toe whilst arranging all their finery. The chairs conserved at first their scroll backs, but gradually the rectangular back, either plain or upholstered with woven fabric according to the quality of the chair, became the most usual form. We should note here the appearance of the curved back chair *en gondole* or gondola-shaped, so pleasing to the eye and appealing to feminine taste. Fine quality examples are to be seen in Josephine's dressing room at Fontainebleau and in Marie-Louise's boudoir at Compiègne.

In refurnishing the former royal residences, which had been emptied of their contents at the Revolution, Napoleon was reviving the grand policy so successfully pursued by the Bourbons in favour of the furniture industry. Although the Tuileries and Saint-Cloud are no more, for they were burned down or destroyed in 1870, the Châteaux of Fontainebleau, Compiègne, Trianon, and the palaces of the Elysée and of Prince Eugène de Beauharnais in Paris still bear witness today to the tremendous efforts made by those in charge of the Imperial furnishings, the *Garde-Meuble Impérial*. That excellent body was not only responsible for the furnishing of those residences, but also supervised the execution of all orders given to a selected number of cabinet-makers and bronze sculptors. To give an example of this activity, which was rewarding in more than one sense, the general inventory of the *Mobilier de la Couronne* between 1810 and 1811 records the expenditure of between 13 and 17 million francs on furniture for the various imperial palaces.[7] Over half a million francs were paid to Jacob-Desmalter for furniture supplied to the Palais des Tuileries alone during the Napoleonic reign. It was an epoch of particular brilliance and at the same time a period in which the art of the cabinet-maker achieved its final flowering.

900
901

901

6 D. Ledoux-Lebard, *Les Ebénistes parisiens* (1795–1830). Paris, 1951, p. 205.
7 *Archives Nationales de Paris (Papiers de Garde-Meuble).*

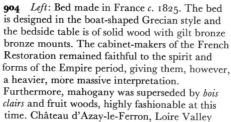

904 *Left*: Bed made in France *c.* 1825. The bed is designed in the boat-shaped Grecian style and the bedside table is of solid wood with gilt bronze bronze mounts. The cabinet-makers of the French Restoration remained faithful to the spirit and forms of the Empire period, giving them, however, a heavier, more massive interpretation. Furthermore, mahogany was superseded by *bois clairs* and fruit woods, highly fashionable at this time. Château d'Azay-le-Ferron, Loire Valley

905 *Right*: Bed in the shape of a shallow basket *(Lit en corbeille)* from La Mésangère's *Collection de Meubles et Objets de goût*. Bibliothèque Nationale, Paris

906 *Below left*: Commode of maplewood made in Paris *c.* 1825, enclosed by two doors. As in other pieces of this period, the general form is heavier, while the wood is thinner as a result of improved methods of sawing boards and cutting veneers. Even the gilt bronze mounts are more attenuated. Signed by Fischer, cabinet-maker of the Faubourg Saint-Antoine. Musée des Arts Décoratifs, Paris

907 *Below*: *Méridienne*, or day bed, of mahogany made in France *c.* 1830. The comfortable, bourgeois simplicity of such pieces made them very popular in France at the time of Napoleon, and again during the Restoration. Sometimes the lower end could be let down on hinges to a horizontal position. Musée des Arts Décoratifs, Paris

Restoration and the July Monarchy (1815-30-48)

French furniture managed at first to preserve its rich vitality, thanks to the exceptional lustre it acquired under the Napoleonic Empire, and to such advantages as the experience of the cabinet-makers, the quality of the designs and the improvement in tools. But all that was soon left behind, after 1815, by inevitable advances in the field of technique.

909 Henceforth, the use of steam power brought a reduction in labour costs, but what was undoubtedly a great advance in method led, on the other hand, to a lowering of artistic standards. Yet the use of machinery allowed for improvement in the system of sawing boards for furniture as well as in the exacting process of

906 slicing veneers. For this reason, particular interest was shown in the choice of indigenous woods and in the decorative effects of various grains and markings, effects which are characteristic of the finest examples of Charles X or Louis-Philippe furniture. The

910 young, sensitive Duchesse de Berry, daughter-in-law of Charles X, has been given the credit of introducing the fashion for *bois clairs*, notably birds-eye maple, so attractive for its dazzling

911 blonde hue, but this theory is doubted, if not disproved by historians. Another new feature was the gradual disappearance of bronze mounts. Often so massive during the Napoleonic epoch, these were now sometimes replaced by discreet inlays of materials such as ebony, brass, pewter, or even painted porcelain. The

commode and bed belonging to the actress Melle Mars, and made in about 1825 by Benard, were inlaid with porcelain plaques painted with mythological scenes.

This change of spirit in the art of furniture-making was accentuated by the increasing number of industrial exhibitions, and that of 1819, held in the Louvre, had profound consequences. These exhibitions demonstrated the supremacy of technique to the detriment of art, but at the same time they brought within the reach of the general public a type of furniture better suited to their need for comfort and simple elegance. The rise of the middle-class under the Bourbon Restoration and the July Monarchy, was by no means the least factor in this movement of widespread industrialisation. Rented apartments made their appearance and for these furniture was needed which was both simple and distinctive.

In this new situation, who was to provide the designs for interiors and furniture? It was, in fact, no longer the architect but the ornamentalist. The famous prints of La Mésangère continued to be published right up until 1835 in Paris. Their example stimulated the zeal of a few valiant craftsmen such as the upholsterer, T. Bodin in 1815, the designer Santi in 1828,[8] the furniture designer Michel Jamsen in 1835,[9] and the upholsterer and manufacturer Alphonse Giroux in about 1840[10]. A cabinet-

[8] *Modèles de meubles et de décorations intérieures pour l'ameublement . . . dessinés par M. Santi et gravés par Mme. Soyer*, Paris, 1828 (72 plates).

[9] *Ouvrage sur l'ébénisterie, dédié aux fabricants . . . avec échelle de proportions*, Paris, 1835 (illustrated).

[10] *Meubles et Fantaisies*, Paris, *c.* 1840 (illustrated).

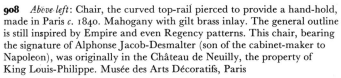

908 *Above left*: Chair, the curved top-rail pierced to provide a hand-hold, made in Paris *c.* 1840. Mahogany with gilt brass inlay. The general outline is still inspired by Empire and even Regency patterns. This chair, bearing the signature of Alphonse Jacob-Desmalter (son of the cabinet-maker to Napoleon), was originally in the Château de Neuilly, the property of King Louis-Philippe. Musée des Arts Décoratifs, Paris

909 *Above centre*: Chair with a curved back, the splat in the form of a palmette, made in Paris *c.* 1835. Mahogany, with tapestry cover. This piece shows how the Empire style became debased and clumsy, in spite of the quality of the materials and the new advances in technique. Musée des Arts Décoratifs, Paris

910 *Above right*: A room in the Pavillon de Marsan, in the apartments of the Duchesse de Berry. Watercolour by Auguste Garneray (1785-1824). Musée des Arts Décoratifs, Paris

911 *Right*: Armchair and chair of maplewood inlaid with purplewood made in France, *c.* 1830. A fashion for indigenous woods, especially for *bois clairs*, came into being during the reign of Charles X. The armchair on the left is known as a *fauteuil à gondole* because of the boat-shaped back. The chair on the right, with the arcaded back, shows the persistent influence of the Gothic taste. Musée des Arts Décoratifs, Paris

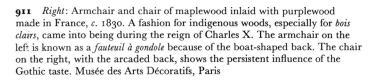

912 *Above*: Armchair and chair of mahogany, on the left a *fauteuil à gondole* (see also illustration 911) with front legs of cabriole form. The right-hand chair has a back composed of diagonally intersecting bars. Both are characteristic of the 1840s and these patterns were very popular with the rich middle classes. Musée des Arts Décoratifs, Paris

913 *Right*: Two chairs, made in France *c.* 1840, in carved wood, one in the so-called 'cathedral' style which reflected the renewed and highly romantic interest in the Middle Ages. Musée des Arts Décoratifs, Paris

914 *Above*: Design for a Gothic Room *c.* 1830 by A. Chenavard. Musée des Arts Décoratifs, Paris

915 *Above right*: Cylinder-top desk, 1830–40, veneered with a burr wood and with gilt bronze mounts. The columns and sphinxes stress the architectural character of this splendid piece which provides yet another example of Neo-Classical taste persisting in France long after the fall of the Napoleonic Empire. Attributed to the Parisian cabinet-maker, Lemarchand. Musée Carnavalet, Paris

916 *Below*: Lady's writing-table with shelf, in mahogany inlaid with lime and sycamore, made in Paris *c.* 1835–40. The form is derived, ultimately, from the *bonheur du jour* of the Louis XVI period. The marquetry is of an exceptionally high standard. Musée des Arts Décoratifs, Paris

917 *Below*: Sideboard, made in France, *c.* 1840–5, of mahogany with turned supports, pierced panels and a mirrored back. The style is eclectic and one can no longer clearly distinguish the various influences that have left their mark on this piece of dining-room furniture. It is, however, very well made. Musée des Arts Décoratifs, Paris

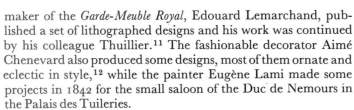

915   maker of the *Garde-Meuble Royal*, Edouard Lemarchand, published a set of lithographed designs and his work was continued by his colleague Thuillier.[11] The fashionable decorator Aimé Chenevard also produced some designs, most of them ornate and eclectic in style,[12] while the painter Eugène Lami made some projects in 1842 for the small saloon of the Duc de Nemours in the Palais des Tuileries.

From these publications, which provide such interesting sources for the study of the history of French furniture, it is evident that manufacturers now aimed, with the help of machinery, at executing their work more rapidly. Cost prices were lowered but the quality of the materials employed was inferior.

Variety, inventiveness and a concern for comfort characterised the furniture made between 1830–40, in contrast to the rigorous architectural perfection of Empire furniture. The resultant manner was really a debasement of the principles employed under Napoleon by Percier and Fontaine. For a long time after 1815, however, an echo of the Empire style lingered on, although 909   the massive forms became somewhat thickened. This lingering aftermath of Neo-Classicism, represented by the works of the elder Jacob-Desmalter and of his son Alphonse, of P.A. Bellangé, Lemarchand and others was to be engulfed in the turbulent spirit of Romanticism, itself perhaps a reincarnation of the Baroque.

[11] *Cabinet de dessins de fauteuils . . . d'après le sieur Thuillier, menuisier-ébéniste . . . par Thre.* Pasquier, Paris, n.d. (54 plates). The original designs, collected together by Lemarchand are in the Library of the Musée des Arts Décoratifs, Paris.

[12] *Album de l'ornemaniste, receuil d'ornements dans tous les genres et dans tous les styles,* Paris, 1836.

Underlying this period of Romanticism, several currents which left their mark on new trends in furniture can be distinguished. Apart from Naturalism, with its direct allusions to Nature's products such as flowers and fruit, and the Orientalism, which attracted more attention after the French advances into Algeria in 1830, there was also a revived interest in the Middle Ages. Medievalism was, of course, wholly in keeping with that age of widespread erudition and archaeological exploration, and it reflects, too, the literary influence of Victor Hugo's *Notre-Dame de Paris*. The 'Gothic' taste, ironically known as *troubadour,* left its picturesque mark on a number of interiors both in middle-class 920 and princely houses, such as Princesse Marie d'Orléans' oratory in the Tuileries, and the *salon* designed by Aimé Chenavard, 914 both astonishing in their meticulous attention to detail.

The eclectic nature of this style was taken even further under Louis-Philippe. Decorators and cabinet-makers now took to imitating, or rather interpreting, the French Renaissance of the second half of the 16th century, sharing the same retrospective passion for pediments, columns and reliefs with Classical figures.

So many and such diverse tendencies all in one epoch indicate a lack of artistic direction. Taste in furniture was corrupted by abusive imitation. To make matters worse, official patronage was no more than a memory. Louis XVIII was not interested in new innovations and, with his sense of economy, was quite content to live in the palaces so lavishly furnished by Napoleon. Charles X was equally, but not quite so obviously indifferent. But Caroline, Duchesse de Berry, showed sensitivity in the pieces she ordered from contemporary cabinet-makers for her own apartments in the Pavillon de Marsan, in the Tuileries and for 910 her château at Rosny. As for Louis-Philippe, he had the good

918 *Left*: Upright pianoforte of ebony with gilt bronze mounts, by Colin, made in France, *c.* 1840. The fashion for mahogany and light-coloured woods was superseded by a fashion for dark woods. These contrasted with the brilliance of the mounts and brought out the effects of light on the mouldings. Musée des Arts Décoratifs, Paris

919 *Below left*: The study of Queen Marie-Amélie at the Tuileries *c.* 1840, gouache by Jean-Charles Develly. Archives de la Manufacture de Sèvres

920 *Below*: Prie-dieu of carved wood in the 'troubadour' style, the back decorated with a painted panel, *c.* 1840. The interest in archaeology and the rediscovery of the Middle Ages inspired the use of Gothic motifs and their adaptation to furniture. Château de Chantilly

sense to appoint Fontaine, Percier's collaborator, as his chief architect, and in this way he maintained a certain traditionalism. An example is the carved and gilt throne, the front legs ornamented with winged griffins, supplied to the Palais Royal in 1831 by Jacob-Desmalter's son for the price of 1,000 francs.[13]

918   The craze for *bois clairs* was succeeded by a return to popularity of mahogany and, in about 1840, by the fashion for dark woods. Ebony, oak and stained pear were then used. Panels of *verre églomisé*, porcelain plaques and mother-of-pearl were introduced to offset the somewhat forbidding aspect of the wood. The same period witnessed the success of the charming japanned pieces painted with bouquets of flowers in polychrome on a black ground and sometimes enriched with mother-of-pearl.

902   We come now to the principal types of furniture. At the beginning of the Restoration, the influence of the Empire, as we have already seen, still persisted and assured the continuation of 18th-century practices. Chairs, nevertheless, gradually abandoned their Napoleonic formality to attain a lighter and more supple charm. Chair backs were to retain the rectangular or round-topped form for a long time, the central part being orna-
912 mented as a rule by crossbars which were very popular with the
908 middle-classes. A pierced opening allowing for a hand-grip was a frequent feature on the top rail of the fashionable gondola-shaped chair backs. And at the height of the Gothic taste, chair backs, carved in the form of Gothic tracery with crocketted
913 pinnacles, *à la cathédrale* became widespread in Paris. The front legs of chairs, also changed in shape, the upper part forming a
912 more or less prominent volute and the lower a baluster outline. This type of chair was all the rage from about 1830–45. Arm supports were often in the form of dolphins, swans or cornu-

copiae. X-shaped stools still found high favour, and Madame Récamier had some in her bedroom at Abbaye-aux-Bois. Finally the appearance, under Charles X, of the comfortable *Voltaire* armchair with its high, scrolled back deserves note.

  The popular *méridienne* was still appreciated for its graceful, 907 curving lines, while settees, like simple divans, were stuffed over with either plain or flowered fabrics. This upholstered style extended to beds, which were adorned with the heavily draped 910 canopies shown in Santi's designs. As in the earlier period, these beds were boat-shaped or else rectilinear, the headboards orna- 904 mented with columns or pilasters.

  Cheval-glasses, screens, jardinières and occasional tables were always present in contemporary interiors while standing shelves and *dessertes* or sideboards were also popular for the display of 917 curios. Dressing-tables were made of 'polished mahogany of swan's neck form, with bronze handles and oval mirror, the top of white marble' to quote an example supplied in 1831 by Lesage for the bedroom of Queen Marie-Amélie in the Palais Royal.[14] Commodes lost their ornamental carving and adopted gentle curves in place of sharp angles; some were designed in the English manner, with drawers enclosed behind doors.

  Considered as a whole, this middle-class furniture is curiously like that made in Austria in about 1830, in the *Biedermeier* style, a development which anticipated the internationalism which was to become apparent well before the middle of the 19th century.

[13] *Archives Nationales de Paris, (Papiers du Garde-Meuble)*.
[14] Idem.

921 *Above*: Upright piano, *c.* 1850, by Roller and Blanchet *fils*, decorated with marquetry and with gilt bronze mounts. The marquetry is of outstanding brilliance but the preoccupation with detailed ornament is so obtrusive that the purpose of the piece is almost overlooked. Château de Chantilly

922 *Above*: Upholstered armchair by Jeanselme, an illustration from Pasquier's *Cahier de Dessins d'ameublement*, published *c.* 1840. Bibliothèque Nationale, Paris.

924 *Below*: *Buffet* composed of two superimposed parts decorated with marquetry in the Louis XV style with baskets of flowers suspended by ribbons on a tulipwood ground, made in Paris by Grohé, *c.* 1845. The disproportionate heaviness of the upper section is rendered less apparent by the brilliant quality of the cabinet-maker's work. Château de Chantilly

923 *Above*: Two chairs of ebonised wood inlaid with mother-of-pearl. Made in Paris *c.* 1850. The use of iridescent shell was still fashionable under Napoleon III. Musée des Arts Décoratifs, Paris

925 *Right*: *Confidents* by Jeanselme, an illustration from Pasquier's *Cahier de Dessins d'ameublement*. Bibliothèque Nationale, Paris

The Second Empire (1848-70)

With the advent of Napoleon III, furniture entered a phase of little aesthetic merit, but although, paradoxically, it was also one in which a distinctive, homogeneous style developed. The newly-found national prosperity and the growth of industry made possible a new way of living, even more bourgeois than hitherto, which was perfectly embodied by the Universal Exhibition of 1867, held in the Champ-de-Mars. This new manner was to continue even into the early years of the Third Republic.

The Second Empire witnessed the triumph of revivalism and the dominance of the upholsterer. Once the enthusiasm for the Gothic had died down, craftsmen proceeded, quite willingly and unhindered by any particular concern for accuracy, to produce rehashes of all the various styles that had been the pride of 16th-, 17th- and 18th-century France. Authentic details borrowed from the Henri II, Louis XIV, Louis XV and Louis XVI styles were incorporated in designs for furniture. Such pieces were generally irreproachably made and were almost always veneered with fine quality wood. Soon, pieces in the Boulle manner: *cabinets d'entre deux*, or cabinets flanked by a set of shelves at each end, of ebony inlaid with arabesques in gilt brass on an imitation shell ground, were essential features in the smart *salons*. Frédéric Roux supplied some superb examples for the Imperial apartments in the Tuileries. The Louis XV Rococo style inspired

some other equally splendid works, often veneered in rosewood, inlaid with Sèvres porcelain plaques, and with bronze mounts; the style was particularly favoured by the rich bourgeoisie and by the numerous readers of an important illustrated periodical, *Le Magasin Pittoresque*, founded in 1833. Towards the end of Napoleon III's reign, the Louis XVI style was by far the most popular, on account of the Empress Eugénie's delight in memories of Marie-Antoinette. Nor was Orientalism forgotten, for certain costly pieces of furniture executed after 1860 were lacquered in the Chinese taste.

As for upholsterers, they enjoyed a dominant role in equalling or even eclipsing cabinet-makers in importance. Their new fame was declared at the famous 1867 exhibition where the majority of the exhibitors of fine quality cabinet furniture, such as Fourdinois and Jeanselme, also described themselves as upholsterers. In effect, the taste for draped hangings and for various kinds of curtains, trimmings and fittings, had never been taken as far as it was now to be. Hence the extraordinary profusion of upholstered seats. Known by such charming names as *pouffes*, *crapauds* or low armchairs and *confidantes à deux places*, *indiscrets à trois places* and *canapés de l'amitié*, all were forms of settees for two or three people. They evoked, like the voluminous crinolines of the ladies, an atmosphere of 'pneumatic bliss'. *La Dame aux Camélias* no doubt enjoyed the soft yielding comfort of these seats and so too the enigmatic Countess of Castiglione. A new type of occasional chair lacquered or gilt, with caned or upholstered seat, would be placed invitingly around small tables. This convenient piece of furniture, so suitable for informal social occasions, was well received in spite of its rather spindly appearance.

In these years of such wide disparities of style, revealing both

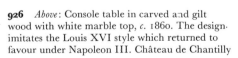

926 *Above*: Console table in carved and gilt wood with white marble top, *c.* 1860. The design imitates the Louis XVI style which returned to favour under Napoleon III. Château de Chantilly

927 *Above right*: Cabinet or *meuble d'appui* of ebony with gilt bronze mounts, *c.* 1860. The central decorative feature on the door, representing a flowering tree, is composed of hard stones. The cabinet-maker is unknown but the design is Louis XVI in spirit. Château de Compiègne

928 *Left*: Upholstered stool or 'pouffe', *c.* 1860. The legs, of carved and gilt wood, simulate knotted rope. This curious piece by Fournier, so provocatively illogical, inspired the glass factory at Baccarat at this period to produce some glass seats. Château de Compiègne

929 *Right*: Low armchair or *chauffeuse* in the Louis XV style, *c.* 1860. Ebony, upholstered in flowered cretonne. This type of chair was placed either beside or in front of the fire. Musée des Arts Décoratifs, Paris

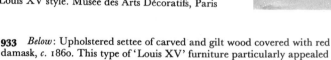

930 *Above*: A selection of chairs, with caned or upholstered seats from Pasquier's *Cahier de Dessins d'ameublement*. Bibliothèque Nationale, Paris

932 *Below*: Cabinet or *meuble d'appui* of tulipwood, *c.* 1860, with gilt bronze mounts and set with porcelain plaques in the manner of the late 18th century. This piece is one of a pair. Musée des Arts Décoratifs, Paris

931 *Right*: Upholstered chair of ebony with a pierced, medallion-shaped back, *c.* 1860. In this piece the interest in cushioned comfort is paramount and hides the lack of invention, for both the outlines and decorative features imitate the Louis XV style. Musée des Arts Décoratifs, Paris

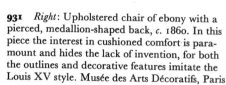

933 *Below*: Upholstered settee of carved and gilt wood covered with red damask, *c.* 1860. This type of 'Louis XV' furniture particularly appealed to the monied middle classes and was found throughout France. Musée des Arts Décoratifs, Paris

utter lack of invention and yet extraordinary ingenuity, there were no outstanding figures. But there were excellent ornamental designers noted for their daring originality, who did much to sustain the applied arts in industry. We will only refer here to the most important.

These were Jean Feuchère, who died in 1852 but whose pupil Jules Klagmann was admired by his generation, and the inventive Liénard, the author of *Spécimens de la décoration et de l'ornementation au XIXe siècle* (Liège, 1866). We might add, in passing, some leading architects who had a part in the development of this composite style: Mauguin, who was particularly fond of ebony, and designed the furniture for the Hôtel de la Païva, erected on the Champs-Elysées; Charles Rossigneux, who designed the furniture for the *Villa Pompéienne*, built in 1860 in the Avenue Montaigne for Prince Napoleon; Lefuel, commissioned by the French sovereigns to refurnish the interior of the Tuileries; and finally Viollet-le-Duc, restorer of châteaux and of Gothic cathedrals, who decorated the Imperial railway carriage, presented by the *Compagnie des Chemins de Fer d'Orléans*, and designed for it the furniture for the dining room and for the dressing-room of Napoleon III's wife.

These select few kept the cabinet-makers and upholsterers well provided with designs for luxury pieces. But it was otherwise in the ordinary furniture industry where quality was lacking as an inevitable result of mechanisation. Busy clients were in the habit of consulting the price lists of the big shops to find cheaper beds, tables, wardrobes with mirrors and other such utilitarian pieces which were turned out more quickly. This process of vulgarisation, together with the competition provided by the iron furniture of the Pihet brothers and Gandillot, hastened the

935

decay of the noble art of cabinet-making.

Finally, an innovation in the method of furnishing Second Empire houses is worthy of note. It became the practice to furnish each room with pieces designed in a style appropriate to the surroundings, a custom which reflected the eclecticism which was *de rigueur* at the mid-19th century. The Henri II style was considered suitable for dining rooms, Boulle or Rococo furniture belonged in the various *salons*, austere pieces in ebony or rosewood provided a masculine note in libraries and smoking rooms, while upholstery and draped hangings were for feminine boudoirs and for bedrooms. This purely conventional ruling prevailed for a long time even in houses furnished after 1870.

934

End of the 19th Century and Art Nouveau

Already by the mid-century, the excessive eclecticism of the applied arts had provoked a healthy reaction which aimed to bring out the 'beautiful in the useful'. Comte Léon de Laborde in France, like John Ruskin in England,[15] believed mechanisation to be a serious hindrance to the evolution of the crafts and

[15] In 1856 De Laborde published a work which has remained famous: *De l'Union des Arts et de l'Industrie* (Paris, 2 vols.). On page 400 we read: 'Industry needs guidance, and apprentices need more enlightened masters.'

934 *Above*: Painting by Delacroix of a bedroom in the house of the Comte de Mornay. The room was planned by the diplomat himself and in its unorthodox yet intimate arrangement reflects his personal approach to comfortable living. The general character is still that of the First Empire although the effect is very much lighter. Louvre, Paris

935 *Right*: Tall ebony cabinet with gilt bronze ornaments in the Renaissance style, *c.* 1865. The piece was made for Madame de Païva's house on the Champs-Elysées in Paris. Musée des Arts Décoratifs, Paris

preached a return to nature and to the values of good workmanship. In his work of restoring historical buildings, Viollet-le-Duc had already taught the use of plant forms, while Ruprich-Robert published his *Flore Ornementale* in 1866. This desire for a new approach was developed quite quickly, giving rise to Symbolism in France and to the Pre-Raphaelite movement in England, countries that were both ready for an art form freed from ties with the past.

Was furniture design after 1870 to escape at last from the marasmus into which it had sunk for want of new inspiration? Was it really to develop in a way made possible by the new ideals? Not, alas, as yet. It continued to pillage the past without restraint, evincing, in even greater measure, a vulgarity and lack of discernment due rather to current fashion than to the insensitivity of the cabinet-makers themselves. All types of furniture were executed with unimpeachable technical ability. The designs hitherto exploited, mainly Louis XV and Louis XVI, were augmented by those of the Empire. At the Universal Exhibition in Paris in 1878, pastiche remained the order of the day, as it still was later at the 1884 and 1889 Exhibitions, but the tremendous skill of the manufacturers was a compensating factor. The *salons* of the Princess Mathilde, frequented by the most brilliant people of the day, were filled with an incongruous medley of furniture although they were not without a certain sense of picturesque comfort. Most rich and middle-class bourgeois interiors, on the other hand, remained stolidly the same in their attempt to imitate former styles. A century had already passed since the suppression of the Guilds whose regulations might have been able to ensure some artistic unity within the craft, as well as a sense of tradition.

Faced with such confusion and, in particular, with the abuses

of mass production, the crusade led by Laborde and Ruskin in favour of a revival of the crafts, as well as the teachings of Viollet-le-Duc, was ultimately to bear fruit. Schools of applied art were founded in the town and even in the country in order to re-educate new generations of craftsmen.

The *Union Centrale des Beaux-Arts appliqués à l'Industrie* started at the time of the retrospective Exhibition of 1865 in Paris, became in 1877 the *Union Centrale des Arts décoratifs*. Its policy, at once social and utilitarian, was to bring together artist and industrialist, designer and manufacturer. In other words, it promoted the democratisation of culture, without abjuring the glories of rich materials and the pursuit of pure forms. It was an attempt to put into practice the concept of William Morris, one of Ruskin's disciples, of an 'art for the people by the people'.

All these efforts resulted in an aesthetic revolution in the domain of interior decoration and furniture. This almost unhoped for transformation took place shortly after the Universal Exhibition of 1889 in Paris, an exhibition which witnessed the revival of floral designs as well as the inauguration of the Eiffel Tower. The change was brought about through various international influences, such as that of William Morris and Arthur H. Mackmurdo in England, Henry Van de Velde in Belgium, Louis C. Tiffany in the United States, to mention only the principal initiators of the Modern Style. The role of France was no less decisive, thanks to the contributions of the theoretician Eugène Grasset, the glass-worker Emile Gallé, founder of the School of Nancy, and the Hamburg dealer S. Bing. Grasset was more a teacher of decorative art than an original designer but some interiors and furniture of his survive, still rather ornate, which he designed between 1879 and 1881 for his friend the

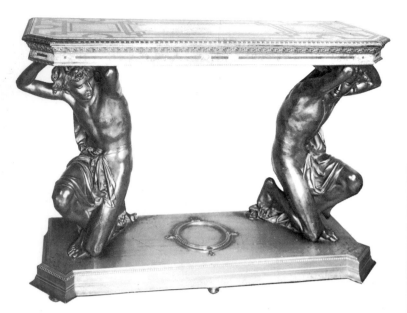

936 *Above*: Console table supported on bronze sculptured figures, partly gilt, the top of marble and semi-precious stones of various colours, *c.* 1865. This superbly elegant piece was made by the sculptor, Dalou for Madame de Païva's house on the Champs-Elysées in Paris. Musée des Arts Décoratifs, Paris

937 *Above*: The Empress Eugènie's bedroom at Saint Cloud. Watercolour by F. de Fournier. Château de Compiègne

939 *Below*: Boudoir of the Princesse Mathilde, 1859, by Charles Giraud, showing a typical Second Empire interior. Château de Compiègne

938 *Left*: *Indiscret* or upholstered settee, *c.* 1860, arranged as three linked armchairs and very fashionable in Paris at the time of the Second Empire. Armchairs upholstered both at the back and the front admirably evoke the atmosphere of bolstered comfort created by the cosy interiors of the time of Napoleon III. Musée des Arts Décoratifs, Paris

photo-engraver, Charles Gillot. Like Grasset, Emile Gallé designed few pieces of furniture, but his work in wood, like that in glass and sometimes in metal, reveals a high degree of originality or a sense of poetry in interpreting nature, particularly plant forms. He was chiefly interested in the decorative aspect of design and had little concern for mass and volume. But he opened the way for the Modern Style of 1900 and anticipated the decisive experimental work of the sculptor Alexandre Charpentier, the architect Hector Guimard, the expert in so many of the decorative arts Louis Majorelle, and other leading artists. To these names should be added those of jewellery designers such as René Lalique, book illustrators, and even poster artists.

The name of S. Bing is more closely associated with this renaissance of French furniture. Ensconced in Paris, where he was concerned with the acquisition of works of art from the Far East, he transformed his shop in the Rue de Provence into an art centre, of which the trade name of *Art Nouveau* was seized upon to designate the new style of the time. With the collaboration of Eugène Gaillard, Colonna, George de Feure, Bing amassed a collection of paintings, objets d'art, furniture and textiles for the decoration of modern interiors. In 1895, the first exhibitions of this kind, the *Salon de l'Art Nouveau*, showed furniture which brought shrieks of horror from Edmond de Goncourt who hastened to condemn 'the delirious rantings of ugliness'.

What exactly were the characteristics of *Art Nouveau* during the last decade of the century? First and foremost, a completely new type of ornament, chiefly drawn from the rich store of nature's resources using plants and flowers in sinuous curves and convolutions. These elegantly winding stalks and leaves, stylised and yet strangely naturalistic, with their undulating and interweaving tendrils, bring to mind 18th-century Rococo. The Symbolist movement, international influences and literature helped to spread the new taste, which was in fact short-lived in France, 'thirty years at most and scarcely more than ten years in places where it took on vital importance'.[16] In the year 1900, *Art Nouveau* received official sanction, in the shape of the Universal Exhibition in Paris, and the craze reached its dizziest heights.

In general, the elongated proportions of the furniture of this period are often marred by an over-rational treatment of structure; this excess of logic was the outcome of Viollet-le-Duc's principles. Furniture dating from 1800-90 does not entirely escape the old predilection for pastiche and archaeology, while that of 1890-1900 on the contrary, presents a homogeneous style and reveals a sound knowledge of carpentry. The true charm of these latter pieces lies in their imaginative originality, in sharp contrast to the preceding conceptions of design. One of the most spectacular achievements was the Castel Béranger, a block of exclusive flats, completed about 1896 by the architect Guimard, in the smart Auteuil district of Paris. The whole of this enterprise, the exterior architecture, interior decoration, furniture, lamps and bronzes, was conceived in the same unified style.

[16] Nikolaus Pevsner, Introduction to the exhibition catalogue *Les Sources du XXe siécle*, Paris, Musée National d'Art moderne, 1960-61, p. LI.

941 *Right*: Music-stand (one of a pair) of polished yoke-elm, made in Paris, 1901. This piece, by the sculptor and decorator Alexander Charpentier, has all the casual, light-hearted elegance so typical of the *Belle Epoque*. Musée des Arts Décoratifs, Paris

942 *Below*: *Guéridon* or side table, made in Paris in 1902, with trilobate top and three supports in the form of water-lilies. Mahogany and varnished tamarind with bronze gilt mounts. This characteristic work by Louis Majorelle (a friend of Emile Gallé of the Nancy School) has an imaginative freshness far removed from eclectic pieces of earlier years. Musée des Arts Décoratifs, Paris

940 *Above*: Wardrobe of carved pearwood, made in Paris, 1900. Designed by the architect-decorator Hector Guimard in the 'Modern Style', the pure and supple lines with their gentle curves are somewhat reminiscent of certain 18th-century Rococo pieces. Musée des Arts Décoratifs, Paris

The Origins of the Modern Movement

Soon after the triumph of 1900, the fervour of *Art Nouveau* abated. Although the style soon ceased to exercise its spell over the general public, it had opened new perspectives for French furniture. With the beginning of the 20th century came a period of intense experiment which was soon to lead to the modern furniture of today.

In these years a new type of patronage developed. Production was henceforth to serve the needs of two different kinds of buyer, the discerning few and the ordinary public, and it was the task of the designers to satisfy the divergent tastes of these two groups. This duality is very characteristic of the period, but it was the desire of the élite for original pieces which was ultimately to prove the more important stimulant.

An interesting development was the new link established between designers and manufacturers although the latter often persisted in clinging to facile imitations of antique furniture. A significant example of this encouraging cooperation was the appointment in 1912 of René Guilleré, founder of the *Société des Artistes Décorateurs*, to the staff of the *Grand Magasins du Printemps*, the big chain store which opened departments for furniture and modern art. Later Maurice Dufrène became attached to the *Galeries Lafayette* and Paul Follot to the *Bon Marché* store.[17]

It would be a mistake to overlook the importance of the annual and bi-annual industrial exhibitions when the work of craftsmen in wood was accorded greater respect, and a high standard in both luxury and standard furniture was encouraged. The *Société des Artistes Décorateurs*, founded in Paris in 1901, has already been mentioned. In 1903, Frantz Jourdain founded the *Salon d'Automne*, at which rooms were set apart for the attractive display of furniture in settings which successfully evoked the atmosphere of everyday life. Under the impetus of these young and dynamic movements, the public authorities were soon persuaded to lend their support by making purchases, offering prizes and, better still, by periodically refurnishing ministerial offices, embassies and even municipal buildings.

One of the most fruitful consequences of such governmental or official backing, was the organisation in Paris of an industrial exhibition of the decorative arts. Planned in 1916, but put off until 1922 on account of the First World War, the exhibition finally took place in 1925 on the banks of the Seine.

Competition from abroad also proved to have a salutary effect in fostering a sense of pride and emulation among the French cabinet-makers. In 1910, in fact, the *Salon d'Automne* made room on its stands for the vigorous craftsmen of the Munich *Werkbund*.

[17] Pierre Olmer, *Le Mobilier français d'aujourd'hui* (1910–25), Paris, 1926, p. 20.

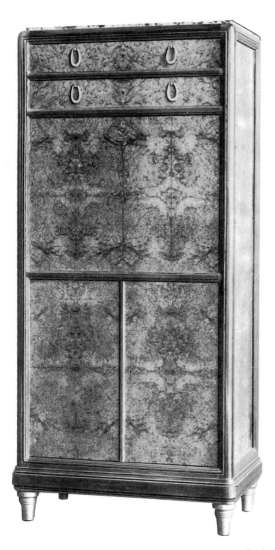

943 *Above*: Fall-front secretaire of mimosa-wood made in Paris, 1914. This piece, with its pure lines and balanced proportion, is given added value by the quality of the veneers. It is the work of Léon Jallot, one of the best cabinet-makers of the time. Musée des Arts Décoratifs, Paris

944 *Above right*: Settee exhibited at the 1911 *Salon des Artistes Décorateurs* in Paris. South-American rosewood. The restraint of the design, bold, plain outlines and balanced proportion are characteristic of this piece by Eugène Gaillard. Musée des Arts Décoratifs, Paris

945 *Right*: Dining-room in the house of Monsieur Masson in Nancy, designed by Eugène Vallin, between 1903 and 1905. The ensemble is characteristic and full of originality, reconciling the logic of constructive form with elements taken from nature. Musée de l'Ecole de Nancy

The whims of fashion continued, as always, to influence the trends in decorative art. In 1909, for example, when Diaghilev's *Ballets Russes* were performing and Léon Bakst was appearing at the Châtelet, the world of furniture and interior decoration was invaded by bright and often violent colours, reflecting the current nostalgia for the Orient. And at the instigation of the dress designer, Paul Poiret, black slate or marble slabs supported on four balls, appeared in a number of drawing rooms to serve as low tables.

At the very beginning of this 1901–16 period, when modern French design was gradually taking shape, the early pieces of furniture still reflected the 'macaroni style' of *Art Nouveau* with their heavily moulded woodwork, although admittedly they were designed by veterans of the last years of the 19th century. Among the most celebrated of these are Bellery-Desfontaines, Alexandre Charpentier, Eugène Gaillard, Hector Guimard, Georges Hoentschell, Louis Majorelle, the brothers Selmersheim and Eugène Vallin.

A sharp reaction set in after 1910. The younger cabinet-makers and furniture designers, trained by their immediate predecessors, reverted to simple lines, pure forms, and a more exact sense of proportion. Fine woods, used singly or in subtle combination, served as a pretext for simple, sober pieces of furniture, logically constructed, but carefully studied down to the slightest curve. Sometimes this stylistic simplicity can be attributed to the influence of industrial design in, say, motor cars or transatlantic liners. The new trend certainly reflects a deliberate change of artistic intention quite apart from the growing concern for middle-class informality. It is strange to remark that the rounded chairs of this period recall those of the early 19th century, particularly of Louis-Philippe and *Biedermeier*. If the plant motifs, so dear to cabinet-makers around 1900, had disappeared completely, ornamental ivory inlays, on the other hand, appear on most of the luxury furniture, for the delight of the connoisseur.

During the years 1910–16, the new generation was represented by rational and restrained designers: Maurice Dufrêne, Paul Follot, Mathieu Gallerey, André Groult, Léon Jallot, Gustave Jaulmes, Abel Landry, Henri Rapin, and the future partners Louis Süe-André Mare. To these men of differing talents, we can also add the name of Emile Ruhlmann, a sensitive cabinet-maker with a clear sense of style. Discovered in 1913, Ruhlmann attracted the interest of the élite with his pieces designed without ornamentation other than a simple moulding or a cartouche inlaid in ivory or sharkskin, making the fullest use of the beautiful surfaces of precious woods, such as Macassar ebony. Often architectural in form, his creations are nevertheless eminently functional.

Emile Ruhlmann was considered a master cabinet-maker, not only on account of his remarkable ability, but also because of the influence which he exercised over contemporary and later artists and craftsmen. He takes his place in the long line of great Parisian cabinet-makers, whose outstanding craftsmanship and high traditions, consistently maintained, have made French furniture of surpassing excellence.

941, 940
944, 942
945

943

AMERICA 1815-1918

Joseph T. Butler

Introduction

The 19th century in the United States, as in other parts of the world, was a period of rapid progress and change. The Industrial Revolution, with its accompanying improvements in transport and communication, was being fully realised by the end of the first quarter of the century. It resulted in the growth of a new furniture industry. The apprenticeship system, whereby young craftsmen had learned under the guidance of a master cabinet-maker, who was himself responsible for the finished piece and often for its original conception, was now replaced by the shop method. Workers learned to tend machines, each being allotted an impersonal mechanical task, rather than training in some time-honoured craft. Other machines were developed which could plant crops, reap them and sort out the end product.

Progress was also achieved in popular education. Rather than being the reserve of the rich, people all over the United States could read and write and books and periodicals became widely distributed. Scientific progress brought about vast improvements in the practice of medicine, and the development of new insecticides and fertilisers revolutionised the world of the farmer. The 19th century was the period of America's westward movement and the settlers carried with them the newly discovered practices of the Eastern seaboard. The East and West drew closer together as roads improved, and travel on waterways became surer and more swift. With the movement westward went ideals of democracy, for never did a century witness such progress in realising human equality.

This then, in briefest suggestion, was the climate which influenced furniture design in the United States during the 19th century. Essentially, the furniture produced during this period may be divided into two large groups. The first, and most important, is the furniture which was designed and executed under the influence of historical revivals; the second is the furniture which sought to escape from the currently fashionable revival and exhibited experimental techniques which helped to form the background to 20th-century taste.

Historical revivals occurred successively in one form or another throughout the entire 19th century and into the 20th. There was a desire not just to borrow the design motifs, but actually to reproduce furniture from different ages and cultures. From the Greek and Roman revivals at the end of the first quarter of the century through to the Oriental vogue of 1900, virtually no design vocabulary was left untouched. Sometimes the pieces were reasonable copies of an earlier form; in other instances elements were borrowed from a number of historical sources and the resulting eclectic product had little relation to the design of any specific period. The machine was a dominant factor because various ornaments could thereby be mass-produced and then combined.

The machine also encouraged the development of 'experimental' furniture, sometimes made from materials other than wood—iron, wire, horn, etc. Sometimes it incorporated a mechanical device such as a spring or it could be converted from one form into another. The one essential characteristic which all furniture in this category demonstrates is that it is outside of the mainstream of the historical revivals. This does not mean that certain elements were not influenced by current fashions. They might well be, but the piece could still be considered experimental because of some other characteristic. This, then, is the method which has been used to divide the material of this essay —the two categories mentioned above, plus a third and final section dealing with the period 1900-18.

The Historical Revivals

It was to Classical Greek and Roman antiquity that designers first turned for inspiration. In Federal furniture, Classical motifs and devices were applied to furniture forms, and while these too derived from antiquity, they were not slavish copies.

The second phase of Classical influence began in about 1810-15. It is referred to in America as the Empire style which attempted actually to reproduce in an archaeological sense the furniture of Classical Greece and Rome. New York might claim to be the first city in which this style flourished. Many French cabinet-makers migrated to New York after the French Revolution, bringing with them the design vocabulary which Percier and Fontaine had developed to adorn the apartments and palaces of the Emperor Napoleon. Such typical Greco-Roman motifs as cornucopiae, anthemion and acanthus leaves, eagles, dolphins and swans, lyres and harps, and the monopodium were the basis of this style. Actual antique furniture forms were also copied; two of the most important being the *klismos* chair, which consisted of a horizontal cresting member crowning vertical stiles and legs which flare outward in a sabre fashion, and the curule or X-shaped base for a bench or chair. Closely linked with Greco-Roman influence was that of Egypt, which resulted from Napoleon's campaign in North Africa. Egyptian motifs from this culture such as scarabs, lotus flowers and hieroglyphs all became popular.

When the French cabinet-makers arrived in New York they found one particular cabinet-maker, the Scot, Duncan Phyfe (1768-1854) well established. He was working in New York by 1795 and produced superb furniture in the Federal style for wealthy patrons. His workshop on Partition Street employed a variant of the factory method in which different craftsmen were used to carve, turn and assemble. Certainly Phyfe was the most important single name in establishing the so-called Empire style in America. His furniture in this manner was expertly made, generally of mahogany, the carving was of the highest quality, and his interpretation of elements borrowed from the English Regency was so individual that Phyfe can be credited with having evolved a highly personal style. Since Phyfe did not close his shop until 1847, his latest productions, such as Voltaire chairs, reflect the curved lines of the dawning Rococo revival. Close to Phyfe's work was that of another New York cabinet-maker, Michael Allison (active 1800-45) whose work shows strong Phyfe influence.

One of the most important French cabinet-makers was Charles-Honoré Lannuier (1779-1819) who migrated to New York in 1803. He was conversant with the French Directoire and Empire styles and produced examples strongly influenced by them. Much of the Lannuier furniture is more elaborate than Phyfe's and it is often characterised by the use of metal mounts in the French manner. These mounts were imported from France and no examples or documents have yet come to light to prove that any were made in the United States. Joseph Brauwers (active 1814-15) was another New York cabinet-maker who made use of metal mounts.

In the 18th century, there had always been a certain time lag in transmitting furniture styles from Europe to the United States. By the 19th century communications had so speeded up that in 1830 a third Classical influence was felt in America, coming this time from England rather than France. In 1828 George Smith published in London his *Cabinet-maker and Upholsterer's Guide* which was quickly imported by Americans. It contained plates showing furniture in the Greco-Roman style, with a new emphasis on massive forms which earlier Regency models did not possess.

948
951
946
947
947
948

946   *Left: Empire Parlor, c.* 1830, watercolour by Alexander Jackson Davis. Both the interior architecture and the formal, academic character of the furniture are typical of early 19th-century Classicism in America. New York Historical Society, New York City

947   *Right:* Side chair of mahogany, *c.* 1810–20, made by the New York City cabinet-maker Duncan Phyfe. The Roman *curule* or X-base was one of the Classical forms adopted by Phyfe, who also made lyre-back chairs with sabre legs. The deep seat rail ornamented with horizontal reeding is characteristic of his work. This example was made for the Pearsall family of New York. Museum of the City of New York

948   *Above:* Card table of mahogany inlaid with brass, *c.* 1815, made in New York City by Charles-Honoré Lannuier. The gilt bronze mounts were probably imported from France. The legs and winged chimera supports are painted in black and partly gilt. The table belongs to a set made for James Bosley, a Baltimore merchant, while a similar set by the same maker came from the Van Rensselaer Manor House near Albany. Maryland Historical Society

949   *Above right:* Card table of mahogany, probably made by a New York cabinet-maker. The device of the swans' necks had been earlier used by Charles-Honoré Lannuier but the legs, composed of lion paws, linked to the base by a richly carved acanthus bracket, suggest a date of about 1830. Author's Collection

950   *Right:* Wardrobe of mahogany made in New York, *c.* 1830–5. The free-standing columns support the projecting cornice which bears elaborate stencilled decoration. In general conception, the design of the piece belongs to the late Classical revival, but the panelled doors, incorporating Gothic arches, betray the advent of Victorian taste. A similar wardrobe is illustrated in an engraved advertisement published in New York in 1833 by the firm of Joseph Meeks and Sons. Museum of the City of New York

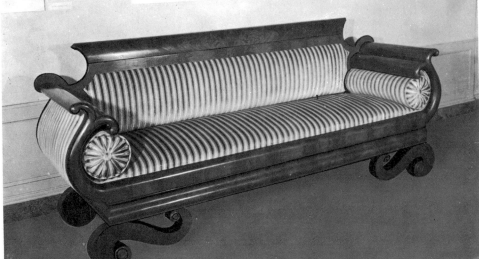

951   *Left: The Tea Party,· c.* 1820, by Henry Sargent. A typical Empire room arrangement, with centre table and seat furniture against the wall, is shown here. The furniture is closely based on French prototypes, or may even be French. Museum of Fine Arts, Boston

952   *Above:* Sofa of mahogany, *c.* 1835–40. The last or debased phase of Classicism is to be observed in this piece. Scrolls form the dominant members and the unadorned surfaces are in the tradition of French Restoration design. Lyman Allyn Museum, Connecticut

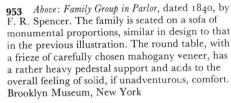

953 *Above*: *Family Group in Parlor*, dated 1840, by F. R. Spencer. The family is seated on a sofa of monumental proportions, similar in design to that in the previous illustration. The round table, with a frieze of carefully chosen mahogany veneer, has a rather heavy pedestal support and adds to the overall feeling of solid, if unadventurous, comfort. Brooklyn Museum, New York

954 *Left*: Card table of veneered mahogany *c.* 1835–45. This piece represents the final phase of the Classical revival and recalls the designs published in Baltimore by John Hall in 1840 which were included in the advertisement issued by the New York firm of Joseph Meeks and Sons in 1833. New York Historical Society, New York City

955 *Below left*: Table of pine and fruitwood, *c.* 1830–50, made at one of the Shaker communities. All superfluous ornament has been eliminated and only the basic functional members remain. The tripod base is an elegant simplification of a standard Classical type. Collection: Mr and Mrs John D. Rockefeller 3rd

956 *Below*: Side chair of hickory and maple, painted black with gilt stencilled decoration, made *c.* 1825–30, by Lambert Hitchcock at Hitchcocksville, Connecticut. Hitchcock marketed these chairs extensively all over the United States. This example bears the stencilled signature of the firm. Henry Ford Museum, Dearborn, Michigan

Generally the furniture of the period was of mahogany and it was sometimes elaborately stencilled with fruit, floral and other Classical decoration. 949

Another form, shortly after 1830, derived from French Restoration design. This is characterised by the use of scroll supports and plain, unbroken and undecorated surfaces. 'C' and 'S' scrolls began to dominate all furniture forms heralding the fourth and final phase in America—the debased Classical style. New York 950, 952 remained the first centre for the production of this furniture and 953 the firm of Joseph Meeks and Sons (1797–1868) was the leading cabinet-workshop of the day. The Meeks firm published an important advertisement in 1833 which showed 41 pieces of furniture being produced by the firm at the time. Chairs were of the Restoration gondola type; side, pier and card tables were sup- 954 ported by scrolls in varying positions; and the French Empire bed appeared, stripped of all its Classical ornament.

It was John Hall, however, who codified the furniture of this style and in 1840 in Baltimore published America's first furniture pattern-book, *The Cabinet Maker's Assistant*. The 198 plates in this book all testify to Hall's belief that the elliptical curve was the most beautiful of shapes. The scrolls which he advocated could be cut with a power saw and combined in various ways. 954 Cabinet-makers from all parts of America—from Boston to New Orleans and as far west as the Mississippi River welcomed Hall's suggestions. Veneering was one of its chief characteristics; this was generally of mahogany or walnut over a soft wood base. The last phase of Classicism was popular into the 1850s. Writing in this year, America's first great arbiter of taste, Andrew Jackson Downing (1815–52) strongly advocated this style which he called 'Grecian' in his *Architecture of Country Houses* published in New York. He also stated that it was most popular for private houses at the time.

Beginning in about 1835 and lasting into the second half of the century, came two other furniture developments which are more closely allied with the country craftsman than the urban cabinet-makers. One of these was the production of 'fancy' chairs. These were of light construction in the late Sheraton style and generally had caned or rush seats and painted decoration. The entire body of the chair was painted a plain colour and highlights were often picked out in gold with the cresting rail or centre slat painted with a landscape, figurative or floral scene. Probably the most famous American chairs of this type were produced by Lambert Hitchcock (1795–1852) at his factory in Hitchcocksville, Con- 956 necticut. The members of these chairs were machine turned and then combined on an assembly line into a finished product. They were stencilled with the name of the factory. Chairs of this type were made at many places in the Eastern United States, and they are often signed with their makers' names.

The second development which should be noted was the furniture produced by a religious sect, the Shakers. At their settlements in New England and New York they evolved a handmade type of furniture which combined stick construction with a complete elimination of all decorative detail. Their pieces were reduced to bare essentials and the result was furniture with a strong 955 ascetic feeling. The same forms, with little change, continued to be produced into the 20th century.

Returning again to the mainstream of stylistic development, it was the Gothic revival which next caught the imagination of furniture designers. This was a style which saw a great flurry of popularity in England in the 18th and 19th centuries. However, in the United States, it was infinitely more popular as an architectural style and the small amount of furniture which survives today testifies to the fact that it never really caught on. In 1850 Downing, in his *Architecture of Country Houses*, confirmed this lack of popularity, suggesting that Gothic furniture was often too elaborate although it was acceptable for use in halls or libraries.

It is probable that Gothic revival furniture first began to be made in the United States during the second quarter of the century and continued until about 1860. The design elements which distinguish it are the use of pointed arches, crockets, finials, rosettes, heraldic devices and elaborate tracery. The earliest pieces combined various of these elements into what were basically Classical forms. Because of its essentially architectural nature, 957 it is not surprising that much of the best furniture was designed by architects. Alexander J. Davis was one of the most successful

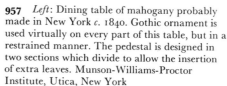

957 *Left*: Dining table of mahogany probably made in New York *c.* 1840. Gothic ornament is used virtually on every part of this table, but in a restrained manner. The pedestal is designed in two sections which divide to allow the insertion of extra leaves. Munson-Williams-Proctor Institute, Utica, New York

958 *Right*: Side chair of rosewood and mahogany made in New York *c.* 1845. The features of the Elizabethan revival which resulted in strangely eclectic pieces inspired by late 17th-century rather than 16th-century examples, included turned stiles and front legs. The centre panel is elaborately carved in a manner which remotely suggests an emasculated version of a Daniel Marot design. The needlework seat cover is original. Museum of the City of New York

959 *Far left*: *Portrait of Nicholas Longworth Ward as a Child*, 1858, by Lilly Martin Spencer. The child stands before a high-backed chair which has turned stiles and carving on the cresting characteristic of the Elizabethan revival. It is similar in form to the chair in the previous illustration. Newark Museum, Newark, New Jersey, Marcus L. Ward Bequest

960 *Left*: Sewing table made of poplar, painted black, with decorative scrolls and birds in gold and flower sprays in polychrome. New York *c.* 1850. Cottage furniture of this type was considered by A. J. Downing in his *Architecture of Country Houses* (1850) to be highly suitable for rural surroundings. Author's Collection

of these and many of his designs were executed by Richard Byrnes of White Plains, New York. John Jelliff of Newark, New Jersey also produced much successful furniture in this style. The most common surviving pieces in this manner are chairs, cabinet pieces and beds.

Another style which enjoyed limited popularity from about 1830 until 1860 was called Elizabethan by contemporary writers, although the design elements were borrowed from the reigns of Charles I and II, rather than from that of Queen Elizabeth. The most common example was the high-backed or *prie-dieu* chair which usually had spiral stiles in the Baroque manner with elaborately carved back panels. The low seats were often covered in fine needlework, also sometimes incorporating elements from Carolean design. Downing illustrates three chairs of this type.

Closely allied with the Elizabethan revival was the mass-produced furniture which enjoyed wide popularity in the United States. This was known as cottage furniture and its use was highly recommended by Downing because of its beauty, simplicity and low cost. Many bedroom suites of this type were produced. They were of soft wood, painted a flat colour, and often decorated with floral motifs. Features from the repertoire of 17th-century ornament were included; split spindles were applied to the front of cabinet pieces and ball-and-spool turning was used in the supports of tables. Turned furniture of this type is popularly called after the famous Swedish singer, Jenny Lind. Cottage furniture was the

only manifestation of Elizabethan which enjoyed considerable vogue in the United States.

The one style which dominated all others in importance and popularity at the middle of the century was the Rococo. It was first revived in English pattern-books of the 1830s and was certainly transplanted to America by 1845. It looked back to the court of Louis XV, borrowing the cabriole leg, 'S' scroll, shell carving, and asymmetrical ornament. One difference in interpretation between the cabriole leg of the 18th and 19th centuries is that the rear legs on a chair of the latter date were generally shaped in a round reverse curve with chamfered sides rather than the true cabriole form. Naturalistic carving on the furniture frame was much heavier than in the 18th century, with human figures, birds, flowers and fruit upon the cresting.

This style was mass-produced more than any other in America. Carved ornament was machine-produced and applied to the frame, often with little consideration to the overall effect. Known as 'Antique French' it was greatly favoured by Downing because of its lightness of form, and he suggested that it was suitable for use in boudoirs and parlours.

While ordinary Rococo revival furniture was being widely produced throughout the country, one man above all stood out in New York City as the leading exponent of the style—John Henry Belter (1804–63). Because of the technical innovations which he introduced, it would be possible to include Belter in the

958, 959

960

961

961 *Right*: Slipper chair made of laminated rosewood by John Henry Belter in New York City *c.* 1855-60. The back, which is composed of Rococo scrolls and naturalistic carving, illustrates the virtuosity of this craftsman whose invention it was to use laminated wood. Author's Collection

962 *Below*: Sofa made of laminated rosewood in New York City *c.* 1850-60 by John Henry Belter. This piece is part of a set. The Renaissance pediment is separate and is applied to the centre of the cresting rail. Metropolitan Museum of Art, Gift of Mr and Mrs Lowell Ross Burch and Miss Jean McLean Morron, 1951

963 *Below right*: Card table of rosewood made in New York City *c.* 1850-5 by Charles A. Baudouine. One of a pair which can be fitted together to create, as the original bill describes it, a 'multiform-table'. The handling of the C scrolls which form the legs of this piece suggests a much better understanding of 18th-century form and proportion than was usual among 19th-century New-Rococo designers. Munson-Williams-Proctor Institute, Utica, New York

second section of this essay, but since his creations are essentially concerned with graceful interpretations of the Rococo style, it seems best to include him here. Belter was born in Würtemberg, Germany, where he received training as a cabinet-maker; he migrated to the United States and is known to have been working in New York in 1844. He replaced Phyfe as the city's most fashionable cabinet-maker.

Belter's furniture is distinguished by its delicate, lacy, naturalistic carving which could only be achieved by using laminated panels. The process which he eventually patented, involved glueing together layers of wood, one-sixteenth of an inch thick in such a way that the grain of one layer ran in an opposite direction to that of the next. The panels varied in number from six to eight, and in exceptional pieces from three to sixteen. Belter then steamed these panels in moulds so that they could be bent into any desired shape. Rosewood was the favourite material, although oak and ebonised hardwood were also used. When particularly elaborate ornament was required, it was carved from solid pieces of hardwood and applied to the frame. The earliest pieces of Belter furniture with their free, curving outlines evoke the manner of Louis XV. As his style developed in the late 40s and 50s, it became more taut, drawing upon elements from other design vocabularies such as those of Louis XIV and Louis XVI. In his final period, he preferred to borrow from Renaissance sources. The intricate carving of some of his pieces places them among the

most elaborate produced in the United States. While the ornament sometimes becomes depressing, the quality of the craftsmanship is undeniable.

Although Belter patented his processes of laminating and steaming, there were other craftsmen in the middle of the century who made furniture with only slight variations which escaped the restrictions of patent law. In New York, Charles A. Baudoine ran a vertical seam through the centre of his laminated panels, but his work closely resembles Belter's. In Philadelphia, George Henkels used similar devices in laminated furniture. Some other important cabinet-makers who worked in the Rococo idiom were the Meeks Brothers, previously mentioned, Leon Marcotte and Gustave Herter in New York, S. S. Johns in Cincinnati, Ohio, and François Seignoret and Prudent Mallard in New Orleans, Louisiana. Two of the important innovations in furniture forms at this time were the balloon-back chair and triple crested sofa. The side chair backs looked literally like old-fashioned balloons and when three of these were placed side by side and upholstered over, they produced a sofa with three cresting pieces.

Another style which developed simultaneously with the Rococo, but did not share its popularity, was the Louis XIV. This style was massive and heavy and was most commonly used for cupboards. Elements were borrowed from Baroque design, and the broken pediment, free-standing heroic figures and geometric detail were its characteristic features. The exhibits at the Exhibition of 1851 at the Crystal Palace and the New York Exposition of 1853 showed many examples, but generally only cabinet pieces were made in this style and little survives today.

By the 1860s novelty seemed to reign supreme. There had been a certain amount of eclecticism earlier in the century but now the design elements became confused. While some new revivals did evolve during the last forty years of the century, they were generally fanciful rather than academic. One of the most important revivals which was highly popular in 1865 was the Louis XVI. This style had been popular in France in the 1850s and would appear to have been as pronounced there and in the United States as it was in England. Although the design vocabulary was borrowed from 18th-century French sources, the resulting product was generally heavier and more squat than its prototype. Oval backs, round tapering legs, straight stiles, and arm supports were all included. Delicate medallions and bows were inlaid with holly, ebony and mother-of-pearl; some pieces were even inlaid with painted porcelain plaques. Mahogany was the favourite wood and it was sometimes ebonised and picked out in gilt. Many of the cabinet-makers previously mentioned as working in the Rococo revival style now adopted the Louis XVI as it became popular. These included Jelliff of Newark and Henkels of Philadelphia, and the Herter Brothers, the Sypher firm, Marcotte, and Thomas Brooks in New York City. In one form or another, it was a popular style until the end of the century and late pieces from the 90s were often made of light walnut and bore a close resemblance to French prototypes.

Cabinet-makers began to turn to the Renaissance for inspiration in the 1860s. A style known as the 'French Renaissance' was mentioned by Downing in the 1850s but it was not dominant until ten years later. The broken pediment, acorn turning, applied medallions and busts, and tapering baluster legs were all important ingredients. Walnut was the favourite wood and large burled panels were used to contrast with the light brown background colour. Marcotte and G. Hunzinger were the chief exponents of the style in New York, although it was in Grand Rapids, Michigan that the greatest quantities of this furniture were produced from the 70s until the end of the century. Grand Rapids bedroom suites are characterised by a particularly gloomy grandeur.

During the 1870s the craze for the antique struck America and collecting became a preoccupation of even the ordinary household. An indiscriminate combination of objects from many cultures and eras was displayed. Along with the collecting craze came an interest in America's colonial past and after the Philadelphia Centennial Exposition of 1876, a large number of reproductions of American furniture of the 18th century began to be made. Although many of the reproduced pieces were extremely well made, it is generally easy to distinguish them from their prototypes through differences in proportion, detail and construction.

Orientalism became a dominant note in the 80s and 90s. Near Eastern objects, as well as those from China and Japan were chosen for smoking rooms. The 'Turkish corner' became an important feature even of modest households. This was an arrangement of pillows, Oriental rugs and usually a divan, set in a corner of a room, often under a tent-like canopy; potted plants and exotic Oriental accessories completed the picture. It was only natural that furniture should be designed for use in these rooms. Furniture of the Moorish or 'Saracenic' type, as it was called, was completely dominated by the art of the upholsterer. Generally no wooden member was visible and an elaborate arrangement of coil springs (to be treated later) was covered by upholstery which was tufted, deeply fringed and tasselled.

By the end of the century eclecticism reigned supreme. The exhibits of the Chicago Columbian Exposition (1893) provide an interesting commentary on taste. Elements from different sources were now so indiscriminately combined that it was sometimes impossible to determine what the designer's original intention might have been. Furniture was so elaborate that every surface was often covered with ornament, drawn from dissimilar sources. Any idea of an archaeologically sound restatement of an earlier form, which had been common in the early part of the century, had now been lost.

965
966
967
968
969
970
971

964 *Above*: The Thomas Cole room at the Munson-Williams-Proctor Institute. On the right can be seen a mahogany armchair painted white and gilt. It is covered in a red silk damask, a reproduction of the original upholstery, and the sumptuous, padded luxury is a typical aspect of mid-19th-century taste. New York *c.* 1845. The side chair *en suite* is of the balloon type, most popular in the United States between 1870 and 1898. The chairs and the piano, part of a large parlour set which includes a centre table and a sofa, were designed by Richard Upjohn for the Robert Kelly house in New York City. The paintings on the right-hand wall illustrating the 'Voyage of Life', are by Thomas Cole.

965 *Left*: Armchair of ebonised mahogany, with gilt decoration, made in New York *c.* 1875. This Louis XVI revival piece shows how heavy the 19th-century interpretation of the late 18th-century style could sometimes be. Museum of the City of New York

966 *Below*: *Portrait of Lucy Hopper in her Paris Apartment*, 1876 by Edward Lamson Henry. Borrowings from the vocabulary of French Louis XVI design can be seen in the chairs shown. The cluttered and gloomy aspect of the room is typical of the 1870s. Newark Museum, New Jersey, Purchase, 1959, Wallace M. Scudder Bequest

967 *Above left*: Sideboard of walnut made in Philadelphia *c*. 1870 by Daniel Pabst. The top is of marble. This heavy piece, resting on a plinth, includes applied carving of leaves and flowers, treated naturalistically, and also Renaissance motifs such as scrolling brackets, bosses, urns and strapwork Philadelphia Museum of Art

969 *Left*: *Not at Home*, *c*. 1890, by Jonathan Eastman Johnson. Eclecticism has reached its height in this interior. In the hall is an 18th-century tall clock while through the archway, the decorative frieze running round the walls suggests an Oriental mood, reinforced by the casual use of loose textile coverings. The armchair and stool are both in the so-called Renaissance style, while the newel post has Tudor features. Brooklyn Museum, New York

968 *Above*: Walnut bed, part of a bedroom suite made by the Berkey and Gay Company of Grand Rapids, Michigan, *c*. 1876. The ponderous quality of this piece, with the tall headboard surmounted by a broken pediment, is typical of the Renaissance revival style. This set was probably exhibited at the 1876 Centennial Exposition in Philadelphia. Grand Rapids Public Museum

971 *Below*: *In the Studio*, *c*. 1880, by William Merritt Chase. This studio is furnished with pieces deriving from very different origins. The artist's 'props' include a collection of antiques, while the large oak press cupboard was probably one of those many pieces which were made up at the time, often partly out of authentic elements, to satisfy contemporary demand. Brooklyn Museum, New York

970 *Below left*: Smoking room in the Turkish style from the John D. Rockefeller house on West 53rd Street in New York City, *c*. 1880. This is one of the most complete interiors in the so-called Saracenic or Turkish taste to survive. Brooklyn Museum, New York

972

972 *Left*: Cast-iron garden seat stamped E. T. Barnum, Detroit, Michigan, *c*. 1885. Cast-iron furniture, particularly for outdoor use or for halls had been produced in England since the beginning of Queen Victoria's reign and was also made in America before the middle of the century. This example, with its scrolling vine leaves and grapes recalls John Henry Belter's frequent use of the same motif in his laminated furniture of the 1850s. Henry Ford Museum, Dearborn, Michigan

973 *Right*: Side chair of papier mâché painted black and gold and inlaid with mother-of-pearl, probably made in England *c*. 1850. Papier mâché chairs were popular in America although little is known about their manufacture. This example unexpectedly and doubtless fortuitously, recalls Oriental lacquer chairs or their English copies of the late 17th century. Museum of the City of New York

974 *Far left*: Rocking chair with a strap metal frame painted to imitate tortoiseshell. Traditionally thought to have been made by Peter Cooper at his iron foundry at Trenton, New Jersey, *c*. 1860–70. Stylistically this chair follows its English and French prototypes. A rocking chair in tube metal was, in fact, shown by an English maker, R. W. Winfield, at the Great Exhibition of 1851. Cooper Union Museum, New York

975 *Left*: Garden chair made of twisted wire and iron, *c*. 1870. The back is in a restrained variant of the balloon form while the profusion of Rococo scrolls lends it an airy lightness. Author's Collection

Furniture using new techniques

In addition to producing the profusion of carved ornament which so typified the eclectic taste of the end of the century, the machine was also assisting craftsmen in producing furniture of a highly original and experimental type. This has been seen in the innovations of John Henry Belter.

Closely linked with the work of Belter was that of the Austrian, Michael Thonet (1796–1871). By 1840 he was experimenting with lamination and bending by steam and by 1850 he had perfected a method for bending birch rods into fanciful shapes. The furniture made from this was known as bentwood and the curvilinear shapes generally followed the Rococo tradition. This furniture was shipped in pieces and was then screwed together. Although primarily a European product, bentwood was imported in great quantities into the United States and it found its imitators there as well.

Another new material which was primarily European but was used in great quantity in America was papier mâché. Improvements in pressing and moulding machinery made it possible to create furniture from this substance by 1850. Papier mâché is made from paper pulp or strips of paper which are forced to-

973

gether under great pressure; the resultant product is durable if it is kept free from damp. The surfaces were covered with coats of lacquer and further decorated with gilt and polychrome painting, often with inlays of mother-of-pearl. England and France were the great centres for the manufacture of this ware, but it was started in a small way in the United States at Litchfield, Connecticut.

Metal was another material which served far-sighted designers in the creation of experimental furniture. The iron industry made rapid advances during the first half of the century and casting processes were greatly improved. Now castings of a much larger size could be achieved and it was possible to make whole components of furniture in one piece. These elements were assembled with braces and screws. The centres of the iron industry were Boston, New York and Baltimore although a number of foundries began to open up in the Mid-West.

From iron to wire. New machinery gave a great impetus to this industry and small, delicate pieces of furniture were manufactured from wire. As with the cast iron, this furniture was primarily intended for outdoor use. Although the designs often reflect the Rococo idiom, they have great charm and originality.

Hollow metal tubing was also used for making furniture. It had been used in England as early as the 1830s and by the 1840s similar examples were being produced in France. The most popular of these was a rocking chair which generally had a sling

972

975

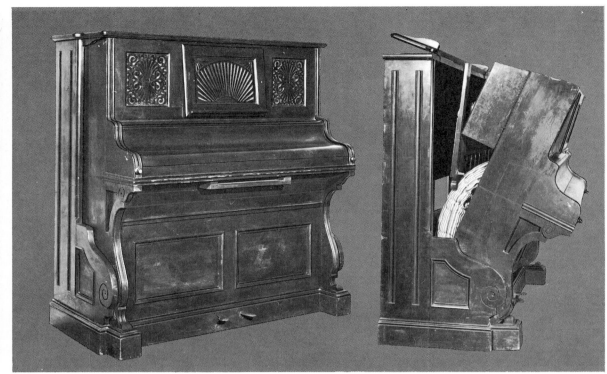

976, 977 *Far left and left*: The piano-bed was one of the most curious of all late 19th-century furniture forms. This example was made *c.* 1870 and the cabinet is so well made that it might be taken for an actual piano. The top lifts, the front falls, and a bed extends forth. Collection: Miss Elinor Merrell

978 *Below left*: Turkish frame chair of which the back, arms and seat are internally sprung by means of spiral coils. This example, which was made *c.* 1880 indicates the growing importance of the upholsterer. Collection: Miss Elinor Merrell

979 *Below centre*: Centripetal spring chair possibly made by the American Chair Company, Troy, New York, *c.* 1850. The back is of metal elaborately painted. The base is of cast-iron. A spring is concealed under the seat which allows the chair to recline and then snap back into place. Collection: Miss Elinor Merrell

980 *Below*: Chair of antlers made in the second half of the 19th century. The antlers have been carefully chosen so that they naturally follow the shape of the chair. Such furniture was very popular, especially during the last quarter of the 19th century. Collection: Miss Elinor Merrell

seat of cloth or carpet. A unique American variant of this survives in a rocking chair which is believed to have been made by the industrialist and philanthropist Peter Cooper.

Probably the most unusual pieces of furniture of all, however, were those which used some mechanical device in their construction. The United States Patent Office records reveal that thousands of patents were taken out between the 1860s and the end of the century. Some contained movable parts so that a chair could convert into a bed with several intermediary stages for sitting and reclining. One of the most curious was a piano-bed, a cabinet closely resembling a piano which could be opened and a bed extended from it.

One of the greatest innovations of the century was the perfection of the metal coil spring. When springs could be combined into a frame which was then upholstered over, it produced an infinitely more comfortable seat then the padding which had been used for so many hundreds of years. With coil springs, the Turkish frame chair was developed. The whole frame of these chairs was of metal except for the four legs and a connecting member which were generally wood. The entire piece was elaborately upholstered, with tufting and fringes a dominant feature. Centripetal spring chairs were popular in the 1850s and 60s. An example made by the American chair Company of Troy, New York was one of the few American pieces illustrated in the catalogue of the Crystal Palace Exhibition. These chairs combined a heavy metal spring into their bases under the seat. This allowed the chair to recline with pressure from the sitter's back, and then to snap back into place. The spring chair was the forerunner of the typewriter chair.

A final category of furniture which broke new ground, and was especially popular during the century was that made from natural organic materials. Pieces of this type were generally made for country houses and were often intended for outdoor use. The simplest was furniture made from the branches or roots of trees. The elements were combined in such a way that they fitted the contour of a piece of furniture and were then nailed together. Many have a highly grotesque appearance. Rattan or cane was imported into the United States from the East Indies in great quantity and made up in all the large cities along the Eastern seaboard. The rattan was woven around a wooden frame and the results were often quite fanciful and elaborate. Bamboo was also used and was made into furniture which had a light, delicate appearance. Probably the most fantastic of all was the furniture made from animal horns. The exploration and settlement of the west aroused great interest in the animals to be found there, so furniture made from horns became popular. As with natural wood, the horns were studied to see how they would best conform to the outline of the desired piece. Thus, new materials, along with improved technical processes and mechanical ingenuity, all helped to develop new forms of 19th-century furniture.

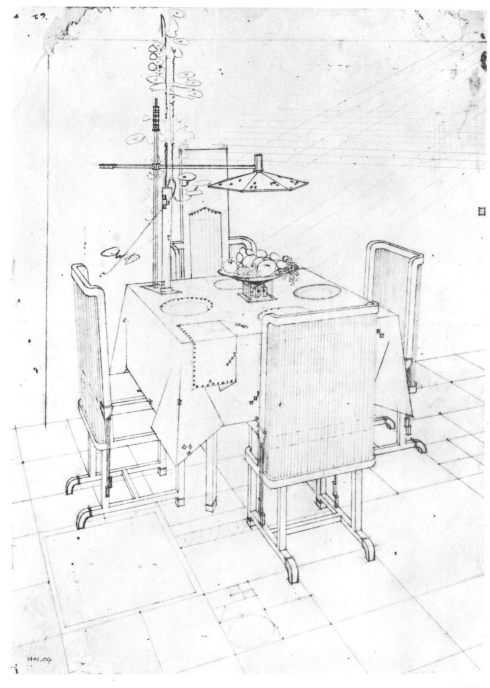

Furniture Design 1900-18

In general, it might be said that the spirit of eclecticism prevailed throughout the first eighteen years of the 20th century. Much cheap and shoddy furniture was produced which had wide popular appeal. There were, however, a few designers who produced furniture of merit during the period.

The English Arts and Crafts Movement had been taken up in the United States at the end of the 19th century. This movement advocated the return to the skills of the craftsman and an honest use of materials. One of America's chief advocates was Elbert Hubbard (1856-1915) who established a community of craftsmen at East Aurora, New York. In addition to printing and binding, his group also designed and made furniture. These pieces, mostly made about 1900, were of a simple, massive nature, generally rectilinear and unadorned. Hubbard was not alone, for groups of craftsmen were active in a number of other places in the East.

The furniture produced by great architects at the end of the 19th century had an influence on the early years of the 20th. Stanford White (1853-1906) is a good example. A great advocate of 'the grandeur of Europe', White designed furniture which was based upon European prototypes.

One name above all stands out, however. Frank Lloyd Wright's furniture was designed to be an integral part of the surrounding architecture—it was to blend with it rather than stand out from it. From his metal chair for the Larkin Building at Buffalo, New York, of 1904, to his wooden frame chair of the following year or his chair and table for the Midway Gardens at Chicago, Illinois of 1914, Wright always reveals himself as a master innovator. His reduction of the elements of furniture to their bare essentials, anticipates the direction which furniture design was to take in the later years of the 20th century.

981
982
983

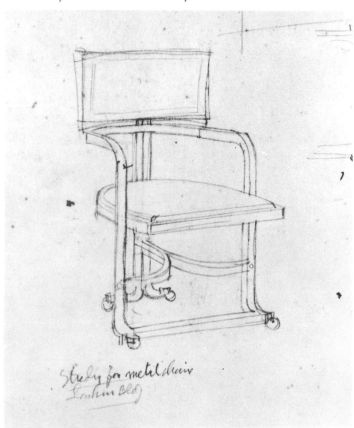

981 *Above*: Design for a table and chairs by Frank Lloyd Wright for the Midway Gardens at Chicago, Illinois, 1914. The furniture in this drawing becomes an integral part of the architectural setting. Reproduced from *The Drawings of Frank Lloyd Wright*, Horizon Press, New York, 1962

982 *Left*: Design for a metal chair by Frank Lloyd Wright for the Larkin Building in Buffalo, New York, 1904. Wright here evolves a form which, with variations, has since become standard. Reproduced from *The Drawings of Frank Lloyd Wright*, Horizon Press, New York, 1962

983 *Right*: Designs for a wooden chair by Frank Lloyd Wright executed in 1905. Here the basic form is reduced to a cube. Reproduced from *The Drawings of Frank Lloyd Wright*, Horizon Press, New York, 1962

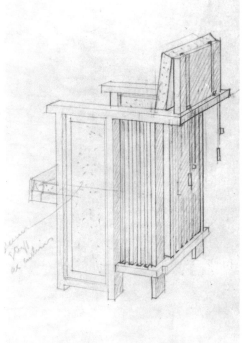

GERMANY

P. W. Meister

The Empire style quickly spread beyond the frontiers of France to the German territories and, indeed, throughout Europe. Developing from the Classicism of Louis XVI, the new style achieved an air of academic formality in shedding any sense of feminine elegance and concentrating upon severe lines and often somewhat heavy forms. The use of dark woods, usually mahogany, contrasting, in the case of Court furniture, with gilt bronze mounts, stressed the sombre aspect of the pieces. Late 18th-century types of furniture survived, modified in shape and decoration to reflect the intellectual excitement aroused by a more exact knowledge of the ancient Greek world. The only piece which was new in conception was the *psyché*, or cheval-glass, already a fashionable novelty in France and adopted with equal enthusiasm in Germany.

In the early 19th century many State rooms in the great German palaces were re-furnished. For the Würzburg Residenz, for example Johann Valentin Raab provided furniture which was less severe in manner than that of contemporary Parisian cabinet-makers and gave more prominence to carved and gilt decorative features. For the Berlin palaces David Roentgen provided superb pieces in the Empire style, richly ornamented with his characteristic fluting. In Vienna, on the other hand, cabinet-makers favoured the use of finely cast and chased gilt bronze mounts. Johann Haertl was among those who were to develop original types of writing-cabinet, such as the lyre-shaped cabinet and the round secretaire, based upon the form of a Classical temple. But neither of these were to outlast the period.

The Empire style itself barely survived the last years of Imperial power. The war had impoverished the middle classes, and building for the Courts in general was brought to a standstill; simple and practical furniture was all that was demanded. From the severe contours of Empire furniture a more relaxed and intimate middle-class style was evolved, known by the name of *Biedermeier*.

Deriving from Classical example, it suited in form, proportion and in reticence of decoration, the modest size and unostentatious needs of comfortable bourgeois houses. Plain surfaces and neat contours were sought after and there were few gilt bronze mounts. This accent on practical requirements lent more importance to seat furniture, and rather less to those pieces which were decorative rather than functional in purpose. Even in the rooms of the well-to-do middle classes, the furniture was sparse and limited in type. The deep, rectangular sofa with high back and ends, supported on straight or sabre legs, was a dominant item. Sometimes, in place of legs, the sofa support consisted of a solid base carved at the ends in the form of scrolls. The greater concern for usefulness and comfort encouraged a less formal arrangement of rooms. A round table was often placed in front of the sofa and chairs were set about it. Indeed, the presence of a niche, into which a sofa of curved shape could be fitted, was a convenient means of avoiding rigid angularity. Deep armchairs, a lighter type of armchair and chairs with simple pierced backs, were used *en suite*, the opulent upholstery revealing a new appreciation of informal ease. Textile coverings included plain or striped velvets or silks to match the wall hangings. Long mirrors, reaching from the floor to the ceiling, reflected the unassuming, almost casually arranged rooms, in which a piano had become a familiar feature. China cabinets had their place in this atmosphere of practical well-being and many varieties of work table, while writing tables, cabinets and secretaires were essential to an age so devoted to letter-writing and the keeping of journals. As a centre of middle-class affluence, Vienna supported large numbers of cabinet-makers. But the factory of Josef Danhauser was the most important concern. Capable of producing every type of furnishing, it flourished from 1804 until the death of Danhauser in 1830. The younger Josef Danhauser then succeeded his father, but he was ultimately to devote himself exclusively to his career as a painter and the factory went into liquidation in 1838. Only

984, 985 Two mahogany chairs, *c.* 1800, North Germany. The influence of English late 18th-century designs is clear in these plain, square-backed examples. Museum für Kunsthandwerk, Frankfurt-am-Main

986 Round table of citrus wood, with silver mounts, resting on a central support composed of three swans rising from a scrolled base. The table belongs to a suite of furniture ordered from Johann Valentin Raab for the rooms in the Würzburg Residenz furnished between 1808 and 1812 for the use of the Grand Duke Ferdinand of Tuscany.

987 *Above*: Mahogany table with gilt bronze mounts, the top of semi-precious stone, *c.* 1800, Vienna. The quality of the bronzes and the neat elegance of the table, with the legs set at the canted corners, are typical of the Viennese Empire style. Museum für Kunsthandwerk, Frankfurt-am-Main

988 *Above right*: Watercolour by Johann Erdmann Hummel (1769-1852), Berlin, *c.* 1820-5, showing an interior in the *Biedermeier* style, the sparsely furnished room containing furniture of prim, almost rigid simplicity. Museum für Kunsthandwerk, Frankfurt-am-Main

989 *Right*: This suite of furniture was designed by the Hamburg architect, Alexis de Chateauneuf (1799-1853), for a house he built in the *Neuer Jungfernstieg* in Hamburg *(Abendrotsches Haus)* in 1835. The room and its furnishings are now in the Hamburg Museum für Kunst und Gewerbe.

in Berlin was a great artistic personality at work; through his buildings, as well as through his designs for furniture and interiors for the royal palaces, Karl Friedrich Schinkel changed the appearance of the city and of fashionable furniture. He was, in fact, the creator of the Prussian Neo-Classical style. Combining aesthetic and functional needs, his pieces included Classical and Gothic features and were more original and interesting than any other German furniture of the period.

Leo von Klenze, previously Court architect in Kassel to King Jerome, worked in Munich, whence he came in 1816 at the invitation of Ludwig I of Bavaria. As an architect he made an important contribution. But he also designed interiors and furniture. Partly influenced by Percier and Fontaine, these reflect a romantic delight both in Greek architecture and decoration, and in Italian Renaissance features. North German furniture in the *Biedermeier* style closely resembles English furniture of the early 19th century and is elegant and simple. Almost always of dark mahogany, it was upholstered in black horsehair. In the West and the South light coloured fruit-woods, especially cherry, were favoured and outlines were accentuated by inlay of ebony or ebonised fruit-wood.

The *Biedermeier* style could so easily have led to a functional style had other influences not been at work. But, alas, Romanticism re-discovered the German Middle Ages and the Gothic world and its effects were naturally reflected in architecture and furniture design. 'Gothic' furniture, ornamented with Gothic architectural forms, in contrast to the simply shaped *Biedermeier* furniture, already anticipated the calamity of historicism.

The so-called 'Second Rococo' period found bold expression in terms of furniture styles in Germany and Austria in the mid-19th century. The revived Rococo style was widespread in Vienna. The first signs appeared in 1835 and after 1840 the earlier *Biedermeier* simplicity had vanished in favour of curving forms in imitation of French example. The new fashion from France found ready acceptance in conservative Vienna where the mid-18th-century traditions had never wholly faded. In Vienna itself the Court and the nobility led the way in approving a luscious display of Rococo revivalism. The Liechtenstein palace was re-decorated between 1842 and 1847 in this manner by the firm of Carl Leistler and Son who were to receive praise for their exhibits at the Great Exhibition in London in 1851. When in the years 1840-50 voices were raised deploring false romanticism

and the misplaced historical styles, no heed was taken. After 1871, the nouveau-riche middle classes in all the German territories no longer demanded well-designed furniture, but sought 'Renaissance' and 'Baroque' pieces, which were now being mass-produced at prices to suit every purse.

Only in the last decade of the 19th century under the stimulus of England, France and Belgium was there any attempt in Germany to free furniture from spurious 'antique' styles. Among a group of Munich artists, Hermann Obrist (1863-1927) produced designs for embroidery, dating from 1893, already expressing the mood of Art Nouveau, while in the following years art exhibitions stimulated in Germany an individual reaction to this positive, yet languid style. The Munich circle included August Endell (1871-1925), whose façade of the Elvira Photographic Studio of 1897-8 was revolutionary in its use of abstract ornament. Endell's furniture was both of traditional materials, such as elm, and also of forged steel. In the meantime, the Belgian artist Henri van de Velde, had exhibited his work in Dresden in 1897. The poor reception his achievements had earned in Brussels encouraged him to settle in Germany in 1899 where he practised as an architect and designer. For a time he was Professor at the School of Decorative Arts at Weimar and was artistic adviser to Wilhelm Ernst, Grand Duke of Saxe-Weimar. Depending upon form rather than ornament, van de Velde's furniture reflects the influence of the English Arts and Crafts Movement, the sweeping lines uniting his pieces into one continuous flow.

The reaction to the use of sinuous curves and floral motifs, from which Art Nouveau had first derived its strength, occurred in Vienna. Otto Wagner (1841-1918), Olbrich (1867-1908) and ultimately Josef Hoffmann (1870-1955) all declared their faith in functionalism. Although Hoffmann himself was not wholly opposed to ornament, his Palais Stoclet at Brussels demonstrates the use of bold verticals and horizontals. Hoffmann was one of the founders of the *Wiener Werkstätte* in 1903, an organisation for the production and sale of works of art for the people. A similar undertaking, the *Deutsche Werkstätte* at Hellerau near Dresden was also working in the first years of the century on the production of inexpensive furniture. In 1906 it was Richard Riemerschmid whose energy encouraged the manufacture of well-designed machine-made furniture, where the real problem of combining art and industry was boldly faced.

992

994

993, 996

1022

995

990   *Far left*: Lady's worktable of spherical shape, veneered with rosewood, shown with the lid open. The border is inlaid with signs of the Zodiac. In the *Biedermeier* period in Vienna fashionable taste demanded unusual shapes and fine craftsmanship. Collection: Dr Walter Formanek, Vienna

991   *Left*: Secretaire veneered with mahogany, with gilt bronze mounts, *c.* 1820. This piece with its monumental simplicity and broad, plain surfaces, made for the palace of Charlottenburg, Berlin, still echoes the grandeur of the Empire period.

992   *Below*: Bed, veneered with pearwood, designed by Friedrich Schinkel for the bedroom of Queen Louise in the palace of Charlottenburg, Berlin. Schinkel (1781–1841) was the most important German architect of the Romantic period. In his furniture designs he developed a personal style in which elegance was combined with functional needs.

993   *Left*: Bookcase designed by August Endell *c.* 1895. The seaweed-like forms recall the fantastic red and turquoise stucco ornament Endell used on the façade of the Maison Elvira at Munich.

994   *Right*: Engraving of a bookcase made of carved limewood with panels of satinwood, designed and manufactured by the firm of M. Leistler of Vienna and exhibited at the Great Exhibition of 1851 in London.

995   *Below*: Study in the Palais Stoclet, Brussels, designed by the Viennese architect, Josef Hoffman between 1905–11. Hoffmann had founded the *Wiener Werkstätte* in 1903 and this room illustrates his theories, which sought to combine pure form with functional needs, rejecting the languid and decorative lines of Art Nouveau. He adhered, nevertheless, to the Art Nouveau principle of unity of design in architecture, interiors and furniture.

996   *Below*: Elm washstand designed by August Endell *c.* 1899. All superfluous ornament has been eliminated and the bold proportions and plain lines, combined with a respect for the natural grain of the wood, bring to mind the spirit of Chinese cabinet-making of the Ming period.

SCANDINAVIA

Peter Thornton

The Scandinavian countries had enjoyed almost continual peace and considerable prosperity during the second half of the 18th century, but the wars waged by the French revolutionary forces and then by Napoleon were to change all that. The extensive and profitable sea-borne trade which Sweden and Denmark-Norway had built up during the century was first severely reduced by the loss of foreign markets, denied to them by one or other of the combatants, and was then almost stifled by the English blockade of the Continental ports, as this became increasingly effective. Incensed by the frequent searches to which their ships were being submitted by the navies of the combating powers, the Danes and the Swedes joined with Russia in a pact of armed neutrality designed to protect their shipping, by means of naval action, from these continual frustrations. England, whose naval forces were already at full stretch, could not afford to allow this alliance to develop. In the year 1801 the British fleet swept down the Sound and destroyed a large part of the Danish fleet at anchor in the Roads off Copenhagen. Denmark would still have preferred to remain neutral. But six years later, as her intentions were unclear, the British Government, fearing that Denmark with her still potent fleet would join France, issued an ultimatum, to which no satisfactory answer was given. The resulting bombardment and destruction of a large part of Copenhagen and the neutralisation of the Danish fleet were harsh but effective measures which ensured that Denmark and the other Scandinavian countries remained on the touchlines of the long drawn-out conflict between England and France. Understandably, these episodes gave rise to a great deal of animosity towards the British. All these misfortunes, moreover, were instrumental in bringing the Danish-Norwegian economy to such a pass that the State went bankrupt in 1813.

The Swedes suffered less. They had taken heed of the treatment meted out to Denmark and stayed clear of any actual alliances with France. However, ruling circles in Sweden remained on the whole sympathetic to France, and when the Swedes found themselves without a suitable heir to the throne, they invited one of Napoleon's marshals to become Crown Prince, thus establishing the Bernadotte dynasty which still rules Sweden today. In spite of this, Sweden now joined England and the Allies and was rewarded by being given suzerainty over Norway which, under the peace treaty, Denmark was forced to cede as a punishment for the part she had played in the war.

Contact with the outside world, and particularly with England, had become difficult during the long period of hostilities, and English influence thus waned, although the sturdy simplicity which characterises English 18th-century furniture was still reflected in much middle-class Scandinavian furniture for several decades. Bulky furniture was of course one of the first things that ceased to reach Scandinavia from England; small wares continued to come in for rather longer. 'One day we may well be able to do without English gloves, English silk stockings and English shoes, just as we have become increasingly able to do

997 Typical Danish Empire commode of about 1810-15. This still echoes the form of commodes like that shown in illustration 659. The flanking columns have been eliminated (they are occasionally found on more ambitious pieces until about 1820) and the decoration now consists of a panel of marquetry in satinwood and a sunken lunette apparently veneered with alder-root burr (see illustration 662). Note the slightly arched underside of the plinth. Arched details and lunettes are commonly found on Danish Empire furniture, (see illustration 998). Characteristically, the drawers are lined with oak while the carcase is of pine. The whole is veneered with mahogany. Egetoftegaard, Helsinge, Denmark

998 Danish furniture from the second decade of the 19th century. The curious sofa with built-in pedestals is peculiar to Denmark and Norway at this period. The pedestals, presumably inspired by those made to accompany English sideboards, could hold a dinner service, plate and glassware— necessary because, in all but the smartest Danish houses, there was still no dining-room, and food was eaten at a sofa table in the drawing room. The cast-iron stove and standing desk are both common features of Scandinavian interiors. The sofa table has rather more marked French Empire characteristics than usual; otherwise the furniture is typical of the so-called Danish Empire style. Nationalmuseet, Copenhagen

1000 *Above*: Danish Empire bureau-cabinet, *c.* 1810–20, known as a *chatol*, with cylinder top to its retractable writing slide—the latter containing shallow compartments with sliding tops. The cupboards in the top are fitted to hold cutlery and glassware—a reminder that at this period Danes ate in the drawing room where such a *chatol* was the principal piece of furniture. This cabinet is of oak, veneered with mahogany; the doors are of solid mahogany. The Germanic heaviness of this attractive piece contrasts with the simplicity of the lightweight, English-inspired chairs which are of later date (*c.* 1830–35). Egetoftegaard, Helsinge, Denmark

999 *Above*: Swedish fall-front chiffonier made in 1811 by the Stockholm cabinet-maker Johan Petter Berg. The decorative herms and columns seem to reflect the influence—more marked in Sweden—of the French Empire style. The marquetry shell and the gallery are clearly of English inspiration. The form is greatly indebted to the style created by Iwersson (see illustration 664). Nordiska Museet, Stockholm

1001 *Right*: A view of the Yellow Room at Rosendal Castle, built for the King of Sweden in the 1820s. The style adopted here is much closer to French Empire than anything produced in Denmark. The furniture was largely designed by the Court cabinet-maker Lorentz Wilhelm Lundelius (1787–1859) and made in Stockholm. Rosendal Slott, Stockholm. Reproduced by Gracious Permission of H.M. the King of Sweden

1002 *Below*: According to an inscription on its back, this chair in the French style was made in 1857, for a long-established firm of workers in ivory and tortoiseshell, from a sycamore (or maple) tree that had stood in their yard. The chair is exceptionally well made and probably comes from the workshops of one of the leading Copenhagen furniture makers, perhaps the Court Chairmaker, C. B. Hansen. Messrs. I. G. Schwartz & Son, Copenhagen

1003 *Below right*: A gathering in a Danish artist's house in 1843. The furniture was all designed by the artist himself—the sculptor Hermann Freund (d. 1840; his widow is seated on the sofa). A number of well known artists at the Copenhagen Academy designed furniture for their own use, from about 1780 until well into the second half of the 19th century, in an extreme and very self-conscious form of Neo-Classicism. Kobberstiksamlingen, Statens Museum for Kunst, Copenhagen

without English furniture', wrote a Danish official, in 1803. The anti-British feeling aroused in Denmark and Norway as a result of the English attacks on Copenhagen helped to make these deprivations easier to bear. What is more, the lack of English competition gave considerable encouragement to the Danish and Norwegian craftsmen, many of whom were by this time very competent and well versed in their trade. Such foreign furniture as was required at this period in Scandinavia had now for the most part to come from the Continent. As a result, a strong German influence now came to bear on Scandinavian furniture, particularly on that made in Denmark and Norway. Intermingled with this came English and French forms at second hand, incorporated in German furniture. Admiration for Napoleon as a person also led quite a number of people, especially in Sweden, to adopt the French Empire style direct. From a fusion of a modified form of this style with a German version of the late 18th century Classical idiom, all under the purging influence of an inherent preference for simplicity (simplicity anyway became a necessity due to the privations of the war and the subsequent economic difficulties), the Danes evolved a charming style of their own which is not quite like anything found elsewhere, although it was of course quickly transmitted to their cousins in Norway and across the Sound into southern Sweden and eventually to Stockholm itself. For lack of a better term this is usually called the Danish Empire style.

997,
998, 1000

Since mahogany was difficult to obtain during the war, the Scandinavians made use of some of their native woods—alder, maple, ash and, notably, birch. Birch served as a passable imitation of satinwood from which they made some pleasing light-coloured furniture that is sometimes decorated with marquetry details in a dark wood. When mahogany became available again after the war, much Scandinavian Empire furniture came to be veneered with this exotic wood. In Denmark and Norway this mahogany furniture is often relieved by panels of marquetry decoration in the light-coloured birchwood. This decoration was at first intended as a substitute for the gilt bronze ornaments of the French Empire style, but later became an accepted form of ornament in its own right. When the Scandinavians did use metal mounts at this period, they were usually of pressed brass sheet. They could also be carved in wood and gilt, as had been the general Scandinavian practice in the 18th century. The carcases of their cabinet furniture were almost always of high quality pine and only rarely of oak.

998

The Classical idiom to which the Danes adhered so tenaciously was given a further lease of life in Denmark under the guidance of Gustav Friedrich Hetsch who, as Professor at the Academy and as a prominent decorator and designer of ornaments had very considerable influence on his contemporaries during the second quarter of the 19th century. Hetsch had studied under Percier in Paris and thus favoured a rather fussy form of Neo-

1004   Gilt centre table in the Neo-Rococo taste, in the Amalienborg Palace. It is the work of the firms of C. B. Hansen and J. G. Lund. Although produced as late as 1864, the long-lived Danish preference for Classical forms is still given expression in the curious urn placed at the crossing of the stretchers. Amalienborg Palace, Copenhagen. Reproduced by Gracious Permission of H.M. the King of Denmark

1005   *Above*: Drawing of the Blue Saloon at the Royal Palace of Amalienborg, Copenhagen, 1866-7. The gilt furniture in the Neo-Louis XVI style was made by the Court furniture makers, C. B. Hansen and J. G. Lund who showed a similar chair at the Great Exhibition in London in 1851. At the piano are seated two sisters of Princess Alexandra, who three years earlier had married the Prince of Wales. Det Kongelige Bibliotek, Copenhagen

1006   *Left*: Even when 19th-century interior decoration was at its stuffiest—in the 1880s—an inherent good taste seems to have prevailed in many Scandinavian homes. In spite of the clutter of furnishings in several disparate styles, this Swedish drawing room has a definite and welcoming charm. Otherwise there is nothing specially Scandinavian about this room—except the tiled stove.

1007   *Right*: Mid-19th-century armchair in the Neo-Renaissance taste, bearing the Danish Royal Arms used by King Christian IX (1863-1906). It was made before 1864 when the King took it with him to his new apartments in the Amalienborg Palace (see illustration 1005). Furniture in the Neo-Renaissance style was deemed especially suitable for men's studies and smoking rooms. The Royal Collections, Rosenborg Castle, Copenhagen

1008 *Above*: Corner of the main room in the Swedish artist Carl Larsson's house in the small village of Sundborn, some 130 miles north-west of Stockholm, as drawn by himself and published in his picture book, *Ett Hem* (A Home) in 1899. The rooms were decorated by Larsson to suit his own taste for light and bright surroundings. Interesting are the runners (made with strips of rag interwoven) arranged to run round the room on the bare boards; the painted chairs of 18th-century form with their striped loose covers, the antique mirror, the stove and the pot plants.

1009 *Below*: Furniture in the *Art Nouveau* style made by the Norwegian artist Gerhard Munthe (1849-1929) in 1895 for a hotel near Oslo. (These are actually copies, made a few years later). The colours are black and white, with pale yellow rays, all on a white ground glazed with a greenish varnish. Munthe had studied painting at Düsseldorf and Munich but turned later to designing for the applied arts, in which field he was influenced not only by the contemporary Danish *Art Nouveau* idioms but by ancient Nordic art and by the strong, lively and naive traditions of Scandinavian peasant decoration. Vestlandske Kunstindustrimuseum, Bergen

1010 *Below*: The White Drawing Room in the house of the Swedish artist Alf Wallander (1862-1914), showing the Scandinavian *Art Nouveau* style as handled by one of its principal exponents, early in the present century. Wallander became Artistic Director to the Rörstrand Porcelain Factory in 1896. For all their attenuation and modish line, the form of the white painted chairs clearly derives from Swedish late 18th-century examples. Such chairs were much favoured in Scandinavian houses during the first quarter of the present century.

Classicism. The Hetsch style, known in Denmark as 'Late-Empire' or, misleadingly, as the 'Christian VIII style', prevailed until the middle of the century. The light-coloured marquetry decoration of the earlier phase was now replaced by applied ornament of mahogany, either carved, or moulded from sawdust. Chairs often had ornamental transverse splats carved with scrolls of a half-round section.

In Sweden, a purer form of the French Empire style was adopted, especially in Court circles, but this too gave way to a Swedish equivalent of the Hetsch 'Late-Empire' style. However, the Swedes were much quicker to react against Neo-Classicism. The Neo-Gothic style makes its appearance already in about 1820, and in 1828 a Neo-Gothic room was set up in the Stockholm Palace. It would also seem that the Neo-Rococo style made its appearance earlier in Sweden than in Denmark, but the picture becomes confused as an increasing number of engraved designs became available towards the middle of the century, and as fashion magazines introduced new ideas to an ever-widening public. New fashions now came to be quickly disseminated and the Scandinavian furniture makers produced their share of Neo-Renaissance, Neo-Baroque, Neo-Louis Seize, pseudo-Islamic and the rest. Such national characteristics as may have been present in earlier Scandinavian furniture were now obliterated. As happened elsewhere, increasing mechanisation wrought a general decline in craftsmanship, but some of the best Stockholm and Copenhagen manufacturers managed to maintain a remarkably high standard in their products. Indeed, there was no lengthy interruption of the tradition of fine craftsmanship like that suffered by the major industrial countries, so that when the handicraft revival movement got under way towards the end of the century, the quality of good Scandinavian furniture was still high. The well-deserved reputation which the best modern Scandinavian furniture now enjoys may well in part be due to this fact. Another important factor which has contributed to this excellence is that it has long been common for Scandinavian artists and architects to try their hand at furniture design; the comparative smallness of the communities in which they practise, together with the resultant contact there continually is between artists and craftsmen of various kinds, has made the rapid and fruitful exchange of ideas much easier.

The oppressiveness of the over-stuffed, befringed, plushy interiors with the myriad of small ornaments and pot plants, had become so great at the end of the century that a reaction against it was bound to set in—as it had already done in England. A leading exponent of this reaction was the painter Carl Larsson who published three or four books of charming drawings and water-colours showing scenes in his own house. One of these books (published in German) was entitled '*Let Some Light In!*' Larsson's interiors are indeed light and airy, and the colours are bright. He could never get entirely away from the prevailing historicism of his day, so one notes Renaissance and Gothic features in his schemes of decoration (he also made free use of genuine and quite unpretentious antiques) but the conscious programme of reform that he introduced was the basis for some of the best elements in modern Scandinavian interior decoration. Larsson did not design sophisticated furniture himself but his example affected the thinking of a whole generation, and his influence has been immense throughout Scandinavia and Germany.

Larsson was not an exponent of Art Nouveau, although some of the ornamental motifs he used have obvious associations with this style. Stronger links with Art Nouveau may, on the other hand, be found in the work of other Scandinavians, notably in the furniture designed by that strange artist Gerhard Munthe, which has its chief inspiration in the romantic 'Old-Norse' (*Fornordisk*) movement. No actual Viking furniture had been discovered when this movement came into being in the 1870s, but Viking decoration was known from carvings in stone and on the medieval wooden churches. The 'Viking style' had its innings as part of the spate of 19th-century stylistic revivals, and traces of this interest in the spirited Nordic ornament may still be found in Scandinavian art of the early 20th century, especially in the so-called *Skønvirke* style which was so named after the title of a journal that appeared in 1918, long after the style had had its heyday.

1001

1005, 1004
1007

1002

1008

1009

THE LOW COUNTRIES

Th. H. Lunsingh Scheurleer

The Empire style reached maturity in the Netherlands when, in 1808, King Louis Napoleon gave instructions for the Town Hall in Amsterdam to be converted into the Royal Palace and to be decorated and furnished appropriately. This 17th-century building was duly equipped with palatial state rooms and these were furnished with many hundreds of new articles of furniture, executed in the ruling French Empire style. Most of these pieces were supplied by Dutch craftsmen. One of the most important was Carel Breytspraak. Son of a German cabinet-maker who had settled in Holland, he presented his masterpiece to the Amsterdam Guild of Cabinet-Makers in 1795 and died as early as 1810. He made a roll-top desk for the King's bedroom in the new Palace and in 1809 he provided a commode, a secretaire, a chiffonier and a dressing table, all of mahogany with gilt bronze mounts, for the apartments of the Crown Prince. In accordance with the severe yet sparse elegance of the Empire style, Breytspraak liked to introduce Classical features in the form of gilt bronze mounts on broad, smooth, flat surfaces. But the mahogany veneers on his cabinet pieces are always set in recessed panels and the natural figure of the wood is thus given a framework which accentuates its subtle rhythms. Breytspraak also showed originality in the shape of the legs on his pieces and in his choice of mounts.

Innumerable chairs and sofas were ordered for the Palace at Amsterdam. Most of these were supplied by the upholsterer, Joseph Cuel, who must have ordered the seat furniture from a cabinet-workshop before upholstering it and supplying it to his royal customer.

Dutch cabinet-makers derived their knowledge of the Empire style not only from imported French furniture, but very considerably from the standard work on the subject by Percier and Fontaine, whose '*Recueil des décorations intérieures*' was published in instalments in 1801. La Mésangère's '*Meubles et objets de goût*' which first appeared in 1802 and clearly reveals the influence of Percier and Fontaine, must also have been frequently consulted in the Netherlands.

Even after the fall of the Empire, the fundamental principles of the Empire style persisted for some considerable time. This was very evident when, after 1815, alterations at the Royal Palace at The Hague carried out by the order of King William I, necessitated the re-furnishing of the State apartments. The carved and gilt chairs, ornamented with late Empire motifs, retain an air of Napoleonic grandeur. One of the important suppliers to the Palace was G. Nordanus, a cabinet-maker of The Hague. In 1818 he provided numerous pieces of furniture including dressing tables, secretaires and chiffoniers, all of mahogany and sometimes enlivened by panels of flower marquetry.

Classical features still persisted into the second quarter of the 19th century, although woods of lighter colour, such as maple and burr-walnut were fashionable. It is this well-proportioned, neatly made furniture in the late Empire or *Biedemeier* style which has always been appreciated for its elegant modesty. But before long such quiet outlines and simple surfaces were to be outmoded in favour of the exuberant confidence of 19th century eclecticism.

The abolition of the Guilds at the beginning of the 19th century, and the appearance of the machine, had very serious effects on the production of furniture. The smaller workshops still relied upon manual skill but furniture factories were being built, using mechanisation to provide for the needs of the expanding middle-classes. The first to be established was that of the Horrix Brothers. It was founded at the Hague in 1853 by Matthijs and Willem Horrix, who had been trained in their father's workshop before being apprenticed in Paris. They had returned from France in 1842. Their factory was immediately successful and was soon employing 250 workers, each specialising in one particular activity in the manufacture of furniture. There was a photo-

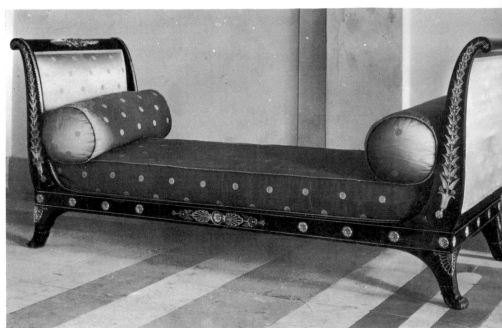

1011 Commode veneered with mahogany and ornamented with gilt bronze mounts, supplied to the Royal Palace in Amsterdam by Carel Breytspraak (*d.* 1810), in 1809. Breytspraak provided a number of pieces in the Empire style to the order of King Louis Napoleon for the newly furnished palace, which had formerly been the Town Hall in Amsterdam.

1012 Sofa veneered with mahogany and ornamented with gilt bronze mounts, supplied in 1810 by the upholsterer, Joseph Cuel, for the bedroom of Queen Hortense in the newly-furnished Royal Palace in Amsterdam.

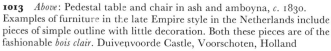

1013 *Above*: Pedestal table and chair in ash and amboyna, *c.* 1830. Examples of furniture in the late Empire style in the Netherlands include pieces of simple outline with little decoration. Both these pieces are of the fashionable *bois clair*. Duivenvoorde Castle, Voorschoten, Holland

1014 *Above right*: Armchair of carved and gilt wood in the late Empire style, ordered in about 1818 by King William I for the State apartments in the Royal Palace of Noordeinde at the Hague.

1015 *Above, far right*: Armchair, the frame carved and pierced in the revived Rococo manner, *c.* 1870. The upholstery is original. The chair was made at the furniture factory of the Horrix Brothers, founded at the Hague in 1853. Private Collection, Holland

1016 *Above left*: Engraving of a bedstead of carved ebony in the 'Renaissance Style', designed and manufactured by the Belgian firm of M. Roulé of Antwerp and shown at the Great Exhibition of 1851 in London. The piece is international in its revivalist manner, but in choosing ebony the Antwerp maker was using a wood which had been employed with particular success in the 17th century by the cabinet-makers of the city.

1017 *Above right*: Drawing room of about 1880. Eclecticism was the rule in the mid-19th century in the Netherlands, as elsewhere. Rooms were crowded; furniture was elaborately carved and richly upholstered and expressed the romantic passion for historical revivalism. Stedelijk Museum, Amsterdam

1018 *Left*: Oak buffet designed by the Dutch architect, H. P. Berlage, *c.* 1900. The panels in low relief, representing stylised animals, birds and fish, are by M. J. Hack. Gemeente Museum, The Hague

1019 *Right*: Tea table of oak inlaid with ebony and ivory, designed by the Dutch architect, K. P. C. de Bazel, *c.* 1905. The simple forms and construction accord with the new aims of creating good design by means of honest craftsmanship. Stedelijk Museum, Amsterdam graphic studio attached to the factory, where pieces were photographed for inclusion in catalogues and for record purposes. Many hundreds of such photographs have been preserved and it is evident that the range of production was considerable. It included furniture in the Gothic and in the French style and also such modern devices as *pouffes* or cushion stools and *crapauds* the new low armchairs, which reflected the middle-class need for expansive comfort. Matthijs was the more gifted of the two brothers and had already shown his talent in Paris, where some of his furniture designs had appeared in the '*Garde meuble ancien et moderne*' of 1840. His son, of the same name, also served his apprenticeship in Paris and was later entrusted with the artistic direction of the firm, but family disagreements forced the business into liquidation in 1890.

Towards the end of the 19th century there developed a reaction against the unrestrained imitation of earlier styles. English theories, expressed in the writings of William Morris, Walter Crane and Lewis F. Day, were of decisive influence in encouraging the growth of new movements concerned with good design and honest craftsmanship. The Netherlands architect, H. P. Berlage (1856–1934) was a distinguished pioneer. His most important work, the Amsterdam Exchange, was built between 1897 and 1903, while he also played a significant part as a furniture designer. As a writer, his theories on the need for logical construction and for integrity of workmanship enjoyed respect and authority. They are clearly reflected in his furniture: his oak buffet, illustrated here, eschews any ornament which might blurr the clear outlines of the structure; the verticals and horizontals are boldly defined and the hinges upon which the doors are hung claim honest recognition of their purpose. Much of Berlage's furniture, which from a technical point of view is exemplary, was created in the Amsterdam atelier known as '*Het Binnenhuis*' (The Interior).

The architect, K. P. C. de Bazel, (1869–1923) was also one of the reformers of furniture design in the late 19th and early 20th century. As a young man he had been apprenticed to a joiner at The Hague and later worked as an architect and designer at Amsterdam. His early designs show a preoccupation with Assyrian and Egyptian art, but his mature work, reflecting the theories of the Arts and Crafts movement in England, is somewhat freer than that of Berlage.

In introducing Javanese Batik designs, the Dutch made an original contribution to the new international currents of the early years of the century. It was C. A. Lion Cachet (1864–1945) who first concentrated on this decorative technique. He used woods of contrasting colour and in combining them with Batik work, gave his furniture an unusually rich appearance.

In 1908 Lion Cachet collaborated with two artists, J. W. Dijsselhof and Theodoor Nieuwenhuis, in founding a studio in Amsterdam, where the design of furniture and interiors was their main concern. But if the work of Dutch architects and designers at this period reflected the influence of the English Arts and Crafts movement, it was in Belgium that Art Nouveau was to find its full expression. In this highly developed industrial country, a newly-founded Socialist party came into power in 1885. Brussels provided a background of challenging intellectualism, nurturing an atmosphere of experiment, and encouraging a fresh approach towards the arts. This new movement, primarily concerned with decoration, sought to break from the past. Developing the sinuous plant forms already used by Mackmurdo in Britain, Victor Horta (1891–1917) designed in 1892 for M. Tassel in the Rue Paul-Emile-Janson in Brussels a house in which not only new materials—iron and glass— were used but in which long curving lines were the dominant feature. Other private houses were included among his subsequent commissions, the Hôtel Autrique in 1893 and the Hôtel Solvay in 1895, in which every detail of the furnishing earned his attention and was marked by the new aesthetic conception. Not only architects, but also painters were to devote themselves to designing interiors and furniture. Henri van de Velde (1863–1957) had been attracted to this aspect of art by the theories of William Morris. His own house at Uccle, near Brussels, which he planned and furnished after his own designs in 1895, was conceived in the new style and it was van de Velde's work, carried out in Germany after his move there in 1899, which was to stimulate German architects and designers.

1020 Armchair of rosewood, the seat and back ornamented with Batik decoration, designed by C. A. Lion Cachet, *c.* 1900. This Dutch artist was the first to introduce ornamental motifs inspired by Indonesian designs. Gemeente Museum, The Hague.

1021 Chair of beech and pearwood, the back painted with stylised flowers and leaves in black, grey and purple, by the Dutch artist and designer, G. W. Dijsselhof, *c.* 1900. Dijsselhof had studied in Berlin, Vienna and Paris and was also influenced by the theories of William Morris. Stedelijk Museum, Amsterdam

1022 *Above*: Oak desk designed by the Belgian architect, Henri van de Velde in 1896. Four examples of this desk were executed, one of which belonged to the famous critic and art historian, J. Meier Graefe. The taut play of lines uniting two opposing curves and the sweeping grandeur of the composition are characteristic of van de Velde's personal style. Germanisches Nationalmuseum, Nuremberg

1023 *Below*: The dining room of the Hôtel Solvay, 224 Avenue Louise, Brussels. The room and furniture were designed by the Belgian architect, Victor Horta, between 1895 and 1900. Every detail of the house was planned by Horta, down to the door and bell handles, so that structure and decoration are united in a sense of flowing rhythm.

ITALY

Hugh Honour

Sphinxes, Grecian and Egyptian caryatids, lion-paw feet and other motifs of the Empire style began to make their appearance in Italy well in advance of Napoleon's army. Before the end of the 18th century the Rococo curves had been ironed out of Italian furniture, even in Venice where this style persisted long after it had fallen out of fashion in France and England. But it was not until the first years of the 19th century that Italians whole-heartedly accepted the full Empire style—with its sober lines, its solid forms and its plain polished wood surfaces. In many ways this type of furniture was unsuited to Italy. It demanded highly skilled craftsmen and wood of the finest quality—neither of which were easy to find—and it provided few opportunities for the sculptors who had hitherto produced most of the best tables, cabinets and chairs made in the peninsula. Nevertheless it became very popular. Rooms and sometimes whole apartments in many of the larger palaces were redecorated and refurnished in the new style. The Empire *chaise longue* became a commonplace in the *salone* and the *psyché* an essential in the boudoir.

The finest of this Empire furniture was produced under Napoleonic patronage. Indeed, Napoleon's relations played a very important part in diffusing the style throughout Italy. Magnificent Empire interiors were created for the Emperor's brothers, Joseph, as King of Naples, and Lucien, as Prince of Canino, and still more notably for his sisters, Elisa Baciocchi in Lucca and Florence, Pauline Borghese in Rome and Caroline Murat in Naples. The lead of the Imperial siblings was naturally followed by remoter connections, like Eugène Beauharnais, and the various generals and administrators. Like all good Frenchmen, the Bonapartes believed that taste was a French monopoly and they therefore looked to Paris for direction in interior decoration. Where possible they bought furniture from Jacob and other Parisian *ébénistes*, their silver from Biennais and their porcelain from the Sèvres factory.

Elisa Baciocchi, Grand Duchess of Tuscany, went further by importing French craftsmen and setting up a furniture workshop in which they could impart their skills to Italians. Many rooms in the Palazzo Pitti, Florence, are monuments to the success of this experiment, for it is now difficult to distinguish which of the pieces of furniture in them are of French and which of Italian make. Several of the more interesting pieces are indeed the work of a Florentine named Giovanni Socchi—some attractive and unusual commodes in the form of drums and a pair of ingenious oval tables which open to form attached chairs and writing tables. It seems that gilt bronze mounts were imported from France for the decoration of Italian-made furniture—and this, of course, increases the difficulty of establishing the origin of a particular piece.

Although Italians had regarded the Napoleonic regime in Italy with mixed feelings, they did not abandon the Empire style after the restorations of 1815. Empire furniture loaded with Napoleonic features retained its place in the palaces of the restored rulers. What is more extraordinary, it came to be regarded as an established form of palatial decoration even in Naples and the Kingdom of Sardinia. Much of the 'Empire' style furniture now to be seen in the royal palaces of Naples, Genoa and Turin was made after 1815. In course of time, however, the style became heavier and more florid, gilt wood replaced the plain polished surfaces of true Empire furniture, carved decorations returned to favour. Some handsome chairs made by an Englishman named Peters working for the Savoy court in the 1840s reveal the way in which the Empire style was elaborated at this period. The magnificent suite of gilt bronze and gilt wood furniture designed by the painter Pelagio Palagi for the Council Chamber of the Palazzo Reale, Turin, still more strongly reveals the Italian tendency to treat furniture as decorative sculpture. In private villas and palaces the Empire style continued to enjoy popularity during the third and fourth decades of the 19th century. In the 1820s a Sienese architect, appropriately named Agostino Fantastici, was designing furniture which incorporated Classical and Egyptian motifs of a strongly Empire flavour.

The Gothic Revival spread to Italy soon after the Napoleonic wars. Its influence was not as great as it was in England, France or Germany. But in the 1820s several complete Gothic rooms were created, with frescoed landscapes glimpsed through ogee arches on the walls, and they were filled with crocketted furniture. There is a rather heavier Gothic room dating from the

1024 *Left*: Writing table of mahogany, 1807, by Giovanni Socchi, shown open. Socchi was a Florentine cabinet-maker patronised by Napoleon's sister Elisa Baciocchi. He closely imitated the French Empire style. On this table the mounts are of ormolu, but a similar table made by Socchi has gilt wood mounts. The contraption is opened by a single lock; the chair being drawn out first. By pulling the brass handles the writing platform slides forwards, the two halves of the top divide and slide sideways, and the paper-rack rises. Although ingenious pieces of furniture like this were often made in France no other Italian examples are known. Palazzo Pitti, Florence

1025 *Right*: Table in the Egyptian taste designed by the architect Agostino Fantastici in the 1820s and made in Siena. Fantastici made designs for several pieces of furniture in a late Empire style; his drawings are preserved in the Siena Public Library. Villa Bianchi-Bandinelli, Siena

1026 *Left*: Centre table of gilt bronze, designed by Pelagio Palagi, 1836, and cast at the Viscari foundry in Milan. It was on this table, designed for the Council Chamber of the Palazzo Reale, that King Carlo Alberto signed the statute of the Piedmontese constitution in 1848. Palazzo Reale, Turin

1027 *Right*: The Council Chamber of Palazzo Reale, Turin, 1835-40, designed by Pelagio Palagi. A romantic evocation of Antiquity, the style contrasts sharply with the Neo-Classicism of the late 18th century. The room provides the last notable example of the Italian passion for sculptural furniture.

1028 *Above*: Ballroom in Palazzo di Capodimonte, Naples, 1835-8, decorated by Salvatore Giusti. The Bonaparte family established the Empire style as the most appropriate for the decoration of palaces in Italy, where it persisted long after their fall.

1031 *Below*: Side table of mahogany with gilt bronze and gilt plaster mounts. Although in the international Empire style, this table probably dates from after the Restoration of 1815. Palazzo Pitti, Florence

1029 *Above*: Chair of carved and gilt wood, *c.* 1840-50. This is one of several pieces of furniture made by an Anglo-Italian cabinet-maker named Peters who was working for the House of Savoy in the 1840s. Palazzo Balbi-Durazzo, Genoa

1030 *Above right*: Chair of carved and gilt wood, *c.* 1815-30. This chair, made after the Restoration of 1815, is of a type which came into fashion in the Empire period and remained popular until well into the 19th century. Palazzo Pitti, Florence

1032 *Below*: The Gothic room in the Museo Sartorio, Trieste. This room was created in the 1850s when Trieste was still a part of the Austrian Empire. The furniture is of a type made in Italy at the same period.

1033 *Above*: The dining room in Villa del Poggio a Caiano, near Florence. A room in a Renaissance villa furnished in the taste of the 1870s, it reveals the current demand for richness, upholstered comfort and reminiscences of Italy's glorious past.

1034 *Above*: A room in Museo Stibbert, Florence. An example of the eclectic style of furnishing which came into vogue after the mid-19th century. This room is in the villa which Frederick Stibbert, an English eccentric, built to contain his vast magpie hoard of *objets d'art et de vertu* dating from many periods.
1035 *Below*: The reading room in the Hotel Grande Bretagne, Bellagio, on Lake Como, *c.* 1900. Comfortable furniture of this type seems to have been made mainly for hotels which began to assume a place of importance in the history of Italian architecture and decoration towards the end of the 19th century.

1850s and distinctly 'High Victorian' in feeling, in the Museo Sartorio, Trieste. In a similar style is the little *saletta di Dante*, lit by stained glass windows, in the Museo Poldi-Pezzoli, Milan.

In the days of the Risorgimento, however, it was less the Gothic than the early Renaissance style that inspired Italian taste. During the struggle for unity and even after it had been achieved under the King of Sardinia, Italians looked back to the greatest period of their history in which, of course, the House of Savoy had played no part of importance. And they created a revivalist style called the Dantesque, with a lavish use of X-chairs upholstered in red plush, heavily carved wooden tables and agonisingly uncomfortable wooden stools. The designs for much of this furniture were derived from late medieval and early Renaissance paintings. But in Dantesque rooms such reproductions often jostled genuine *cassoni* of the 15th and 16th centuries.

Generally speaking the Dantesque style was a middle-class vogue, even as the Risorgimento was a middle-class movement. The great families of Naples, Rome, Florence and Venice, many of them now impoverished, preferred to dwell on their more recent splendours and to recall amongst their Baroque furnishings the grandeurs of the *Ancien Régime*. It is largely for this reason that the most grandiose pieces of mid-19th-century furniture were made almost exclusively for the palaces of members of the House of Savoy.

Many houses, especially those of the middle classes, were furnished mainly with chairs and tables barely distinguishable from those of contemporary England and France. A certain individuality appeared, however, in the design of the wrought iron bedsteads which were made mainly in Liguria and Tuscany and which have recently became very fashionable. With their elaborately curved heads and feet, painted and gilded and sometimes set with charming little landscape panels, they are indeed among the most immediately attractive pieces of Italian furniture of the period.

Towards the end of the 19th century, Italian houses revealed several different styles of furniture and decoration. In the palaces and villas of the ancient aristocracy, furniture dating from the 18th century and earlier predominated—there was little need to add to the accumulation which they possessed. Then there were houses belonging to collectors, either Italians or, more usually, expatriate Englishmen like Frederick Stibbert, John Temple-Leader or, at the beginning of the present century, Herbert Horne, who accumulated hoards of old furniture and not a few 19th-century reproductions and fakes. The Villa Stibbert, which has been left more or less as it was when its owner bequeathed it to the city of Florence in 1907, provides a notable example of this eclectic style of furnishing. Middle-class homes were furnished in a style differing little from that popular in contemporary England—though they might contain such a nationalistic piece as a knobbly walnut X-chair or a heavily carved fake Renaissance table. Further down the social scale, the peasant's farmhouse was as sparsely furnished as most palaces had been in the Renaissance—with a few simple tables and chairs and a *cassone* or two of designs which had remained popular since the 16th century.

The fashion for Art Nouveau which reached Italy early in the 20th century (notably by way of the 1902 exhibition in Turin) under the names 'Liberty' and *Floreale*, did little to alter this pattern of furnishing. A few Italians, generally the rich and eccentric, bought Art Nouveau furniture, just as a few built themselves Art Nouveau houses. But no furniture to put beside that designed by Mackintosh, Gallé and Horta was created in Italy, although a great deal of mass-produced furniture in a watered down Art Nouveau style was made in the 1920s. This movement affected the Italian hotel more than the Italian home—as, for example, the Villa Igeia, Palermo, which boasts an Art Nouveau dining room. This is not altogether surprising. Hotels were probably the largest, most expensive and most numerous of the non-ecclesiastical buildings erected in late 19th-century Italy. Built to cater for a predominantly foreign clientele of wealthy travellers, they naturally reflected in their furnishings and architecture the international hotel style which eddied outwards from Paris and the various fashionable German spas. Thus a new standard of well-upholstered comfort was created, to be reflected in the interior decoration of houses in many parts of Europe.

SPAIN AND PORTUGAL

Andrew Ciechanowiecki

For Spain the 19th century was a period of acute internal tension. It opened with enslavement under Napoleon and the shameful double abdication of Charles IV and his son Ferdinand (1808), only redeemed by the heroic struggle of the Spanish people. It was in fact in Spain and not on the plains of Russia that the French Empire received its mortal wound. The French, however hated, brought with them new political and social ideas which caught on like wildfire, producing a liberal movement in the country. The struggle between the new progressive policies and the reactionary ones of the restored king, Ferdinand VII (1814-33), were complicated by problems of succession. Under Isabella II (1833-68) the constitutional difficulties culminated in civil war. It was only during the reigns of Alfonso XII (1875-85) and Alfonso XIII (1886-1931), that Spain found peace to develop economically and culturally in spite of the loss of her last colonial possessions in 1898.

The chief characteristics of early 19th-century Spanish furniture are virtually those of the close of the preceding period. The graceful early Neo-Classical designs of the 1780s gave place to a more massive and ponderous style, usually called *Fernandino*. Early examples were strongly influenced by French *Directoire* furniture, soon to become heavier and richer still in an adaptation of the *Empire*. However short-lived was the actual Bona-

partist rule in Spain, the impact of imperial decoration was extremely strong and was to last until about 1830. Spanish Empire furniture, usually of mahogany, enriched with numerous bronze mounts or carved and gilt elements, is certainly heavier than its French prototypes, showing also more fantasy and exuberance in the combination of the various Classical motifs. They can seldom boast of really good craftsmanship in the carving and bronzes.

Chairs are *en gondole* with legs shaped as crossed cornucopiae, as dolphins or swans, sometimes with pierced backs. Others have lyres or bunches of arrows to decorate the splats. Simpler models which became popular towards 1820 dispensed with carving and gilding, concentrating on the quality of the design. Large, heavy sofas were popular, usually supported by carved and gilt figures, amongst which one can find sphinxes, and, of course, swans. In one case carved galleons form the supports and arms of an Empire sofa. With the advent of Romanticism, Gothic features appeared in the furniture of about 1830, together with a return to French fashions of the 18th century. This style, called *Isabellino*—is the Spanish version of Louis-Philippe and the Second Empire style. It is more exuberant and colourful than its northern counterparts. Some armchairs are richly adorned with carved and gilt *putti*, others are painted or inlaid with mother-of-pearl. Rose-

1037

1036

1038

1036 *Right*: Mahogany desk with carved and gilt supports in the form of swans, *c.* 1820, in the King's study in the Royal Palace, Madrid. It betrays the weaknesses of the later 'Fernandino' style. Palacio Nacional, Madrid

1037 *Below*: The antechamber to the Gasparini rooms at the Royal Palace in Madrid was redecorated in the 'Fernandino' style. The circular sofa of mahogany with carved and gilt applied decoration and sumptuous upholstery is typical of the early 19th century. Palacio Nacional, Madrid

1038, 1039 *Below centre*: Spanish carved mahogany chair, partly gilt, in the late 'Fernandino' style which bridges the gap between the earlier Neo-Classical phase and the Neo-Baroque of the subsequent 'Isabellino' style. Museo Romantico, Madrid. *Below right*: This exuberantly carved and gilt armchair and footstool, both upholstered with gold embroidered velvet, follows earlier Spanish tradition in a spirit which is wholly of the mid-19th century. Museo de Artes Decorativas, Madrid

wood with bronze mounts was also much used.

Next to the drawing room suite of large sofa and armchairs with side chairs, the occasional table was a favourite of the period. It developed from the elegant bronze *guéridons* inlaid with Buen Retiro porcelain of the *Fernandino*, into Neo-Baroque examples of all shapes and sizes. This Neo-Baroque which covered every piece of furniture with elaborate ornamentation gave place in about 1870 to a return of fashion for Spanish furniture of the 16th and 17th centuries until finally the Art Nouveau movement in Madrid and Barcelona produced something as new and revolutionary as the 20th century which was just beginning.

In Portugal the brutality of the French occupation forces had not managed to dim the attraction of French political theory. Returning to Portugal in 1821, after a self-imposed exile of fourteen years in Brazil, the former Regent, now King John VI (1816–26) faced overwhelming political difficulties. Constitutional problems finally caused civil war under Queen Maria II (1826–53) and acute political crises during the reigns of her successors Pedro V (1853–61), Luis I (1861–89) and Carlos I (1889–1908), bringing about the final collapse of the monarchy in 1910.

The French Empire style was very influential in the first years of the century. Lisbon craftsmen produced pieces which are heavier than French examples and often lacking their elegance. After the liberation from the French in 1811, English influence was again felt. Regency furniture, particularly Trafalgar chairs, became popular, and even some Sheraton designs were still imitated. After 1820 chairs became simpler, closely resembling those of the German *Biedermeier*. The German consorts of Queen Maria II encouraged Germanic influences: the Queen's Classic-al throne is nearer to Klenze than to Percier or Fontaine and the furnishing of that folly, Peña palace, is closely related to many German houses of the period. But while the international eclectic Neo-Baroque was later fostered by Queen Maria Pia of Savoy, her father-in-law, the artist-King Ferdinand, consort of Maria II, and Carlos I brought about a revival of Portuguese traditional furniture of the 17th and 18th centuries. From their well meaning antiquarianism issued the flood of Neo-17th-century and Neo-John V furniture, which still fills many Portuguese houses today.

The 19th century was the century of independence for Latin America, starting with the deposition of the Spanish Viceroy in Buenos Aires in 1810. The continent, not always divided into friendly units, was free by 1826, and the only anomaly amongst the various republics, the Empire of Brazil, ceased to exist in 1889. Many emigrants reached South America from Europe, infusing their new environments with the cultural elements of their native lands, thus changing traditional patterns.

Not having had any direct contact with France, Latin America has no Empire furniture, Neo-Classicism in Brazil being a variant of European 18th-century designs, created there during the residence of the Portuguese royal family (1808–21). The new republics adapted simplified Neo-Classical styles, or copied English Regency furniture with which trade had made them familiar. As prosperity grew, houses became filled with local examples of *Isabellino* furniture, made out of local wood and sometimes inlaid with mother-of-pearl. The former exuberance of decoration, which marked the survival of a native tradition disappears now in a full stylistic conformity with European and North American counterparts.

1040 *Above*: The taste in early 19th-century Portugal for furniture in the French Empire style is well expressed in this bedroom in the Royal Palace of Queluz. All the furniture is of mahogany with either gilt bronze mounts or with decorative motifs of carved and gilt wood. Palacio Nacional de Queluz, Portugal

1042 *Below*: Mid-19th-century Brazilian chair made of jacaranda, and carved with the Imperial arms of Brazil. Chairs of this type were common to much of Europe and North America, but this example reflects the South American delight in exuberant carving. Palacio Itamaraty, Rio de Janeiro

1041 *Above*: Queen Maria Pia's bedroom in the Royal Palace at Lisbon hung with dark blue damask. The black Neo-Baroque furniture, white damask curtains and upholstered armchairs evoke the atmosphere of extravagant comfort fostered by the Court. Palacio Nacional de Ajuda, Lisbon

1043 *Below left*: Chair designed by Antonio Gaudi y Cornet for the Casa Calvet in Barcelona upon which the Catalan architect was working between 1898 and 1904. As Gaudi's buildings rely upon massive, undulating forms, his furniture too avoids harsh angles. This chair recalls the human skeleton in its grim originality.

1044 *Below*: A colonial version of the Portuguese style of the turn of the century can be seen in this Brazilian interior dating from the early 19th century, clearly influenced by fashions brought over by the Portuguese Court. The chairs are derived from the '*doiradinhas*'; the bed is an adaptation of a Portuguese prototype. Museu de Inconfidencia, Ouro Preto, State of Minas Gerais

RUSSIA

Bozenna Maszkowska

The Russian victory over Napoleon in 1812 freed the country at last from the threat of foreign invasion. Much of the land was devastated. But a feeling of exhilaration was in the air, and a desire to rebuild, and to erect new and splendid houses, was a natural sequel to the years of uncertainty and destruction. During the reign of Tsar Alexander I (1801–25) foreign architects were invited to Russia, among them the Swiss Thomas de Thomon, and the Italian Carlo Rossi. Russian architects, too, such as Zacharov and Voronikhin, adopted features of the Classical revival already established in France and England.

Furniture continued, as in the previous century, to be largely derivative. The Hermitage collection includes, for example, a large number of sets of chairs made of mahogany and dating from about 1800. These show an interesting compromise between the designs of the French cabinet-maker, Jacob Desmalter and those of Sheraton in England. They were made by Russian craftsmen in St. Petersburg.

Simplicity and symmetry were the dominant characteristics of early 19th-century interiors, and furniture shared these features although it was perhaps heavier than elsewhere. The quality of the veneering is high, and the workmanship of the finer pieces stands comparison with the best from France.

In the early 19th century the Russian workshops continued to produce attractive furniture in *bois clair*, enriched with other woods of contrasting colour. Birch, from the forests of Karelia, was used to satisfy this taste for light woods which Russian patrons, like their contemporaries in France and England, adopted. Much of this type of Russian furniture differs little from that produced at the time in Central Europe. The vast quantities of Empire and *Biedermeier* produced, shared common characteristics and a high quality of workmanship with pieces made abroad. But only if they have been preserved in houses for which they were originally made, and for which records still exist, can pieces conclusively be termed 'Russian'.

The general decline in the applied arts in mid-19th-century Europe also affected Russia. Here, too, great factories were to replace the workshops of the cabinet-makers. Eclectic furniture was turned out in large quantities, and the level of craftsmanship dropped. Towards the end of the century, however, certain efforts were made to restore standards of craftsmanship. A movement to encourage traditional Russian cottage industries, carving, ceramics and weaving, occurred during the period 1895–1905. As in England, the revival of hand crafts was achieved by minority groups, such as that centred around Prince Savva Ivanovich Mamontov who had a colony of painters, woodworkers and metalworkers on his estate at Abramtsevo. Although in this Russian equivalent of the Arts and Crafts movement certain features of Art Nouveau can be discerned—an interest in plant motifs and two dimensional patterns—the essential character of the early Russian modern style is reflected rather in Diaghilev's and Benois' admiration for the romantic Rococo of Rastrelli's Tsarskoe Selo.

1045 *Above*: The Tiepolo Room at Arkhangelskoe Palace near Moscow, also called the Venetian Room. Like the Rotunda Drawing Room, (see illustration 1047), it was damaged by fire in 1820 and subsequently redecorated by Tiurin. The mirror is in the French Empire manner, being divided vertically into three parts by pilasters surmounted by Egyptian heads. The mahogany chairs are in the later *Biedermeier* style.

1046 *Left*: Armchair displaying strong French influence, designed in 1804 by Andrei Voronikhin. Voronikhin was responsible for the rebuilding of the palace of Pavlovsk after its damage during the Napoleonic wars, and he also designed the new furniture. The carved busts and feet of this chair are painted and patinated in imitation of antique bronze, and contrast with the bright gilt of the wing-shaped armpieces.

1047 *Right*: The Rotunda Drawing Room at Arkhangelskoe designed by the architect De Guernes for Prince Yusupov between 1797 and 1799. The furniture and decoration date from 1820 and were carried out by Tiurin after damage by fire. The stove on the right, is built to look like a fireplace. It has a large mirror above it and a pair of candlesticks and a bust are placed on the false mantelpiece.

1048 *Right*: The drawing room at Abramtsevo near Moscow, a house built for Prince Savva Ivanovich Mamontov, a wealthy patron of the arts. The day-bed with its flanking cabinets was probably made at the Mamontov workshop organised by the painter Polenov, and dates from the late 19th century.

1049 *Below*: Armchair, *c.* 1820, veneered in birch, with a simple inlay of a darker wood. This piece with its lyre-shaped splat shows English and French influence, and is probably of provincial manufacture.

1050 *Above right*: Study in the Palmer's House, Leningrad, 1907-8. Art Nouveau furniture in Russia possesses certain features which distinguish it from Western Art Nouveau. The Neo-Classical decoration on the writing desk and on the back of the barrel-shaped chair contrasts strangely with the freer forms of the light fittings. The desk itself is of simple rectangular structure but curiously heavy in its proportions.

1051 *Right*: The dining room at Arkhangelskoe near Moscow. The set of chairs is in the so-called 'Russian style' which was fashionable during the second half of the 19th century. After a long period in which fashions from abroad had been imitated, there was a revival of interest in purely Russian decoration, a revival fostered by such people as Mamontov, and Princess Tenisheva. The ornamentation of the chairs is reminiscent of 17th-century Russian church architecture. As in all the reception rooms of Arkhangelskoe, there is a fine floor of inlaid woods.

POLAND

Bozenna Maszkowska

In the first half of the 19th century, Polish cabinet-making flourished. Napoleon's wars of expansion had brought a promise of liberty and independence to Poland and the French Directoire and Empire styles were consequently regarded with admiring approval. Neo-Gothic decoration was also fashionable.

Neo-Classical furniture of the Grand Duchy of Warsaw, and of the Congress Kingdom (1815–31), forms a separate national style evolved both from English and French example. The so-called 'Simmler furniture' and that of the workshop of the brothers Friedrich and Johann Daniel Heurich belong to this period. They are characterised by lightness of proportion and elegance of line not unlike German *Biedermeier*. In spite of the simplicity, however, the traditional Polish liking for carved detail sometimes emerges.

In the two remaining partitioned territories, the influence of Vienna on the great centres of Lwow and Cracow and that of Berlin on the Poznan district is apparent. In the Grand Duchy of Lithuania the important cabinet-making centre was Vilno, where massive and heavy proportions are characteristic. Besides mahogany and light veneers such as ash, poplar and especially birch, yew, elm and thuya also became popular. Black oak and plane were used for decorative marquetry.

Traditional furniture, usually veneered with ash, but sometimes in fruitwood or lime, was still made in manorial workshops on both large and small estates throughout the century and indeed almost up to the Second World War.

After a period in which the cabinet-making firms in the larger towns were providing mainly eclectic pieces, a revival of the art of the cabinet-maker occurred at the turn of the 19th century. The centre of the new movement was Cracow. Here three guild associations of artist-craftsmen were founded, known as the 'Sztuka' Art Association, the Polish Applied Art Group *(Polska Sztuka Stosowana)* and the Cracow Workshops *(Warsztaty Kratkowskie)*. The last continued to operate as the Warsaw 'Ład' group. This movement parallels the Arts and Crafts Movement in England. The so-called 'Zakopane' style manifested itself in interiors, furniture and other crafts. It was created about 1886 by Stanislaw Witkiewicz who sought to evolve a new national style on the basis of southern Polish folk art (Podhale). In Poland, as in other European countries, it was in such movements, which endeavoured to reform design, that the modern style found its origins.

1052 *Above*: The Neo-Gothic Room at Tylmanowa, 1840. Neo-Gothic interiors were fashionable in Poland from the 1880s onwards. The decoration is Oriental, rather than the more usual Northern Gothic. The furniture, produced at Cracow, is typical of the mid-19th century.

1053 *Above*: The Pompeian Room at Łańcut Castle, *c*. 1800. The wall decoration is a combination of bright printed wallpaper, and inset panels with hand-painted Pompeian scenes in gouache. The settees were made in Warsaw *c*. 1800 in the 'English taste'. The simulated bamboo chairs are English. Łańcut, like many other great houses in Poland, has magnificent wooden floors inlaid with contrasting woods in geometric patterns.

1054 *Above*: Interior of the artist's house in Warsaw by Alexander Kokular, *c*. 1830. The walls are covered with the artist's canvases, and the chairs are a Polish adaptation of *Biedermeier*.

1055 *Far left*: The round drawing room at the Villa Zarzecze in Little Poland. The villa was built by Christian-Peter Aigner in 1817–20 for the Countess Morska. This lithograph was published in Vienna in 1836.

1056 *Left*: Armchair of the early 19th century, pearwood veneer on pine. It is light, graceful but unpretentious, and typical of Polish country house furniture at that period. Kielce Museum

Whiling away the summer, detail of a painting by Li Kuan-tao of the early 14th century, showing a scholar reclining on a *k'ang* with a stool and tables. William Rockhill Nelson Gallery, Kansas City

VIII THE FAR EAST

CHINA

Margaret Medley

The arts of the Orient have always fascinated the West. Chinese lacquered cabinets and screens, no less than Chinese porcelain, were increasingly admired, sought after and imitated in Europe from the end of the 16th century. Much late 17th- and early 18th-century Dutch and English furniture survives to witness the delight with which new ideas from China were received. But the Rococo 'vision of Cathay' which grew out of this early enthusiasm was as misleading as it was charming. While the 19th century, in its turn, produced in the early decades, *chinoiserie* furniture of picturesque charm, it made no contribution towards a more realistic understanding of the virtues of Chinese furniture. The elaborately lacquered, multi-shelved cabinets and frail bamboo pieces of the Victorian era, which pretended to copy the Chinese, were not at all the type of furniture that we should fairly expect of an ancient civilisation and a nation with a long experience of woodworking. The highly-developed techniques of joinery in China are probably only equalled in the East by those of Japan and perhaps Korea, all three countries having been accustomed to working in wood from the earliest times. It is just these qualities of subtle craftsmanship together with a sure understanding of form and a respect for quiet restraint which characterise the best Chinese furniture and which have never been truly appreciated.

For the early history of Chinese furniture we are dependent upon archaeological materials, paintings and illustrated books; there is very little information to be found in literary sources. It is clear from the meagre resources at present available, that furniture was already well developed in the Han dynasty (206 B.C.–A.D. 221), for low platforms called *k'ang* were used for page 275 sleeping and reclining on, and were accompanied by occasional tables and stools. Sometime in the latter part of this period, the chair was introduced and as a consequence the sitting and reclining level became higher; tables and stools followed suit.

By the T'ang dynasty (A.D. 618–906) most furniture forms were well developed, and there was apparently already a marked distinction between furniture for ordinary household use, and that for the imperial palaces. The former was often simple and strictly utilitarian. The latter tended to be massive and richly ornamented and in later times had very elaborate surface decoration. While conservative taste has ensured that the same principles of construction and, indeed, the same basic forms, have been retained through the ages, the finest examples of Chinese furniture to survive are those made between the 15th and the 18th centuries, that is through the Ming dynasty (1368–1644) and into the earlier part of the Ch'ing dynasty (1644–1911). The best pieces are undoubtedly those of plain hardwood of simple, uncluttered form with well matured, polished surfaces.

Furniture in China has been made from many different woods according to local taste. The most admired and valued timbers are those known as *hua-li mu*, *tzu-t'an* and *huang-hua-li*. These are the best hardwoods and have been identified by different specialists with such a wide variety of species that they should perhaps be regarded as generic terms, since all three can be identified with *Pterocarpus indicus* (rosewood) and its varieties. One fine wood, with unusual figuring and a marked grain, is called by the Chinese *chi-ch'ih mu* or 'chicken wing wood'. This is a greyish brown timber that matures to a dark coffee colour, and has been variously identified as *Cassia siamea* and its varieties, and as *Ormosia* and its varieties; the latter includes the 'Red Bean' of central and west China. Some of the *Pterocarpus* woods were imported from Indonesia and South East Asia, but some came from

1057 *Left*: Bed of *huang-li-hua* wood, 16th century. The posts and openwork are all concave moulded, only the base has convex moulding on the leading edges. Originally the bed was hung with curtains. Philadelphia Museum of Art

1058 *Above*: Ch'uang, couch of rosewood and chestnut, late 18th or early 19th century. The heavy horse hoof feet are mitred into the shaped apron. The finely woven matting seat is stretched over boards, and originally would also have had a silk cover, and cushions. Philadelphia Museum of Art

1059 *Above*: Detail of a painting showing a schoolroom where the master sleeps and the children take advantage of the chance to play. Attributed to the Sung dynasty (A.D. 960-1279). Stools and table are both of very common form.

The clamps on the underside are dovetailed in, as the one being balanced suggests. The master sits in an armchair. From a former private collection in Shanghai

1060 *Above*: Carved red-lacquer table, 15th century with the mark of the Hsüan-te period, 1426-35. This is an extremely fine example of the kind of furniture and lacquer that was made under imperial patronage in the Ming dynasty. Collection: Mr and Mrs Fritz Low-Beer, New York

1061 *Below*: Chinese Palace Hall. This shows something of the formal arrangement, as well as the splendour of lacquered furniture. Entry is from the left through the south side; the Emperor would face one. Philadelphia Museum of Art

south-western and south-central China. Differences of climate between the north and south have influenced the use of materials. In the warmer south, where people can live more outside, bamboo furniture was common and was regarded as expendable. Lacquered furniture, on the other hand, more popular in the south than in the north, was preferred for permanent use, because it was resistent to insect attack. Similar in form to that of hardwood, it was sometimes painted in colours or gilt or perhaps inlaid with white or stained ivory, mother-of-pearl, hardstone or coloured glass. As a practical defence against damage by insects, the underside of much early furniture, lined with soft woods, was lacquered, the visible surfaces of hardwood being virtually impervious to this evil.

A unique feature of Chinese furniture is the total absence of nails and dowels; when dowels are present it generally means that a repair has been made. The construction is based entirely on a mortice and tenon principle, with a limited use of dovetailing and a minimal use of glue. There are two practical reasons for this. Jointing had to withstand humidity and temperature changes, which can be from one extreme to another over short periods of time, while furniture had to be taken apart for removal from one premises to another.

The intricate interlocking structure is concealed where possible, so that the beauty of the timber and the formal balance can be appreciated without distracting elements. A satisfying feature is the use of simple bevelling and beading, and a delight in convex edges, or in some fine early pieces, a slight concavity. Rounded members were cut and sculptured by hand and were never turned. A curved section was carved from a single block of hardwood wherever possible. If joins had to be made, they were not concealed, although they were achieved unobtrusively. The use of veneer was not common and was probably a late development though there are exceptions. On the other hand, there was a liking for combining different woods in a single piece, and also for the use in tables, chairs and stools, of finely-woven cane surfaces or decorative stone in the horizontal plane. A restrained use of metal mounts, of pale brass alloy is found on chests, cupboards, and tables fitted with drawers. In the best pieces they are countersunk to lie nearly flush with the polished surface.

Chinese traditions concerning the arrangement and use of furniture have always differed fundamentally from those of Europe. On formal occasions the place of honour in any room or pavilion was that furthest from the door and to the left or east side of the host, who faced south across the reception area towards the door, or folding screens. The furniture was set against the walls. Two chairs, with or without arms and with a small table between, often formed groups of three pieces designed as a unit, the table sometimes serving as a stand for a work of art, or for bowls of sweetmeats. Even in less formal rooms the furniture was placed against the walls or at a strict right-angle to them. It was never slanted out or carelessly grouped in the central floor area. At meal-times a round or square table was brought into any room in which it was decided to eat, the Chinese having no room specifically set aside for this purpose. Such dining tables were suitable for only eight or ten people since it was important that everyone should be able to reach all the main dishes, placed in the centre, with their chopsticks. In later times, for really large feasts, tables were often hired from catering establishments but the guests always sat at tables ranged round the sides of the room in groups of eight or ten.

Chinese tables generally appear rather unusual to European eyes, but once their function in relation to the formal architectural plan of a room is understood, they are more readily appreciated. The very low *k'ang* table was originally intended for use on the *k'ang* or platform upon which one sat to read or write or even recline. The early *k'ang* is fundamentally a box-framed structure with elegantly designed openings in the sides. *K'ang* tables followed the same pattern but later examples are without base stretchers.

Higher and larger tables were used with low stools for sitting round at meals. Those over the usual European height of about two foot six inches, are of two types. The first are the square or round tables intended for eating. Square tables are usually called *Pa-hsien cho*, or 'tables for the Eight Immortals'. The guests sat round these on chairs which had built-in footrests so that their

1071

1057

1058
1066

1068

1061

1073

1062, 1069

page 275

1062 *Above*: Rare rosewood, cabriole legged *k'ang* table, 15th century. The cabriole leg has a long history in China; it does not, however, have any connection with the ball-and-claw type. Collection: Miss Alice Boney, New York

1063 *Right*: Box-frame side table in *huang-hua-li* wood, with small horse hoof feet, late 16th century. When it was found that base stretchers were not essential to the stability of the table they were eliminated, and the hoof foot developed to give weight to the design. Collection: R. Hatfield Ellsworth Esq., New York

1064 *Below*: Rosewood *(Dalbergia)* side table, late 17th century. This is an unusually handsome example of a trestle frame table. The slightly splayed, as well as inclined legs, counterbalance in lightness the weight given by the massive carved panels that replace the usual double stretchers. The elegant brackets at the ends are inset. Philadelphia Museum of Art

1065 *Below right*: Trestle-type side table in *huang-hua-li* wood, 17th-18th century. This is a refined example of a classic type, and is the Ch'ing dynasty equivalent of the kind shown in illustration 1059. The legs are not circular in section, but show a subtle elipse; this, since they are hand worked with a spoke-shave type of tool, is not surprising. William Rockhill Nelson Gallery, Kansas City

1066 *Below*: Chair with finely woven bamboo matting seat. *Huang-hua-li* wood, 16th century. Box frame chairs are common, but this example is a very rare variation with a horse hoof foot. The single broad splat in the back curves in comfortably. The front stretcher extends beyond the leading edge of the front framework to form a stout footrest. Collection: R. Hatfield Ellsworth Esq., New York

1067 *Below*: One of four *huang-hua-li* wood chairs, late 16th or early 17th century. This unusual and elegant round-backed chair has been carved to resemble bamboo. Only the foot rail has been left plain. William Rockhill Nelson Gallery, Kansas City

1068 *Below*: Pair of chests with hat cupboards veneered with *huang-hua-li* on a walnut carcase, c. 1600. The hat cupboards on top are removable. This small pair of cupboards owe their distinction to the use of good grain and the extreme simplicity of the mounts. Collection: R. Hatfield Ellsworth Esq., New York

1069 *Above*: K'ang table in *huang-hua-li* wood, early 17th century. William Rockhill Nelson Gallery, Kansas City

1071 *Below*: One of a pair of dark brown lacquered wood chairs with decoration painted in gold lacquer, 17th century. This is a delightful example of a more southern style, with ornament of a less functional nature than is usual. The seat would have had a silk covered cushion placed upon it. Royal Ontario Museum, Canada

1072 *Right*: Late 17th-century lacquered chest-on-chest, Ch'ing dynasty (1644-1911). The black ground is inset with ivory, mother-of-pearl, glass and hardstones and is painted red, white and gold. The upper chest has handles allowing it to be lifted off. Victoria and Albert Museum, London

1073 *Below*: Chinese scholar's study. An early 19th-century arrangement of the contemporary furniture. Space is allowed for the placing of extra tables for painting, or for setting up a musical instrument. Symmetry and asymmetry combine in a pleasing informal arrangement. Philadelphia Museum of Art

1070 *Below*: Table of unusual melon shape, *c.* 1650. Ta-li Fu in the Province of Yünnan in south-west China is famous for its decorative marble of green, grey and white. Known as *Ta-li-shih* it is often used for decorative insets in tables, chairs and screens. Private Collection

feet were clear of the draughty polished brick floor. The second type of rather high table is of narrow, rectangular shape. It was intended either to be placed along a wall or used as a base for the *ch'in* or lute, or tables might be made in pairs and placed symmetrically along the east and west walls of a formal room, to which the main entrance was on the south side. In less formal rooms these side tables could be arranged along the walls with a carefully calculated asymmetry. In structure, tables are either based on a box form, or have developed from a trestle type. The box type often display monumental qualities, especially when the subtle, curved legs terminate in horse-hoof feet. But late examples became heavy and often ornate. The trestle type is the reverse, for it is often light and subtle. The delicately inward inclination of the leg units and the high stretchers placed close to the apron contribute towards a rational and elegant composition. In late examples or in tables of unusually large size the stretchers may be replaced by carved panels. Ornamentation of the apron, whether of the box or trestle type, is generally restrained and enhances the well proportioned functional character of the design. [1063] [1064] [1065]

The great range of cupboards and chests suggest that as much as possible was placed under cover. Clothes for example, were laid away in chests and were never kept in drawers. Books and the scholar's working materials, such as ink sticks, brushes, brush-rests and paper, were all stored away in cupboards. Each treasured jade or other work of art was preserved in its own neatly made box and stored in a chest. Household crockery was also stacked in cupboards that might contain both drawers and shelves. Shelves were usually made of soft wood, the surface lacquered as a protection against insect attack. [1068] [1072]

The principles of pairing and arrangement already discussed also applied to cupboards, chests and sideboards. In these the embellishment is often to be found in the metal mounts and their placing in relation to each other. The only cupboards intended to stand alone are those in which the side walls are inclined inwards towards the top, but even so their placing is carefully related to other objects in the room. [1068] [1072]

Chairs are of three kinds, a rigid box-frame base with straight back and arms, a similar frame but with a swinging curved back; this is often called an abbot's chair. And finally a collapsible chair with round or straight back. The straight-backed chair with a single wide splat up the back often has a pleasingly designed yoke-like top rail. These are probably earlier in date than the squarer type, which later became heavier, with back and sides elaborately carved or painted. Occasionally decorative panels of well-marked marble or polychrome enamelled porcelain are set in the back and arms. An armchair was always regarded as a seat of honour and as such was usually reserved for men. In Sung times (A.D. 960-1279), in fact, it was regarded as most improper for women to sit on chairs, and, indeed, it is significant that in Chinese paintings and illustrations women are always shown on stools and not on chairs. [1066] [1071]

It is only with the great twelve-fold screens of the late 17th century and later that bright colours were introduced as a decorative feature. Some screens were painted, but more popular were the lacquer screens which came to be known in the West as Coromandel screens. These lend themselves particularly well to bright colours that show up clearly against the dignified restraint of plain black and brown polished lacquer. Symbolism plays an important part in much of the decoration of these screens and elaborate punning is common, conveying, as it so often does, wishes for health, wealth, happiness, long life and numerous progeny. This same kind of elaboration occurs also on much of the massive carved lacquer furniture intended for the palaces, the best of which would seem to date from the 17th and 18th centuries.

While every kind of Chinese furniture had its proper use, there was also the added refinement that the right sort of furniture should be used at the proper time of the year and in the correct surroundings. Bamboo furniture, for example, was made for summer use, and especially for out-of-doors. Little survives today, but the designs show the same regard for proportion, simple dignity and function as may be seen in more formal furniture. This is indeed the outstanding characteristic of Chinese furniture which has been so long overlooked in the West and could well be studied with the same attention that we bring to European furniture.

JAPAN

J. Hillier

In Japanese painting, as in Chinese, it is an axiom to 'take care of the voids'. An awareness of space has also influenced the Japanese in planning their houses and in designing and arranging their furniture. It is coupled with an innate flair for decoration that marks all their arts, whether painting, lacquer, pottery, textiles or metalwork. The frequency of earthquakes dictated the generally light, wooden, one-storey construction of their houses, and also, correspondingly, the sparsity of the permanent solid furniture. Accustomed to sitting and sleeping on the floor, they needed neither tables, chairs nor beds of Western type and in general the objects of daily use, such as armrests, writing tables, book chests and cabinets, are small, low and unobtrusive.

In their thus, to us, empty rooms, the walls become of paramount significance and here the Japanese possess a singular advantage: the walls, internal and external, are invariably moveable. The light paper-covered framework called *shōji* and the more solidly constructed *fusuma*, the latter often with painted panels, make the divisions between rooms. They slide in grooves and not only provide a means of entrance and exit, like doors, and a source of light, in place of glazed windows, but also allow the rooms to be varied in size and shape. Externally, the *shōji*, shielded by overhanging eaves, may give on to a garden which is designed as an extension to the living room. A wide verandah, the *engawa*, projects directly from the floor level out under the boughs of the trees or the arbour of wisteria. When closed, the paper-covered *shōji* filter the light and give a soft suffused penumbra which tempers the blankness of the walls and adds to the feeling of quiet serenity. The *fusuma*, being solid, were one of the accepted areas for decoration, and quite often striking effects were achieved by encrusting the natural wood, *paulownia* or similar bold-grained species, with painting or ceramic.

In western countries, before central heating changed the pattern, the fireplace was a central feature of one wall, a focal point governing the orientation of the furniture. In the Japanese house, heating is by means of a charcoal burner in a container which can be moved from place to place. Typically too, artificial lighting is from an oil lamp in a paper-covered stand, *(andon)* although naturally, even in houses which are otherwise traditional, fixed electric lights have largely supplanted them.

Since the 14th century it has been normal in Japan, and still is, to cover the floors with *tatami*. These are mats of rice-straw and rushes, each approximately six feet by three. (The sizes of the rooms are expressed by the numbers of mats they accommodate.) Castle, mansion, *cha-shitsu* (the hut for the Tea Ceremony), and the normal dwelling are alike in their use of the *tatami* floor covering. The restrained colour and cleanliness of these mats, helped by the practice of leaving shoes outside, gives the interiors a cool freshness.

Another structural feature of a typical Japanese room is the *tokonoma*. This is a small alcove set apart for exhibiting a particular painting or work of art, with perhaps a complementary flower or driftwood arrangement, placed there for an occasion and frequently changed.

Everything tends to create an impression of mobility, for a room may constantly be altered in shape and arrangement. With such fundamental differences of design between a Japanese room and a typical western interior, where stability was sought and the furniture was part of a formal arrangement, it is to be expected that Japanese furniture is of an entirely different order from that of the west, even though some things, like the screen, have been adopted here.

The screen is, of course, another feature which suggests impermanency in the aspect of an interior. Devised originally to divide the large halls of great houses or palaces into separate compart-

(margin references: 1084, 1090, 1079, 1077, 1087, 1079, 1083)

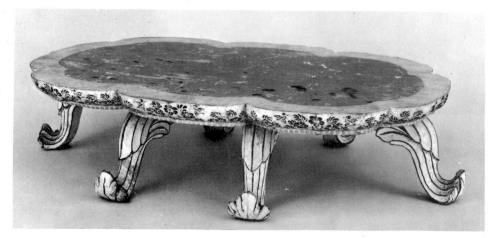

1074 *Above*: Eight-lobed stand, *hinoki* wood painted gold and silver, 8th century. In the Shōsoin Depository, or Treasure House, objects of every kind are preserved, placed there as the relics of Emperor Shomu after his death in A.D. 756. There have been later additions to the storehouse but much of the contents dates from the 8th–12th centuries. This stand is considered to be among the earliest examples. Although probably of ritualistic Buddhist usage, there is little doubt that other similar tables were in domestic use. Shosoin Depository, Nara, Japan

1075 *Above*: Low stand of painted *hinoki* wood, 8th century. The board is foliated with twenty-four lobes and is covered with a pad of twill silk. The eight legs are painted white, yellow, green, purple, and red. Like the previous illustration this stand was probably used for presenting offerings to the Buddha at temple services. Shōsoin Depository, Nara, Japan

1076 *Below*: Chest of lacquered wood, 10th–11th century. The phoenix medallion design is inlaid in shell, a process introduced from China in the 7th century. For centuries after the first major invasion of Chinese design, the objects of daily use in Japan were closely modelled on those of the continent, and this chest is of decided Chinese pattern. National Museum, Tokyo

1078 *Above*: Chest-of-drawers for poem books, late 16th century. Of lacquered wood with metal fittings, it is decorated with a design of autumn grasses and flowers. Manuscript volumes, often with illustrations painted by prominent artists, were kept in chests of this type. This piece was owned by the great Generalissimo Hideyoshi. National Museum, Tokyo

1080 *Below*: 17th-century cabinet of lacquered wood, with metal fittings. Cabinets vary in shape and in the arrangement of shelves, some being almost completely enclosed with sliding doors, others largely open. They owe their striking effect to the superb applied design, for which the Japanese have always shown an innate gift. The design illustrates scenes from the Genji Romance. National Museum, Tokyo

1077 *Top of page*: A typical *cha-shitsu*, tea-room, showing the effectiveness of subtle proportions and composition, the simple, austere decoration, *tatami* on the floor and calligraphy hanging in the *tokonoma* or alcove. The use of natural wood including a twisted wistaria root should be noted. The origin of many houses such as this can be traced back to the Muromachi period, 15th–16th century. Kodansha, Tokyo

1079 *Above*: Another tea-house interior, with display of calligraphy and a single stone in the *tokonoma*. The splendid iron vessel on the left is the *hibachi* or charcoal fire. Kodansha, Tokyo

1081 *Left*: 17th-century mirror stand, lacquered wood with metal fittings. National Museum, Tokyo

1082 *Right*: Four-drawer cabinet with door, in gold and brown lacquer with shell inlay and silver mounts. Late 16th century. The metalwork, especially the lock-plate, shows signs of Portuguese influence, which is also traceable in other spheres in the 16th century. The design is typical of the Momoyama period, characterised by a richly ornate style and the use of sumptuous materials. Victoria and Albert Museum, London

1083 *Above left*: Dressing-room and bedroom of 1692, from a woodcut illustration to a book of instructions to women on how to run a house (*Essentials for Ladies* by Naemura Johaku). The upper picture shows a dressing-room, with *kimono* and towel racks, and a mirror stand draped with a cover; the lower is the bedroom with coverlets and pillows spread on the *tatami*, and a shielding screen. The *tokonoma* with hanging picture is at rear. Author's Collection

1084 *Above*: Corner of a room with a writing-table at which a girl is seated reading a scroll. Behind her are the painted sliding *fusuma* and in front of a bell-shaped opening is a carved lacquered stand. From a book by an unknown artist: *A series of famous crests*, 1744. Author's Collection

1087 *Below*: Interior, 1723. From a picture book by Sukenobu. This print illustrates the Japanese practice of sitting on *tatami*. The maid is placing the oil lamp in the stand, with its shield of transparent paper. There is little furniture, except for storage chests. Author's Collection

1085 *Above*: Kimono rack of lacquered wood with metal fittings. This simple, elegant and unchanging shape goes back many hundreds of years and can be seen in scrolls of the 11th century. This example is probably late 18th century. The joints and ends were invariably decorated with chased metalwork, as in this instance and the two feet were of a heavy enough wood to ensure stability. Ashmolean Museum, Oxford

1086 *Below*: Detail of the kimono rack shown above. Ashmolean Museum, Oxford

1088 *Above*: Two-fold screen dated 1784, with a painting of wistaria by one of the greatest of Japanese painters, Maruyama Ōkyō. The screen is of a stout paper on a slender wooden frame. City Art Gallery, Bristol

1089 *Below*: A low table that serves as armrest, writing- and reading-table. In this painting by Eishi of a courtesan and her maid, dating from about 1795-8, the table is of a simple lacquered type of Chinese pattern. Collection: Ralph Harari, London

ments, they are used, too, in rooms of more modest size. They are intended as shields against draughts, to which Japanese houses by their very construction are prone, and they also give privacy. But apart from their functional importance, they also provide further opportunities for interior decoration. These screens, (*byōbu*) are six-leaf, four-leaf or two-leaf, often as much as six feet in height, and sometimes used in pairs. The frames are of planed and lacquered wood decorated, if at all, with small metal ornaments to disguise the joints. Invariably, the fabric is stout paper. Screens were the accepted vehicle for decorative painting, a field in which the Japanese have made a significant contribution to world art. The screens, and the paintings on the *fusuma*, are the counterpart to the murals of western interior decoration. But neither is static in the way that a wall painting must be, for the *fusuma* slide from side to side in the floor-channels, and the *byōbu* are both transportable and capable of a concertina movement which allows their decorated surfaces to be seen from different angles. Other screens are the *tsuitate*, a standing single-leaf screen that is again a vehicle for varied applied decoration, and the *sudare*, a blind of split bamboo that can be rolled up when not in use.

Most of the free-standing furniture is small and a great deal is of lacquered wood. No nation, not even the Chinese, has achieved the supreme quality of lacquer work perfected by the Japanese and the material is so durable that examples from the 8th century onwards survive. The shapes of these lacquer pieces—armrest, writing table, sword-rack, cabinet and *etagère*—are unexceptional, but the surface decoration is of an unparalleled beauty and originality, and one sees the virtue of the plain and unadorned walls and of the *tatami* in showing off such splendidly ornamented objects. There is a constant delight in such contrasts between the natural and the sophisticated in all Japanese arts: and in the house, the superb craftsmanship of the pieces of furniture is set off against the posts of unworked and unvarnished wood, the hand made texture of the stout paper of the *shōji* and the homely straw mats. In this connection, mention must be made of the extensive use of textiles. In Japan sumptuous brocades and silks are placed directly on to the *tatami* for sitting on, or used as coverlets against the cold. The rich colour and variety of these textiles help to satisfy that need of the Japanese to bring textural contrasts into their interiors. Different materials are grouped together so that one acts as a foil to the other: the brittle lustre of a shell makes us feel the depth and penetrability of wood, the falling petal the enduring hardness of granite. Such themes are the essence of the art of driftwood arrangement and, more subtly, of *ikebana*, flower arrangement.

The 'art of the room' is no empty phrase in relation to the Japanese. A living room is not a medley of objects of use in a haphazard setting but a careful arrangement of a few finely made and decorated objects set against a neutral background, itself not static, the whole composed with the same attention to contrasting forms and textures as is displayed in the driftwood compositions. The geometrical austerity of the walls, the *shōji* and *fusuma*, the harmony of the varying rectangles, is entirely to the modern taste: it has been suggested, not too fancifully perhaps, the Mondrian may well have been inspired by a recollection of pictures of Japanese interiors. Their furniture, apart possibly from certain types of shelved cabinet and the elegant kimono-rack, have had little apparent influence outside Japan, but the sophisticated use of materials, the sense of proportion, the restrained composition, the implication of mobility, the filtered light playing on subtly alternating textures, all these have had, and will probably increasingly have, a deep influence on interior decoration throughout the world.

1088

1078, 1080
1081, 1082

1083

1085

1090 *Left*: A room in one of the *Green Houses* where men are waiting to make their overtures to the courtesans. The drawing shows clearly the sliding *shōji* and *fusuma* and the absence of any large solid pieces of furniture. From the famous *Annals of the Green Houses*, a picture book by Utamaro, dated 1804. British Museum, London

THE MIDDLE EAST, INDIA AND SOUTH EAST ASIA

Anthony Christie

For the historian of furniture those parts of Asia which lie between the hinterland of the eastern Mediterranean and the South China Sea are chiefly of negative interest. For here we find regions in which high civilisations developed without any apparent need to develop furniture. Life tended to be lived at ground level, upon mats and rugs with little more than cushions to give support and perhaps a low table to carry a toilet set, a mirror, or, less often, food. The reasons for this are not clear, unless we are to assume that the tradition of tent-dwelling nomads, all of whose gear was designed for easy transport upon the pack animals, remained the ideal in South Asia.

To this general absence of furniture there is one notable exception, for the throne, chair or stool occurs universally from the earliest historical period to the present day. These objects served both as physical supports and as symbols of authority. The throne was the attribute of gods and kings: the commonalty squatted upon the floor. Among earlier representations there is scarcely ever more than one seated figure, whose seat takes one of a number of forms, from a simple bench to an elaborate high-backed chair with a cushion, turned legs and decorative features.

In early seals and ritual scenes from Mesopotamia there may be a stand in front of the principal figure, bearing a tree or some other sacred object. Such stands have been found on house sites in the Middle East and the valley of the River Indus. In Sumer before the First Dynasty of Ur (early in the 3rd millenium) scenes of feasting are shown upon cylinder seals. In these the seated figures are usually on backless stools, often sharing a drink from a common vessel by means of drinking tubes. Contemporary sites in the Indus valley provide little certain evidence of furniture but one celebrated seal shows what appears to be a god seated on a throne. It has been claimed by some investigators that both chairs and tables are represented in the pictographs from the Indus valley inscriptions. But there is no direct evidence for beds or couches, nor even for chests, although the deep recesses in the walls were probably fitted with wooden shelves. It is also likely that large pottery vessels were used as 'cupboards', a practice which persists in Northern Pakistan to the present day.

A second type of royal seat was apparently used in Sumer. The king, Gudea, is portrayed in a kind of tub chair, related, it would seem, to a seat with a rounded back depicted on reliefs from Telloh in Iraq and perhaps also on objects from the Royal Graves at Ur. This style of seat is of interest, for when at last we find Indian scenes depicting seated figures some are shown in similar chairs.

At a later stage in the history of the Middle East, sites such as Nimrud and Nineveh provide evidence of further developments in the form of the throne and chair. A relief of the Assyrian King Ashur-nasir-pal (884–860 B.C.) shows the king on a backless stool with turned legs, his feet resting upon a footstool. The seat has animal-head terminals and what are probably bronze ornaments, since such have been found in excavations. There is also evidence to suggest that ivory decorative panels were employed by furniture makers. Two hundred years later King Ashur-bani-pal is shown reclining on a day-bed and drinking with his queen who sits on a high-backed chair of a kind which elsewhere would be occupied by the king himself. This relief, which shows two styles of table, is a splendid illustration of an Assyrian *fête champêtre,* with attendants bearing foodstuffs or waving their fly wisks over the royal couple, while in the background a harpist provides music on an instrument exactly like that used by his pre-

1092

1093

1094

1095

1096

1091 *Left*: Terracotta plaque showing a seated figure playing a harp. The folding stool appears to have a cushion upon it, and the two legs are linked by a cord. From the Diyala river region, east of Baghdad, *c.* 2025–1700 B.C. Oriental Institute, Chicago

1092 *Below*: Line drawing from a cylinder seal impression showing an enthroned lion receiving tribute from other animals, one of which carries a harp. The lion sits upon a backless throne with animal legs. The apron is carved and pierced. From the Royal Cemetery at Ur, 3500–2800 B.C.

1093 *Below*: Impressions from cylinder seals, showing seated figures drinking from common vessels by means of tubes. Seats and tables are of various forms, sometimes of bent wood, sometimes rectangular with diagonal crossed supports. Ur, first half of the 3rd millennium B.C. British Museum, London

1094 *Left*: Carved granite figure of Gudea, patesi of Lagash, Neo-Sumerian, *c.* 2100 B.C. Although Gudea appears to sit upon a barrel-shaped seat, an open, four-legged stool is indicated in relief, and it is probable that the seat was a simple stool which the carver was unable to render realistically in such intractible material. On his lap Gudea has the architects' plan for the city. From Telloh, Iraq. Louvre, Paris

1095 *Right*: Relief from the palace at Nimrud, Iraq, showing King Ashur-nasir-pal II of Assyria (883–859 B.C.) seated upon a backless throne, the ends of the seat rails carved as bulls' heads. A deep fringe hangs from the cushion between carved legs. The King's footstool has lion-paw feet and a stout stretcher. British Museum, London

1096 *Right*: King Ashur-bani-pal of Assyria (668–631 B.C.) is shown feasting with his queen, after the defeat of his enemy the King of Elaur, whose head hangs from a nearby tree. The King reclines on a high couch which would also serve as a throne. It has a mattress and bolster and elaborately carved legs and stretcher. The table legs combine symbolic features with realistically carved lion paws. The musician on the left is playing a harp similar to the one from Diyala (see illustration 1091) nearly two thousand years earlier. From the palace at Nineveh, Iraq. British Museum, London

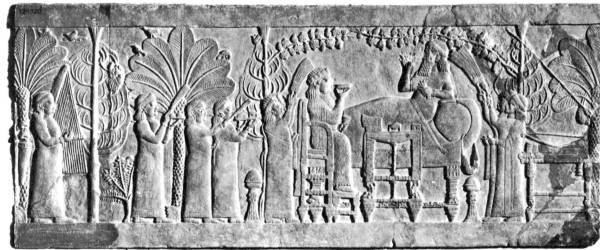

1097 *Above*: Sassanian silver plate illustrating another royal banquet. The presence of guests is indicated symbolically by garlands, while the boars' heads denote the cause of celebration. The day-bed is piled high with cushions and a folding stool stands beside it. 5th century A.D. Walters Art Gallery, Baltimore

1098 *Right*: Darius, King of Persia is shown giving audience to a high Court official. His throne and footstool are of regal magnificence, and it is interesting to see again the combination of turned elements with lion-paw feet (see illustration 1096). From the Treasury at Persepolis, now in the Teheran Museum.

1099 *Above left*: Stone relief illustrating Queen Maya's dream. She dreams that she is conceiving the Buddha, symbolised by a white elephant entering her side. The queen's couch is set in a recess and is flanked by pilasters which are inspired by Roman example. Gandhara School, *c.* 2nd century A.D. British Museum, London

1100 *Above right*: Relief showing the Mugha Pakkha Jataka story of an earlier existence of the Buddha. A ruler and his wife occupy a backed couch-throne with substantial turned legs, while the women of the Court sit on cushions, pouffes and round-backed chairs. Amaravati, South India. 2nd century A.D. British Museum, London

1101 *Left*: Enthroned Buddha as king. The throne is also a lotus, so that only the back is treated naturalistically. On each side are other figures, two of whom are seated on stool-thrones in a European pose with their legs down, as opposed to cross-legged. At the top a bed supports the dead Buddha. 9th–10th century A.D. British Museum, London

1102 *Right*: Indian painting showing a maidservant making a bed. The bed is raised on six bell-shaped feet of painted wood, but the richness is provided not by the bed itself but by the decorative textiles which cover the bed, and the striped and tasselled bolsters which adorn it. Punjab Hills, Nurpur School, *c.* 1720. Victoria and Albert Museum, London

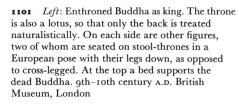

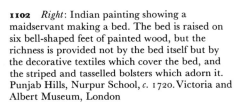

1103 *Left*: Lady playing a vina to a pair of deer. She is seated on a backless cushioned seat with a polygonal footstool. Punjab Hills, Kulu School, *c.* 1700. Victoria and Albert Museum, London

1104 *Right*: Royal lovers on a high-backed throne supported on four legs. A large deep bolster supports their backs. With its deep frieze below the seat rail and polygonal shape, this throne is similar in general appearance to the Golden Throne of Ranjit Singh (see illustration 1108). Central Indian painting of the early 18th century. Victoria and Albert Museum, London

1105 *Left*: Mughal cabinet of the late 17th century, decorated with a marquetry of ebony and ivory. Based upon a European form, even to the cushioned frieze below the cornice, this piece was probably made for European use. Victoria and Albert Museum, London

1106 *Above*: Detail from the cabinet shown in the previous illustration. Although the cabinet is European in form the ivory decoration is purely Mughal. Here a ruler is depicted reclining on a canopied day-bed, receiving gifts. The feet of the bed are similar to those shown on the throne (illustration 1108) and the backless seat (1103). Victoria and Albert Museum, London

1091
1098 decessor at Diyala two thousand years earlier. At Persepolis King Darius is shown seated upon a high-backed chair of state, his feet on a footstool; both chair and stool show elaborate turned work but in general their relation with earlier Assyrian styles seems clear, particularly in the treatment of the motif where the stretcher bar joins the legs.

1097 More than a thousand years later a Sassanian silver bowl shows another royal banquet, at which king and queen share a couch. Here the occasion celebrated is a successful royal hunt where the boar's head motif replaces the head of the enemy king in the scene from Nineveh.

In the earliest Buddhist reliefs in India, which do not pre-date the 2nd century B.C., the throne occurs in various forms. Its appearance is usually symbolic and it alludes to the mystical presence of the Buddha. Such thrones have a flat, rectangular seat, supported on four legs with perhaps an upright back and no arms. Later the Buddha himself is shown upon a throne, of flat seat type supported on animal legs. The first representations of
1099 beds date from the 1st Century A.D. These have a wooden frame with turned legs and are covered with a mattress.

The normal sitting position upon the Indian throne seat is with the legs crossed so that the whole body, including the legs
1101 and feet, is on the platform of the throne. This is in contrast to the style of sitting in the Middle East where the feet hang down to the floor. This posture is also found in Indian images, but it is significant that, unlike other postures, it does not appear to have a Sanskrit name, and a tradition has grown up of describing images seated thus as being seated 'in the European manner'. (Similarly, in Burmese, the western-type chair is called *kala-taing*, 'foreigner sits'). Indian practice does, however, admit of a posture in which one leg is allowed to dangle over the edge of the throne to be supported on a separate footstool in a 'position of royal ease'. The bed on which the dying Buddha is shown in reliefs from northern India is clearly designed also to serve as a
1099 divan with a stool to support the dangling leg.

A relief now in the British Museum shows the story of an earlier existence of the Buddha in which he was born as a prince who renounced all luxuries. His despairing parents surrounded him with all worldly pleasures but the prince remained unmoved until his father resolved to dispose of him as unfit to be a prince. At this point the prince revealed his true power and by his example converted his parents and people to asceticism. The Court with its dancing girls is depicted on the relief. The king is

seated on a wide 'sofa', with his son beside him. Girls sit upon 1100 pouffes and also upon tub chairs strangely similar to those from the Middle East of very much earlier date.

Elaborate cane or bamboo chairs seem to have been well established in southern India by the 2nd–3rd centuries A.D., and literary sources now add some more information to our pictorial evidence for furniture. Thus the *Kamasutra* gives an account of a room suitable for a wealthy young man-about-town. This has a divan and a soft bed, with a canopy and pillows, a small table for perfumes and make-up, a chest for clothes and jewellery, a spittoon and a table for drawing. Other sources recommend a birdcage. Such a tradition persists and paintings from the 13th to the 19th century show very similar rooms as suitable for amorous *Plate facing* encounters. It is, however, noticeable that the room of a wealthy *page 288* citizen too, was very simple: furniture has little place in it. In India, even the coming of the Mughals in the 16th century made little difference. For the poor a mat upon the floor or simply a floor of mud and cow-dung smoothed flat had to serve for seat and bed alike, and still does.

The simplicity of Indian furniture is equalled or even exceeded by that of the various countries of South-East Asia which have been strongly influenced by India since the beginning of the Christian era. Here too the throne is almost alone as an article of furniture and it retains its symbolic role. Even today in the *kraton,* the royal enclosure, of Jogjakarta in central Java, the mystical presence of the ruler is indicated by an empty throne in the open audience chamber above which a lamp burns perpetually. The *kraton* servants and officials crouch deferentially as they pass in front of it, as they would do were the sultan seated upon it. From earlier periods of Javanese history the monuments which survive provide a valuable source of information about everyday life, for although much of the material upon which the reliefs were based was of Indian origin, the artists based the *mise-en-scène* upon the life which they saw around them. Even when the story required a palace throne room, nothing more elaborate than a canopied platform is usually shown, a similar platform serving as a bed. A few pots for drinking water and for use as spittoons complete the furnishings.

To judge from the evidence of the reliefs and the accounts of Cambodia left to us in Chinese sources things were no different there. The traveller, Chou Ta-kuan, who spent the years 1296–7 A.D. in Cambodia, has left us an account of a Cambodian household which could well describe any South-East Asian home:

1107 *Above*: Armchair of ivory following a late 18th-century English form. English designs were given to Indian craftsmen who often followed them most faithfully. There was a thriving export business in such chairs. Victoria and Albert Museum, London

1108 *Below*: The Golden Throne of Ranjit Singh, Sikh Maharaja of the Punjab (1780–1839). The polygonal throne is of traditional form, which had continued in use for over a century. (Compare illustration 1104.) The conical feet are also typical, (see 1102, 1103, 1104). The upper section can be lifted off the base by the gold handles. Victoria and Albert Museum, London

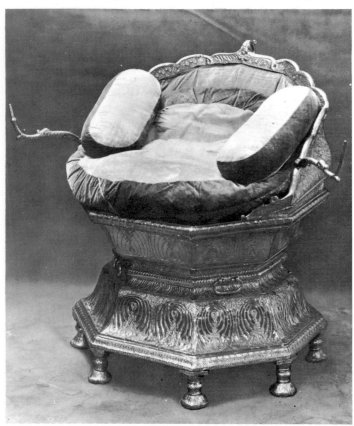

'Middle-class citizens have a house without table, seat, basin or bucket. To cook their rice they use an earthenware pot: a similar vessel serves for the curry. Three stones set in the ground form the hearth and coconut-shells act as ladles. To serve the rice they use Chinese earthenware or copper spoons. The curry is served on leaves which are fixed together: even when the curry is juicy they do not leak. They also make leaf spoons for drinking the juice. When the meal is finished, the leaves are thrown away. They use the same objects even when making offerings to the spirits and to the Buddha. They keep a tin or an earthenware bowl full of water at their side when eating in which to dip their hands. This is because they eat rice with their fingers and need to rinse them occasionally so that it does not stick. They drink wine from tin goblets: the poor use earthenware bowls. Silver and sometimes gold vessels are found in the houses of the nobles and the rich. At festivals large numbers of gold vessels of all shapes and sizes are used. On the floor they spread Chinese mats or the skins of tiger, panther, deer or buck; they also use reed mats. In recent years they have started to use low tables, a few inches high. They sleep on mats spread on the floor, though recently a few people have begun to use low beds which are usually made by Chinese. They cover their table utensils with a piece of cloth: in the palace they use gold brocade which is given by foreign merchants. They do not use rice-mills but husk the grain in mortars.'

Simple stools were sometimes used by market traders who otherwise sat on the bamboo platforms upon which their wares were displayed. A royal figure may be displayed upon a folding stool of a type which occurred many centuries earlier in the Middle East and seems to have been widely distributed throughout Eurasia. When thrones are shown they derive from the Indian sofa type and it is from a modified form of this that the Buddhist monk today preaches his sermon.

More recently in Cambodia, as elsewhere in mainland South-East Asia, a tradition has grown of making lacquered wooden cabinets to hold sacred books and the like. Such cabinets seem to have been modelled upon Chinese originals though their decoration may now be wholly South-East Asian. Lacquer wares, of Chinese origin, have been developed, notably in Burma since the 13th century, as containers for everything from toilet articles and combs to switches of false hair and to store the elaborate dress turbans which formal dress required. Lacquer, too, served for food containers and drinking vessels as well as for the ubiquitous spittoons. The rattan baskets, used to contain clothes and the like in simple houses without cupboards, might also be varnished with lacquer. Under Chinese and European influences standing cupboards and chests of lacquered or varnished wood have come gradually into use, but it is still normal to keep what is not in immediate use in bundles or baskets, hung from the walls or perched upon the rafters.

Chinese influences have already been noted as the main source for innovations in the furniture of pre-colonial times. Chinese joiners made much of the colonial furniture in South-East Asia, often from Sino-European pattern-books. In India native craftsmen soon learnt to make what the Europeans needed. In one 1106, 1107 country alone, Viet-nam, part of whose present territory formed a political and cultural province of China for the first millenium of the Christian era, Chinese concepts of furniture provided the standard and Chinese styles prevailed. Here beds, tables, stools and chairs, with screens and wooden panelling, were to be found, the styles changing with those of China itself. Even after China had finally been defeated and Viet-nam achieved independence, the houses of mandarins and merchants continued to be furnished in a manner befitting their grades in China. But in the villages and among the hill-peoples, life continued to be upon the verandah floor by day and upon the sleeping mats spread on the room floor by night: such furniture as there was, was for gods and kings.

Painting of the Nurpur School, Punjab Hills *c.*1800 showing the Hindu God, Krishna approaching his love, Radha. Radha sits upon a deep wide throne, on bell-shaped feet, the back and arm pieces scalloped and outward-curving. There is an attractive carpet upon the floor and similar material covers the doorways, rolled and tied high during the day. Victoria and Albert Museum, London.

'Red-blue chair', 1917, by Gerrit Rietveld, Stedelijk Museum, Amsterdam. This armchair was designed during the First World War by a leading member of the Dutch *de Stijl* group as a deliberate break with existing traditions. In itself and in its aspirations this design may seem archaic to our eyes, yet it marks the beginning of what we now call modern design.

Storage Cases by Charles Eames, manufactured by the Herman Miller Furniture Co. In 1950 Eames developed a series of storage units in neutral coloured woods with bright metal frames which can be combined in many different ways. This illustration shows one possible arrangement, in which the extreme simplicity of the parts, and their light airy appearance are characteristic of this designer's work for mass production.

Chair of teak, oak and cane, 1949, by Hans Wegner, manufactured by Johannes Hansen. This is a modest, unpretentious chair, but with extraordinary appeal and of faultless design. It has a sturdy stance, a seat and curved back promising comfort; but the secret lies in the flow of the modelled forms, the subtly changing curves and surfaces, satisfying for their own sake, but given meaning by function.

IX THE TWENTIETH CENTURY

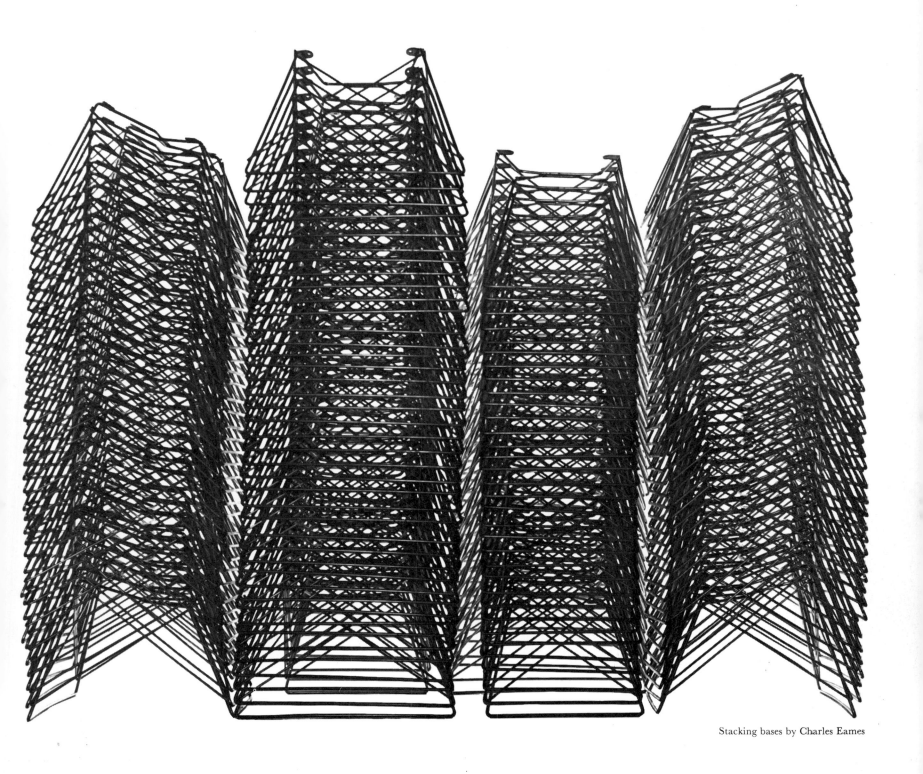

Stacking bases by Charles Eames

THE TWENTIETH CENTURY

Herwin Schaefer

It is somewhat hazardous to speak of modern furniture as though we were certain just what this means in terms of style and could determine the exact moment of its birth. We can do neither quite precisely. Apart from the fact that modern furniture has a history of at least fifty years in which there has naturally been development and change, it may vary considerably and yet be truly modern and this has been the case particularly during the last fifteen years. It can move between organic and geometric. It can use traditional materials, techniques and forms and draw its design inspiration from them, or it can determinedly employ only the newest technological means and achieve appropriately new results. Nevertheless, there are qualities of design which are generally characteristic of modern furniture, whether made in the 1920s or 60s, by hand or machine, of wood or plastic, and it is these which help us to define the style.

Modern furniture design is concerned with essential form. This form may emphasise structural or sculptural qualities, but it is always abstract. It is never copied from nature, and it is neither symbolic nor ornamented. Modern technology and economy demand that products give maximum value with minimum expenditure. Thus, ideally, more comfort and convenience are achieved by using less material. This material should be light in weight and colour, and smooth and hard in texture, using as few joints as possible, so that the manufacturing process is simple. Modern abstract, pure form is often thought of as being merely functional and as deriving only from technological advances. But this is hardly the case, for function can be satisfied by many forms, and modern technology can produce any form. The use of abstract form is rather the result of a larger movement embracing all the visual arts. The genesis of modern design coincides almost exactly with the birth of abstract painting and sculpture, and the spiritual values that Kandinsky and others sought in their paintings also inspired the first designers of modern furniture. The fact that furniture made today by hand and of traditional materials is devoid of ornament or symbolism and conforms to the canons of abstract design, attests to this common formal approach.

The quality of newness is often sought by designers and critics of modern furniture. This is because of the conscious effort to break away from the historical styles of the 19th century. The insistence on forms which had no reference to past styles marked the beginning of the modern movement before the turn of the century and has remained one of its principle aims. But a more compelling reason today for newness in design is that our age of technology has a unique character which should be reflected in our environment. To many designers and critics, newness represents, therefore, a probing search for forms at once removed from the past and adjusted to the technological and social realities of today.

A less defensible reason for seeking newness in design is the result of economic pressure. We must buy in order to keep our machines running and employment stable, and industry persuades us that we must be up-to-date and always have the newest designs of furniture as well as of automobiles and many other things. However, this feverish search for novelty imposed by the industrial cycle has not contributed to the formation of the modern style, but has become a consideration only much more recently; in fact, this urgency for newness is in distinct contradiction to much of the earlier doctrine of modern design which still regarded durability as essential. The fact that this compulsion for continuous change is gaining momentum means that we are entering a new phase and that we can look back on the modern style as something of the past.

Where are the beginnings of modern design? At the turn of the century Art Nouveau contributed towards a new start, but was not itself that starting point. Forward-looking in its rejection of the past and in its insistence on originality, Art Nouveau, in spite of many enthusiastic statements made at the time, failed to come to grips with the central problem of design in our time, that of large-scale machine production. It was therefore not ready to

1109 Sideboard of painted wood made in 1919 by Gerrit Rietveld (born 1888), a member of the Dutch *de Stijl* group. There is none of the structural disguise of the pre-war world. These are bare statements, deliberately revealing construction, using standard elements to facilitate mass production. 'Archaic' to our eyes, this piece marks the beginning of what we call modern design. Stedelijk Museum, Amsterdam

1110 Armchair of chromium-plated steel tubing and canvas designed in 1925 by Marcel Breuer (born 1902). This light, airy chair of tubular steel seems a logical development from the more 'primitive' wooden structure of Rietveld. Given new materials and an experimental and pragmatic approach to design many new and unprecedented forms were inevitable.

1111 *Above*: Side chair, the first cantilevered chair, designed in 1926 by Mies van der Rohe (born 1886). The inherent strength of the tubular metal allows the designer to discard the traditional four legs, and to cantilever his chair from two supports, thus giving resilience and comfort, without the weight and multiplicity of parts needed in traditional joinery. This idea was tried out by several designers in the mid-20s, but never so elegantly as by Mies van der Rohe in this beautifully curved example. Collection: The Museum of Modern Art, New York. Manufacturer: Thonet, Germany

1112 *Above*: Side chair of chromium-plated steel tubing, wood and cane, designed by Marcel Breuer in 1928. More practical than the Mies example, Breuer's cantilevered chair became the prototype for countless versions in the following years. The lightness, clarity and frugality of the design is very much in keeping with the aspirations of the period. Collection: The Museum of Modern Art, New York

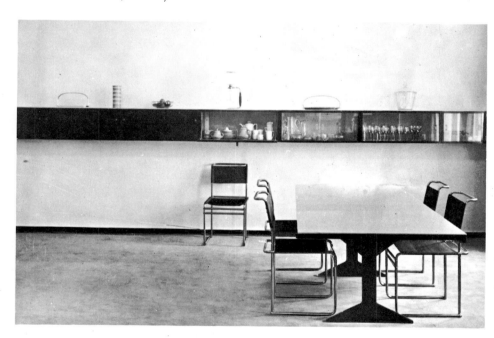

1113 *Above*: Piscator apartment, Berlin, designed by Marcel Breuer in 1927. Piscator was one of Berlin's most famous avant-garde theatrical directors of the 20s. Breuer's interior shows his passion for clarity and precision, lightness and spaciousness, with never a superfluous detail.

1114 *Below*: Unit furniture designed by Walter Gropius (born 1883) in 1927 for the Feder Store in Berlin. Economic mass production inevitably involves standardisation but variety can be achieved by providing a number of units on a modular basis which can be combined in a number of ways. This principle has since been used by many designers.

produce or even advocate the abstract, impersonal form which we now associate with modern machine production.

The cataclysm of the First World War marked the turning point. The breakdown of social values and structures was accompanied by disillusion and poverty, but also by a desire to experiment. There were three centres where decisive contributions were made in this initial phase: Holland, Germany and France. Holland, spared by the war, has the priority in terms of time. *Plate facing page 289* There, Gerrit Rietveld worked during the war years on designs which were more radical than anything seen before. Not only 1109 were all reminiscences of past, traditional styles eliminated, but it was as though no chair, no sideboard had ever existed before, and these objects were newly conceived. Only rectangular cubic forms were used, and they were not joined, but were carefully, almost tentatively set one next to the other. An impression of lightness and clarity was created, leaving each member distinct and separate, but also suggesting the provisional rather than the final, an experiment rather than a solution.

Rietveld was a constructivist and a member of a group which explained its theories in a magazine called *de Stijl*, a name which has since been applied to the group itself. The constructivist ideal was based upon abstract, rectangular forms, using only the primary colours of red, blue and yellow. Their form language was cubism, but the interpretation and significance they gave these forms was their own and are more important in the history of design than the forms themselves. They used abstract, geometric forms which had for them spiritual and philosophical connotations. They persuaded themselves that their choice of form was made not on an aesthetic but on a spiritual level and that they would further human development from materialism to spirituality. They believed that by total abstraction and simplification, art and design would achieve a universal harmony and appeal and would help to transform an individualistic, materialistic society into a spiritual, idealistic, and socialistic civilisation. These constructivist designs represent the modern style at its purest and most uncompromising. They are like primitive archetypes which are the starting point of all changes and accretions. We have today developed new ideas, and yet we feel a kinship with these early designs and later development is unthinkable without them.

The Utopia of the *de Stijl* group was not realised in the 20s, but its basic ideas were fruitfully adopted and incorporated in the teaching of a new design school, known as the *Bauhaus*, which became the focal point of the new movement soon after the war in Germany. Under the leadership of its first director, Walter Gropius, it revolutionised the training of designers. Here the desirability of invention and newness was paramount and the study of the past cast out. The students were taught to search probe, and experiment, and to seek a solution which would fulfill functional requirements and be a rational result of the materials and tools employed. The method taught was so fundamentally right for the time that the work of the *Bauhaus* staff and students made its influence felt all over the world. It was here that Marcel Breuer first experimented with metal furniture, suggested by the curved metal tubing of his bicycle handlebars. In 1924-5 he used non-resilient chrome tubing to construct a number of totally new models, notably an armchair which was related in its 1110 formal language to the earlier constructivist chair of Rietveld. Like Rietveld's chair, it emphasised structure, relying on similar parallel and angular forms, but Breuer used new and lighter materials, gleaming metal for the frame and canvas instead of upholstery. One continuous piece of bent tubular steel formed the basic frame, and front and back were connected by runners along the floor on both sides, in place of the conventional legs.

Certain features of this chair anticipated two cantilever chairs both designed in 1927 by architects. The Dutchman, Mart Stam's chair of non-resilient tubular steel rests on the floor with a U-shaped section. The front rises to support the seat and back cantilevered from this front support. This chair demonstrated for the first time the possibilities inherent in the strength of the new material used. In the same year Mies van der Rohe designed a cantilevered chair of thinner resilient tubular steel in which the front support was given a sweeping, semicircular form. 1111

In 1928 Breuer designed a resilient cantilevered chair of tubular steel which was manufactured by the Thonet firm. Simple

1115, 1116 *Above and above right*: The Barcelona chair was designed by Mies van der Rohe (born 1886) in 1929 for the German pavilion at the International Exhibition held in Barcelona in that year. Industrial techniques are here combined with natural materials and scrupulous craftsmanship to produce furniture of Classical simplicity and elegance. On the left the chair is shown with other related pieces by Mies in the house built by Philip Johnson for himself in 1949 at New Canaan, Connecticut, where it appears as much of our time and environment as it was of the 20s. The chair is now manufactured by Knoll Associates Inc.

1117, 1118, 1119 Le Corbusier (Charles-Edouard Jeanneret, born 1888) in collaboration with Pierre Jeanneret and Charlotte Perriand. *Below*: Armchair with adjustable back, 1929, of chromium-plated steel tubing and black canvas. *Right*: Adjustable *chaise longue*, 1927, of chromium-plated steel tubing, oval steel tubes and sheets painted green and black, grey jersey and black leather. *Below right*: Interior: *L'Unité d'habitation*, shown at the *Salon d'Automne des Artistes Décorateurs* in 1929. Le Corbusier's chair is a clear example of functional design—there is no striving after effects. His ideal is furniture which will perform an anonymous function within an architectural framework. Adjustability and versatility are as important to the individual pieces as to the interior as a whole. Armchair and *chaise longue*, collection: Museum of Modern Art, New York, gift of the manufacturer: Thonet Frères, France. Photograph, interior: Museum of Modern Art, New York

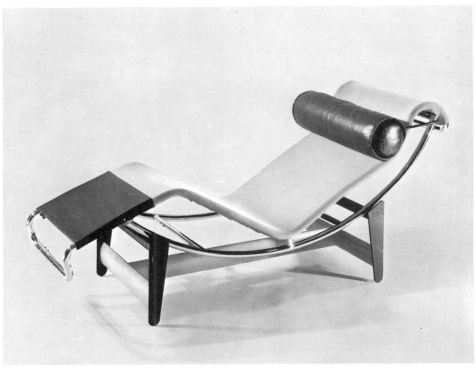

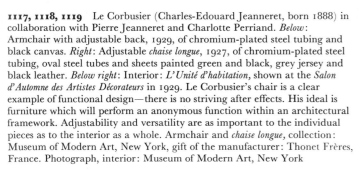

1120 *Above left*: Interior of the Paul R. Hanna House, Palo Alto, California, designed in 1937 by Frank Lloyd Wright (1869–1959). In direct contrast to the European concept of furniture as anonymous and functional equipment, Lloyd Wright designed furniture individually for each house, carefully suiting the form to the setting.

1121 *Above right*: Interior, the Health House, Los Angeles, California, 1927–29 by Richard Neutra (born Austria 1892). The severe rectangular planes of the room have European connotations, although the ample seating and furnishing materials are characteristically American.

1122, 1123 *Right and left*: Desk comprising a table with pedestal drawer unit of Cuban mahogany designed in 1933 by the Danish architect Kaare Klint (1888–1954). Folding stool of ash and sail cloth also by Klint. Less revolutionary than designers elsewhere in Europe, Klint held to traditional forms, methods and materials. His pioneer work in the 30s has guided much subsequent Scandinavian design. Both pieces manufactured by Rud. Rasmussens Snedkerier.

and useful, it became a universally accepted prototype. Here maximum comfort as well as a perfection of form were achieved with minimum materials, effort and cost. It consisted of only one piece of continuously curved metal tubing and two pieces of canvas; it eliminated costly joints, complicated construction and upholstery, and as a design seemed to have permanent validity.

In the following years tubular steel and other forms of metal were used extensively, not only out of doors, as had been done earlier, but also inside the house. The material lent itself to the urge to reduce all form to the barest, most austere minimum, which was then called functional. This interest in function could result in rather grim-looking furniture and interiors, but when handled sensitively it could also achieve extreme elegance. Tubular steel was used not only for chairs, but for stacking stools, tables, desks, and beautifully simple beds. Breuer designed all these, as well as some cabinets which, in their perfect detail and proportion were most satisfying. They possess an architectural, finite character, the individual parts being standardised so that the units could be combined in innumerable ways.

In 1929 Mies van der Rohe designed his celebrated Barcelona chair, so named after the international exhibition held in that city, for which Mies designed the German Pavilion where this chair was displayed. It is perhaps the most beautiful modern chair, for it would be difficult to find its peer. In profile it consists of two crossing curves of steel bars, the single curve of the back

crossing the reverse curve of the seat to form an expressive linear pattern. The seat is of leather straps supporting welted leather-covered cushions. Meticulous in its proportion and detail, the chair must be executed with impeccable craftsmanship to achieve its essential elegance. It is manufactured today by Knoll Associates in Europe as well as in America.

In France during these same years Le Corbusier and his associate Charlotte Perriand designed metal furniture which is closely related to that produced in Germany. An armchair with a tubular steel frame is similar to Breuer's early experiment. Here too stretched fabric is used for seat, back and armrests, but on a frame which is at once less complicated, more logical and direct, but also less pregnant of future development.

While designers in Germany worked with curiosity and ingenuity to find solutions for the new possibilities afforded by industry, they remained concerned with integrity under all circumstances, and their interest lay mainly in the creation of the design itself. Le Corbusier, on the other hand, saw the problem of design not as an isolated one, but as a technical, social and economic problem for which a generally applicable solution could be found. He replaced the term furniture with a new one: equipment, thereby not only abandoning tradition, but also all the usual associations with individual, personal and limited use. He reduced all furniture to three categories: chairs, tables, and open or enclosed shelves and went on to design standard forms

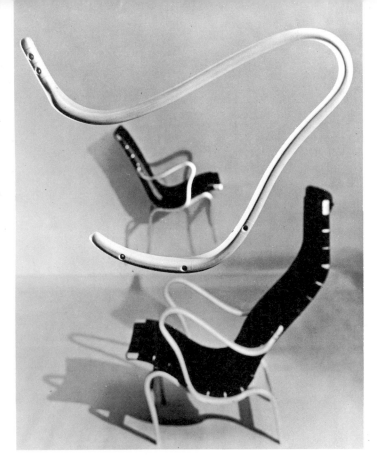

1124, 1125 *Above and below:* Lounge chair of laminated bent birchwood, 1940, and dining table by the Swedish designer Bruno Mathsson (born 1907). Wood, the traditional material, is here manipulated by an industrial process to produce something lighter and stronger than could have been achieved by hand craft.

1126 *Below:* Lounge chair and table, 1935, by Marcel Breuer, made by the Isokon Furniture Company, London. In the early 30s Breuer left Germany and came to Britain. Here, he too was to experiment with bent laminated wood. Both pieces of furniture are instructive examples of the economy and rationale of the technique. The table consists of a simple piece of cut out and bent laminated wood. The base, frame and armrests of the chair are ingeniously cut from strips of laminated wood rising and curving to support the body in comfort. The two side frames are braced by the bent plywood of the seat itself.

for each category: a multi-use table, standardised sectional cabinets and chairs for various purposes, working, relaxing, a *chaise longue*, an easy chair, a pivotal chair, and a *fauteuil*—and then never concerned himself with the problem again. This equipment could be used in any of his architectural settings and in fact it contributed to the architectonic effect. It was, of course, not equipment as we are apt to think of it in terms, for example, of 'well designed' refrigerators, but it was 'equipment' in a nobler sense for an architecture of purity and rationality. In practice he frequently combined his own designs with the light and linear design of the bentwood armchair by Thonet, originally designed in about 1870 and in production for over 50 years when Le Corbusier raised it from anonymity. His standardised cabinets, which could be fitted along walls or left free-standing, were allocated wherever needed in the house for varying purposes. They could be the same colour as the wall to maintain a clean, unbroken plane, or painted a contrasting colour to form a bold plastic element.

In addition to mobile furniture, open shelves of concrete often appear in Le Corbusier's interiors as an integral part of the architectonic setting. They represent furniture in a new sense, for they are fully integrated with the architecture. They have been freed from the stigma of being 'artistic', and from the emotional demands of the 'artistic' object. Equipment in the house was to be a commonplace, part of the machine for living, so that man, disencumbered of 'personal' possessions, could turn his thoughts to nobler things.

This frugality is in marked contrast to the practice of Frank Lloyd Wright in America. Wright demanded the 'integral' design, which meant that all furniture was to be designed by the architect as a natural part of the whole building. But while Le Corbusier designed standardised universal 'equipment' which could be used in all houses equally well, Wright saw each house as a particular creation and his furniture suited each one individually. We can refer to 'the' Le Corbusier table or cabinet, or 'the' Le Corsubier chair, but we can only choose an example by Wright and illustrate with it one solution of a particular artistic problem. Any other would be equally valid but notably different. In making furniture an integral part of an overall artistic solution, he often treated tables, benches, desks and cabinets as structural details of the building itself and even where they are not built in, they appeared to be. Architectural forms were repeated in movable furnishings, so that a house of hexagonal shape, such as the Hanna House, has polygonal tables, ottomans and chair seats, and even polygonal beds and sofas. A rectangular plan resulted in box-like ottomans and coffee tables; and in a house of circular plan, tables, chairs and seats are circular with arms shaped as segments of circles. The furniture is almost always enriched with ornamental detail, usually again repeating the central motif of the house.

Though his designs are romantically individualistic, organic rather than technical, and thereby opposed to a fundamental tendency of our time, much of his furniture convinces by the sheer artistic quality of the total design. But his concern for aesthetically pleasing design has not always led to practical results. A number of his clients have confessed that his furniture has proved too impractical, too uncomfortable, and has been replaced, over the years, by Danish or other suitable pieces. In his tendency to integrate furniture with its background he, as well as Le Corbusier, anticipated developments which are much more pronounced today than they were in the 20s and 30s. Wright was alone in preferring the particular problem, the individual solution, at a time when the generally applicable form was concerning most architects.

In this respect he is related to designers in Scandinavia, though here the emphasis is somewhat different. The Scandinavian countries have contributed notably to the development of modern furniture design in traditional terms, relying on organic forms and using materials and techniques adapted from earlier craft practices. But even in Scandinavia a conscious renewal was necessary, since industrialisation had interrupted craft traditions. Revitalised in the 20s and 30s, craftsmen's and designers' organisations played a major role in creating a fresh approach towards traditional values, encompassing industrialisation and revealing a definite concern for social needs.

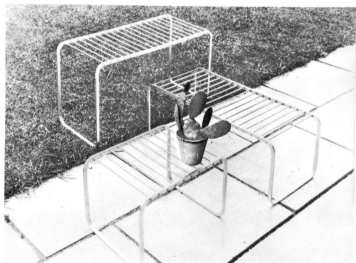

1127, 1128 *Above left*: Armchair, *c.* 1934, of laminated bent frame, the plywood seat and back being in one piece. *Above*: Stacking stools, 1938, both by the Finnish architect Alvar Aalto (born 1898). Forms as unprecedented and modern as those of Breuer's and Mies's metal furniture are here achieved in wood by bending plywood and laminated strips. The silky, glowing colour and beautiful grain of Finnish birch enhance all Aalto's furniture.

1129 *Left*: Tables of aluminium rods, 1933, by Marcel Breuer. Having created many new forms in stainless steel tubing, Breuer designed a group of aluminium rod furniture in 1933 of which these graceful yet sturdy little tables are the most memorable.

In Denmark, Kaare Klint is the great innovator of the 20s and 30s, but in a very different sense from Breuer. Klint renewed, he did not invent. He took the best features of late 18th-century English furniture as well as from other periods and countries, China and Egypt for example, eliminated their stylistic characteristics and produced 'timeless' forms with both functional and traditional appeal.

Klint began his career as an associate of the architect Carl Petersen, who built a small provincial art gallery in Faaborg in 1912–15, for which Klint designed the furniture. In 1924, when a professorship in furniture design was established at the architectural school of the Academy of Fine Arts in Copenhagen, Kaare Klint was appointed to it. In marked contrast to the teaching at the *Bauhaus*, his students were required to study the forms of the past and to profit by them. His own designs do not reveal a craving for newness, but are a restatement of classic solutions combining comfort and dignified simplicity which we have come to regard as typically Scandinavian. He was interested in rational proportions, and his tables, chairs and cupboards were standardised in size and measurements in accord with practical needs. For Klint, good design was not an end in itself, nor was he concerned exclusively with mastering technical problems—he wanted to serve his public. All his designs were executed with a sensitivity for material and an attention to detail which only a long tradition of craftsmanship can give.

Wood is also used by two other notable Scandinavian designers, but in new ways and with new techniques. Karl Bruno Mathsson in Sweden uses bent laminated wood particularly for chair frames to create fluid curved shapes of extraordinary grace and litheness. Webbing composed of a paper compound is employed on his curved frames, so that bulk, weight and expense are reduced to a minimum. More luxurious upholstered pads as well as arms may be bought with the chair or added later, since the arms are simply and visibly attached by screws. His tables are supported by legs which open like petals at the top to widen their support and add stability. His designs also include a construction of pole and shelves braced from floor to ceiling, an ingenious combination which serves as book shelf, magazine rack and writing desk.

In Finland, Alvar Aalto makes use of wood in dramatically new ways. In 1932 he produced a chair with a seat and back of one continuous piece of bent plywood resting on a frame of tubular metal clearly indebted to Breuer's chair. But soon he made his furniture entirely of wood, using solid wood, laminated wood and ingenious combinations of the two. His tables, desks, cabinets, chairs and stools rest on solid wood legs which separate at the knee into laminated curves and run either part way or connect horizontally with the opposite leg. This unusual construction gives not only a light and strong knee joint but also greater stability. The cantilever principle introduced by Mies and Breuer

A3501

CONVERSATION

1130, 1131 *Left and above*: Prize-winning drawing in the Museum of Modern Art's Organic Design Competition by Charles Eames and Eero Saarinen. Armchair, side chair and unit cases on benches, 1940, by Eames and Saarinen. Although the foundations for the design and production of modern furniture were laid in Europe, notably in Germany in the 20s, America entered the field decisively with the prize-winning designs of Eames and Saarinen for a competiton held just before World War II. Here the basic trend, the reduction of parts, is followed, and plywood is moulded into a multi-curved shell, a step which anticipates the use of plastics soon after the war. A comparison between the design and the executed chair is interesting. Wartime shortages meant that wooden legs had to replace the originally planned aluminium ones, and production difficulties led to a less fluent overall form. The modular case units following the European lead, can be combined in various ways. Drawing, collection: Museum of Modern Art, New York. Gift of the designers. Photograph, armchair, unit cases, etc: Museum of Modern Art, New York

1132, 1133 *Right and far right*: Side chairs, 1946, by Charles Eames (born 1907), of moulded walnut plywood and metal rods. In both cases back and seat are attached to the base by means of rubber discs which allow spring and slight adjustment and movement between the parts, and thus greater comfort. Both versions are developed from the Organic Design Competition prize-winning chairs of 1940.

1134 *Below*: Storage units, 1950, by Charles Eames, of plywood, coloured plastic panels, and metal rods. These units are designed to be economic, light in weight, and, in their many combinations, infinitely versatile.

1135 *Below*: Armchairs of moulded plastic reinforced with glass fibre, 1950, with various bases by Charles Eames. This chair form is the result of the experiment for the Museum of Modern Art Competition of 1948 for low cost seating. It makes use of very strong, durable, high quality materials developed during World War II. The chair is in one piece, fabricated in one operation. A detail of one base is shown in illustration 1138, opposite.

in metal tubing is used by Aalto entirely in laminated wood, taking advantage of the resilience, strength and lightness inherent in bent laminated wood, and also of the great abundance of wood in Finland.

The traditions of the Arts and Crafts Movement in Britain had earlier encouraged reforms on the Continent, while the work of such inspired designers as A. H. Mackmurdo, C. F. A. Voysey and C. R. Mackintosh had rendered a vital service to the development of European design. By the late 20s and 30s England turned to the Continent for inspiration, and the more daring International Style was introduced through various publications and exhibitions. In 1929 and 1930 the Studio Yearbook *Decorative Art* provided an amazingly complete survey of continental developments in architecture, interiors and furniture. But even then Serge Chermayeff, Wells Coates and Betty Joel were designing in the new idiom, using metal in adaptations of the graceful linear designs of the originators on the Continent, or strong, massive but simplified cubic designs in the case of Coates. An *Exhibition of British Industrial Art in Relation to the Home* at Dorland Hall in 1933 brought these designs to the attention of the public, and in the same year the *Architectural Review* sponsored an exhibition of Finnish furniture—mostly by Aalto—at Fortnum and Mason's of which the editor devoutly hoped that 'for England it might at last spell death to the fake Queen Anne.'

Meanwhile, Germany, which had been the centre for so much of the new development, had become increasingly intolerant of its most creative spirits, and in 1933 with the coming of the Nazi party, many of them left the country and contributed to the spread of the modern movement elsewhere. Breuer, during a short stay in Paris in 1933, participated in a design competition for aluminium furniture in which his group of designs won two first prizes. The designs exploit the properties of aluminium, its lightness, strength, and resilience, as logically as his earlier designs had made use of the properties of steel tubing. The chairs rest on runners which divide and rise in four supports, but the supports are brought forward and leave a wider base strip at the back which counterbalances the semi-cantilevered seat, thus giving springiness with stability. This construction seems most logical in the form-fitting lounge chairs, but is awkward in the straight chairs and armchairs. Stacking tables of aluminium rods are the most delicate and charming items of this group. 1129

In 1935 Breuer went to England and designed a group of bentwood furniture for the London firm of Isokon. The pieces have a close formal and technical relationship to the Paris aluminium group. In a reclining chair of bentwood, with runners rising to form supports and armrests, he achieved an organic form of elegant curved lines in which the structural frame is nevertheless very clearly and sharply set off against the softer outline of the cushioned surface on which the sitter rests. The mechanics are 1126

1136 *Above*: Folding tables, 1947, by Charles Eames. The thin but strong plywood tops are treated to withstand alcohol and other liquids. They are fixed on thin metal rod legs, held firm by hairpin-like braces. Legs and braces fold under the table into a flat package. The height, proportions and the beauty and economy of materials and structure are most satisfying.

1137 *Above right*: Upholstered lounge chair and ottoman, by Charles Eames. A large, generous chair of moulded plywood on a metal base, with soft leather cushions stuffed with feathers. In this luxury chair too, all parts are allowed a little movement in relation to each other, and in addition both main units are mounted on swivels for maximum ease and comfort.

1138 *Below*: (see caption **1135**)

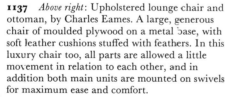

1139 *Above*: Storage units, 1950, by the English designers, Clive Latimer and Robin Day (both born 1915), which won the prize in the Museum of Modern Art's Competition for low cost furniture. Here bent plywood is used, constituting a shell which hangs in a tubular metal frame well off the floor. The shell is fitted either with a drop flap or with sliding glass doors.

1140 *Right*: Stacking chair of light alloy, die cast frame with bent plywood, 1948 by the English designer J. W. Leonard (born 1905), for the Educational Supply Association. Leonard combines bent wood—a Scandinavian feature—with the metal frame first introduced in Germany, to produce a chair of curved seat and backrest fixed to a light metal frame.

1141 *Far right*: Demountable side chair of cast aluminium, 1947 by the English designer Ernest Race (1913-63). The cast aluminium frame gives this chair a slim tensile appearance. It can be unscrewed and packed flat for easy transport. Awarded a Gold Medal at the X Triennale, Milan, and selected for the design index of the Council of Industrial Design, London

1142 *Below*: Armchairs and table, 1948, by Eero Saarinen (1910-1961), manufactured by Knoll Associates Inc. The chair is of moulded plastic, foam rubber, and upholstery fabric, on a base of metal rods. A descendant of the 1940 prize-winning design by Eames and Saarinen, (see illustrations 1130, 1131) this chair gives maximum comfort, with minimum weight and bulk.

1143 *Below right*: Wire chairs, 1952, by the sculptor Harry Bertoia (born Italy 1915). Bertoia designs chairs consisting of wire mesh shells resting on frames of thin metal rods. The chairs are manufactured by Knoll Associates Inc. and are shown here in an ensemble of their furniture in the Knoll Chicago Showrooms. The hanging cupboards on the far wall are by Florence Knoll.

no longer as obtrusive as they had been in the previous decade. In a set of stacking tables of bent plywood he reached an ingenious solution of utmost economy of material and technique, which has proved very influential.

The rational approach, the sparse, clean abstract form became an international style, the Modern Style from Central Europe to Japan and America. In the United States it was introduced by Richard Neutra, by Howe and Lescaze, and by Percival Goodman and others, but here as in England the style was being adopted, not created. In the same years of the 30s Walter Gropius, Marcel Breuer, Moholy-Nagy, and Albers were the most prominent of the *Bauhaus* masters to migrate to America and assume important teaching positions in the field of design, not without ·profound effect in the ensuing decades.

Between the two World Wars America came to the fore in an interesting experiment which was to make its full impact only in the post-war years. In 1940 the Museum of Modern Art in New York inaugurated a competition for 'Organic Design in Home Furnishings', in which two young architects, Eero Saarinen and Charles Eames, won the first prizes for seating and other living-room furniture. Their designs for chairs were revolutionary, for they united seat, back and armrests in a single shell form made of strips of veneer and glue, laminated in a cast iron mould. This shell form was covered with a thin rubber pad and then fabric. It

provided continuous contact and support for the sitter with a minimum of materials. Though the chair legs were to be of aluminium, in production wooden legs had to be substituted. Saarinen and Eames also collaborated in designing a group of tables and storage cases for which they also won first prize. All cases were designed on an eighteen-inch module, thus making possible a great variety of combinations. The cases were designed to stand on benches which could also serve as seats or plant stands and thereby add to the versatility of the series. Arrangements had been made for the manufacture and marketing of the winning designs of the competition, but the war soon put an end to all furniture making, and it was not until afterwards that the significance of their work became apparent.

In 1946 Eames produced his now justly famous chair design of two pieces of plywood moulded to fit the body comfortably, and shock-mounted by means of thick rubber discs onto a spider thin frame of chrome rods. The legs could be of metal or wood, while the chair could be wide or narrow, high or low, integrally coloured or covered with foam rubber or hide, or the grain of the wood could be left exposed. This design and all his later designs were manufactured by the Herman Miller Furniture Company. This firm helped him in his early experiments and became one of America's leading manufacturers of modern furniture in the post-war decades.

1144 *Above*: Executive Office for the Trident Oil Company, New York by Florence Knoll and the Knoll planning unit, in a building designed by Mies van der Rohe. From small beginnings in New York, Knoll Associates have grown in scope and importance to become a highly influential international concern. They have always sought out and manufactured the best designs from all over the world.

1145, 1146 *Right*: Low coffee table with steel frame and plate glass top by William Armbruster, manufactured by the Edgewood Furniture Corporation. *Below*: Table of movable sections of laminated wood, and herculite glass top designed by the sculptor Isamu Noguchi in 1940, photographed in the house of A. Conger Goodyear on Long Island, New York, a house built by Edward D. Stone. Armbruster's table emphasises the clarity and precision that we associate with an age of technology, while Noguchi's table, essentially a piece of sculpture, is a romantic individual creation. The parts can be moved at will, to produce differing relationships between the forms.

1147, 1148 *Right and far right*: Two chairs based on the traditional Windsor type by George Nakashima (born 1913). Hand-made furniture by individual craftsmen is rare in America. Nakashima takes simple, vernacular forms, refining them to bring them into the modern idiom, but retaining their sturdiness and simplicity.

1149, 1150 *Below*: Armchair of teak and hide, 1949, by Finn Juhl (born 1912), manufactured by Niels Vodder. *Below right*: Bed of teak and oak, 1950, by Finn Juhl, manufactured by Baker Furniture, Inc., Holland, Michigan. The chair shows Juhl's liking for diagonal line and free forms. The bed, on the other hand, is severe and restrained. The subtly tapering members and the use of contrasting materials give his work especial interest.

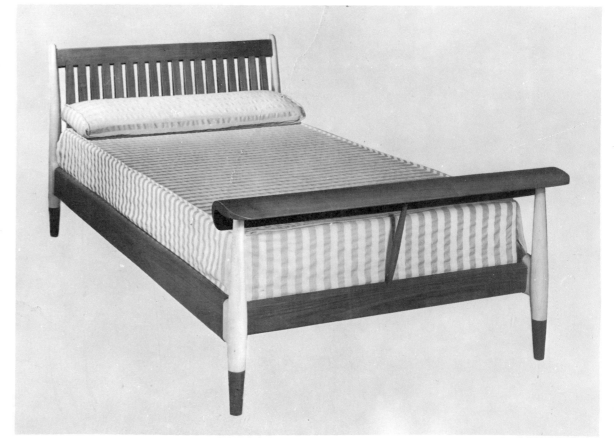

1151 *Right*: Storage units of teak with brass mounts, 1953, by the Danish designer Børge Mogenson (born 1914). Manufactured by P. Lauritsen. The pleasing effect achieved by combining brass with fine wood, is no new discovery. Here traditional materials are used in a traditional way, but with great subtlety both of proportion and in the placing of the brasses. Aesthetically most satisfactory, the units are also extremely practical.

1152 *Above*: The Danish architect Verner Panton's half-spheric glass-house in Copenhagen was built as a showroom for the firm of Pluslinje which produces Panton's furniture. Within can be seen his series of cone chairs, made in two forms, upholstered or with a wire frame.

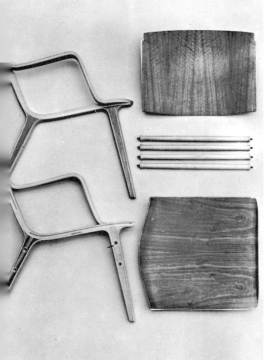

1153, 1154 *Left and far left*: Armchair of moulded plywood, 1950, by Peter Hvidt and O. Mölgaard Nielsen. Manufactured by Fritz Hansens Eft, Copenhagen. Although much of the fame of Danish furniture rests on traditionally hand-made pieces, fine furniture is also increasingly being made by industrial methods which are often in themselves of exceptional interest. This chair has a side frame of beech veneer over a mahogany core, the broad laminated strips are cut in the middle section, one side being drawn upwards to form an armrest while the other is bent downwards to form the frame for seat and back. Seat and back are moulded plywood sheets which are inserted in grooves in the side frames. These chairs have none of the shortcomings so often characteristic of pieces designed for mass production and easy shipping.

In 1948 the Museum of Modern Art in New York sponsored an 'International Competition for Low Cost Furniture' in which **1135** Eames again won a prize, this time for a moulded fibreglass chair, which was actually a fulfillment of the ideas developed by Eames and Saarinen in their prize-winning design of the 1940 competition. Integrally coloured plastic with the addition of fibreglass is moulded into a shell of complicated curves, of a soft, smooth finish, but great strength and durability. A variety of bases, legs, **1138** pedestals or rockers, of varying heights can be used, so that the chair can serve a number of purposes.

In the same competition English designers also scored a notable success. Robin Day and Clive Latimer won first prize for their **1139** storage cases of plywood shells which tapered from a wide base to a narrow top and were hung from tubular metal supports, well off the ground for easy access and cleaning.

In 1949-50, as a development of his and Saarinen's pre-war case designs, Eames designed storage units of a few standardised **1134** parts which can be assembled in a number of different ways for different purposes. In place of conventional cabinet-making, Eames used continuous vertical aluminium angles, with diagonal bracings of round metal rods to form a frame. Horizontal

Plate facing page 289

slabs of plywood are slid in as shelves, to which coloured sliding panels or drawers can be added. All the components are taken from stock industrial production, but are assembled with a fine

feeling for scale and colour to produce a gay, light series of storage pieces, intended for easy maintenance and visual and practical enjoyment.

Eames has also produced a series of folding tables with ply- **1136** wood and plastic tops and a simply but cleverly braced system of metal legs. The thinness of plywood top and the unencumbered metal rod legs give these tables a wonderfully light, floating quality. Equally practical and delightful in design is a screen of moulded plywood sections which can be folded into a small space. In recent years he has designed wire mesh chairs, aluminium furniture and a most luxurious leather-upholstered chair of **1137** modern plywood on a metal swivel base, a new version of the old fashioned lounge chair with footstool. It is made of bent plywood veneered with rosewood. Foam rubber upholstery is added and a down filling with a black leather cover.

Eero Saarinen also drew on the experience he gained in the pre-war competition when he introduced his so-called 'womb' chair soon after the war. It is also a shell of fibreglass and resins, **1142** but of very generous, wide proportions, covered with foam rubber padding and fabric and mounted on a metal rod cradle. This design was followed a few years later by his pedestal chair, a startling and elegant shape composed of a shell of plastic and fibreglass mounted on a single aluminium pedestal.

In all these designs the aim is to reduce the number of parts

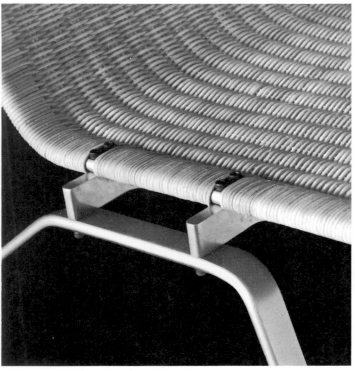

1155, 1156, 1157 *Above and above right*: Chair of steel straps with cane or canvas, 1957. *Right*: Folding stool of dull chromium-plated steel, with canvas or leather, 1960. Both designed by the Danish architect Poul Kjaerholm (born 1929), and manufactured by E. Kold Christensen A/S. Kjaerholm's furniture is uncompromising in its directness. Yet he manages to bring to the hard industrial materials, steel and glass, a subtlety and refinement usually associated only with wood and hand craft. The spare elegance of steel structure is complemented by the soft richness of leather and cane. It is particularly interesting to compare Klint's stool of wood and sailcloth (illustration 1122) with Kjaerholm's steel and leather version.

1158 *Below*: Interior in a house at Rungsted Kyst, Denmark by the architects Poul and Hanne Kjaerholm. Sofas, table and folding stools by Poul Kjaerholm.

1159, 1160 *Far left*: Stacking chair, 1953, of moulded plywood and three legs of steel tubing by Arne Jacobsen (born 1902). *Above*: Dining table and further development of the stacking chair, 1957, of moulded plywood throughout. All manufactured by Fritz Hansens Eft. Inexpensive everyday chairs can also have visual qualities which are both imaginative and amusing. These are like free forms in a collage, yet every detail is rational and functional. As chairs, they are among the numerous descendants of Charles Eames's moulded plywood chair (see illustration 1132) but the freedom with which the process is used shows how much it has become a common practice and common property.

1161 *Left*: Side chair with a seat of plastic filament by Gio Ponti (born 1891). A vernacular chair, a traditional product of the town of Chiavari near Genoa, it is refined and adjusted for economic mass production by one of Italy's foremost modern architect-designers. A comparison of this with the individually hand-made vernacular chairs by Nakashima (illustrations 1147, 1148) and the equally light and open-structured chair by Charles Eames (illustration 1135) which is entirely based on industrial materials and methods, is very instructive.

and minimise the manufacturing process. Clearly the ultimate aim is the one-piece chair made in one single operation, and though it has not been manufactured, it has been designed by Mies van der Rohe, whose drawings of 1947 show just such a chair in two different versions.

The designs of Saarinen are carried out by Knoll Associates, who also manufacture the old, classic designs of Mies as well as those of younger designers from all over the world. Amongst others, Harry Bertoia, the American sculptor, has designed a series of chairs, stools and tables of wire mesh and rods, while the French designer, Andre Dupré, has produced a beautifully simple chair of chromium-plated steel frame and interlaced cord. Florence Knoll, the widow of the founder of the firm, has herself designed tables, beds and cabinets for the firm, all with a crisp, clean geometric character, often made of beautiful woods and other natural materials in combination with metal. The same clarity is also apparent in interiors designed by the firm, often by Florence Knoll herself, and then heightened by dramatic use of colour and softened by fabrics, paintings, sculpture and flowers. Interiors by Knoll, usually with furniture by a number of different designers, give a convincing and harmonious impression representing perhaps the most successful interpretation of the austere, industrially oriented modern style of the mid-century.

Similar to the Knoll pieces is a table by William Armbruster of square black metal rods forming the most simple frame into which a sheet of plate glass is set. This linear geometric design of almost mechanical perfection, is apparently devoid of weight and mass. It represents reduction to the barest essentials, and for that reason may appear cold and austere to those who seek traditional qualities in furniture.

In contrast there is the interesting table by the Japanese-American Isamu Noguchi which consists of a freeform sheet of plate glass on a sculptured wooden base of two parts which can be rearranged to change the form at will. While Armbruster's table makes a fine, but severely regular pattern in space, Noguchi's is a bold and romantic form that satisfies quite different demands.

As in the 1930s, so again in the post-war period Scandinavia supplied balance and softened the impact of industrial designs by offering furniture in traditional materials and of more traditional design. Since the war Denmark has produced the most refined designs and the highest level of craftsmanship. Exhibitions as well as craft, design and trade organisations have all helped to maintain this high quality, because of their vigilant and strict selection. Though modern furniture is produced in factories as well as in small craft workshops, it is the handsome product of the latter which is most admired and most eagerly accepted on the inter-

1143

1144

Plates facing page 304

1145

1146

1151
1154
1150

national scene. Industrially produced furniture of steel and plywood or plastics, such as the very graceful and at the same time sensible and economic little chair of moulded plywood and tripod steel rod base by Arne Jacobsen, or the clear, simple, logical chair of steel bands and woven cane by Poul Kjaerholm, is admirable but perhaps less interesting, because this type of design has been used in other countries and is not exclusive to Denmark. The qualities of refined craftsmanship, on the other hand, are outstanding. The satiny sheen of a wood surface as well as the strength, stability and smoothness of a joint, or the sculptural form of a member, are exciting because they are so rare in our industrial society. We enjoy the qualities of craftsmanship precisely because thay are not dominant in our time.

1160
1156

Plate facing
page 305

It is significant that we expect craftsmanship to limit itself to the same abstract forms, devoid of decoration, symbols or reference to past styles, which have been devised for machine production. But in using abstract forms, craftsmanship is more inclined to express itself in organic rather than geometric terms, and these are usually quiet rather than emphatic in mood. The use of natural materials such as wood, softens the visual effect, and furniture of this type evokes an atmosphere of warmth in an interior. Hand-made furniture of wood in basically traditional shapes suggests durability and appeals to tastes which have not yet accepted rapid obsolescence. With few exceptions—perhaps the Barcelona chair—all metal or plastic pieces seem expendable because they have become consumer goods in our industrial system. They are, in fact, items of 'equipment', shiny and bright, new and smart today, but uneconomic to repair once the initial perfection is marred by cracks, dents or loose parts.

The general standard in Denmark is high, but among many admirable designers and craftsmen Hans Wegner and his master cabinet-maker Johannes Hansen, and Arne Jacobsen and his cabinet-maker, Fritz Hansens, stand out.

Hans Wegner has designed a classic chair which is nevertheless essentially modest. Besides being eminently functional it is most satisfying aesthetically, and has been very influential ever since its first appearance in 1949. The tapered legs rise from floor to top rail, supporting the seat frame at mid-height. The curved top rail gives the chair its distinction. It is composed of three parts, joined together in saw-tooth joints, which in themselves are expressive and decorative. Though much of the work is done with power tools, the shaping, carving and finishing of this top rail must be done by hand.

Plate facing
page 289

Wegner has designed tables, cabinets, beds, tea trolleys, all of equal quality, always with a fine sculptural sense, a clean, expressive form, and always executed with impeccable craftsmanship by Johannes Hansen.

Finn Juhl's designs are more complex, more probing and more daring, and for that reason perhaps less successful in the field of hand-made furniture which by its very nature demands a quiet acceptance of continuity with tradition. He likes diagonal bracings and other unorthodox forms, but his work too, is distinguished by its sculptural quality and fine use of wood. An

1149

1162 *Above*: Living room of the Entenza house with built-in seating by Charles Eames and Eero Saarinen. The sitting area in the large living room of this California house designed by two of America's outstanding architects, is so composed that the two sides of the periphery consist of a built-in sofa, thus making the seating arrangement an integral part of the architecture. Furniture has not been eliminated entirely; the chair on the right and the round coffee table are characteristic light weight and airy pieces by Charles Eames, while the low outdoor furniture of metal rods and stretched string is by Hendrick van Keppel and Taylor Green.

1163 *Below*: Study for a country house, 1961, by the German architect Walter Brune. A particularly fine example of built-in cabinets and drawers. Although such 'storage walls' are manufactured and sold in America much as a wardrobe used to be, this is a custom-built wall of fine materials and excellent workmanship. The ceiling is of larchwood, the floor of marble tiles. There is a sound-proofed door in the cabinet wall.

Pedestal table and chairs by Eero Saarinen, manufactured by Knoll Associates, New York. The seat and back units of the chairs are of moulded plastic reinforced with fibreglass, and the bases are of cast aluminium. Foam rubber cushions, fabric covered, are fixed to the seats. The table top is of white plastic laminate, and the base, as with the chairs, is of cast aluminium. This series constitutes perhaps the most striking example of synthetic materials and mass production methods in use to achieve furniture of distinction

Executive office designed and furnished for *Look* Magazine, New York, by Knoll Associates Inc. The interior of the office is divided into two areas by means of recessed channel ceiling dividers and vertical uprights on the two side walls, giving definition to the working and lounge areas, without losing a sense of space. The low circular table is by Eero Saarinen, the lounge chairs and desk by Florence Knoll.

ensemble of his furniture creates a cheerful, light atmosphere, made interesting by the unusual forms and combinations he uses.

A rare instance of craftsmanship in America is that of George Nakashima, an architect of Japanese ancestry trained at the Massachusetts Institute of Technology, who settled in a village in Pennsylvania to make furniture. Nakashima draws on Japanese traditions of design for some of his pieces, for example in using light and dark wood for contrast and in leaving one edge of a table top the free form of a tree trunk. But above all he is both modest and workmanlike. He refers to himself as a 'woodworker'. He has also drawn on Shaker tradition and on other simple vernacular designs. His 'Captain's' chair, a version of the Windsor chair, reinterprets that traditional piece in modern terms. It was for a time manufactured by Knoll Associates, but while Nakashima's own work delights the eye and the hand, the manufactured version fails because even the minute changes in form and finish were enough to remove its distinction.

It remains to mention Italy where there has been much post-war activity in the field of design. Many Italian designers are producing startling, dramatic and daring forms. An armchair by Gio Ponti has a faint hint of tradition about it but its racy, taut design gives it an exciting quality while at the same time promising great comfort. The chair of curved forms, moulded of solid birch by Carlo Mollino is reminiscent of flowers, plants, stems and petals—and Art Nouveau.

One phenomenon should be mentioned in discussing modern furniture and that is its disappearance. Much that was once universally part of the furnishing of a room has disappeared through technical changes, such as heating stoves, radiators, or light fixtures, and the tendency evident in the work of Wright and Le Corbusier continues. The built-in closet in place of the wardrobe has been known for some time and is a logical development in a bedroom. But sideboards, radios, book cases, and storage units of all kinds are also increasingly built in. In fact the only thing that remains, that seems irreducible, is the chair, and even that has been eliminated in the so-called 'conversation pits', perhaps the descendants of the inglenooks of the turn of the century, where built-in benches surrounded the fireplace. The elimination of superfluities is a modern need dictated by lack of space and service, both of which have become costly rarities. Such furniture as is needed takes up less space and requires less maintenance if it is built in. But this in turn deflates the whole concept of furniture. There is a danger that we may cease to regard it as a work of art. Instead it could become mere 'equipment' serving us anonymously and efficiently, but no longer delighting or even interesting us.

Starting with faith and dogma and a very narrowly prescribed form language, the 1920s and 30s were the exciting decades in which the modern style developed, while the post-war years saw its acceptance, and the creation of variations upon original themes. We now have a multiplicity and a permissiveness of form, ranging from the quiet, refined traditional craftsmanship of Scandinavia to the exhilarating, technically oriented designs of international industry. Design is never fixed and stable, but always changing. One phase merges into the next, creating new forms which often surprise and delight. To define these as a new style we must wait for the perspective of experience.

1164, 1165 *Above*: Living room in the Mossberg House, South Bend, Indiana, 1952, by Frank Lloyd Wright. *Below*: Lounge pit in the Palladian House, 1958, by Eero Saarinen, Alexander Girard and Kevin Roche. While the built-in furniture in the living room by Frank Lloyd Wright retains its identity, in the lounge pit by Saarinen and Girard it becomes part of the building itself. The elimination of independent pieces of furniture in favour of built-in equipment is a logical development in which complete interiors are the direct result of architecture; pure structure, pure colour, pure materials. Any separate piece of furniture seems almost anachronistic.

Finn Juhl recently designed a new series of office furniture for the manufacturers France & Son of Hillerød. It comprises tables, shelves, cabinets and various chairs. Juhl received the Design Award of the American Institute of Interior Design in January 1964 for the desk, which combines severe but subtle lines with impeccable craftsmanship.

Interior showing the 'egg' chair (on the right) and the 'swan chair' and sofa by Arne Jacobsen, both manufactured by the firm of Fritz Hansens Eft., who have collaborated with Jacobsen for twenty-five years. The 'swan' was designed for the SAS Hotel in Copenhagen in 1958 and has been enormously successful ever since.

Primitive Furniture

1166   *Left*: One of the most widely distributed objects in primitive societies is the headrest. This very simple type, made of a length of bamboo, supported on wooden struts comes from Tonga and dates from the 19th century. British Museum, London

1167   *Left*: Headrests in primitive societies were used to keep a sleeper's head from the floor in the absence of a bed. In many societies the head is treated with special reverence and has to be kept from contamination by the ground. Some headrests are highly decorated and this example from Kararau, New Guinea, has supports in the form of animal heads. It dates from the late 19th century but is of a type still in use today. British Museum, London

1169   *Below*: This rather different variety of headrest from Finschhafen, New Guinea is only 6¼ inches high and is made of carved wood, the decoration including a double mask and eyes, presumably as a protection to the sleeper against evil. It dates from the late 19th century but is of a type still in use today. British Museum, London

1168   *Left*: In Africa especially, the stool of a chief is a sacred object in which power is implicit. This quartz example has a dignity which stems from its simplicity. It was brought from Ife, the sacred city of the Yoruba tribe of Western Nigeria, in the late 19th century and is of traditional form, although of unknown date. British Museum, London

1170   *Below*: This ancient, ceremonial stool of the Arawaks was found in a cave in Carpenters Mountain, Jamaica, and dates from before 1400 A.D. It is of carved wood and represents a recumbent figure. Among the Arawak of the Caribbean, seats often took animal or human form. British Museum, London

1171   *Below right*: This chief's throne is carved from the solid section of a tree trunk and is slightly elliptical rather than round. It dates from the early 20th century and comes from the Bamileke tribe, Cameroun. British Museum, London

1172 *Left*: Ceremonial stool of wood, mounted with sheets of embossed silver, said to have belonged to a Queen Mother of the Angruman tribe in Ashanti, Ghana. This stool dates from the late 19th century. British Museum, London

1173 *Right*: Ceremonial stool of carved wood, dating from the late 19th century, from the Bini tribe, Benin City, Nigeria. This type of stool is still in use today. British Museum, London

1174 *Left below*: Carved panel from a wooden door or screen, dating from the early 20th century, from the Yoruba tribe, Western Nigeria. The scene shows a chief seated upon a throne, which is modelled on a European folding camp-chair. Some stools follow European prototypes in this manner, perhaps in the hope that their possessors will inherit the power of the white man British Museum, London

1175 *Right*: Ceremonial chair of carved wood with a leather seat from the Bajokwe tribe, on the Congolese-Angolan border. This chief's chair, dating from the early 20th century is another example based upon European prototypes. It adheres, however, to the smaller proportions of a typical stool, for it is not much more than 30 inches high. British Museum, London

1176 *Below left*: The development of a comprehensive range of furniture among primitive societies seems to relate to the emergence of an urban culture. Containers for articles of value, from small boxes to great chests occur and this example, carved in imitation of basket work comes from Benin City, Nigeria. It dates from the 19th century or perhaps earlier. A few such chests are still in use in chiefs' households. British Museum, London

1177 *Below right*: Platforms or tables for the preparation of food or for offerings to the gods and spirits occur in primitive societies. This wooden table, from the Pelew Islands in the Pacific, served to display such offerings, which the Master fisherman in each community would make to the sea, in order to ensure a good catch. The table is inlaid with clam shell, ground into triangular and rosette shapes. British Museum, London

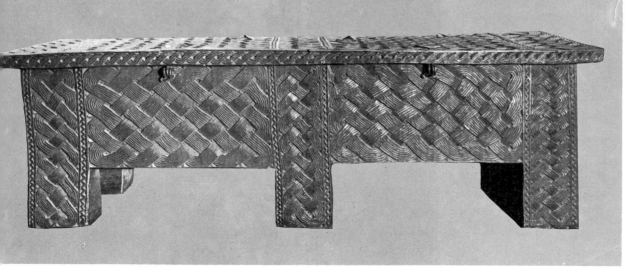

GLOSSARY

Acanthus. Formalised leaf used in Classical ornament, particularly on Corinthian capitals; frequently found on furniture as carved decoration.

Acroter. Pedestals, at the centre or sides of a pediment, to support sculptured figures; sometimes also loosely used to describe the figures themselves.

Ailettes. Shoulder appendages, usually rectangular, forming part of medieval armour. Laced to the sides of the shoulders and projecting up on either side of the head, ailettes were of flimsy material and were probably heraldic or even purely ornamental in purpose.

Amorini. (It.). Cupids, much used as carved ornament on furniture from the Renaissance onwards.

Andirons. A pair of iron bars, usually ornamented at the front end by a vertical member, placed at each side of the hearth and upon which the burning logs were supported; also known as fire-dogs.

Antefix. Corner ornaments on ancient sarcophagi, also adopted as decorative features on late 18th- and early 19th-century cabinet furniture.

Anthemion. Ornament of Greek origin based on the honeysuckle.

Apron piece. Ornamental member below the seat rail of a chair or settee, sometimes joining the legs at the junction with the rail; also used on side tables, stands, chests-of-drawers, etc.

Arabesque. Ornament of flowing lines composed of foliage, scrolls or animal forms, used for the decoration of borders or panels.

Arcading. Carved decoration composed of a series of arches supported on columns or pilasters.

Architrave. In furniture of Classical form, the lowest point of the entablature, the lintel above the columns.

Art Nouveau. Style of decoration which first appeared in England in the 1880s but was developed in Europe, especially in Belgium, France and Germany, in the early 1890s, then to survive some twenty years. Traditional motifs were eschewed and, instead, plant forms, waves or flame-like shapes were reflected in languid, sinuous curves expressing a new sense of abandon. The style was known in Germany as *Jugenstil,* in Austria as *Sezession* and in Italy as *Le Stile Liberty.*

Auricular ornament. Form of decoration known in Germany as *Knorpelwerk,* in which parts of the human skeleton, surrounded by membrane and fleshy forms, were used, sometimes, as the name implies, suggesting the curving lines of the human ear. These gristly motifs appear first to have been developed by the Dutch goldsmiths, Paulus and Adam Van Vianen in the first decade of the 17th century and were inspired by contemporary studies of anatomy. They were rapidly adopted as a form of decoration by carvers and cabinet-makers and did not lose popularity until the third quarter of the century.

Ball foot. Round, ball-shaped foot forming the terminal for turned legs or the support to a cabinet or cupboard, particularly in the late 17th century.

Baluster. Turned member of columnar form, straight, twisted, tapered or vase-shaped.

Banding. Decorative border or edging on furniture. *Cross-banding* is a border of veneer in which the grain runs across the band. *Herring-bone* or *feather banding* is composed of strips of veneer set diagonally, suggesting the appearance of a feather or the back-bone of a fish.

Baroque style. Style, based upon Classical example, which originated in Italy *c.* 1600 and gradually spread through Europe; characterised by dynamic movement, the use of rich, symmetrical, sculptured forms and bold contrasts of colour.

Bascinet. Light, conical helmet of the 14th and early 15th centuries, usually worn with a mail curtain laced to the lower edge, protecting the throat and neck.

Bas-relief. Panel or frieze depicting decorative or ornamental subjects, carved or moulded in low relief.

Bead. Small moulding of semi-circular section; or adjacent semi-spheres, resembling strips of beads.

Bead and real. Decorative border consisting of carved or inlaid alternating round and oblong forms.

Bell-flower. American term for a conventional hanging flower bud of three or five petals used in repeated and diminishing pattern.

Bentwood. Wood steamed and bent to form the structural members of chairs, etc.; first developed in the early 19th and widely extended in the 20th century.

Bergère. (Fr.). Large, embracing armchair with upholstered sides, popular in France in the Louis XV period and later. In England in the 18th century, these chairs were known as 'burjairs' or 'barjairs'.

Biedermeier. (Ger.). Style of furniture and decoration current in the German territories *c.* 1815 to 1848 in which simplicity of line and decoration was combined with a regard for function.

Block front. Term used to describe a technical method of constructing the fronts of case furniture, such as chests-of-drawers or cabinets, developed in America and especially in New England in the 18th century. Inspired by Northern European Baroque prototypes, block fronts are composed of three flattened curves, the central of concave and the two outer of convex shape.

Blocking. See BLOCK FRONT.

Boiserie. (Fr.). Carved wood panelling.

Bolection moulding. Raised moulding of ogee shape surrounding a panel.

Bombé. (Fr.). Convex, bulging; descriptive particularly of Rococo case furniture with outward-swelling front and sides.

Bonnet scrolls. An American term describing a curved and scrolled pediment on a bookcase, cabinet or tallboy.

Boulle. (Fr.). Term loosely used to describe a form of marquetry particularly associated with the French cabinet-maker, André-Charles Boulle (1642–1732). Veneers of tortoiseshell and brass, sometimes combined with other materials, such as pewter, copper, mother-of-pearl, or stained horn, were used. Thin sheets of brass and tortoiseshell, glued together, were cut into various patterns. These were then separated, and by combining them in different ways they could be used to create two distinct marquetries. *Première-partie* describes that in which the pattern in brass is set in the ground of tortoiseshell, while *contre-partie* refers to the alternative arrangement in which the pattern is in tortoiseshell, set in the ground of brass. This system of applying marquetry was not, in fact, invented but was developed by Boulle and was used in France throughout the 18th and the 19th centuries and was copied elsewhere in Europe.

Bracket. Member projecting from vertical surface to provide horizontal support.

Bracket foot. Squared foot supporting the underframing of case furniture.

Brattishing. A carved and pierced cresting found on 16th-century screens or panelling.

Breakfront. Term used to describe a bookcase or cabinet in which the central section projects beyond the lateral sections.

'Buhl'-work. See BOULLE.

Bulb. The bulb-like part of the turned supports of furniture; of Flemish origin; commonly found on tables, court cupboards, etc., in the 16th and early 17th centuries.

Bun foot. Flattened ball foot.

Cabochon ornament. Raised oval ornament, resembling a polished, uncut gem.

Cabriole leg. Curving outwards at knee, inwards below the knee, and outwards again at the foot; terminating in feet of varied forms—hoof, club, paw, bun, claw-and-ball, scroll, etc.

Candelabrum. A branched candlestick.

Canted. Chamfered or bevelled surface.

Cantilever. A projecting support or arm, carrying a load at the free end or evenly distributed along the projecting part. The cantilever principle involves the subjection to tensile stress of the upper half of the thickness of such a support, thus elongating the fibres, while the lower half is subjected to compressive stress, which tends to crush the fibres.

Capital. The upper part of a column or pilaster, conforming in Classical architecture to the Greek (Doric, Ionic and Corinthian) and Roman (Tuscan and Composite) orders.

Carcase. The body of a piece of furniture to which veneers are applied.

Cartouche. Tablet in form of a scroll with curled edges, often bearing an inscription, a monogram or a coat-of-arms. Used as a decorative motif in the centre of apron pieces or pediments.

Caryatid. Sculptured support to an entablature or moulding in form of a female figure.

Cavetto. Concave moulding, hollowed out to form quadrant of circle in section.

Certosina work. (It.). Inlays made of polygonal tesserae of wood, bone, metal and mother-of-pearl, so called because the work required such patience, not because it was made by Carthusian nuns. Popular in 15th-century Lombardy and Venetia, it was occasionally applied to *cassone* in these districts in the 16th century as well. Sometimes humbler chests were painted in imitation of *certosina* work.

Chaise longue. A chair with an elongated seat.

Chamfered. A bevelled or smoothed-off surface or edge; also 'canted' or 'splayed'.

Channelling. Parallel grooving.

Chequer ornament. Ornamental inlay of alternating squares of light and dark woods.

Chimera. A fabulous animal, with either a lion or goat's body and legs, eagle's wings and a serpent's tail, used originally in Greek and Roman ornament.

Chinoiserie. Free and fanciful rendering, in Western terms, of features adopted from the decorative repertoire of Chinese ornament. European admiration for Chinese porcelain, lacquer, textiles and wallpapers had grown rapidly in the course of the 17th century. Before the mid-18th century such motifs as latticework, frets, pagodas, bells or figures of Chinamen appeared, as an aspect of Rococo taste, in the stucco decoration of ceilings or walls and as decorative features on furniture.

Chip carving. Shallow carved ornament usually composed of geometrical patterns, drawn with the aid of a pair of compasses and chipped out.

Churrigueresque. Spanish version of Baroque.

Classical. Greek or Roman and their derivatives.

Claw-and-ball foot. Terminal to a cabriole leg in form of a paw or claw clutching a ball; of Oriental derivation; widely used in England and the Netherlands in the second quarter of the 18th century and in America in the mid-18th century.

Club foot. The commonest and simplest terminal to the cabriole leg, resembling a club head; when set on a disc, known as a pad foot.

Cock beading. Small astragal moulding applied to edges of drawer fronts.

Coiffeuse. (Fr.). French armchair the top-rail of the back curving downwards in the centre to enable the hair to be dressed.

Console. Variety of bracket, resembling a scroll, supporting the frieze or cornice of a piece of cabinet furniture. Also applied to a table standing against a wall, supported by two bracket-shaped legs.

Contre-partie. (Fr.). See BOULLE.

Coquillage. (Fr.). Ornament in the form of a shell, popular in the Rococo period; often found in the centre of the seat rail of chairs and settees, on the knees of cabriole legs, etc.

Corbel. Bracket projecting as a horizontal support.

Cornice. Moulded projection surmounting a frieze; the top member of an entablature.

'Coromandel' lacquer. A variety of lacquer, imported into Europe in the late 17th century and later, in which the design was incised into the surface.

Counter-table. A table with an under compartment thought to have been used for reckoning accounts with counters disposed on a marked scale.

Cove. Concave or hollow moulding.

Cresting. Decorative top rail of a chair or settee or decorative termination for a piece of cabinet furniture, composed of pierced work or carving.

Crocket. A projecting ornament, in the form of buds or leaves, used in medieval architecture and consequently also furniture, and found, for example, on the sides of pinnacles, buttresses and gables.

Cross-banding. See BANDING.

Curule. Roman chair, used by the 'curule' or higher magistrates, with curved legs and no back so that it could be folded.

Cushion frieze. See FRIEZE.

Cusp. Projecting point on a foiled Gothic arch, roundel, etc.

Demi-lune. (Fr.). Crescent-shaped.

Dentil. Moulding carved to form series of small rectangular blocks or teeth, with narrow gaps between.

Diaper. Ornament composed of small squares or lozenges forming an all-over pattern.

Dovetail. A joint used in woodwork, in which fan-shaped tongues projecting from one member fit into corresponding fan-shaped slots cut in a second member.

Dowel. Wooden peg used for joining wood.

Drop-front. See FALL-FRONT.

Drop-in seat. Upholstered chair seat which can be lifted from the chair and which is supported upon corner brackets within the chair-frame.

Ebonised wood. Stained black to imitate ebony.

Egg-and-dart. Ornament of Greek origin, generally found carved on ovolo mouldings, consisting of alternate raised oval and dart shapes.

Egyptian taste. In Europe and subsequently in America the revival of Egyptian decorative motifs was stimulated by Napoleon's Egyptian campaign of 1798 and the publication of Baron Dominque-Vivant Denon's account of Egyptian antiquities: *Voyage dans la Basse et Haute Egypte*. Ornamental features which were consequently adopted included sphinxes and lotus leaves.

Entablature. In Classical architecture, everything above the columns, i.e. architrave, frieze and cornice.

En suite. (Fr.). As a matching set.

Escutcheon. Armorial shield popular on 18th-century furniture as the central ornament of a pediment; term also used for the ornamental plate surrounding a keyhole.

Faience. Glazed quartz frit, i.e. calcined mixture of sand and fluxes as materials for glass-making, used in ancient Egypt to decorate furniture; name later (from Faenza in Italy) applied to glazed earthenware.

Fall-front. Writing-board of a desk, lowered to form the writing surface. Also known as drop-front.

Fauteuil en cabriolet. (Fr.). Louis XV and Louis XVI armchair in which the upholstered back is slightly curved and shaped to the human body.

Feather banding. See BANDING.

Fielded panel. A raised panel with bevelled edges.

Fillet. Narrow flat band between mouldings, especially between the flutes of a column.

Finial. Knob, often vase-shaped, used as a crowning ornament on furniture; also found on the intersection of stretchers joining legs of chairs, tables, etc.

Flamboyant style. In architecture, and consequently also in furniture, the last stage of the Gothic in France, beginning in the late 14th century. It is characterised by sinuous curves in window and panel tracery, suggesting flame-like forms.

Fluting. Decoration of parallel grooves, concave and semi-circular in section, on Classical columns and friezes.

Footpace. Footrest.

Frets. Angular patterns, either pierced as in the galleries on tables, etc., or cut in the solid or applied, on friezes. legs, etc.

Frieze. Horizontal section below a cornice. A cushion frieze is of convex profile.

Gadrooning. A border ornament of curved or straight radiating lobes; also known as *nulling* and *lobing*.

Geometric dipylon vases. (Gr.). Dipylon, a cemetery in Athens was excavated in recent years, and many large Attic Geometric vases of the later 8th century B.C. were found there. The Geometric style in vase decoration is characterised by the use of narrow horizontal bands of minute ornament, rows of repeated figures, and geometric shapes such as triangles, lozenges and circles. A constantly recurring feature is the maeander or key-pattern.

Genoa velvet. See VELVET.

Gesso. A composition, often of chalk and parchment size, applied to furniture as foundation upon which gilding or silvering could be applied.

Gilding. The decoration of surfaces with gold leaf. Woodwork was first coated with gesso before being gilded.

Gongorism. An affected literary style introduced into Spanish literature by the poet Góngora y Argote (1561–1627).

Gothic style. A style first developed in France in the mid-12th century, spreading over Europe, where it remained dominant until the Renaissance. It is characterised in architecture by pointed arches, flying buttresses, ribs, vaults and tracery in windows. The furniture of the period is also ornamented with such typical architectural features.

Griffin (Griffon, Gryphon). Fabulous creature of Classical origin with an eagle's head and wings on a lion's body.

Grisaille. (Fr.). Painting in various tints of grey representing objects in relief.

Groove-and-tongue. A carved decoration composed of a narrow channel sunk in a surface and partially filled with a convex moulding in the shape of a tongue.

Grotesques. Decorative design used on friezes, panels and pilasters, composed of such motifs as trailing leaves, anthemion, urns and fantastic creatures. These decorative designs were of Classical origin and were imitated and developed by Renaissance artists. As they had first been discovered on the walls of Roman ruins, or *grotti*, they came to be known as *groteschi*, hence grotesques.

Guilloche. Carved ornament of Classical derivation consisting of interlaced circles.

Halfa grass. The North African name of a species of Esparto grass.

Haulberk. A mail shirt.

Headboard. Head of a bedstead rising behind the pillow.

Herring-bone banding. See BANDING.

Hipping or hip joint. Extension of the cabriole leg above the seat rail of a chair.

Honeysuckle motif. See ANTHEMION.

Hoof foot. Common terminal of the early cabriole leg in the form of a hoof. (Fr. *pied de biche*).

Husk ornament. Ornament resembling the husk of a wheat used in repeated and diminishing pattern, particularly on Neo-Classical furniture.

Hydria. (Gr.). Pottery, or sometimes bronze water jug of urn shape, with broad base and narrow mouth.

Impost. Upper course of a pillar, often projecting in the form of a moulding supporting the foot of an arch.

Inlay. A surface decoration created by insetting into the solid wood a pattern or representation composed of differently coloured woods or other materials, such as ivory or horn. Inlay is recessed into a solid carcase, as opposed to marquetry, which is a veneer.

Intaglio. Incised carving or engraving on a hard material such as a gem.

Intarsia—or tarsia. Italian term to describe inlay or marquetry. A type of geometrical intarsia is found, for example, on Venetian 15th-century chests. At the same time, Florence was famous for intarsia panels representing pictorial scenes, while perspective views of real or imaginary architecture were popular in Italy as a whole in the late 15th and 16th centuries. At this period too, intarsia panels for walls or furniture were skilfully produced in South German workshops.

Japan Work. A term used in England and America to describe lacquer made in imitation of Oriental lacquer. Both Chinese and Oriental lacquer was widely collected by European patrons in the late 17th and earlier part of the 18th centuries but the Japanese was of higher quality. As demand exceeded supply, European craftsmen were quick to provide for the fashion by their own efforts. English japan work was often in bright colours such as scarlet or yellow and much of it was exported, particularly to Portugal. Normally designs were raised on the surface, but inferior work was merely varnished.

Key pattern (Greek fret). Repetitive pattern, of Classical origin, composed of lines set at right angles, usually applied to frieze or border.

Knee-hole desk. Desk with central section, containing a small cupboard or drawers, recessed to allow space for the writer's knees.

'Knulled' foot. See KNURL FOOT.

Knurl foot. Curled inwards.

Krater. (Gr.). A large vase with wide mouth for serving wine at banquets.

Kylix. (Gr.). A wide shallow drinking vessel with two handles, on a foot of varying height.

Lacquer. Essentially, decoration in coloured varnishes of Oriental origin; loosely applied (with japan) to European substitutes.

Ladderback chair. Modern term for a chair with back composed of horizontal slats or rails.

Lambrequin. Ornamental drapery, sometimes copied in wood, with a scalloped lower edge.

Laminated. Composed of layers of the same or alternating materials, such as plywood or plywood faced with plastic sheets.

Linenfold. Modern name for style of panel decoration, probably originating in Flanders in the late 15th century, and much used in the first half of the 16th century on panelled furniture, in which the carved ornament has the appearance of folded linen.

Lion monopodium. See MONOPODIUM.

Lotus ornament. The 'water-lily of the Nile' used in ancient Egyptian decoration and revived in Europe in the early 19th century when, during the Napoleonic campaign in North Africa, a new interest in Egypt arose.

Lucchese silk. Silk woven at Lucca in Italy.

Lunette. Carved, inlaid or painted pattern of semicircular form.

Mannerist style. A style evolved in Italy in the second decade of the 16th century as a reaction against the Classical tenets of the Renaissance. As a Court art, adopted at Fontainebleau, it spread throughout Europe, rejecting Classical proportions and eschewing naturalistic forms.

Marlborough leg. English term for a straight square or square tapering leg, sometimes with a plinth foot. Used on American furniture from the mid-18th century, often with the inside edge chamfered.

Marquetry. Decorative veneer of wood or other materials, such as ivory or mother-of-pearl, in which thin sheets are cut into delicate patterns and applied to the carcase. Floral marquetry, composed of trailing leaves and flowers and sometimes including birds and butterflies, was a special feature of Dutch and French cabinet-making from the mid-17th century and was quickly copied elsewhere. In the 18th century the Parisian cabinet-makers set a new standard in the art of marquetry which was the admiration of all Europe.

Masterpiece. Piece of work by which a craftsman gained from his guild the recognised rank of 'master'.

Mensa lunata, sigmoid. (L.). Crescent-shaped table.

Mitre joint. The corner joint of mouldings framing a panel, each edge of the join cut at an angle of 45°.

Modillion. Projecting brackets in pediment and below cornice of furniture of architectural character.

Moghul. Indian Muslim dynasty of Mongol Turks reigning in India between 1525 and 1827.

Monopodium. Support for tables, etc., in the form of an animal's head and body with a single leg and foot; of Classical origin, revived in the late 18th and early 19th centuries.

Mortice. Cavity into which a projecting tenon is fitted to join two pieces of wood. (Mortice and tenon joint).

Moulding. Projecting band shaped in section, often with continuous patterning.

Mudéjar style. (Sp.). Hispano-Mauresque style of the late 15th century evolved in Spain as a result of the influence of Moorish craftsmen who remained in the country after the fall of Granada.

Mule chest. Chest with a plinth in which are two or three drawers.

Neo-Classical style. Style evolved in France and England in the third quarter of the 18th century and quickly adopted elsewhere in Europe and America, inspired by an increasingly informed knowledge of Roman and also of Greek art.

Ogee moulding. Moulding of double curvature, concave below and convex above.

Ogival. Having the form of an ogive or pointed arch.

Ormolu. English term, derived from the French but not, in fact, used in France, to describe decorative objects and furniture mounts of cast and gilt bronze or brass. The French term is *bronze doré* while in England, gilt bronze is an alternative description.

Ovolo. Convex moulding of quarter-circle section.

Oyster veneers. Veneers cut transversely from very small branches of walnut, laburnum, olive and other trees, showing the whorled pattern of the graining and laid side by side, a method developed in Holland in the second half of the 17th century.

Pad foot. Resembling club foot, but set on a disc.

'Paintbrush' foot. American term to describe the foot of a chair or table curled inwards in resemblance of a paintbrush; otherwise known as tassel foot, or Spanish foot *(pe de pincel)*.

Palmette. Ornament of formalised palm leaf, of Classical derivation, often resembling a spread fan.

Papier-mâché. Process of ancient Eastern origin, later developed in France and elsewhere, by which specially prepared paper pulp, mixed with other ingredients, is pressed, moulded and baked into a hard substance used in furniture and capable of taking a high polish.

Papyrus culm. Stem of the paper reed, *Cyperus Papyrus* cultivated in ancient times in the Delta of Egypt.

Parcel gilt. Partly gilt.

Parquetry. A form of veneer, creating a geometrical pattern.

Passementerie. Lace-work or trimming.

Patera. A motif of Classical origin, consisting of a round or oval decoration; much used in the Neo-Classical period, applied, carved, inlaid or painted.

Pedestal. In architecture a moulded base supporting a column. In terms of furniture, a solid support for a lamp or a decorative object. Pedestal desks are those in which the top is supported on two side sections containing drawers. Pedestal tables are supported on a single pillar or column.

Pediment. Member of triangular or curved form surmounting a Classical cornice. When 'broken', the lines of the pediment are stopped before reaching the apex.

Penwork. A method of decorating furniture in which designs in black are drawn with a pen on a light-coloured ground, the surrounding wood being stained black; popular in England at the Regency period.

Perpendicular style. In architecture, and consequently also in furniture, the latest style in English Gothic, dating from about the mid-14th century until the Renaissance. Characterised by vertical lines in window tracery, wall surfaces displaying traceried panels in which vertical lines are dominant and the moulded profiles tend to be flat, and the appearance of the four-centred or Tudor arch. Decorative details became less naturalistic and are often purely conventional.

Piano nobile. (It.). The first floor of a palace or fine house, accommodating the state rooms. The term was also adopted in England.

Pied de biche. (Fr.). See HOOF FOOT.

Pier wall. Section of wall between windows; hence pier glass, pier table, etc.

Pietre dure. (It.). Ornamental work in hard stone (e.g. jasper, agate), originating in Florence in the late 16th century. Widely used for table tops and decorative cabinets from that period.

Pilaster. Flattened column, rectangular in section.

Plateresque. Descriptive of exuberant early Renaissance decoration on Spanish furniture; name first applied to such decoration on silver *(plata)*.

Plinth. Base of a piece of furniture; plinth or spade foot of tapered rectangular shape found as leg terminal.

Point de hongrie. (Fr.). An all-over canvas embroidery of zigzag designs.

Première-partie. (Fr.). See BOULLE.

Press. A cupboard.

Putto. (It.). Naked male infant much used as a decorative motif on furniture from the Renaissance.

Quadrant drawer. A drawer which is the fourth part of a circle in plan and swings outward on a pivot when opened.

Quartetto tables. Sheraton used this term in *The Cabinet Dictionary* (1803) to describe a nest of four small tables.

Rebate. Groove of rectangular section on the edge of a door, drawer, etc.

Reeding. Convex moulding resembling series of reeds; opposite of fluting.

Régence period. (Fr.). Term most commonly used to describe the years between 1715 and 1723 when Philippe, Duc d'Orléans, was Regent of France during the minority of Louis XV.

Repoussé. (Fr.). Method of making a design in relief in metalwork by hammering from behind so that the decoration projects.

Rococo. (Rocaille). Derived from the French *rocaille*, the term describes a style which originated in France in the early 18th century and spread throughout Europe. A decorative style conceived at first in terms of flowing arabesques, it developed in the second quarter and in the mid-18th century a more sculptural, volatile manner, in which motifs based on shell and rock forms, foliage, flowers, sprightly animals, 'C' scrolls and tortuous curves were combined with fantasy and charm.

Roll-top desk. A desk closed by means of a flexible shutter of convex shape composed of strips of wood. See also TAMBOUR FRONT.

Roll-work. See STRAPWORK.

Romanesque. Style currently in Europe in the 11th and 12th centuries characterised by the round arch inspired by Classical example.

Roundel. Ornament occupying a circular space.

Sabre leg. A leg curved in resemblance of a cavalry sabre.

Saut de lit. (Fr.). Bedside stool.

Scagliola. (It.). Composition of plaster and glue, to which small pieces of marble were added, coloured to imitate marble and other ornamental stone; capable of taking a very high polish.

Scallop. See COQUILLAGE.

Sconce. Wall light.

Scriptor. An old term for a fall-front writing cabinet of the type introduced into England in the reign of Charles II.

Serpentine form. A profile composed of a convex curve, flanked by two concave curves.

Shell. See COQUILLAGE.

Soffit. The underside of an arch or lintel.

Sopraporta. (It.). Ornamental panel over a door.

Spade foot. See PLINTH.

Spandrel. The triangular section between two arches.

Sphinx. Hybrid monster with the head of a woman and the body of a lion.

Splat. Vertical member between the uprights of a chair back; often pierced or shaped.

Split baluster or spindle. Turned member split lengthwise and applied as matched decoration on furniture.

Split spindle. See SPLIT BALUSTER.

Spoon-back. American term to describe a 'Queen Anne' chair with a back curved like a spoon to give comfort to the sitter.

Stile. Vertical section of the frame of panelling into which the horizontal section (rail) is fitted.

Strapwork. Decoration composed of interlacing bands or straps sometimes combined with foliage. A popular ornament in Northern Europe in the second half of the 16th and early 17th centuries. Late 17th-century Baroque ornament also included a delicate form of foliate strapwork based upon the designs of the French designer, Jean Bérain.

Stretcher. Horizontal bar joining and strengthening the legs of chairs or tables.

Stringing. Inlay in form of fine lines, usually in wood, but sometimes in metal.

Stucco. (It.). Plaster.

Stucco lustro. (It.). Plaster imitating marble.

Studiolo. (It.). Small study (room).

Sunburst motif. Ornamental motif resembling the rays of the sun sometimes resembling a mask.

Tambour front. A roll front or shutter made of narrow strips of wood glued to a canvas backing, and used for desk tops, etc.

Tenon. See MORTICE.

Term. A statue or bust representing the upper part of the body, sometimes without arms, and terminating below in a pillar or pedestal.

Terrazza. (It.). Terrace.

Tester. Wooden canopy, particularly over a bedstead.

'Thrown' chair. 16th-century chair with triangular seat and arms, the legs and back composed of turned members.

Torchère. (Fr.). Portable stand, known also as a candlestand or *guéridon*, for candlestick, candelabrum or lamp.

Tracery. Intersecting rib-work in the upper part of a Gothic window, or in panels and screens.

Trefoil. An ornament suggesting a three-lobed leaf.

Trompe l'oeil. (Fr.). A pictorial technique, using perspective and foreshortening, to deceive the eye and heighten the impression of reality.

Troubadour style. (Ironic) description in France in the 19th century of furniture in the revived Gothic style.

Trumeau. (Fr.). Pier or pier-glass.

Turkey work. Upholstery of even, deep pile formed by knotting wools on a canvas base, in imitation of Turkey carpets. In use from the 16th century onwards.

Turning. Until about 1700 turning was an outstanding feature of chair and table legs. It was executed on a foot-operated pole lathe and the turner's chisel determined the final shape. Baluster turning resulted in turned members of various columnar shapes (see BALUSTER). Ball and Spool turning and Bobbin turning were other popular 17th-century characteristics, the members imitating the shapes of spools or bobbins. Twist or Spiral turning, resembling 'barley sugar', was sometimes known by this latter name.

Turqueries. (Fr.). Free rendering in Western terms of what was thought to represent Turkish taste.

Velvet. Woven silk material with a plush pile surface. The richest fabrics are those of Genoese and Utrecht manufacture.

Veneer. Thin sheet of wood glued to the carcase of furniture for decorative effect; formerly sawn by hand, now cut by machine.

Verre eglomisé. (Fr.). Method of decorating glass by painting on the underside and then backing the glass with metal (usually gold or silver) foil. Though this process is named after J.-B. Glomy, French designer of the 18th century, it is of much greater antiquity.

Vernis Martin. (Fr.). Term used generically to describe varnishes and lacquers used for furniture and interiors in France in the 18th century. The four Martin brothers developed a method of lacquering (patent 1730, renewed 1744) which brought them Court patronage and widespread fame. They used many colours, but their green lacquer was the most celebrated.

Vitrine. (Fr.). Display or china cabinet.

Vitruvian scroll. (wave pattern). Border decoration of Classical origin composed of a band of convoluted scrolls.

'Voltaire' chair. Mid-19th-century upholstered armchair with high, scrolled back.

Volute. Spiral scroll, particularly associated with Ionic capital.

Wainscot. Name originally used in medieval England for imported timber suitable for wagon (wain) construction, and thus for furniture and panelling; more strictly applied in America to panelling and panelled furniture.

Wine cellaret. A deep drawer in a sideboard fitted for bottles. The term is also used to describe a wine cooler.

READING LIST

International

Eames, Penelope. *Furniture in England, France and the Netherlands from the Twelfth to the Fifteenth Century.* London, 1977.
Holzhausen, W. *Lackkunst in Europa.* Cologne, 1958.
Honour, Hugh. *Chinoiserie. The Vision of Cathay.* London, 1961.
Musée National d'Art Moderne. *Les Sources du XXᵉ siècle. Les Arts en Europe de 1884 à 1914.* Exhibition catalogue. Paris, 1960.
Reitlinger, Gerald. *The Economics of Taste. Vol II: The Rise and Fall of Objets d'Art Prices since 1750.* London, 1963.
Thornton, Peter. *Interior Decoration in England, France and Holland.* London, 1978.

America

Bjerkoe, Ethel Hall. *The Cabinetmakers of America.* Garden City, NY, New York, 1957.
Comstock, Helen. *American Furniture: Seventeenth, Eighteenth and Nineteenth Century Styles.* New York, 1962.
Downs, Joseph. *American Furniture, Queen Anne and Chippendale periods, in the Henry Francis du Pont Winterthur Museum.* New York, 1952.
Drexler, Arthur. *The Drawings of Frank Lloyd Wright.* New York, 1962.
Fales, Dean A. *American Painted Furniture, 1660-1880.* New York, 1972.
Kane, Patricia E. *300 Years of American Seating Furniture.* Boston, 1976.
Montgomery, Charles. *American Furniture, The Federal Period in the Henry Francis du Pont Winterthur Museum.* New York, 1966.
Newark Museum. *Classical America, 1815-1845.* Newark, New Jersey, 1963.
Nutting, Wallace. *Furniture Treasury* (mostly of American origin). 3 vols, New York, 1948-9.

China

Ecke, Gustav. *Chinese Domestic Furniture.* (Reprint) Rutland, Vermont, Tokyo, and Hong Kong, 1963.
Ellsworth, Robert Hatfield. *Chinese Furniture: Hardwood Examples of the Ming and early Ch'ing Dynasties.* London, 1971.
Kates, George N. *Chinese Household Furniture.* New York, 1948 and 1962.
Luzzatto-Bilitz, Oscar. *Lacche orientali.* Milan, 1966.

Egypt

British Museum. *A General Introductory Guide to the Egyptian Collections in the British Museum.* 1964.
Carter, H. *The Tomb of Tut-ankh-Amen.* 3 vols, London, 1923-33.
Erman, A. and Ranke, H. *Aegypten und Aegyptisches Leben im Altertum.* 2nd ed., Tübingen, 1923.
Lucas, A. *Ancient Egyptian Materials and Industries.* 4th ed. (J.R. Harris), London, 1962.
Quibell, J.E. *The Tomb of Yuaa and Thuiu.* Cairo, 1908.
Schiaparelli, E. *Relazione sui lavori della missione archaeologica Italiana in Egitto, II, La tomba intatta dell'architetto Cha.* Turin, 1927.

England

Agius, Pauline. *British Furniture, 1880-1915.* London, 1978.
Aslin, Elizabeth. *19th Century English Furniture.* London, 1962.
Beard, Geoffrey. *Georgian Craftsmen and Their Work.* London, 1966.
Bøe, Alf. *From Gothic Revival to Functional Form.* Oslo and Oxford, 1957.
Coleridge, Anthony. *The Chippendale Period in English Furniture.* London, 1966.
Edwards, Ralph. *Georgian Furniture.* Victoria and Albert Museum, 2nd ed., London, 1958. (Ed.) *Hepplewhite Furniture Designs.* Reprint with preface by Ralph Edwards. London, 1947. *Sheraton Furniture Designs.* Reprint with preface by Ralph Edwards. London, 1949. *Thomas Chippendale: The Gentleman and Cabinet-maker's Director.* Reprint of the 3rd ed., introduction by Ralph Edwards. Bonn, 1957. *William Ince. The Universal System of Household Furniture.* Reprint with preface by Ralph Edwards. London, 1960. *The Shorter Dictionary of English Furniture from the Middle Ages to the late Georgian Period.* London, 1964. *English Chairs.* Victoria and Albert Museum. 2nd ed., London, 1965.
Edwards, Ralph and Jourdain, Margaret. *Georgian Cabinet-makers c.1700-1800 – A New and Revised Edition.* London, 1955.
Fastnedge, Ralph. *Sheraton Furniture.* London, 1962. (Ed.) *Shearer Furniture Designs from the Cabinet-Makers' London Book of Prices 1788.* Reprint with preface by Ralph Fastnedge. London, 1962.
Fowler, John and Cornforth, John. *English Decoration in the 18th Century.* London, 1974.
Gilbert, Christopher. *Furniture at Temple Newsam House and Lotherton Hall.* 2 vols, London, 1978. *The Life and Work of Thomas Chippendale.* 2 vols, London, 1978.
Gloag, John. *Georgian Grace: A Social History of Design, 1660-1830.* London, 1956. *English Furniture in the Irwin Untermyer Collection.* Introduction by John Gloag. Notes and comments by Yvonne Hackenbroch. London, 1958. *The Englishman's Chair: Origins, design and social history of seat furniture in England.* London, 1964. *English Furniture.* 5th ed., London, 1965.
Harris, Eileen. *The Furniture of Robert Adam.* London, 1963.
Harris, John. *Regency Furniture Designs from Contemporary Source Books, 1803-1826.* London, 1961.
Hayward, Helena. *Thomas Johnson and English Rococo.* London, 1964.
Hayward, Helena and Kirkham, Pat. *William and John Linnell, Eighteenth-Century London Furniture Makers.* 2 vols, London, 1968.
Hayward, J.F. *Chests of Drawers and Commodes.* Victoria and Albert Museum. London, 1960. *Tables.* Victoria and Albert Museum. London, 1961. *English Cabinets.* Victoria and Albert Museum. London, 1964.
Heal, Sir Ambrose. *London Furniture Makers from the Restoration to the Victorian Era.* London, 1953.
Jervis, Simon. *Victorian Furniture.* London, 1968. *Printed Furniture Designs before 1650.* London, 1974.
Joy, Edward. *English Furniture, 1800-1851.* London, 1977.
Macquoid, Percy and Edwards, Ralph. *The Dictionary of English Furniture.* 2nd ed., revised by Ralph Edwards. 3 vols, London, 1960.
Madsen, Tschudi. *Sources of Art Nouveau.* Oslo, 1956.
Mercer, Eric. *Furniture 700-1700 (The Social History of the Decorative Arts series).* London, 1969.
Molesworth, H.D. (Ed.) *A Treatise of Japanning and Varnishing (1688) by John Stalker and George Parker.* Reprint with introduction by H.D. Molesworth. London, 1960.
Musgrave, Clifford. *Regency Furniture.* London, 1961. *Adam and Hepplewhite and Other Neo-classical Furniture.* London, 1966.
Schmutzler, Robert. *Art Nouveau.* London, 1964.
Symonds, R.W. *Furniture Making in Seventeenth and Eighteenth century England.* London, 1955.
Thornton, Peter. *The Furnishing and Decoration of Ham House.* London, 1980.
Tomlin, Maurice. *Catalogue of Adam period Furniture.* Victoria and Albert Museum. London, 1972.
Ward-Jackson, Peter. *English Furniture Designs of the Eighteenth Century.* London, 1958.
Wills, Geoffrey. *English Looking-glasses.* London, 1965. *English Furniture, 1550-1760.* London, 1971. *English Furniture, 1760-1900.* London, 1971. *Craftsmen and Cabinet-Makers of Classic English Furniture.* London, 1974.
Wolsey, S.W. and Luff, R.W.P. *Furniture in England: The Age of the Joiner.* London, 1968.

France

Brunhammer, Yvonne et de Fayet, Monique. *Meubles et Ensembles Époques Régence et Louis XV. Meubles et Ensembles Époque Louis XVI. Meubles et Ensembles Époques Directoire et Empire.* 4 vols, Paris, 1965. *Meubles et Ensembles Époques Moyen Âge et Renaissance.* Paris, 1966.
Coll. Connaissance Des Arts. *Le XVIIᵉ Siècle Français.* Paris, 1958. *Grands Artisans d'Autrefois: Les Ébénistes du XVIIIᵉ Siècle Français.* Paris, 1963.
Devinoy, Pierre et Janneau, Guillaume. *Le Meuble Léger en France.* Paris, 1952.
Devinoy, P., Jarry, M., et Janneau, G. *Le Siège en France du Moyen Âge à Nos Jours.* Paris, 1948.
De Fayet, Monique. *Meubles et Ensembles: Moyen Âge et Renaissance.* Paris, 1961.
Du Colombier, Pierre. *Le Style Henri IV-Louis XIII.* Paris, 1941.
Eriksen, Svend. *Early Neo-Classicism in France.* London, 1974.
Grandjean, Serge. *Empire Furniture, 1800-1825.* London, 1966.
Janneau, Guillaume. *Les Meubles.* Vol I, Paris, 1949.
Jarry, Madeleine. *Le Siège Français de Louis XII à Napoléon III.* Paris, 1958.
Keim, Albert. *La Décoration et Le Mobilier à l'époque Romantique et Sous le Second Empire.* Paris, 1929.
Ledoux-Lebard, Denise. *Les Ébénistes Parisiens (1795-1830).* Paris, 1951.
Ledoux-Lebard, R.G. et C. *La Décoration et L'ameublement de La Chambre de Mme Recamier sous le Consulat in Gazette des Beaux-Arts.* Paris, October 1952 and May-June 1955.
Lefuel, H. *François-Georges-Honoré-Jacob-Desmalter, ébéniste de Napoleon Ier et de Louis XVIII.* Paris, 1925.
Martin, Henry. *Le Style Louis XIV.* Paris, 1947.
Mauricheau-Beaupré. *Le XVIIᵉ Siècle, lère et 2ème période.* 2 vols, Paris, 1946 and 1947.
Moussinac, Leon. *Le Meuble Français Moderne.* Paris, 1925.
Niclausse, Juliette. *Thomire, Fondeur-ciseleur.* Paris, 1947.
Percier, Charles, et Fontaine, Pierre François, Léonard. *Recueil de Décorations Intérieures.* 1st ed., Paris, 1801, and 2nd ed. (illustrated), Paris, 1812.
Robiquet, Jacques. *L'Art et Le Goût sous la Restauration.* Paris, 1928.
de Salverte, Comte François. *Le Meuble Français d'après Les Ornemanistes de 1660 à 1789.* Paris, 1930. *Les Ébénistes du XVIIIᵉ Siècle.* 3rd ed., Paris, 1934.
Tardieu, Suzanne. *Meubles Régionaux Datés.* Paris, 1950.
Theunissen, André. *Meubles et Sièges du XVIIIᵉ Siècle.* Paris, 1934.
Verlet, Pierre. *Le Style Louis XV.* Paris, 1942. *Le Mobilier Royal Français.* 2 vols, Paris, 1945-55. *The Frick Collection,* Volume XI. New York, 1956. *Les Meubles du XVIIIᵉ Siècle.* 2 vols, Paris, 1956. *L'Art du mueble à Paris au XVIIIᵉ siècle.* Paris, 1958. *French Furniture and Interior Decoration of the 18th Century.* London, 1967.
Viaux, Jacqueline. *Le Meuble en France.* Paris, 1962.
Wallace Collection Catalogues. *Furniture* by F.J.B. Watson. London, 1956.
Watson, F.J.B. *Louis XVI Furniture.* London, 1960.
Weigert, R.A. *Le Style Louis XIV.* Paris, 1941.

Germany

Arens, F.V. *Meisterrisse und Möbel der Mainzer Schreiner.* Mainz, 1955. *Deutsche Werkstätten-Möbel.* Hellerau, 1936.
Falke, Otto von. (Ed.) *Deutsche Möbel des Mittelalters und der Renaissance.* Stuttgart, 1924.
Himmelheber, G. *Biedermeier Furniture* (trans. and ed. by Jervis, S.). London, 1974.
Huth, Hans. *Friderizianische Möbel.* Darmstadt, 1958. *Roentgen Furniture.*
Kreisel, Heinrich. *Fränkische Rokokomöbel.* Darmstadt, 1956. *Die Kunst des Deutschen Möbels. Vol I: Von Möbels der Anfangen bis sum Hochbarock.* Munich, 1968. *Vol II: Spätbarock und Rokoko.* Munich, 1970. *Vol III: Klassizismus, Historismus, Jugendstil.* Munich, 1973.
Möller, Liselotte. *Der Wrangelschrank und die Verwandten Süddeutschen Intarsienmöbel des 16 Jahrhunderts.* Berlin, 1956.
Schmitz, Hermann. (Ed.) *Deutsche Möbel des Barock und Rokoko.* Stuttgart, 1923.
Schönen, Paul. *Aachener und Lütticher Möbel des 18 Jahrhunderts.* Berlin, 1942.
Sievers, J. *Karl Friedrich Schinkel. Lebenswerk. Die Möbel.* Berlin, 1950.
Trachsler, Walter. *Renaissance-Möbel der Deutschsprachigen Schweiz um 1520 bis 1570 aus dem Schweizerischen Landesmuseum.* Berne, 1959.
Wernitz, G. (Ed.) *Historische Möbel und Innenräume.* Berlin, Deutsche Bauakademie, 1956.

Greece and Rome

Deonna, Waldemar. *Le Mobilier Délien.* Athens, 1938.
Liversidge, Joan. *Furniture in Roman Britain.* London, 1955.
Richter, G.M.A. *Ancient Furniture: A history of Greek, Etruscan and Roman furniture.* Oxford, 1926.

Italy

Alberici, Clelia. *Il Mobile Lombardo.* Milan, 1969.
Baccheschi, Edi. *Il Mobile Veneziano del Settecento.* Milan, 1962. *Mobili Laccati del Settecento Veneziano.* Milan, 1962. *Mobili Intarsiarti del Sei e Settecento in Italia.* 1964. *Mobili Italiani del Rinascimento.* Milan, 1964.
Brosio, Valentino. *Mobili Italiani dell'Ottocento.* Milan, 1962. *Ambienti Italiani dell'Ottocento.* Milan, 1963.
Canonero, Lelio. *Barocchetto Genovese.* Milan, 1962.
Del Puglia, Raffaella. *Mobili e Ambienti Italiani dal Gotico al Floreale.* 2 vols, Milan, 1963.
Gonzales-Palaçios, Alvar. *Il Mobile nei Secoli. Italia.* 3 vols, Milan, 1969.
Levy, Saul. *Il Mobile Veneziano del Settecento.* Milan, 1964. *Lacche Veneziane Settecentesche.* 2 vols, Milan, 1967.
Mariacher, Giovanni. *Ambienti Italiani del Cinquecento.* Milan, 1962.
Mazzariol, Giuseppe. *Mobili Italiani del Seicento e del Settecento.* Milan, 1963.
Morazzoni, Giuseppe. *Il Mobilio Italiano.* Florence, 1940. *Il Mobile Genovese.* Milan, 1949. *Il Mobile Intarsiato di Giuseppe Maggiolini.* Milan, 1953. *Il Mobile Neoclassico Italiano.* Milan, 1955. *Il Mobile Veneziano.* Milan, 1958. *Ambienti Italiani del Seicento e Settecento.* Milan, 1964.
Odom, William M. *A History of Italian Furniture from the Fourteenth to the Early Nineteenth Centuries.* New York, 1966/7.
Palazzina di Stupinigi, Turin. Exhibition catalogue: *Mostra del Barocco Piedmontese: Mobili e intagli.* Vol. III, ed. Vittorio Viale. Turin, 1964.
Pignatti, Terisio. *Lo Stile dei Mobili.* Milan, 1951. *Mobili Italiani del Rinascimento.* Milan, 1961.
Tinti, Mario. *Il Mobilio Fiorentino.* Milan, 1929.

Japan

Ishimoto, T. and Ishimoto, K. *The Japanese House: Its Interior and Exterior.* New York, 1963.
Luzzatto-Bilitz, Oscar. *Lacche orientali.* Milan, 1966.
Taut, B.R. *Houses and People of Japan.* Tokyo, 1938. *This is Japan.* Tokyo, 1954.

The Low Countries

Berendsen, Anne. *Het Nederlandse Interieur.* Utrecht, 1950.
Catalogus van Meubelen en Betimmeringen in het Rijksmuseum. 3rd ed., Amsterdam, 1962.
Denuce, Jan. *Kunstuitvoer in de 17de eeuw te Antwerpen.* Antwerp, 1931.
Jonge, C.H. de, and Vogelsang, W. *Holländische Möbel und Raumkunst von 1650-1780.* The Hague, 1922.
Lunsingh Scheurleer, Th. H. *Van haardvuur tot Beeldscherm.* Amsterdam, 1952.
Philippe, J.F.E. *Le Mobilier Liégeois Moyen Âge – XIXᵉ siècle.* Liège, 1962.
Pluym, Willem van der. *Vijf Eeuwen Binnenhuis en Meubels in Nederland, 1450-1950.* Amsterdam, 1954.
Singleton, Esther. *Dutch and Flemish Furniture.* London, 1907.
Staring, A. *De Hollanders Thuis.* The Hague, 1956.

Poland

Arps-Aubert, R. *Sächsische Barockmöbel, 1700-1770.* Berlin, 1939.
Malicki, Longin. *Sztuka Ludowa Pomorza Gdańskiego na tle zbiorów Muzeum – Pomorskiago w Gdansku.* Warsaw, 1962.
Mankowski, Tadensz and Gebethner, Stanislaw. *Przewodnik po Dziale Sztuki Zdobniczej, Muzeum Narodowe w Warszawie.* 2nd ed., Warsaw, 1938.
Maszkowska, Bozenna. *Z Dziejów Polskiego Meblarstwa Okresu Óswiecenia.* Warsaw, 1956.
Sienicki, Stefan. *Meble Kolbuszowskie.* Warsaw, 1938. *Wnetrza Mieszkalne.* Warsaw, 1962.

Russia

Cherikover, L.Z. *Bykovaka Mebel' Russkogo Klassitsizma Kontsa XVIII Nachala XIX v.v.* Moscow, 1954.
Grabar, Igor, E. *Istoriya Russkagho Iskusstwa.* Vol. III – Istoriya architekturui; Petersburgskaja architektura v XVIII i XIX v., Moscow, c.1912.
Ivanov, D.D. *Iskusstvo mebeli.* Moscow, 1924. *Bol'shaia Sovetskaia Entsiklopedia.* Vol XXVI, 2nd ed., Moscow, 1954.
Popova, Z.P. *Russkaya Mebel' Konets XVIII Veka.* Moscow, 1957.

Scandinavia

Clemmensen, Tove. *Møbler paa Clausholm, Langesø og Holstenshuus.* Copenhagen, 1946. *Danish Furniture of the 18th Century.* Copenhagen, 1948. *Signerede Arbejder af Københavnske Snedkere. In Københavns Snedkerlaug Gennem Fire Hundrede år, 1554-1954.* Copenhagen, 1954. *Danske Møbler.* Copenhagen, 1963.
Clemmensen, Tove and Mackeprang, M. *Christian IX's Palae på Amalienborg, 1750-1906.* Copenhagen, 1956.
Fett, Harry. *Baenk og Stol i Norge.* 2 vols, Kristiania, 1907.
Fischer, Ernst. *Svenska Möbler i Bild.* 2 vols, Stockholm, 1931 and 1950.
Henschen, I. and Blomberg, S. *Svenskt Möbellexikon.* 3 vols, Malmö, 1961.
Lagerquist, Marshall. *Svenska stolar.* Gothenberg, 1946. *Rokokomöbler Signerade av Ebenister och Schatullmakare i Stockholm.* Stockholm, 1949. *Georg Haupt, Ebéniste du Roi.* Stockholm, 1979.
Lassen, Erik. *Danske Møbler: Den Klassike Periode.* Copenhagen, 1958.
Lexow, J.H. *Bergenske Empiremøbler.* Bergen, 1948.
Slomann, Vilhelm. *Nyklassisismen og de Danske Møbler fra det 18de Århundre.* In Arbok of the Kunstindustrimuseum, Oslo, 1931-2.
Stavenow-Hidemark, Elisabet. *Svensk Jugend.* Stockholm, 1964.
Tunander, B. and I. *Köpa Möbler på Auktion.* Västeras, 1963.
Wallin, Sigurd. *Nordiska Musseets Möbler.* Stockholm, 1931-5.

Spain and Portugal

Bueno, Luis Perez. *El Meuble.* Barcelona, 1930. New ed. 1950.
Burr, Grace H. *Hispanic Furniture.* New York, 1941. Enlarged ed. 1964.
Carrillo y Gariel, Abelardo. *Meuble Mexicano.* Mexico, 1948.
Domenech, Raphaël. *Meubles Antinguos Españoles.* Barcelona, 1921.
Enriquez, Maria Dolores. *El Meuble Español en los Siglos XV, XVI, XVIII. Madrid, 1951.*
de Fayet, Monique. *Meubles et Ensembles. Renaissance espagnole.* Paris, 1961.
Feduchi, Luis M. *El Meuble en España.* Vol I and II *El Palacio Nacional.* Madrid, 1949. Vol IV *Los Museos Arqueologico y Valencia de Don Juan.* Madrid, 1950. Vol V *El Hospital de Afuera.* Madrid, 1950. *Antología de la Silla Española.* Madrid, 1957.
Guimaraes, Alfredo and Sardoeira, Albano. *Mobiliário Artístico Portugues. Vol I: Lamego.* Oporto, 1924.
Nascimento, J.F. da Silva. *Leitos e Camilhas Portugueses.* Lisbon, 1950.
Pinto, A. Cardoso. *Cadeiras Portugueses.* Lisbon, 1952.
Rodriguez de Rivas, Mariano. *El Museo Romantico.* Madrid, 1950.
Taullard, Alfredo. *El Meuble colonial Sudoamericano.* Buenos Aires, 1954.

The Twentieth Century

Agius, Pauline. *British Furniture 1880-1915.* London, 1978.
Aloi, Roberto. *L'Arredamento Moderno.* Milan, 1950, and later vols.
Brosio, Valentino. *Lo Stile Liberty in Italia.* Milan, 1967.
Carney, Clive. (Ed.) *International Interiors and Design.* Sydney, 1960.
Giedion, Sigfried. *Mechanization takes Command.* New York, 1948.
Hard af Segerstad, Ulf. *Modern Scandinavian Furniture.* London, 1963.
Hatje, Gerd. *New Furniture.* New York, 1953, and later vols.
Logie, Gordon. *Furniture from Machines.* London, 1947.
Nelson, George. *Living Spaces.* New York, 1952. *Chairs.* New York, 1953. *Storage.* New York, 1954.
Russell, Sir Gordon. *Furniture.* Rev ed., London, 1964.
Young, D. and B. *Furniture in Britain Today.* London, 1964.

ACKNOWLEDGMENTS

THE PUBLISHERS WISH TO EXPRESS THEIR THANKS TO THE FOLLOWING FOR THEIR PERMISSION TO REPRODUCE SUBJECTS FROM THEIR COLLECTIONS:

H.M. the Queen 287, 296, 304, 308, 319, 320, 322, 499, H.R.H. the Princess Royal 510, 511, 512, H.M. the King of Denmark 353, 644, 645, 1004, 1007, H.M. the Queen of the Netherlands 1011, 1012, 1014, H.M. the King of Sweden 646, 653, 654, 1001.

Alvar Aalto 1127, 1128, William Armbruster 1145, Harry Bertoia 1143, Marcel Breuer 1110, 1112, 1113, 1126, 1129, Walter Brune 1163, Le Corbusier 1117, 1118, 1119, Robin Day 1139, Charles Eames, 1130, 1131, 1132, 1133, 1134, 1135, 1136, 1137, 1138, 1162, *illus. p.* 289, *pl. f. p.* 289 (below left), Walter Gropius 1114, Peter Hvidt & O. Mölgaard Nielsen 1153, 1154, Arne Jacobsen 1159, 1160, *pl. f. p.* 305 (below), Finn Juhl 1149, 1150, *pl. f. p.* 305 (above), Poul Kjaerholm 1158, Bruno Mathsson 1124, 1125, Mies van der Rohe 1111, 1115, 1116, Børge Mogensen 1151, George Nakashima 1147, 1148, Richard Neutra 1121, Isamu Noguchi 1146, Verner Panton 1152, Gio Ponti 1161, Gerrit Rietveld 1109, Hans Wegner, *pl. f. p.* 289 (below right).

Abramtsevo, Moscow 1048, Accademia, Venice, *pl. f. p.* 48, Norman Adams Ltd., London 526, 528, 530, The Lords of the Admiralty, Admiralty House, London 764, Alte Pinakothek, Munich, *pl. f. p.* 33 (below), American Museum in Britain, Claverton, Somerset 691, Sir Colin Anderson, London 870, S. Fabrizio Apolloni, Rome 572, Archives de la Manufacture de Sèvres 919, Arkhangelskoe Palace, Moscow 1045, 1047, 1051, Ashmolean Museum, Oxford 1085, 1086, Lady Ashton, London 794, 795, Badisches Landesmuseum, Karlsruhe 542, Baltimore Museum of Art, Maryland 743, Bath Club, London 771, Bayerisches Nationalmuseum, Munich 86, 134, 144, 340, 345, Bayerisches Verwaltung der Staatlichen Schlösser, Gärten und Seen, Munich, 556, 567, Biblioteca Laurenziana, Florence, *pl. f. p.* 32 (above left), Biblioteca Nazionale, Turin 574, Bibliothèque de l'Arsenal, Paris 258, Bibliothèque Nationale, Paris 112, 120, 121, 127, 129, 130, 244, 263, 266, 267, 270, 271, 273, 280, 894, 905, 922, 925, 930, Birmingham City Museum and Art Gallery 188, Miss Alice Boney, New York 1062, Bradford Town Hall, Yorkshire 847, John Brandon-Jones Esq., 869, 872, Bristol City Art Gallery 1088, British Museum, London 10, 12, 17, 18, 19, 29, 51, 78, 83, 84, 1090, 1093, 1095, 1096, 1099, 1100, 1101, 1166, 1167, 1168, 1169, 1170, 1171, 1172, 1173, 1174, 1175, 1176, 1177, Princess A. de Broglie, Paris 439, The Brooklyn Museum, New York 376, 953, 969, 970, 971, The Duke of Brunswick 354, The Duke of Buccleuch 289, 312, Burg Eltz, Moselle, 338, Joseph T. Butler Esq., New York 949, 960, 961, 975, D. Celesta Cabral, Evora 367, Cairo Museum, Egypt 3, 5, 6, 7, 8, 9, 11, 14, 15, 16, *pls. f. p.* 16, Caisse Nationale des Monuments Historiques 899, Mrs G. H. M. Carfrae 789, Casa Calvet, Barcelona 1043, Centraal Museum, Utrecht 166, Charlecote Park, Warwickshire 783, Château d'Azay-le-Ferron, Loire Valley 904, Château de Champs, *pls. f. p.* 113, Château de Chantilly 920, 921, 924, 926, Château de Compiègne 927, 928, 937, 939, Château de la Roche-Pichemer 254, Château de Talcy 251, The Trustees of the Chatsworth Collection, Chatsworth, Derbyshire 299, Cheadle and Gatley Urban District Council 785, Lord Cholmondeley, Houghton Hall, Norfolk, *pl. f. p.* 129, Christie, Manson & Woods Ltd., London 293, 323, 326, 327, Mr & Mrs Lansdell K. Christie, U.S.A. 724, Church Commissioners, London 183, 184, Clermont Club, London 829, Colonial Williamsburg, U.S.A. 682, 706, 709, Colonel N. R. Colville 291, Connecticut Historical Society 689, Cooper Union Museum, New York 974, T. Cottrell-Dormer Esq., Rousham House, Oxfordshire 468, 506, Sir Hugh Dawson, Bart., London 324, 328, 329, 330, 331, 332, 333, Dithmarscher Landesmuseum, Meldorf, Germany 143, Michael Dormer Esq., London 303, Duivenvoorde Castle, Voorschoten, Holland 1013, Durham University Library 49, Egetoftegaard, Helsinge, Denmark 997, 1000, R. Hatfield Ellsworth, New York 1063, 1066, 1068, C. J. A. Evelyn Esq., 215, 216, The Marquess of Exeter 300, Syndics of the Fitzwilliam Museum, Cambridge 585, John Fleming Esq., Italy 586, Fondazione Giorgio Cini, Venice 218, 221, Dr Walter Formanek, Vienna 990, Mrs Mary Francis 884, Frank Lloyd Wright Foundation, U.S.A. 981, 982, 983, Frans Hals Museum, Haarlem 635, Frick Collection, New York 94, 95, 114, 125, Fundación Tavera-Lerma, Toledo 189, 195, Galleria Borghese, Rome 101, 590, Gemeente Museum The Hague 1018, 1020, Germanisches Nationalmuseum, Nuremberg 136, 335, 336, 1022, Girard College, U.S.A. 741, Glasgow Art Gallery and Museum (Burrell Collection) 48, 311, Glasgow School of Art 877, Glasgow University 875, 876, Wardens of the Goldsmiths' Company, Goldsmiths' Hall, London 772, Göteberg Museum, Sweden 400, Grand Rapids Public Museum, Michigan 968, Ralph Harari Esq., London 1089, M. Harris & Sons, London 748, Mrs Helena Hayward, London 768, J. F. Hayward Esq., London 482, Henry Ford Museum, Dearborn, Michigan 379, 380, 688, 956, 972, H. F. du Pont Winterthur Museum, Delaware, 375, 378, 381, 382, 685, 693, 694, 695, 696, 699, 701, 702, 707, 708, 710, 712, 714, 716, 717, 721, 722, 725, 729, 730, 736, 738, 739, 740, 746, 747, *pls. f. pp.* 177 (above), 192 (above right and below), J. Hillier Esq., Surrey 1083, 1084, 1087, *pl. f. p.* 225 (below), Hispanic Society of America, New York 194, 196, 199, 202, 360, 361, 619, Historisches Museum, Basle 139, 154, Historisches Museum, Dresden 146, Historisk Museum, University of Bergen 650, Prince Hohenlohe, Schloss Neuerstein 346, 347, Hôtel Grande Bretagne, Bellagio 1034, Hôtel Lambert, Paris 255, Hôtel Lauzun, Paris, *pls. f. pp.* 96, 97 (below), Hôtel Solvay, Brussels 1023, Hôtel de Sully, Paris, *pl. f. p.* 97 (above right), Mrs Wallace Hughes, Sussex 790, John Hunt Esq., Co. Dublin, *pl. f. p.* 32 (above right), Christopher Hussey Esq., Scotney Castle, Kent 781, Instituto de Valencia de Don Juan, Madrid 77, Istituto Bancario San Paulo di Torino, *pl. f. p.* 161, H. W. Keil, Broadway, Worcestershire 177, 182, Kielce Museum, Poland 1056, Knoll Associates Inc., *pls. f. p.* 304, Kodansha, Tokyo 1077, 1079, Det Kongelige Bibliotek, Copenhagen 1005, Kunsthistorisches Museum, Vienna 128, Kunstindustrimuseet, Copenhagen 649, 659, 661, Kunstindustrimuseet, Oslo 640, Kuskowo Palace, Russia 674, Łańcut Castle, Poland 670, 1053, Nicolas Landau, Paris 124, 246, 250, 252, 264, 269, 275, Landesmuseum Joanneum, Graz, Austria 149, Landesmuseum für Kunst und Kulturgeschichte, Münster 140, 141, Lefuel, Paris 456, 457, 458, 459, 460, 461, The Earl of Leicester, Holkham Hall, Norfolk, 467, Lady Lever Art Gallery, Port Sunlight, Cheshire 462, 472, 497, Michael Levi Esq., 775, Alexander Lewis Esq., London 502, Jas. A. Lewis & Son, London 306, 471, 758, 759, Library Company of Philadelphia 703, 705, Linley House, Bath 479, The Marquess of Linlithgow, Hopetoun House, Linlithgow 295, London County Council 476, 477, Mr & Mrs Fritz Low-Beer 1060, Lyman Allen Museum, Connecticut 952, Mainfränkisches Museum, Würzburg 541, Mallett & Son, Ltd., London 520, 523, 524, Maryland Historical Society, U.S.A. 948, Sir Andrew McTaggart 883, Miss Elinor Merrell, New York 976, 977, 978, 979, 980, Metropolitan Museum of Art, New York 98, 690, 700, 713, 734, 735, 742, 744, 962, *pl. f. p.* 177 (below), (Cloisters Collection) *illus. p.* 25, *pl. f. p.* 33 (above), (Irwin Untermyer Collection) 465, 466, 498, Municipal Museum, Portalegre, Portugal 203, Munson-Williams Proctor Institute, Utica, New York 957, 963, 964, Musée des Arts Décoratifs, Paris 105, 106, 107, 108, 113, 116, 122, 123, 245, 249, 253, 256, 272, 274, 277, 283, 285, 384, 386, 393, 394, 396, 397, 406, 407, 411, 422, 423, 424, 427, 430, 433, 442, 445, 446, 453, 454, 893, 903, 906, 907, 908, 909, 910, 911, 912, 913, 914, 916, 917, 918, 923, 929, 931, 932, 933, 935, 936, 938, 940, 941, 942, 943, 944, Musée de Beaux Arts, Tours 408, Musée Carnavalet, Paris 56, 915, Musée de Cluny, Paris 58, 110, 131, Musée Curtius, Liège, 158, Musée de l'Ecole de Nancy 945, Musée du Louvre, Paris 13, 109, 117, 257, 385, 387, 389, 390, 391, 392, 395, 413, 414, 426, 431, 432, 436, 440, 443, 895, 896, 897, 901, 902, 934, 1094, Musée de Lyon 119, Musée de Malmaison, France 892, 898, *pl. f. p.* 193, Musée National de Fontainebleau, France 451, 891, 900, Musée Nissim de Camondo, Paris 404, 405, 412, 416, 419, 420, 421, 428, 429, 434, 438, 444, 447, 448, 449, 455, *pls. f. p.* 128, Musée de Strasbourg 261, 262, Musée de Valère, Sion, Switzerland 46, Musée de Versailles, 276, *illus. p.* 65, Musées Royaux d'Art et d'Histoire, Brussels 630, Museo Arcivescovile, Ravenna 41, Museo degli Argenti, Palazzo Pitti, Florence 219, Museo Arqueologico, Madrid 201, Museo de Artes Decorativas, Barcelona 197, Museo de Artes Decorativas, Madrid 87, 190, 191, 192, 193, 358, 359, 362, 363, 602, 1039, Museo di Capodimonte, Naples 102, Museo Civico, Belluno 224, Museo Civico, Bologna, *illus. p.* 19, Museo Civico d'Arte Antica, Turin 207, 214, Museo Civico d'Arte del Castello Sforzesco, Milan 66, 595, Museo dei Conservatori, Rome 26, Museo Correr, Venice 579, Museo des Descalzas Reales, Madrid 204, Museo Etrusco Gregoriano, Vatican, Rome 25, Museo Historico Nacional, Buenos Aires 621, Museo Horne, Florence 93, Museo Nazionale, Florence 96, Museo Nazionale, Naples, 20, 23, 24, 34, *illus. p.* 9, Museo del Opificio delle Pietre Dure, Florence 596, *pl. f. p.* 64, Museo di Palazzo Venezia, Rome 100, Museo Poldi-Pezzoli, Milan 92, Museo Romantico, Madrid 1038, Museo Sartorio, Trieste 1032, Museo Stibbert, Florence 1034, Museu Escola de Artes Decorativas, Lisbon 369, 611, 613, 615, 616, Museu Guerra Junqueira, Oporto 365, 370, Museu de Inconfidencia, Ouro Preto, State of Minas Gerais 1044, Museu Nacional de Arte Antiga, Lisbon 75, 364, 368, 606, 607, 608, 609, 610, 614, Museu Soares dos Reis, Oporto 366, Museum Boymans van Beuningen, Rotterdam 163, Museum of the City of New York 947, 950, 958, 965, 973, Museum of Decorative Art, Oslo 126, Museum of Fine Arts, Boston 374, 951, *pl. f. p.* 192 (above left), (M. & M. Karolik Collection) 711, 719, 722, 728, 731, 732, 737, Museum für Kunsthandwerk, Dresden 554, 555, Museum für Kunsthandwerk, Frankfurt-am-Main 534, 536, 537, 539, 549, 553, 558, 563, 564, 569, 570, 571, 984, 985, 987, 988, Museum für Kunst und Gewerbe, Hamburg 351, 565, 989, The Museum of Modern Art, New York 1111, 1112, 1117, 1118, 1130, Narodni Galerie, Prague 55, 80, National Gallery, London 63, 70, Nationalmuseet, Copenhagen 642, 643, 658, 660, 998, National Museum, Athens 21, 22, Nationalmuseum, Stockholm 281, 284, National Museum, Tokyo 1076, 1078, 1080, 1081, National Museum, Warsaw 665, 671, 672, 673, The National Trust, Great Britain 301, 309, 488, 513, 515, 757, *pls. f. pp.* 144, 145, Neues Schloss, Bayreuth 547, Newark Museum, New Jersey 959, 966, New Hampshire Historical Society (Prentis Collection) 686, 687, Sir Ralph Newman, Bart., Mamhead, Devonshire 778, New York Historical Society, New York City 946, 954, New York State Historical Association, Cooperstown, New York 377, Neiborów Palace, Warsaw 666, 680, Nordiska Museet, Stockholm 152, 639, 641, 651, 657, 662, 663, 664, 999, (Svindersvik) 652, The Duke of Northumberland, Alnwick Castle 803, 806, Old Deerfield, Massachusetts 692, 697, Oriental Institute, University of Chicago 1091, Ospedale del Ceppo, Pistoia 82, Palacio Itamaraty, Rio de Janeiro 618, 1042, Palacio Nacional, Madrid 598, 599, 600, 601, 603, 604, 1036, 1037, Palacio Nacional de Ajuda, Lisbon 1041, Palacio Nacional de Queluz, Portugal 1040, Palais Stoclet, Brussels 995, Palazzo Altieri, Rome 597, Palazzo Balbi-Durazzo, Genoa 584, 589, 1029, Palazzo Brignole, Genoa 225, Palazzo di Capodimonte, Naples 1028, Palazzo Colonna, Rome 210, 217, Palazzo Davanzati, Florence 61, 97, Palazzo della Farnesina, Rome 91, Palazzo Pitti, Florence 206, 227, 1024, 1030, 1031, Palazzo del Quirinale, Rome 576, Palazzo Reale, Turin 211, 212, 591, 1026, 1027, Palazzo Rezzonico, Venice 222, 223, 575, 578, 580, 582, 583, Palazzo Sacchetti, Rome 226, 577, Palazzo Serristori, Florence 573, Palazzo Spada, Rome 213, Palazzo di Stupinigi, Turin 592, Palazzo Vecchio, Florence 89, Eric Pasold Esq., London 348, 349, 522, The Earl of Pembroke, Wilton House, 290, 302, 307, 334, Pennsylvania University 715, S. Celedonio Pereda, Lima, Peru 371, Philadelphia Museum of Art 683, 684, 698, 704, 967, 1057, 1058, 1061, 1064, 1073, *pl. f. p.* 49 (below), (Foulc Collection) 111, 115, S. Vascancelos Porto, Oporto 617, The Earl of Radnor, Longford Castle 145, 147, Reform Club, London 774, Residenz, Ansbach 540, 543, Residenz, Bamberg 544, 546, Residenz, Würzburg 533, 545, 986, Residenzmuseum, Munich 343, 344, 559, 562, Residenzschloss, Brunswick 535, Residenzschloss, Fulda, *pl. f. p.* 160, Mr & Mrs John D. Rockefeller 3rd, New York 955, Rhode Island Historical Society 718, Rijksmuseum, Amsterdam 157, 159, 161, 164, 165, 167, 168, 169, 170, 171, 228, 229, 230, 231, 232, 233, 235, 236, 237, 238, 239, 240, 241, 242, 388, 399, 402, 417, 418, 441, 622, 623, 624, 625, 626, 627, 628, 629, 633, 636, 637, 638, *pls. f. pp.* 80, 81, Rijksmuseum Kam, Nijmegen, Holland 30, 31, Rijksmuseum van Oudheden, Leiden 35, Royal Institute of British Architects, London 784, 786, 865, Royal Ontario Museum, Canada 1071, Royal Palace, Madrid *pl. f. p.* 176, Royal Pavilion, Brighton 749, 750, 753, 755, 756, 765, 766, 767, 769, Rzeszów Museum, Poland 669, Lord Sackville, Knole, Sevenoaks 288, Sanssouci, Potsdam 551, 552, Schleswig Holsteinisches Landesmuseum, Germany 150, 151, Schloss Berchtesgaden, Bavaria 560, Schloss Schönbrunn, Vienna 557, Graf von Schönborn-Wiesentheid, Schloss Pommersfelden, Germany 71, 356, 357, 561, I. G. Schwartz & Son, Copenhagen 1002, Schweizerische Landesmuseum, Zürich 155, 339, Shōsoin Depository, Nara, Japan 1074, 1075, Skokloster Castle, Sweden 352, Sir John Soane's Museum, London 516, S. Russell de Sousa, Oporto 612, Staatliche Museen, Berlin 27, 32, 133, 138, Stadtisches Museum, Wiesbaden 69, Stadtmuseum, Cologne 538, Stadtschloss, Potsdam 548, State Historical Museum, Moscow 676, State Library, Munich 44, State Library, Trier, Germany 45, Statens Museum for Kunst, Kobberstiksamlingen, Copenhagen 1003, Stedelijk Museum, Amsterdam 1017, 1019, 1021, 1109, *pl. f. p.* 289 (above), Rev. C. E. Steward, Berkshire 829, Mr & Mrs Stanley Stone 720, Francis Stonor Esq., London 220, Colonel N. V. Stopford-Sackville 294, 297, 298, Teheran Museum 1098, Temple Newsam House, Leeds 469, Toledo Museum of Art, Ohio 464, La Torre Lastres, Lima, Peru 373, Trier Museum, Germany 35, Twickel Castle, Holland 234, Tylmanowa, Poland 1052, Upsala University, Sweden 153, Vatican Library, Rome 594, Verwaltung der Staatlichen Schlösser und Gärten, Berlin 341, 550, 566, 991, 992, Vestlankske Kunstindustrimuseum, Bergen 1009, Victoria and Albert Museum, London 59, 60, 62, 64, 65, 67, 68, 73, 79, 85, 88, 103, 181, 187, 198, 200, 310, 313, 314, 318, 321, 325, 372, 470, 471, 474, 475, 480, 483, 485, 487, 490, 500, 508, 587, 656, 679, 681, 760, 788, 792, 797, 798, 801, 808, 809, 813, 818, 822, 825, 826, 835, 836, 837, 838, 845, 848, 853, 854, 855, 856, 857, 862, 863, 868, 880, 886, 888, 889, 1072, 1082, 1102, 1103, 1104, 1105, 1106, 1107, 1108, *pls. f. pp.* 65, 112, 224, 225 (above), 288, (Ham House) 286, 292, 305, 315, 316, (Osterley Park) 514, 517, 518, 519, *Endpapers*, Villa Bianchi-Bandinelli, Siena 593, 1025, Villa Lechi, Montirone, Brescia, 588, Villa del Poggio a Caiano, Florence 1033, Vodroffsvej, Copenhagen 1152, Walker Art Gallery, Liverpool 463, Wallace Collection, London 104, 208, 209, 383, 409, 410, 415, 425, 437, Walters Art Gallery, Baltimore 40, 1097, Waring & Gillow (Contracts) Ltd., London 814, 815, 816, 828, Warsaw University 667, 668, The Marquis of Waterford, Curraghmore, Co. Waterford 501, Baron Jens Wedell-Meergaard, Svenstrup Castle, Denmark 648, Mrs James West, Alscot Park, Warwickshire 796, Mrs Giles Whiting, New York 745, William Morris Gallery, Walthamstow 841, 859, 860, 861, William Rockhill Nelson Gallery of Art, Kansas City, 1065, 1067, 1069, *illus. p.* 275, Temple Williams Ltd., London 525, 529, 531, 532, 751, 752, 754, 761, 763, Madame Lopez-Willshaw, Paris 268, 278, 279, 282, *pl. f. p.* 97 (above left), Wittumspalais, Weimar 568, S. W. Wolsey, Ltd., London 173, 174, 175, 176, 178, 179, 180, 185, 186, Dr D. C. Wren, Gloucestershire 843, Yale University (Mabel Brady Garven Collection) 726, 727.

PHOTOGRAPHS WERE KINDLY PROVIDED BY THE FOLLOWING:

Colour: Amilcare Pizzi, S.p.A., Milan *pl. f. p.* 161, Bavaria-Verlag, Munich *pl. f. p.* 160, C. H. Cannings, London *pl. f. p.* 288, Country Life, London *pl. f. p.* 129, Editions de Presse Filmée d'Art, Paris *pl. f. p.* 49 (above), Foto Ferruzzi, Venice *pl. f. p.* 32 (below), John R. Freeman, London *pls. f. pp.* 65, 112, 225, Giraudon, Paris *pl. f. p.* 33 (below), Green Studio, Dublin *pl. f. p.* 32 (above right), Erik Hansen, Copenhagen *pl. f. p.* 289 (below right), H. F. du Pont Winterthur Museum, Delaware *pls. f. pp.* 177 (above), 192 (above right and below), Michael Holford, London *pl. f. p.* 144, Denis Hughes Gilbey, London *pl. f. p.* 17 (below), Jacqueline Hyde, Paris *pls. f. pp.* 96, 97 (above right and below), 113, 128, F. L. Kenett, London *Frontispiece and pls. f. p.* 16, Kersting, London *pls. f. pp.* 145, 224, Knoll Associates Inc., New York *pls. f. p.* 304, Metropolitan Museum of Art, New York *pl. f. p.* 33 (above), Musée de Malmaison, France *pl. f. p.* 193, Museum of Fine Arts, Boston *pl. f. p.* 192 (above left), Philadelphia Museum of Art *pl. f. p.* 49 (below), George Rainbird Ltd., London *Frontispiece and pls. f. p.* 16, Rijksmuseum, Amsterdam *pls. f. pp.* 80, 81, Royal Palace, Madrid *pl. f. p.* 176, Scala, Florence *pls. f. pp.* 32 (above left), 48, 64, Louis Schnakenburg, Copenhagen *pl. f. p.* 305 (above), Stedelijk Museum, Amsterdam *pl. f. p.* 289 (above), Strywing, Copenhagen *pl. f. p.* 305 (below), Taylor & Dull, New York *pl. f. p.* 177 (below), Viewpoint Projects, London *pl. f. p.* 17 (above).

Black and White: A.C.L., Brussels 72, 158, 630, Helène Adant, Paris 406, 420, 430, 433, 434, 903, Afrodisio Aguado, Madrid 191, 192, 193, 362, 363, 598, 599, 601, 602, 605, 1036, 1039, Agraci, Paris 892, 898, Alinari, Florence 20, 25, 26, 28, 33, 34, 37, 38, 41, 61, 82, 89, 91, 93, 100, 206, 213, 219, 225, 1030, *illus. pp.* 9, 19, Allegri, Brescia 588, American Museum in Britain, Claverton, Somerset 691, Ananta & Haagen, Amsterdam 635, Anderson, Rome 36, 205, 217, Antikvarisk Topografiska Arkivet, Stockholm 43, 657, Archives de la Manufacture de Sèvres 919, Archives Photographiques, Paris 105, 110, 119, 131, 243, 251, 408, 426, 436, 440, Artek, Helsinki 1127, 1128, Ashmolean Museum, Oxford 1085, 1086, Badisches Landesmuseum, Karlsruhe 542, F. Barsotti, Florence 573, E. Baumann, Bad Reichenhall, Germany 560, Bayerisches Nationalmuseum, Munich 86, 134, 144, 340, 345, Bayerische Verwaltung der Staatlichen Schlösser, Gärten Und Seen, Munich 567, Biblioteca Nazionale, Turin 574, Bibliothèque Nationale, Paris 112, 120, 121, 127, 129, 130, 266, 267, 270, 271, 273, 280, 894, 905, 922, 925, 930, Bildarchiv Foto Marburg, Germany 2, 5, 21, 22, 44, 45, 46, 47, 54, 71, 81, 197, 338, 355, 568, 995, *illus. p.* 25, Bildarchiv Meyer, Vienna 557, Boudot-Lamotte, Paris 533, 556, 1023, *illus. p.* 109, Bristol City Art Gallery 1088, British Museum, London 10, 12, 17, 18, 19, 29, 51, 78, 83, 84, 1090, 1093, 1095, 1096, 1099, 1100, 1101, 1166, 1167, 1168, 1169, 1170, 1171, 1172, 1173, 1174, 1175, 1176, 1177, Brogi, Florence 92, 96, 97, 99, 1033, 1034, 1035, Brooklyn Museum, New York 376, 953, 969, 970, 971, Bulloz, Paris 56, Caisse National des Monuments Historiques, Paris 899, Centraal Museum, Utrecht 166, C.F.E., Paris 456, 457, 458, 459, 460, 461, Ronald A. Chapman, London 348, 349, 522, Chicago University, Oriental Institute 1091, Chomon-Perino, Turin 592, Christoph, Hamburg 1158, Colonial Williamsburg, U.S.A. 682, Connaissance des Arts, Paris 254, 255, Connecticut Historical Society 689, Cooper Union Museum, New York 974, Council of Industrial Design, London 1140, Country Life, London 501, 778, 781, Deutsche Fotothek, Dresden 146, 554, 555, Dithmarscher Landesmuseum, Meldorf 143, Frank Dobinson, Brighton 750, 766, Durham University Library 49, Charles Eames, U.S.A. 1132, 1133, 1134, 1135, 1136, 1137, 1138, *illus. p.* 289, Irena Elgas-Markiewicz, Warsaw 670, 1053, English Life Publications Ltd., Derby 510, 511, Claude Esparcieux, Fontainebleau 891, 900, Fine Art Engravers Ltd., London 767, 775, Bill Finney, Concord, New Hampshire 687, Günther Fischer, Hanover 354, Fondazione Giorgio Cini, Venice 90, 224, Raymond Fortt, London 471, 474, 526, 528, 529, 530, 531, 532, 748, 751, 752, 754, 758, 759, 761, 763, 765, Foto Gelderland, Nijmegen 30, 31, Fotostudio Positief, Amsterdam 162, 634, Foto Technische Dienst, Rotterdam 163, Foto Visentini Guglielmo, Venice 221, John R. Freeman, London 145, 147, 181, 183, 184, 188, 220, 487, 516, 679, 681, 803, 806, 870, 1072, Freitas, Evora 367, Frick Collection, New York 94, 95, 114, 125, Gabinetto Fotografico Nazionale, Rome 101, 210, 572, 590, 597, Gasparini, Genoa 584, 589, 1029, Gemeente Museum, The Hague 1018, 1020, Germanisches Nationalmuseum, Nuremberg 136, 335, 336, 1022, E. & N. Gibbs, London 185, 499, 523, 525, 756, 785, Giraudon, Paris 42, 52, 53, 117, 118, 244, 247, 248, 257, 258, 259, 260, 261, 262, University of Glasgow 874, 876, Glasgow Art Gallery and Museum 48, 311, Göteberg Museum, Sweden 400, Griffith Institute, Ashmolean Museum, Oxford 3, 7, 8, 9, 11, 16, Leo Gundermann, Würzburg 540, 541, 543, 544, 545, 546, 547, 986, Carlfred Halbach, Ratingen 1163, Erik Hansen, Copenhagen 1122, 1123, 1149, 1153, 1154, Heal & Son Ltd., London 873, Helmer-Petersen, Copenhagen 1155, 1156, 1157, Henry Ford Museum, Dearborn, Michigan 379, 380, 688, 956, 972, Hess, Rio de Janeiro 618, 1042, 1044, H. F. du Pont Winterthur Museum, Delaware 375, 378, 381, 382, 685, 693, 694, 695, 696, 699, 701, 702, 707, 708, 710, 712, 714, 716, 717, 721, 723, 725, 729, 730, 736, 738, 739, 740, 746, 747, L. H. Hildyard, London 173, 174, 175, 176, 178, 179, 180, 186, 482, 768, Hirmer Verlag, Munich 356, 357, Hispanic Society of America, New York 194, 196, 199, 202, 360, 361, 619, Historisches Museum, Basle 139, 154, Historisk Museum, Bergen 650, Hohenlohe Museum, Germany 346, 347, Michael Holford, London 87, 190, 198, 200, 303, 324, 328, 329, 330, 331, 332, 333, 358, 359, 804, 811, 831, 1038, *illus. p.* 65, G. William Holland, Pennsylvania 1147, 1148, Horizon Press, New York 981, 982, 983, Hutin, Compiègne 927, 928, 937, 939, Jacqueline Hyde, Paris 124, 246, 250, 252, 263, 264, 268, 269, 275, 278, 279, 282, 385, 387, 389, 390, 391, 392, 395, 413, 414, 429, 431, 432, 448, 920, 921, 924, 926, Instituto de Valencia de Don Juan, Madrid 77, Kersting, London 74, 301, 309, 467, 468, 488, 506, 757, 771, 772, 773, 782, 783, 792, 794, 795, 796, 798, 801, 802, 805, 807, 818, 819, 826, 837, 838, 845, 853, 855, 856, 858, 862, 863, Kielce Museum, Poland 1056, Sylvain Knecht, Tours 904, Knoll Associates Inc., New York 1142, 1143, 1144, Kodansha, Tokyo 1077, 1079, Det Kongelige Bibliotek, Copenhagen 1005, E. Koztowska, Warsaw 680, E. Koziowskie-Tomszyk, Warsaw 668, Kunsthistorisches Museum, Vienna 128, Kunstindustrimuseet, Copenhagen 659, 661, Kunstindustrimuseet, Oslo 640, 649, Landesmuseum Joanneum, Graz, Austria 149, Landesmuseum für Kunst und Kulturgeschichte, Münster 140, 141, Giorgio Laurati, Florence 1031, Lady Lever Art Gallery, Port Sunlight, Cheshire 462, 472, 497, Alexander Lewis, London 502, Library Company of Philadelphia 703, 705, Libros Horizonte, Lisbon 203, London County Council 476, 477, Lott, Nancy 945, Lyman Allyn Museum, Connecticut 952, Lino Manfrotto, Bassano del Grappa, Italy 586, Maryland Historical Society 948, Mas, Barcelona 50, 76, 189, 195, 201, 600, 1043, Karl Mathsson, Varnamo, Sweden 1125, Elfriede Mejchar, Vienna 990, Metropolitan Museum of Art, New York 98, 465, 466, 498, 690, 700, 713, 734, 735, 742, 744, 962, Holmes I. Mettee Studio, Baltimore 743, Tom Molland, Plymouth 513, 515, Munson Williams Proctor Institute, Utica, New York 957, 963, 964, Musée des Arts Décoratifs, Paris 106, 107, 108, 113, 116, 122, 123, 245, 249, 253, 256, 265, 272, 274, 277, 283, 285, 384, 386, 393, 394, 396, 397, 398, 401, 403, 407, 411, 422, 423, 424, 427, 435, 439, 442, 445, 446, 450, 452, 453, 454, 893, 906, 907, 908, 909, 910, 911, 912, 913, 914, 916, 917, 918, 923, 929, 931, 932, 933, 935, 936, 938, 940, 941, 942, 943, 944, Musée Carnavalet, Paris 915, Musée de Cluny, Paris 58, Musée du Louvre, Paris 13, 109, 443, 895, 896, 897, 901, 902, 1094, Musée National de Fontainebleau 451, Musée Nissim de Camondo, Paris 404, 405, 412, 416, 419, 421, 428, 438, 444, 447, 449, 455, Museo Civico d'Arte Antica, Turin 207, 214, Museo Civico d'Arte del Castello Sforzesco, Milan 595, Museo Correr, Venice 579, Museo des Descalzas Reales, Madrid 204, Museu Escola de Artes Decorativas, Lisbon 613, Museum of the City of New York 947, 950, 958, 965, 973, Museum of Decorative Art, Oslo 126, Museum of Fine Arts, Boston 374, 711, 719, 722, 728, 731, 732, 737, 951, Museum für Kunst and Gewerbe, Hamburg 351, 565, 989, Museum für Kunsthandwerk, Frankfurt-am-Main 534, 536, 537, 539, 549, 553, 558, 563, 564, 569, 570, 571, 984, 985, 987, 988, The Museum of Modern Art, New York 1111, 1112, 1117, 1118, 1119, 1130, 1131, Narodni Galerie, Prague 55, 80, National Buildings Record, London 879, National Gallery, London 63, 70, Nationalmuseet, Copenhagen 642, 643, 658, 660, 998, Nationalmuseum, Stockholm 281, 284, National Museum, Tokyo 1076, 1078, 1080, 1081, National Museum, Warsaw 673, Newark Museum, New Jersey, U.S.A. 959, 966, Sidney W. Newbery, London 512, New Hampshire Historical Society 686, New York Historical Society, New York City 946, 954, New York State Historical Association, Cooperstown, New York 377, Nordiska Museet, Stockholm 152, 639, 641, 647, 651, 652, 655, 662, 663, 664, 999, 1010, Mario Novaïs, Lisbon 369, Palazzo Pitti, Florence 1024, Palazzo del Quirinale, Rome 576, Palazzo Rezzonico, Venice 222, 223, 575, 578, 580, 582, 583, Patrimonio Nacional, Madrid 603, 604, 1037, Pennsylvania University 715, Mario Perotti, Milan 66, Peuser, S.A., Beunos Aires 371, 373, 620, 621, Philadelphia Museum of Art 111, 115, 683, 684, 698, 704, 741, 955, 967, 1057, 1058, 1061, 1064, 1073, A. Cardoso Pinto 204, 607, Rampazzi, Turin 211, 212, 591, 1026, 1027, Jan H. Reimers, Bergen 1009, Residenzmuseum, Munich 343, 344, 559, 562, Residenzschloss, Brunswick 535, Rheinisches Bildarchiv, Cologne 538, Rhode Island Historical Society 718, Rijksmuseum, Amsterdam 157, 159, 161, 164, 165, 167, 168, 169, 170, 171, 172, 228, 229, 230, 231, 232, 233, 234, 235, 236, 237, 238, 239, 240, 241, 242, 388, 399, 402, 417, 418, 441, 622, 623, 624, 625, 626, 627, 628, 629, 633, 636, 637, 638, 1014, Rijksmuseum van Oudheden, Leiden 35, Robinson Studio, Grand Rapids, Michigan 968, Rodriguez, Toledo 189, 195, A. Rokicki, Poland 669, Romanowski, Warsaw 666, 667, Rossi, Venice 218, Rota, Trieste 1032, Thurman Rotan, New York 949, 960, 961, 975, Royal Academy of Arts, London 287, 288, 289, 291, 294, 297, 298, 299, 300, 302, 312, Royal Institute of British Architects, London 784, 786, 864, 865, Royal Ontario Museum, Canada 1071, David Royter, New York 1145, John D. Schiff, New York 1060, Schleswig Holsteinisches Landesmuseum 150, 151, Schweizerische Landesmuseum, Zurich 155, 339, Tom Scott, Edinburgh 295, Service de Documentation Photographique des Musées Nationaux, Versailles 276, 934, Shōsoin Depository, Nara, Japan 1074, 1075, Julius Shulman, U.S.A. 1162, J. F. da Silva Nascimento 612, Soprintendenza alle Antichita della Campania, Naples 23, 24, 102, 1028, Soprintendenza alle Galerie di Firenze 227, 596, Staatliche Museen, Berlin 27, 32, 133, 138, Stadtisches Museum, Wiesbaden 69, Stadtschloss, Potsdam 548, Statens Museum für Kunst, Copenhagen 1003, Stearn & Sons (Cambridge) Ltd. 585, Stedelijk Museum, Amsterdam 1017, 1019, 1021, 1109, Dr Franz Stoedtner, Dusseldorf 993, 996, Ezra Stoller Associates, New York 1115, 1116, 1146, 1164, 1165, Strywing, Copenhagen 1160, Roger Sturtevant, California 1120, Sundahl, Stockholm 1124, Swiderski, Warsaw 665, 671, 672, Tass, Moscow 675, 676, 677, 678, 1046, 1048, 1049, 1051, Taylor & Dull, New York 692, 697, Teheran Museum 1098, Temple Newsam House, Leeds 469, Teofilo Rego, Oporto 370, Thomas Photos, Oxford 215, 216, Toledo Museum of Art, Ohio 464, Bertram Unné, Harrogate 510, 511, Upsala University, Sweden 153, Valentine, Dundee 777, Vasari, Rome 226, 577, Vatican Library, Rome 594, Verwaltung der Staatlichen Schlösser und Gärten, Berlin 341, 550, 566, 991, 992, Victoria & Albert Museum, London 59, 60, 62, 64, 65, 67, 68, 73, 79, 85, 88, 103, 187, 286, 292, 305, 310, 313, 314, 315, 316, 318, 321, 325, 372, 470, 475, 478, 480, 481, 483, 484, 485, 490, 493, 494, 496, 500, 507, 508, 514, 517, 518, 519, 587, 656, 760, 788, 797, 808, 809, 813, 822, 825, 834, 835, 836, 848, 854, 857, 868, 875, 877, 880, 881, 882, 883, 884, 885, 886, 888, 889, 890, 1082, 1102, 1103, 1104, 1105, 1106, 1107, 1108, *illus. p.* 201, *Endpapers*, Vodroffsvej, Copenhagen 1152, Walker Art Gallery, Liverpool 463, Wallace Collection, London 104, 208, 209, 383, 409, 410, 415, 425, 437, Walters Art Gallery, Baltimore 40, 1097, Waring & Gillow (Contracts) Ltd., London 814, 815, 816, 828, Delmore Wenzel, Colonial Williamsburg 706, 709, William Morris Gallery, Walthamstow 841, 859, 860, 861, William Rockhill Nelson Gallery of Art, Kansas City 1065, 1067, 1069, *illus. p.* 275, Ole Woldbye, Copenhagen 997, 1000, 1002, C. H. Wood (Bradford) Ltd. 847, Roger Wood, London 6, Yale University, U.S.A. 726, 727.

Paul Hamlyn Ltd. are grateful to the following publishers for permission to reproduce illustrations from their books:

N. de G. Davies, *The Tomb of Rekhmirē, Thebes*; Metropolitan Museum of Art, New York, illustration 1, which also appears on the half-title. N. M. Davies & A. H. Gardiner, *Ancient Egyptian Paintings*; Chicago University, Oriental Institute, illustration 4.

INDEX